D1141268

INTELLECTUAL PROPERTY
LAW
IN IRELAND

To my dear Máire

(S.S.)

To K.K.

(R.C.)

INTELLECTUAL PROPERTY LAW IN IRELAND

by

Robert Clark

BA, LLM, Ph D, Barrister-at-law (King's Inns)
Associate Professor in Law, University College Dublin

and

Shane Smyth

BCL, BSc, Solicitor, Partner, F.R. Kelly & Co.

Butterworths

Ireland	Butterworth (Ireland) Ltd, 26 Upper Ormond Quay, DUBLIN 7
United Kingdom	Butterworths a Division of Reed Elsevier (UK) Ltd, Halsbury House, 35 Chancery Lane, LONDON WC2A 1EL and 4 Hill Street, EDINBURGH EH2 3JZ
India	Butterworths India, New Delhi, INDIA
Australia	Butterworths Pty Ltd, SYDNEY, MELBOURNE, BRISBANE, ADELAIDE, PERTH, CANBERRA and HOBART
Canada	Butterworths Canada Ltd, TORONTO and VANCOUVER
Malaysia	Malayan Law Journal Sdn Bhd, KUALA LUMPUR
New Zealand	Butterworths of New Zealand Ltd, WELLINGTON and AUCKLAND
Puerto Rico	Butterworths of Puerto Rico Inc, SAN JUAN
Singapore	Reed Elsevier (Singapore) Ltd, SINGAPORE
South Africa	Butterworths Legal Publishers (Pty) Ltd, DURBAN
USA	Michie, CHARLOTTESVILLE, Virginia

A CIP Catalogue record for this book is available from the British Library.

ISBN 1 85475 1247

Printed in Ireland by Microprint, Dublin.

Foreword

The law in relation to intellectual property has changed radically in the last few years. The Patents Act 1992, the Trade Marks Act 1996 and the implementation of a number of European Community directives in relation to copyright has brought Ireland into line with Europe in many respects. In addition, the whole scope of intellectual property has widened enormously with developments in technology, and perhaps it can also be said that the concept of intellectual property has changed. It now embraces a much more inclusive philosophy with a more equitable outlook, taking into account both the rights of the owner of the intellectual property to be fairly remunerated for his or her endeavour, and the rights or needs of the public to have access to and the benefit of the subject matter of such property.

It is, accordingly, fitting that two people from different backgrounds should come together to produce the first Irish textbook to deal with intellectual property in its entirety. Bob Clarke has a vast academic knowledge of intellectual property law and combines it with an enquiring mind which is very necessary to understand a changing concept. Shane Smyth, as well as being a lawyer, has all the practical experience gained over many years as a partner in the largest patent and trade mark agents in the country. In this book the union of the academic and the practitioner has given birth to an off spring which has the best of both, well researched and learned on the one hand and practical and all-embracing on the other.

I am particularly glad to see that the authors have dealt with intellectual property in a wide sense and have not restricted themselves to a commentary on various sections of legislation. They have considered in detail the large number of international conventions, treaties and agreements which now exist, and have placed our national provisions fairly and squarely in the context of European Community law and of international law generally. The traditional, somewhat insular, view of the subject in Ireland has thankfully been abandoned, and there is a serious attempt to foresee the world-wide problems which the 21st century will bring in this field.

It is not for a foreword to consider the details of a work such as this, that is for the critics and the commentators. Suffice it to say that it is an invaluable contribution which fills a huge void in Irish legal literature. In my view there would be a *prima facie* case of professional negligence against any solicitor, barrister, trade mark or patent agent - and perhaps even any judge, if such a cause of action could arise against a judge - who does not have this book in their library.

Mr Justice Brian McCracken
The High Court
Dublin 7
25 June 1997

Preface

It is appropriate to begin this Preface by thanking Mr Justice McCracken for his words of support, encouragement and complimentary remarks. His interest in our work has been an inspiration. We have tried to provide an Irish readership with a general textbook in the hope that we can throw light into areas of law and practice that have hitherto been neglected by other writers. Martin Tierney's excellent monograph, *Irish Trade Marks: Law and Practice* is now ten years old and the analysis therein has been overtaken by the new Act. Numerous areas of intellectual property law are increasingly attracting attention from others - eg Paul Lavery's recent book, *Commercial Secrets* - but the production of our new work, providing an overview of the law, will hopefully meet a long felt gap in Irish legal literature.

Something must be said about the timing of this book. While recent patents and trade mark legislation has enabled us to produce a work that is truly up-to-date, we have been constantly aware of the difficulties presented by the forthcoming Copyright Bill. The drafting of both the heads of a Bill and the Bill itself are, we understand, going on *in tandem*. One choice was to wait until those procedures had ended or to go to press now. We chose the latter option because of the uncertainty surrounding the issue of completion of the drafting work. However, the features of much of the new legislation are known, shaped as it is by both EU legislation and other external pressures and influences. It is hoped that, in writing much of the copyright material in a thematic manner, we will allow readers some insights into how the law will change in the years ahead. Our emphasis on the work completed by WIPO in Geneva in December 1996 is inspired by the same rationale. Although our intention is to highlight Irish law and practice, it is conceded that Irish case-law in certain key areas is sparse. Wherever possible, we have tried to use relevant case-law from other jurisdictions that share in the common law tradition but we do not presume to have produced an international legal encyclopedia on intellectual property law.

Thanks are due to our publishers, Butterworths (Ireland) Ltd, and in particular to Louise Leavy and Gerard Coakley who have been supportive in terms of their time, advice, patience and logistical support. Their enthusiasm for this project has never waned despite our prevarications on just when it would be safe to stop sketching this hyperactive subject. Our families too have also suffered but they can take comfort in the fact that a second edition is probably several years away! His partners and associates in FR Kelly & Co have indulged Shane Smyth to an outrageous degree, a debt he gratefully acknowledges. He is also grateful to Norma O'Donoghue who typed much of the manuscript.

This book purports to be up-to-date as of 31 March 1997 but some later materials have been included when they have been available to us.

Bob Clark

Shane Smyth   30 June 1997

Table of Contents

Chapter 11 Protected Works - Literary and Artistic Works

Chapter 12 Protected Works - Neighbouring Rights, State Copyright, Performers' Rights

Chapter 13 The Protection of Computer Programs as Copyright Works

Chapter 14 Databases

Chapter 19 Moral Rights and the Droit de Suite

Chapter 20 Copyright - Irish Legislative Developments in the Twentieth Century

Chapter 21 Semiconductor Chip Protection

Chapter 22 Industrial Designs

Chapter 23 The Duty of Confidence

Chapter 24 Remedies in Tort

Chapter 25 Introduction to Trade Mark Law

Chapter 26 Irish Trade Mark Law and International Conventions

Chapter 27 The Community Trade Mark

Chapter 28 Trade Marks Act 1996 - Registrability

Chapter 29 Trade Marks Act 1996: Absolute Grounds for Refusal of Registration

Chapter 30 Trade Marks Act 1996: Relative Grounds for Refusal of Registration

Chapter 31 Trade Marks Act 1996: Infringement and Remedies

Chapter 32 Trade Marks Act 1996: Limitations On Rights Conferred

Chapter 33 Trade Marks Act 1996: Registration Procedure and Ownership

Chapter 34 Trade Marks Act 1996 - Revocation and Invalidity

Chapter 35 Certification and Collective Marks

Chapter 36 Geographical Indications and Appellations of Origin

Chapter 37 Taxation and Intellectual Property Rights

A

C

D

L

N

O

P

Q

R

T

U

Table of Abbreviations

CA 1963	Copyright Act 1963
CPC	Community Patents Convention
ECJ	European Court of Justice
EPC	European Patent Convention
EPO	European Patent Office
GATT	General Agreement on Tariffs on Trade
OHIM	Office for the Harmonisation of the Internal Market
PA 1992	Patents Act 1992
PCT	Patent Co-Operation Treaty
SPC	Supplementary Protection Certificate
TLT	Trademark Law Treaty
TRIPS	Agreement on Trade Related Aspects of Intellectual Property
UPOV	*Union Pour La Protection des Obtentions Végétales* (Convention for the Protection of New Varieties of Plants)
WIPO	World Intellectual Property Organisation
WTO Agreement	World Trade Organisation Agreement

Chapter 1

Patents: A Brief History and Introduction

[1.01] The utilisation of the patent system by Irish nationals and entities has been relatively low. This could easily be put down to a lack of inventiveness, but it can probably be attributed to a lack of awareness of the importance of a system which rewards even a low level of inventiveness with monopoly rights and which can often be the only effective way of protecting innovation. The early laws of Ireland, the Brehon laws, recognised copyright[1] but not the concept of a protective right for inventions. As far back as 1474, the Venetians established a form of patent law which granted protection for a ten year term. During the reign of James I (1566-1625), the Brehon laws were abolished and the common law of England became legally established in Ireland. The Statute of Monopolies 1623[2] was the first English statute which specifically referred to patents for inventions and with which many analogies can be drawn with modern patent legislation. Under s 6, a 14 year patent monopoly was granted to "any manner of new manufactures"[3] and "to the true and first inventor and inventors of such manufactures".[4] There were, of course, limitations imposed on this monopoly right including a statement that they could not be used in a manner "contrary to the law nor mischievous to the State by raising prices of commodities at home or hurt of trade, or generally inconvenient". Again, these are concepts very similar to current legislation which provides as an exception to patentability, inventions, the publication or exploitation of which would be contrary to public order or morality,[5] and which also provides for compulsory licences in a broad range of circumstances.[6]

[1.02] An example of the early grant of a monopoly right in Ireland was that given to William Wood on 12 July 1722[7] relating to the manufacture of copper coins for Ireland. This patent was later to be rescinded but not before Mr Wood

---

1. See Ch 9.
2. The statute was actually passed on 25 May 1624.
3. See PA 1964, s 2 and definition of invention.
4. See PA 1964, s 6(1)(a).
5. PA 1992 s 10(a), but the section goes on to say that the "exploitation shall not be deemed to be so contrary only because it is prohibited by law".
6. PA 1992, s 70.
7. AB Tomkins, *A Short Historical Revision of the Law on the Protection of Industrial Property in Ireland* (Transactions of the Chartered Institute of Patent Agents, Vol 87 1968-9 CIPA p cii.

received a substantial compensation.[8] Prior to 1852, the cost, delay and cumbersome procedure for obtaining the grant of letters patent was considered to be prohibitive but by modern day standards, the delay for example of six months in 1850 would now be considered as insignificant. The relative cost was, however, sizeable.[9]

[1.03] The Patent Law Amendment Act 1852[10] established a single Patent Office for England, Scotland and Ireland and from which a single granted patent gave protection for Great Britain, Ireland, the Channel Islands and the Isle of Man. The effect of this Act was to dramatically increase the number of patents, no doubt encouraged by the significant decease in the cost of obtaining a patent. The Act did, however, introduce the concept of renewal fees to keep a patent in force, ie £50 to be paid before the end of the third year and £100 before the end of the seventh, part of these fees was a stamp duty. Renewals are now a feature of the patent laws of most jurisdictions. An Act of 1853 substituted stamp duties for the Patent Office fees.[11]

[1.04] Another feature which has filtered through to modern legislation is that which allows for pre-application disclosure at certain exhibitions.[12] The Industrial Exhibitions Act 1865[13] allowed for the filing of a patent application subsequent to disclosure at a duly certified industrial exhibition. Although not repealing s 6 of the Statute of Monopolies, the Patents, Designs & Trade Marks Act 1883[14] radically reformed patent law. The Board of Trade was empowered to order a compulsory licence on grounds very similar to those contained in s 70(2)(a),(b),(d) of the Patents Act 1992 and the preceding statute, the Patents Act 1964.[15] Importantly, the 1883 Act introduced the examination of patent applications by specially trained examiners in the Patent Office, whose duties included examination as to the sufficiency of disclosure in the patent specification.

[1.05] Certain grounds of opposition were allowed under the 1883 Act, namely, 'obtaining', 'prior patenting', 'interference' and conflict with a pending, and hence unpublished patent application. This third ground imposed a duty on an examiner to report if a second application comprising the same invention was

---

8. Henry JP Murdoch, *Invention and the Irish Patent System* (University of Dublin - Administrative Research Bureau, 1971).
9. Neil Davenport, *The United Kingdom Patent System* (Kenneth Mason, 1979).
10. 15 & 16 Vict c 83.
11. 16 & 17 Vict c 5.
12. PA 1992, s 12(1)(b).
13. 28 & 29 Vict c 3.
14. 46 & 47 Vict c 57.
15. No 12 of 1964.

filed during the pendancy of an earlier application but was abolished by the Patents, Designs & Trade Marks (Amendment) Act 1885.[16]

[1.06] Irish legislation contains detailed provisions regarding the registration of patent agents, who may act as a patent agent and the maintenance and control of the Register of Patent Agents.[17] The origins of such lie in an Act of 1888[18] and the Register of Patent Agents Rules 1889.

[1.07] A feature of the Patents Act 1902[19] was a provision for the introduction of examination as to the novelty of an invention involving a search which was restricted to British patent specifications up to 50 years old. Such novelty searches did not actually commence until 1905. It is common for a patent infringement action to be met with a counterclaim of invalidity of the patent. Until the Patents and Designs Act 1907,[20] any such claim had to be made by a separate petition for revocation. Under the 1907 Act, invalidity could be a counterclaim by way of defence to the infringement proceedings.[21] Because patent protection confers rights, even against an innocent infringer, the 1907 Act provided a limitation on liability for damages for patent infringement in the case of parties who could prove that they had no reason to know of the existence of the patent. This provision, together with a statement that the words 'patent' or 'patented' without the number of the patent on the product did not infer such knowledge, is still part of the law.[22] The last piece of patent legislation before the founding of the State was the Patents and Designs Act 1919[23] which increased the normal term of a patent from 14 years to 16 years and it was not until the Patents Act 1992 that this became 20 years. The 1919 Act also provided that a patentee could offer a licence as of right and to encourage such, a patent so endorsed, paid only half of the normal renewal fees.

[1.08] The establishment of the Irish Free State (Saorstát Éireann) in 1921 put the position regarding patents into a vacuum. No mention was made of patents in the Irish Free State Constitution 1922 or in the Treaty forming part of the Constitution. Provided there was no inconsistency with the Constitution, the laws in force in the Irish Free State at the time of the coming into operation of the Constitution continued to be of full force and effect until repeal or amendment by enactment of the Oireachtas.[24] Such repeal did not take place

---

16. 48 & 49 Vict c 63.
17. PA 1992, Part X.
18. 51 & 52 Vict c 50.
19. 2 Ed 7 c 34.
20. 7 Ed 7 c 29.
21. PA 1992, s 61(1)(a).
22. PA 1992, s 49(1).
23. 9 & 10 Geo 5 c 80.
24. Article 73 of the Constitution of the Irish Free State (Saorstát na hÉireann) Act 1927.

until 1927 and since the foundation of the Irish Free State there have been three major statutes dealing with the patent system:

1. The Industrial and Commercial Property (Protection) Act 1927,[25]
2. The Patents Act 1964,[26]
3. The Patents Act 1992.[27]

The 1927 Act also dealt with trade marks, designs and copyright. Part II of the Act which deals with patents came into operation on 1 October 1927, repealing the existing UK legislation as it applied in the Irish Free State and setting up an independent Irish Patents Office.

[1.09] Unlike the current Patents Act 1992, the 1927 Act included a definition of invention,[28] namely:

> any new and useful art, process, machine, manufacture or composition of matter, or any new and useful improvement in any art, process, machine, manufacture or composition of matter, and includes an alleged invention.

This definition was repeated in the 1964 Act[29] but with the addition of the words "and also any new method or process of testing applicable to the improvement or control of manufacture". Under the 1927 Act, if the invention was published or made available to the public before the date of application in any document published in the State or prior to the establishment of the State in the United Kingdom, then this was a ground of opposition[30] to a patent and also for revocation.[31]

[1.10] The 1964 Act contained an anomaly whereby publication in the State was a ground of opposition[32] but in revocation proceedings publication was not limited to that within the State.[33] There was also a broad definition of 'published' as "made available to the public by the written or spoken word or by public use, or in any other way".[34] Because of the provisions in the 1927 Act limiting publication to such within the State, it was possible for inventions which had been already been patented in other jurisdictions to be validly

---

25. No 16 of 1927.
26. No 12 of 1964.
27. No 1 of 1992.
28. Industrial and Commercial Property (Protection) Act 1927, s 3.
29. PA 1964, s 2.
30. Industrial and Commercial Property (Protection) Act 1927, s 24.
31. Industrial and Commercial Property (Protection) Act 1927, ss 41, 42.
32. PA 1964, s 19(1)(b).
33. PA 1964, s 34(1)(e).
34. PA 1964, s 2.

patented in the State by "the first party to introduce or import the invention into the Irish Free State".[35]

[1.11] Although the 1927 Act established the Irish Patents Office with examiners to whom every application for patent was to be referred,[36] there was still an onus on an applicant to furnish what became known as evidence of novelty. The examiners considered the application in a number of ways, including whether the invention was fairly described and whether the complete specification was substantially the same as that described in the provisional specification.[37] In addition, an 'investigation' was carried out to ascertain whether the invention was claimed or described in a prior application made in the State.[38] The obligation imposed on an applicant by way of evidence of novelty was to show that the invention was not claimed or described in any earlier British patent specification published in the State pursuant to an application for a British patent made during the period commencing 50 years before the date of the application for a patent in the State and ending on 1 October 1927.[39] The evidence of novelty could take the form of a copy of an accepted equivalent British patent application or a statutory declaration from an Irish registered patent agent or British patent agent stating that, having carried out the required search and investigation, the invention was not wholly or in part claimed or described in an earlier British patent specification. Since disclosure of an invention prior to filing was grounds for refusal, opposition or revocation of a patent, a procedure arose for the filing of a provisional patent application which was a relatively simple procedure and which provided a date, ie the filing date from which disclosure could take place without prejudice to the outcome or validity of a patent. The complete specification had to be lodged within nine months from the date of filing of the provisional specification.[40]

[1.12] The 1927 Act was amended in 1929[41] and 1957.[42] The 1929 Act allowed for an assignment of patent rights to a Minister[43] and the 1957 Act included provisions for the inventor 'to be mentioned' in the patent.[44] There was not, however, a complete review of patent legislation until the Patents Act 1964, which commenced on 1 July 1966. The 1964 Act was very similar to the UK

---

35. See F Lysaght, *Patents, Designs and Trade Marks in the Irish Free State* (1931).
36. Industrial and Commercial Property (Protection) Act 1927, s 14.
37. Industrial and Commercial Property (Protection) Act 1927, s 17.
38. Industrial and Commercial Property (Protection) Act 1927, ss 20 and 21.
39. Industrial and Commercial Property (Protection) Act 1927, s 19.
40. Industrial and Commercial Property (Protection) Act 1927, s 16.
41. Industrial and Commercial Property (Protection) (Amendment) Act 1929 (No 13 of 1929).
42. Industrial and Commercial Property (Protection) (Amendment) Act 1957 (No 13 of 1957).
43. Industrial and Commercial Property (Protection) (Amendment) Act 1929, s 6.
44. Industrial and Commercial Property (Protection) (Amendment) Act 1957, s 2.

Patents Act 1949 and hence case law under the corresponding sections of the UK Act were of persuasive authority. It is not true, however, to state that the 1964 Act is a mirror image of the UK 1949 Act. By way of example, s 32(1)(e) of the UK Act provided for revocation of a patent on the ground that the invention was "not new having regard to what was known or used ... in the United Kingdom" whereas s 34(1)(e) of the Irish Act used the words "is not new having regard to what was published", without any limitation on the need for such disclosure to take place in the State, ie universal novelty. In this regard, the Irish legislation, by its definition of publication, conformed to Article 4(2) of the Strasbourg Convention on the Unification of Certain Points of Substantive Law on Patents for Invention.[45] In a report presented to the UK Parliament in 1970, it was concluded that the novelty criteria should be universal.[46]

[1.13] Defining what was patentable had to take into account not just the definition of 'invention'[47] but also whether or not the application claimed as an invention:

    (a) was anything obviously contrary to well established natural laws;

    (b) the use of which would be contrary to public order or morality; or

    (c) a substance capable of being used as food or medicine which is a mixture of known ingredients possessing only the aggregate of the known properties of the ingredients, or a process producing such a substance by mere admixture.[48]

Section 8 provided for the filing of a provisional specification to be completed within twelve months with a possible extension to fifteen months. An applicant had to file the results of an investigation, ie a novelty search, to show that the invention claimed in the complete specification was novel.[49] There were strict requirements as to the form that this evidence of novelty could take.[50] In addition to the evidence of novelty, the examiner searched as to publication in the State before the date of filing of the applicant's complete specification in any other document.[51] The term of a patent under the 1964 Act was 16 years from the date of filing of the complete specification subject to payment of renewal

---

[45.] Concluded on 27 November 1963 and entered into force on 1 August 1980. See para **[2.25]** *et seq, post.*

[46.] *Report of the Committee to Examine the Patent System and Patent Law* (Chairman - Mal Banks).

[47.] PA 1964, s 2.

[48.] PA 1964, s 15.

[49.] PA 1964, s 8(6).

[50.] Rule 27 of the Patent Rules 1965; Rule 6 of the Patent Amendment Rules 1970; Rule 2 of the Patent Amendment (No 2) Rules 1978; Rule 2 of the Patent Amendment Rules 1979.

[51.] PA 1964, s 12(2).

fees. Most High Court proceedings under the 1964 Act were applications under s 27 to extend the term of a patent. Most of these applications were heard by Costello J and related to pharmaceutical patents where, because of the strict regulatory requirements, there was a long delay in launching the drug. The principles upon which the High Court exercised its discretion to extend the term of a patent were stated in *Fleming's Patent,*[52] namely:

(1) was the invention one of more than ordinary utility?

(2) had the patentee been adequately remunerated? and

(3) was the absence of remuneration due to no fault of the patentee?

[1.14] These principles were applied in *JR Geigy AG*[53] and Costello J gave a ten year extension. This was unusual, however, and most extensions granted were for a period of five years.[54] In the case of *Fison's Petition*[55] an extension of term was refused by the High Court and this decision was upheld by the Supreme Court. The basis for the refusal was that "the figures for the world-wide sales of this product, which have been very extensive, show that the patentee has been adequately, even handsomely, remunerated". It was recognised that it was correct to offset against profits in Ireland, a portion of the research and development costs. In considering remuneration, the primary concern was the position in the Irish market but that nevertheless, the world-wide remuneration may be taken into account.[56] Under the Patent Rules 1965, it was also possible to present the petition to the Controller[57] but this was rarely done in practice.

[1.15] Although the Patents Act 1992 contains extensive provisions regarding compulsory licences,[58] s 42 of the 1964 Act contained a special provision in respect of patents relating to food, medicine or to medical, surgical or other remedial devices. The Controller was obliged to grant a licence unless, having regard to the desirability of encouraging inventors and the growth and development of industry and to such other matters as he considered relevant, there were good reasons for refusing the application. It could, of course, be argued that the very existence of this section encouraged the voluntary licensing of pharmaceutical patents but for whatever reason, the section was not utilised in practice. Several applications were made under the corresponding s 41 of the

---

52. 35 RPC 55.
53. [1982] FSR 278.
54. *Science Union Patent* High Court, unrep, 14 May 1987, Costello J; *John Wyeth & Brother's Patent* [1985] RPC 545, Costello J.
55. [1984] FSR 59.
56. *Minerals & Chemical Corporation's Patent Extension* High Court, unrep, 2 February 1982, Costello J.
57. Rules 65-68
58. PA 1992, ss 70 & 71.

UK Patents Act 1949 where it was established *inter alia* that a licence to supply a market by importation should not be granted[59] but the situation may be different if the patentee is supplying the home market by importation.[60] The British courts have also given guidelines as to how to calculate an appropriate royalty based on the criteria that the product should be available to the public at the lowest prices consistent with the patentee deriving a reasonable advantage from their patent rights.[61]

[1.16] Shortly before the introduction of the Patents Act 1992, an Irish based generic pharmaceutical manufacturer, Clonmel Healthcare Limited made applications for licences under s 42 of the 1964 Act in respect of a number of patents. Since there is no corresponding section in the 1992 Act, the applicant sought to avail of the transitional provisions of the 1992 Act which states that any application for a licence under s 42 of the 1964 Act which was pending at the commencement of the 1992 Act shall be decided under the provisions of the 1964 Act.[62] The Controller did order a compulsory licence in respect of two patents on 2 June 1995 but on appeal to the High Court the orders were rescinded.[63] Carroll J held that the TRIPS Agreement which is part of the World Trade Organisation Agreement, obliged the Controller to refuse to grant compulsory licences pursuant to s 42 of the Patents Act 1964. Although the Controller had heard the applications[64] prior to the entry into force of TRIPS,[65] his decision was rendered subsequently.[66]

---

59. *FARMERS Marketing Patent* [1966] RPC 546.
60. *Hoffmann-La Roche's Patent* [1969] RPC 504; [1971] 1 FSR 522.
61. *Geigy's Patent* [1964] RPC 391 and *Farbwerke Hoecht's Patent* [1973] RPC 253.
62. PA 1964, First Schedule, s 13.
63. *Allen & Hanburys Ltd and Glaxo Group Ltd v The Controller and Clonmel Healthcare Ltd*, [1997] FSR 1.
64. July/September 1994.
65. 1 January 1995.
66. June 1995. This case is currently under appeal to the Supreme Court.

Chapter 2

The Irish Patent System and International Conventions

[2.01] As stated in the explanatory memorandum to the Patents Bill 1991, the principal objectives of the new legislation included the updating of the law so to bring it into line with the laws applying generally in other European countries and to enable ratification of two international agreements concerning patents, namely, the European Patent Convention and the Patent Co-Operation Treaty. These agreements are designed to facilitate an applicant who wishes to file patent applications in a number of jurisdictions but the first real attempt at such which still survives is the International Convention for the Protection of Industrial Property or, as it is commonly known, the Paris Convention or Union.

PARIS CONVENTION

[2.02] The Paris Convention was signed in Paris on 20 March 1883 by eleven countries.[1] The UK was not one of the eleven countries but acceded to the Convention on 17 March 1884 and ratified it on 6 June 1884. Since UK patent legislation was at that time applicable in Ireland, it could be said that the provisions of the Paris Convention had effect in Ireland from its infancy. The Convention has been revised at Brussels (1900), Washington (1911), The Hague (1925), London (1934), Lisbon (1958) and Stockholm (1967).

[2.03] Although the Irish Free State was established on 6 December 1921, it was not until 4 December 1925 that the State formally acceded to the Convention[2] and is currently bound by the Stockholm revision.[3] The countries to which the Convention applies are said to constitute a Union for the Protection of Industrial Property and Article 1(2), which lists the forms of industrial property, includes at the head of the list, patents. The Convention also applies to various kinds of "industrial patents" recognised by Member States. Hence, there can be no doubt that short term patents also fall within the provisions of the Convention.

[1.] Belgium, Brazil, France, Guatemala, Italy, Netherlands, Portugal, El Salvador, Serbia, Spain and Switzerland.

[2.] For circumstances surrounding accession, see Henry JP Murdoch, *Invention and the Irish Patent System* (1971, University of Dublin - Administrative Research Bureau) pp 37-39.

[3.] Articles 1-12 of the Convention came into force on 19 May 1970 and Articles 13-30 on 26 April 1970.

[2.04] The fundamental principle of the Convention is that nationals of any Member State enjoy the same protection as that afforded to nationals of that particular State and no requirement as to domicile or establishment may be imposed as a prerequisite "for the enjoyment of any industrial property rights". Irish patent law does provide that in proceedings under the legislation, the Controller must be provided with an address for service in the State[4] but such a provision is permitted under the Convention.[5] Foreign nationals are discriminated against under Irish patent law by the requirement that they must be represented by a duly authorised patent agent[6] and so cannot represent themselves. Again, however, this is permitted under the Convention.[7] Nationals of non-Member States enjoy the same protection as nationals of Member States if they are domiciled or have a real and effective industrial or commercial establishment in the territory of any one of the countries of the Union.[8] Article 4 of the Convention has important practical application and provides for priority rights. In relation to patents, a person who has filed a patent application in one Convention country is entitled, when filing in other Convention countries, to claim the priority date of the first application, provided that the subsequent applications are filed within twelve months of the first application.

[2.05] In calculating the twelve months, the actual day of filing is not included. If, in a country where priority is claimed, the twelve month period falls on an official holiday or a day upon which that national Patent Office is closed, the period is extended until the first following working day.[9] This twelve month period enables an applicant to file just a single patent application in a Convention country and delay the filing of further patent applications in other Convention countries without risking invalidity on the grounds, for example, of prior publication.[10] Since the later applications are regarded as if they had been filed on the same day as the first application, rights are preserved against third parties who may, for example, file a patent application in respect of the same invention in a Convention country between the priority date and the expiry of the twelve month period.

[2.06] Section 25 of the 1992 Act (which deals with priority rights) does not state the period to be twelve months but allows for the period to be prescribed.

---

4. Patents Rules 1992, r 92.
5. Article 2(3).
6. Patents Rules 1992, r 93.
7. Article 2(3).
8. Article 3.
9. Article 4C(3).
10. PA 1992, s 27(2).

This is sensible since priority periods have changed.[11] Rule 21(1) of the Patents Rules 1992 prescribes a priority period of twelve months.

[2.07] If one or more priority dates are claimed, this must be declared when filing the Convention application, indicating the date(s) and the country or countries in which the application(s) were made.[12] Rule 22 of the Patents Rules 1992 states that this information must be provided in the prescribed Form No 1 which is scheduled in the Rules and headed "Request for the grant of a patent". The filing number of each application from which priority is claimed must also be indicated but this can be done after the filing date if necessary.

[2.08] A certified copy of each priority application must also be filed together with an English language translation of such document, if appropriate.[13] The priority application is generally certified by the relevant national patent office. This certified priority document must be filed by the end of the sixteenth month from the earliest priority date with a maximum of a further one month extension available. A longer period of 21 months after the priority date is allowed for the translation of the priority document.[14] If the formalities for claiming the priority date are not complied with, it does not mean the loss of the application but the loss of the right of priority.[15]

[2.09] Section 26(2) of the 1992 Act allows for the claiming of multiple priority dates as provided in Article 4(F) of the Paris Convention. Priority dates may arise from applications filed in differing countries. Time limits run from the earliest priority date. It is also possible for multiple priorities to be claimed for any one claim. A priority date is not lost simply because an application contains one or more elements that were not included in the application from which priority is claimed. There must, however, be what is termed in the Convention as "unity of invention within the meaning of the law of the country". The right of priority will only extend to those elements which have been included in the priority application(s).[16]

[2.10] Irish law provides that:

> if certain elements of the invention for which priority is claimed do not appear among the claims formulated in the previous application, priority may nonetheless be granted if the documents of the previous application as a whole specifically disclosed such elements.[17]

[11.] Previously seven months.
[12.] Article 4D(1).
[13.] PA 1992, s 26(1) and r 22(2).
[14.] Rule 22(3).
[15.] Article 4D(4).
[16.] Section 26(3).
[17.] PA 1992, s 26(4); Article 4(H).

[2.11] Article 4(G) of the Paris Convention provides that where an application is shown to contain more than one invention, then it may be divided into one or more divisional applications as appropriate and the benefit of any priority will still apply. This is reflected in s 24 of the 1992 Act which also provides that, to benefit from a priority right, the subject matter must not extend beyond the content of the earlier application as filed. Certain countries, but not Ireland, operate a system which allows for what is termed an inventor's certificate. Such a certificate means that where the government of that country utilise the invention then the inventor would be rewarded if, for example, there were resultant savings to that government. As would be expected, these certificates were attractive in countries where most industry was in State control. Thus, for example, in the former Soviet Union, most applications by Soviet nationals were for inventors' certificates.[18] A priority right can be claimed from an inventor's certificate.

[2.12] The Convention does not prescribe a uniform duration for patent rights and leaves such to national laws. What is provided, however, is that the benefit of priority should not affect the duration.[19] Section 36 of the 1992 Act states the duration to be twenty years from "the date of filing of the patent application" and not from the priority date. This is one of the reasons for the tendency to file applications claiming priority very close to the twelve month anniversary date.

[2.13] The right of an inventor to be mentioned as such in a patent, although enshrined in the Convention,[20] is not a provision utilised very much in practice either under former legislation[21] or the current Act.[22]

[2.14] Although the grant of a patent may be refused in cases where the publication or exploitation of such would be contrary to public order or morality,[23] there are limitations on how broadly this can be construed. The Convention states that refusal or invalidity of a patent cannot occur "on the ground that the sale of the patented product or of a product obtained by means of a patented process is subject to restrictions or limitations resulting from the domestic law".[24] This is reflected in the 1992 Act by the proviso that exploitation shall not be deemed to be contrary to public order or morality only because it is prohibited by law. The former legislation did not contain such a

---

18. In 1968, 106,620 applications were made for inventors' certificates, only 158 of which were by foreign nationals. In the same year, there were only 3,808 patent applications.
19. Article 4 *bis*.
20. Article 4 *ter*.
21. PA 1964, s 21.
22. PA 1992, s 17.
23. PA 1992, s 10(a).
24. Article 4 *quater*.

proviso and, under such, the Irish Patents Office did refuse applications for inventions which were described as abortifacients for human use. In fact, s 15 of the 1964 Act empowered the Controller with a discretion in this regard and, as an alternative to refusal, an insertion could be made in the complete patent specification of a disclaimer in respect of use which would be in any manner contrary to law. No such discretion exists under s 10 of the 1992 Act and it remains to be seen as to what circumstances would lead to refusal of a patent on these grounds or indeed an application for revocation on the grounds that the subject matter is not patentable.[25]

[2.15] The Convention allows Member States to legislate for the granting of compulsory licences[26] and in limited cases, the forfeiture of the patent. The provisions are designed to prevent "abuses" of patent rights. Apart from a statement that a failure to work or possibly sufficiently work the patent, there is no indication as to what might constitute such an abuse. It was left to Member States to define abuse for themselves.[27] Section 39 of the 1964 Act specifically stated "the grounds deemed to constitute an abuse of monopoly rights". These grounds are repeated in s 70 of the 1992 Act but a statement that they are deemed to constitute an abuse is notably absent. It is now necessary to consider compulsory licences in the context of EU law and Article 31 of the TRIPS Agreement.

[2.16] The earliest time at which application for a compulsory licence can be made is three years from the publication of notice of grant[28] which in order to comply with the Convention must not be before the date of the grant of the patent or prior to a period of four years from the date of filing of the patent application. The proprietor of a patent may oppose the grant of a compulsory licence[29] and the Convention provides that the application "shall be refused if the patentee justifies his inaction by legitimate reasons".[30]

[2.17] Any compulsory licence which is granted must be non-exclusive and non-transferable.[31] The Convention also specifically disallows the granting of a sub-licence, except with that part of the enterprise or goodwill which exploits such licence.

---

25. Section 58(a).
26. Article 5.
27. Article 5A(2).
28. PA 1992, s 70(1).
29. PA 1992, s 73.
30. Article 5A(4).
31. PA 1992, s 70(3)(d); Article 5A(4).

[2.18] Although the Convention does allow Member States to provide for the forfeiture of a patent in cases where the grant of a compulsory licence would not be sufficient to prevent an abuse of the patent right, this provision is not part of Irish patent law.

[2.19] There is no requirement of any marking of goods by way of mention of a patent number in order to enforce patent rights[32] but the failure to include such will mean that damages or an account of profits will not be awarded against an innocent infringer.[33]

[2.20] Another important time period provided for in the Convention is a grace period of not less than six months within which to pay outstanding renewal fees.[34] Section 36(3) of the 1992 Act allows a maximum six month extension with additional fees payable for each month of extension.[35] Within two years from the date on which a patent lapses, application can be made to restore a patent.[36]

[2.21] Section 42(d) and (e) of the 1992 Act provides that the rights conferred by a patent do not extend to visiting vessels, aircraft or land vehicles. These rights must be reciprocated to Irish registered vessels, aircraft or land vehicles temporarily in another Member State.[37]

[2.22] The importation of a product obtained directly by a process which is the subject matter of a patent is an infringement.[38] Article 11 of the Convention imposes an obligation on Member States to grant temporary protection to patentable inventions exhibited at official or officially recognised international exhibitions. Since pre-application disclosure destroys the novelty in what might otherwise be a patentable invention, this provision allows for disclosure at certain exhibitions without prejudicing novelty.[39] Ireland is not a party to the Convention on International Exhibitions signed at Paris on 22 November 1928[40] but recognises exhibitions under the auspices of such as a non-prejudicial disclosure.

[2.23] Each Member State of the Convention must provide a Central Office to enable the public to obtain details of patents and to regularly publish an official

---

[32.] Article 5D.

[33.] PA 1992, s 49(1).

[34.] Article 5 *bis*.

[35.] Patents Rules 1992, Schedule I, Item No 15.

[36.] PA 1992, s 37.

[37.] Article 5 *ter*.

[38.] PA 1992, s 40(c); Article 5 *quater*.

[39.] Patents Rules 1992, r 5; PA 1992, s 12.

[40.] Amended and supplemented by Protocols of 10 May 1948, 16 November 1966 and 30 November 1972.

periodical paper. However, in relation to patents, the only information which it specifically states must be included in such a publication is the names of the owners of the patents granted with a short designation of the patented inventions.[41] The Patents Office Journal is published fortnightly. Prior to publication under s 28 of the 1992 Act, the only information obtainable from the Journal is the name of the applicant, the title of the invention, the date of application, the priority claimed and the number assigned to the application by the Irish Patents Office. An indication is also provided, by use of the letter "S", that an application is for a short term patent.

[2.24] Although the Convention does not deal with many substantive matters of patent law such as criteria for patentability, it has remained in place with most countries concluding separate and further agreements in addition to and not in contravention of the Convention.[42] Member countries include all of the major industrial countries of the world.[43]

STRASBOURG CONVENTION

[2.25] Ireland was the first country to ratify the Strasbourg Convention on The Unification of Certain Points of Substantive Law on Patents For Inventions[44] which came into force on 1 August 1980. There are just eleven Member States[45] and the Convention is only open for signature by Member States of the Council of Europe. The principal aim of the Convention was to create common criteria as to the patentability of inventions on issues such as novelty, inventive step and how to resolve conflicts concerning concurrent applications.

[2.26] Article 1 states:

> patents shall be granted for any inventions which are susceptible of industrial application, which are new and which involve an inventive step. An invention which does not comply with these conditions shall not be the subject of a valid patent.

The criteria for patentability are stated in s 9 of the 1992 Act and Article 52 of the European Patent Convention. However, the criteria in relation to a short term patent under s 63(4) are different, namely:

> an invention shall be patentable ... if it is new and susceptible of industrial application provided it is not clearly lacking an inventive step.

---

41. Article 12.
42. Article 19.
43. Including all EU countries.
44. 27 November 1963.
45. France, Denmark, Germany, Ireland, Italy, Liechtenstein, Luxembourg, Netherlands, Sweden, Switzerland and the United Kingdom.

The question which immediately arises is that of the apparent conflict with the above criteria, particularly since, under Article 1, a patent declared invalid because the invention does not comply with the conditions shall be considered invalid *ab initio*. In the Patents Bill 1991, as initiated, there was no requirement for an inventive step in respect of a short term patent. This would have meant that valid short term patents could have existed for an invention which was clearly obvious. Germany also operates a petty patent system which allows for a different standard of inventive step but these are identified as utility models and not patents.

[2.27] The exceptions to patentability in s 10 of the 1992 Act namely, inventions contrary to public order or morality and plant or animal varieties, are provided for in Article 2 of the Convention. The Convention provides no definition of invention but in Article 3 there is a broad interpretation of the words "susceptible of industrial application", namely, if the invention "can be made or used in any kind of industry including agriculture".[46] Article 12 allows for exclusion of horticultural and agricultural processes from patentability for a period of ten years but there was no such exclusion in the 1964 Act.

[2.28] Under the Convention, the term used to refer to the knowledge against which novelty and inventive step must be considered is "the state of the art"[47] which is broadly defined[48] and is not limited to the state of the art in Ireland. Thus universal novelty is required. Contracting States may also provide that the state of the art includes prior concurrent patent applications even though unpublished. This option has been exercised under s 11(3) of the 1992 Act for consideration of novelty only. Article 11(2) of the Paris Convention does not allow the exhibiting of an invention at an officially recognised international exhibition to extend the twelve month priority period which may be claimed. However, the Strasbourg Convention provides that such exhibiting may not be considered as disclosure, provided the patent application is filed within six months of such disclosure.[49] Another form of non-prejudicial disclosure and subject to the same six month time constraint is where there has been "an evident abuse in relation to the applicant or his legal predecessor".[50] Section 12(1)(a) of the 1992 Act does not use these words and, as a consequence, could possibly be considered as unnecessarily limiting. The words used, namely "a breach of confidence or agreement in relation to, or the unlawful obtaining of the matter constituting, the invention"[51]would presumably be considered as

---

46. PA 1992, s 14.
47. Article 4; PA 1992, s 11.
48. Article 4(2); PA 1992, s 11(2).
49. Article 4(4)(b); PA 1992, s 12(1)(b).
50. Article 4(4)(a).
51. PA 1992, s 12(1)(a).

evident abuses. The further and quite separate requirement that a patentable invention must also involve an inventive step[52] is judged by what is not obvious having regard to the state of the art.[53] However, as allowed for in the Convention, s 13 of the 1992 Act does not include unpublished prior concurrent applications as part of the state of the art in deciding whether or not there is an inventive step.

[2.29] In return for the monopoly rights granted by a State, the description of the invention "must disclose the invention in a manner sufficiently clear and complete for it to be carried out by a person skilled in the art".[54] The extent of the protection conferred by a patent shall be determined by the terms of the claims but the Convention requires that a patent application contain a description of the invention with the necessary drawings referred to therein and one or more claims defining the protection applied for.[55]

STRASBOURG AGREEMENT CONCERNING THE INTERNATIONAL PATENT CLASSIFICATION[56]

[2.30] A previous European Convention on the International Classification of Patents for Inventions was signed in 1954 and came into force in August 1955. Its objective was the adoption of a uniform system of classification for patents, inventor's certificates, utility models and utility certificates. This Convention was denounced by Ireland in a letter dated 24 March 1972 and the denunciation became operative on 7 October 1975. The Agreement of Strasbourg Concerning International Patent Classification entered into force on 7 October 1975, thus replacing the earlier Convention. The latest edition of the classification is the Sixth Edition which became operative on 1 January 1995.

[2.31] In the foreword, it is stated that the classification has as its primary purpose the establishment of an effective search tool for the retrieval of patent documents by Patent Offices and other users in order to establish the novelty and evaluate the inventive step (including the assessment of technical advance and useful results or utility) of patent applications. The classification contains eight sections indicated by the letters A-H and these sections are divided into classes which are themselves further divided into sub-classes and grouped.[57] Along with the United Kingdom and a number of other countries, Ireland has declared that it does not undertake to include certain classification symbols on

---

[52.] Different criteria apply to a short term patent: PA 1992, s 63(4).
[53.] Article 5; PA 1992, s 13.
[54.] Article 8(2); PA 1992, s 19(1).
[55.] Article 8(1); PA 1992, s 18(2).
[56.] 24 March 1971.
[57.] See Guide, *Survey Of Classes And Summary Of Main Groups* (WIPO).

documents laid open for public inspection and in notices relating thereto.[58] Parties to the Strasbourg Agreement include Japan, the United States of America, Australia and all EU countries except Greece.

EUROPEAN PATENT CONVENTION

[2.32] The European Patent Convention (EPC) was signed by Ireland and 14 other European countries in Munich on 5 October 1973 but was not ratified by Ireland until 1 May 1992 pursuant to the 1992 Act, the effective date was 1 August 1992. There are now 18 Member States, namely all of the EU countries, Switzerland, Liechtenstein and Monaco. There are also five Non-Contracting States to the EPC but which may still be designated by virtue of extension agreements. These countries are Slovenia, Lithuania, Latvia, Albania and Romania. The effect of such designation is to extend the protection conferred by a European patent to these countries.

[2.33] The principal objective of the EPC is to enable a patent applicant to secure patent rights in a number of European countries by way of a single application and prosecution before a centralised office, the European Patent Office (EPO). Prior to the EPC, a separate application had to be made and prosecuted before the national Patent Office of each country in which patent protection was required. If protection was required in a large number of countries, the procedure was both expensive and cumbersome.

[2.34] Instead of a plurality of applications, the EPC enables the filing of a single application which, by way of designation, can cover all Contracting States. The EPC can be utilised by non-Contracting States and in fact among the major users are US and Japanese corporations. Prior to 1 August 1992, an Irish individual or entity could file an application at the EPO but any person wishing to secure patent protection in Ireland had to file a separate patent application at the Irish Patents Office. Now, there is a choice of filing either at the Irish Patents Office or before the EPO, designating Ireland. The national patent laws of Contracting States remain in place.

[2.35] Although the EPC enables the filing and prosecution to grant of a single application, ultimately the grant of what is called a European patent[59] does not result in one unitary patent having federal effect but a bundle of patents. The effect of s 119 of the 1992 Act is that a European patent designating the State is treated in the same way as if it were an Irish patent granted directly by the Irish Patents Office. There are also instances where an EPC application designating

---

58. Article 4(4)(i).
59. Article 2(1).

the State can (on compliance with certain conditions) be converted into what is effectively an Irish patent application.[60]

Procedure Before The European Patent Office

[2.36] The EPO has its seat in Munich with branch offices in the Hague and Berlin. European patent applications can be filed at any of these locations or at the national Patent Office of a Contracting State. In this way, European Patent applications, except divisional patent applications, can be filed at the Irish Patents Office.[61] There is also an EPO sub-office in Vienna but applications cannot be filed through that office.

[2.37] A European patent application can be filed in any of the three official working languages of the EPO (English, French or German)[62] and is first considered in the Hague. The receiving section initially examines whether or not the filing requirements have been met[63] and as to formal requirements.[64] Subsequently, a novelty search is carried out relating to the state of the known art and a search report issues.[65] The search report contains a classification in accordance with the Strasbourg Convention.[66] The search report is transmitted to the applicant together with copies of any cited documents. Under Article 82, a European patent application must relate to one invention only or to a group of inventions so linked as to form a single general inventive concept. If it is found that this requirement has not been met, a search report will be drawn up only for the invention (or group) first claimed. Further search fees are payable in respect of a search for each additional invention.

[2.38] Publication of a European patent application takes place as soon as possible after 18 months from filing or from the earliest priority date if priority is claimed.[67] This publication contains the description, the claims, the abstract and any drawings as filed. Also published in an annex are the search report and, on the front cover, the abstract in so far as these are available at the time of termination of the preparations for publication.

[2.39] Details of the States designated are specified in the published application. Earlier publication can be requested but there cannot be a postponement. To prevent publication, it is necessary to formally withdraw the application or have

---

[60]. PA 1992, s 122.
[61]. PA 1992, s 120(7).
[62]. Article 14.
[63]. Article 90.
[64]. Article 91.
[65]. Article 92.
[66]. Paras **[2.30]** and **[2.31]** *supra.*
[67]. Article 93.

such finally refused before termination of the technical preparations for publication. Upon publication, there is no opposition procedure but any third party may submit written observations concerning the patentability of the invention. The third party has no right of audience and is not officially informed as to the effect of the observations. However, by inspecting the file the third party can determine the effects of observations and submit futher observations for as long as the application is pending. Under s 56 of the 1992 Act, damages can be recovered for infringement from the date of publication,[68] subject to translation requirements where appropriate.

[2.40] At the time of filing the application, examination is automatically requested. However, examination cannot commence until the examination fee has been paid. The examination fee must be paid within six months of the date on which the publication of the search report is mentioned in the European Patent Bulletin. Substantive examination then takes place and the examiner will consider whether or not the invention meets the requirements of the EPC[69] including, but not limited to, novelty and inventive step[70] and as to whether or not the invention is patentable subject matter.[71] The applicant is invited to make 'observations' and amendments can be made to the description, claims and drawings. If the examining division decides to grant a patent, it informs the applicant of the text on which grant will be based and the applicant must indicate approval or otherwise of the text within a specified period. Grant and printing fees must then be paid and a translation of the claims into the two further official languages must also be filed. Grant is not effective until the date on which it is published in the European Patent Bulletin.[72] From publication, there follows a nine month period within which any person may give notice of opposition. The opposition applies to the European patent in all of the Contracting States in which the patent has effect.[73]

[2.41] The grounds of opposition are stated in Article 100 and are as follows:

    (a) that the invention is not susceptible of industrial application, is not new and/or does not involve an inventive step;

    (b) that the invention is not patentable subject matter;[74]

[68.] Articles 64 & 67.
[69.] Article 96.
[70.] Article 52(1).
[71.] Article 52(2).
[72.] Article 97(4).
[73.] Article 99.
[74.] Article 52 & Article 53(b).

(c) the publication or exploitation of the invention would be contrary to public order or morality; [75]

(d) insufficient disclosure of the invention;

(e) the subject matter of the European patent extends beyond the content of the application as filed or, if the patent was granted on a divisional application, goes beyond the contents of the parent patent application as filed.

The opposition division of the EPO considers the opposition and again invites observations from the parties "as often as necessary".[76]

[2.42] During opposition, the patentee may be invited to amend the description, claims and drawings. The claims of the patent may not be amended in such a way as to extend the protection conferred. A third party may intervene in opposition proceedings if it can prove that infringement proceedings relating to an opposed European patent have been instituted against that party or that the owner of an opposed European patent has requested that the third party cease alleged infringement of the patent and that proceedings have been instituted before a Court ruling that there is no infringement.[77] The opposition division may revoke the patent, reject the opposition or maintain the patent in amended form. Appeal structures are in place in respect of refusal of the application at first instance as well as opposition proceedings. The appeal is to a Board of Appeal and must be filed within two months of the date of notification of the decision appealed from.[78]

[2.43] After publication of the mention of grant, a European patent starts its life in each of the Contracting States which have been designated[79] and has the same rights as those conferred by a national patent granted in a designated State.[80] Infringement of a European patent is dealt with under national law. Most countries require the filing of a translation of the patent into one of its official languages. The minimum period which must be allowed for such a translation is three months. Rule 83 of the Irish Patents Rules 1992 provides for a six month period and payment of a fee. Where a translation is not filed by the due date, the European patent shall be deemed to be void *ab initio* in that State.[81]

[75.] Article 53(a).
[76.] Article 101(2).
[77.] Article 105.
[78.] Article 108.
[79.] Article 64.
[80.] PA 1992, s 119.
[81.] Article 65(3); PA 1992, s 119(7).

[2.44] Under Article 63, the term of a European patent is 20 years from the date of filing of the application. A Contracting State can extend the term of a European patent under the same conditions as those applying to its national patents in order to take into account a state of war or similar emergency conditions affecting that State. This Article has been revised by an Act of 17 December 1991 and allows for the possibility of an extended term of duration of European patents whose subject matter is a product or a process of manufacturing a product or a use of a product which has to undergo an administrative authorisation procedure required by law before it can be put on the market.[82]

[2.45] Under EC Regulation No 1768/92 of 18 June 1992, concerning the Creation of a Supplementary Protection Certificate (SPC) for Medicinal Products, which has an effective date of 2 January 1993, EU Member States must allow for the duration of patents for medicinal products to be extended for a period equal to that which has elapsed between the date of filing the patent application and the date of grant of the first marketing authorisation in the EU, less five years. The maximum period for which this supplementary protection certificate can be granted is five years. On 23 July 1996, the Council of Ministers adopted Regulation EC/1610/96 concerning the creation of a supplementary protection certificate (SPC) for plant protection products, eg herbicides, fungicides and insecticides.

[2.46] In order to maintain a European patent application in force, it is necessary to pay annual renewal fees. Under Article 86, these fees are due in respect of the third year and each subsequent year, calculated from the date of filing of the application. The obligation to pay renewal fees terminates with the payment of the renewal fee due in respect of the year in which the mention of the grant of the European patent is published. After grant, a European patent is subject to payment of national annuities in the countries in which the patent is to be maintained.[83]

[2.47] A European patent application may be filed by any national or legal person or any body equivalent to a legal person by virtue of the national law of the applicant's country.[84] There is no requirement for nationality of or residence in a Contracting country. The right to a European patent belongs to the inventor or his successor in title.[85] If the inventor is an employee, the right to a European patent is determined by the law of the State in which the employee is mainly

---

[82] OJEPO 1-2/1992, p 7.
[83] Patents Rules 1992, r 34.
[84] Article 58.
[85] Article 60.

employed. If this cannot be established, the applicable law is that of the State in which the employer has its place of business to which the employee is attached. The inventor(s) must be identified and if the applicant is not the inventor or is not the sole inventor, there must be a statement indicating how the right to apply arose.[86] A European patent application can be assigned and such an assignment must be in writing.[87] In order to be effective, an assignment of a European patent application must be recorded in the EPO. After grant, assignment and recordal of such is governed by national laws.[88] A European patent application may be licensed in whole or in part for the whole or part of the territories of the designated Contracting States.[89]

Unpatentable Subject Matter

[2.48] It is specifically stated in Article 53[90] of the EPC that European patents shall not be granted in respect of:

(a) inventions the publication or exploitation of which would be contrary to "*ordre public*" or morality, provided that the exploitation shall not be deemed to be so contrary merely because it is prohibited by law or regulation in some or all of the Contracting States; and

(b) plant or animal varieties or essentially biological processes for the production of plants or animals; this provision does not apply to microbiological processes or the products thereof.

Article 52(4) also denies patentability to methods for treatment of the human or animal body by surgery or therapy and diagnostic methods practised on the human or animal body. Such methods are not considered to be susceptible of industrial application. However, products, in particular substances or compositions, for use in any of these methods are patentable sometimes even if these products were already known *per se* for use in any different method.

Criteria For Patentability

[2.49] European patents are granted for any inventions which are susceptible of industrial application, which are new and which involve an inventive step.[91] The following are not regarded as inventions:[92]

(a) discoveries, scientific theories and mathematical methods;

---

86. Article 81.
87. Article 72.
88. PA 1992, s 85.
89. Article 73.
90. PA 1992, s 10.
91. Article 52(1); PA 1992, s 9(1).
92. Article 52(2); PA 1992, s 9(2).

(b) aesthetic creations;

(c) schemes, rules and methods for performing mental acts, playing games or doing business, and programs for computers;

(d) presentations of information.

These exclusions only apply to the extent to which a European patent application or patent relates to such subject matter or activities as such.[93]

Computer Programs

[2.50] Originally, it was considered that an invention would be unpatentable if the novelty and inventive step lay completely in the computer program involved. Revised EPO guidelines[94] now adopt a more liberal approach. It is stated that a computer program claimed by itself or as a record on a carrier is unpatentable, irrespective of its content and the situation is not normally changed when the computer program is loaded into a known computer. However, program controlled machines and program controlled manufacturing and control processes are provided as examples of normally patentable subject matter. The combination of a known computer and a new program loaded into it could be patentable if the program causes the computer to operate in a new way from a technical point of view. What is required is a technical contribution to the known art and the essential ingredient in decisions before the EPO has been "technical effect". In the *Vicom* decision[95] in 1986, the EPO Technical Board of Appeal considered an application relating to a method and apparatus for improving the quality and speeding up of the processing of picture information. There was no novel end product but a process for manipulating electrical signals representing the picture in accordance with steps expressed mathematically. The Board decided that:

(a) even if the idea underlying an invention may be considered to reside in a mathematical method, a claim directed to a technical process in which the method is used, does not seek protection for the mathematical method as such; and

(b) an invention which would be patentable in accordance with conventional patentable criteria should not be excluded from protection by the mere fact that for its implementation, modern technical means in the form of a computer program are used.

Decisive to this decision was the technical contribution the invention as a whole made to the known art.

---

93. Article 52(3); PA 1992, s 9(3).
94. C-IV 2.3.
95. [1987] EPOR 66.

[2.51] The *Vicom* application was accepted with claims directed to a "method of digitally filtering data". In the *Koch & Sterzel Application*,[96] the EPO Technical Board of Appeal considered the patentability of an x-ray apparatus controlled by a computer program to ensure optimum exposure with sufficient protection against overloading of the x-ray tube within a given routine. It was held that it was not necessary "to weigh up the technical and non-technical features of a claim". A mix of such features may be patentable if they interact so as to solve a technical problem. However, a number of IBM applications have been refused because they related to non-technical subject matter, namely, document abstracting and retrieving,[97] linguistic expression processing[98] and spell checking.[99]

Micro-Biological Processes

[2.52] Article 53(b) which excludes patentability for plant or animal varieties or essentially biological processes for the production of plants or animals but permits patenting of microbiological processes or the products thereof is almost identical to the wording in Article 2(b) of the Strasbourg Convention 1963. Micro-organisms as such may be patented by a European patent. The words 'microbiological processes' include traditional processes using micro-organisms (but not essentially biological processes) and techniques of genetic engineering. Among patentable inventions are genetically engineered micro-organisms such as bacteria and viruses. Essentially biological processes would include processes such as sexual reproduction. If the invention concerns a microbiological process or the product thereof and involves the use of a micro-organism which is not available to the public and which cannot be described in the European patent application in such a manner as to enable the invention to be carried out by a person skilled in the art, a culture of the micro-organism must be deposited with a recognised depositary institute. The Institute must hold the status of international depositary authority under the Budapest Treaty on the International Recognition of the Deposit of Micro-organisms for the purpose of Patent Procedure (1977).[100]

Plant And Animal Varieties

[2.53] The unpatentability of plant varieties is due essentially to the existence of an alternative form of protection under the Convention for the Protection of New Varieties of Plants (UPOV - *Union Pour La Protection Des Obtentions*

96. [1988] 2 EPOR 72.
97. T22/85 - IBM/System for Abstracting Document.
98. T52/85 - IBM/Linguistic Expression Processing.
99. T121/85 - IBM/System for Spell Checking.
100. Patents Rules 1992 r 14.

Végétales), 1961 as revised.[101] The practice of the EPO is to construe exclusions from patentability narrowly. Under the UPOV Convention, a new variety must be distinct, uniform and stable. Hence, samples within the variety must be clearly distinguishable from previously known varieties, different samples within the variety must be similar and the variety must breed true over a number of generations. If these conditions are not complied with, then the EPO is inclined to accept such as not being a plant variety and hence as patentable and only plants in the genetically fixed form of a plant variety are excluded from patentability.[102]

[2.54] Animal varieties are not patentable but this does not imply that a European patent cannot be granted for an animal. In the US, a patent was granted to Harvard University in relation to mice in which a particular gene had been introduced in order that the mice would develop a tumour. These were sold to laboratories as an aid to cancer research. The Examining Division in the EPO rejected the corresponding European application[103] on the grounds that animals are not patentable. The Technical Board of Appeal reversed the decision and sent the case back to the Examining Division to reconsider whether the application fell within the specific Article 53 exception including as to whether or not the invention was contrary to public order or morality. The Examining Division decided that the invention did not fall within any of the specific exclusions and allowed the patent but at the same time, decided that the invention assisted the research into cancer, had no real threat to the environment and it would reduce the overall level of animal suffering by reducing the number of animals required in conventional laboratory testing. It was stressed that in other cases of transgenic animals, a different decision might be reached.

Novelty

[2.55] Article 52 of the EPC repeats Article 1 of the Strasbourg Convention and states that European patents shall be granted for any inventions which are susceptible of industrial application, which are new and which involve an inventive step. An invention is considered new if it does not form part of the state of the art.[104] The state of the art is everything made available to the public on a universal basis prior to the filing/priority date.[105] Even prior dated unpublished European patent applications are considered to be part of the state

---

[101.] Plant Varieties (Proprietary Rights) Act 1980, (Commencement) Order 1981 (SI 22/1981). See para **[3.21]** *et seq.*

[102.] *Propagating Material/Ciba Geigy* [1984] OJEPO 112. *Hybrid Plants/Lubrizol* [1990] EPOR 173.

[103.] *Harvard/Onco Mouse* [1990] EPOR 501.

[104.] Article 54(1).

[105.] Article 54(2).

of the art in so far as the Contracting States designated in the later application are the same as those designated in the earlier application.[106] Again, in a similar fashion to the Strasbourg Convention, the EPC allows for certain "non-prejudicial disclosure" provided such disclosure does not occur more than six months prior to the filing of the European patent application.[107] These are as a consequence of:

(a) an evident abuse in relation to the applicant or his legal predecessor, or

(b) the fact that the applicant or his legal predecessor displayed the invention at an official, or officially recognised, international exhibition falling within the terms of the Convention of Paris on International Exhibitions of 22 November 1928, as revised on 30 November 1972.

In relation to (b), the applicant must, at the time of application, state that there has been such a display and, within four months of application, produce a certificate from the authority responsible for the protection of industrial property at that exhibition.

Priority Rights

[2.56] In keeping with the Paris Convention for the Protection of Industrial Property, a European patent application may claim priority[108] by means of a declaration of priority to be lodged on filing. The date and country of the basic application must be identified. Priority may also be claimed from an earlier European patent application. This is called internal priority.

Privilege and Immunities of the European Patent Organisation

[2.57] Under the European Patent Organisation (Designation and Immunities) Order 1996[109] the privileges and immunities of the European Patent Organisation under the EPC and the Protocol on the privileges and immunities of the European Patent Organisation have been implemented pursuant to the Diplomatic Relations and Immunities Acts 1967 and 1976.

PATENT CO-OPERATION TREATY

[2.58] The Patent Co-Operation Treaty (PCT) was concluded in Washington on 19 June 1970 and ratified by Ireland with effect from 1 August 1992. Under Article 1 of the PCT which is entitled "Establishment of a Union", it is stated

---

106. Article 54(3) and 54(4).
107. Article 55; PA 1992, s 12(1).
108. Article 87; PA 1992, s 25(1).
109. SI 392/1996.

that the Union is for co-operation in the filing, searching and examination of applications for the protection of inventions and for rendering special technical services. The Union is called The International Patent Co-Operation Union. The word "international" is somewhat of a misnomer. There are over 90 members including all EU countries but the PCT does not result in any international patent. The PCT is administered by the World Intellectual Property Organisation (WIPO) based in Geneva. The PCT is divided into two "chapters" and enables the filing of a single application designating as many Member States as desired.

PCT - Chapter I

[2.59] The 'international application' only needs to be filed in a single language and at a single Patent Office which is called the receiving office.[110]

[2.60] Priority can be claimed under the Paris Convention for the Protection of Industrial Property.[111] Subject to compliance with certain formalities, the receiving office accords as the international filing date, the date of receipt of the international application.[112] The receiving office then transmits a copy of the application to the International Bureau of WIPO and a further copy to the International Searching Authority.[113] The objective of the International Searching Authority is to discover any relevant prior art[114] and the search is made on the basis of the claims, with due regard to the description and any drawings. A search report is drawn up listing all of the documents which have any bearing on the patentability of the invention. The search report is sent to the applicant and the International Bureau of WIPO. In the light of the search report, an applicant has a single opportunity to voluntarily amend the claims.[115]

[2.61] Approximately 18 months after the priority date, the International Bureau publishes the specification as filed and the search report and forwards the application and the search report to the National Patent Offices of each Member State designated, unless that requirement has been waived. The application now becomes, in effect, a number of separate patent applications, one in each designated country, and these are prosecuted before the National Patent Offices or the EPO. Entry into the national phases must take place within twenty months of the priority date or the filing date, whichever is the earlier.[116] It is also

---

110. Article 10.
111. Article 8.
112. Article 11.
113. Article 12.
114. Article 15(2).
115. Article 19.
116. Article 22.

possible to apply for a European patent through the filing of an international patent application under the PCT.

PCT - Chapter II

[2.62] If desired, the Chapter II phase must be requested within nineteen months of the priority date, or the filing date of the PCT application, whichever is the earlier.

[2.63] Chapter II provides a system that allows patent applicants in countries which have agreed to be bound by this chapter to request preliminary examination by an International Preliminary Examining Authority. This examination, which is stated to be non-binding, is as to novelty, inventive step and whether the claimed invention is industrially applicable.[117]

[2.64] Only one country, namely Spain, has declared that it is not bound by Chapter II. Liechtenstein and Switzerland made such declarations which have now been withdrawn. The US had also made such a declaration which has also been withdrawn.[118]

[2.65] The applicant will receive at least one written opinion listing any objections and is given a time period within which a response may be filed, together with any amendments, if appropriate. Within the prescribed time period, the examination report is drawn up.

[2.66] The examination report is transmitted to the applicant and to the International Bureau. Having elected for Chapter II, an applicant can enter the national/regional phase within 30 months of the priority date.

[2.67] The advantages of the PCT system are that, at a relatively low cost, it can delay the considerable expense of filing national or regional applications. This is important in many cases where cashflow problems arise in the early stages of a new product's life cycle. Translation costs do not arise until the national and/or regional filings.[119]

[2.68] It is also the experience of many patent practitioners that applicants may decide on foreign patent applications towards the very end of the twelve month priority period. In some cases, so late that translation(s) within the time scale allowed would not be possible. In these cases, the PCT system is a valuable tool. Ultimately, if applications are pursued, the PCT system does create an additional expenditure but there has been a deferral of patenting expenses, ie up to 30 months (Chapter II) as opposed to the normal twelve month priority

---

[117.] Article 33.
[118.] With effect from 1 July 1987.
[119.] Article 39.

period. Forbairt, which is the Irish State body responsible for funding certain patenting programs often utilises the PCT system.

Designation

[2.69] Under Article 45(2) of the PCT, it is stated that:

> the national law of the said designated or elected State may provide that any designation or election of such State in the International application shall have the effect of an indication of the wish to obtain a regional patent under the regional patent treaty.

One such regional patent treaty is the EPC. Ireland, together with France, Greece, Belgium, Italy, the Netherlands and Monaco have opted for this provision and so have excluded the grant of national patents on PCT applications. If patent protection for Ireland is desired via a PCT route, this can only be done by designating Ireland in a European patent application. It is not possible to apply for a national Irish patent by filing an international patent application under the PCT.[120]

COMMUNITY PATENT CONVENTION

[2.70] By way of amendment to Article 29 of the Irish Constitution and following a Referendum,[121] the Eleventh Amendment of the Constitution Act 1992 introduced as Article 29.4.6° a provision that:

> The State may ratify the Agreement relating to Community Patents drawn up between the Member States of the Communities and done at Luxembourg on the 15th day of December, 1989.[122]

The Community Patent Convention (CPC) has been signed by all Members States of the EU and is open to accession by all States in the future becoming members of the EU. The CPC is not yet in force and requires ratification by all Member States. Under Article 142 of the EPC, it is provided that any group of Contracting States, which has provided by a special agreement that a European patent granted for those States has a unitary character throughout their territories, may provide that a European patent may only be granted jointly in respect of all of those States.

[2.71] The entry into force of the CPC has been identified by the Commission of European Communities as necessary for the completion of the internal market under the EEC Treaty. The objective is to remove the distortion of competition which may result from the territorial aspect of national patent rights. Under the

---

120. PA 1992, s 127(1).
121. Held on 18 June 1992.
122. 89/695/EEC.

CPC, this is achieved by establishing a community patent system and whereby a European patent granted by the EPO will have a unitary and autonomous character throughout the EU. As stated in the White Paper on the Treaty of European Union, the introduction of a Community patent system as envisaged by the Agreement would have a number of consequences:

- Community patents would be granted on the basis of a single application for each such patent made to the European Patent Office in Munich;

- Annual renewal fees would be payable in a single payment to that office;

- A single patent licence agreement for a Community patent could be established for the internal market under the EEC Treaty; and

- Community patents would be subject to the common system of law set down in the agreement.

[2.72] The unitary effect of a Community patent means that it could be granted, transferred, revoked or allowed to lapse only in respect of the whole of the EU.[123] Under the current CPC, infringement is a matter to be tried in national courts[124] although application for revocation of a Community patent is filed at the EPO.[125]

[2.73] There have been a number of resolutions to the CPC, two of which have recognised the inconsistencies that can result from issues of infringement of a Community patent being decided in national courts. The resolution on the centralisation in each Contracting State of jurisdiction in actions for infringement of Community patents calls for judges experienced in such actions in all Contracting States and centralisation of first instance jurisdiction to guarantee that actions will be dealt with by judges experienced in this field. An example of the problems which can arise can be seen in the *Epilady* case[126] where the English Patents Court refused an interlocutory injunction because of the absence of an arguable case that there was an infringement and in an identical action in Germany, infringement was held to exist. The English Court of Appeal reversed the decision and granted the injunction taking cognisance of the German decision when deciding as to whether or not there was an arguable case. The German courts on appeal removed the injunction. Then at the full hearing, the English Patents Court held there was no infringement but the

---

[123] Article 2(2).
[124] Article 69.
[125] Article 56.
[126] *Improver Corp v Remington Consumer Products Ltd* [1989] RPC 69.

German court took the opposite view. In opposition proceedings before the EPO, it was then held that the patent be revoked.

[2.74] At a diplomatic conference in Brussels in 1985, agreement was reached to provide for appeals from "Community Patent Courts" at first instance, such as the Irish High Court, to be taken to a common Patent Appeal Court (COPAC).[127] A further diplomatic conference in Luxembourg in December 1989 concluded a package of documents concerning the common Patent Appeal Court and the protocol on the settlement of litigation concerning the infringement and validity of community patents. These form the Agreement relating to community patents and which are identified in the new Article 29.4.6° of the Irish Constitution.

[2.75] The creation of a centralised litigation procedure at this appellate level caused constitutional problems because effectively, decisions relating to property rights in the State would be dealt with by a court not established and judges not appointed in a manner provided for under the Constitution.[128] Article 29.4.5° of the Constitution provides that:

> No provision of this Constitution invalidates laws enacted, acts done or measures adopted by the State which are necessitated by the obligations of membership of the European Union or of the Communities or prevents laws enacted, acts done or measures adopted by the European Union or the Communities or by institutions thereof, or by bodies competent under the Treaties establishing the Communities, from having the force of law in the State.

[2.76] However, the CPC is an intergovernmental agreement outside the legal framework of the European Community treaties and would not fall within the ambit of this Article, hence the need for the Referendum and the Eleventh Amendment of the Constitution Act 1992.

BUDAPEST TREATY

[2.77] The Budapest Treaty on the International Recognition of the Deposit of Micro-Organisms for the Purposes of Patent Procedure (1977) has not yet been ratified by Ireland. The Treaty entered into force for the first five countries, ie, Bulgaria, France, Hungary, Japan and the United States on 19 August 1980 and is now in force in over 20 countries including the United Kingdom. The basis of the Treaty is that Member States are bound to recognise the deposit of a micro-organism with any depositary institution which has the status of international depositary authority under the Treaty. Such recognition includes the recognition of the fact and date of the deposit as indicated by the international depositary

---

[127.] Protocol on the Settlement of Litigation Concerning the Infringement and Validity of Community Patents.

[128.] Constitution of Ireland, Article 34.

authority as well as the recognition of the fact that what is furnished as a sample is a sample of the deposited micro-organism.

[2.78] On 26 August 1980, the EPO filed the declaration specified in Article 9 of the Treaty. This declaration states that the EPO accepts the obligation of recognition provided for in Article 3(1)(a) of the Treaty, the obligations concerning the requirements in Article 3(2) and all the effects of the provisions of the Treaty and the Regulations applicable to inter-governmental industrial property organisations.

[2.79] Although not yet ratified, the Treaty is referred to in rule 14 of the Patents Rules 1992 and which also refers to certain forms provided for by the Regulations under the Treaty. Rule 14 provides for the depositing of a culture of a micro-organism with a depositary institution and the recognition of such. The definition of a depositary institute under rule 14(21) means the State will almost certainly recognise the status of all international depositary authorities established under the Treaty because such would:

    (a) carry out the function of receiving, accepting and storing micro-organisms and the furnishing of samples thereof; and

    (b) conduct its affairs in so far as they relate to the carrying out of those functions in an objective and impartial manner.

TRIPS

[2.80] TRIPS is the acronym used to refer to the Agreement on Trade Related Aspects of Intellectual Property Rights. TRIPS is part of the World Trade Organisation Agreement (WTO Agreement) which was formally signed by the State on 15 April 1994 and ratified on 15 November 1994. Following Council Decision No 94/900/EEC on 30 December 1994, the EU, Ireland and other EU Member States deposited instruments of ratification. The WTO Agreement including TRIPS, entered into force on 1 January 1995 although Article 65(1) of TRIPS does contain a one year transitional grace period.

[2.81] The objective of TRIPS as part of the negotiations to revise GATT and as stated in the preamble, is to reduce distortions and impediments to international trade by promoting effective and adequate protection of intellectual property rights and by ensuring that measures and procedures to enforce intellectual property rights do not themselves become barriers to legitimate trade. This is achieved in the main by identifying minimum standards to which each State must adhere. The provisions dealing with patents are contained in Part II, s 5 (Articles 27-34) of TRIPS.

[2.82] In general, the Irish Patents Act 1992 is in compliance with the minimum thresholds imposed by TRIPS except in respect of the working requirements and compulsory licensing provisions. Article 27.1 of TRIPS states that "patents shall be available and patent rights enjoyable without discrimination as to the place of invention, the field of technology and whether products are imported or locally produced". This was considered by the Irish High Court in *Allen and Hanburys Limited and Glaxo Group Limited v The Controller and Clonmel Healthcare Limited*[129] and it was conceded that s 42 of the 1964 Act which allowed for a compulsory licence in respect of certain stated categories of invention, was indeed discriminatory. Section 70(3)(f) of the 1992 Act is also a provision that is specific to patents relating to food and medicine in identifying that, in settling the terms of a compulsory licence for such:

> the Controller shall endeavour to secure that food and medicine shall be available to the public at the lowest prices consistent with the proprietors of patents deriving reasonable remuneration having regard to the nature of the invention.

Article 31 of TRIPS does allow for a compulsory licence, ie use without authorisation of the right holder but with certain in-built safeguards. Under Article 31(b), except in the case of a national emergency, other circumstances of extreme urgency or public non-commercial use, it is necessary for a licence to be sought from the right holder on reasonable commercial terms and conditions and that such efforts have not been successful within a reasonable period of time. Although Article 31(k) does allow the provision in Article 31(b) to be negated where use is required to remedy a practice which has been determined as anti-competitive, it is readily apparent that the provisions allowing for a compulsory licence in s 70 of the 1992 Act are broader than those allowed for under TRIPS.

[2.83] Article 34 deals with the burden of proof in the case of process patents for new products and is already reflected in s 46 of the 1992 Act in providing that the same product when produced without the consent of the patent owner shall, in the absence of proof to the contrary, be deemed to have been obtained by the patented process. In Article 34, this can arise in circumstances where either:

(a) the product obtained by the patented process is new; or

(b) there is a substantial likelihood that the identical product was made by the process and the owner of the patent has been unable through reasonable efforts to determine the process actually used.

[2.84] Patentable subject matter is identified in Article 27 as requiring inventions to be new, involve an inventive step and be capable of industrial application.[130] The rights which must be conferred by a patent in Article 28 are already in place in Irish law by virtue of s 40 of the 1992 Act.

---

129. [1997] FSR 1.

130. PA 1992, s 9(1).

Chapter 3

The Patents Act 1992 - Patentability

INTRODUCTION

[3.01] The Patents Act 1992 ('the 1992 Act') came into operation on 1 August 1992 under the Patents Act 1992 (Commencement) Order 1992[1] signed on 17 June 1992 by the then Minister for Industry and Commerce, Desmond O'Malley. The 1992 Act enabled ratification of the EPC and PCT and subject to the transitional provisions, repealed the Patents Act 1964 ('the 1964 Act')[2] and the Patents (Amendment) Act 1966.[3] Unlike the 1964 Act, there is no definition of invention. There are, however, new criteria as to what is patentable. There is no longer an opposition procedure and the patent term under the new Act is 20 years[4] with no provision for an extended term. The Act also introduces the completely new concept of a short term patent. Also new to Irish law is the payment of annual maintenance fees on patent applications and a broader definition of infringement which embraces indirect use of an invention. From a practical point of view, the Controller also hoped to streamline the system for examination and effectively remove the backlog of patent applications which on 1 August 1992 was approximately five to six years in arrears. This backlog inevitably will be removed because of the greatly reduced number of Irish national patent applications as a consequence of ratification of the EPC.[5] In addition, the 1992 Act also imposes a minimal obligation on the Irish Patents Office towards examination.

[3.02] It should be noted that the Irish draftsman did not copy or even mimic closely the UK Patents Act 1977. The UK Patents Act 1977, in s 130(7) provides that many sections of the Act are framed so as to have, as nearly as practicable, the same effect in the UK as the corresponding provisions of the EPC, CPC and the PCT have in the territories to which those conventions apply. The effect of this is that in interpreting those sections identified, due weight must be given to the relevant provisions of the EPC, CPC and PCT and to their *travaux preparatoires* such as official minutes of the conferences which led to

---

1. SI 181/1992.
2. SI 12/1964.
3. SI 9/1966.
4. Previously 16 years under the 1964 Act.
5. In 1991, there were 4,580 patent applications filed in the Irish Patents Office. In 1995 there were only 990 applications filed, of which 628 applications were for short term patents.

the wording adopted.[6] This was deemed necessary because the UK draftsman added their own gloss and altered the wording to put such into UK statute format. No similar catch-all provision is contained in the 1992 Act and the Irish draftsman closely followed the wording of the EPC and CPC. Thus, while decisions in the English courts on the interpretation of corresponding sections in the UK Act will be of importance, the Irish courts may instead look to decisions in other European countries which have legislation that in many cases is more likely to correspond to that of our own. In *Wavin Pipes Limited v The Hepworth Iron Company Limited*,[7] Costello J observed that "it had obviously been found helpful to base a great deal of Irish patent law on the law as it had evolved in England both as a result of judicial decisions and statutory enactment" but was prepared to find that differences did exist in the revocation sections of the old British Patents Act 1949 and the Irish Patents Act 1964. In addition, Costello J obtained assistance in the interpretation of the 1964 Act from an examination of the parliamentary history of the Act. In doing so, he followed the Supreme Court decision in *Bourke v Attorney General and Wymes*[8] which examined the *travaux preparatoires* of the European Convention on Extradition (1957) and formed the view that:

> "if the Courts can properly look at the history of the adoption of an International Convention for the purpose of ascertaining the meaning of the words used in it, there would appear to be no reason in principle why in appropriate cases, they should not be free when construing the words of a statute to obtain assistance from the history of its enactment by Parliament."

[3.03] Section 129 of the 1992 Act specifically provides that both judicial notice and notice by the Controller shall be taken of the EPC, PCT and when ratified, the CPC. This includes decisions or opinions of "a competent authority" under the EPC. In *Genentech Inc's Patent*,[9] Mustill LJ gave this a restrictive interpretation by stating that this provision is directed to evidentiary matters, ie, the proof of matters that might otherwise have had to be proved as foreign law. It does not give to rulings of other courts any greater status than they would otherwise have possessed. The EPO enlarged Board of Appeal would be considered a competent authority and under the corresponding UK section, judicial notice has been taken of their decisions.[10]

---

6. *Fothergill v Monarch Airlines* [1980] 2 All ER 696.
7. [1982] FSR 32.
8. [1972] IR 36.
9. [1989] RPC 147, at 266
10. *John Wyeth's and Schering's Applications* [1985] RPC 545.

WHAT INVENTIONS ARE PATENTABLE?

[3.04] Chapter II of the 1992 Act deals with patentability and conforms to Articles 52 to 57 of the EPC and Articles 1 to 5 of the Strasbourg Convention 1963. The 1964 Act included a definition of an invention as:

> ... any new and useful art, process, machine, manufacture or composition of matter, or any new and useful improvement in any art, process, machine, manufacture or composition of matter, and includes an alleged invention and also any new method or process of testing applicable to the improvement or control of manufacture.

The 1992 Act has no such definition, it simply states in s 9(1) that an invention shall be patentable if it is susceptible of industrial application, is new and involves an inventive step and then specifically identifies in ss 9(2), 9(3) and 10 what is not to be considered as an invention and what are unpatentable inventions. These are:

(a) a discovery, scientific theory or a mathematical method;

(b) an aesthetic creation;

(c) a scheme, rule or method for performing a mental act, playing a game or doing business, or a program for a computer;

(d) the presentation of information;

(e) a method for treatment of the human or animal body by surgery or therapy;

(f) a diagnostic method practised on the human or animal body;

(g) a plant or animal variety or an essentially biological process for the production of plants or animals other than a microbiological process or the products thereof; and

(h) an invention whose publication or exploitation would be contrary to public order or morality.

Patentability is excluded for subject matter or activities in (a) to (d) "only to the extent to which a patent application or patent relates to such subject matter or activities as such".[11]

Discovery, scientific theory or mathematical method

[3.05] In the case of *Reynolds v Herbert Smith & Co Ltd*,[12] Buckley J drew the following distinction between discovery and invention:

---

11. PA 1992, s 9(3).
12. (1903) 20 RPC 123, at 126.

"discovery adds to the amount of human knowledge, but it does so only by lifting the veil and disclosing something which before had been unseen or dimly seen. Invention also adds to human knowledge, but not merely by disclosing something. Invention necessarily involves also the suggestion of an act to be done, and it must be an act which results in a new product, or a new result, or a new process, or a new combination for producing an old product or an old result."

Thus although a discovery is not patentable, a product or process making use of such could be. The term "mere discovery" is used to describe the discovery of a new advantage for an old article or process and is also unpatentable. Therefore, in *Adhesive Dry Mounting Company Ltd v Trapp & Co*,[13] it was held that the idea of using an old material for an entirely new purpose, not being analogous to a purpose for which it had theretofore been used, may be good subject matter, but such idea, however ingenious, can hardly justify a claim for the material itself.

[3.06] Even without the specific exclusion which is contained in the 1992 Act, mathematical methods have long been held to be unpatentable. In *Young v Rosenthal*,[14] it was succinctly put by Grove J who gave the following example: "supposing a person discovered that three angles of a triangle are equal to two right angles, that is an abstract discovery and would not be the subject of a patent". In *LIPS' Application*,[15] a claim for a ship's propeller was refused because it differed from the prior art only by the process of calculation by which its profile was determined and the only novelty alleged was the mental process by which the propeller blade thickness at different radical positions was determined.

Aesthetic creations

[3.07] The words 'aesthetic creations' are those used in Article 52(2)(b) of the EPC. In the UK Patents Act 1977, the words used are "a literary, dramatic, musical or artistic work or any other aesthetic creation whatsoever". The Irish Copyright Act 1963 does not define aesthetic and in fact copyright can subsist in, for example, an artistic work irrespective of its artistic quality[16] and drawings of purely functional objects can enjoy copyright subject to the Copyright (Amendment) Act 1987. It is possible for patent and copyright protection to exist in the same product. An object of aesthetic creation may be registerable as a design having visual appeal under the Industrial and Commercial Property (Protection) Act 1927.[17]

---

13. (1910) 27 RPC 341.
14. (1884) RPC 29, at 31.
15. [1959] RPC 35.
16. CA 1963, s 9(1)(a).
17. No 16/1927 - s 3 (definition of a design).

Schemes, rules or method of performing a mental act, playing a game or doing business

[3.08] The exclusion from patentability of a scheme, rule or method for performing a mental act, playing a game or doing business is attributable to the view that these are the proper subject of copyright law. Again, the boundaries between patent and copyright law can and do overlap and so, for example, the rules for a board game can enjoy copyright protection as a literary work and simultaneously patent protection can exist for the game apparatus, that is the pieces and the board, to be played in accordance with the rules.[18] The game of *Monopoly* was patented as are a multiplicity of other board games. In *Cobianchi's Application*,[19] a patent was allowed for a special pack of cards designed for playing canasta, the main novelty being that the symbols shown in two colours on an ordinary pack of cards were replaced by pips or other markings in two colours, ie, a new pack of cards for playing an old game. Although this decision hinges on the old definition of an invention as a "manner of new manufacture", the proviso in s 9(3) of the 1992 Act is likely to have brought about the same result since it is not the rules *per se* which were being patented and such in any event were known. The border line is sometimes very narrow since the rules, although not patentable *per se*, are taken into account when deciding on novelty. A patent for a new arrangement of markings on the playing surface of a roulette game was refused.[20] Ingenuity or usefulness does not make a scheme or plan patentable[21] nor does the implementation of new workforce practices or the better utilisation of manpower.[22] In refusing the grant of a patent for an invention entitled "method of notation in writing music for pianos, organs and other musical instruments",[23] it was recognised that it is impossible to lay down a guiding principle but it appears that this case was decided on the basis of a lack of any technical aspect. This decision was distinguished in *Pitman's Application*[24] where a patent was allowed for a method and means of teaching the pronunciation of a language since in relation to its recommended use in a speaking machine a definite mechanical purpose was apparent.

[18.] Notes of official rulings (1926) 43 RPC Appendix i.
[19.] (1953) 70 RPC 199.
[20.] *Kent & Thanet Casinos Ltd v Bailey's School of Dancing Ltd* [1968] RPC 318.
[21.] *Ward's Application* (1912) 29 RPC 79 - refusing a patent for a system of indexing.
[22.] *Quigley's Application* [1977] FSR 373 (Australian decision).
[23.] *C's Application* (1920) 37 RPC 247.
[24.] [1969] RPC 646.

Presentation of information

[3.09] In relation to the issue of the presentation of information, in *Johnson's Application*,[25] a patent was refused because the different colouring of fertilisers used to distinguish one from another was considered as adding nothing to the efficiency of the fertiliser. This can be contrasted with *ITS Rubber Limited's Application*[26] which related to a squash ball characterised by being blue in colour and which aided vision. It was held that the colouring added a desirable characteristic and could be considered a manner of new manufacture. The subject matter was not the presentation of information as such since the objective of the colouring achieved more than the mere purpose of differentiating different categories of squash ball.

Computer programs

[3.10] The exclusion of computer programs as such from patentability is taken from Articles 52(2)(c) and 52(3) of the EPC.[27] Similar wording is adopted in the UK Patents Act 1977.[28] Prior to the EU Software Directive, it was assumed that programs enjoyed copyright protection as a literary work and even in the UK and other countries where this has been clear for a number of years, a large number of patents have been granted for inventions in which the program is an integral part and in some cases, the only novel feature. The pursuit of patent protection for software related inventions is attributable to the broader scope of protection than that existing under copyright law. In addition to decisions of the EPO, the UK courts have also considered these provisions in detail. In *Merrill Lynch Inc's Application*,[29] Falconer J in the Patents Court considered an application in respect of a data processing system for implementing an automated trading market for securities. Also at issue was whether or not the application should be refused on the basis that it merely related to a method of doing business. In holding that there was no patentable subject matter because of lack of novelty in anything other than the computer program, a narrow and restrictive approach was taken even in the face of the *Vicom* decision of the EPO.[30] In *Genentech Inc's Patent*,[31] Dillon LJ in the Court of Appeal did not accept the reasoning of Falconer J and described such as "a drastic change from English law as previously understood" quoting with approval the statement of Whitford J in the UK Patents Court, namely "it is trite law that you cannot patent

---

[25.] (1930) 47 RPC 361.
[26.] [1979] RPC 318.
[27.] See paras **[2.50]** and **[2.51]**.
[28.] UK Patents Act 1977, s 1(2)(c).
[29.] [1988] RPC 1.
[30.] [1987] EPOR 66.
[31.] [1989] RPC 147, at 240.

a discovery, but if on the basis of that discovery, you can tell people how it can be usefully employed, then a patentable invention may result".[32] While critical of Falconer J's reasoning, the Court of Appeal made it clear that they were not voicing disagreement with the decision in the *Merrill Lynch* case, stating that:

> "it would be nonsense for the Act to forbid the patenting of a computer program, and yet permit the patenting of a floppy disc containing a computer program, or an ordinary computer when programmed with the program".[33]

[3.11] In the Court of Appeal in *Merrill Lynch's Application*[34] Fox LJ quoted with approval the statement in the *Vicom* decision that "decisive is what technical contribution the invention makes to the known art", going on to say "there must ... be some technical advance on the prior art in the form of a new result (eg a substantial increase in processing speed as in *Vicom*)". The Court of Appeal dismissed the appeal, agreeing that there was not a patentable invention.

[3.12] In *Gale's Application*,[35] the applicant had discovered an improved method of calculating the square root of a number with the aid of a computer. The Court of Appeal rejected the claim holding that it was:

> "in substance a claim to a computer program, being the particular instructions embodied in a conventional type of ROM circuitry, and those instructions do not represent a technical process outside the computer or a solution to a technical problem within the computer."

The Court of Appeal also rejected the proposition that the prohibition against the patenting of computer programs as such could be circumvented by incorporating a program in a floppy disk.

[3.13] In *Fujitsu Ltd*[36] Laddie J reviewed the existing law in the context of software which assisted chemists to design new chemical compounds by enabling a computer operator to depict on his screen the crystal structure of two known chemicals. The two images could be rotated and their scales adjusted, so as to align the face of one with a complementary face of the other. It was possible to use the resulting picture as a blueprint for a new hybrid 'designer' chemical. Essentially the invention was the software which enabled the computer to be used as a tool to assist in the designing of new chemicals. Laddie J set out guiding principles and stated that the exclusion to patentability applied regardless of whether the subject matter is technical or non-technical. Focus was not to be directed to the control of the computer by the program, but to what the

---

[32.] [1987] RPC 553, at 566 - *Genentech Inc's Patent* - Whitford J in the Patents Court.

[33.] [1989] RPC 147, at 240 - *Genentech Inc's Patent*.

[34.] [1989] RPC 561, at 569.

[35.] [1991] RPC 305, at 328.

[36.] [1996] RPC 511.

computer, so controlled, is doing. Laddie J held that the software left the operator to decide what data to work on, how to assess the results and which, if any results should be used. The invention was held to be abstract and its effect determined by the personal skill and assessment of the operator. In substance, it was a scheme or method of performing a mental act and as such was unpatentable.

[3.14] A summary of the UK cases shows a movement towards the views of the EPO ie the claimed invention must be viewed in its entirety to ascertain whether or not it addresses a technical problem as opposed to being simply an improvement in programming by the creation of new algorithms. The question is whether the software (non-technical features) is essential to the achievement of a technical effect.

Medical treatments

[3.15] Section 9(4) of the 1992 Act which deals with methods for treatment of the human or animal body by surgery or therapy and diagnostic methods practised on the human body does not state these are not inventions. They may be regarded as an invention but not of a type susceptible of industrial application and are therefore unpatentable under s 9(1). Short term patents for such would also appear to be precluded[37] and if obtained, can be revoked.[38] This exclusion does not apply to a product, in particular a substance or composition, for use in any such method. The *Banks Report*[39] considered the possibility of patentability of known compounds in a known form which could be used against a disease for which it was not previously thought to be effective. It was considered that the extension of patent protection in this way would result, in effect, in patents for the treatment of human beings, since a claim for such an invention would have to specify the condition against which the compound was effective and to include instructions for its use. This was considered to be undesirable.

[3.16] Under the 1964 Act, methods for the medical treatment of human beings were considered unpatentable because they fell outside the definition of an invention by virtue of not being a manufacture. In *C & W's Application*,[40] a patent was refused for a process of extracting lead from persons suffering from lead poisoning. It was considered that the question to be asked is whether the process is something to be used in the making of an object that is or may be of commercial value or is a process adapted to that end. In *Neva Corporation's Application*,[41] the principle that a process for the treatment of the human body

---

37. PA 1992, s 63(4).
38. PA 1992, ss 58, 67.
39. (1970) Cmnd 4407.
40. (1914) 31 RPC 235.
41. [1968] RPC 481.

could not be a manner of manufacture, was confirmed by the refusal of an application in respect of a method of inducing loss of pain sensibility by sound recording.

[3.17] The courts focus in on the word 'medical' and consider such as being limited to treatments of a curative nature. A patent was allowed for a method of contraception[42] and a method of defence against a human assailant by the injection of a painful non-lethal chemical irritant.[43] In the Australian case of *Joos v Commissioner of Patents*,[44] Barwick CJ allowed a patent for a process of improving the strength and elasticity of human hair observing that "the process here is clearly cosmetic, in high contradistinction to a separate prophylactic or therapeutic medical process". In *Bio-Digital Sciences Inc's Application*,[45] a patent was allowed for a method of testing cells and it was confirmed that medical treatment must be regarded as a narrow term which should be confined to the cure or prevention of disease. In *Puharich and Lawrence's Application*,[46] a patent was allowed for a hearing aid even though an operation was required for the insertion of the receiving device.

[3.18] In relation to veterinary treatment, again there is a narrow interpretation. Thus, in *Swift's Application*,[47] a patent for injecting animals with a meat tenderising enzyme was allowed.

[3.19] The word 'therapy' embraces both curative and prophylactic treatments such as immunisation. In *Unilever Limited (Davis's) Application*,[48] Falconer J also refused to draw any distinction between the prophylactic treatment of diseases in human beings and animals. This interpretation of the word 'therapy' has also been applied by the EPO.[49] In *Pigs 1/Wellcome*,[50] the EPO refused to grant a patent for a method of curing mange mites in pigs even though the treatment could be carried out by farmers in general and did not require the services of a veterinary surgeon.

[3.20] Although s 9(4) of the 1992 Act states that surgical, therapeutic or diagnostic methods practised on the human body are not patentable, it also indicates that this does not apply to new products, particularly substances or compositions, for use in such methods. For example, in the case of a substance

---

[42] *Organon Laboratories' Application* [1970] RPC 574.
[43] *Palmer's Application* [1970] RPC 597.
[44] [1973] RPC 59.
[45] [1973] RPC 668.
[46] [1965] RPC 395.
[47] [1962] RPC 37.
[48] [1983] RPC 219.
[49] *Pigs II/Duphar* [1988] 1 EPOR 10.
[50] [1988] 1 EPOR 1.

or composition which is already known but has no known pharmacological activity, a patent may be obtained for the substance or composition for use as a medicament or for use in a specified medical treatment. This is known as first medical use and can be protected by way of purpose-limited product claims of the general format:

> Substance/composition X for use as a medicament.

A new medical indication of a known drug, ie a second or subsequent medical indication, can also be patented. Protection is available by way of purpose-limited process claims, also known as Swiss-type claims, of the following format:

> Use of substance/composition X for the manufacture of a medicament for the treatment/prophylaxis of disease Y.

Such claims have been allowed by the EPO following a decision of the Enlarged Board of Appeal of the EPO.[51]

Plant Variety Protection

[3.21] Apart from broadening the prospect of patent protection available for new strains of plant material produced by way of genetic engineering, the International Community has sponsored a number of attempts to secure agreements that are intended to source intellectual property rights for the producers of "new" varieties of plants, when the reproduction of those plants is a further intended use of these plants. The most important international instrument is the International Convention for the Protection of New Varieties of Plants ('the UPOV Convention'), which was first agreed in 1961 and revised in 1972, 1978 and 1991. It is this document, specifically the 1978 revision, signed by Ireland on 27 September 1979 that forms the basis of existing Irish statute law in the form of the Plant Varieties (Proprietary Rights) Act 1980, although certain aspects of the 1991 Revision[52] and the introduction of a EU Regulation on Community Plant Variety Rights[53] make a review and revision of the 1980 Act something of an inevitability. It should be noted that GATT/TRIPS allow WTO members to address biological process protection via patents or a *sui generis* system.[54]

---

51. Known as claims in 'Swiss form': *Second Medical Indication/Eisai* OJ EPO 3/1985 64.
52. But see Article 3 of the 1991 Revision which directs existing Member States to apply the 1991 rules.
53. Council Regulation 2100/94/EC.
54. TRIPS, Article 27.3.(b).

The 1980 Act

[3.22] In introducing the Plant Varieties (Proprietary Rights) Bill 1979 to Dáil Éireann,[55] the Minister for Agriculture, Mrs Hussey, explained that the production of new plant variety was the result of a substantial investment in terms of time, skill and financial expenditure. Some strains took around 15 years to create. This effort was not always compensated for via the sale of the resultant propagating material alone, for upon such sale others could replicate the work of the originator and market that reproductive material, and it was this realisation that caused the UPOV Convention to emerge at international level. The Minister asserted the need for Ireland to ratify the Convention and in particular the central principle that the propagating material of new plant varieties may be produced or marketed by the breeder of that variety, or by others, only with the breeder's prior authorisation and in accordance with the conditions set by the breeder.[56] The Minister conceded that Governmental interest in such a scheme was the result of pressure from both the EEC (only Luxembourg and Ireland had no such system in place) and by pressure from the agricultural sector who feared that if a system of remuneration were not in place, foreign breeders might decide to blacklist exports to Ireland. The Minister also indicated that a national law system would make domestic production of strains of plant more likely in a regulated legal environment. The 1980 Act replaced a number of bilateral agreements (eg between Irish producers and groups like the Holland Producers Association) that had worked satisfactorily, albeit as instruments of private law.

[3.23] The breeder's right is a sole right to produce, for marketing purposes and to export or import, any reproductive material[57] of the variety for which rights are granted, or the sole right to licence others to do so.[58] This right is however controlled by the prospect of a compulsory licensing mechanism,[59] which can be used to prevent the breeder from unreasonably restricting the distribution of the said reproductive material.[60] The right is related to the distribution of reproductive material and does not apply to plant varieties to be utilised for making foodstuffs or the composting of vegetable material, for example.

[3.24] However, the system of protection is quite bureaucratic and formalistic. The system of protection depends upon a Ministerial decision to recognise a genus or species of plant. Once this decision is taken and communicated in the form of a statutory instrument, the scheme thus propounded allows breeders to

---

55. 318, Dáil Debates, Col 373-6.
56. See Article 14 of the 1991 Convention.
57. Defined in s 1.
58. Section 4(5) and (6).
59. Section 8.
60. Section 8(1).

obtain protection based upon the commercial needs and characteristics of the plant and the market for that plant. The minimum period for protection is set at 15 years under the Act although the 1991 revision to UPOV raises this to 20 years.[61] The minimum period for trees and vines is set at 25 years in the 1991 revision, 18 years in the 1980 Act.[62] Initially, protection was to be available to wheat, oats, barley, potatoes, ryegrass and white clover,[63] but recent schemes have been put in place to cover certain trees and flowering plants such as Norway Maple, whitebeam, sunflower, paper daisy, as well as soft core fruits such as raspberry and other *rubus* plants.[64]

[3.25] The criteria for protection are that the variety must be new, distinct, uniform and stable.[65] These factors have a precise meaning and are not to be confused with the criteria for patent protection. The variety is new if at the date of filing the application, propagating or harvested material of the variety has not been sold or otherwise disposed of to others, by or with the consent of the breeder, for exploitation purposes, within the previous year in the country of filing, or within four years of that filing in any other territory.[66] Thus, a "new" variety can include existing or newly discovered plant varieties, as long as the person who files this kind of "discovery" application can lodge a requisite amount of propagating material.[67] The distinctiveness criteria is set by Article 7 of the UPOV Convention and this requires that the variety be "clearly distinguishable from any other variety whose existence is a matter of common knowledge at the time of filing the application."[68] The variety must be clearly distinguishable by one or more important morphological, physiological or other characteristic from any other variety and this can be satisfied for example by showing that the variety is highly resistant to mildew while apparently having no other distinctive feature *vis-à-vis* other plants of this variety.[69] The distinctions must be "important" and the fact that other UPOV countries have granted applications will not assist in a determination.[70] The question of the uniformity of the variety is tested in the light of the variations that may be expected from the particular features of its propagation,[71] while Article 9 of the

---

61. Note that SI 78/1993 extended protection for potatoes from 20 to 25 years.
62. Section 4(10).
63. See SI 23/1981, the Principal Regulation, but substantially amended and added to since then.
64. SI 369/1992, SI 332/1993 and SI 393/1994.
65. UPOV Convention, Article 5; 1980 Act, s 5 and First Schedule.
66. UPOV Convention, Article 6 (six years in the case of vines or trees); 1980 Act, First Schedule. On the meaning of sale, see *Re Sunworld Inc & Registrar* (1995) 33 IPR 106.
67. 320 Dáil Debates, 452-463.
68. 1980 Act, First Schedule, para 1.
69. *Maris-Druid Spring Barley* [1968] FSR 559.
70. *L Daehnfelt Ltd v Controller* [1976] FSR 95.
71. UPOV Convention Article 8; 1980 Act, First Schedule, para 3.

UPOV Convention requires that the variety will be deemed to be stable if its relevant characteristics remain unchanged after each repeated propagation, or in the case of a particular cycle of propagation, after each cycle.[72]

[3.26] The testing of applications is the function of the Department of Agriculture and Food. The 1980 Act sets up the post of Controller of Plant Breeders' Rights who has specific powers and functions under the Act. Once a scheme has been established, a breeder will register a variety within that scheme as long as the criteria set out above can be met. A name for the variety is registered and exclusivity is given for that name, but if a name is proposed which is likely to cause confusion, including confusion with a trade mark or trade name, the name of the variety may be denied registration.[73] Once registered however, infringement of rights in that name can be actionable by the breeder.

[3.27] There are grounds upon which a plant right may be revoked. These include prior commercialisation, lack of distinctiveness, failure to supply reproductive material when so required, incorrect information at the time of application and failure to pay the necessary fees.[74] These matter are for the Controller to decide upon. A third party has no general right to challenge or seek revocation on the ground of an alleged lack of distinctiveness, for example.

[3.28] Notices concerning the schemes in place are publicised in the form of a Government Publication, *The Official Journal of Plant Varieties*.[75] It is the role of the Controller of Plant Breeders' Rights to process applications made for plant breeders rights under the Act whenever a scheme has been put in place by the Minister[76] and it is the Controller who investigates and tests the legal[77] and botanical[78] merits of the application. Assignments and other dealings in the right are to be notified to the Controller who registers such dealings in accordance with s 17 of the 1980 Act.

Later Developments

[3.29] The area of plant breeders' rights, which is essentially technical and arcane, can provoke substantial debate. The fact that plant discoveries may invoke protection causes much political resentment in the non-developed world, who fear that loss of species, increasing concentration of propagation

---

72. 1980 Act, First Schedule, para 4.
73. Section 12.
74. Section 11.
75. 1980 Act, s 19. The most recent issue is Issue 32, published 1.1.97 (Ref A/76/32).
76. 1980 Act, s 4.
77. 1980 Act, s 5.
78. 1980 Act, s 3(13) and s 5.

technology into the hands of western multi-national companies, and general strengthening of the breeders' monopoly, will impoverish Third World farming communities. Some attempts at balance are maintained by permitting reverse engineering[79] and by allowing the farmers an exemption whereby farmers may reserve seed from produce raised on their own lands for a successive sowing of the crop.[80] Loss of species and the dangers associated with monoculture are legitimate concerns for world farming, particularly when indigenous genetic diversity is lost, but it is argued by some supporters of legal protection that these serious dangers are not the result of plant breeding laws, for many Third World countries simply do not grant protection.[81]

[3.30] It seems that what is often in dispute is the right of research establishments in the Developed World to regulate the agricultural and trading patterns of other countries, and the fear the genetic uniformity may not be in anyone's long-term interest, least of all those farming in the developing world. These issues are complex and transcend the narrow focus of plant breeders' rights via *sui generis* protection methods.

The EU Council Regulation 1994[82]

[3.31] This Regulation, closely modelled on the UPOV Convention, seeks to put forward a parallel system of Community law that can co-exist with national law regimes but will allow for the grant of industrial property rights which are valid throughout the Community. While the principle of Community exhaustion applies in this field, recent ECJ judgments give a limited field of application to Article 85 of the Treaty of Rome and the intent behind this Regulation is to provide a high level of Community-wide protection that will ultimately mean that the Community Plant Variety Office will displace national systems. This is made particularly clear by Article 92 of the Regulation.

Biotechnological inventions

[3.32] As discussed above, plant variety rights arise under the Plant Varieties (Proprietary Rights) Act 1980. The exception to patentability which arises under s 10(b) of the 1992 Act is taken from Article 53(b) of the EPC.[83] This specific exception was not contained in the 1964 Act but both animals and plants were not considered to be a manufacture or composition of matter within the definition of an invention.[84] This exception to patentability applies to varieties only and for example, a plant or animal treated by a patentable process can be

---

79. UPOV Convention, Article 15(1) (Compulsory).
80. UPOV Convention, Article 15(2) (optional), not taken up in the 1980 Act.
81. Eg, Dworkin [1983] EIPR 270.
82. (EC) No 2100/94.
83. See para **[2.52]**.
84. *Rank Hovis McDougall v Controller* [1978] FSR 588, see para **[3.35]** *infra*.

patentable.[85] Under the UPOV Convention, Member States are obliged to grant either a plant breeder's right or a patent but not both. Many countries have separate plant breeders' rights legislation and it is the existence of such which allows for the exclusion from patentability. Similar to the position in other countries, protection under the 1980 Act imposes strict requirements when claiming a new variety. Consequently there was a tendency to grant a patent unless the subject matter was deemed a variety under the UPOV Convention.

[3.33] In the case of *Plant Genetic Systems/Glutamine Synthetase Inhibitors*[86] the patent under opposition was a method of making plants resistant to a herbicide by inserting a transgene. The technical board of appeal of the EPO stated that a plant variety is a plant grouping within a single botanical taxon of the lowest known rank which, irrespective of whether it is protectable under the UPOV Convention, is characterised by at least one single transmissible character distinguishing it from other plant groupings and which is sufficiently homogeneous and stable in its own characteristics. The claimed subject matter applied to genetically altered plants which remain stable with regard to their altered, and thus characterising characteristics, since this character is transmitted from generation to generation in the plants and their seeds. The starting material was derived from known plant varieties and the genetically altered plants were essentially derived varieties and fell within the definition of a plant variety under the UPOV Convention. The claimed plants were held to fall within the exclusion from patentability under Article 53(b) of the EPC and the resulting plants were also held not to be the product of a microbiological process.

[3.34] Processes for treating plants are patentable. In *Lenard's Application,*[87] a patent was refused in respect of an improved pruning method for meeting or offsetting the advance of disease in clove trees even though Lloyd-Jacob J described such as unfortunate given the great advance in the culture of clove trees and the ingenuity involved. However, this decision was under the old UK Patents Act 1949 and hence the requirement that the method be a manner of manufacture. This requirement no longer exists under the 1992 Act. This case was distinguished in the Australian decision *NRDC's Application*[88] where a patent was allowed for a selective herbicide on the grounds that the process in question was only one for altering the conditions of growth, so that the contemplated end result would not be a result of the process but would be the inevitable result of that which was inherent in the plant. Where micro-organisms are employed, it is seen as analogous to a chemical process, in that, given the

---

[85.] *Hybrid Plants/Lubrizol* [1990] EPOR 173.
[86.] [1995] EPOR 357 (T 356/93).
[87.] (1954) 71 RPC 190.
[88.] [1961] RPC 134, at 147

micro-organisms and the appropriate conditions, the desired result inevitably follows from the working of the process.

[3.35] In the High Court in the case of *Rank Hovis McDougall Limited v The Controller*,[89] McWilliam J considered an application for a patent for a naturally occurring micro-organism and for methods for its production. The matter fell for consideration under the 1964 Act and thus the definition of invention and s 9(7) which stated that "where a Complete Specification claims a new substance, the claim shall be construed as not extending to that substance when found in nature". The particular micro-organism under consideration provided edible protein and it was accepted that the strain of micro-organism was produced by an elaborate process which did not occur naturally. However, the micro-organism was viewed as a form of life. Even though a British patent had been granted in respect of the same organism, McWilliam J upheld the decision of the Controller and refused the application. It was held that the words 'manufacture' and 'composition' appearing in the definition of invention had to be distinguished from 'grow' or 'cause to grow' and since micro-organisms were composed of living cells which had been grown, they did not fall within the definition of invention. It was also held to be an unaltered substance occurring in nature and fell within the s 9(7) exclusion. Article 2(b) of the Strasbourg Convention[90] specifically provides that the exclusion from patentability does not extend to micro-biological processes and the products thereof. In *Wavin Pipes Limited v The Hepworth Iron Company*,[91] Costello J pointed out that it was clear from the Dáil Debates that one of the objectives of the 1964 Act was to adhere to the Strasbourg Convention. It was clear that there was an inconsistency and even before the 1992 Act, the Irish Patents Office had relaxed its practice of prohibiting claims to living micro-organisms *per se*. In particular, following the US Supreme Court case of *Diamond v Chackarbarty*,[92] the Patents Office recognised a distinction between unaltered micro-organisms occurring in nature and micro-organisms altered by human intervention. Section 10(b) of the 1992 Act includes the provision in Article 2(b) of the Strasbourg Convention and Article 53(b) of the EPC and the exclusion relating to plant or animal varieties does not extend to microbiological processes or the products thereof.

[3.36] At EU level, there is a proposal for a Council Directive on the legal protection of biotechnological inventions.[93] It is not intended to create a *sui generis* form of protection but to ensure that the Member States provide

---

[89.] [1978] FSR 588.

[90.] See paras **[2.25]-[2.29]**.

[91.] [1982] FSR 32, at 38.

[92.] 206 USPQ 193 (1980).

[93.] Draft Directive - Prosposal for European Parliament and Council Directive on Legal Protection of Biotechnological Inventions Com (95) 661.

protection for biotechnological inventions under their patent laws and to provide for harmonisation in relation to matters such as the scope of protection, deposit and access. It is proposed that if the holder of a plant breeder's right can only exercise his rights by infringement of a national patent, then a licence of right shall be accorded upon payment of reasonable royalties.

[3.37] In *Biogen Inc v Medeva plc*[94] the House of Lords considered the validity of a patent for products of genetic engineering or "recombinant DNA technology" which consisted of altering the DNA of suitable cells to produce a protein which in nature occurs in another organism. The patent was held to be invalid on grounds which included the excessive breadth of the claimed invention due to the fact that the same results could have been produced by different means. The House of Lords cautioned on the need not to stifle research and competition by allowing an inventor who had discovered a way of achieving an obviously desirable goal to monopolise every other way of doing so.

Public order and morality

[3.38] Section 10(a) which excludes from patentability inventions which are contrary to public order or morality repeats the wording in Article 53(a) of the EPC except that '*ordre public*' is not translated as public order in the EPC. The EPO guidelines[95] explain that the purpose of the exclusion is to prevent the patenting of inventions likely to induce riot or public disorder or to lead to criminal or other generally offensive behaviour. It is to be invoked only in rare and extreme cases and the obvious example of a letter bomb is given. The EPO guidelines suggest applying the test of whether it is probable that the public in general would regard the invention as so abhorrent that the grant of patent rights would be inconceivable. Because exploitation of an invention is contrary to Irish law does not mean the invention is contrary to public order or morality. A patented product could be manufactured in Ireland for export to other countries in which use of the invention is allowed. The 1964 Act also contained a similar exclusion[96] and previously claims for contraceptives were refused. The Patents Office could refuse an application for an invention which is described as an abortifacient for human use. However, since the EPO do not refuse such, there could be valid patents in Ireland which may have been refused if an applicant had attempted to proceed by way of a national patent application. Section 34(1)(k) of the 1964 Act contained a provision that a patent could be revoked on the ground that the primary or intended use or exercise of the invention was contrary to public order or morality. However, even under broader wording, a

---

94. [1997] RPC 1.
95. C-IV, 3.1-3.3.
96. PA 1964, s 15(1)(b).

patent in the UK was allowed for a game which could be used for unlawful gambling on the grounds that there was a degree of skill involved and hence the game was not necessarily used for gambling.[97] Article 53(a) of the EPC has been considered in the context of the patenting of a genetically engineered mouse[98] and whether such was immoral or contrary to *ordre public*. The mouse was intended for use in relation to research on treating cancer in humans and would reduce the number of animals normally needed in such research. Given the EPO guidelines, it is not surprising that the EPO decided that since the advantages were considerable, they outweighed any possible disadvantage and the invention was not so abhorrent that the grant of a patent would be inconceivable. A patent was thus granted and is currently under opposition.

NOVELTY

[3.39] Section 11(1) of the 1992 Act states simply that an invention shall be considered to be new if it does not form part of the state of the art. An invention must be new in order to be patentable.[99] This simple statement repeats the words of Article 54(1) of the EPC. The state of the art is broadly defined in s 11(2). It includes everything made available to the public anywhere in the world, ie absolute novelty. It can be by means of written or oral description, by use, or in any other way. If the invention is made available to the public before the date of filing of the patent application the novelty is destroyed.[100] In the 1964 Act, the term 'state of the art' was not used but there was a broad definition of published as made available to the public by the written or spoken word or by public use, or in any other way.[101] There was an anomaly in the 1964 Act whereby in revocation proceedings, a patent could be revoked if the invention was published anywhere in the world prior to the priority date of the claim[102] but in opposition proceedings, account could only be taken of prior publication in the State, ie local novelty.[103]

[3.40] In *Wavin Pipes Limited v The Hepworth Iron Company Limited*,[104] Costello J considered a revocation action in which one of the grounds was lack of novelty. The patentee argued that several of the patents which had been cited as part of the prior art were inadmissible because they were not published in the Republic of Ireland before the priority date. Costello J rejected this argument

---

[97.] *Pessers and Moody v Hayden & Co* (1909) 26 RPC 58.
[98.] *Harvard/Onco-Mouse* [1991] EPOR 501.
[99.] PA 1992, s 9(1).
[100.] Defined in s 2 to include a priority date.
[101.] PA 1964, s 2.
[102.] PA 1964, s 34(1)(e).
[103.] PA 1964, s 19(1)(b), (c), (d).
[104.] [1982] FSR 32.

concluding that the omission of the words 'within the State' from the s 34 revocation provisions must have been deliberate and accordingly, publication was not limited to what had been made available to the Irish public. Furthermore, regard was made to the parliamentary history of the Act and the State's intention to introduce the concept of absolute novelty in accordance with its international obligations, ie, the Strasbourg Convention on the Unification of Certain Points of Substantive Law on Patents of Invention. The rationale behind the refusal to allow a patent in respect of an invention which forms part of the state of the art lies in the fact that if the invention has already been made available to the public, then a patent is of no advantage to the public, the disclosure having already taken place. As far back as 1885 and in the case of *Humpherson v Syer*,[105] Bowen LJ held that there was prior publication where information had been communicated to any member of the public who was free in law or equity to use it as he pleased. In a similar vein, Fry LJ considered the relevant question to be whether it is the fair conclusion from the evidence that some English people, under no obligation to secrecy arising from confidence or good faith towards the patentee, knew of the invention at the date when the plaintiff took out his patent. In the case of *Bristol-Myers Application*,[106] it was reiterated that communication even to a single member of the public without an inhibiting fetter was enough to amount to making available to the public. A further example of the courts' willingness to find that an invention has been made available to the public is to attach great significance to actual availability. Thus, in the case of *Dalrymple's Application*,[107] a bulletin issued to members of a trade association which was marked "Confidential - Not to be Published" and "All Rights Reserved - Private and Confidential. The bulletin is issued to you as a member, its contents are strictly confidential and must not be disclosed to non-members" was still held to be published. The bulletin had been sent to 1,079 members and elsewhere.

[3.41] In *Monsanto Company (Brignac's) Application*,[108] a bulletin which was issued to the applicant's own salesmen was held to be published. On the facts, the salesmen were considered to be members of the public. There was no fetter upon the salesmen in respect of the information in the bulletin.

[3.42] Under the 1964 Act in deciding whether or not an invention was published in an earlier document, the High Court[109] applied the test of Sachs LJ

---

105. (1887) 4 RPC 407.
106. [1969] RPC 146.
107. [1957] RPC 449.
108. [1971] RPC 153.
109. *Wavin Pipes v The Hepworth Iron Co* [1982] FSR 32.

in *General Tire and Rubber Company v Firestone Tyre and Rubber Company*, namely:

"The earlier publication and the patentee's claim must each be construed as they would be at the respective relevant dates by a reader skilled in the art to which they relate having regard to the state of knowledge in such art at the relevant date. The construction of these documents is a function of the Court, being a matter of law, but, since documents of this nature are almost certain to contain technical material, the Court must, by evidence, be put in the position of a person of the kind to whom the document is addressed, that is to say, a person skilled in the relevant art at the relevant date ... when the prior inventor's publication and the patentee's claim have respectively been construed by the Court in the light of all properly admissible evidence as to technical matters, the meaning of words and expressions used in the art and so forth, the question whether the patentee's claim is new ... falls to be decided as a question of fact. If the prior inventor's publication contains a clear description of, or clear instructions to do or make, something that would infringe the patentee's claim if carried out after the grant of the patentee's patent, the patentee's claim will have been shown to lack the necessary novelty, that is to say, it will have been anticipated".[110]

[3.43] In *Windsurfing International Inc v Tabur Marine (GB) Ltd*,[111] Oliver J stated the reasoning behind what is termed anticipation, namely that it would be wrong to enable the patentee to prevent a man from doing what he has lawfully done before the patent was granted. In that case, the defendant's counter-claim to infringement cited as a ground for revocation a prior use of the invention some ten years earlier. This use was a sailboard built and used by a then 12 year old boy in close proximity and visible to people in a caravan site. It was held that such prior use even of a short duration was anticipation. In the case of *Quantel Ltd v Spaceward Microsystems Ltd*,[112] it was held that demonstrations of a prototype of the claimed invention at an exhibition were not disclosure because no one was allowed near the actual computer and no engineering description was provided. The public could see the computer in operation but its circuitry was concealed and the public had not been enabled to practice the actual invention for themselves.

[3.44] A test for anticipation which is often applied is what is termed the post infringement or right to work test. Simply stated, this means that anything which would infringe a patent would also anticipate that patent if published before the priority date of the patent. This test was applied by Lord Diplock in *Bristol-Myers Co (Johnson's) Application*[113] where it was stated that:

---

110. [1972] RPC 457, at 485.
111. [1985] RPC 59, at 77.
112. [1990] RPC 83.
113. [1975] RPC 127, at 156.

"the right of a trader to go on dealing by way of trade in any man-made substance in which he had dealt before, without impediment by a monopoly in that substance granted to any other person, was not dependent upon his knowledge of its composition or how it could be made".

However, in the case of *Asahi's Application*,[114] it was held that matter comprised in the state of the art had to be the subject of an enabling disclosure, ie a disclosure to the public of such type as would enable the working of the invention by a person skilled in the art. In *Pall Corporation v Commercial Hydraulics (Bedford) Ltd*,[115] it was held that the supply prior to the priority date of test samples for customer evaluation had not made the invention available to the public because the nature of the samples had not been disclosed and this was not apparently ascertainable by examination. In the case of *C Van Der Lely NV v Bamfords Ltd*,[116] what was at issue was whether or not a photograph was clear enough to amount to a disclosure. The alleged invention related to a hay raking machine in which the rake wheels were driven by contact with the ground. It was argued that there could not be anticipation unless this was shown clearly and unmistakably. This was rejected by Lord Reid who saw no practical difference between a definite statement of fact and material from which the skilled man would clearly infer its existence. The question was whether the typical skilled man would infer that it was ground driven from the photograph and it was held that the photograph amounted to anticipation even though the features were not explicitly disclosed in the photograph. This test in which the courts put themselves in the position of a skilled technician was also applied in *Dow Chemical AG v Spence Bryson & Co Ltd*[117] but the prior art must still contain clear and unmistakable directions to do what the patentee claims to have invented.[118] Sometimes at issue is the question of mosaics of documents in the context of assessing novelty. This is the piecing together of a number of prior documents in order to produce an anticipation of the invention.[119] The EPO guidelines make it quite clear that in considering novelty (as distinct from inventive step), it is not permissible to combine separate items of prior art together. However, if a primary document refers explicitly to another document as, for example, in providing more detailed information on certain features, the import of the latter may be regarded as incorporated into the document containing the reference.

---

[114] [1991] RPC 485.
[115] [1990] FSR 329.
[116] [1963] RPC 61.
[117] [1984] RPC 359, at 399-400.
[118] *General Tire v Firestone* [1972] RPC 457, at 486. *Ward's Applications* [1986] RPC 50.
[119] *Von Heyden v Neustadt* 50 LJ Ch 126, at 128.

[3.45] Also when considering novelty, regard must be had to the possible effect of a prior concurrent application. Under s 11(3) of the 1992 Act which corresponds to Article 54(3) of the EPC, the state of the art includes the content of an Irish patent application of earlier priority. This provision is designed to protect against double patenting and although limited to patent applications published under s 28 of the 1992 Act, is not limited to Irish national applications. Under s 120(1) & (2), patent applications published under s 28 include European patents designating the State. There is also an additional provision in s 127(5) that an international application designating the State (which is deemed to be an application for a European patent designating the State) which is published under the Patent Co-operation Treaty (PCT) is only to be treated as published under s 11(3) when a copy has been supplied to the EPO in English, French or German and the relevant fee under the EPC has been paid. This sub-s (5) was not in the Patents Bill as initiated. It was argued by Peter Barry TD that if sub-s (5) was not included, a PCT application would be part of the state of the art against an Irish application of later priority date even if the PCT application was published after the date of the Irish application in some language such as Japanese, Russian or Mongolian and even if the fees were never paid to the EPO to bring the PCT application into effect as a European application.[120] The Dutch Patent Office, in considering their equivalent to s 11(3) held that account must be taken not only of the literal text of the earlier application but also of anything which an average person skilled in the art, interpreting what he had read, would have regarded as part of the earlier application.[121] If prior art falls within the relevant claim, there is lack of novelty irrespective of whether or not the later application discloses advantages.[122]

[3.46] The provisions of s 11(4) allow for the patenting of a substance or composition used in the treatment of the human or animal body even if previously known for some other purpose as long as that purpose is not comprised in the state of the art. An area of contention in relation to this provision is that pertaining to what is called second or subsequent medical use, ie a patenting of a known drug in respect of a second or subsequent new medical use. The German courts have adopted a very liberal attitude and have held that there is no prohibition against claims for a second or subsequent medical use. The Swiss Patent Office, deciding on this issue, allowed a claim in respect of the use of a known compound for the manufacture of a medicament for the treatment of a disease even though this compound had previously been used in the treatment of a different disease. This approach has been followed by the

---

[120.] 413 Dáil Debates Cols 1268-1270 and 414 Dáil Debates Cols 176-177.
[121.] [1981] FSR 356 - Netherlands Patent Office, Dec No 14,633.
[122.] *EI Du Pont's (Witsiepe's) Application* [1982] FSR 303.

enlarged Board of Appeal of the EPO[123] and by the British[124] and Swedish courts.[125]

NON-PREJUDICIAL DISCLOSURES

[3.47] Non-prejudicial disclosures are limited to just two instances and these are identified in s 12. Both instances require that the disclosure at issue must have taken place not more than six months before the date of filing of the application. The first instance relates to circumstances in which there has been a breach of confidence, agreement or the unlawful obtaining of an applicant's invention. A somewhat similar provision in relation to obtaining existed under s 47 of the 1964 Act. It is interesting to note that the wording used does not correspond to Article 55(1)(a) of the EPC which refers to an evident abuse in relation to the applicant or his legal predecessor. In addition, the EPO opposition division has held that under Article 55(1), the six month grace period runs from the priority date and not the actual date of filing.[126]

[3.48] In *Gallay Ltd's Application*,[127] Lloyd-Jacob J considered a drawing sent to Rolls Royce who had approached the opponents with an insulation problem. The drawing was of an insulating component and there was no explicit request for confidential treatment. An order was subsequently placed for the component shown. It was held that even if not forwarded in confidence but in the ordinary course of business, this was not decisive. It was necessary to look further and in particular at the nature of the business and the circumstances surrounding the transaction. In that case, Rolls Royce were considered to be partners with the opponents in a design project and were therefore deemed to have had a duty of confidence. In following this case in *James Industries Ltd's Patent*,[128] it can be seen that if there is disclosure of confidential information for a specific purpose then this will normally be deemed to be imparted in confidence and the recipient is duty bound not to use the information for any other purpose. The disclosing party has a legal right to prevent use of the information for the recipient's own purposes.[129] In *Tecalemit Limited's Application*,[130] it was alleged that a pamphlet in a company library where it was available to technical staff amounted to disclosure. It was held that inspection by personnel of a technical department

---

[123.] *Esai's Application* [1985] OJEPO 64.

[124.] *John Wyeth and Brother Limited's Application* [1985] RPC 545.

[125.] *Hydropyridine* (1988) 19 IIC 815.

[126.] *Passoni/Stand Structure* [1982] EPOR 79.

[127.] [1959] RPC 141.

[128.] [1987] RPC 235. See also *Saltman Eng v Campbell* (1948) 65 RPC 203 and *Strachan & Henshaw Ltd v Pakcel* (1949) 66 RPC 49.

[129.] *Humpherson v Syer* (1887) 4 RPC 407.

[130.] [1967] FSR 387.

was not inspection by members of the public and there was consequently no disclosure.

[3.49] Lord Parker in *Bristol-Myers' Application*[131] followed a Court of Appeal decision in *Formento v Mentmore*[132] and rejected the contention that publication depends either upon anything in the nature of a dedication to the public or upon the degree of dissemination of the information alleged to have been published. On the contrary, if the information, whether in documentary form or in the form of the invention itself, has been communicated to a single member of the public without inhibiting fetter that is enough to amount to a making available to the public. The mere receipt of information by an employee from a third party does not infer confidentiality in circumstances where the employer was free to publish the information or make use of it as it wished. There is an onus on the party relying on s 12(1)(a) to show there has been a breach of confidence.[133] The second instance of a non-prejudicial disclosure relates to display at certain exhibitions.[134] The exhibitor must file a supporting certificate issued by the authority responsible for the protection of industrial property at that exhibition[135] within four months of the date of filing of the patent application. The certificate must state the opening date of the exhibition and the date of first disclosure.

INVENTIVE STEP

[3.50] In most cases which are litigated, the invention has not been directly anticipated and hence is novel but what is at issue is whether or not prior art can be inferred to be part of the state of the art as being obvious.[136] Under s 9 of the 1992 Act, in order for an invention to be patentable, it must involve an inventive step. The criterion used in relation to short term patents is that the invention must not be clearly lacking an inventive step.[137] Although novelty and inventive step are separate criteria, they are interrelated. The question of whether or not there is inventive step only arises if there is novelty.[138] As in the case of novelty, regard must be had to the state of the art. The existence of an inventive step is judged by determining whether the invention as claimed would be obvious to a person skilled in the art at the priority/filing date of the application. The EPO guidelines define 'obvious' as that which does not go beyond the normal progress of technology but merely follows plainly or logically from the prior art,

---

131. [1969] RPC 146, at 155.
132. [1956] RPC 87.
133. *Microsonic's Application* [1984] RPC 29.
134. Article 4(4)(b) - Strasbourg Convention.
135. Patent Rules 1992 r 5.
136. PA 1992, s 13. *Molins v Industrial Machinery Co Ltd* (1938) 55 RPC 31.
137. PA 1992, s 63(4).
138. EPO Guidelines C-IV 9.1.

ie something which does not involve the exercise of any skill or ability beyond that to be expected of the person skilled in the art.[139] The guidelines then go on to indicate various ways in which a skilled person may arrive at an invention, namely:

(a) the formulation of an idea or of a problem to be solved (the solution being obvious once the problem is clearly stated);

Example:

The problem of indicating to the driver of a motor vehicle at night the line of the road ahead by using the light from the vehicle itself. As soon as the problem is stated in this form the technical solution, ie the provision of reflective markings along the road surface, appears simple and obvious.

(b) the devising of a solution to a known problem;

Example:

The problem of permanently marking farm animals such as cows without causing pain to the animals or damage to the hide has existed since farming began. The solution ('freeze-branding') consists in applying the discovery that the hide can be permanently depigmented by freezing.

(c) the arrival at an insight into the cause of an observed phenomenon (the practical use of this phenomenon then being obvious).

Example:

The agreeable flavour of butter is found to be caused by minute quantities of a particular compound. As soon as this insight has been arrived at, the technical application comprising of the addition of this compound to margarine is obvious.

[3.51] The 1964 Act allowed for opposition on the ground that the invention "is obvious and clearly does not involve an inventive step".[140] Revocation was also provided on the same terms but the word 'clearly' was not used.[141] Since the question at issue was essentially one of obviousness, cases under the 1964 Act and the corresponding UK Patents Act are still important. However, the inclusion of the word 'clearly' in opposition proceedings meant that if there was any doubt, it had to be resolved in favour of the applicant.[142] The word 'clearly'

---

[139] EPO Guidelines C-IV 9.3.
[140] PA 1964, s 19(1)(e).
[141] PA 1964, s 34(1)(f).
[142] *Electric and Musical Industries (Clarke's) Application* [1970] RPC 5.

appears in s 63(4) of the 1992 Act in relation to the consideration of the patentability of short term patents only.

[3.52] In considering the British cases, Costello J in the High Court in *Beecham Group Limited v Bristol-Myers Company*[143] held that the Controller's task was not that of adjudicating a dispute between two rival litigants but a statutory duty to decide whether or not monopoly rights which affect the public should be granted. In the same case, it was held that for the purpose of obviousness, regard should be taken of the whole contents of Irish patent applications bearing an earlier priority date even though not published. Section 13 of the 1992 Act makes it clear that for the purposes of considering inventive step, no regard should be had of unpublished contents of a patent application. Budd J in *Rawls v Irish Tyre and Rubber Services Ltd*[144] reviewed the British cases and from them summarised:

> "the tests to be applied as to the characteristics and quality of ingenuity which distinguish invention from workshop improvement are these:- Has the improvement been a commercial success? Has it supplied a want? Has the problem awaited a solution for many years and is the device novel and superior to that which has gone before? Is it widely used and is it used in preference to alternative devices? It is apparent that the mere simplicity of the device is no objection and a very slight advance, something approaching to a scintilla, will suffice to support the invention. Moreover, an *ex post facto* approach and analysis of the invention is to be guarded against, because it is so easy to say after the event that the whole thing was perfectly obvious in the popular sense of the word."

[3.53] In *Windsurfing International Inc v Tabur Marine (GB) Ltd*[145] Oliver J identified four steps to be taken in the determination of any issue as to obviousness, namely:

(1) Identification of the inventive concept embodied in the patent in suit;

(2) Inputing to a normally skilled but unimaginative addressee what was common general knowledge in the art at the priority date;

(3) Identifying the differences if any between the matter cited as being 'known or used' and the alleged invention;

(4) Deciding whether those differences, viewed without any knowledge of the alleged invention, constituted steps which would have been obvious to the skilled man or whether they required any degree of invention.

[143.] High Court, unrep, 13 March 1981 (1979/328/Sp).
[144.] [1960] IR 11, at 30.
[145.] [1985] RPC 59, at 73-74.

[3.54] The British courts have adopted variations on what is called the *Cripps* question. This question was originally formulated in *Sharpe & Dohme Inc v Boots Pure Drug Co Ltd*[146] and can be summarised as asking whether it was for all practical purposes obvious to any skilled worker in the respective field given the state of knowledge existing at the date of the patent (which consists of the literature then available to that person and their general knowledge) that they could make the invention claimed. Variations of this question can be seen in the case of *Olin Mathieson Chemical v Biorex*,[147] as "would the notional research group at the relevant date in the circumstances ... directly be led as a matter of course to try the invention in the expectation that it might produce a useful desired result". In *Technograph Printed Circuits v Mills & Rockley (Electronics) Ltd*[148], the *Cripps* question was essentially not *could* the skilled worker make the invention but *would* such a skilled person make the invention? The EPO adopted what has been called the problem and solution approach as seen in *Metal Refining/BASF*[149] where the Appeal Board stated:

> "When assessing inventive step, it is not a question of the subjective achievement of the inventor. It is rather the objective which has to be assessed. Objectivity in the assessment of inventive step is achieved by starting out from the objectively prevailing state of the art, in the light of which the problem is determined which the invention addresses and solves from an objective point of view and consideration is given to the question of the obviousness of the disclosed solution to this problem as seen by the man skilled in the art and having those capabilities which can be objectively expected of him. This also avoids the retrospective approach."

[3.55] One of the criteria for assessing obviousness used by Costello J in *Wavin Pipes v Hepworth Iron*[150] was the alleged invention's commercial success. It was stressed, however, that this is not a determining factor but is of assistance on the question of obviousness. In *Samuel Parkes & Co Ltd v Cocker Brothers Ltd*,[151] it was stated that when it has been found that the problem has awaited solution for many years and that the device is in fact novel and superior to what had gone before and has been widely used and indeed in preference to alternative devices, it is practically impossible to say that there is not that scintilla of invention necessary to support the patent. This question of the scintilla of invention also finds its way into Costello J's judgment in the *Wavin Pipes* case in an acceptance that even if a very slight advance on the prior art is found, there

---

146. (1928) 45 RPC 153, at 173.
147. [1970] RPC 157.
148. [1969] RPC 395, at 404.
149. [1983] OJEPO 133.
150. [1982] FSR 32, at 48.
151. (1929) 46 RPC 241.

cannot be obviousness. What is important is whether the advance is technically or practically obvious and is not a question of being commercially obvious. The skilled man is not to be taken as applying his mind to the commercial consequences[152] and in particular, whether it would have appeared commercially worthwhile to exploit the invention.[153] It is important to guard against *ex post facto* analysis[154] as it is always easy to see how to arrive at an invention once it is known, using pieces of prior art selected with knowledge of the invention.[155] The question of obviousness must be answered without any knowledge of the alleged invention.[156]

[3.56] What is meant by a person skilled in the art is not defined in the 1992 Act and these words did not exist in the 1964 Act. The EPO guidelines state that:

> "the person skilled in the art should be presumed to be an ordinary practitioner aware of what was common general knowledge in the art at the relevant date. He should also be presumed to have had access to everything in the state of the art ... and to have had at his disposal the normal means and capacity for routine work and experimentation. If the problem prompts the person skilled in the art to seek its solution in another technical field, the specialist in that field is the person qualified to solve the problem."[157]

In *Technograph Printed Circuits Ltd v Mills & Rockley (Electronics) Ltd*,[158] Lord Reid described this hypothetical person as:

> "a skilled technician who is well acquainted with workshop technique and who has carefully read the relevant literature. He is supposed to have an unlimited capacity to assimilate the contents of, it may be, scores of specifications but to be incapable of a scintilla of invention. When dealing with obviousness, unlike novelty, it is permissible to make a mosaic out of relevant documents, but it must be a mosaic which can be put together by an unimaginative man with no inventive capacity."

In certain areas of technology, it is permissible to view this notional person not as a single individual but as a group or team whose combination of multi-disciplinary skills would be employed.[159]

---

152. *Hallen Co v Brabantia* [1991] RPC 195.
153. *Windsurfing International Inc v Tabur Marine (GB) Ltd* [1985] RPC 59.
154. *Wavin Pipes Ltd v Hepworth Iron Co Ltd* [1982] FSR 32, at 48.
155. *Southco v Dzus* [1990] RPC 587.
156. *Shoketsu's Patent* [1992] FSR 184; *Windsurfing International Inc v Tabur Marine (GB) Ltd* [1985] RPC 59, at 73.
157. C IV 9.6.
158. [1972] RPC 346, at 355.
159. *General Tire v Firestone* [1972] RPC 457; *Genentech's Patent* [1989] RPC 147.

[3.57] An example of forming a mosaic of the state of the art in order to prove obviousness can be seen in the case of *Allmanna Svenska v Burntisland*[160] where it was held that the substitution in a marine engine of an electro-dynamic coupling described in one patent specification for a geared diesel drive described in another specification, although novel, was still obvious. The decision in this case is hard to reconcile with the court's reluctance to accept a mosaic of documents where at least one document is not within the general knowledge of a skilled person. This can be seen from the statement of Lord Reid[161] that "it must be a mosaic which can be put together by an unimaginative man with no inventive capacity". It is easier for a court to accept a mosaic if one document contains a reference to the other. The longer separate parts of an invention have been known from different documents but have not been combined, the more difficult it is to argue that the combination of the documents is obvious.[162]

[3.58] It is part of the state of the art if the information which had been disclosed enabled the public to know the product under a description sufficient to work the invention. Products need not be known under their chemical description in order to be part of the state of the art. If a recipe which inevitably produced a substance was part of the state of the art, so was the substance as made by that recipe.[163]

INDUSTRIAL APPLICATION

[3.59] A patentable invention must be susceptible of industrial application and s 14 of the 1992 Act states that such susceptibility arises if the invention can be made or used in any kind of industry, including agriculture. This corresponds to Article 57 of the EPC and differs from the UK Patents Act 1977 which uses the words 'capable of' as opposed to 'susceptible of'. Although this is a new provision in Irish patent legislation, the 1964 Act did contain a definition of invention but which is almost certainly narrower since an invention can be susceptible of industrial application even if not an "art, process, machine, manufacture or composition of matter".[164]

[3.60] The word 'industry' should be given a broad meaning. As stated in the EPO guidelines,[165] it should be understood as including any physical activity of 'technical character', ie, an activity which belongs to the useful or practical arts

---

[160] (1952) 69 RPC 63.

[161] *Ibid* at 125.

[162] *Mitsubishi/Endless Power Transmission Belt* [1987] 3 EPOR 120.

[163] *Merrell Dow Pharmaceuticals Inc v HN Norton & Co Ltd* [1996] RPC 76.

[164] PA 1964, s 2.

[165] C IV 4.1.

as distinct from the aesthetic arts; it does not necessarily imply the use of a machine or the manufacture of an article and could cover, eg a process for dispersing fog, or a process for converting energy from one form to another. There are very few inventions which would not be excluded under ss 9 and 10 and yet, would fail to fall under s 14. However, one such type of invention would be articles or processes alleged to operate in a manner clearly contrary to well established physical laws, eg, a perpetual motion machine.

Chapter 4

Patents Act 1992 - Acquisition of Patent Rights

PATENT APPLICATIONS

[4.01] The Statute of Monopolies 1623 provided for the grant of a patent to the "true and first inventor and inventors" of new manufactures and the Patents Act 1964 stated that an applicant had to be the true and first inventor or their assignee[1] with an exception made in the case of a personal representative.[2] Section 15 of the Patents Act 1992 contains no such limitation but this must be read in conjunction with s 16 which states that "the right to a patent shall belong to the inventor or his successor in title" and with a particular provision concerning employee inventions. There is no limitation on the number of co-applicants and there are special provisions relating to the co-ownership of patent applications[3] and the substitution of applicants.[4] Even though an applicant may not be the inventor, it is still necessary to identify the inventors within sixteen months of the earliest priority date.[5] Where the applicant(s) is/are not the inventor(s), it is also necessary to indicate the derivation of title.[6] The sometimes difficult task of determining the inventor(s) is not greatly helped by the definition of an inventor[7] who is stated to be "the actual deviser of an invention". The principal problem of identification lies in instances where there are large teams of individuals involved in research and development. In such cases, the applicant should use his best endeavours to identify the actual devisers of the invention. Although s 17(2) states that it is identification of the inventor(s) in accordance with the belief of the applicant which is important, presumably this belief must be reasonably held. Failure to provide details of the inventor(s) and the derivation of title within sixteen months from the priority date means that the patent application is deemed abandoned. In *Nippon Piston Ring Co Ltd's Application*,[8] two applications were refused for failure adequately to identify the applicants' right to apply. It was, however, accepted that the

---

1. Section 6(1).
2. Section 6(4).
3. Section 80.
4. Section 85.
5. Patents Rules 1992, r 6.
6. Section 17(2); Patents Rules, r 6(1).
7. Section 2.
8. [1987] RPC 120.

requirement to identify the inventor(s) had been satisfied by supplying a certified copy of the priority document which did name the inventor.

[4.02] Sections 17(1) and 17(3) make provision for one or more inventors to be mentioned and for their deletion. A person alleging that they ought to have been mentioned or that an inventor is incorrectly mentioned must discharge the onus of proof by setting out fully the facts relied on. The Controller sends a copy of the application and the evidence to the applicant or proprietor of the patent, the identified inventor(s) and to every other person whose interests the Controller considers may be affected by the application. A counter statement may be filed within three months of the receipt of the documents.[9] Under UK patent law, there is provision for employee inventors to receive certain compensation in the case of a patent which is of outstanding benefit to the employer. The identification of an employee as an inventor lends credence to any claim for such compensation. Irish patent law has no similar provision and judging from the experience under the 1964 Act there are likely to be very few applications for mention as an inventor.

[4.03] It is, of course, quite conceivable that several people independently and simultaneously create the same invention. They may all be inventors but ownership resides in the person whose patent application has the earlier date of filing and provided prior publication has taken place.[10]

Employer/Employee Situations

[4.04] If an inventor is an employee, the right to a patent is determined in accordance with the law of the State in which the employee is wholly or mainly employed or, if the identity of such State cannot be determined, in accordance with the law of the State in which the employer has his place of business to which the employee is attached.[11] The same provision also exists in Article 60(1) of the EPC governing the right to a European patent. Unlike the situation in the UK Patents Act 1977, the Irish legislation does not set out any criteria for determining the ownership of employer/employee inventions. Although the situation in Ireland is governed by the common law, s 39 of the UK Patents Act 1977 is of value in that it reflects the common law position that an invention made by an employee belongs to an employer where:

    (a) it was made in the course of the normal duties of the employee or in the course of duties falling outside his normal duties, but specifically assigned to him, and the circumstances in either case were such that

---

[9.] Rules 7(1), 7(2) and 7(3).
[10.] Section 16(2).
[11.] Section 16(1).

an invention might reasonably be expected to result from the carrying out of his duties; or

(b) the invention was made in the course of the duties of the employee and, at the time of making the invention, because of the nature of his duties and the particular responsibilities arising from the nature of his duties, he had a special obligation to further the interests of the employer's undertaking.

[4.05] In the absence of an express provision to the contrary, the common law imports an implied term that an employee is a trustee of his employer in relation to an invention made in the course of that person's duty as an employee. In *Patchett v Sterling Engineering Co Ltd*,[12] the inventor was employed as the appellant's chief designer. Lord Reid stated:

> "it is, in my judgement, inherent in the legal relationship of master and servant that any product of the work which the servant is paid to do belongs to the master".

The implied term can only be displaced by an agreement having legal force to the contrary effect since, again as stated by Lord Reid:

> "of course, as the relationship of master and servant is constituted by contract, the parties can, if they choose, alter or vary the normal incidents of the relationship, but they can only do that by express agreement or by an agreement which can be implied from the facts of the case."

[4.06] Whether an invention was made by the inventor in the course of his duty as employee is often difficult to determine and is a question of fact in each case. In *Loewy's Application*,[13] the inventor although described as a consulting engineer was held to be an employee. The tests applied in reaching a conclusion are whether the inventor was or was not employed to make the invention or whether the invention was made in the course of employment in which it was part of the employee's duty to make.

[4.07] The UK Bank's Report into the patent system and patent law[14] quotes from the judgment of Danckwerts J in *Fine Industrial Commodities Limited v Powling*[15] that:

> "the mere existence of a contract of service does not in itself disqualify the officer or employee from taking out a patent for an invention made by him during his term of service, even though the invention may relate to subject-matter germane to, and useful for, his employers in their business, and even

---

12. (1955) 72 RPC 50.
13. (1959) 69 RPC 3.
14. Cmnd 4407 p 132-133.
15. (1954) 53 RPC 253, at 257.

though the employee may have made use of his employer's time and servants and materials in bringing his invention to completion, and may have allowed his employers to use the invention while he was in their employment. But all the circumstances must be considered in each case. It is very material to see what is the nature of the inventor's position in regard to the business."

It was pointed out that:

"in the *Powling* case, the employee was the managing director of the employing company and was held to be a trustee for the company of his interest in the invention. It seems to be generally true to say that directors of companies and managers of businesses to whom no specific duties are allocated have a general duty to forward the interests of the company or business and will accordingly hold any inventions made during their employment (at least so far as they relate to the relevant business) in trust for the employer".

[4.08] In the case of *Electrolux Ltd v Hudson & Others*,[16] the defendants were husband and wife and the husband was employed as a senior storekeeper. Outside working hours the couple devised an adapter for use in vacuum cleaners and without using the materials of their employer. The standard conditions of employment included a clause to the effect that the discovery of any process, invention or improvement relating to articles not only manufactured by the plaintiff but by any of its associated companies in the United Kingdom or elsewhere had to be fully disclosed to the plaintiff who had first option over such. It was held by Whitford J that it was doubtful whether such a provision was appropriate or reasonable even for a research worker employed by the plaintiff but that in any event, there was no implied term because the husband's duties were such that he was not employed to invent. While it was necessary to serve his employer with good faith and fidelity, this did not mean that he could not take part in activities that might be harmful to the business of the plaintiff. In *Mellor v William Beardmore & Co Ltd*,[17] it was pointed out that notwithstanding that an inventor has used his employer's time and materials to aid him in completing the invention, the resulting patent could still belong to the employee. Where an employee is obliged by the terms of his employment to use his industry, skill, ingenuity and inventive ability to solve a technical problem, then the invention is held in trust for the employer because essentially that person has been employed to invent.[18] In *Harris's Patent*,[19] the employee/inventor was employed purely as a manager and salesman of a company engaged in the sale of valves under licence and there was no research and development carried out

---

16. [1977] FSR 312.
17. (1927) 44 RPC 175.
18. *British Reinforced Concrete v Lind* (1917) 34 RPC 101; *Adamson v Kenworthy* (1932) RPC 57.
19. [1985] RPC 19.

by it. It was held that his duties were such that the invention was not made in circumstances that it might reasonably have been expected from his normal duties. This decision was made on the basis of the legislative provisions in the UK Patents Act 1977 and it was stated that this may not necessarily embody the common law, which is used when deciding the position under Irish law.

[4.09] Section 53 of the Patents Act 1964 contained a specific provision which allowed the Court or the Controller to determine disputes between an employer and employee and in certain cases, apportion between them the benefit of the invention. There is no similar provision in the 1992 Act. Section 81 allows the Court to determine ownership and apportion such but this is limited to a two year time period from the date of grant of the patent unless the patentee knew that he was not entitled and s 81 is not specific to the employer/employee situation.

Form of Application

[4.10] An Irish patent application must be filed at the Irish Patents Office.[20] The request for the grant of a patent must be made on Form No 1[21] which is scheduled to the Patent Rules 1992[22] and must be accompanied by the requisite official fee.[23] The title of the invention appearing in the request for grant must be the same as the title in the specification.[24] The specification forming part of the patent application must commence with the title of the invention (which should be brief and indicate the matter to which the invention relates), continue with the description of the invention followed by the claim or claims and drawings, if any, in that order.[25]

[4.11] Since the title of the invention appears in the Official Journal shortly after the application is made, it may be important for an applicant to ensure that the title, while complying with the requirement of indicating the matter to which the invention relates, does not disclose information which it is desired, should not be published before the rest of the specification. The European Patent Office (EPO) Rules state that the title should clearly and concisely state the technical designation of the invention and should exclude all fancy names.

[4.12] The description of the invention which can be aided by drawings must disclose the invention in a manner sufficiently clear and complete for it to be carried out by a person skilled in the art.[26] This fictional person is also used in

---

[20.] Currently situated at 45 Merrion Square, Dublin 2 but scheduled to move to Kilkenny shortly.
[21.] See Schedule II - Patent Rules 1992 (SI 179/1992).
[22.] Section 18; Patent Rules, r 8.
[23.] Under the Patent Rules 1992 the fee payable is £117.
[24.] Rule 9.
[25.] Rule 10.
[26.] Section 19(1).

deciding whether or not there is an inventive step.[27] In the Irish High Court decision in *Rawls v Irish Tyre and Rubber Services Limited*,[28] Budd J approved of the reasoning of Lord Shaw in *British Thomson-Houston Co Ltd v Corona Lamp Works Ltd*[29] that the reader of a specification must be taken to be:

> "ordinarily intelligent and versed in the subject matter. Such a reader must be supposed to bring his stock of intelligence and knowledge to bear upon the document. If he is able to understand what the invention is and can produce the object and achieve the manufacture by the help of the written and drawn page, then the subject-matter of the invention does not fall because of vagueness."

[4.13] In addition, in construing a patent specification, its claims should be given a purposive construction rather than a literal one.[30] The person skilled in the art and to whom the specification is addressed is to possess no more than average knowledge. As stated in *Edison and Swan v Holland*,[31] it is:

> "to persons having a reasonably competent knowledge of what was known before on the subject to which this patent relates and having reasonably competent skill in the practical mode of doing what was then known".

Unlike the former position under the Patents Act 1964, an applicant is not required to disclose the best known method of performing the invention except in the case of a short term patent where under s 63(7)(b)(i) the applicant must describe the best method of performing the invention..

Micro-organisms

[4.14] There are special conditions concerning applications relating to inventions which require for their performance the use of micro-organisms.[32] The conditions set out in Rule 14 of the Patent Rules 1992 apply where the micro-organisms used in the invention are not available to the public at the date of filing and it cannot be described in the specification in such a manner as to enable the invention to be performed by a person skilled in the art. The conditions involve depositing a culture of the micro-organism in a depositary institution no later than the actual filing date of the application.[33] Details of the name of the depositary institution, the date of the deposit and the accession number of the deposit must be given in the specification. The giving of this information constitutes an unreserved and irrevocable consent to the depositary

---

[27.] Section 13.
[28.] [1960] IR 11, at 57.
[29.] [1922] 39 RPC 49, at 89.
[30.] *Wavin Pipes v Hepworth* [1982] FSR 32, at 53; *Catanic Components Ltd v Hill and Smith Ltd* [1981] FSR 60, at 65-66.
[31.] (1889) 6 RPC 243, at 280.
[32.] Section 19(2).
[33.] Rule 14(2).

institution to make the culture available on receipt of a certificate from the Controller.[34] Scheduled to the Patent Rules 1992 is the text of the prescribed request for the Controller's certificate authorising the release of the sample of the micro-organism. This Form must be filed in duplicate together with that required under the regulations to the Budapest Treaty on the International Recognition of the Deposit of Micro-Organisms for the Purposes of Patent Procedure.[35] The request must include an undertaking not to make the culture, or any culture derived from it, available to any other person and secondly, not to use the culture otherwise than for experimental purposes relating to the subject matter of the invention. The undertakings can be varied by way of agreement[36] and are not required of any Minister pursuant to the right to use an invention for the service of the State under s 77 of the Patents Act 1992. The undertaking not to make the culture, or any culture derived from the micro-organism available to the public, does not apply where it is necessary to give effect to a licence of right[37] or a compulsory licence.[38]

[4.15] Provided the preparations for publication of a patent application under s 28 have not been completed, an applicant can give notice that the sample of the micro-organism is only to be made available to an expert.[39] In these circumstances, a request for the Controller's certificate authorising release to an expert must contain full particulars of the nominated expert[40] who must also provide the undertakings vis-à-vis non-availability to other persons and non-use for other than experimental purposes relating to the subject matter of the invention.

[4.16] Rule 14(17) also provides that an applicant or proprietor may make a new deposit or to transfer the deposit to another institute in cases where the depositary institute can no longer satisfy a request for release and has notified the applicant accordingly. This must be done within three months of the receipt of such notification or of the depository institution ceasing to perform the functions of a depositary institution or to conduct its activities as such in an objective and impartial manner and requires a declaration that the culture so deposited is of the same micro-organism as the culture originally deposited. There must also be an amendment to the specification to indicate the accession

---

[34.] Rule 14(4).
[35.] Schedule II - Form No 6; see paras **[2.77]-[2.79]**.
[36.] Rule 14(11).
[37.] Section 68 - Rule 14(12).
[38.] Section 70 - Rule 14(12).
[39.] Rule 14(13).
[40.] Form No 8; Rule 14(16)(a).

number of the transferred or new deposit and, where applicable, the name of the depositary institution with which the deposit has been made.

THE CLAIMS

[4.17] A patent specification must contain one or more claims. Under s 20 of the Patents Act 1992, the claims must define the matter for which protection is sought, be clear and concise and be supported by the description. The extent of the protection conferred by the patent/patent application is determined essentially by the terms of the claims.[41] Novelty and inventiveness are also determined by the reference to the claims. When drafting claims, a patent agent strives to obtain the broadest possible protection for the invention, so that a patent cannot be avoided by making minor changes. In some instances, however, a claim must be very narrow in scope in order to distinguish the invention as claimed from what is already known. Since what is not claimed is disclaimed, the wording of a claim is extremely important.

[4.18] Claims essentially fall into two categories. Firstly, claims to a physical entity which are often called product claims and secondly, process claims which are applicable to all kinds of activities in which the use of some material product for effecting the process is implied. The activity may be exercised upon material products, upon energy, upon other processes (as in control processes) or upon living things.[42] Under s 34(1)(i) of the Patents Act 1964, it was a ground for the revocation of a patent that the scope of any claim of the complete specification was not sufficiently and clearly defined or that any claim of the complete specification was not fairly based on the matter disclosed in the specification.

[4.19] The grounds for revocation in the 1992 Act are set out in s 58 and do not include failure to comply with s 20. Thus, a patent cannot be revoked on the ground that the claims are not clear and concise and are not supported by the description.[43] The onus is on the Patents Office during examination to refuse the application if the claims are too wide or include matter not disclosed in the specification. Although this does lead to the position that mistakes of the Patents Office in allowing a claim which is too wide cannot later be put right, this seems to have been a deliberate decision of the parliamentary draftsman who would have had the benefit of the Court of Appeal decision in *Genentech Inc's Patent* and the regrets of Mustill LJ that even as guardians of the public interest, their hands were tied. In addition, given the very limited examination undertaken by the Irish Patents Office and since in most cases, a nationally filed Irish patent

---

41. Section 45.
42. EPO Guidelines - Part C (Ch III) 3.1.
43. *Genentech Inc's Patent* [1989] RPC 147.

application is likely to conform to a granted European or British patent, it would be extremely rare that an objection would arise under s 20, particularly as Article 84 of the EPC and s 14(5) of the UK Patents Act 1977 have equivalent provisions. Even though the claims must be supported by the description, it was made clear by Kenny J in the Irish High Court decision of *Farbwerke Hoechst AG v Intercontinental Pharmaceutical (Eire) Ltd*[44] that it is not permissible to supplement the claims by referring to the specification although it may be referred to as an indication of the sense in which words are used and as giving the technical background against which the claims have been formulated.

[4.20] Claims may be drafted in terms of the result to be achieved by the invention.[45] However, as made clear in *No-Fume Ltd v Pitchford*,[46] the claim must mention those features which must be chosen to enable the result to be achieved and the description must explain to a person skilled in the art how to conduct tests in order to find out how to achieve the result and to know that the result has been achieved. The EPO Guidelines[47] state that claims which define the invention in terms of the result to be achieved may be allowed if the invention can only be defined in such terms and if the result is one which can be directly and positively verified by tests or procedures adequately specified in the description and involving nothing more than trial and error. The important question is what is clear and concise to a person skilled in the art. An imprecise term may still be clear to a skilled person.[48]

[4.21] The question of whether or not a claim was supported by the description was discussed in the case of *Glatt's Application*.[49] The description referred to in s 20 is the description of the invention found in the specification which has been filed in support of the application and the claims must be within the contemplation of the inventor at the time of filing. The word 'support' requires the description to be the base which can fairly entitle the patentee to a monopoly of the width claimed.[50]

Unity of Invention

[4.22] A patent application must relate to one invention only or to a group of inventions so linked as to form a single general inventive concept.[51] Subject to this provision, a patent application may contain two or more independent claims

---

44. [1968] FSR 187, at 197.
45. *Hughes Tool Company v Ingersoll Rand Company Limited* [1977] FSR 406.
46. (1935) 52 RPC 231.
47. C-111 4.7.
48. *British Thomson v Corona* (1922) 39 RPC 49.
49. [1983] RPC 122.
50. *Schering Biotech's Application* [1993] RPC 249.
51. Section 21.

in the same category (product, process, apparatus or use) where it is not appropriate, having regard to the subject-matter of the application, to cover this subject-matter by a single claim.[52] Any claim stating the essential features of an invention may be followed by one or more claims concerning particular embodiments of that invention.[53] Section 21(2) states that rules may be provided for treating two or more inventions as being so linked as to form a single inventive concept. Rule 17 allows for one and the same patent application to include:

(a) in addition to an independent claim for a product, an independent claim for a process specially adapted for the manufacture of the product, and an independent claim for a use of the product; or

(b) in addition to an independent claim for a process, an independent claim for an apparatus or means specifically designed for carrying out the process; or

(c) in addition to an independent claim for a product, an independent claim for a process specially adapted for the manufacture of the product, and an independent claim for an apparatus or means specifically designed for carrying out the process.

The question of what is a single invention is a question of fact. In *Celanese Corp Application*,[54] it was held that claims to intermediate and final chemical products did not relate to a single invention.

[4.23] The validity of a patent cannot be challenged on the ground that it relates to more than one invention. If, during examination, there is an objection that the application relates to more than one invention, the applicant can amend the specification and delete or amend the claims. The applicant may also file another patent application in respect of the additional invention, ie, a divisional application.[55] This can also be done voluntarily. It is extremely important, however, that the subject matter of the divisional application does not extend beyond the content of the earlier (parent) application as filed because this is a ground for revocation under s 58(c). The divisional application may be filed within two months of amendment of the earlier (parent) application following:

(1) a search report;

[52.] Rule 11(1).
[53.] Rule 11(2).
[54.] (1952) 69 RPC 22.
[55.] Section 24.

(2) the grant of a patent which is being utilised as evidence in support of the earlier application, provided the request to pay the grant fee has not been issued in either case; or

(3) at any time before grant under s 32.[56]

If there has been no amendment of the earlier application or the amendment of the earlier application does not fall within the above, then a divisional application may be filed at any time after filing of the earlier application except after refusal, withdrawal, deemed withdrawal of the earlier application, or after the applicant has been requested to pay the fee for the grant of a patent in respect of the invention to which that application relates.[57] A divisional patent application is deemed to have been filed on the date of filing of the earlier application and is entitled to any priority claimed, if appropriate. In all other respects, a divisional application proceeds as an independent substantive application. Since the reality of the Irish patent system is that there is little or no examination under the provisions of s 21, patents may be granted in respect of applications claiming more than one invention. Although a division of a corresponding EPC or UK application may have been required, the resulting patents may be used as combined evidence under s 30 and an objection is unlikely to arise.

ABSTRACT

[4.24] The filing of an abstract was not a requirement under Irish patent legislation prior to the 1992 Act. Under Rule 13 of the Patents Rules 1992 the abstract must commence with the title of the invention and contain a concise summary of the matter contained in the specification. The abstract must indicate the technical field to which the invention pertains and be drafted in such a way so as to allow an understanding of the technical problem, the gist of the solution to that problem by means of the invention and the principal use or uses of the invention. Where appropriate, it should contain the chemical formula which, among those contained in the specification, best characterises the invention. Not to be included are statements on the alleged merits or value of the invention or on its speculative application. The abstract should preferably contain fewer than one hundred and fifty words. The purpose of the abstract is that it should constitute an efficient instrument for the purposes of searching in the particular field by making it possible to assess whether there is a need for consulting the patent application itself.[58] Section 22 states that the abstract shall only serve for use as technical information. It is not be to used for any other purpose and does

---

[56.] Rule 20(1).
[57.] Rule 20(1).
[58.] Rule 13(5).

not form part of the state of the art against a subsequently filed co-pending application under s 11(3). It is important not to rely on the disclosure solely in an abstract when amending a specification. The EPO has refused to allow an abstract to be used as a basis for overcoming an objection that an amendment to an application constituted subject matter which extended beyond the content of the application as filed.[59] The Controller has power to reframe the abstract if he forms the view that it does not adequately fulfil its purpose. Against this decision of the Controller, there is no appeal.[60]

FILING DATES AND PRIORITY

[4.25] While s 18 lays down the requirements for an application for a patent under the 1992 Act all of those requirements need not be complied with on the initial filing of the application. Section 23 lays down the minimum requirements to establish a filing date, namely the payment of the official filing fee and documentation containing (a) an indication that a patent is sought, (b) information identifying the applicant and (c) a description of the invention even though such may not comply with the Act or Rules. There is provision for the Minister to prescribe for the late payment of filing fees but the current patent rules do not allow for late payment. Unlike the provisions of Article 80 of the EPC, a filing date can be established without the inclusion of any claims and this is similar to the position under the Patents Act 1964 which did not require the inclusion of claim(s) in a Provisional Patent Application. Under r 95, it is necessary that documentation in a foreign language be accompanied by a translation and this would include the need for a translation of the description as filed.[61]

[4.26] Subsections (3) and (4) of s 23 deal with the question of drawings which are referred to in the application but which have been omitted from the documentation at the date of filing. Rule 18 provides for a one month grace period from official notification and within which to make a request to treat the drawings as having been filed on the date of filing the application. If there is no request, any reference to the drawings is deemed to be deleted.

[4.27] Under rule 19, the claims and the abstract can be filed within twelve months from the date of filing or, if priority has been claimed, from the date of priority. A divisional application is deemed to have the date of the parent application.[62] There is also provision for the High Court to determine a question of entitlement to a granted patent. If it is found that a patent was granted to a

---

[59.] See s 58(c); see *Identification System/Bull* [1989] 6 EPOR 344.
[60.] Section 96(1).
[61.] See *Rohde and Schwarz's Application* [1980] RPC 155.
[62.] Section 24.

person not entitled and revocation is ordered, then the party who had sought revocation can make a new application and such will be given the date of filing of the revoked patent.[63] In this instance and that of a divisional application, after expiry of the period of twelve months allowed for in r 19, the requirements must be met at the actual filing date of the new application or divisional application, as the case may be.

[4.28] The Paris Convention for the Protection of Industrial Property[64] to which most countries adhere, allows for persons who have filed in a convention country to claim this date when filing a corresponding patent application in further convention countries. There is a twelve month priority period within which to file such further applications. The effect of claiming priority is best illustrated by an example. If a patent application is filed in Britain on 2 January 1995 and a corresponding application in respect of the same invention is filed in Ireland in December 1995, then provided the requisite formalities are complied with and priority claimed, the Irish application will be given the priority date of 2 January 1995. The importance and effect of such a provision is that there is a twelve month period from filing and within which disclosure can take place without invalidating any subsequent patent because novelty and inventiveness will be determined with reference to the priority date. If priority is claimed, publication of the invention will take place 18 months after the priority date thus moving forward the date from which the contents of a patent specification are treated as being available to the public.[65]

[4.29] Section 25 provides that priority can also be claimed from an application in a convention country for a utility model, a utility certificate or an inventor's certificate. The applicant claiming priority does not have to be the same applicant as that in the priority country but can be a successor in title. There is also no requirement for a successful outcome to the application from which priority is claimed.

[4.30] The 12 month priority period is prescribed in rule 21(1) and commences on the date following the date of filing of the previous application whose priority is claimed. Outside this period the right of priority is normally lost. However, under rule 21(2), if an applicant can show that despite all due care, the application could not have been filed within the 12 months, there is prescribed a period of not later than 14 months from the date of filing the earlier application. It is possible for an application to be filed and then withdrawn, abandoned or even refused and to then subsequently re-file the application and claim priority

---

[63.] Section 81.
[64.] See Ch 2, paras **[2.02]-[2.24]**.
[65.] Section 28.

from this second application provided that the first application has not been published and that there are no rights outstanding. An applicant must be sure that there has been no public disclosure prior to filing the second application. Otherwise the invention would be considered to be part of the state of the art and not novel.[66]

[4.31] If priority is to be claimed, then an applicant must declare such[67] and Form No 1 relating to a request for the grant of a patent and which is scheduled to the Rules, must indicate the date of the previous filing, the state in or for which it was made and the application number, if available.[68] It is also necessary to file a certified copy of the previous application, ie, the priority document. This can be done within 16 months of the priority date with a possible further extension of one month. The certification must be by the authority (usually the National Patent Office) which received the previous application and includes a certificate stating the date of filing.[69] An English translation of the priority document is required within 21 months of the priority date when the basic application is in a language other than English or Irish.[70] Where the claimed priority date is from an application filed under the 1964 or 1992 Patents Act or an International application for a patent designating the state which is filed at the Irish Patents Office, then instead of filing a certified copy of the previous application, an applicant may simply request the Controller to include such a document with the patent application.

[4.32] It is also possible to claim priority from an application filed under the EPC even if Ireland has not been designated. In relation to an EPC application designating Ireland, the procedural requirements for claiming priority are deemed to have been complied with, provided the requirements of r 38(1) to (3) of the implementing regulations to the EPC have been met. It is possible to claim multiple priorities even originating from different states. However, the 12 month period cannot be extended by making further applications and claiming priority from such. The time limit runs from the earliest date of priority.[71]

[4.33] The right of priority only extends to those elements of a patent application which are included in the application(s) whose priority is claimed.[72] This should be apparent from the claims but priority may still be allowed if the documents as a whole, specifically disclosed such elements.[73] Under the 1964 Act the same

---

66. Section 11.
67. Section 26.
68. Rule 22(1).
69. Rule 22(2).
70. Rule 22(3).
71. Section 26(2).
72. Section 26(3).
73. Section 26(4).

question was answered on the basis of whether the claim was fairly based on the matter disclosed in the specification.[74] The new criteria should probably be considered to be stricter and more likely to equate to the test applied by the EPO under Article 123(2) of the EPC dealing with amendment of a European patent application and which states an amendment cannot contain subject matter which extends beyond the content of the application as filed. The test which is stated in EPO Guidelines C-V, 2.4 is that:

> the subject matter of the claim must be derivable directly and unambiguously from the disclosure of the invention in the priority document when account is taken of any features implicit to a person skilled in the art in what is expressly mentioned in the document.

In *Stauffer Chemical Company's Application*,[75] Buckley LJ in considering the matter under the "fairly based" criteria of earlier legislation observed that if a new feature were a development along the same line of thought which constitutes or underlies the invention described in the earlier document, then priority might be claimed. However if the additional feature involved a new inventive step or brought something new into the combination which represented a departure from the idea of the invention described in the earlier document, it could not.

PUBLICATION OF THE PATENT APPLICATION

[4.34] When an Irish patent application is filed at the Patents Office, within approximately four weeks of filing, brief particulars are published in the fortnightly Patents Office Journal. The particulars are provided for in r 65 and are as follows:

(a) the name of the applicant;

(b) the title of the invention;

(c) the date of filing;

(d) the date and country of any priority claimed;

(e) the number of the application given by the Patents Office and the use of a letter "S" to indicate if the application is in respect of a short term patent.

The first two numerals indicate the year of filing. If an application is for a divisional, the date of filing and any priority date of the parent application will also be indicated. This is the only information publicly available until publication of the application, which is as soon as practicable after the expiry of

---

74. PA 1964, s 10.
75. [1977] RPC 33.

eighteen months from the date of filing, or, if priority is claimed from the date of priority. An applicant can, however, request earlier publication.[76]

[4.35] The information to be made publicly available is unclear in that rule 23 simply states that it should include the description, claims, drawings (if any) and abstract as fil∪d. If there has been an amendment of the claims prior to termination of the technical preparations for publication, both the original claims and the new or amended claims are published. If available, the statement of inventorship[77] and a copy of any priority document is also published together with all translations. A patent application is not published if, before the termination of the technical preparations for publication, it has been finally refused or withdrawn or has been deemed to have been withdrawn.[78]

[4.36] Under r 23(3), it is for the Controller to determine when the technical preparations for publication of the application are to be treated as having been completed. However, in *Intera Corporation's Application*,[79] the Court of Appeal ordered an application not to be published and pointed out that each case had to be determined objectively on a case by case basis. In *Peabody International's Application*,[80] an application to stop publication was refused, it being held that preparations for publication were completed by the Patent Office on the day when the folio of documents for the application had been made ready for collection by the printer.

[4.37] Applications which are published under s 28 are advertised in the Patents Office Journal. The advertisement lists the applications becoming open to public inspection as from the date of issue of the Journal. The information in the advertisement is the application number, name of applicant, title of invention and the date of filing of the application or the earliest priority date claimed. Also included for search purposes are code marks showing the primary index under the International Patent Classification. The Controller can omit from the published patent application, statements or other matter contrary to public order or morality. Also, statements disparaging the products or processes of any particular person other than the applicant, or the merits or validity of applications or patents of any such person can be omitted. Mere comparison with the prior art is not considered to be disparaging *per se*.[81] There is no appeal from the Controller's decision in relation to decisions to omit such statements.[82]

---

76. Section 28.
77. The Rules incorrectly state such to be under s 14(2). This should presumably be s 17(2).
78. Section 28(2).
79. [1986] RPC 459.
80. [1986] RPC 521.
81. Section 28(5).
82. Section 96.

PROCEDURE UP TO GRANT

[4.38] In the explanatory memorandum to the Patents Bill 1991 it was stated that:

> before the Bill was prepared, the procedure for examination and grant of patents under the present law was reviewed as there was concern about the large and growing backlog of applications awaiting examination in the Patents Office. It was clear that by continuing to follow present procedures, there was no prospect of either eliminating the present backlog in the foreseeable future or avoiding future backlogs. Accordingly, the present Bill now contains new provisions regarding examination which will both be adequate and speed up examination considerably.

In 1991, there were delays in the order of six years in the examination of applications. It is true that the new procedures which are not dramatically different from those under the 1964 Act are likely to streamline the procedure to grant but the reduction in the backlog is more likely to be attributable to a substantial reduction in the number of nationally filed Irish patent applications following ratification of the EPC.

[4.39] The procedures leave open to an applicant a number of options. Under s 29 an applicant can prosecute the application by means of a search report requested from the Irish Patents Office on payment of the appropriate search fee. The request for such a search report and the fee must be submitted within 21 months from filing or if claimed, the priority date. In the case of a divisional application filed on or after the 21 months from the filing date of the parent case, the request must be submitted on the actual filing date of the divisional application.[83] The search is not in fact carried out by the Irish Patents Office but with the approval of the Minister by the UK Patents Office.

[4.40] A patent application must include one or more claims and it is on the basis of such claim(s) that the search is undertaken. If it transpires in the course of the search that an application claims more than one invention, the search is conducted only in relation to the first invention specified in the claim(s). If the applicant wishes a search to be carried out in respect of any additional invention, then a request and further fee must be submitted within one month of the date of issue by the Controller to the applicant of the search report relating to the first invention.[84]

[4.41] The search report is sent to the applicant who has a two month period from issuance to advise the Controller if the application is to be withdrawn.[85]

---

[83] Rule 24(1).
[84] Section 29(2); r 24(3).
[85] Rule 24(4).

The consequence of non-withdrawal is that the report is published. If the application is maintained (in the light of the search report(s)), the applicant has four months within which to submit amendments to the application or to advise the Controller that no amendment is considered necessary. If this is not done, the Controller may refuse the application.[86]

[4.42] An alternative to requesting a search report lies in s 30 and if applicable, an applicant can avail of the option of submitting to the Controller a statement that an application for the same invention has been made in the UK, Germany, the EPO or under the PCT. This statement must be made within 21 months of the date of filing or priority date if claimed. In addition to the statement, there must subsequently be filed evidence in the form of the search results issued on the relevant patent application or the grant of a patent from such. The form of evidence and the time limits for filing such under r 27 are as follows:

SOURCE	FORM	TIME LIMIT
(1) EPC	Copy of published European patent application and related search report or a copy of the published specification of the granted European patent.	Within two months of the publication of the search report or of the specification.
(2) PCT	Copy of the published International application and the related search report.	Within two months of publication of the search report.
(3) UK Patent Office	Copy of the published application and related search report or a copy of the published specification of the granted patent.	Within two months of the publication of the application or of the receipt by the applicant of the search report (whichever is the later), or within two months of the publication of the specification.

[86.] Section 29(4).

(4) German Patent Office (Deutsches Patentamt)	Copy of the published application and related search report or a copy of the published specification of the granted patent (Patentschrift)	Within two months of publication of the search report or of the specification.
(5) Countries where searches are carried out by the EPO.	Copy of the published application and related search report of the EPO.	Within two months of the publication of the search report.

The fifth source of evidence is provided for in r 27(1)(e) but there is an inconsistency because r 26 which lists the prescribed sources does not include such. This omission is likely to be regarded as an error and the inconsistency resolved in favour of an applicant relying on such a source. Belgium is an example of a country whose national Patent Office has its searches carried out under the auspices of the EPO. An extension of the time limit for filing the evidence under r 27 may be allowed by the Controller if a request for such is made and the official fee is paid within the extended period specified in the request.

[4.43] Section 30(2) also states that if requested, an applicant must furnish details of foreign applications for the same invention. The time limit for furnishing such information is six months from the request and what is required is a list of all such applications and a copy of the report showing the result of any search made in relation to such applications. [87] The Controller can also specifically request a statement as to whether such applications are still pending, have been accepted, are withdrawn or deemed to have been withdrawn or have been refused. It should be noted that the request for such information does not appear to be limited to instances where an applicant is relying on a foreign specification or search report under s 30(1). When the evidence under s 30(1) has been filed, there is a two month time limit within which to notify the Controller of any withdrawal. Failure to withdraw means that the evidence will be published.[88] If there has been no withdrawal and the applicant is relying on the results of a search of a corresponding foreign application, ie, s 30(1)(a), then the Controller issues a notification that the applicant has an opportunity to amend the application in the light of that evidence. The applicant has four months from notification either to submit amendments or a statement that no

---

[87.] Rule 25.
[88.] Section 30(3); r 28(1).

amendment is considered necessary failing which the application may be refused.[89] Similarly, if the evidence is based on the grant of a corresponding foreign patent, ie, s 30(1)(b), there is a four month period from notification within which to submit amendments to the specification so that the subject matter claimed therein does not extend beyond that of the evidence.[90] Again, an applicant must make the required amendment or advise the Controller that such is not considered necessary.

[4.44] Any amendment under ss 29(4) or 30(4) and (5) or the furnishing of a statement that no amendment is considered necessary must be submitted by a patent agent.[91] There is no provision for such to be done by an applicant. The extremely limited examination that will be carried out by the Irish Patents Office can be seen in s 31(1) and the proviso that the Controller will not raise an objection because of non-compliance with ss 9(1) (unpatentability), 11 (lack of novelty), 13 (lacking inventive step), 14 (no industrial application), 19 (no clear and complete disclosure) or 20 (unclear or inconcise claims). The onus to ensure compliance with these substantive issues is with the applicant whose incentive for compliance is that failure to do so could lead to successful grounds for revocation under s 58.

[4.45] It should be noted, however, that the presence of claim(s) which do not define the matter in a clear and concise form and which are not supported by the description[92] are not included in the grounds for revocation and therefore it may be extremely difficult for a third party to establish the scope of protection. There is provision for including in Rules, examination of these substantive matters and objection for non-compliance[93] but this is only likely to arise if the current procedure leads to an abuse of the patent system.

[4.46] If, following the limited examination, the Controller requests compliance with requirements, then a time limit for dealing with the official action is indicated in the communication from the Controller. Failure to comply may lead to refusal of the application.[94] There is also a provision in s 31(5) which disallows double patenting. In cases where there are two or more applications for the same invention with the same filing or priority date by the same applicant or his successor in title, the Controller may refuse to grant a patent in respect of more than one of the applications. This may arise, for example, in the case of a nationally filed application before the Irish Patents Office and a second EPO

---

89. Section 30(4); r 28(2).
90. Section 30(5); r 28(2).
91. Section 30(6); r 28(3).
92. Section 20.
93. Section 31(2).
94. Section 31(1).

application designating Ireland. The words "may refuse" suggest that the Controller has a discretion. However, in the case of *IBM (Barclay & Bigar's) Application*,[95] the UK Patents Office held that the second application must be refused.

[4.47] If all formalities have been satisfied, the Controller will request payment of a grant fee. The fee must be paid within four months of the request with a possible three month extension. Failure to pay the fee means that the application is deemed to be withdrawn.[96] Once the grant fee and appropriate renewals have been paid, then a certificate of grant of a patent issues as per Form No 3 annexed to the Rules. A notice of grant is also published in the Patents Office Journal and the Controller also publishes a specification of the patent containing the description, claims and drawings (if any) and such matters which appear to the Controller at his discretion to be useful or important.[97] This, for example, could include information concerning foreign patent applications which the Controller may have sought under s 30(2).

[4.48] In addition to an amendment of an application under ss 29 or 30 following a search report or the grant of a corresponding foreign patent, an applicant is allowed to amend of their own volition.[98] Under s 32(3) the Controller may refuse to accept such amendment if it is considered that it should have been properly made under s 29 or s 30 and presumably, within the time limits prescribed under these sections. The Rules also impose restrictions on amendments made of an applicant's own volition and such amendment of the description, claims or drawings can only be made in accordance with the Rules.[99] If made prior to the time limits imposed under ss 29 and 30, then amendment of the description, claims and drawings can only take place once.[100] After making amendments under ss 29 and 30 or if there has been no such amendment and the time limit has expired, then amendment of the description, claims or drawings at an applicant's own volition can only be made with the consent of the Controller following the filing of an application for leave to amend[101] which must give the reasons for desiring amendment.

[95.] [1983] RPC 283.
[96.] Section 31(3); r 29.
[97.] Section 34.
[98.] Section 32(1).
[99.] Rule 31(5).
[100.] Rule 31(1).
[101.] Rule 31(2).

[4.49] Any amendment of a patent application is invalid to the extent that it extends the subject matter disclosed in the application as filed.[102] This is a ground for revocation under s 58(c). The EPO guidelines[103] state that:

> an amendment should be regarded as introducing subject matter which extends beyond the content of the application as filed, and therefore is unallowable, if the overall change in the content of the application (whether by way of addition, alteration or exclusion) results in the skilled person being presented with information which is not directly and unambiguously derivable from that previously presented by the application, even when account is taken of matter which is implicit to a person skilled in the art in what has been expressly mentioned.

In *Van Der Lely's Application*,[104] a divisional application was refused because the disclosure extended beyond that of the parent application. Falconer J accepted the Comptroller's view that the fundamental principle in determining additional subject matter is to decide whether one document presents the informed reader with information relevant to the invention which the other document does not. In *Ward's Application*,[105] it was held that matter must not be disclosed which extends, in the sense of enlarging upon, the original disclosure, ie, which increases the specificity or particularisation of that disclosure. It would appear that unless an amended claim is supported by the unamended specification, the disclosure must have been extended.[106] Ambiguities are usually construed against an applicant. If a specification states, expressly or by implication, that a particular feature is essential, the applicant will normally be held to that.[107] In *Southco Inc v Dzus Fastener Europe Ltd*,[108] the Court of Appeal held that even though the main claim of the granted patent was worded differently from the application, it was allowable because it did not add fresh subject matter to the application even though there was a possible broadening of the claim.

[4.50] An application can be withdrawn at any time before grant. This must be a clear and unqualified statement of withdrawal if publication is to be avoided and it is advisable to request official confirmation that the withdrawal is effective and to give sufficient time to ensure that preparations for publication have not been completed.[109] Once publication takes place, the contents of the application

---

102. Section 32(2).
103. C-VI, 5.4; Article 123(2).
104. [1987] RPC 61.
105. [1986] RPC 50.
106. *Raychem Ltd's Application* [1986] RPC 547.
107. *Harding's Patent* [1988] RPC 515.
108. [1992] RPC 299. See also *AC Edwards v Acme Signs & Displays Ltd* [1992] RPC 131.
109. *Intera's Application* [1986] RPC 459.

become part of the state of the art when considering novelty. Priority rights can still be claimed from an application which has been withdrawn or refused[110] but no other rights remain.[111] Under s 34(3) a lapsed patent application can be restored on the same grounds as those for restoring a patent under s 37.

SHORT TERM PATENTS

[4.51] A short term patent is a totally new concept under Irish law and it did not exist under the Patents Act 1964 or the Industrial and Commercial Property (Protection Act) 1927. An explanation as to why such was introduced was given on the explanatory memorandum to the Patents Bill 1991 as follows:

> The provisions here are completely new to Irish law and were devised in the interests of the small inventor who may find that a full term patent is unnecessary for his particular invention. Experience has shown that small innovators and individual inventors find the task of obtaining a full patent costly and time consuming and, therefore, a disincentive to protecting inventions. Short term patents will be capable of being obtained without undue official obstacles and lower official fees will apply. The period of protection will be 10 years which will particularly suit less technologically complex inventions which by their nature, will not have very long life cycles but which nevertheless have an important place in the whole process of industrial innovation and in encouraging the start-up of new projects.

[4.52] The concept of a system for securing a petty patent to ensure that a short term monopoly protection can be obtained easily and inexpensively for small articles or simple inventions is not new and, for example, such exists under Australian law but with a different structure. Germany and some other countries have protection for what is termed a "utility model" and which again provides for a shorter term of protection but in return, a simplified and speedier registration.

[4.53] Probably the best way of looking at the provisions governing a short term patent is to look at how they differ from that of a regular or full term patent. Firstly, as the name suggests, it has a shorter duration, namely ten years[112] as opposed to the usual twenty year term. Secondly, the criteria governing patentability are that the invention must be new, susceptible of industrial application and not clearly lacking an inventive step. In the Patents Bill 1991 as initiated, what was proposed was a short term patent for an invention which did not involve an inventive step. This would have meant that valid patents could have existed for inventions which were clearly obvious. What exists in s 63(4) is

---

[110.] Section 33(2)(b).
[111.] Section 33(2)(c).
[112.] Section 63(1).

simply a less onerous requirement for patentability, namely that the invention is not clearly obvious. There is, of course, a very fine line to be drawn between what is and what is not obvious, being a question of degree in each case. Many inventions seem in retrospect to be very simple but since the courts have long recognised that simplicity should not be confused with obviousness, it may well be that the difference will not in fact prove significant. However, in relation to a short term patent, it is probably true to say there is no longer a requirement that in order to maintain a patent, there must be a substantial exercise of the inventive power or inventive faculty.[113]

[4.54] Importantly, a short term patent requires disclosure of the best method of performing the invention known to the applicant.[114] This differs considerably from the provisions relating to sufficiency of disclosure for a normal patent, which is that the invention as disclosed must be sufficiently clear and complete for it to be carried out by a person skilled in the art.[115] The words "best method of performing" in fact appear in the revocation grounds under the 1964 Act[116] and guidance as to interpretation can be obtained from this source. It is essentially a question of the good faith of the applicant. As stated by Pollock CB in *Tetley v Easton*:[117]

"a man has no right to patent a principle and then give to the public the humblest instrument that can be made from his principle and to reserve to himself all the better part of it".

[4.55] However, this is not restricted to cases of dishonest conduct in withholding information from the public. It covers any case in which the applicant has not disclosed the best method known to him of performing the invention, whatever the reason for the omission.[118] In the case of a body corporate, the relevant knowledge is that of the person who gave instruction for the application, and controlled it on the company's behalf, properly instructed so as to be in possession of the relevant information. The question of the date on which the determination of "best method" is to be decided has not been dealt with by the Irish courts. In the UK there have been contrasting decisions in *American Cyanamid Company v Ethicon Limited*[119] where it was held that there was no obligation on an applicant to incorporate in the complete specification improvements made after the filing of the priority application. In *Monsanto Co v*

---

113. *Williams v NYE* (1890) 7 RPC 62.
114. Section 63(7)(b)(i).
115. Section 19(1).
116. Section 34(1)(h) - PA 1964.
117. (1833) 2 EI & BI 956.
118. *Du Pont De Nemours v Enka BV* [1988] FSR 69.
119. [1979] RPC 215.

Maxwell Hart (London) Ltd,[120] the relevant date of knowledge of the best method was held to be the period shortly before the filing of the complete specification. In *American Cyanamid Company v Berk Pharmaceuticals Limited,*[121] the patent was revoked because the specification was held not to describe the best method of performing the invention known to the patentee. Certain strains of micro-organisms were known by the patentee to produce higher yields and were not disclosed.

[4.56] A short term patent may include a maximum of five claims.[122] The claims must be clear and supported by the description. Although s 20 dealing with claims pertaining to a full term patent also states that a claim should be 'concise' the absence of such a requirement for a short term patent is unlikely to be of any consequence. There is, however, a requirement for an application for a short term patent to be accompanied by any drawing referred to in the description.[123] It is not possible to hold both an ordinary patent and a short term patent for the same invention.[124]

[4.57] A short term patent is not examined *vis-à-vis* the existing state of the art and there is no requirement to submit any evidence of patentability by way of grant of an equivalent patent in other jurisdictions or search results in other jurisdictions.[125] In effect, this means that a short term patent can be obtained in respect of an invention which is not novel or which is totally lacking in any inventive step. The *quid pro quo* of securing a short term patent is that in order to enforce such against third parties by way of an action for infringement, it is at that stage necessary to carry out a prior art search. This search is by way of a request accompanied by a fee to the Controller who in fact commissions the UK Patent Office to carry out the search as to the state of the art and prepare a report as to the results. The resulting search report is sent both to the proprietor of the short term patent and the alleged infringer[126] and is also published.[127] Instead of requesting a search report, it is possible to submit the results of a search carried out in the UK or Germany or by the EPO or WIPO in respect of the same invention. A copy of a corresponding European, UK or German patent can also be used instead of a search report. Again, this evidence is published and a copy must be sent by the proprietor to the alleged infringer.[128] Essentially, these

---

120. [1981] RPC 201.
121. [1976] RPC 231.
122. Section 63(7)(b)(ii).
123. Section 63(7)(b)(iii).
124. Section 64.
125. Section 65.
126. Section 66(1)(b).
127. Section 66(2).
128. Section 66(3).

requirements are imposed so that alleged infringers will be able to consider the actual validity of the patent and counterclaim for revocation if appropriate. Because of the ease with which a short term patent is granted as opposed to the rigours of securing a normal patent, it is entirely justified that the proprietor of a short term patent be obliged to furnish the results of a state of the art search in respect of the invention before infringement proceedings can be instituted.

[4.58] It is also possible for a search to be requested by a person other than the proprietor of a short term patent.[129] Such a person must show to the satisfaction of the Controller the following:

(a) that there are grounds to suspect that the invention is not new or is clearly lacking an inventive step; and

(b) that because of the person's legitimate business interests, it would, in all the circumstances, be reasonable that a search report be prepared.[130]

Infringement proceedings on foot of a short term patent can be brought before the Circuit Court irrespective of the amount of a claim.[131]

[4.59] The grounds for revocation of a short term patent are the same as those for a normal patent but include an additional ground that the claims of the specification of the patent are not supported by the description.[132] Section 20 of the Patents Act 1992 also imposes this requirement but an objection under this provision can only be raised pre-grant and thus the onus lies with the Patent Office. In *Glatt's Application*,[133] a divisional application was rejected on the grounds that the claims were not supported by the description, the principle being that third parties should not have to face monopolies which were neither clearly sought nor founded by the inventor at the date of filing, but which were conceived later and claimed *post hoc*. In *Protoned BV's Application*,[134] the claim referred to two types of spring, one of which was stated to be a "mechanical compression spring". The applicant sought to delete the word "compression". The deletion was not allowed because it had the effect of adding a whole range of springs not described in the body of the specification.

[129.] Section 66(6).
[130.] Rule 45(2).
[131.] Section 66(4).
[132.] Section 67.
[133.] [1983] RPC 122.
[134.] [1983] FSR 110.

Chapter 5

Patents Act 1992 - Maintenance and Dealings in Patents

RENEWAL FEES

[5.01] Under the Patents Act 1964 there were no renewal fees payable during the pendency of an application. The Patent Rules 1965 provided for annual renewal fees at the expiration of the fourth year from the date of the patent.[1] Certainly, during the latter years of the Patents Act 1964, it was rare that a patent would be sealed within this period and the Rules allowed for payment of outstanding accumulated annuities at any time before the expiration of three months from the date of sealing the patent. The Patents Act 1992 follows the EPC model and for patent applications filed from 1 August 1992, annual renewal fees are payable on pending applications.

[5.02] Rules 33(8) and 34 prescribe that renewal fees are payable in respect of the third and each subsequent year calculated from the date of filing of the patent application. A renewal fee is payable on or before the last day of the month in which such year commences. Thus, for example, if a patent application was filed on 5 August 1993, the renewal fee for the third year would be payable on or before 31 August 1995 and annually thereafter. In relation to patent applications filed prior to 1 August 1992, ie, under the 1964 Act, no renewals are payable until the application proceeds to grant. From the issue of the certificate of grant, there is a three month period within which to pay accumulated annuities.

[5.03] When a divisional application is filed after the expiry of the second year from the date of the parent application, accumulated renewal fees are paid at the time of filing the divisional application. Renewal fees cannot be validly paid more than four months before the date on which they fall due.[2] When paid, the Controller issues a renewal certificate. The prescribed period for payment of a renewal fee can be extended, subject to a maximum extension of six months, provided the necessary extension fees are paid.[3] This extension is a requirement under Article 5 *bis* of the Paris International Convention. A court may refuse to

---

[1.] Rule 61.
[2.] Rules 33(2) and 34(3).
[3.] Sections 35(2) and 36(3).

award damages for infringement during any extended period and before the renewal fee is paid.[4]

[5.04] In the case of a European patent application designating the State, renewal fees from the third year are paid to the EPO under Article 86(1) of the EPC. The renewal fees are only paid to the Irish Patents Office in respect of years which follow that in which the mention of the grant of the patent is published in the European Patent Bulletin. Where a renewal fee is due within two months of such publication, it may be paid within those two months.[5] Where the period for paying a renewal fee has expired, rule 34(5) imposes an obligation on the Controller to send a reminder to the address for service not later than six weeks after the last day for payment. The reminder must also advise of the consequence of non-payment, ie the lapsing of the patent.

DURATION OF A PATENT

[5.05] Under the 1964 Act, an Irish patent remained in force for sixteen years from the date of filing of the complete specification and provided renewal fees were paid. Section 27 of the 1964 Act allowed a patentee to petition either the High Court or the Controller for an extension of the term of a patent. If it appeared to the Court or the Controller that the patentee had been inadequately remunerated by the patent, the term could be extended for a further term not exceeding five years, or, in exceptional cases, ten years. In making a decision, regard was had to the nature and merits of the invention in relation to the public, to the profits made by the patentee as such, and to all the circumstances of the case. In *JR Geigy AG's Patent*,[6] the Irish High Court followed the principles in *Fleming's Patent*[7] and asked itself the following questions:

    (a) is the invention one of more than ordinary utility?

    (b) has the patentee been adequately remunerated? and

    (c) is the absence of remuneration due to no fault of the patentee?

There were a number of petitions presented, mostly these were to the High Court. In almost all cases, the extensions sought were in relation to pharmaceutical or veterinary patents where there were delays in the introduction of the product onto the market because of delays in obtaining regulatory approval from the Drugs Advisory Board. While these cases are now of academic interest only, because the 1992 Act does not allow for an extended term, one must have regard to the transitional provisions of the 1992 Act and to

---

[4.] Section 49(2).
[5.] Rule 34(2).
[6.] [1982] FSR 278.
[7.] (1918) 35 RPC 55.

the European Communities (Supplementary Protection Certificate) Regulations 1993.[8]

[5.06] Under s 36 of the 1992 Act, a patent shall, subject to payment of renewal fees "continue in force until the end of the period of twenty years beginning with the date of filing of the patent application". This twenty year period is in keeping with that which exists in most countries and under the EPC. Article 33 of TRIPS imposes a minimum duration of 20 years. The transitional provisions[9] effectively extended the term of a patent from 16 to 20 years for all patents granted under the 1964 Act and in force on 1 August 1992 subject to the payment of renewal fees for the additional term. If a patent had already been extended following a petition under the 1964 Act, a patentee could not avail of the additional term under the 1992 Act. After 1 August 1992, no petitions for an extension could be presented under the 1964 Act. In cases where a patent expired prior to 1 August 1992 and a petition under the 1964 Act had been presented prior to 1 August 1992, a patentee could elect to withdraw the petition and be granted four additional years as of right. However, this applied only in cases of an unopposed petition. If the petition was opposed, then the extension would be decided on its merits in accordance with s 27 of the 1964 Act.

Supplementary Protection Certificate

[5.07] On 18 June 1992, EU Regulation No 1768/92 was adopted, the purpose of which was to provide for the creation of a Supplementary Protection Certificate ('SPC') for medicinal products for human or animal use.[10] This Regulation was given effect on 5 May 1993 by the European Communities (Supplementary Protection Certificate) Regulations 1993[11] and deemed to have come into operation on 2 January 1993.

[5.08] The problem for patentees with patents for medicinal products is stated in the preamble to the Regulation, namely:

> the period that elapses between the filing of an application for a patent for a new medicinal product and authorisation to place the medicinal product on the market makes the period of effective protection under the Patent insufficient to cover the investment put into the research.

The purpose of the Regulation is to compensate patentees for the period during which they could not exploit the invention, due to the need to obtain regulatory

---

8. SI 125/1993.
9. First Schedule, s 2.
10. Council Regulation (EEC) 1768/92 of 18 June 1992; OJ 1992/L182/1.
11. SI 125/1993.

approval. This compensation takes the form of the grant of an SPC which extends the patent term in respect of the product which is the subject of the SPC.

[5.09] Under Regulation No 1768/92, an SPC can only be granted for a medicinal product for human or animal use. The term 'medicinal product' is defined in the Regulation as meaning:

> any substances or a combination of substances presented for treating or preventing disease in human beings or animals and any substances or combination of substances which may be administered to human beings or animals with a view to making a medical diagnosis or to restoring, correcting or modifying physiological functions in humans or in animals.

A product can be an active ingredient or combination of active ingredients of a medicinal product and includes the pharmaceutically acceptable salts, esters or the like of the active ingredient, provided such are covered by the basic patent.

[5.10] An SPC must be filed within six months of the date of the marketing authorisation in the relevant State or within six months of the date of grant of the patent, whichever is the later.

[5.11] Under transitional provisions contained in Article 19 of Regulation No 1768/92, any product which on 2 January 1993 was protected by a valid basic patent and for which the first authorisation to place it on the market as a medicinal product in the Community (except Spain, Portugal or Greece) was obtained after 1 January 1985,[12] may be granted an SPC. To avail of this transitional provision, an application was required before 2 July 1993.

[5.12] An SPC takes effect when the patent expires and has a term equal to the period which elapsed between the date on which the application for the patent was lodged and the date of the first authorisation to place the product on the market in the Community, reduced by five years. The maximum duration of an SPC is five years. It is necessary to pay annual renewal fees in Ireland during the term of the SPC. The date of the first marketing authorisation in the EU determines the SPC term in all Member States.

[5.13] The subject matter of SPC protection is identified in Article 4 of the Regulation and extends only to the product covered by the authorisation to place the corresponding medicinal product on the market and for any use of the product as a medicinal product that has been authorised before the expiry of the SPC. Given the fact that a product is defined as the active ingredient, if a patent only contains claims to a process for making or using an active ingredient, then the SPC is limited to the product *per se* as produced by the patented process or to the patented medical use in the marketing authorisation.

---

12. 1 January 1982 in Belgium and Italy; 1 January 1988 in Denmark and Germany.

[5.14] An SPC is granted to the holder of the basic patent or his successor in title but there is no requirement that such must also be the holder of the marketing authorisation. In many cases, a licensee may be responsible for marketing and the securing of regulatory approval.

[5.15] A request for grant of an SPC on foot of an Irish patent is made before the Irish Patents Office in accordance with a form annexed to the statutory instrument.[13] The request must include a copy of the authorisation to place the product on the Irish market and in which the product is identified, containing in particular, the number and date of the authorisation and a summary of the product's characteristics. If this is not the first authorisation in the European Union, details of the country which granted the first authorisation, the authorisation number, the authorisation date, the identity of the product thus authorised and the legal provision under which such authorisation took place must be indicated in the form of request.

[5.16] Obviously, third parties need to have knowledge of what is effectively the extension of the term of a patent. It is specifically provided that the Patent Office Journal will publish details of an application for an SPC, any grant, refusal or lapsing or subsequent invalidity. In addition, the Register must include the fact that a request for an SPC has been filed, any grant and its duration, rejection, withdrawal and invalidity. In relation to renewal fees, the Register should indicate payment or lapsing through non-payment, any restoration or invalidity. If market authorisation is withdrawn, an SPC shall lapse under Article 14(d) but only for so long as the period of withdrawal. Any termination of the lapsing is also published.

[5.17] An application for a declaration of invalidity of an SPC can be made to the Controller or the Court[14] although Article 15 of the Regulation states that the action should be taken "before the body responsible under national law for the revocation of the corresponding basic patent", ie, the Irish Patents Office. An appeal lies to the High Court.[15] The grounds of invalidity are stated in Article 15, namely:

(a) the grant was contrary to the conditions for obtaining an SPC under Article 3;

(b) the basic patent has lapsed before its lawful term expires; and

(c) the basic patent is revoked or limited to the extent that the product for which the Certificate was granted would no longer be protected by

---

[13.] First Schedule - SI 125/1993.

[14.] Rule 11 - SI 125/1993.

[15.] Article 17.

the claims of the basic patent or, after the basic patent has expired, grounds for revocation exist which would have justified such revocation or limitation.

Under Article 63 of the EPC, the term of a patent is fixed at 20 years from the date of filing of the application. The only exception being a possible extension to take into account a state of war or similar emergency conditions. A conference of the contracting States on the revision of Article 63 was held in Munich on 16-17 December 1991, following which the EPC was revised to allow for patent term extension. The revised Article 63 permits members to extend European patents in cases of national emergency or to compensate for marketing delays due to an administrative authorisation procedure required by law before a product can be marketed. This could, for example, include agricultural chemicals or aircraft and is not limited to the EU Regulation No 1768/92.

[5.18] On 23 July 1996, the Council of Ministers adopted Regulation EC/1610/96 concerning the creation of an SPC for plant protection products ie, herbicides, fungicides and insecticides. This Regulation was published on 8 August 1996 and consequently entered into force on 8 February 1997. The duration of the plant protection SPC is equal to the period which elapsed between the filing date of the basic patent and the date of the first authorisation to place the product on the market in the Community, reduced by five years. The maximum period allowable is five years from the end of the lawful term of the basic patent. Procedures under the Regulation are specifically stated to be equally valid *mutatis mutandis* with the equivalent provisions in the medicinal products SPC Regulation No EEC/1768/92. Article 4 of the Regulation states:

> Within the limits of the protection conferred by the basic patent, the protection conferred by a certificate shall extend only to the product covered by the authorisations to place the corresponding plant protection product on the market and for any use of the product as a plant protection product that has been authorised before the expiry of the certificate.

Thus, the SPC protects not only the precise subject matter of the authorisation but also modifications which do not alter the product's activity eg, salts or esters, provided such are covered by the basic patent. The SPC arises irrespective of who has obtained the product authorisation. A plant protection product SPC application must be filed within six months from the date of the grant of the first marketing authorisation or the grant of the basic patent, whichever is the later. Under Article 3.2 the holder of more than one patent for the same product cannot be granted more than one certificate for that product. However, where two or more applications concerning the same product and emanating from two or more holders of different patents are pending, one certificate for this product may be issued to each of these holders.

RESTORATION OF A PATENT

[5.19] Section 29 of the 1964 Act provided that where a patent had lapsed by failure to pay a renewal fee, application could be made by the patentee, within three years of the date on which the patent ceased to have effect, for the restoration of the patent. If the Controller was satisfied that the failure to pay the renewal fee was unintentional and that no undue delay had occurred in the making or prosecution of the application for restoration, then an order for restoration was granted. Section 37 of the 1992 Act also allows for restoration of a lapsed patent and a patent application[16] but the time limit for such an application for restoration is two years from the date on which the patent lapsed. The application can be made by the person who was the proprietor of the patent or their personal representative. Where the patent is held by two or more persons jointly, the application may, with the leave of the Controller, be made by one of the joint owners without joining the others. It was held in *Dynamics Research and Manufacturing Inc's Patent*[17] that the mere application for payment of a renewal fee cannot be regarded as an application for restoration. Rule 35 prescribes the information to be included in an application for restoration and as to be expected, the circumstances which led to the failure to pay the renewal fee must be identified. From the evidence, the Controller must satisfy himself that the failure to pay the renewal fee was *prima facie* unintentional, that reasonable care had been taken to ensure payment within the prescribed period and that there had been no undue delay in the making of the application. One of the most common reasons for failure to pay a renewal fee is the lack of funds but this is viewed as an intentional decision. What is reasonable care means more than a normal system used to pay accounts and a person:

> "must be prepared to set up a system containing safeguards more sufficient than those used to ensure that, for example, cheques to meet everyday accounts are sent when they should be".[18]

Proper supervision is required and in *Tekdata Ltd's Application*,[19] the failure of a managing director to check that an accounts team was properly carrying out his instructions was held to be a lack of reasonable care. It is now common for patentees to rely on the services of specialist computer renewal agencies and entrusting the payment of renewal fees to such or to patent agents is the norm.

---

16. Section 35(3).
17. [1980] RPC 179.
18. *Convex Ltd's Patent* [1980] RPC 423, at 432.
19. [1985] RPC 201.

However, such agencies and patent agents, unless they receive standing instructions to renew or unless instructed to the contrary, must look for renewal instructions on an annual basis. Patentees are obliged to have in place a system for dealing with requests and reminders for such instructions. A patentee can, however, rely on the services of a professional such as a solicitor[20] or a recognised renewal agency appropriately selected, qualified and experienced to carry out clear and unambiguous instructions.[21] In *Ling's Patent*,[22] it was held to be sufficient for a patentee to rely on the reminder from the Patents Office provided there was no failure to take adequate care to notify the Patents Office of a change of address.

[5.20] If upon assessing the evidence, the Controller is not satisfied that a *prima facie* case has been made, he must inform the applicant who has a one month time period within which to request a hearing.[23] If the Controller finds that there is a *prima facie* case, the application is advertised in the Official Journal and there is a two month period from advertisement within which opposition can be lodged. The opposition procedure is set out in rule 36 and following the filing of a formal Notice of Opposition which must state the ground(s) of opposition to restoration and which must be lodged in duplicate with the Controller, a copy of such is sent to the applicant for restoration. From receipt, the applicant must, within three months, file a counter-statement stating the grounds upon which the opposition is resisted. Again, this is filed in duplicate with the Controller who sends a copy to the opponent. Rule 36(6) goes on to state that the Controller may give such directions as he may think fit with regard to the subsequent procedure but this must include the right of a party to apply for and attend a hearing before the Controller.[24]

[5.21] If restoration is allowed, the unpaid renewal fees must be paid together with an additional penalty. However, more importantly, conditions are imposed which are designed to protect a third party who in good faith acted in the belief that a patent or patent application had lapsed and irrespective of whether or not that third party had opposed the application for restoration.

[5.22] The conditions consequent upon restoration are set out in rule 38 and if not complied with by the patentee, the Controller can revoke the order for restoration.[25] The imposition of the conditions arise in circumstances where a person between the date of lapsing and the application for restoration "began in

---

20. *Frazer's Patent* [1981] RPC 53.
21. *Textron Inc's Patent* [1989] RPC 441.
22. [1981] RPC 86.
23. Rule 35(2).
24. Rule 67(1).
25. Section 37(7).

good faith to do an act which would constitute an infringement" or "made in good faith effective and serious preparations to do such an act". The conditions are that such a person has a right to continue the act and therefore has a defence to an infringement action. The rights are personal and cannot be licensed.[26] If the act was done, or the preparations made in the course of a business, such a person may authorise other partners in the business to continue, assign that right or transmit it on death (in the case of a body corporate on dissolution) provided that this is done as part of the acquisition of that part of the business in the course of which the necessary act or the preparations therefor, were done. These rights conferred extend to any subsequent third party dealing with a product which has been disposed of under these rights.

[5.23] It might be thought that these safeguards were sufficient and that consequently, the Controller should, when in doubt, decide in favour of an applicant for restoration. However, in the UK case of *Dynamics Research & Manufacturing Inc's Patent,*[27] the Assistant Controller had cause to consider similar sections of the UK Act and observed that although they gave some protection, he was:

> "not satisfied that they give full protection against a third party who has acted in some way or another in the thought that a patent is dead and gone forever without hope of resurrection. He might be wishing to expand into further developments of the invention, he might have arranged mergers, and so on, on the assumption that he would be able to work the patent and made all sorts of commercial arrangements. I am not a businessman, I cannot envisage the ramifications of them, but the possibilities are there".

[5.24] The worries expressed by the Assistant Controller were unlikely to be justified because of the words 'good faith' appearing in rule 38 since it is hard to envisage a set of circumstances in which a third party would be acting in bad faith as presumably, it would be relying on the position as stated in the Register, ie, the lapsing of the patent before acting. The problems are in the words 'continue' and 'began'. The word 'continue', if given a literal interpretation, could mean that the nature and extent of the act could not be varied. If a person has, for example, commissioned detailed, lengthy, expensive, financial and marketing projections and reports, the position of such a person is uncertain. He has begun effective and serious preparations but what acts is he allowed to continue? Whitford J considered that the Assistant Controller was overly worried about the inadequacy of safeguards for third parties but applicants for restoration have a heavy onus to discharge.

[26.] Rule 38(2).
[27.] [1980] RPC 179.

AMENDMENT OF PATENT SPECIFICATION AFTER GRANT

[5.25] Under s 38, the Controller possesses a discretionary power to allow the proprietor of a patent to amend the specification of a patent. There are also special provisions which deal with the correction of an error in a patent specification.[28]

[5.26] Rule 39 which governs the procedure for requesting an amendment after grant does not require an explanation of the reasons for seeking amendment. However, because the Controller's power is discretionary, it would appear that the Controller could call for such an explanation so as to determine whether or not to exercise his discretion in favour of an applicant. In the UK Patent Office decision in *Waddington Ltd's Application*,[29] an explanation was given that amendment was required because of prior art which had only recently come to the attention of the applicant. However, the applicant refused to disclose the prior art. It was held that it was necessary for the Controller to have particulars of that prior art so that he could take it into account in the exercise of his discretion. If there are proceedings before the Court or the Controller in which the validity of the patent has been or may be put at issue, amendment is not possible.[30] However, in such proceedings, the proprietor may, at the discretion of the Court or Controller, be allowed to amend the patent specification with the added proviso of possible conditions being imposed. These include, but are not limited to, advertisement of the amendment and costs and expenses to the party challenging the validity.[31] In *Chevron's Patent*,[32] it was stated by Graham J that:

> "it is essential that those seeking amendment should realise that they have a heavy onus to discharge and can only expect to do so if they have full evidence to prove their case and put the whole story before the Court".

[5.27] It is dangerous for a patentee knowingly and deliberately to obtain claims of unjustified width because such could be viewed as "covetous" claiming and could result in the refusal of an application for amendment.[33] Likewise, if a patentee's attention is drawn to the fact that a claim is unjustifiably wide and does not take proper steps by amendment to remedy the position within a reasonable period of time, then an application for amendment may be refused. In the case of *Autoliv Development Ab's Patent*,[34] there was a delay of four years before seeking amendment and after learning of the anticipating art. This was

---

28. Section 110.
29. [1986] RPC 158.
30. Section 38(1).
31. Section 38(2).
32. [1970] RPC 580.
33. *Imperial Chemical Industries Ltd (Whyte's) Patent* [1978] RPC 11.
34. [1988] RPC 425.

held to be a culpable delay and was such as to cause the discretion to be exercised against the applicant for amendment. In patent litigation, the Court must examine the circumstances in detail before allowing amendment. If the evidence establishes that the patentee was aware of deficiencies in the specification but did not take any action to remedy such, it is improper for amendment to be allowed.[35] In *Bristol Myers Company v Manon Freres*,[36] amendment was allowed despite a long delay, it being held that the lapse of time between the knowledge of a potentially damaging citation and the application to amend is only fatal if the patentee must always have known that his claim could not have been supported against the earlier citation. Because there must be full disclosure in an application for amendment, it is possible that a patentee may be reluctant to proceed because of the disclosure of privileged documents being used, for example, in other jurisdictions. Consequently, in *Bonzel v Intervention Ltd*,[37] the Court allowed the hearing of certain evidence *in camera* and imposed an injunction against the use of certain documents other than in the amendment proceedings at issue.

[5.28] A summary of the tests applied are conveniently stated in the case of *Smith, Kline & French Laboratories Limited v Evans Medical Limited*[38] and the statement of Aldous J that:

> "The discretion as to whether or not to allow amendment is a wide one and the cases illustrate some principles which are applicable to the present case. First, the onus to establish that amendment should be allowed is upon the patentee and full disclosure must be made of all relevant matters. If there is a failure to disclose all the relevant matters, amendment will be refused. Secondly, amendment will be allowed provided the amendments are permitted under the Act and no circumstances arise which would lead the Court to refuse the amendment. Thirdly, it is in the public interest that amendment is sought promptly. Thus, in cases where a patentee delays for an unreasonable period before seeking amendment, it will not be allowed unless the patentee shows reasonable grounds for his delay. Such includes cases where a patentee believed that amendment was not necessary and had reasonable grounds for that belief. Fourthly, a patentee who seeks to obtain an unfair advantage from a patent, which he knows or should have known should be amended, will not be allowed to amend. Such a case is where a patentee threatens an infringer with his unamended patent after he knows or should have known of the need to

---

[35] *Chrome-Alloying Co. Ltd. v Metal Diffusions Ltd* [1962] RPC 33. *Western Electric v Racal-Milgo* [1981] RPC 253.
[36] [1973] RPC 836.
[37] [1991] RPC 553.
[38] [1989] FSR 561, at 569.

amend. Fifthly, the Court is concerned with the conduct of the patentee and not with the merit of the invention".

This was approved in *Hsiung's Patent*[39] where it was also held that where the question of discretion has already been litigated and decided against a patentee seeking an amendment of his patent, that ground would apply to all future applications to permit amendments. A patentee should not be allowed an opportunity to formulate a different amendment.

[5.29] If an application for amendment is deemed acceptable, the Court or the Controller can require advertisement of the proposed amendment. It is likely that at a very minimum, advertisement in the Patents Office Journal will be imposed. From advertisement, there is a three month opposition period.[40] If an application for amendment is made to the Court, the applicant must notify the Controller who is entitled to appear and be heard. The effective date of an amendment is the date of the grant of the patent[41] and the amendment is invalid to the extent that it extends the subject matter disclosed in the application as filed or the protection conferred by the patent.[42]

SURRENDER OF A PATENT

[5.30] Section 39 of the 1992 Act includes a provision for the voluntary surrender of a patent by way of written notice to the Controller. The application is described as an "offer" to surrender and the proprietor must declare the reasons for making such an offer. In addition, the proprietor must furnish a declaration that no action for infringement or for the revocation of the patent is pending in any Court.[43] The offer is advertised in the Patent Office Journal and within three months from advertisement, the surrender may be opposed "by any person". It appears that no *locus standi* is required, unlike the situation under s 36 of the 1964 Act which limited opposition to "any person interested". Rule 40(3)(c) requires the opponent to give reasons for opposing surrender but this could, for example, be the public interest. A bar to opposition would exist if the action was frivolous, vexatious or blackmailing.[44] The most likely opponent would be a licensee.

[5.31] If the Controller is satisfied that a patent may be properly surrendered, he may accept the offer. Under s 39(5), the patent ceases to have effect from the date on which the notice of acceptance is published in the Patents Office

---

39. [1992] RPC 497.
40. Rule 39(2).
41. Section 38(4).
42. See s 58(c) and (d) - grounds for revocation.
43. Rule 40(1).
44. *Braun's Application* [1981] RPC 355.

Journal. However, no infringement action or compensation for State use arises for acts done earlier. The effect, however, is to make the surrender *ex nunc* which means that a licensee cannot claim the return of royalties paid earlier. Section 60(2) of the 1992 Act requires the Controller to revoke a patent in circumstances where there exists for the same invention a nationally filed Irish patent and a European patent designating the State. Because surrender does not amount to revocation, a surrender would not be sufficient to overcome an objection under s 60(2).[45]

PATENTS AS A PROPERTY RIGHT

[5.32] A patent or patent application is a personal property right and consequently may be assigned, licensed or charged by way of a mortgage. Section 85(1) of the 1992 Act, by the use of the word "shall", imposes a statutory obligation to record changes in ownership or an interest in a patent or a patent application once published. The penalty for non-recordal is that a document in respect of which there has been no recordal will only be admitted in any court as evidence of title if the court so directs.[46] In the 1964 Act, there were increased official fees for late recordal but this is no longer the position under the 1992 Act. The statutory obligation appears to have little teeth and, for example, a patentee could simply record the change in ownership if and when the need arises. There are, however, delays in recordal before the Irish Patents Office and if an interlocutory or even interim injunction is necessary, and the court refuses to admit a document of title, the delays may prejudice the patentee. Similarly, the holder of an exclusive licence may also be delayed in instituting an infringement action under s 51. A licensee also has an added incentive for recordal in order to be put on notice such as, for example, in a situation where the patentee makes application for an entry in respect of licences of right.[47] Recordal no longer requires the furnishing of the original assignment document, and a certified copy will suffice.[48] When recordal takes place, the Register identifies particulars of the instruments in respect of which recordal has been made.[49]

[5.33] Section 99 of the Companies Act 1963 as amended by s 122 of the Companies (Amendment) Act 1990, requires that a company must register with the Registrar of Companies certain specified charges. Failure to comply means that the charge will be void as against the liquidator and any creditor of the

---

45. *IBM (Barclay & Biger) Application* [1983] RPC 283.
46. Section 85(7).
47. Section 68(1).
48. Rule 58(1); s 85(6).
49. Section 85(3).

company. The provision applies to a charge on a patent or a licence under a patent.

Co-Ownership

[5.34] Unless specifically agreed to the contrary, two or more persons who hold a patent application or to whom a patent has been granted, hold such as tenants in common in equal shares.[50] Thus, the ownership of a deceased patentee's share in a patent devolves on their personal representative. If the existence of an agreement is not established, the patentees are entitled to equal shares in the patent no matter what their individual efforts amounted to in relation to the whole.[51] Every registered co-owner is entitled by himself or his agents to work the patented invention for his own benefit without accounting to the other(s) unless there is an agreement to the contrary. An agent does not include an independent contractor or the partner of a co-owner.[52] One co-owner cannot licence the patent or assign any share in the patent without the consent of all other co-owners.[53] The supplier to a co-owner who might otherwise be considered an indirect infringer under s 41(1) is not deemed to be an infringer.[54] Also exempt from infringement are persons acquiring a patented product from one co-owner only.[55] Such a person may deal with the product as if purchased from a sole patentee. One co-owner can sue for infringement joining the other co-owner(s) as party to the proceedings.[56]

Courts' authority to determine ownership

[5.35] Under s 16(1), the right to a patent belongs to the inventor(s), their successor(s) in title or in certain cases, to an employer. An application to revoke a patent can be made on the grounds that there was a lack of entitlement.[57] If such an action is taken, it must be by a person who has referred the matter to the High Court and where entitlement in their favour has been determined.[58] The application to the High Court is made under s 81(1). There is a time limit of two years from grant unless it can be shown that the patentee knew at the date of grant that he was not entitled to be granted the patent.[59] A Court will have to determine whether the test as to knowledge is subjective or objective. It is

---

[50.] Section 80(1).
[51.] *Florey's Patent* [1962] RPC 186.
[52.] *Howard & Bullough v Tweedales & Smalley* (1895) 12 RPC 519.
[53.] Section 80(3).
[54.] Section 80(4).
[55.] Section 80(5).
[56.] Section 48.
[57.] Section 58(e).
[58.] Section 57(2).
[59.] Section 81(2).

probably not sufficient that the referring party has previously simply alleged proprietorship to the patentee. No order can be made which affects the mutual rights and obligations of trustees or of personal representatives.[60]

[5.36] If a Court finds that a patent was granted to a person not entitled in whole or in part, then the entitled party can make application[61] to revoke the patent or part of the patent. In such a case, the Court may permit the person or persons making the revocation application to make a new application for a patent which will be treated as having been made on the same date as the original patent application.[62] A replacement application cannot proceed if it contains any additional matter over that contained in the original patent application.[63] An example of where the referrer failed to establish entitlement in substitution of the original application is *Norris's Patent*.[64] However, it was held that there had been a contribution to a significant aspect of the invention and therefore an entitlement to become a joint proprietor of the granted patent.

[5.37] If a court order directs a change in ownership, then the position *vis-à-vis* a licensee or any other third party rights is determined by whether or not there has been a complete change in ownership or if the new proprietor(s) include some or all of the old proprietor(s).[65] In the latter instance, any existing licences or other rights appear to continue in force unless contractually otherwise provided. If there has been a complete change in ownership, then any licence or other rights in force prior to the transfer lapse as and from the date of registration of the new proprietors. In this event, previous proprietor(s) or licensee(s) who had acted in good faith and before the proceedings had used or made serious preparations to use the patent in the State, may continue to use as a non- exclusive licensee. A request for grant of this licence must be made by the previous proprietor within two months and if by a licensee within four months of being notified by the Controller of the court order which transferred the patent.[66] Failing agreement between the parties, the terms of the licence can be settled by the Controller with the criteria that both the period and terms must be reasonable, presumably to both parties.[67]

---

[60]. Section 81(3).
[61]. Section 57.
[62]. Section 81(4).
[63]. Section 81(5); *X Ltd's Application* [1982] FSR 143.
[64]. [1988] RPC 159.
[65]. Section 82(1).
[66]. Rule 54.
[67]. Section 82(3).

THE REGISTER

[5.38] No details are entered on the Register until the patent application is published which is eighteen months after the filing date or the priority date, if earlier.[68] The Register details to be made publicly available are:[69]

(a) particulars of the applicant(s), their address for service and the inventor(s);

(b) the number and date of application;

(c) the details of the priority claim;

(d) the date of publication;

(e) the date on which an application is refused, withdrawn or has lapsed;

(f) the date on which notice of the grant of the patent is published;

(g) particulars of patentee(s) and address for service if different from applicant(s); and

(h) particulars of any interest or title in a patent.

There is a prohibition in s 84(5) on entry in the Register of a notice of any trust whether express, implied or constructive and the Controller is not affected by any such notice. However, it was held in *Kakkar v Szelke*,[70] that a document which affected the proprietorship of a patent, whether by creating trusts or otherwise, is not excluded from entry in the Register. Until a patent application is published, documents or information can only be secured with the consent of the applicant[71] unless it is to advise of withdrawal, bibliographic information or information required to be furnished to the European Patent Office. Shortly after a patent application is filed, the following information is published in the Patents Office Journal namely:

(a) The name of the applicant;

(b) The title of the invention;

(c) The date of application;

(d) Details of priority claimed, if any;

(e) Whether or not the application is for a short term patent. This is identified by the letter 'S';

(f) The number given to the application.

[68.] Section 28
[69.] Rule 55.
[70.] [1989] FSR 225.
[71.] Section 88(2).

[5.39] Rule 64 prescribes information which the Controller is also obliged to furnish upon request. This includes whether or not a search report has been published, the form of evidence of novelty submitted and whether there has been an application for restoration.

[5.40] An aggrieved party may, at their option, apply either to the court or the Controller to amend the Register.[72] The cause of complaint by an applicant may be the non-insertion in or omission from the Register of any entry or any entry made in the Register without sufficient cause or wrongly remaining in the Register or an error or defect in the Register. The Controller may apply to the court on his own motion in the case of fraud in the registration or transmission of a patent application or a patent.[73] In *Beecham Group Limited v Bristol Myers Company*,[74] the patentee failed to rectify the Register to delete a priority date claimed for the patent. It was held that the proprietor himself was not an aggrieved person. However, an aggrieved person may have some proprietary interest in the patent.[75]

[5.41] It is possible to apply to the Controller for a search[76] to be carried out as to novelty only or novelty and inventive step. A request for a search must be accompanied by a sufficiently full and detailed description (including drawings where appropriate) of the product, process or apparatus to be searched.[77] If possible, the sub-class or group units of the International Patent Classification should be identified. The search is carried out among Irish patents and published applications, UK applications and complete specifications published within the previous thirty years, published PCT and European patent applications which are in English or for which English language abstracts are available.

---

72. Sections 86(1) and 86(7).
73. Section 86(5).
74. [1979] IR 330.
75. *Manning's Patent* (1903) 20 RPC 74.
76. Section 89.
77. Rule 66.

Chapter 6

Patents Act 1992 - Infringements and Remedies

RIGHTS CONFERRED

[6.01] Under the Patents Act 1964 it was an infringement of a patent for any person, without the licence of the patentee, to make, use, exercise or vend the invention in the State. Section 40 of the Patents Act 1992 deals with the question of substantive or direct infringement while s 41 introduces a new concept of contributory or indirect infringement. The wording in s 40 corresponds to that existing in Article 25 of the Community Patent Convention (CPC) and classifies infringing acts according to whether the invention is (a) a product; (b) a process; or (c) the product of a process. If and when the CPC comes into force, the fact that the wording does correspond will assist the Irish courts. The UK Patents Act 1977 adopts different wording but even so, the UK courts have been obliged to take cognisance of a further legislative provision[1] whereby the UK equivalent to s 40 is "so framed as to have, as nearly as practicable, the same effects ... as the corresponding provisions of the Community Patent Convention".[2]

[6.02] Under the transitional provisions,[3] a patent granted under the 1964 Act will have the same effect as a patent granted under the 1992 Act. Thus, any claim for infringement after 1 August 1992 will be dealt with under the new provisions irrespective of the date of the patent. However, there is an absence of any transitional provisions dealing with claims for infringement which occurred before 1 August 1992. This would suggest that claims for infringement that occurred pre-1 August 1992 must be dealt with under the 1964 Act. This is an important factor given that the 1992 Act displaces many of the concepts under the 1964 Act and in particular, the large volume of UK cases which interpreted the corresponding provisions in the UK.[4]

[6.03] The territorial scope is limited to infringement taking place in the State. In the UK case of *Kalman v PCL Packaging*,[5] the Patents Court held that both an offer and the subsequent disposal needed to take place in the UK before infringement occurred. This, however, results from the wording 'offer to

---

[1.] UK Patent Act 1977, s 130(7).
[2.] See *Smith Kline & French v Harbottle* [1980] RPC 363.
[3.] Patents Act 1992, First Schedule, s 1.
[4.] See *Genentech Inc's Patent* [1989] RPC 147.
[5.] [1982] FSR 406.

dispose' which is different from that in s 40. It appears from s 40 that a simple offer in the State can amount to an infringement and there is no reason why magazines which are printed abroad but which circulate in Ireland could not include advertisements which would amount to infringement in the State. If the advertisement specifically stated that the offer was not open to residents in the State, then a claim to infringement might be avoided. It is also quite permissible to serve proceedings outside the State against a party who is infringing in the State.[6] There are no equivalent provisions in patent law to European Regulation Nos 3295/94 and 367/95[7] which enable the customs authorities to seize trade mark infringing goods at the point of entry. In *Morton-Norwich Products Inc v Intercen*[8] Graham J dealt with the question of joint tortfeasors and stated that it was clear that two persons who agree on common action, in the course of and to the furtherance of which one of them commits a tort in this country are joint tortfeasors. The effect of this was that provided a tort was committed in the jurisdiction and it was proved that the defendants had a common design to commit it, then it does not matter that a person sued has not himself committed within the jurisdiction any act which, taken by itself, could be said to amount to several infringements.[9] In *Unilever plc v Gillette (UK) Ltd*,[10] a defendant's foreign parent company was joined as a co-defendant since the patentee was able to show a good arguable case that the two companies had acted in concert pursuant to a common design resulting in infringement. The mere fact of a parent and subsidiary relationship does not show a common design. It is the extent of the control actually exercised or the involvement which are the determining factors.[11] A plaintiff who has been injured by a number of joint tortfeasors can choose whom to sue, including a defendant outside of the jurisdiction.[12]

[6.04] A third party does not infringe where it has a consent from the proprietor and there is nothing to say that such a consent need be in writing and thus it may be an implied consent. In *Betts v Willmott*,[13] it was established that an implied licence to use or re-sell a patented product arises in the case of an ordinary sale of the product. There is also an implied right to repair a patented product provided that such repairs do not amount to the manufacture of a new product.

---

6. *Electric Furnace Co v Selas Corporation of America* [1987] RPC 23.
7. SI 48/1996.
8. [1978] RPC 501.
9. See also *Puschner v Tom Palmer (Scotland) Ltd. & Another* [1989] RPC 430.
10. [1989] RPC 583.
11. *Intel Corporation v General Instrument Corporation* [1991] RPC 235.
12. *Molnlycke v Procter & Gamble* [1992] RPC 21. *Lubrizol Corporation v Esso Petroleum Company Ltd* [1992] RPC 467.
13. (1871) LR 6 Ch 239.

In *Solar Thompson Engineering Co Ltd v Barton*,[14] it was made clear that the implied licence extends to a right to have the repairs carried out by a third party, such as a contractor, who can also utilise drawings even though protected under copyright. The repair must be a genuine one and not a replacement of the product disguised as a repair.[15] Also, the ambit of an implied licence for modifying a patented product is no wider than that for repairing it.[16] An implied licence can also arise by virtue of the failure of a proprietor to take earlier action.[17]

Direct Infringement

[6.05] Under s 40(a) of the 1992 Act, infringement of a patent relating to a product can arise in a number of ways, namely making, offering, putting on the market, using, importing or stocking the product for those purposes. This should be read in conjunction with s 46(1) whereby in relation to a patent in respect of a process for obtaining a new product, if the same product is produced by an unauthorised party, it is deemed to have been obtained by the same process and is thus an infringement. The onus falls on a defendant to rebut this presumption. The effect of this provision is that if, for example, a product is treated by using a patented process, then it would be extremely difficult for a third party to make the resultant new product without infringement occurring.

[6.06] In *Hoffmann-La Roche v Harris Pharmaceutical Ltd*,[18] Whitford J held that possession with the intention of using the products for trade purposes and for the securing of a profit amounts to an infringement, whether the dealing proposed is a dealing with a customer in the country or with an export customer. This was a decision on wording equivalent to that in the Patents Act 1964, ie, making, using, exercising or vending the invention, but would still appear to extend the scope of protection beyond that identified in the legislative provisions and even Whitford J identified the need to protect the rights of a mere carrier against too broad an interpretation of his decision. In *Smith Kline Corp v DDSA Pharmaceuticals Ltd*,[19] the defendant had imported a pharmaceutical product into the UK in bulk for tableting. It was intended to export it in its entirety to Nigeria. It was held that importing even with a view to subsequent export was an infringement and it was not incumbent on a plaintiff to show that it has suffered commercial loss.

---

14. [1977] RPC 537.
15. *Sirdar Rubber v Wallington Weston* (1907) 24 RPC 539.
16. *Dellareed Ltd v Delkim Developments* [1988] FSR 329.
17. *Habib Bank Ltd. v Habib Bank AG* [1982] RPC 1.
18. [1977] FSR 200.
19. [1978] FSR 109.

[6.07] In the case of *Upjohn Company v T Kerfoot & Co Ltd*,[20] the defendant had applied to the UK Authorities (DHSS) for a product licence in respect of a pharmaceutical product. It was alleged that this included data obtained by tests on the product which may have been carried out abroad. It was held that while such amounted to a step towards commercial use, it did not amount to an infringement.

[6.08] The New Zealand Court of Appeal distinguished the *Upjohn* case, stating that while it supported the contention that the submission of data obtained from tests is not an infringement, it does not warrant a conclusion that the supply of a sample is not an infringement.[21] In reviewing the earlier decided cases, it was considered that they set the permissible use at the submission of an application and accompanying data to a regulatory authority. However, the sending of an embodiment of an invention to a government authority for approval was a use of the invention since by doing so the defendant acted for the commercial advantage or as a springboard, in order to be prepared to launch into the market when the patent expired.

[6.09] It is, of course, sometimes difficult for a plaintiff to secure information on the identity of an infringer. In *Norwich Pharmacal v The Commissioners of Customs and Excise*,[22] it was held that an action for discovery lies even against a non-infringer in order to identify infringers. Such an order would be made if the defendant was so mixed up in the transaction which *prima facie* constitutes an infringement of the patent that he is under a duty to aid the patentee to prevent further loss to his intellectual property by disclosing the name of the supplier.[23]

[6.10] Under s 40(b), the use of a process claimed in a patent is an infringement as is offering the process for use in the State, including in circumstances where it should have been obvious to a reasonable person that such would infringe. It is only in the case of an act consisting of offering the process for use that knowledge or imputed knowledge is a requirement for a direct infringement. In *Kalman v PCL Packaging (UK) Ltd*,[24] it was held that an offer to sell abroad equipment for working a patented process in the UK, was not in itself offering the process for use in the UK.

---

20. [1988] FSR 1.
21. *Smith Kline & French Laboratories Ltd v Douglas Pharmaceuticals Ltd* [1991] FSR 522.
22. [1974] RPC 101.
23. See also *Smith Kline & French Laboratories Ltd v Global Pharmaceuticals* [1986] RPC 394 and *Societe Romanaise v British Shoe Corporation* [1991] FSR 1.
24. [1982] FSR 406.

[6.11] In the case of *Furr v CD Truline (Building Products) Ltd*,[25] the defendants directed purchasers to use the articles in a way which was not the way stated in the method claim. It was held that the defendants could not be said to have offered a process for use since they clearly did not intend that the articles should be used in the claimed way.

[6.12] Article 64(2) of the EPC states that if the subject matter of the European patent is a process, the protection conferred by the patent shall extend to the products directly obtained by such process. This is reflected in s 40(c) which classifies an infringing act to include offering, putting on the market, using or importing, or stocking for those purposes a product obtained by a patented process.

Indirect Infringement

[6.13] The Patents Act 1964 did not contain any specific provision concerning indirect or sometimes called contributory infringement and which is now found in s 41 of the 1992 Act. However, where there is a concerted design by two persons to infringe, then both may be liable as joint tortfeasors.[26] However, in *Belegging v Witten Industrial Diamonds*,[27] the English Court of Appeal held that the selling of a commercial commodity to someone who, with the knowledge of the vendor, intended to use it in a patented product was not in itself an infringement. Neither did supply for that sole purpose amount to procuring an infringement, Buckley LJ stating that "facilitating the doing of an act is obviously different from procuring the doing of the act" but that if the defendants had procured, counselled and/or aided other persons to infringe, "this may perhaps amount to an allegation of indirect infringement by the defendants themselves, but I am inclined to think that it is a claim in respect of a distinct, suggested tort of procuring infringement by others (based on the principle enunciated by Erle J in *Lumley v Gye*)".[28] In *Dow Chemicals v Spence Bryson*,[29] it was held that where the second defendant persuaded and induced the first defendant to adopt the patented process in order to secure the first defendant's order for a supply of latex used in the process, and also provided the necessary technical assistance in establishing the process, this amounted to procuring an infringement.

[25.] [1985] FSR 553.
[26.] *Morton-Norwich Products Ltd v Intercen Ltd* [1978] RPC 501.
[27.] [1979] FSR 59.
[28.] (1853) 2 E & B 216, at 231.
[29.] [1982] FSR 598.

[6.14] The wording in s 41(1) is taken from the CPC[30] and it enables a patentee to take action against any person who supplies or offers to supply any of the means, relating to an essential element of the invention, for putting the invention into effect. Thus, for example, the case of *Innes v Short and Beal*[31] would clearly fall within this provision. In that case the plaintiff was the patentee of an invention for using zinc powder to prevent corrosion in steam boilers. The defendant formerly sold the zinc powder under an agency agreement. The agency agreement terminated but the defendant continued to sell the zinc powder. Although an injunction was granted to restrain the defendant from selling powdered zinc with an invitation to the purchasers to use it so as to infringe the patent, this was based on an inducement to infringe. The provisions in s 41(1) do not require there to be such inducement although there must be knowledge that the 'means' in question are suitable for the infringing purpose. This knowledge can be inferred where it would be "obvious in the circumstances to a reasonable person". In *Furr v CD Truline (Building Products) Ltd*[32] an interlocutory injunction was refused, it being held that the defendant had not intended its articles to be used in the claimed manner and that it would not have been obvious to a reasonable person that the articles were intended to be used in that manner. An example of a case in which indirect infringement was held to occur is *Helitune Ltd v Stewart Hughes Ltd*,[33] where the patent in suit related to a method of detecting the degree of unbalance of helicopter rotor blades. The plaintiff asserted that there was a direct infringement by the defendant's blade tracker and an indirect infringement by the defendant's offer to supply a part of its tracker to another company. Aldous J in the Patents Court found that the defendant did know and any reasonable man would have known that its part would be used in a system which fell within the patent.

[6.15] The Malaysian High Court case of *Rhone Poulenc v Dikloride Herbicides*[34] related to a patent in respect of compositions for use in regulating plant growth. Certain claims also related to the "treatment of rubber trees to stimulate the flow of latex". The planters using the defendant's product were direct infringers and the defendants who provided their products to the planters were guilty of contributory infringement. It is necessary for the means to be an "essential element of the invention" and this must be a question of fact in each case. The word 'essential' presumably means an element in relation to which an alternative would not suffice in order for the invention to be put into effect.

---

30. CPC, Article 26.
31. (1898) 15 RPC 449.
32. [1985] FSR 553.
33. [1991] FSR 171.
34. [1988] FSR 282.

[6.16] Indirect or contributory infringement does not apply when the 'means' are 'staple commercial products' except where the supply or offer is made for the purpose of inducing the person supplied to do an act which constitutes a direct infringement.[35] The key words are staple commercial product and there is no definition of such. A similar provision exists in US patent law and guidelines may be obtained from this source[36] which suggest a meaning akin to raw materials of a type which are generally available or a commodity of commerce suitable for uses of which at least some would not amount to an infringement. Under s 41(3) a person entitled to exploit an invention under these provisions does not include private users of the invention, those experimenting with the invention or pharmacists making up prescriptions. The issue of contributory infringement in relation to use for experimental purposes arose in *Monsanto Co v Stauffer Chemical Co Ltd*[37] and the UK Patents Court expressed the view that supply of the patented herbicide product known as 'Touchdown' was an infringement even if the activities of the person to whom the product was supplied was to use such for experimental purposes. The Court of Appeal went on to say by way of *obiter* that there was force in such an argument but did not rule on the issue.

LIMITATIONS ON PATENT RIGHTS

[6.17] Sections 42 and 43 of the 1992 Act impose a number of limitations on the extent of the rights granted.

Private and Non-Commercial Purposes

[6.18] Under s 42(a), "acts done privately for non-commercial purposes" do not infringe. This provision was considered in *Smith Kline & French Laboratories v Evans Medical Ltd.*[38] The defendant had conducted in-house experiments to support evidence in opposition to an amendment of the patent sought by the plaintiff patentee. Aldous J, in the Patents Court, examined the word 'privately' even though it was accepted that the experiment was indeed carried out privately in this instance. It was stated that:

> "as this subsection goes on to exclude acts done for commercial purposes, the word 'privately' includes commercial and non-commercial situations. This word is not, in my view, synonymous with 'secret' or 'confidential' and would include acts which were secret or confidential or were not. This word appears to me to be used as the opposite of 'publicly' and to be used in the sense of denoting that the act was done for the person's own use. This construction of

---

[35.] Section 41(2).
[36.] C Baillie, 'Contributory Infringement in the US' (1980-81) 10 CIPA 56.
[37.] [1985] RPC 515.
[38.] [1989] FSR 513.

the word 'privately' is consistent with the rest of the subsection which provides
that even if the acts are done privately in the sense of for the person's own use,
there will be infringement if the acts are done for commercial purposes."

Since the act in this case was done privately, the dispute turned on whether it
was done for purposes which were commercial. Although the stated sole
purpose of the experiment was to produce evidence for the amendment
proceedings, it was accepted that in carrying out the experiment, the defendants
acquired information which would be useful in commercial production. It was
held that experiments done for the legal proceedings were not done for
commercial purposes but if the experiment had a dual purpose which included
the obtaining of commercial experience, then the exclusion did not apply. On the
facts it was held that there was an issue to be tried. However, the test is
subjective and if all the purposes are non-commercial, it is irrelevant that
knowledge gained might be of commercial benefit.

Experimental Purposes

[6.19] Acts done for experimental purposes do not infringe if they relate to the
subject matter of the patented invention. In *Monsanto Co v Stauffer Chemical
Co*,[39] the Court of Appeal held that trials carried out in order to discover
something unknown or to test a hypothesis or even in order to find out whether
something which is known to work in specific conditions, eg, of soil or weather,
will work in different conditions, can fairly be regarded as experiments.
However, trials carried out in order to demonstrate to a third party that a product
works or, in order to amass information to satisfy a third party, whether a
customer or a regulatory body, that the product works as its maker claims, are
not to be regarded as acts done for experimental purposes. The section not only
requires the act to be done for experimental purposes, but also that the purposes
relate to the subject matter of the invention, ie, an invention covered the patent
in respect of which infringement is alleged. Thus experiments performed for the
purpose of invalidating some other patent will not be excluded.[40]

Extemporaneous Preparation of Medicines

[6.20] No infringement arises where there is extemporaneous preparation of a
medicine in a pharmacy for individual cases where such is in accordance with a
medical prescription issued by a registered medical practitioner. Also excluded
from infringement are acts concerning the medicine so prepared.[41] Unlike the
situation under the equivalent UK provision,[42] there is no exclusion for

---

[39.] [1985] RPC 515.
[40.] *Smith Kline & French v Evans Medical Ltd* [1989] FSR 513.
[41.] Section 42(c).
[42.] UK Patents Act 1977, s 60(5)(c).

prescriptions issuing from a dental practitioner. The exclusion does not extend to veterinary preparations. The provision is taken from Article 27(c) of the CPC although the CPC does not require the prescription to be that of a registered medical practitioner. The word 'extemporaneous' means on the spur of the moment or without prior notice, so medicines which are prepared prior to a specific request are not exempt such as, for example, bulk preparation of a common prescription. It is unclear whether or not the medical practitioner must be registered in this country.

Vessels, Aircraft or Land Vehicles

[6.21] There are specific provisions exempting the use of patented inventions on certain vessels, aircraft or land vehicles temporarily or accidentally entering the State.[43] In the case of a vessel, this includes entry in the territorial waters of the State, the extent of such territorial protection also being identified in s 117. The exemption does not apply to vessels registered in the State. The wording corresponds to Article 27(d) and (e) of the CPC. The vessel must be registered in a Member State of the Paris Convention. Certain 'Flag of Convenience' countries are not members such as, for example, Taiwan. It is also necessary that the invention be used exclusively for the needs of the vessel which includes the vessel's machinery, tackle, gear and other accessories.

Limitations Under EU Law

[6.22] Article 29.4.3° of the Irish Constitution specifically states that:

> No provision of this Constitution invalidates laws enacted, acts done or measures adopted by the State necessitated by the obligations of membership of the European Union or of the Communities, or prevents laws enacted, acts done or measures adopted by the European Union or the Communities or by institutions thereof, or by bodies competent under the Treaties establishing the Communities, from having the force of law in the State.

Given the superiority of EU law over domestic legislation, it was not necessary for the 1992 Act[44] to state as it does that the rights conferred by a patent do not extend to prevent acts which under the Treaty of Rome could not be prevented by the proprietor.

[6.23] Article 222 of the Treaty of Rome states that the Treaty shall not in any way prejudice the rules in Member States governing the system of property ownership. However, while the Treaty does not affect the existence of patent and other intellectual property rights, there are situations in which the exercise

---

[43.] Section 42(d) & (e).
[44.] Section 43.

of such rights must be restricted. The ECJ has distinguished between the existence of intellectual property rights and their exercise.[45]

[6.24] Patent rights were considered in the case of *Parke Davis & Co v Probel and Centrafarm*.[46] In that case, Parke Davis held a patent in the Netherlands. There was no corresponding patent in Italy where at that time, it was not possible to secure a patent in respect of pharmaceutical products. The drug was produced in Italy and imported by Centrafarm into the Netherlands. Parke Davis sought an injunction to stop infringement in the Netherlands. It was argued by Centrafarm that the granting of an injunction would create an obstacle to free movement throughout the Community. It was nonetheless held that Parke Davis were not prevented under Article 85 of the Treaty of Rome from blocking the import of a competing drug manufactured in Italy where there was no patent protection and where Parke Davis had not marketed the drug. The important factor in this case was not the absence of a system for patent protection in one Member State but the fact that the imported product had not been put on the Italian market by the patentee or with his consent.

[6.25] Distinguishing between the existence of intellectual property rights and their exercise, it was considered that in the absence of some agreement, decision or concerted practice which prevented, restricted or distorted competition, then the exercise of such rights did not fall within Article 85(1). In relation to an abuse of a dominant position under Article 86, the charging of higher prices in one Member State as opposed to another does not necessarily show an abuse. Costs in marketing and patenting can vary from State to State and it is not unreasonable that an attempt be made to recoup such on a State by State basis.

[6.26] Article 30 of the Treaty of Rome states that quantitative restrictions on imports and all measures having equivalent effect between Member States are not permitted. However, under Article 36, such prohibitions or restrictions are allowed on the grounds of the protection of industrial and commercial property where they are not "a means of arbitrary discrimination or a disguised restriction on trade between Member States". Thus, in the copyright case of *Deutsche Grammophon v Metro*,[47] the ECJ held that Article 36 only permitted derogations from Article 30 "to the extent to which they are justified for the purpose of safeguarding rights which constitute the specific subject matter of such property".

---

[45]. *Consten and Grundig-Verkaufs GmbH v EC Commission* [1966] ECR 299.
[46]. [1968] ECR 55.
[47]. [1971] ECR 487.

Doctrine of Exhaustion

[6.27] In *Centrafarm v Sterling Drug*,[48] the ECJ described the specific subject matter of a patent as:

> "The guarantee that the patentee, to reward the creative effort of the inventor, has the exclusive right to use an invention with a view to manufacturing industrial products and putting them into circulation for the first time, either directly or by the grant of licences to third parties, as well as the right to oppose infringements".

The words 'for the first time' are a reference to the doctrine of the 'exhaustion' of rights which was laid down in the *Deutsche Grammophon* case.[49] Simply put, this doctrine means that patent rights cannot be used to prevent the import of goods which have been marketed by the patentee or with his consent in another Member State. The application of this doctrine in the patent field can be found in the case of *Merck & Co Inc v Stephar BV*.[50] The plaintiff held a patent in the Netherlands for a pharmaceutical product which the plaintiff also sold in Italy. Similar to the situation in *Parke Davis v Probel*[51] no patent existed in Italy because Italian law did not allow for such. The defendant, attracted by the lower prices in Italy, acquired the product and sold it in the Netherlands. The European Court of Justice held that the patentee's rights were exhausted when the goods were sold in Italy and stated:

> "The substance of a patent right lies essentially in according the inventor an exclusive right of first placing the product on the market. That right of first placing a product on the market enables the inventor, by allowing him a monopoly in exploiting his product, to obtain the reward for his creative effort without, however, guaranteeing that he will obtain such a reward in all circumstances.

> It is for the proprietor of the patent to decide, in the light of all the circumstances, under what conditions he will market his product, including the possibility of marketing it in a Member State where the law does not provide patent protection for the product in question. If he decides to do so, he must then accept the consequences of his choice as regards the free movement of the product within the common market, which is a fundamental principal forming part of the legal and economic circumstances which must be taken into account by the proprietor of the patent in determining the manner in which his exclusive right will be exercised".

[48.] [1974] ECR 1147.
[49.] [1971] ECR 487.
[50.] [1981] ECR 2063.
[51.] [1968] ECR 55.

[6.28] In *Pharmon BV v Hoechst AG*,[52] the ECJ emphasised the need for a consent by the patentee before his rights are exhausted. In that case, Hoechst held patents for the drug 'frusemide' in both the UK and the Netherlands. In the UK, the drug was the subject of a compulsory licence. A UK company who had obtained such a licence produced and sold the drug to Pharmon who imported it into the Netherlands. The Court held that where a patented product was the subject of a compulsory licence, the patentee could not be said to have made a free choice about where the product should be first marketed in the EU. Therefore, the patentee was entitled to prevent importation even though there was a prohibition against export in the terms of the compulsory licence.

[6.29] The issue of consent was further considered in *Allen & Hanbury v Generics (UK) Ltd*.[53] In that case, the patent for the drug 'salbutamol' was subject to licences of right in the UK under transitional provisions of the UK Patents Act 1977. Generics imported the drug from Italy where it was not patented, arguing that they were entitled to do so under a licence of right. The patentee argued that the licence of right did not include a right to import. The effect of the licensing of right provisions is to remove the ability of a patentee to oppose third party use but merely retained the right to a fair return by way of royalties. It was held that the patent right was not exhausted against foreign imports to the extent necessary to ensure the patentee the same rights as against domestic producers, ie, the right to a fair return. Because UK law distinguished between domestic producers who could secure a licence as of right and importers who could be refused such a licence, it had to be considered whether or not such a discrimination was justified under Article 36. The prohibition on imports could only be justified if it:

> "is necessary in order to ensure that the proprietor of such a patent has, *vis-à-vis* importers, the same rights as he enjoys as against producers who manufacture the product in the national territory, that is to say the right to a fair return from his patent".

The Court found that no such prohibition was necessary for this purpose and the authorities could not prevent the licensee of right from importing products from other Member States. Effectively, therefore, the ECJ rejected the rights of the patent holder in favour of the rules of non-discrimination in the Treaty.

[6.30] Applying the doctrine of common origin, if patent rights of common origin are owned by different persons in particular Member States, a patentee cannot rely on a national patent to prevent the importation of goods lawfully marketed under a patent by a patentee in another Member State.[54]

---

52. [1985] ECR 2281.
53. [1988] ECR 1245; [1988] FSR 312.

Abuse of a dominant position

[6.31] Article 86 of the Treaty of Rome prohibits an "abuse of a dominant position". Since a patent is a form of monopoly, it may inevitably put a patentee in a dominant position. However, it is only when it is abused that there is a prohibition. An example of such an abuse is identified in Article 86(d) as:

> making the conclusion of contracts subject to acceptance by the other parties of supplementary obligations which, by their nature or according to commercial usage, have no connection with the subject of such contracts.

Thus, a patent licensee should not be compelled as part of the licence to buy unpatented goods. Also, any unfair commercial practice on the part of a dominant enterprise intended to eliminate, discipline or deter small companies is potentially an abuse of the monopoly right.[55]

[6.32] Rather contrasting views can be seen in the cases of *Volvo AB v Eric Veng (UK) Ltd*[56] and *Magill v ITP, BBC and RTE*.[57] In the first of these cases, the Court had to consider the issue of car body panels and whether or not car manufacturers could use intellectual property rights to prevent the manufacture of competing spare body panels. It was held that an abuse would arise only if the owner of the rights neither sold the goods itself nor licensed others to do so. The charge of an excessive price would also amount to an abuse. The European Court stated:

> "It must however be noted that the exercise of an exclusive right by the proprietor of a registered design in respect of car body panels may be prohibited by Article 86 if it involves, on the part of an undertaking holding a dominant position, certain abusive conduct such as the arbitrary refusal to supply spare parts to independent repairers, the fixing of prices for spare parts at an unfair level or a decision no longer to produce spare parts for a particular model even though many cars of that model are still in circulation provided that such conduct is liable to affect trade between Member States".

This is hard to reconcile with the *Magill* case and the finding that broadcasters in preventing publishers from meeting substantial potential demand for alternative listings were abusing a dominant position which they held by virtue of copyright.

[6.33] It is not always easy to establish whether a party is in a dominant position. In *Hugin v EC Commission*,[58] it was held that an approximate twelve per cent

---

54. *Van Zuylen Freres v Hag AG* [1974] ECR 731; *Terrapin v Terranova* [1976] ECR 1039.
55. *Engineering & Chemical Supplies v Akzo* [1986] 3 CMLR 273.
56. [1988] ECR 621.
57. [1989] 4 CMLR 757.
58. [1979] ECR 1869.

share of the EU market in respect of cash registers did not put Hugin in a dominant position. Again, spare parts were at issue. There was considered to be a dominant position in respect of recondition and repair of Hugin registers because in the main, the spare parts for the Hugin registers were not interchangeable with spare parts for other registers.

[6.34] In *Eurofix and Bauco v Hilti AG*,[59] the defendant was fined by the Commission for abuse of a dominant position by attempting to control the supply of unpatented nails for use with its patented fastening guns. Hilti's attempt to justify its behaviour on the grounds of safety and reliability failed. In addition, one of the many categories of conduct which were held to constitute a breach was the frustrating and delaying of legitimately available licences of right under the defendant's patents. The defendant had demanded excessive royalty payments.

[6.35] Another example of an abuse can be seen in the case of *Elopak Italia Srl v Tetra Pak*.[60] The EC Commission imposed a fine of 75 million ECUs for activities which were aimed at eliminating competition by imposing unduly binding terms in sales and leasing contracts and discriminatory and predatory pricing. In *Pitney Bowes Inc v Francotyp-Postalia*,[61] the English High Court made it clear that a refusal to grant a licence on reasonable terms was not itself an abuse and interestingly, Hoffmann J found some substance in the argument that patent rights may have to be considered differently because of the compulsory licensing provisions under UK law.

Block Exemptions

[6.36] Provisions of a licence agreement which come within Article 85(1) of the Treaty of Rome as being incompatible with the Common Market are void unless the agreement is notified to the EC Commission and an exemption granted under Article 85(3). Since intellectual property licence agreements often contain restrictions on competition in one form or another, the Commission has from an early date, indicated a list of clauses commonly found in patent licences which are not to be considered objectionable. The Commission has issued a number of block exemption regulations for different types of licences including patent licence agreements. The Patent Exemption Regulation[62] was principally concerned with the licensing of patents with or without associated know-how and was originally due to expire on 31 December 1994 but was extended pending adoption of the Technology Transfer Block Exemption Regulation.[63]

---

59. [1989] 4 CMLR 677.
60. [1992] 4 CMLR 551; Summary [1992] FSR 542.
61. [1991] FSR 72.
62. Regulation 2349/84; OJ 1984 No. L219/15; [1985] FSR 191.

The Regulations provide for automatic exemption of agreements containing certain provisions which are known as 'white clauses' provided certain other provisions known as 'black clauses' are not present. Agreements with provisions by way of restrictions which have neither white nor black clauses may be exempted under an opposition procedure whereby the agreement is notified to the Commission and the Commission decides not to oppose such exemption within six months. Restrictions which were not exempted by the Regulation either automatically or under the opposition procedure, could still be notified for individual exemption. Although the Patent Exemption Regulation No 2349/84 applied to agreements combining the licensing of patents and know-how, Article 9 of the preamble provided that the patents must be necessary for the achievement of the objects of the licensed technology. In addition, the licensed product must have been protected in all of the Member States to which the licence applies. The effect of this is to reduce the scope of the Regulation. There was, however, a further Regulation called the Know-How Block Exemption Regulation[64] which covered not only purely know-how agreements but also the majority of patent and know-how licences not covered by the patent exemption Regulation.[65]

[6.37] Regulation No 240/96 is a block exemption regulation relating to technology transfer agreements. It became effective on 1 April 1996 and replaced both the Patent Licensing Block Exemption Regulation No 2349/84 and the Know-How Licensing Block Exemption Regulation which were not due to expire until December 1999. Regulation No 240/96 applies to pure patent licences, pure know-how licences and mixed patent/know-how licences. Also embraced are licence agreements providing for the licensing of other intellectual property rights including trade marks, design rights, and copyright where such are ancillary.

[6.38] The rationale behind Regulation No 240/96, as with its predecessors, is that certain contractual provisions in licence agreements although generally restrictive of competition nevertheless have positive attributes which fall within Article 85(3). In Regulation 240/96 these include one or more of the following obligations:

(1) an obligation on the licensor not to licence other undertakings to exploit the licensed technology in the licensed territory;

(2) an obligation on the licensor not to exploit the licensed technology in the licensed territory himself;

---

63. Regulation No 240/96; OJ 1996 L 31/2.
64. Regulation No 556/89; OJ 1989 L 61/1 as amended [1993] OJ L21/8.
65. Paragraph 2 of the Preamble; Article 1(7)(6).

(3) an obligation on the licensee not to exploit the licensed technology in the territory of the licensor within the Common Market;

(4) an obligation on the licensee not to manufacture or use the licensed product, or use the licensed process, in territories within the Common Market which are licensed to other licensees;

(5) an obligation on the licensee not to pursue an active policy of putting the licensed product on the market in the territories within the Common Market which are licensed to other licensees, and in particular not to engage in advertising specifically aimed at those territories or to establish any branch or maintain a distribution depot there;

(6) an obligation on the licensee not to put the licensed product on the market in the territories licensed to other licensees within the Common Market in response to unsolicited orders;

(7) an obligation on the licensee to use only the licensor's trade mark or get up to distinguish the licensed product during the term of the agreement, provided that the licensee is not prevented from identifying himself as the manufacturer of the licensed products;

(8) an obligation on the licensee to limit his production of the licensed product to the quantities he requires in manufacturing his own products and to sell the licensed product only as an integral part of or a replacement part of his own products or otherwise in connection with the sale of his own products, provided that such quantities are freely determined by the licensee.

[6.39] The exemption of these obligations is subject to various provisos which vary depending on whether the agreement is a pure patent licence, pure know-how licence or a mixed patent and know-how licensing agreement. Article 2 of Regulation No 240/96 contains a list of clauses which are stated to be generally not restrictive of competition. This 'white list' of clauses is extensive and includes by way of example, an obligation on the licensee not to grant sub-licences or assign the licence, minimum quality standards and minimum royalty and production obligations. The white list is broader than in previous Regulations and allows a licensor the right to terminate the agreement if the licensee contests the secret or substantial nature of the licensed know-how or challenges the validity of licensed patents within the Common Market belonging to the licensor or undertakings connected with the licensor.

[6.40] The Regulation further identifies by way of a 'black list' clauses which will make the Regulation inapplicable. This black list includes clause(s) whereby one party is restricted in the determination of prices, components of prices or discounts for the licensed products and non-compete restrictions. Because a clause is not on the black list does not mean that it is permissible *per se*. There may still be a need for individual notification to the Commission or alternatively, it is possible to avail of an opposition procedure. Under the opposition procedure an agreement containing anything but black listed clauses may be notified to the Commission and deemed automatically exempt if the Commission takes no action within a specified four month period.

[6.41] Under Article 7 of the Regulation, the Commission may withdraw the benefit of the Regulation where it finds in a particular case that an agreement exempted by the Regulation nevertheless has certain effects which are incompatible with the conditions laid down in Article 85(3) of the Treaty. Examples given include where the effect of the agreement is to prevent the licensed products from being exposed to effective competition in the licensed territory from identical goods or services or from goods or services considered by users as interchangeable or substitutable in view of their characteristics, price and intended use, which may in particular occur where the licensee's market share exceeds 40 per cent.

PATENT APPLICATIONS AND INFRINGEMENT

[6.42] Under s 26 of the 1964 Act, it was specifically stated that no proceedings could be taken in respect of an infringement committed before the date of the publication of the complete specification, which occurred on acceptance. However, no infringement action could be taken until after grant.[66] Section 44 of the 1992 Act now provisionally provides protection from the date of first publication of the specification, ie, 18 months from the earliest priority date and 18 months after the date of application where priority has not been claimed. A patent application prior to publication cannot be used as a basis for an infringement action. Nor when granted, can damages be secured for infringement during this period. From this date, there lies a claim for damages but under s 56, a patent must be granted before proceedings for infringement can be taken.

[6.43] The words 'provisionally confer' in s 44 appear in Article 67 of the EPC. It is a requirement under Article 67 of the EPC that the State provide for an applicant from the date of publication of the European patent application, an ability to claim reasonable compensation from any person who has used the invention in the State in circumstances where that person would be liable under national law for infringement of a national patent. Under s 56(3) of the 1992 Act, damages may be reduced if it would not have been reasonable to expect,

---

66. PA 1964, s 25.

from a consideration of the published application, that the ultimate patent would be infringed. With this in mind, an applicant should file a patent application with a set of claims of differing scope in order that the application contains at least a single claim that will be valid and infringed.

[6.44] In the case of a European patent application designating the State and which has been published by the EPO in French or German, relief under s 56 is dependant upon the filing and publication of an English translation of the claims. An exception arises in cases where an applicant has sent the translation to the person alleged to be infringing.[67] If a patent application is withdrawn, deemed to have been withdrawn or finally refused, then no claim of infringement can arise.[68]

Scope of Protection

[6.45] The scope of protection conferred by a patent or a patent application is determined by the wording of the claims.[69] The description and drawings can be used to interpret the claims. This provision corresponds to Article 69 of the EPC. Section 45(3) of the 1992 Act states that in interpreting this provision, a court must have regard to the directions contained in the Protocol on the interpretation of Article 69 of the EPC. This Protocol is in fact scheduled to the 1992 Act and by way of directions to the interpretation of s 45 states that:

> Section 45 should not be interpreted in the sense that the extent of the protection conferred by a patent is to be understood as that defined by the strict, literal meaning of the wording used in the claims, the description and drawings being employed only for the purpose of resolving an ambiguity found in the claims. Neither should it be interpreted in the sense that the claims serve only as a guideline and that the actual protection conferred may extend to what, from a consideration of the description and drawings by a person skilled in the art, the patentee has contemplated. On the contrary, it is to be interpreted as defining a position between these extremes which combines a fair protection for the patentee with a reasonable degree of certainty for third parties.

The Protocol was intended to enter a middle ground between what was at least perceived as the extreme English literal approach and the equally extreme German guideline approach. In practice, however, the English courts have adopted the view that the pronouncement of Lord Diplock in *Catnic Components Ltd v Hill & Smith Ltd*[70] conforms to the Protocol. In the *Catnic* case, the patent related to steel lintels, and Claim 1 required that a rear member

---

[67.] PA 1992, s 120(6).
[68.] PA 1992, s 44(2).
[69.] Section 45(1).
[70.] [1982] RPC 183.

of the lintel should 'extend vertically'. The lintel produced by the defendants differed only from that claim, in that the rear member, instead of being vertical, was inclined slightly to the vertical. The House of Lords held that, on the basis of a purposive rather than a literal construction, the patent was infringed. Lord Diplock considered the *Pith and Marrow Doctrine*[71] under which a patent could be held to be infringed if a defendant takes the pith and marrow of the invention even if he does not meet all the requirements of the claims and against this had to consider the principle expressed by Lord Upjohn in *Rodi & Weinberger AG v Henry Showell*[72] that "the essential integers (of the claims) having been ascertained, the infringing article must be considered. To constitute infringement the article must take each and every one of the essential integers of the claim". In *Catanic*, Lord Diplock stated the approach to be followed in these terms:[73]

> "A patent specification is a unilateral statement by the patentee, in words of his own choosing, addressed to those likely to have a practical interest in the subject matter of his invention (ie, 'skilled in the art'), by which he informs them what he claims to be the essential features of the new product or process for which the letters patent grant him a monopoly. It is those novel features only that he claims to be essential that constitute the so-called 'Pith and Marrow' of the claim. A patent specification should be given a purposive construction rather than a purely literal one derived from applying to it the kind of meticulous verbal analysis in which lawyers are too often tempted by their training to indulge. The question in each case is: whether persons with practical knowledge and experience of the kind of work in which the invention was intended to be used, would understand that strict compliance with a particular descriptive word or phrase appearing in a claim was intended by the patentee to be an essential requirement of the invention so that any variant would fall outside the monopoly claimed, even though it could have no material effect upon the way the invention worked".

[6.46] In *Improver Corp v Remington Consumer Products Ltd*,[74] the Court of Appeal held the statement of Lord Diplock correctly indicates the same approach to construction as is indicated in the Protocol on the interpretation of Article 69 of the EPC. The UK Patents Court has suggested that the tests applied by Lord Diplock can be broken down into three questions:[75]

---

71. Lord Cairns in *Clark v Adie* (1877) 2 App Cas 315, at 320.
72. [1969] RPC 367, at 391.
73. [1982] RPC at 242-243.
74. [1989] RPC 69.
75. *SouthCo Inc v Dzus Fastener Europe Ltd* [1990] RPC 587; *AC Edwards Ltd v Acme Signs* [1990] RPC 621.

(1) Does the variant have a material effect upon the way the invention worked? If it does, then there is no infringement.

(2) If the variant has no material effect upon the way the invention worked, would that be obvious to the skilled addressee? If not, then there is no infringement.

(3) Upon the assumption that questions (1) and (2) are answered in the affirmative, does the specification make it obvious to the skilled addressee that the variant could not have been intended to be excluded from the ambit of the claim? If so, there would be infringement.

The Irish courts have not had cause to consider this matter under the 1992 Act and the Protocol. However, Costello J in the High Court, in the case of *Wavin Pipes Limited v The Hepworth Iron Company Limited*[76] did apply Lord Diplock's statement and also in assistance drew attention to words quoted with approval by Kenny J in *Fabwerke Hoechst Aktiengesellschaft v Intercontinental Pharmaceutical (Eire) Ltd*[77] to the effect that a patentee who describes an invention in the body of a specification obtains no monopoly unless it is claimed in the claim. A claim is a portion of the specification which fulfils a separate and distinct function. It alone defines the monopoly and the patentee is under a statutory obligation to state in the claims clearly and distinctly what is the invention which he desires to protect.[78]

[6.47] The *Farbwerke* case is an example of the doctrine of equivalents occurring where a defendant replaces an inessential integer of a claim with an obvious equivalent. It was held by the Irish High Court that the defendant's starting material which was butylamine sulphate was chemically equivalent to the plaintiff's starting material, butylamine, in the process described in the specification, since any technician who failed to get a result with butylamine might be expected to try butylamine sulphate, even though not mentioned in the patent. This decision was made under the 1964 Act. It is usual in many continental European countries to include obvious equivalents within the scope of protection but this would appear to be at variance with a strict interpretation of s 45(1) which specifically states that the extent of protection is to be defined by the claims. However, given s 45(3), it is not such a strict approach which must be applied and the decision in *Fabwerke* may well have been the same under the 1992 Act. An example of the German approach can be found in the *Formstein* case[79] where the German Supreme Court also considered the Protocol

---

76. [1982] FSR 32.
77. [1968] FSR 187.
78. *Electric and Musical Industries Limited v Lisson Limited* [1939] 56 RPC 23.
79. [1991] RPC 597.

on Article 69 and concluded that the decisive factor was the scope of the invention as it was appreciated by a person skilled in the art. The question asked by the German Supreme Court was:

> "whether a person skilled in the art, has managed, on the basis of the invention protected by the claims, to solve the problem solved by the invention using methods which have the same effect, ie, has achieved the desired result with other means which lead to the same result. Solutions which a person of normal skill in the art, on the basis of the invention described in the claims, and the aid of his specialist knowledge, can discover to have the same effect, will ordinarily be within the protection of the patent".

In the UK Patents Court, Aldous J in *Bonzel v Intervention Ltd*[80] considered the word 'near' and construed such according to the perception of the skilled man in the light of the problem which the invention set out to solve. In *Willemijn Houdstermaatschappij v Madge Networks Ltd*,[81] there was held to be no infringement because the alleged infringement was considered to be outside the wording of the claim. The wording had a material effect on the manner of operation and this would have been obvious to a skilled addressee.

[6.48] The situation prior to grant is dealt with in s 45(2) of the 1992 Act. Prior to grant, it is possible to secure claims which are wider in scope than the published claims. Consequently, it is provided that the extent of protection prior to grant is determined by the claims published under s 28, ie, publication which occurs within 18 months of filing or of the priority date. Claims as amended should not extend the scope of disclosure of the application otherwise any subsequent patent is liable to revocation.[82]

[6.49] There is, of course, a difficult decison for a patent applicant between securing widely worded claims which will provide a broader scope of protection but which increases the likelihood of a defendant being able to successfully argue invalidity on the grounds of anticipation as forming part of the state of the art or obviousness. The Courts in the UK have applied the statement of Lord Moulton in *Gillette Safety Razor v Angio-American Trading Co*[83] in which he stated:

> "I am of opinion that in this case, the defendant's right to succeed can be established without an examination of the terms of the specification of the plaintiff's letters patent. I am aware that such a mode of deciding a patent case is unusual, but from the point of view of the public, it is important that this

---

[80] [1991] RPC 553.
[81] [1992] RPC 386.
[82] PA 1992, s 58(c).
[83] (1913) 30 RPC 465, at 480.

method of viewing their rights should not be overlooked. In practical life, it is often the only safeguard to the manufacturer. It is impossible for an ordinary member of the public to keep watch on all the numerous patents which are taken out and to ascertain the validity and scope of their claims, but he is entitled to feel secure if he knows that that which he is doing differs from that which has been done of old only in non-patentable variations, such as the substitution of mechanical equivalents or changes of material shape or size. The defence that 'the alleged infringement was not novel at the date of the plaintiff's letters patent' is a good defence in law and it would sometimes obviate the great length and expense of the patent cases if the defendant could and would put forth his case in this form, and thus spare himself the trouble of demonstrating on which horn of the well-known dilemma the plaintiff had impaled himself, invalidity or non-infringement".

[6.50] This has become known as the *Gillette defence*. Since this mode of deciding a patent case is unusual, it must be strictly proved.[84] If a defendant can prove that the act complained of was merely what was disclosed in a publication which could be relied on against the validity of the patent, without any substantial or patentable variation having been made, he has a good defence.[85]

Burden of Proof

[6.51] The onus of proving infringement normally lies with the plaintiff who can be either a patentee or an exclusive licensee.[86] Evidence of infringement must be obtained and exhibited in a form admissible under the general laws of evidence. Thus, an affidavit should be secured from a person who obtains the infringing product and who can verify the source, time and manner of purchase, exhibiting receipts, invoices or delivery notes. If the product is analysed, examined or experimented with, these facts should also be evidenced. Details of storage should be given if there is even only a slight possibility that the condition of the product may be affected.

[6.52] If the invention is a process for obtaining a new product, the burden of proof can shift to a defendant. If the same product is produced, there is an assumption that such a product is made by the patented process, unless the contrary is proved.[87] The onus is on a defendant to show non-infringement. Under s 40(c), it is an infringement to offer, put on the market, use, import, or stock a product obtained directly by a process protected by a patent.

[6.53] It is not clear what is meant by the same product. It could be argued that this means an identical product but if an analogy is drawn with trade mark law, it

---

[84.] *Hickman v Andrews* [1983] RPC 147.
[85.] *Terrell on the Law of Patents* (13th Ed) p 170.
[86.] Section 51.
[87.] Section 46(1).

may extend, for example, to products of the same description. The German Federal Supreme Court has already had to tackle this issue in relation to a chemical product which was not identical but which was held to be a product of the same composition.[88]

[6.54] In circumstances where a defendant must show non-infringement, there is in some circumstances, a danger that a defendant would be forced to disclose manufacturing or business secrets in so doing. Indeed, a plaintiff might pursue an action with this very objective in mind. Hence, s 46(2) provides an important safeguard whereby a defendant can, at the court's discretion, hear the defendant's evidence in the absence of any other party to the proceedings. The factors to be considered by a court in deciding whether or not to exercise its discretion in favour of the defendant are stated in s 46(3) and the court must be satisfied as to the defendant's possession of a manufacturing or commercial secret, the secret information would enable the burden of proof to be discharged and that it would be unreasonable to require disclosure.

[6.55] Rather than exclude a plaintiff fully, a court could presumably exercise its discretion by limiting disclosure to, for example, the plaintiff's solicitor or counsel or to selected individuals upon terms aimed at securing that there will not either be use or further disclosure of the information in ways which might prejudice a defendant.[89] In *Centri-Spray Corp v Cera International*,[90] an order was made permitting the plaintiff's employee to inspect drawings subject to an undertaking not to make use of information disclosed therein. The plaintiff was not allowed to take away the drawings or to take copies. In *Roussel Uclaf v ICI*,[91] the defendant was faced with the dilemma of protecting clearly valuable proprietary information and at the same time, giving the plaintiff an opportunity to inspect materials which would have a considerable bearing on its case. In the circumstances, limited disclosure was ordered to a single nominee of the plaintiff and with undertakings incorporated in an order of the court.

REMEDIES

[6.56] The remedies which are available consequent on a finding of patent infringement are specifically identified in s 47 of the 1992 Act. The proceedings must be brought by the proprietor of the patent or an exclusive licensee[92] and except in the case of an infringement of a short term patent,[93] the action must be

---

[88.] *Alkylenediamine 11* (1977) 8 11C 350.
[89.] *Warner-Lambert v Glaxo Laboratories Ltd* [1975] RPC 354.
[90.] [1979] FSR 175.
[91.] [1990] RPC 45.
[92.] Section 51
[93.] Section 66(4).

taken in the High Court. An exclusive licence is defined in s 2 of the 1992 Act and means:

> A licence from a proprietor of or applicant for a patent which confers on the licensee or on the licensee and persons authorised by him, to the exclusion of all other persons (including the proprietor of or applicant for the patent), any right in respect of the invention.

The use of the words 'any right' would suggest an exclusive right could arise in a situation where, for example, the licence was in respect of manufacture only and not use or a licence limited to a particular part of the country. The language would permit a plurality of exclusive licensees to be created in respect of one patent.[94]

[6.57] The distinction must be drawn between a sole licence and an exclusive licence. Under a sole licence, there is no exclusion for the patent proprietor and thus such falls outside the definition. The holder of a sole licence as opposed to an exclusive licence has no right to take an infringement action. No particular form of grant is required to constitute an exclusive licence. The position is in each case a mixed question of law and fact as to whether a licence is in fact exclusive. The fact that a party is appointed an agent to manufacture without others does not amount to an exclusive licence where an ability remains to appoint further agents.[95]

[6.58] A licence can be partly written and partly oral as in the case of *Morton-Norwich Products Inc v Intercen Ltd*.[96] In an exclusive licence, the licensee, in addition to an action for breach of contract, should be in a position to recover damages for infringement by a patent proprietor. In the case of *Pcuk v Diamond Shamrock Industrial Chemicals Ltd*,[97] Falconer J held that a sole licensee was clearly not in a position to take an action for patent infringement but may nevertheless have a claim under the tort of 'interference with business'.[98]

[6.59] An exclusive licensee is entitled to avail of the reliefs for infringement even in cases where there has been non-recordal of the interest on the register. There must, however, be evidence that, at the date of the writ, an exclusive licence is in place.[99] The patentee is entitled to the full set of reliefs even where an exclusive licensee has already obtained relief of their own.[100] The patentee

---

94. *Courtauld's Application* [1956] RPC 208.
95. *Bondax Carpets Ltd v Advance Carpet Tiles* [1993] FSR 162.
96. [1981] FSR 337.
97. [1981] FSR 427.
98. See however *Lonrho v Shell* [1981] 2 All ER 456, at 461.
99. *Procter & Gamble v Peaudouce (UK) Ltd* [1989] FSR 180.
100. *Optical Coating Laboratory Inc v Pilkington PE Ltd* [1993] FSR 310.

must be a party to any proceedings taken by a licensee but if added as a defendant, a patentee has no liability for any costs unless they enter an appearance and take part in the proceedings.[101]

Injunctions and Groundless Threats

[6.60] Section 47(1)(a) does not identify the types of injunction of which a patentee can avail but does state that it should be by way of a restraint on the defendant "from any apprehended act of such infringement". This seems to rule out the possibility of a mandatory as opposed to a prohibitory injunction.

[6.61] Under the Brussels Convention on the Jurisdiction and Enforcement of Judgments in Civil and Commercial Matters 1968, the general rule is that the defendant must be sued in his home State but there is an exemption in matters relating to torts and a defendant may be sued in the country in which the patent infringement takes place. Therefore, an Irish domiciled defendant infringing a British patent may be sued either in Britain or Ireland. A split in proceedings may occur if the validity of a patent is being challenged since such must take place in the courts of the country having jurisdiction over the patent.[102]

[6.62] A cease and desist letter claiming infringement should not issue lightly given the provisions governing 'groundless threats' contained in s 53 of the 1992 Act.

[6.63] While there is no statutory requirement to put an infringer on notice before commencement of proceedings seeking injunctive relief, it is certainly normal to do so. If relief by way of an interlocutory injunction is to be sought, then it is necessary for prompt action. A normal cease and desist letter would identify the patent by way of number, the act alleged to be an infringement and the demands over and above cessation such as damages and handing over of infringing products. In practice, seven to ten days are usually given in any notice to an infringer. Given the complexity of patent litigation and the fact that the only defence is often invalidity of a patent which invariably involves in-depth study as to the 'state of the art', it is quite normal for an alleged infringer to seek a further period of time. While this can often be only reasonable, a patentee must be careful of time constraints which operate when seeking interlocutory relief. A patentee cannot risk entering into lengthy correspondence on invalidity in such circumstances. Acts which continue following a cease and desist letter provide a basis for inferring a deliberate intention to infringe and the likely repetition of such acts in the future.[103]

[101.] Section 51(2).

[102.] See O'Sullivan, 'Cross-Border Jurisdiction in Patent Proceedings in Europe', [1996] 12 EIPR 657.

[103.] *Steiner Products LD v Stevens* [1957] RPC 439.

[6.64] In the case of *Customagic Manufacturing Co Ltd v Headquarter & General Supplies Ltd*,[104] no notice was given and although Plowman J notes this as being very unusual, he felt the circumstances of the case in which the plaintiff had made two 'trap owners' justified the immediate issuance of proceedings. Moreover, if the plaintiff has reason to believe that there is a grave danger that the infringer, if put on notice in the usual way, will destroy evidence of infringement so as to defeat the ends of justice, an *Anton Piller*[105] order, which is usually obtained *ex parte* and may be granted in appropriately serious cases.

[6.65] A practitioner alleging patent infringement on behalf of a client must be particularly cautious given the provisions of s 53[106] of the 1992 Act and whereby such threats if unjustified, could result in an injunction and damages actually being awarded against a patentee. The basis of this provision was well stated by Lindley LJ in *Skinner & Co v Perry*:[107]

> "The legislature desires that threats of patent actions shall not hang over a man's head; that the sword of damages ... should either not be suspended, or should fall at once".

[6.66] It is also no defence that the threats were made in good faith. However, in the case of malicious threats, the common law remedies of malicious falsehood and trade libel are also available.[108]

[6.67] Although the threat must be to take proceedings for infringement, such a threat can take many forms, given the additional words 'or otherwise' following the stated examples of circulars or advertisements in s 53(1).[109] Whether or not a statement amounts to a threat is an objective one determined by whether or not the "language used has been such as would convey to a reasonable man that there was an intention to bring proceedings".[110] In the case of *Luna Advertising Co Ltd v Burnham & Co*,[111] a threat was made by a representative of the defendant calling on a customer of the plaintiff and stating that a sign outside the customer's premises was an infringement and should be removed. Although there was no reference made to solicitors or court proceedings, the discussion had no real meaning except to the person threatened that the threatening party

---

[104.] [1968] FSR 150.
[105.] *Anton Piller KG v Manufacturing Processes Ltd* [1976] RPC 719.
[106.] Remedies for groundless threats.
[107.] [1893] 10 RPC 1.
[108.] *Wren v Weild* (1889) LR 4 QB 727; *Halsey v Brotherhood* (1881) 19 Ch D 388; *Farr v Weatherhead & Harding* (1932) RPC 267.
[109.] *Speedcranes Ltd v Thomson* [1978] RPC 221.
[110.] *C & P Development Co (London) Ltd v Sisabro Novelty Co Ltd* (1953) 70 RPC 277.
[111.] (1928) RPC 258.

has legal rights and intends to enforce them unless the person threatened ceased the alleged infringing act.

[6.68] In *Bristol-Myers Co v Manon Freres Ltd*,[112] a retailer was verbally informed that the patentee would proceed against the defendant manufacturer for infringement. The retailer cancelled its orders. It was held that "the defendant, though not directly threatened, could claim to be aggrieved by that threat". Although the threat was held to be justifiable in this instance, it would otherwise have been actionable. A general warning to the trade is not actionable since a court must be satisfied that a warning finger is pointed against some specific manufacturer, importer or vendor.[113] In *Olin Mathiesen Chemical Corp v Biorex Ltd*,[114] a letter was sent to the Ministry of Health with the objective of trying to ensure that sales to hospitals would be prevented. It was held that such was an actionable threat. In *Bowden Controls v Acco Cable Controls Ltd*,[115] the plaintiff took an action on the basis of a letter written by the defendant to manufacturers in the UK, drawing attention to the result of proceedings in Germany and stating that the patentee had similar patents in all major European vehicle manufacturing countries and intended to enforce its rights. An interlocutory injunction restraining such threats was granted "the fact that it (the letter) is not explicit that patent proceedings will be taken is in no way conclusive as a threat can be veiled or implied just as much as it can be explicit".

[6.69] It is important to note that while the heading to the section uses the words 'groundless threats', such does not appear in the section itself which refers instead to 'unjustifiable' in the sense that infringement of a valid claim is not ultimately established.

[6.70] The reliefs are stated in s 53(2) and are a declaration that the threats are unjustified, an injunction to restrain further threats, and damages. The use of the words 'shall be entitled' does not, however, remove the discretion of a court to refuse the relief. In *Benmax v Austin Motor Co*,[116] Evershed MR refused to grant any relief whatever, rejecting the suggestion of any obligation on the court and stating the words mean nothing more than the plaintiff shall be entitled *prima facie*.[117] In *Cerosa Ltd v Poseidon Industries*,[118] an interlocutory injunction was granted even though infringement proceedings had already commenced.[119]

[112.] [1973] RPC 836.

[113.] *Alpi Pietro v John Wright & Sons* [1972] RPC 125.

[114.] [1970] RPC 157, at 196.

[115.] [1990] RPC 427.

[116.] (1953) 70 RPC 143 & 284.

[117.] See *Tudor Accessories v Somers Ltd* [1960] RPC 215.

[118.] [1973] RPC 882.

[119.] See also *HVE Electric Ltd v Cufflin Holdings Ltd* [1964] RPC 149.

[6.71] Section 53(3) provides that proceedings may not be brought under this section in relation to a threat to bring proceedings for an infringement alleged to consist of making or importing a product for disposal or of using a process. In interpreting a similar provision in s 70 of the UK Patents Act 1977, Oliver LJ supported the view that it was the intention of the legislature that a person, whether a patentee or not, could threaten proceedings with impunity where what is complained of as infringement is the making of a product for disposal.[120] It is not restricted to threats against a primary infringer. However, an example of where s 53(3) could not be availed of, are threats against use[121] or sale.[122]

[6.72] Under s 53(4), a mere notification of the existence of a patent or patent application does not constitute a threat. However, extra caution is necessary because the whole context of the notification is taken into account. In *Reymes-Cole v Elite Hosiery Co Ltd*,[123] a letter was not considered to be a mere notification of the existence of letters patent having regard to the inclusion of the allegation of infringement by a number of firms and the statement of impending proceedings against some of them.

Delivery Up or Destruction

[6.73] The basis for an order under s 47(1)(b) which requires that a defendant deliver up or destroy an infringing product is to protect a patentee from use after expiry of the patent of products made while the patent was still in existence. However, the order cannot be granted except as an adjunct to an interdict. It cannot be granted after the expiry of the patent.[124] The purpose of the order is to make the interdict more effective. The order can be modified where an infringing article can be rendered non-infringing by some alteration or by the removal of some part. Thus, in *Merganthaler Linotype Company v Intertype Ltd*,[125] Russell J stressed the ancillary nature of the relief and that it ought not go beyond what was necessary for protection of the plaintiff. In *Electrical & Musical Industries Ltd v Lissen Ltd*,[126] Luxmoore J refused to order delivery up of a valve which could be used in a non-infringing manner as well as in an infringing manner. In *Codex Corporation v Racal-Milgo Limited*,[127] Whitford J highlighted the care which should be given to the exact form of any order for delivery up or destruction that may be made. It was held to be sufficient to

---

120. *Therm-A-Stor Ltd v Weatherseal Windows Ltd* [1981] FSR 579.
121. *Johnson Electric v Mabuchi-Motor KK* [1986] FSR 280.
122. *Neild v Rockley* [1986] FSR 3.
123. [1964] RPC 255.
124. *Monsanto Company v Stauffer Chemicals* [1988] FSR 57.
125. (1926) 43 RPC 381.
126. (1937) 45 RPC 5.
127. [1984] FSR 87.

deliver up or destroy the elements in the apparatus which caused the act of infringement.

Damages or an Account of Profits

[6.74] A plaintiff in patent infringement proceedings may claim damages in respect of such infringement[128] or an account of profits derived by the defendant[129] but cannot be awarded both.[130]

[6.75] In valuing a claim for damages, Lord Wilberforce in *General Tire & Rubber Co v Firestone Tyre & Rubber Company Ltd*[131] stated that there were two essential principles:

> "first, that the plaintiffs have the burden of proving their loss; second, that the defendants being wrongdoers, damages should be liberally assessed but that the objection is to compensate the plaintiffs and not punish the defendants".

[6.76] Damages are compensatory and not punitive. The measure of damages is to be, so far as possible, that sum of money which will put the injured party in the same position as he would have been in if he had not sustained the wrong. A way of calculating damages in patent infringement proceedings is on the basis of the loss of profits by the proprietor. In cases where the effect of the infringement is to divert sales from the owner of the patent to the infringer, the measure of damages will then normally be the profit which would have been realised by the owner of the patent if the sales had been made by him.[132] However, the court must be satisfied that if infringement had not occurred, the patentee would himself have had the business of the infringing acts.[133] If it is not possible to calculate damages on a loss of profit basis, then it should be possible to be compensated on a notional royalty basis, ie the measure of damages payable will be the sum which the defendant would have paid by way of royalty if instead of acting illegally, he had acted legally.[134] In *Smith, Kline & French Laboratories v Doncaster Pharmaceuticals*,[135] damages were assessed on the basis of the difference between the price a parallel importer of infringing products actually paid for the products and the price he would have had to pay in order to lawfully import the products. It does not appear that a claim of exemplary damages is available to a plaintiff except in very exceptional circumstances.[136]

[128.] Section 47(1)(c).
[129.] Section 47(1)(d).
[130.] Section 47(2).
[131.] [1976] RPC 197.
[132.] *The United Horse-Shoe Co v John Stewart* 13 AC 401.
[133.] *Catnic Components v Hill & Smith Ltd* [1983] FSR 512, at 521.
[134.] *Meters Ltd v Metropolitan Gas Meters* (1911) 28 RPC 157.
[135.] [1989] FSR 401.
[136.] *Morton-Norwich Products Inc v United Chemicals (London) Ltd* [1981] FSR 337.

[6.77] When an infringing article includes patented subject matter as an integral part, all damage caused by that sale will be compensated.[137] In *British Insulated Wire Co Ltd v Dublin United Tramway Co Ltd*[138] it was held that lost profits relating to articles sold with a patented article were not recoverable. However, more recently Jacob J in the *Gerber Garment* case[139] compensated a plaintiff by way of ancillary damages once it was established that the entire loss which included service contracts was forseeably caused by the infringement.

[6.78] The distinction between an account of profits and damages was well explained by Windeyer J in the Australian case of *Colbeam Palmer Ltd v Stock Affiliates Pty Ltd*:[140]

> "by the former the infringer is required to give up his ill-gotten gains to the party whose rights he has infringed; by the latter he is required to compensate the party wronged for the loss he has suffered. The two computations can obviously yield different results, for a plaintiff's loss is not to be measured by the defendant's gain, nor a defendant's gain by the plaintiff's loss. Either may be greater, or less, than the other".

There are, of course, difficulties in computation and it should be reasonable approximation rather than by mathematical exactness and to ensure that neither party receives what justly belongs to the other.[141] Where there are a number of defendants a plaintiff can elect between damages and an account for each defendant.[142]

[6.79] Under s 56(1) of the 1992 Act, damages are recoverable from the date of publication of the application but no action can be brought until the patent is granted. Section 49(2) gives the court a discretion to refuse to award damages in respect of infringements committed during any period in which the patentee is in default of payment of renewal fees. In the case of an innocent infringer under s 49(1), the court cannot award damages or an account of profits. The onus lies on a defendant to show that it was unaware of the existence of the patent. This is often referred to as innocent infringement but this defence does not arise because an infringer is unaware that his actions amount to an infringement but only concerns knowledge as to whether that the patent existed.

[6.80] The onus is heavy and such can be illustrated in the case of *Lancer Boss Ltd v Henley Forklift Co Ltd*[143] where it was held that the defendant should at

---

[137.] *Meters Ltd v Metropolitan Gas Meters Ltd* (1911) 28 RPC 260; *United Horse-Shoe & Nail Co Ltd v Stewart* (1888) 5 RPC 260.

[138.] (1899) 17 RPC 14; *Clement Talbot Ltd v Wilson* (1909) 26 RPC 467.

[139.] *Gerber Garment Technology Inc v Lectra Systems Ltd & Anor* [1995] RPC 383 (case under appeal).

[140.] [1972] RPC 303, at 308.

[141.] *My Kinda Town Ltd v Soll* [1983] RPC 15.

[142.] *Electric Furnace Co v Selas Corporation of America* [1987] RPC 23.

[143.] [1975] RPC 307.

least have appreciated the probability of patents and have carried out investigations in this regard.

[6.81] Graham J, in considering the concluding words corresponding to s 49(2), that marking goods with the word 'patent' or 'patented' was not of itself conclusive of knowledge unless it was accompanied by the number of the relevant patent, held that an objective test was to be applied and gave the following example:

> "Circumstances might however exist in which only a few examples of the plaintiffs' patented goods, though marked with a patent number, had been made and sold at the time of the infringement in question and the defendant might not have seen any of them. If so, it might well not be right to hold that at that time there had been sufficient notification to amount to the existence of reasonable grounds for supposing that a patent existed".

[6.82] A defendant who seeks to avail himself of the protection afforded by s 49(1) must plead and prove complete ignorance of the existence of the patent monopoly during the period in which the wrongful acts were being committed.[144] It is quite common for a patentee to draw a defendant's attention to a patent application and by doing so, it is not possible for a defendant to claim 'this special defence' since it is then "inconceivable that any court could hold that they had any reasonable ground for supposing that this patent did not exist".[145]

[6.83] The defence of innocent infringement was successfully raised in *Lux Traffic Controls Ltd v Pike Signals Ltd*[146] and it was even conceded by the patentee that it should also apply for a reasonable time period after finding out about the patents. Because of this concession, no argument was presented as to whether from the time of notice, a reasonable time period should be given to a defendant within which to investigate the assertions made by an alleged patentee and to cease infringement. However, a court is likely to allow such a period.

[6.84] Section 49(3) provides that in a situation where a patent specification has been amended, no damages will be awarded for the period prior to the date of the decision allowing the amendment unless the court is satisfied that the specification as originally published was framed in good faith and with reasonable skill and knowledge. Similar wording also appears in s 50(2) dealing with the relief available in respect of infringement of a partially valid patent.

[144.] *Benmax v Austin Motor Co Ltd* (1953) RPC 143.
[145.] *Wilbec Plastics Ltd v Wilson Dawes Ltd* [1966] RPC 513.
[146.] [1993] RPC 107.

[6.85] The question of good faith in framing a patent specification is basically in a field of enquiry as to whether the patentee or his agent knew something detrimental to the patent, as applied for in the form in which the specification was framed. In *General Tire & Rubber v Firestone Tyre & Rubber*, Russell LJ commented that if a patent agent puts forward something of which he has no knowledge, which suffers from some fatal imperfection in the patent field, "we do not consider that when the Patent Office accepts it without demur, it can be said that it was framed, otherwise than in good faith. It is, after all, the function of a patent agent to argue in honesty for the width of the application".[147]

[6.86] In *Ronson Products Ltd v A Lewis & Co (Westminster) Ltd*,[148] a patent agent in drafting a specification departed in a material respect from the intention of the applicant despite having all relevant information in his possession. It was held that the admission by the patent agent that the specification was wrong in view of the information in his possession must establish an absence of reasonable skill and knowledge. Accordingly, the onus which is on the patentee had not been discharged. Good faith and reasonable skill and knowledge may be assumed in the patentee's favour in the absence of internal or external evidence to the contrary.[149] The requisite knowledge is the law and practice relating to patent specifications. The fact that with hindsight and following sustained argument and evidence from experts, it can be seen how the patent might have been more clearly drafted does not demonstrate a want of reasonable skill and knowledge.[150] In *Rediffusion Simulation Ltd v Link-Miles Ltd*,[151] Aldous J accepted that a distinction must be drawn between reasonable care and reasonable skill and that the word 'skill' concerned skill in framing the specification as opposed to care in checking for the errors. It was held that a patent agent, in altering a claim, was exercising skill and it should have been a reasonable exercise of that skill to make such consequential amendments as were necessary. Failure to do so resulted in a refusal of damages.

[6.87] The restriction in s 49(3) only relates to damages and therefore, a plaintiff is entitled to an account of profits in respect of infringing acts without being required to prove that the specification as originally published was framed in good faith and with reasonable skill and knowledge.[152]

[6.88] Although ss 40 and 41 of the 1992 Act do not use the word 'infringe', the relief by way of a declaration of infringement and validity under s 47(1)(e)

---

147. [1975] RPC 203.
148. [1963] RPC 103, at p 138.
149. *Molins & Molins v Industrial Machinery Co Ltd* (1938) 55 RPC 31.
150. *Molnlyck & Peaudouce v Proctor & Gamble* [1992] FSR 549, at 606.
151. [1993] FSR 369, at 384.
152. *Codex Corporation v Racal-Milgo Ltd* [1983] RPC 369.

follows as a matter of course in the event of a successful claim, that a third party has committed any of the unauthorised acts. If the validity of a patent has been contested and is found to be wholly or partially valid, then it is normal to request that the declaration contain a certificate of contested validity under s 52(1). The effect of such a declaration is that if in subsequent proceedings for infringement or revocation of that patent, a final order or judgment is made in favour of the party relying on the patent (which can include an exclusive licensee), that party is to be entitled to his costs as between solicitor and own client, "unless the court otherwise directs".[153] The purpose is to avoid the duplication of proceedings contesting the validity of the patent and the incurring of unnecessary costs in trying to fight over matters again which have already been decided in a previous action.

[6.89] In *Letraset International Ltd v Mecanorma Ltd*,[154] Graham J reviewed the large number of earlier cases on this provision and concluded that there was not very much assistance to be derived from them except to the extent that they make it clear that the judge has a discretion as to whether he should grant the plaintiff, solicitor and client costs or only party and party costs. *Prima facie*, a plaintiff, having obtained a certificate of validity in one action, is entitled in a subsequent action to his solicitor and client costs, unless the defendant can persuade the court to make an order to the contrary effect. The onus is clearly on the defendant who must show that there is something in the case which ought to persuade the judge that the normal rule should not apply. When there has effectively been no contest as to the validity of a patent, then it is not usual to grant a certificate. "In a case where the matter has not been thoroughly gone into, the jurisdiction to grant certificates of validity should be exercised with great caution".[155] However, in suitable cases, a court may depart from this general principle. In *New Inverted Incadescent Gas Lamp Co Ltd v Globe Light Ltd*,[156] the validity of the patent was disputed but only upon a certain construction of the specification and accordingly, a certificate was refused. In *Edison & Swan Electric Light Co v Holland*,[157] the court refused the certificate on the grounds that a certificate had been granted in the previous action, and to give one in the action would have been to throw a doubt on the sufficiency of the former certificate. A new certificate may be granted in circumstances where the validity of a patent has been contested on new grounds.[158]

[153.] Section 52(2).

[154.] [1975] FSR 125.

[155.] *Gillette Industries v Bernstein* [1941] 58 RPC 271, at 285.

[156.] (1906) 23 RPC 157.

[157.] (1889) 6 RPC 243.

[158.] *Flour Oxidising Co Ltd v J & R Hutchinson* (1909) 26 RPC 597.

[6.90] The rights and limitations on such rights conferred on the proprietor of a patent also apply to a joint proprietor and includes under s 48(2) a statutory right to sue for infringement without the consent of any other joint proprietor. The other joint proprietors must be made party to the proceedings. If the others are joined as defendants, then they shall not be liable for any costs or expenses unless they enter an appearance and take part in the proceedings. The purpose of such a provision is to ensure that all joint proprietors are on notice of an infringement action on foot of a patent in which they have such joint proprietorship. The provision should be read in conjunction with s 80 which defines the rights and obligations of co-ownership.

[6.91] If in proceedings for infringement of a patent, some of the claims are held to be invalid but other(s) are held to be valid, then an injunction may still be granted.[159] The claims can be considered separately and the invalidity of only some of the claims does not invalidate the whole patent and does not prevent the granting of relief in respect of the claims which are valid.[160] An injunction can be granted without any amendment of the patent although such an amendment may be a condition for granting such relief.[161] The court also has a discretion to grant relief by way of damages or costs.[162] However, the onus is on the plaintiff to prove that the specification of the patent was framed in good faith and with reasonable skill and knowledge. In *Hallen Co v Brabantia (UK) Ltd*,[163] Aldous J considered this provision and held that it imposed upon a plaintiff a duty to prove on the balance of probabilities two things. First, that the specification was framed in good faith. That requires a plaintiff to prove that the specification was framed honestly with a view to obtaining a monopoly to which, on the material known to him, he believed he was entitled. Secondly, that the specification was framed with reasonable skill and knowledge. The words 'skill and knowledge' are a composite phrase relating to the competence employed in framing the specification and require the specification as framed to be in the form in which a person, with reasonable skill in drafting patent specifications and a knowledge of the law and practice relating thereto, would produce. Whether terms should be imposed on allowing a patent to be amended, or some limitation ordered as to the date from which damages would be reckoned, is in the court's discretion depending on the particular facts of each case. The defendant must establish the following:

[159.] Section 50(1).
[160.] *C Van Der Lely NV v Bamfords Ltd* [1964] RPC 54, at 73.
[161.] Section 50(3).
[162.] Section 50(2).
[163.] [1990] FSR 134.

(a) that he received reasonable advice that the patent was not infringed or was invalid;

(b) that he acted on this advice to his detriment; and

(c) that the advice given was based in some way upon the defect to be cured by the amendment.

[6.92] The court should also consider in the public interest the possibility that the defect in the patent could have caused persons not before the court to act to their detriment. If so, it may be proper to allow the amendment only subject to conditions safeguarding the position of such persons. There is no apparent duty upon a patentee to tell the Patent Office of matters that could affect prosecution of a patent application.[164] It is however wise to do so because it could be relevant to the court's exercise of discretion on amendment.

Declaration of Non-Infringement

[6.93] It is possible for a person to secure from the court a declaration that their use of a process or the manufacture, use or sale of a product does not amount to an infringement. In addition, a declaration can also be sought in relation to proposed activities.[165] It is not necessary that the patentee or any exclusive licensee have asserted infringement. The person seeking a declaration from the court must first have written to the patentee or licensee seeking a written acknowledgement corresponding to that sought in a declaration. He must provide full particulars of the process or product in question and there must be a failure by the patentee or licensee to give the acknowledgement sought.

[6.94] Reference is to a patent, and a declaration cannot be sought in respect of a patent application. This provision may be considered as a useful tool for establishing certainty before commencing activities which might be considered infringement. There are, however, two drawbacks, firstly and unless the court otherwise thinks fit, the party seeking the declaration must pay the costs of all parties. Secondly, the validity of a patent cannot be challenged. In both regards the Irish Patents Act differs from s 71 of the UK Patents Act 1977 where unlike the Irish Act, it is also possible to seek a declaration before the Controller.

Right to Continue Use

[6.95] Similar to the position under trade mark law, there is a recognition that rights which are acquired subsequent to a third party usage, cannot be exercised against that party's continued usage. s 55 gives a party certain specified rights of continuance. This arises where in the State before the priority date the third

---

[164.] *Chiron Corporation v Organon Teknika* [1994] FSR 448, at 468.
[165.] Section 54.

party was in good faith committing acts or making effective and serious preparations to do such acts, which would have constituted infringement if the patent had been in force. This provision is necessary given that if such usage is in secret, it is not grounds for revocation.[166] Since to form part of the state of the art, the information given by the user must have been made available to at least one member of the public who is free in law and equity to use it.

[6.96] What is readily apparent is that s 55(1) discriminates in favour of persons whose activities have taken place in the State and this restriction may consequently be questionable under the Treaty of Rome. It is also unclear as to whether or not the use must correspond exactly to the pre-patent usage and, for example, whether or not some minor modifications can be made and still avoid infringement. In *Helitune Ltd v Stewart Hughes Ltd*,[167] Aldous J gave the example of an infringing process and suggested that this might be allowed to continue even though the product or process may subsequently be different to some degree and "the fact that he alters that process after the priority date does not matter". This can be contrasted with the view given in *Lubrizol Corp v Esso Petroleum Co Ltd*[168] that the right was to the continued use of the specific act of commerce and was "not meant to be a charter allowing him to expand into other products and other processes".

[6.97] Section 55(2) allows an assignment of the right of continued use or transmission on death of an individual or dissolution of a body corporate. Authorisation is also given to business partners. A prior user cannot, however, licence a third party to exercise this right of continued use.[169] Any disposal of a patented product by virtue of the right of continued use carries with it an implied licence for further dealings in that product.[170] Section 37(7) also provides for protection by way of continued use in circumstances where a patent lapsed but subsequently restored.

---

[166] *Plg Research Ltd v Ardon International Ltd* [1993] FSR 197; *Merrell Dow Pharmaceuticals Inc v HN Norton & Co Ltd* [1996] RPC 76.
[167] [1991] FSR 171.
[168] [1992] RPC 281.
[169] Section 52(3).
[170] Section 52(4).

Chapter 7

Patents Act 1992 - Revocation and Proceedings before the Controller and Courts

REVOCATION OF A PATENT

[7.01] The grounds for seeking revocation of a patent are specifically stated in s 58 of the 1992 Act. Unlike the 1964 Act, there is no requirement that the party seeking revocation be an interested person. A revocation action can be taken either before the High Court or before the Controller. However, if there are already court proceedings pending in relation to the patent, then it is not possible to take revocation proceedings before the Controller without leave of the High Court.[1] This prohibition is not restricted to instances where the party seeking revocation is also a party to the court proceedings. A factor considered by the courts in deciding whether or not to put a stay on proceedings before the court and allow a revocation action before the Controller to proceed is the expense of court proceedings.[2] In *Gen Set SpA v Mosarc Limited*,[3] a stay was refused where it was considered that both parties could afford court proceedings and that the issue in question was considered to be simple and straightforward and unlikely to be lengthy.

[7.02] Another instance where the High Court may be called upon to determine whether or not to grant a stay is an action for infringement of a European patent and where there is also opposition at the EPO seeking revocation.[4] Under Article 68 of the EPC, if the opposition proceedings are successful, the patent is deemed never to have been in force and consequently, the High Court may be reluctant to waste time in deciding on an issue of infringement knowing that an EPO decision could make such a futile exercise.

[7.03] If there are already revocation proceedings before the Controller, an application cannot be made to the court without the consent of the patentee or unless the Controller certifies in writing that the question of whether the patent should be revoked is one which would more properly be determined by the High Court.[5]

---

1. Section 57(5).
2. *Hawker Siddeley Dynamics Engineering Ltd v Real Time Developments Ltd* [1983] RPC 395.
3. [1985] FSR 302.
4. *Amersham International plc v Corning Ltd* [1987] RPC 53; *Pall Corporation v Commercial Hydraulics* [1989] RPC 703.

[7.04] The procedure governing revocation before the Controller is set out in rule 41 of the Patent Rules 1992 and includes the payment of an official fee. Before seeking revocation, it is normal to give a patentee an opportunity to voluntarily surrender their patent. Failure to do so can be held against the applicant for revocation when deciding on the issue of costs.[6]

[7.05] Section 61(1) of the 1992 Act identifies the circumstances in which the validity of a patent may be put in issue. In most instances of revocation, it would be by way of a defence to infringement proceedings.

[7.06] The first three grounds of revocation under s 58(a), (b) and (c) have corresponding provisions in Articles 100 and 138 of the EPC and are as follows:

(a) that the subject matter of the patent is not patentable under the 1992 Act

[7.07] A literal reading might suggest that this ground was limited to inventions within s 9(2) of the 1992 Act and which because of their nature, were not appropriate to the patent system, ie non-patentable subject matter. This view could be said to be reinforced by s 9(3) where the words "subject matter" appear when referring to inventions classified within sub-s (2). However, such an interpretation would be contrary to what must have been the legislative intention, namely to mimic Article 138(a) of the EPC and therefore, include as grounds for revocation not just excluded subject matter[7] but also lack of novelty,[8] lack of inventive step[9] and inventions not susceptible of industrial application[10] or contrary to public order or morality, or plant or animal varieties,[11] all of which were dealt with earlier.[12]

(b) The specification of the patent does not disclose the invention in a manner sufficiently clear and complete for it to be carried out by a person skilled in the art

[7.08] This is usually referred to as insufficiency and adopts the wording used in s 19(1).[13] Revocation is limited to insufficiency of the specification and thus, for example, the fact that the claims under s 20 are not supported by the description is not a ground for revocation. In *Genentech Inc's Patent*,[14] it was held that the

---

[5.] Section 57(6).
[6.] Rule 42.
[7.] Section 9(2) and (3).
[8.] Section 11.
[9.] Section 13.
[10.] Section 14.
[11.] Section 10.
[12.] See Ch 3.
[13.] See Ch 4, para **[4.12]**.

revocation provisions were a complete code and it was not open to a court to revoke a patent on the grounds that the claim was not supported by the description. The court cannot revoke a patent on the basis that the patent is not sufficiently clear or concise by any standard other than that of a person skilled in the art.[15] Even under the 1964 Act, objections of ambiguity and lack of definiteness in the claims could not be raised under the guise of insufficiency.[16]

[7.09] It is not necessary that the applicant disclose the best method known to him of carrying the invention into effect although the applicant should take care because a failure to disclose the best method may damage a claim to priority such as in the US.

(c) Unlawful extension of disclosure

[7.10] An amendment to a specification cannot add new matter. In *Bonzel v Intervention Ltd*,[17] Aldous J held the decision on whether or not there was extension of disclosure must be made on a comparison of the two documents read through the eyes of a skilled addressee. The task of a court was considered to be threefold:

(i) to ascertain through the eyes of the skilled addressee what was disclosed, both explicitly and implicitly in the application;

(ii) to do the same in respect of the patent as granted; and

(iii) to compare the two disclosures and decide whether subject matter relevant to the invention had been added, whether by deletion or addition. The comparison is strict in the sense that subject matter will be added unless such matter is clearly and unambiguously disclosed in the application either explicitly or implicitly.

The EPO in its guidelines for examination[18] applies a novelty test. In that test, the EPO considers the application as filed and decides whether it would render the claim as sought to be amended invalid because it would not be new.

[7.11] The case of *Southco Inc v Dzus Fastener Europe Ltd*[19] concerned the pre-grant broadening of a claim and referred to a decision by the EPO Technical Board of Appeal where it was held that the replacement or removal of a feature from a claim would not be considered to extend the subject matter provided the skilled person would directly and unambiguously recognise that:

---

14. [1989] RPC 147.
15. *Molnlycke AB v Proctor & Gamble* [1992] FSR 549.
16. *Dual Manufacturing & Engineering Inc's Patent* [1977] RPC189.
17. [1991] RPC 553.
18. EPO C-VI, 5.4
19. [1992] RPC 299.

(1) the feature was not explained as essential in the disclosure;

(2) it is not, as such, indispensable for the function of the invention in the light of the technical problem it serves to solve; and

(3) the replacement or removal requires no real modification of other features to compensate for the change.

(d) the protection conferred by the patent has been extended by an amendment of the application or the specification of the patent

[7.12] This fourth ground of revocation does not correspond exactly to Article 138(1)(d) of the EPC and hence a potentially serious problem may arise for a patentee which presumably the legislature did not intend. Section 58(d) should be read in conjunction with s 32(2). Prior to grant, the claims of a patent application may be widened, provided that the matter does not extend beyond that disclosed in the application. However, after grant, widening of the protection conferred by a patent is prohibited.[20]

[7.13] The problem with s 58(d) lies in relation to the words "of the application". This could be construed to mean that any amendment to the claims of the application which broadens its scope when compared with the claims as originally filed falls foul of s 58(d). This can be contrasted with provisions of the EPC whereby two types of amendment are considered unacceptable:

(i) An amendment which extends the content of the application, ie adds new subject matter to the disclosure of the specification. Such an amendment is unacceptable both before and after grant. This is reflected in ss 32(2), 38(3) and 58(c) of the 1992 Act.

(ii) An amendment which extends the protection conferred by the patent which in effect broadens the scope of the claims of the granted patent. This type of amendment relates to a post-grant activity and is in accordance with s 38 of the 1992 Act. Thus, the wording of s 58(d) does not correctly reflect this circumstance and is essentially a contradiction in terms.

[7.14] The effect of s 58(d) on Irish patents in which amendments have been made when bringing them into conformity with the so-called Evidence of Novelty document derived from, say, a corresponding European Patent application is, that if the claims of the European specification were broadened during the course of prosecution of the European application, then potentially the corresponding Irish patent could be revoked on the basis of s 58(d). It could also be suggested that every national phase Irish patent derived from a European patent application in which the claims were broadened during prosecution is

---

[20.] *Liversidge v British Telecommunications plc* [1991] RPC 229 - s 38(3).

also vulnerable to a revocation action under s 58(d). If clarification be needed, it should be pointed out that an applicant can legitimately broaden the scope of the claims of a European patent application during its prosecution. Of course, there must be sufficient disclosure in the specification and/or drawings (as originally filed) to provide support or basis for claims of broader scope than those originally filed. Such amendments are frequently made.

(e) The proprietor of the patent is not entitled

[7.15] The final ground of revocation under s 58(e) corresponds to Article 138(3)(e) of the EPC. The entitlement is by reference to s 16(1) and resides with the inventor, their successor in title or possibly an employer.[21] This particular ground of revocation is only open to a person who the court has determined to be the entitled party.[22] In addition, it is necessary that the attempt to establish the right was started within two years from grant unless it is shown that the patentee at the time of grant or when the patent was transferred to him, knew he was not entitled to the patent.[23]

[7.16] The onus of proof in revocation proceedings lies on an applicant for revocation but the evidential burden may shift according to the state of evidence during the course of the proceedings. The nature of the issue may affect the kind and the cogency of the evidence necessary to bring the scales down on one side or the other. If something is inherently improbable, more weighty evidence is required to establish that it probably occurred than if it were inherently probable.[24] If the application for revocation is admissable, the Court or Controller must consider whether the grounds for revocation prejudice the maintenance of the patent.[25] If so, the Court or Controller may revoke the patent unconditionally.[26] It is also provided that if the patent is invalid to a limited extent, then the Court or Controller may allow an amendment to the specification.[27] If a European patent designating Ireland is revoked or amended under the EPC, it has the same effect as if such had occurred under the provisions of the 1992 Act.[28]

[7.17] It is possible for the Controller to seek revocation on his own initiative[29] but the basis for such is limited to inventions forming part of the state of the art

---

[21.] Ch 4 para **[4.01]**.
[22.] Section 57(2).
[23.] Section 81(2).
[24.] *Dunlop Holdings Limited* [1979] RPC 523.
[25.] Section 59(1).
[26.] Section 59(2).
[27.] Section 59(3).
[28.] Section 119(4).
[29.] Section 60.

being, (a) the content of a patent application with an earlier priority and (b) double patenting:

(a) Section 11(3) of the 1992 Act provides that the contents of a patent application with an earlier priority, although unpublished, may still be taken into account in determining novelty. Section 60(1) which allows for revocation on this ground at the initiative of the Controller does require the Controller to show both that the prior patent or patent application is indeed part of the state of the art and that as a consequence, the invention is lacking in novelty.

(b) Double patenting arises in a situation where there has been both a national patent granted by the Irish Patents Office alongside a European patent designating Ireland for the same invention granted by the EPO and which having designated Ireland, is treated as a National patent under the 1992 Act.[30] It is possible for an applicant to proceed both nationally and through the European patent route but the applicant must ultimately make an election or risk revocation. A decision can be made at the end of the period for filing opposition to the European application designating Ireland or if any opposition is lodged, the date when such opposition proceedings are finally disposed of. To avoid double patenting, the proprietor should take action before the grant of the patent in accordance with s 36(1), ie the date upon which notice of grant appears in the Official Journal.

[7.18] To decide whether or not an Irish patent and a European patent designating Ireland have been granted for the same invention, it is necessary to look at the claims of the patents, ascertain their scope and conclude whether they are the same. The word "same" does not require identicality but requires practical similarity.[31]

[7.19] If the Controller decides on a revocation action, the proprietor of the patent must be notified and afforded a period of three months to make observations and/or amend the specification.[32]

[7.20] In addition to the grounds of revocation, it is also expressly provided as to the circumstances in which the validity of a patent may be put in issue.[33] These are as follows:

(a) by way of defence to infringement proceedings;

[30.] Section 119(1).
[31.] *Marley Roof Tile Co Ltd's Patent* [1992] FSR 614.
[32.] Rule 43.
[33.] Section 61.

(b) in proceedings relating to threats of infringement;[34]

(c) in proceedings relating to revocation;[35] and

(d) disputes as to the right to use the invention by the State[36]

Specifically excluded from the circumstances where the validity of a patent may be put in issue is where the Controller seeks revocation on his own initiative.[37]

[7.21] The validity of a patent cannot be determined on the grounds of non-entitlement unless the issue has been resolved in "entitlement proceedings" on the question of whether the patent was granted to a person entitled to such.[38]

[7.22] Proceedings in which validity is an issue on the grounds of non-entitlement must be commenced within two years of grant of the patent unless the proprietor of the patent knew at the time of grant or on transfer of the patent to him, that he was not entitled to the patent.

[7.23] The Controller must be given notice of any proceedings before the court where the validity of a patent is put at issue and of the decision of the court in respect of such proceedings.[39]

Costs

[7.24] The Controller is empowered to award such costs as he may consider reasonable.[40] The amounts traditionally awarded have been nominal. Where a defendant seeks to amend a defence by alleging new grounds of invalidity (eg because of prior art just coming to the attention of the defendant) the plaintiff may seek to discontinue the action and recover costs by what is termed an 'Earth Closet' order or *See v Scott Paine*[41] order. The costs recoverable by the plaintiff patentee are those between the time of service of the original particulars of objection and the time of the amended particulars. It is at the discretion of the courts whether or not to allow the amended claim of invalidity but in the past this tended to be automatic and thus a defendant who is forced to carry out lengthy and expensive searches and who may only belatedly identify relevant prior art may find they are left with a large bill of costs. The injustice of such has recently been considered in the cases of *GEC Alsthom Ltd's Patent*[42] where

---

34. Section 53.
35. Section 57.
36. Section 77.
37. Section 61(4).
38. Section 61(2),(3) & s 81.
39. Section 62.
40. Section 91.
41. (1933) 50 RPC 56. See also *Baird v Moule's Patent Earth Closet Co* (1881) 17 Ch D 137, at 139.
42. [1996] FSR 415; see also *Josiah Wedgwood & Sons Ltd v Stained Glass Systems Ltd* High Court, unrep, 16 October 1996, Jacob J).

Laddie J identifed the following factors which the court should take into account when deciding what order to make:

(a) The timetable of the proceedings;

(b) The lateness of the amendment;

(c) The extent to which the patentee has been taken by surprise by the reliance on the new prior art;

(d) The extent to which the defendant has explained the lateness of the amendment. Whether or not the defendant has been diligent in searching as to prior art is a major factor in determining whether or not to make a *See v Scott-Paine* order.

[7.25] If a party to opposition, revocation or licence proceedings before the Controller does not reside or carry on business in the State or elsewhere in the EU,[43] the Controller may require that party to give security for costs. The same power also exists to the High Court and also embraces matters relating to an appeal from any decision of the Controller. In practice, security for costs is only an issue if raised by one of the parties. Non-compliance with a requirement for security can result in the proceedings or appeal being deemed abandoned.

PROCEEDINGS BEFORE THE CONTROLLER OR THE COURT[44]

[7.26] The laws of natural justice require that a person has a right to be heard and s 90 of the 1992 Act specifically provides that in the exercise of any discretionary powers by the Controller, any party that may be adversely affected has a right to be heard.[45] There is a ten day period for application for a hearing from notice of that right by the Controller. Evidence before the Controller is by way of statutory declaration[46] which on appeal will be accepted by the courts in lieu of affidavit evidence. Rule 71 sets out the form which the statutory declaration should take and if executed outside the State, must be made and subscribed before a consular officer, a notary public, judge or magistrate.[47] Rule 73 dispenses with the need for authentication of the seal, signature or capacity of the person taking the declaration. Although the Controller may take evidence *viva voce* in lieu of or in addition to evidence by way of statutory declaration, this rarely occurs in practice. The Controller also has power to summon and examine witnesses, require production of documents and permit Affidavit or other sworn testimony.[48] Non-compliance is an offence[49] and such witnesses are

---

43. Rule 70.
44. PA 1992, Part VIII.
45. Section 90; Rule 68.
46. Section 92(2).
47. Rule 72.
48. Section 92(3).
49. Section 92(6).

entitled to the same immunities and privileges as before a court.[50] Section 94 extends privilege to communications with solicitors or patent agents or a third party instructed by such in relation to any matter concerning the protection of an invention, patent, design or technical information or any matter involving passing off. Although the wording is quite broad, it is limited to "protection" thus leaving it questionable as to privilege in relation to issues such as compulsory licence applications. It also does not extend to any copyright advice which might be given by a patent agent. The extension of privilege to patent agents was deemed necessary, given that patent agents were not recognised as legal advisers and did not come within common law privilege.[51] The Rules of the Superior Courts provide for the discovery of documents which are or have been in a person's possession or power and relating to the proceedings and if privilege is claimed, the court may inspect the document to decide on the validity of the claim of privilege. The existence of confidential information is not itself the basis of a claim to privilege[52] although a court may limit inspection of such to legal or independent advisers.[53] The grounds of privilege are self incrimination, public policy and legal professional privilege. In relation to the latter, documents within s 94 which are privileged are communications between a patent agent and a third party and which have come into existence for the purpose of obtaining or giving advice in relation to pending or contemplated proceedings. The proceedings must actually be in contemplation. In the case of *Rockwell International Corp v Serck Industries Ltd*,[54] Falconer J stated:

> "As I understand the matter, it requires something more than the mere seeking of advice on the part of some party from the patent agent as to whether or not a particular course of action, whether it be making a product or using a process, would or would not infringe or might infringe a patent, or how he can avoid falling within the claims of a particular patent".

[7.27] Following *Re Duncan Garfield v Fay*,[55] there is authority for the proposition that a litigant's privilege arising in proceedings in a foreign court is also an answer to a claim for production of the document in proceedings before the Irish courts. In the case of *Société Française Hoechst v Allied Colloids*,[56] an analysis report was prepared at the instigation of a UK patent agent in connection with French proceedings and was prepared for the conduct of those proceedings. It was held that privilege extended to such. In *Sonic Tape plc's Patent*,[57] the personal recipient of letters from a patent agent was an employee of

---

50. Section 92(5).
51. *Wilden Pump Engineering Co v Fusfield* [1985] FSR 159.
52. *Crompton (Alfred) v Customs & Excise* [1974] AC 405.
53. *Roussel-Uclaf v ICI* [1990] RPC 45.
54. [1987] RPC 89.
55. [1968] 2 All ER 395. See also *Minnesota Mining Co v Rennicks* (UK) Ltd [1991] FSR 97.
56. [1992] FSR 66.

the applicant. After leaving that employment, the recipient sought to make use of copies of the letter in an inventorship dispute. It was held that he had received those letters both in a personal capacity and as a representative of his employer. On this basis, the employer could claim privilege for their contents as against third parties but not as against that person. The question of privilege has also been considered by the ECJ which recognised the confidentiality of written communications between a lawyer and client, provided such are made for the purposes and in the interests of the client's right of defence and they emanate from independent lawyers, ie lawyers who are not bound to the client by a relationship of employment.[58]

---

57. [1987] RPC 251.
58. *Australian Mining & Smelting Europe Ltd. v EC Commission* [1982] 2 CMLR 264.

Chapter 8

Patents Act 1992: Voluntary and Compulsory Licences

LICENCES AS OF RIGHT

[8.01] The proprietor of a patent may, at any time after the grant of the patent, apply to the Controller to indicate that licences as of right are available in respect of the patent.[1] This is a voluntary action by the proprietor. The advantages in taking this course of action are not just that it may attract potential licensees by virtue of publication of the licence as of right but also renewal fees are only one half of that normally payable.[2] On an application for a licence of right, the patentee must satisfy the Controller that he is not precluded by contract from granting licences under the patent.[3] Although it is stated that this must be verified by evidence,[4] there is no indication as to the form of the evidence required in this regard. In practice a simple statement by the patentee that he is not so precluded will suffice. The Controller must give notice of an application to any person entered on the Register as having an interest in the patent. This would clearly include another licensee, a mortgagee or a chargee.

[8.02] The effect of a licence of right entry is that any person may obtain a licence on terms to be agreed between the parties, or in default of agreement, on terms to be settled by the Controller.[5] An application in this regard cannot be made until the licence of right is entered on the Register. A licence granted by the Controller takes effect from the date when terms are settled by the Controller.[6] Terms are settled when the Controller gives his final decision. The applicant can accept those terms and operate the licence without prejudice to any appeal. If an appeal by the applicant seeking more favourable terms succeeds, the effect is that the terms previously settled are varied in the applicant's favour.[7] If the royalty is increased on appeal, it will be backdated to

---

1. Section 68(1).
2. Section 68(2)(d).
3. Section 68(4).
4. Rule 46.
5. Section 68(2)(a).
6. *Allen & Hanbury's Ltd v Generics (UK) Ltd* [1986] RPC 203.
7. *Allen & Hanbury's (Salbutamol) Patent* [1987] RPC 327.

155

the date of the original grant by the Controller by requiring a further royalty payment in respect of the increase.[8]

[8.03] An applicant may apply for a licence of right and still attack the validity of the patent in a defence to infringement proceedings. This does not constitute an admission of liability.[9] An infringer of a licence of right patent may undertake to accept a licence to be settled by the Controller. If this is done, no injunction will be granted and damages will be limited to double what the royalties would have been if the licence had been granted before the earliest infringement.[10]

[8.04] The procedure for application to the Controller for settlement of the terms of a licence of right is governed by rule 47 and may be made by the patentee, an existing licensee or a person requiring a licence. The application should be accompanied by a statement setting out the terms of the licence which the applicant is prepared to accept or grant as the case may be.

[8.05] As stated by Lord Diplock in *Allen & Hanburys Ltd v Generics (UK) Ltd*,[11] the Controller's "discretion to impose limitations and conditions upon what the licence of right authorises the licensee to do is a wide one". It is not restricted to the amount of royalties and security for their payment. Terms that are settled by the Controller cannot, however, impose upon the licensee any positive obligation to do any of the acts so licensed, although such a positive obligation could be imposed by a contract relating to a licence of right granted by agreement between the patentee and licensee. Also the Controller cannot settle terms to be incorporated in any one licence of right which would have the effect of debarring future applicants from applying for a similar licence.

[8.06] In the UK, it was the practice, on a request, to include a prohibition on importation of the patented product, if the patentee himself manufactured that product within the UK.[12] However, the ECJ has ruled that it is contrary to Articles 30 and 36 of the Treaty of Rome to discriminate between manufacturers in the UK and others in the EU. Thus subsequently, terms were varied so as to limit import prohibitions only from outside the EU. In the UK, there has been an amendment to the provision corresponding to s 68(2)(c) which specifically states that if an infringer undertakes to take a licence on settled terms, an injunction can now only be granted in respect of importation "otherwise than

---

8. *Smith Kline & French (Cimetidine) Patents* [1990] RPC 203.
9. *El Du Pont De Nemours & Co (Blades) Patent* [1988] RPC 479.
10. Section 68(2)(c).
11. [1986] RPC 203.
12. *Ciba-Geigy's (FMC's Application)* [1986] RPC 403.

from another Member State of the EEC". This amendment did not appear in the 1992 Act.

[8.07] The ECJ has also held that it is contrary to EU law to prohibit a licensee from importing the patented product from a non EU country where the patentee manufactures the product in the Member State concerned but to authorise importation from non-member countries where the patentee manufactures the product in another Member State.[13] Again in the UK, certain contractual provisions have been refused as part of the terms settled. These include a restriction preventing "passing off"[14] and a requirement that the licensee should not indicate that his product has been licensed or approved by the patentee.[15] Provisions against assignment, sub-licensing or for termination in the event of a take-over of the licensee have been allowed in the UK.[16]

[8.08] There is no guidance in the 1992 Act as to how the Controller is to settle the financial terms of any licence, unlike in the UK where it is stated "that the inventor or any other person beneficially entitled to a patent shall receive reasonable remuneration having regard to the nature of the invention". Presumably, a similar general principle would be adopted by the Controller and the Irish courts. However, in this regard, s 42(2) of the 1964 Act relating to compulsory licences for food and medicines stated the need for patentees to derive a reasonable advantage from their patent right. The question is essentially a consideration of what a willing licensor and a willing licensee would have agreed upon as a reasonable royalty to be paid for the rights granted under the licence as of right.

[8.09] In *JR Geigy's Patent*[17] which was a compulsory licence case, it was held that the royalty fee payable should take into account three factors, namely (1) recovery for research and development costs, (2), recoupment of promotional costs and (3), an appropriate reward element. A further approach in calculating an appropriate royalty and one which is finding more favour is what is termed the 'comparables' approach. This involves simply looking at comparable licences where they exist on the basis that "there is no better guide to what a willing licensor and a willing licensee would agree than what other licensors and licensees have in fact agreed in comparable cases".[18] Less used is a profits available approach. This asks the question as to the likely profits to be earned by the licensee and to then agree a division between the licensor and licensee which

---

13. *Generics (UK) Ltd v Smith Kline & French Laboratories* [1993] FSR 592.
14. *Syntex Corporation's Patent* [1986] RPC 585.
15. *Hilti AG's Patent* [1988] RPC 51.
16. *Allen & Hanburys (Salbutamol) Patent* [1987] RPC 327.
17. [1964] RPC 391.
18. *Smith Kline & French Laboratories (Cimetidine) Patents* [1990] RPC 203.

is, of course, problematic in itself. The different approaches can lead to quite a divergence in the royalty rates.[19] It is, however, accepted that there are 'going rates' in specific industries.[20]

[8.10] An existing licensee under a patent may, subsequent to an entry of a licence of right, apply to the Controller to exchange the licence for a licence of right upon terms to be settled.[21]

[8.11] A licensee under a licence of right and unless an agreed express contractual provision provides otherwise, may issue proceedings for infringement. However, the licensee must first request the patentee to take the proceedings and the patentee must fail to do so within two months of the request. The patentee must be made a defendant but is not liable for costs unless he enters an appearance and takes part in the proceedings.[22]

[8.12] It is possible to cancel a licence of right entry.[23] The patentee must pay the balance of all renewal fees which would otherwise have been payable and the Controller must be satisfied that there are no existing licences or if there are, then there must be a consent to cancellation from the licensees. Also, an interested party may seek cancellation of the licence of right on the grounds that the patentee was precluded by contract from granting licences under the patent.[24] In this regard there is a time period of three months from the making of the relevant entry.[25] Any person may also oppose cancellation within three months from advertisement of the cancellation in the Official Journal.[26]

COMPULSORY LICENCES

[8.13] Unlike s 39(1) of the 1964 Act, the 1992 Act does not use the words "abuse of monopoly rights" in referring to the grounds under which a person may compel the granting of a licence. However, apart from the special provisions relating to foods and medicines in s 42 of the 1964 Act, there has been substantial re-enactment of the compulsory licence provisions.[27]

[8.14] There is no positive requirement on a patentee to work his patent and indeed, he may not be able to do so through lack of resources or for some other reason. However, the compulsory licence provisions are an attempt to ensure

---

[19.] *American Cyanamid Co's (Fenbufen) Patent* [1990] RPC 309.
[20.] *Shiley Inc's Patent* [1988] RPC 97.
[21.] Section 68(2)(b).
[22.] Section 68(3).
[23.] Section 69.
[24.] Section 69(2).
[25.] Rule 48(2).
[26.] Rule 49(1).
[27.] Section 70(1).

that there should be the fullest practical use of the patented invention and that patent rights should be exercised without prejudice to the development of industry. Examples often quoted but rarely substantiated are situations in which a party would either secure a patent or acquire such with a view to hindering a new product and thus maintaining the market for an existing conventional product. However, the compulsory licence provisions also apply in other situations such as where demand for a product is not being met on reasonable terms. Article 31 of TRIPS allows States to provide for use of the subject matter of a patent without the authorisation of the right holder but under certain conditions and with certain safeguards which includes that "such use may only be permitted if, prior to such use, the proposed user has made efforts to obtain authorisation from the right holder on reasonable commercial terms and conditions and that such efforts have not been successful within a reasonable period of time". There is an exception in the case of a national emergency, other circumstances of extreme urgency or in cases of public non-commercial use.

[8.15] A compulsory licence cannot be applied for until after three years from the date of publication of grant of the patent, after which any person may apply for a licence under the patent and/or for an entry to be made on the Register to the effect that licences are available as of right. The grounds on which an application can be made are identified in s 70(2) and the procedure is set out in rules 50-52. The grounds are as follows:

(a) Insufficient domestic working

[8.16] This requires that the patented invention, although being capable of being commercially worked in the State, is not being so worked or to the fullest extent that is reasonably practicable.[28] There is a definition of "commercially worked" as the manufacture of the product or the carrying on of the process in or by means of a definite and substantial establishment or organisation, and on a scale which is adequate and reasonable in all the circumstances.[29] In *Hunter v Fox*,[30] Kenny J found under the provisions of the 1927 Act that although the invention was not being worked on a commercial scale, a satisfactory reason for this had been given, namely that the manufacture of the patented sealing head in this country would have been grossly uneconomic. However, the 1992 Act does not provide for a defence by way of a satisfactory reason for non-working.

[8.17] In *Kamborian's Patent*,[31] consideration was given to what is meant by the expression "fullest extent that is reasonably practicable" and considered this to be the highest rate of production which is practicable and necessary

---

28. Section 70(2)(a).
29. Section 2.
30. [1965] RPC 416.
31. [1961] RPC 403.

substantially to meet the demand. The onus falls upon an applicant and it is therefore necessary to bring evidence to show what the demand for the invention might reasonably be expected to be, and how far short, if at all, production under the patent fails, as far as is practicable to supply the demand.

[8.18] The working required is in relation to "the subject of the patent". If, for example, the patent claims a new improvement in a well known machine, the patentee must manufacture the improvement and not necessarily the whole machine. However, if the patent claims the improvement in combination with a machine consisting of well-known parts, it may be that the patentee must, besides manufacturing the improvement, put together the whole machine in the State, or at any rate the combination claimed.[32] In *Smith Kline & French Laboratoires Ltd (Cimetidine) Patents*,[33] there was importation from Ireland into the UK of raw cimetidine, an important and highly successful drug used in the treatment of duodenal and gastric ulcers. The drug was then formulated in the UK. It was held that since the patent contained both product and process claims, commercial working was not met by the manufacture of the basic ingredient in a foreign country. However, it has now been made clear by the ECJ that it is contrary to Article 30 of the Treaty of Rome to provide for the grant of a compulsory licence where the product is imported from an EU country rather than being manufactured domestically.[34] Essentially, this means that references in s 70 to "the State" should be replaced by a reference to a Member State of the EU.

[8.19] The consideration of the adequacy of manufacture in the State does, no doubt, depend to some extent upon the local demand existing for the article. However, it does not follow that if there is no demand existing, that there is a defence to an application for a compulsory licence.[35] Also the fact that there has at some stage been commercial working is not a defence, if this has ceased.[36]

(b) Failure to meet demand or on reasonable terms or doing so substantially by importation[37]

[8.20] Demand means public demand and not that of an individual person or company.[38] It must also be an actual demand and not merely one which the applicant for a licence hopes and expects to create and if when the licence is

---

[32.] *Lakes Patent* (1909) 26 RPC 443.

[33.] [1990] RPC 203.

[34.] *EC Commission v United Kingdom* [1993] FSR 1. See also s 75(3).

[35.] *Boult's Patent* (1909) 26 RPC 383.

[36.] *Gebhardt's Patent* [1992] RPC 1

[37.] Section 70(2)(b).

[38.] *Robin Electric Lamp Co Ltd* (1915) 32 RPC 202.

obtained.[39] Demand on reasonable terms is that which exists under the prevailing conditions, so that it is irrelevant that price cutting by a licensee might increase the existing demand. As stated by Hoffman J in *Research Corporation's (Carboplatin) Patent*,[40] when considering corresponding UK provisions:

> "demand not being met on reasonable terms, recognises that demand, unless wholly inelastic, must mean demand at a given price. If the price being charged by the patentee or the licensee is reasonable and the demand at that price is being full met, it seems to me irrelevant to say (as one almost invariably could) that the demand would be greater at a lower price. The question is whether in all the circumstances the patentee is charging a reasonable price".

The circumstances would include the right to recoup research costs, fund further research in the public interest and make a profit from their monopoly.

[8.21] The Supreme Court in *Hunter v Fox*[41] held that there was no abuse under the corresponding provision of the 1927 Act and that even though there was a void restrictive clause in an agreement, it did not result in demand not being met on reasonable terms. Such a restrictive clause would now fall foul of s 83 of the 1992 Act.

[8.22] Again, the effect of EU law is that importation from a Member State of the EU should be regarded as equivalent to manufacture in the State.[42] National law which equates a case where a demand for a patented product is satisfied on the domestic market by imports from other Member States (rather than by domestic production) to insufficient exploitation of the patent justifying imposition of a compulsory licence, infringes Article 30 of the Treaty of Rome.

(c) Commercial working hindered by importation of product[43]

[8.23] It is interesting to note that this provision differs from the corresponding UK section which also includes importation of the product of a process protected under the patent. The Irish section is limited to situations of "importation of a product which is protected by the patent".

(d) Refusal to grant licence on reasonable terms[44]

[8.24] This refusal must result in either:

---

39. *Cathro's Application* (1934) 51 RPC 75 and 475.
40. [1990] RPC 663, at 695-6.
41. [1965] RPC 416.
42. *EC Commission v United Kingdom* [1993] FSR 1. See also s 75(3).
43. Section 70(2)(c).
44. Section 70(2)(d).

(i)   an export market not being supplied;

(ii)   the working of another substantial invention being prevented or hindered; or

(iii) the establishment of commercial or industrial activities in the State being unfairly prejudiced.

These provisions were also found in s 39(2)(d) of the 1964 Act and therefore, older cases decided under the corresponding section of the UK Patents Act 1949 are still pertinent. There must have been an absolute refusal by the patentee to grant the licence on reasonable terms.[45] A consideration of what is meant by reasonable terms involves a review "of all the surrounding circumstances including the nature of the invention, the terms of existing licences, if any, the expenditure and liabilities of the patentee in respect of the patent, the requirements of the purchasing public and so on".[46] An insistence that a licensee take out a licence in respect of a group of patents rather than just the particular patent might be reasonable in a given set of circumstances.

[8.25] In the UK Case of *Penn Engineering and Manufacturing Corporation's Patent*,[47] Graham J allowed export of the patented article by the licensee under the terms of a compulsory licence. In this case, there had been no manufacture in the United Kingdom and accordingly and in the further absence of patents in export countries where there was likely to be a market, there was no justification to restrict export since such would prevent working to the fullest extent that was reasonably practicable. It was considered to be incumbent upon the patentee to ask for and justify an export restriction if he wished it to be inserted in a compulsory licence. The Controller, in a decision on 3 July 1995,[48] did not order the inclusion of provisions in a compulsory licence which would allow for export but this was conceded without argument by the applicant for the licence.

[8.26] Under s 70(2)(d)(ii) where a patented invention making a substantial contribution to the art cannot itself be exploited, the Controller will call for the applicant seeking a compulsory licence to cross-licence his own patent on reasonable terms.[49]

[8.27] The phrase "development of commercial or industrial activities" in s 70(2)(d)(iii) includes an increase in the size of a business.[50] In *Monsanto's CCP Patent*,[51] it was held that the onus was on an applicant for a compulsory

45. *Loewe Radio Co Ltd's Application* (1929) 46 RPC 479.
46. *Brownie Wireless Co Ltd's Application* (1929) 46 RPC 457.
47. [1973] RPC 233.
48. *Clonmel Healthcare Limited.*
49. Section 70(3)(c).
50. *Kamborian's Patent* [1961] RPC 403.
51. [1990] FSR 93.

licence to show that the licence offered by the patentee was not on reasonable terms. The mere allegation of advantages in a patent was not in itself conclusive evidence that commercial or industrial activity was being unfairly prejudiced.

(e) Unfairly prejudiced due to unreasonable conditions[52]

[8.28] This arises as a result of conditions imposed by the proprietor on the grant of licences under the patent, or upon the purchase, hire or use of the product or process which is the subject of the patent and whereby the manufacture, use or sale of materials not protected by the patent or the establishment or development of commercial or industrial activities in the State is unfairly prejudiced. In *Monsanto's CPP Patent*,[53] the applicant for a compulsory licence wished to use a solvent. Although this was held to be a material not covered by the patent, it was proposed to import the solvent from France and it was accordingly held that the manufacture of the solvent in the UK was not prejudiced unfairly or otherwise. The applicant had also failed to discharge the onus in the pleadings which asserted that the royalty offered was unreasonable.

(f) Null and void contractual provision[54]

[8.29] Under s 83, certain contractual provisions are unlawful and can be declared null and void. If such a provision relates to the sale or lease of, or licence to use or work any patented product or process, then it is grounds for a compulsory licence. Provisions corresponding to s 83 were considered in *Hunter v Fox*,[55] the Supreme Court held that a consequence of finding such an unlawful clause resulted in the restriction being null and void *ab initio* and consequently should be treated as ineffective and indeed non-existent which means that there could not be an abuse of monopoly rights. This therefore begs the question of whether or not this particular ground could ever be successfully argued.

TERMS OF A COMPULSORY LICENCE OR LICENCE AS OF RIGHT

[8.30] In making a determination on the terms of a licence, the Controller and ultimately the courts are given some guidelines by way of factors which should be taken into account.[56] There are also certain terms which may or must be included in the licence, dependant on the grounds for the compulsory licence.

---

52. Section 70(2)(e).
53. [1990] FSR 93.
54. Section 70(2)(f).
55. [1965] RPC 416.
56. Section 70(4).

[8.31] If the application for a licence is based on inadequate or non-commercial working in the State, the Controller may in fact adjourn the application if the time period to enable working has been insufficient.[57] In *Fette's Patent*,[58] there was a time period of six and a half years during which demand was met by importation. It was only when the application for a licence had begun that the patentee decided to commence local manufacture. It was held that the time period was a substantial proportion of the total life of the patent and that there was no defence to the licence application.

[8.32] A licence granted on the grounds of neglect of exploitation of an export market, may restrict the sale or use by the licensee to such countries as the Controller thinks fit.

[8.33] Section 70(3)(c) which deals with an application where a licence is required to permit the exploitation of a patent (the second patent) which cannot be exploited without infringing another patent[59] should be read in conjunction with Article 31(L) of TRIPS whereby:

(i)   the invention claimed in the second patent shall involve an important technical advance of considerable economic importance in relation to the invention claimed in the first patent;

(ii)   the owner of the first patent shall be entitled to a cross-licence on reasonable terms to use the invention claimed in the second patent; and

(iii)   the use authorised in respect of the first patent shall be non-assignable except with the assignment of the second patent.

[8.34] Any licence granted under the compulsory licence provisions must be both non-exclusive and non-transferable.[60] Since a compulsory licence is predominantly to cater for the domestic market,[61] the Controller can, in the terms of a licence, preclude importation[62] but must, of course, take cognisance of EU law[63] which would not allow a restriction on imports from another EU Member State.

[8.35] Section 70(3)(f) is a special provision dealing with patents relating to food or medicine. Under s 42 of the 1964 Act, a patent in respect of a substance capable of being used as a food or medicine or in the production of food or

---

57. Section 70(3)(a).
58. [1961] RPC 396.
59. Section 70(2)(d)(ii).
60. Section 70(3)(d) and Article 31(d) and (e) of TRIPS.
61. Article 31(8) of TRIPS.
62. Section 70(3)(e).
63. Section 75(3).

medicine was vulnerable to a compulsory licence being granted. Somewhat surprisingly, this provision was not exploited until it was due to be repealed by the 1992 Act. Under the transitional provisions of the 1992 Act,[64] an application commenced under s 42 was dealt with under the 1964 Act. The Controller in *Clonmel Healthcare Limited*[65] did not find s 42 to be incompatible with Ireland's obligations under EU law and declined to refer the matter to the ECJ for a preliminary ruling under Article 177. Although a patent relating to food or medicine is no longer *per se* subject to a compulsory licence, it is a factor in determining the terms of a licence. The statutory obligation of the Controller in this regard is to endeavour to secure that food and medicine are available to the public at the lowest prices consistent with the proprietor of a patent deriving reasonable remuneration having regard to the nature of the invention. In the *Clonmel Healthcare* decision, the Controller accepted the principles laid down in *JR Geigy SA's Patent*[66] which set out the following elements which the royalty should comprise:

(i)   an element to take account of the patentee's expenditure on basic research and development;

(ii)   an element to take account of the benefit which the licensee will derive from the promotion of the pharmaceutical product by the patentee; and

(iii)   an element of profit to provide the patentee with an appropriate return on capital investment involved in basic research and development and in promotion.

[8.36] Reasonable remuneration was, in the view of the Controller, to be determined independently of what the licensee offers or could afford. It was an objective criteria. After hearing expert evidence on the issue, the Controller decided that a 40% royalty figure was appropriate. He then went on to determine the basis of calculation of this figure. The applicant, Clonmel Healthcare Ltd, had proposed that the royalty be a percentage of the patentee's (Glaxo) selling price to wholesalers in Ireland. Glaxo sought a royalty of a fixed, inflation adjusted sum per unit sold or supplied by Clonmel, calculated as a percentage of the Glaxo price to wholesalers at the date of the licence but thereafter, being independent of variations in Glaxo's price. The Controller accepted Glaxo's approach as having the merit of avoiding any possible disputes, at a later stage, between the parties as to net wholesale prices.[67]

[64.] Paragraph 13 - First Schedule.
[65.] Decision of 3 July 1995.
[66.] [1964] RPC 391.
[67.] See also *Allen & Hanbury's (Salbutamol) Patent* [1987] RPC 327.

[8.37] Glaxo had also argued that a licence, if granted, should prevent Clonmel from referring to the patentees, the patents or the licence, in their promotional activities. In response, it was stated:

> "It seems to me that in the course of trade, Clonmel may need to indicate how they are in a position to market a product which is protected by a patent without infringing the patent. For this purpose, it seems to me inevitable that reference must be made to the licence which results from these proceedings and thus to the patents in question. Clonmel may not, of course, market their product in any way which would cause it to be confused with a product of Glaxo and their product will have to carry their own logo; and I have decided to order the insertion of provisions to this effect in the licence".

The Controller held against the inclusion of a most favoured licensee clause considering such to be more appropriate in the case of a voluntary licence.

[8.38] The Controller is required by statute to take into account certain matters when making a decision on the granting and terms of a compulsory licence. These are stated in s 70(4) namely:

(a) the nature of the invention, how long the patent has been granted, and the measures taken by the patentee or any licensee to make full use of the invention;

(b) the ability of the proposed licensee to work the invention to the public advantage;[68] and

(c) the risks to be taken by the proposed licensee in providing capital and working the invention.

[8.39] The Controller is not required to take into account matters subsequent to the application for a compulsory licence. This is not a mandatory requirement on the Controller but it is unlikely that the Controller would accept post-application efforts by the patentee in an attempt to remedy their position. In *Halcon's Patents*,[69] there was a refusal to order discovery of a licence agreement offered subsequent to the filing of an application.

[8.40] As to the obligation of an applicant to show their capacity to work the invention, in the case of *Enviro-Spray Systems Inc's Patent*,[70] it was stated that:

> "It would clearly be unreasonable, before the grant of a licence, to require any applicant to show contracts or firm agreements with anyone for either finance or for the other forms of assistance which would be required to operate a licence. On the other hand, I have to be able to form some estimate of the

---

68. *Monsanto's CCP Patent* [1990] FSR 93.
69. [1989] RPC 1.
70. [1986] RPC 147.

ability of the applicants to work the inventions, at least to the extent of satisfying myself that the applicants are likely to have available to them the various resources, including technical expertise and know-how, which would be necessary to put the inventions into practice in a way which would benefit the public. It is in turn the responsibility of the applicants to explain as far as is reasonable what they expect to do, and also to put me in a position in which I can form some estimate of their likelihood of achieving it".

[8.41] An applicant for a compulsory licence is not prejudiced or estopped by virtue of the fact that they may already be a licensee.[71] A licensee under a compulsory licence has the same power to sue for infringement as a licensee under a licence of right.[72] If the Controller is satisfied that conditions imposed by the patentee on the grant of licences, or on the disposal or use of the patented product or process, unfairly prejudices the manufacture, use or disposal of materials not protected by the patent, he may also order the grant of licences to customers of the applicant.[73] If the applicant is already a licensee, the Controller may amend the existing licence or order it to be cancelled and grant a new licence.[74] An application may also be made by any Minister of the Government for an entry on the Register that a licence as of right is available.[75]

Procedure on Applications for a Compulsory Licence or by A Minister for Entry of a Licence as of Right[76]

[8.42] The applicant must present a *prima facie* case to the Controller. If this is done, the application papers are then served on the patentee and any other interested party entered on the Register. The application is also advertised in the Official Journal. Within three months from advertisement, the application may be opposed by either the patentee or any other person. The parties can agree to the appointment of an arbitrator[77] or the Controller may insist on such if the proceedings require a prolonged examination of documents or any scientific or local investigation which cannot conveniently be carried out by the Controller. If the whole proceedings have been referred to an arbitrator unless otherwise agreed between the parties, an appeal lies from the arbitrator's award to the High Court. However, if the arbitrator is only to rule on a question or issue of fact, the arbitrator reports the finding to the Controller.[78] Before ruling, the Controller is obliged to give the parties an opportunity to be heard.[79] An appeal from the Controller's decision lies to the High Court.[80]

[71.] Section 70(5).
[72.] Section 70(6).
[73.] Section 71(1).
[74.] Section 71(2).
[75.] Section 72.
[76.] Section 73; Rules 50, 51 and 52.
[77.] Section 74(2).
[78.] Section 74(4).
[79.] Rule 67; Section 90.
[80.] Section 96(1).

USE OF INVENTIONS FOR THE SERVICE OF THE STATE

[8.43] A Minister of the Government may acquire rights to a patented invention or to a patent application and can exploit such, including, by granting a licence(s) and forming or promoting an incorporated company to develop, perfect or commercially work the invention.[81]

[8.44] It is permissible for a Minister of the Government, his officers, servants, agents or persons authorised in writing, to use patented inventions for the service of the State and without the consent of the patentee.[82] Certain acts which would otherwise amount to an infringement are not to be considered as such.[83] Service of the State is broadly defined to mean a service financed out of moneys charged on or advanced out of the central fund or moneys provided by the Oireachtas or by a local authority for the purposes of the Local Government Act 1941.[84]

[8.45] The TRIPS Agreement recognises that a State may, in certain circumstances, use a patented invention without the authority of the right holder and on terms which include the right to be paid adequate remuneration taking into account the economic value of the authorisation. The terms governing State use are agreed between the parties or failing which, the matter is referred to the High Court which in turn can refer the whole matter or any question or issue of fact to an arbitrator.[85]

[8.46] Under s 77(4), if the invention prior to the filing or priority date has been recorded in a document by, or been tried by or on behalf of a Minister, then the State may use such royalty free or without any other payment. Evidence of such documentary recordal or the trial may be given to counsel representing the patent applicant/proprietor or to any agreed independent expert where the Minister determines that such disclosure would be detrimental to the public interest.

[8.47] Information as to the extent of State use should be provided by the Minister to the patent applicant or proprietor unless such would be contrary to the public interest.[86]

---

81. Section 76(1).
82. Section 77(1).
83. Section 77(2).
84. Section 77(10).
85. Section 77(6).
86. Section 77(5).

[8.48] If there are proceedings between the Minister and the proprietor of a patent under the provisions governing State use, then the patent can be challenged by the Minister.[87]

[8.49] The rights to State use under s 77 includes a power to dispose of, or sell, or offer to dispose of or sell, any products made in pursuance of such a right which are no longer required for the service of the State.[88] Also covered are persons acquiring such products.[89]

[8.50] There are extended provisions for State use during a period where there is in existence, exceptional circumstances and it is desirable in the interests of the community. In such circumstances, the Government may by order empower the State to use the invention for any purpose which appear to be necessary or expedient for one or more stated reasons which are set out in s 78(1). These reasons include to ensure public safety and the preservation of the State, the maintenance and sufficiency of supplies and services essential to the life or well-being of the community and for assisting in the relief of suffering in any country outside the State that is in grave distress. This would presumably include instances such as a famine. However, included in the reasons, are broadly stated objectives such as for promoting the productivity of commerce and industry including agriculture.

VOID CONDITIONS IN CONTRACTS

[8.51] Section 83 renders null and void certain restrictive conditions in contracts relating to the sale, lease or licence to use or work a patent. This arises firstly where there is a prohibition or limitation of the use of a product supplied by, or of a patented process owned by, anyone other than the supplier or licensor or his nominee. Secondly, where there is a requirement to purchase from the patentee (or his nominee) a product not protected by the patent.

[8.52] However, such conditions can validly be included if the purchaser, lessee or licensee has the option of accepting the contract on reasonable terms without such restrictive conditions and relieve himself of his liability to comply with such conditions on giving the other party three months notice in writing and on payment of compensation or royalty. Section 83(4) makes the inclusion of a condition which is null and void a defence to infringement proceedings while the contract is in force. In *Hunter v Fox*,[90] the Supreme Court held that a scheme of licensing was contrary to the corresponding provision in the 1927 Act. The facts of this case were that Hunter manufactured lids for jam jars and sealing heads for fixing the lids to the jars. They held a patent for the sealing heads but

---

87. Section 77(7).
88. Section 77(8).
89. Section 77(9).
90. [1965] RPC 416.

not in respect of the lids. The sealing heads were leased to Irish jam manufacturers subject to a covenant that the heads remain the property of the patentee and the hirer had no licence to use the sealing heads. However, supplies of lids contained a label licence to use the sealing heads. It was held that the effect of the agreement was to force the hirer of the sealing heads to purchase the lids from Hunter. Accordingly, the agreement between Hunter and the jam manufacturers was illegal and the relevant clause of the agreement was null and void *ab initio*, which meant that jam manufacturers were free to use lids from any source. There is no corresponding provision in the EPC but licence agreements with such a restrictive condition would offend against Article 85 of the Treaty of Rome if they affect trade between Member States. In *Windsurfing International Inc v EC Commission*,[91] the ECJ considered clauses in a patent licence agreement and found objectionable amongst others, a clause limiting a licence to manufacture to a country where a patent existed with the effect that royalties were to be paid even on products sold in parts of the EU where no patent existed.

[8.53] On the basis of Article 85(3), the Commission has issued certain Regulations exempting certain licensing agreements from the application of Article 85(1), including the Technology Transfer Block Exemption Regulation.[92] The block exemption applies to patent and/or know-how licences between two parties that contain one or more obligations that although generally restrictive of competition have positive attributes which fall within Article 85(3). Included in the Regulation are obligations declared to be outside Article 85(1). These are known as the formal exemptions. Other provisions are not caught by Article 85(1) provided that they are generally not restrictive of competition and are referred to as the white list. The black list are obligations in a licence agreement which are definitely not exempted from Article 85(1).

[8.54] It is also provided in s 83(3) that a licence agreement or lease allowing use on working of a patented product or process may be terminated by three months' notice in writing in the event that the relevant patent ceases to have effect. This is irrespective of any contractual agreement to the contrary. Section 83(5) which provides that certain conditions by way of exception are not void, may still fall foul of Article 85 and the Competition Act 1991. These include an agreement containing a clause which prohibits a person from selling goods other than those of a particular person and a contract for hire or use of a patented product which reserves the right to supply new parts or repair. In *Fichera v Flogates Limited*,[93] the provision of the UK Patents Act 1977 corresponding to s 83(5)(d) was held to be wide enough to provide an exception for a clause requiring the replacement of worn as well as damaged parts. A worn part needing to be replaced was considered a part required to keep the patented article in repair.

---

91. [1988] FSR 139.
92. Regulation No 240/96; OJ 1996 L 31/2. See paras **[6.37]** and **[6.38]** *ante*.
93. [1984] RPC 257.

Chapter 9

Introduction to Copyright

COPYRIGHT IN EARLY IRISH LAW

[9.01] The creation of any tangible object can be seen as an expression of skill, effort or individuality which raises in turn issues about ownership of that work, the freedom of others to imitate or utilise the work, or the right of the original creators of the work to control such imitations or uses. While these matters are now regulated by statute, early Irish manuscripts provide a well-known illustration[1] of this kind of conflict. Saint Columcille is recorded as having illicitly copied a gospel manuscript which belonged to Saint Fintan. When Saint Fintan discovered this unauthorised act of reproduction he claimed, before Dairmait, the King of Ireland, ownership of the copy. Dairmait, arguing by analogy, held "for every cow its calf": thus "to every book its copy". Scholars dispute the true outcome of this copyright litigation; under some traditions it is said to have led to the battle of Cúil Dremne. One scholar at least is of the view that the entire "decision" is probably fictitious[2] and *Phillips* is unable to identify any convincing proof that the trial of Columcille was actually about unauthorised copying.

HISTORICAL INTRODUCTION TO STATUTORY COPYRIGHT LAW

[9.02] The development of the modern law of copyright, addressing as it does an entire range of works and products, held in a diverse range of material (and sometimes intangible) formats, is the result of a number of economic, political and cultural factors. It would be a mistake to see copyright simply in terms of parliamentary recognition of an author's right to assert a 'property' in the work in question. Indeed, a brief survey of the development of statutory copyright,[3] particularly in relation to the book trade, reveals a somewhat convoluted political struggle between the Crown and Crown agents, on the one hand, and publishing entrepreneurs, on the other, a struggle within which the author or creator of a work had, at times, only an incidental role.

[1.] See Phillips, *St Columba the Copyright Infringer* [1985] EIPR 350.

[2.] Kelly, *A Guide to Early Irish Law* (1988) (Dublin Inst for Advanced Studies), p 239-40.

[3.] Patterson, *Copyright in Historical Perspective* (1968) (Vanderbilt UP); Kaplan, *An Unhurried View of Copyright* (1967) (Columbia) pp 2-7; Feather [1988] EIPR 377; Saunders [1993] EIPR 452.

[9.03] The right to print not only Crown promulgations like statutes and royal proclamations but also common law books became seen as a part of the Royal Prerogative by the beginning of the sixteenth century, by which time it had devolved to the King's printer. In 1553 Mary I provided that in relation to all existing and future common law books, the right to publish them would be a matter of a separate royal grant, and in 1531 Mary I, by Royal Charter ceded these rights to the Worshipful Company of Stationers of London. The Stationers Company, as an arm of the State, took over functions that had previously been the province of other institutions, in particular the Privy Council which had been engaged in suppressing 'heretical' works imported into the Realm from Northern Europe. Through the Stationers Company, it was possible to regulate the publishing trade, in particular the right to establish presses and publish books and other works. Such a centralised supervisory system was therefore an important mechanism in controlling religious and political dissent.

[9.04] The Stationers Company,[4] the members being stationers or printers, established the practice of allowing its members to register the fact that a certain member had possession of the manuscript of a book and that such a manuscript had been read by the censor. This register of lawfully printed books soon evolved into a form of declaration of right, namely, that once the stationer had his name entered onto the register that stationer had the sole right to print copies of that book, infringement of such a right being a matter to be controlled by way of a fine imposed by the company. The basic equation established by the licensing system, namely, that registration equalled the sole right to make copies, was to survive both the attacks upon the Crown Prerogative and Cromwell's Protectorate, and upon the restoration of the Stuart dynasty the system was reaffirmed in the seventeenth century when the Printing Act 1662 vested censorship functions and pre-publication clearance of manuscripts into the hands of the Secretary of State. However, this legislation, which reaffirmed the power of the copyholders to exclusive rights of publication of works, was not renewed by Parliament when it lapsed in 1695,[5] thereby removing the statutory rights of these early publishers to counteract piracy in printed books and pamphlets. While it appears that publishers were still able to utilise registration procedures and seek some remedy in damages against post-1694 pirates, the effective reliefs of search, seizure and injunction were no longer available in Chancery, although publishers were able to use the rules of the Stationers Company to base a claim of copyright infringement in the 1709 case of *Stationers Company v Partridge*.[6]

---

4. Blagden, *The Stationers Company - A History* (1960).
5. Macaulay, in *History of England* (Vol 3) pp 171-175 (1967, Heron) wrote entertainingly on the effects on the press and publishing trades of the consequences of non-renewal.
6. 4 Burr 2329, 2381, 2402.

[9.05] At this stage it should be noted that the right to make, or authorise, the manufacture of copies in books, was vested in the stationer, or publisher, such a right being proved, or established, *via* registration. The raw material for publication, the manuscript, was acquired by the stationer under a contract, and the idea that the author held or acquired any rights under the instruments which effected the Royal Prerogative, the procedures that had evolved in the Stationers Company, or under the 1662 Act, would be far from the mark. Agitation for recognition by Parliament of 'literary property' rights was successful and the Statute of Anne 1709,[7] gave the owner of a book the legal right to make copies. Both the notion of an owner - the author and his assigns - and the scope of the right - "the sole right and liberty of printing books" - were somewhat imprecise, and while the protection ran for 14 years from first publication, renewable if the owner was still alive at the end of this period for a further 14 years, the registration system and the operation of the anti-piracy provisions by the Stationers Company point to the statutory copyright as being a publishing right. This point is reinforced somewhat by the protection afforded to pre-published works: upon the passage of the Statute of Anne such works were protected for 21 years and in practice these rights were held by persons other than the author or the authors' descendants.

[9.06] With the expiry of the statutory copyrights, particularly in relation to established and profitable literary and learned writers, the publishers attempted to persuade the courts that, apart from statutory copyright, the owners of 'literary property' could utilise common law rights of property to not only protect works from unauthorised publication but also protect 'property' once the statutory copyrights ended. The Court of Chancery remedy of an injunction was available to publishers who objected to pirated versions of works that no longer enjoyed statutory copyright, although cases of this kind do not address directly the issue of whether a common law copyright, perpetual in nature, revived upon expiry of the statutory copyright. The common law cases which address this point accepted that the practice in equity was to grant injunctive relief on the basis of a perpetual copyright[8] and in *Millar v Taylor*[9] a majority of the Court of King's Bench, led by Lord Mansfield, accepted the concept of a perpetual property right which could be used against pirates. However, in *Donaldson v Beckett*[10] it was held[11] that for a published work copyright was a statutory right that did not survive expiry of a statutory right.

---

7. Ransom, *The First Copyright Statute* (1956, U Texas P). Passed in 1709 but effective from 10 April 1710.
8. *Eyre v Walker* (1735); *Molte v Falkner* (1735); *Walthoe v Walker* (1736) 1 Black W 332-1, cited in Saunders [1993] EIPR 452.
9. (1769) 4 Burr 2303; See the earlier case of *Tonson v Collins* (1762) 1 Black W 332.
10. (1774) 2 Bro PC 129.
11. See however *Rooney v Kelly* (1861) 14 Ir CL Rep 138 which stresses that common law remedies survived the Statute of Anne.

[9.07] Apart from copyright in books, there was agitation from other creative forces in society for protection of works against unauthorised reproduction. In 1734[12] Hogarth was successful in obtaining a copyright for engravings which had previously been protected only through a subscription system which was ineffective once authorised copies had been put upon the market. Designs of fabric patterns also secured a limited statutory protection for some two months in 1787 and a year later, protection for sculptures depicting the human figure were available. The Acts of 1734 and 1798 provided protections for 28 years and two periods of 14 years respectively, thus providing a parallel with the copyright afforded to books under the Statute of Anne, this implicitly emphasising that in all three cases it was the work created by the author, the artist/engraver and the sculptor respectively that was worthy of protection. The debate in *Millar v Taylor*[13] while ultimately the issue of perpetual protection was lost, also highlighted copyright as being an author's right rather than an entrepreneur's right.

THE NINETEENTH CENTURY

[9.08] The nineteenth century also further enhanced this identification of copyright as an author's right when the Copyright Act 1814 extended the statutory copyright in published books to one period of 28 years or the author's life, whichever was the longer. As we shall see, the debate about the most suitable period of copyright protection is a contentious one, particularly at the present time, but in the first half of the nineteenth century, Parliament continued with an either/or approach by extending the copyright term in 1842[14] to the author's life and seven years, or 42 years post publication, whichever was the longer. While the authors' right conferred by statute could of course be effectively negated by way of a contractual assignment to a publisher there was no doubt that copyright was, in essence, a statutory right *vis-à-vis* a published work, and that when the statutory period expired, the work fell into the public domain and was thus freely exploitable by anyone, even if the author's dependants had not reaped an adequate return seven years after the author had passed on. Arguments for a longer period were in part based upon the public interest for under the either/or approach, authors were tempted to withhold works for posthumous publication in order to attract the fixed period tariff, thus depriving the public of certain literary works for some time.

[9.09] With the passage of the Copyright Act 1911, the United Kingdom was able to participate fully in the Berne Union, having not only embraced the

---

12. Hyatt-Mayor, *Prints and People* (1971, Metropolitan Museum of Art) pp 550-5.
13. (1769) 4 Burr 2303.
14. Literary Copyright Act 1842.

principle of national treatment and ending both the registration system and extending the period of protection to the Berne minimum of fifty years following the end of the year of death of the author.

COPYRIGHT IN IRELAND

[9.10] In historical terms, Ireland and Scotland were seen as havens of book piracy. Efforts to counteract the piracy of well known titles centred on both the courts[15] and the Irish Parliament[16] and gradually the Westminster Parliament extended the structure of English Copyright Protection Statutes to cover Ireland. With the foundation of the State, however, many of the cultural and economic patterns that had built up over the previous century continued to operate: academic and literary figures still tended to look to British academic presses and commercial publishers to put their works before the world;[17] the Performing Rights Society, established in 1914, still functioned from London for the benefit of Irish composers and music publishers,[18] and even attempts to stimulate the publication of scholarship in the Irish language and early Irish history, for example, were frustrated by the size of the market, publishers' indifference and lack of technical resources.[19] With the establishment of the Irish State on 6 December 1921, Ireland lost all of the administrative structures and bodies that had caused the commercial and industrial property sectors of the economy to function - there was no Patent Office for example, and registration of a design copyright did not take place because there was no administrative body to accept applications for registration. Although the right to assert a copyright was afforded to an author as a common law right, it was only on the passing of the Industrial and Commercial Property (Protection) Act 1927[20] that design registration could take place so as to provide the author with a right to commence an action for breach of artistic design copyright.[21] The most significant feature of the 1927 legislation, Part VI of which reproduced in substantive terms the 1911 Act which itself was repealed,[22] related to a discussion about the basis upon which copyright should be available to a citizen of Saorstát Eireann. Senator Dowdall sought to introduce an amendment which

---

15. *Pope v Curl* (1741) 2 Atk 342; see however *Fisher v Folds* (1838) 1 Jones 12.
16. Print protection arrived via 6 & 7 Vic c 59(1843) as extended in 1852 by 15 & 16 Vic c 12; 5 & 6 Vic c 45 (1842 Act) which extended to Ireland the British copyright system for books.
17. See Senator WB Yeats in 8 Seanad Debates Cols. 599-610.
18. This remained so until 1988 when IMRO was established; total separation occurred in 1995.
19. 8 Seanad Debates Cols 599-610.
20. An earlier Bill had been introduced in 1925 but was withdrawn to allow for revisions which appeared in the 1926 Bill.
21. The provision was retrospective.
22. See paras **[20.01-20.02]** for an account of the relationship between the 1911 Act and the post Treaty period.

would have required Ireland to introduce a manufacturing clause similar to that found in the USA and Canada which would have made the printing of a work (but not necessarily publication) a *sine qua non* for copyright protection. This amendment was defeated, not simply because of difficulties in relation to the Berne Convention, but because the amendment was castigated by WB Yeats in the Seanad as being tantamount to a vote for piracy[23] and likely to lead to the ruination of publishers and the death of academic scholarship in the country. In 1927 legislation was thus able to reconcile substantive law and administrative effectiveness[24] until it was replaced by the Copyright Act 1963 which in turn is about to be replaced by more appropriate legislative and administrative structures.

ECONOMIC AND CULTURAL IMPLICATIONS OF COPYRIGHT

[9.11] While the copyright system does not exactly parallel the patent system by giving the first into the field a statutory monopoly in every case - coincidental or simultaneous creation of two works creates two copyright works with no liability for either author once copying has been disproved[25] - a copyright does give the author, or rightholder, quite substantial and enduring exclusive rights of exploitation. In justifying the scope and duration of statutory copyright, it is customary to defend the monopoly as being dependant upon the need to provide a satisfactory environment for investment and innovation. If works of authorship or derivative works, for example, are not protected then the creative and entrepreneurial sectors of society will have no incentive, or reward, for innovation or cultural or artistic progress. This argument is a powerful one,[26] particularly in the new digital environment where original works such as sound recordings, films and computer programs cost significant amounts to produce but such works can be reproduced with no discernible loss of quality, at a fraction of the original cost, by a counterfeiter. Certainly at the level of international trade relations, the need to provide an economic and legal climate in which certain rogue States tolerated, or even tacitly supported, the counterfeiting of high volume and high value copyright works, was a central motivating factor for the position taken by the developed industrial economies in the Uruguay Round of the GATT. The fact that few commentators would

---

23. 8 Seanad Debates Cols 599-610, 1107-1121.
24. Eg see the background to effective enforcement of performance rights sketched in *PRS v Bray UDC* [1930] IR 509.
25. Landes & Posner (1989) 18 JLS 325 at 344-7.
26. The vibrancy of the Irish music industry and its potential for job creation make calls for improved copyright laws somewhat non-controversial (see, for example, 148 Seanad Debates Col 1747 at 1813), at least until the issue of enforcement of performance rights comes to the fore.

countenance a complete departure from a copyright regime does not mean however that there is some panglossian consensus in favour of the broad levels of protection that generally operate within the Berne Convention tradition.

[9.12] Any monopoly, whether statutory or *de facto*, has distasteful implications but the defenders of copyright in the traditional, paper-based literary fields argue that without an extensive period of copyright protection, and a power to obtain the assignment of copyright from an author to a publisher, it is not possible for the publishing industry to adequately exploit a published book due to the uncertainties of public taste, the ebb and flow of literary fashion, as well as the vagaries of a market in which rival works may appear to compete with, or even supplant, a work.[27] This approach, supported by the publishers of new works, justifies copyright protection for extensive periods of protection on the ground, *inter alia*, that production of unprofitable titles is subsidised by revenue obtained from more successful works and that such a subsidy must endure for a long rather than a short period of time. This argument is often regarded with some scepticism for it tends to treat publishing as an altruistic rather than a commercial activity, and some commentators point to the evidence from countries which have traditionally extended short, but renewable, periods of protection. The leading USA study, got instance, indicated that around 15% of authors thought it worthwhile considering renewal following expiry of the 28 year copyright period.[28]

[9.13] While there will always be some works which will be modern classics and which will sell for whatever period of protection is decided upon, the reality for most works is that their commercial value is exhausted within a few years of initial publication, particularly in relation to academic, technical or scientific works, or new types of work such as computer programs where marketing or related factors such as advances in hardware make the work obsolete.[29] Indeed, *Ricketson* concludes that:

> "longer terms of protection probably do not play any part in the investment decisions of copyright investors such as publishers and the like although there is a need to investigate the effect that the prospect of future exploitation plays in their decisions".[30]

[9.14] It may of course be asked, if copyright protection for most works is a legal reality but an economic pipedream, why does this matter? The answer is of course that the onus lies upon those who assert the need for a copyright to justify

---

[27] Ricketson (1992) 23 IIC 753 at 758-760.

[28] Ringer (1963) 1 *Studies in Copyright* 583.

[29] Some games do enjoy a revival, eg the early *Donkey Kong* games in the 1970s were revived in the 1990s, albeit in more sophisticated form.

[30] [1992] 23 ITC 753, at 766.

that right, for the core of the copyright debate is one of public policy and the public interest. *Macauley's* observation[31] that "monopoly is an evil that must not last a day longer than is necessary and that copyright, being a (necessary) tax on readers for the purpose of giving a bounty to writers", requires society to be vigilant in testing the monopoly which is thus obtained at a substantial social cost.

[9.15] Some commentators point to the fact that copyright keeps up the price of books by granting exclusive rights to one publisher, a matter which is compounded by resale price maintenance under the now mortally wounded Net Book Agreement.[32] Suggestions for the compulsory licensing of copyright works following upon first publication find support from the compulsory licensing provisions of the Berne Convention in relation to sound reproductions of musical works, the powers to republish works within developing countries, not to mention the broader public policy issues that the *Magill*[33] litigation seems to presage.

[9.16] Apart from the purely financial aspects that the monopoly produces, there are important cultural questions that remain at large when copyright is in issue. *Parrinder*[34] and others make the point that when a classic text remains in copyright publishers have no incentive to produce newer, cheaper texts[35] but when such a work falls out of copyright, the public can often expect a range of newer, cheaper printings of the work (as occurred in relation to Joyce's works in the early 1990s). This has significant cost and quality advantages to students, libraries and others. One may also make the point that such public domain texts must also be worth reproducing or the publisher would steer clear of the text at all costs! The significant educational benefits of such printings is not the only cultural benefit from truncated or strictly controlled copyright protection. The estate or literary executor of a deceased author may have a separate agenda. There may be a dislike of either the form or the contents of a particular work, whether it be Richardson's famous nephew[36] or a relative concerned to safeguard the reputation or privacy of a third party, and in such a case the public may be deprived of a work on grounds which may have differing degrees of validity. Sometimes permission to reproduce a work may not appear to be based on particularly strong ground, as occurred recently when permission to perform

---

31. T Macauley, *Speeches on Copyright*, 25.
32. British Publishers Association withdrew on 30 September 1995. *In re Net Book Agreement 1957* Times Law Report, 20 March 1997.
33. [1995] FSR 230; Vinje [1995] EIPR 297.
34. [1993] EIPR 391.
35. Save when the work is serialised for television when a newer, more expensive printing of the text often results.
36. See Macauley's example in the House of Commons, cited by Ricketson [1992] 23 IIC 753, 769.

an extract from *Finnegans Wake* in a London musical recital was withheld by the Joyce Estate (the work having come back into copyright under the Term Directive) on the ground that the permission request inserted an apostrophe between the 'n' and the 's' in 'Finnegans'.[37]

HUMAN MOTIVATION AND THE DISTRIBUTION OF KNOWLEDGE

[9.17] It is often pointed out that authorship, which should be encouraged and promoted within society, is not always subject to the same motivating factors.[38] While the desire to see one's writings in print is a natural human ambition, the deeper reasons for this desire may differ. It may be simply a desire for financial reward, and Dr Johnson remarked that this is the only valid reason - "no man but a blockhead ever wrote, except for money."[39] There are of course areas of book and journal production where the author has no realistic expectation of financial reward; indeed some scientific publishers and journals require a financial contribution, often from the author, before a work can be printed, such is the limited market for even the most erudite work. Here the motivation is scholarship, the search for truth, or the advancement of reputation and career. In such a context, *Breyer*[40] asserts copyright is not a significant element and he argues for the more effective distribution of such works via grants or State subvention, a powerful argument given that most scientific research is publicly funded in any event. In Ireland, the tax exemption[41] given to the income on royalties is intended to provide a stimulus to cultural creation but the Revenue Commissioners have traditionally resisted extending this exemption to school or university texts (as distinct from novels) so this form of non-copyright stimulus does not always operate coherently in such a context. Although the copyright system has its critics, particularly amongst economic rights theorists who argue that copyright can be contrary to the public interest by keeping the cost of published works artificially high,[42] a recent survey by *Landes and Posner*[43] (in which the authors specifically examined the extent to which copyright law can

---

37. "Dead Loss" *The Times* 21 September 1995.
38. Plant (1934) Economica 167: Senator WB Yeats had this to say about the motivation of Irish scholars researching and writing in the fields of Old and Middle Irish: "those books pay the author practically nothing at all. The learned man is satisfied merely that his scholarship should be given to the world" 8 Seanad Debates Col 600 (March 11 1927).
39. Boswell's *Life of Johnson* April 5 1776.
40. (1970) 84 Harv LR 281; contrast Tyerman (1971) 18 UCLA L Rev 1188; and Breyer's riposte at (1972) 20 UCLA Rev 75. Gordon (1989) 41 Stan LR 1343.
41. Finance Act 1969 s 2: See *Revenue Commissioners v Loinsigh* High Court, unrep, 21 December 1994.
42. Eg, Plant (1934) Economica 167: Plant, *The New Commerce in Ideas and Intellectual Property* (1953).
43. (1989) 18 JLS 325.

be explained as a means for promoting efficient allocation of resources) can be said to be broadly supportive of the copyright system. *Landes and Posner* argued that the rights of an owner to prevent others from copying a work represents a trade off between the cost of limiting access to a work against the benefits of providing incentives towards the creation of a work in the first place. In such a context, positive doctrinal elements such as non-protection of ideas *per se*, fair use, and even the length of the protection, are seen as intuitively efficient in economic terms. It may be that *Landes and Posner* overstate their thesis and underestimate the strength of opposition towards an overready assimilation of new economic and technological interests into copyright[44] but an economic defence of authors' rights is particularly opportune at this time.

COPYRIGHT WORKS AND THE RIGHTS OF THEIR CREATOR

[9.18] We have seen that in historical terms copyright evolved somewhat uneasily, from an entrepreneurial right into an author's right which can and often is abridged or transferred by way of contractual licence or contractual assignment. It is nevertheless argued that a copyright is necessary because it provides the author, or creator, of a work with statutory recognition of rights which are inherently based upon the causal link between the author and the work. The difficulty with supporting such a theory is that market forces and society generally does not reward or recognise the effort, imagination or skill that each author brings to bear on a work in any rational way. The author of a successful three minute popular song, which was perhaps composed in under an hour, is likely to net considerably more in terms of fame and income than the author of a scholarly tone that represents a lifetime of endeavour and investigation. This point is side-stepped by those who assert the existence of copyright as an author's right by arguing that the true link is not between the author and the market as an economic relationship but between the author and the work as an expression of human personality. Such a perspective has found expression in the European Court of Justice which has forged together[45] the common law tradition of copyright as an exploitative economic right with the civilian idea that rights in an original work are authors' rights - the *droit d'auteur* - for the Court has said on several occasions, within the context of Article 36 of the Treaty, that the essential function of copyright is to protect the moral rights in the work and ensure a reward for the creative effort in producing a work.

[44.] Breyer (1970) 84 Harv LR 281, Karnell (1995) 26 IIC 193. See also MacQueen (1994) 45 NILQ 30 for a specific discussion on software protection.

[45.] In the most recent instance, Magill [1995] FSR 530.

[9.19] Within the context of Irish statute law however, it must be noted that save for the little used provisions of s 53, which relate to false attribution of authorship, the Copyright Acts do not contain any moral rights protection and the only realistic options available to an author facing mutilation of the author's work (and this often prejudicial or humiliating treatment at the hands of others) are actions for defamation, or breach of contract and the like. The rights of a creator to maintain rights over a work are sometimes described as inherent rights in property but as we have already seen, the publication of works brings such works into the realm of statutory rights only, according to English judicial decisions, and many economic commentators point to the differences between indeterminate and perpetual rights in real property and some tangibles, on the one hand, and the less compelling arguments *vis-à-vis* works of authorship on the other. Nevertheless, one Irish judge has recently stressed that the Irish Constitution does recognise intellectual property as property to be protected under the Constitution, thus opening up some prospect of control for a creator over a work, notwithstanding the non-application or exhaustion of a statutory copyright. In *PPI v Cody and Princes Investments Ltd*,[46] Keane J considered a defence that recorded music that had been publicly performed in the defendant's premises had not been proved to be copyright material:

> "Section 60(4) of the Act of 1963 provides that no right in the nature of copyright 'shall subsist otherwise than by virtue of this Act or of some other enactment in that behalf'. The right of the creator of a literary, dramatic, musical or artistic work not to have his or her creation stolen or plagiarised is a right of private property within the meaning of Articles 40.3.2 and 43.1 of the Constitution, as is the similar right of a person who has employed his or her technical skills and/or capital in the sound recording of a musical work. As such, they can hardly be abolished in their entirety, although it was doubtless within the competence of the Oireachtas to regulate their exercise in the interests of the common good. In addition, and even in the absence of any statutory machinery, it is the duty of the organs of the State, including the courts, to ensure, as best they may, that these rights are protected from unjust attack and, in the case of injustice done, vindicated. The statements in some English authorities that copyright other than by statutory provision ceased to exist with the abolition of common law copyright are not necessarily applicable in Ireland.[47]

COPYRIGHT AND THE COLLECTIVE ENFORCEMENT OF RIGHTS

[9.20] While copyright is clearly an individual right given to a human person in order to encourage and recognise the economic and cultural benefits of creating

---

46. [1994] 2 ILRM 241.
47. [1994] 2 ILRM 241, at 247.

new works, the nature of copyright is in fact a collection of separate rights, the most important being rights to authorise or control physical reproduction of the work and public performance of the work. The first right is clearly important in relation to printed works and works of fine art, for example, while the performance right will be critical for the authors of musical and dramatic works, but there are significant areas of cultural endeavour where both reproduction and performance rights will be of concern to the author. However, the individual nature of the right should not deflect attention from the reality behind the right - they are extremely difficult to enforce on an individual basis. Even in cases where the author assigns copyright to an entity that possesses greater economic clout or expertise - a composer or songwriter assigning copyright to a music publisher for example - problems about detecting levels of use or reproduction make it worthwhile for rightholders to consider collective action to bring about effective enforcement of these rights.[48]

[9.21] In the area of publishing, Irish publishers have established a licensing body, the Irish Copyright Licensing Agency (ICLA). The agency administers the reproduction right for books and periodicals, giving individuals and institutions such as universities and schools the necessary permissions for photocopy and other reproduction activities, the revenue income being distributed to members of CLÉ, the Irish Publishers Association. In the area of musical copyrights, the Irish Music Rights Organisation (IMRO) and Phonographic Performance Ireland (PPI) enforce performance rights in musical works on behalf of composers and music publishers and recording companies respectively. Recognition of the necessity and effectiveness of collective enforcement of rights is a matter of broad international and national agreement. Both the Berne Convention and the GATT recognise these institutions, while the European Union, in the Rental and Lending Directive, expressly authorises collecting societies to administer rental and lending rights on behalf of authors. In a domestic context, however, the role of the music collecting societies in the Irish economy has become a matter of controversy. However, the Competition Authority, while it has ruled that certain aspects of the initial IMRO standard assignment agreement are anti-competitive in nature, has upheld the general effect of compulsory licensing in the context of Irish society as being positive in nature:

> "The notifying parties advanced a number of arguments in support of their claim that the arrangements notified met the above condition [ie, are not anti-competitive and contrary to the public interest]. These arguments may be summarised as follows. Effective protection of performing right (*sic*) is

---

48. Some stronger entertainment units, eg. rock groups, are pressing for a more fragmented approach to performance rights.

extremely labour intensive involving considerable expenditure on administrative and monitoring procedures. In view of the practical difficulties and expense involved, it is only through collective action that creators may ensure effective protection of their performing right. In the absence of the present arrangements, it would be impossible for creators to obtain a just reward for the performance of their works and, in that event, the incentive to produce musical works would be very significantly reduced, or licences to perform music might not so readily be made available, and these would be to the detriment of licensed users and of the general public, as ultimate consumers.

The Authority accepts this reasoning. There are considerable practical difficulties involved in the administration and enforcement of performing rights, particularly in relation to the multiplicity of smaller users, and these difficulties do point to the need for a central collective licensing/ enforcement system on behalf of creators and publishers many of whom are based outside the State. Substantial additional transaction costs would clearly be involved in any multiplicity of systems of administration of performing right based on licensing by individual creators. Compliant users would require a large number of licences while the cost of pursuit for non compliance by individual creators/ publishers would make this activity totally uneconomic except in the case of major users or events. The pursuit of breaches of copyright by smaller users would become totally uneconomic.

The Authority therefore accepts that a collective system of performing right administration involves efficiencies and these would be significant in the generality of cases. Assignment of the performing right to PRS is accepted as improving the provision of services.

Allowing consumers a fair share of the resulting benefit

Users benefit from the improved provision of services. Licensees (ie, the users, such as radio and television broadcasters, discos, public houses etc) benefit from access to the PRS repertoire and from the avoidance of additional transaction costs which would be involved if they had to deal with a multiplicity of licensers. The ultimate consumers, the listening public, also share in this benefit as consumers of the various services, of which music forms part, provided by the intermediary undertakings. Consumers also benefit to the extent that a collective copyright arrangement has resulted in a greater supply and variety of musical works being available than would otherwise be the case. The Authority therefore considers that the collective copyright arrangements allow consumers a fair share of the benefit."[49]

[9.22] However, in many important sectors of the Irish business community, a substantial level of hostility to the music collecting societies can be identified. The broadcasting organisations are in dispute with PPI about the levels of copyright clearance fees charged and the method of assessment; individual users

---

49. Competition Authority, Decision No 326, May 18 1994.

of copyright music, in particular publicans, discotheque owners, hoteliers and shopkeepers have combined to form a representative association which is actively lobbying for a complete review of the copyright licensing system.[50] While disgruntled users of copyright music do not publicly go so far as to call for the abolition of the music copyright system *per se*, the volume of dissatisfaction caused the then Minister of State at the Department of Enterprise and Employment to review certain aspects of copyright law. Critics of the collecting societies describe their activities as resembling 'almost a legalised Mafia operation'[51] and 'parasitic',[52] and while one cannot accept such hyperbole, there is no doubt that the collecting societies have at times been forced onto the defensive[53] because the public perception often tends towards the view that the societies are multinational bodies that exercise monopoly powers. While this is somewhat unrealistic because the societies are made up of individuals who, by and large, do not have any substantial economic or contractual leverage, the societies will have to continue to react to comments that charges are arbitrary and unrealistically high, that the system of collection and distribution of income lacks transparency, particularly in relation to administrative costs, and that collection and enforcement mechanisms are intimidatory or based on using draconian legal measures such as the interlocutory injunction. Recent Competition Authority decisions, however, have broadly endorsed the activities of IMRO however.[54] These matters are considered in depth below.[55]

[50.] See *PPI v Controller* [1995] 2 ILRM 1 (SC).

[51.] 136 Seanad Debates Col 1098 (Senator Maloney).

[52.] *Ibid* Col 1100 (Senator Kiely).

[53.] See the school content debate in 464 *Dáil Debates* Col 806.

[54.] CA/3/91E. Decision No 445 of Authority - 15 November 1995. It is understood that a High Court action revolving around this decision is pending.

[55.] See paras **[15.45]-[15.50]** *post*.

Chapter 10

The Copyright Term

HISTORICAL INTRODUCTION

[10.01] The period of copyright protection under statute has fluctuated over the centuries but the trend has largely been an expansive one. The Statute of Anne initially provided for protection for fourteen years, renewable for a further period of protection. The 1814 legislation provided for a 28 year period or the life of the author, whichever was longer. The 1842 revision extended the period of protection to the life of the author plus seven years, or 42 years, whichever was the longer. The 1911 Act, intended as a measure which allowed the United Kingdom to implement the Berne Convention, required a minimum of 50 years following the death of the author, a period of protection adhered to by the Irish State until 1995. Apart from literary copyright under the statute, the common law has provided substantial protection for unpublished works by fusing together notions of ownership of property and the law of confidence.[1] Injunctive relief has long been available in such cases.[2]

THE COPYRIGHT TERM UNDER THE 1963 ACT[3]

[10.02] In accordance with the Berne Convention, the period of protection for protected works observed the minimum of 50 years pma. However, this general principle cannot be relied upon as a universal rule, for Irish law could produce significant variations on this theme, depending on the nature of the work and the kind of exploitative act which would trigger the running of the copyright term.

[10.03] A distinction was drawn depending upon whether the work was protected under the Berne Convention as an original work in Part II of the Act, or was protected as a related or neighbouring right under Part III of the Act.

---

1. *Perceval v Phipps* (1813) 2 V & B 19; *Jeffreys v Boosey* (1854) 4 HL Cas 815; *Prince Albert v Strange* (1849) 1 M & G 25; *Turner v Robinson* (1860) 10 Ir Ch R 510; *Caird v Sime* (1887) 12 AC 327; *Exchange Telegraph Company v Central News* [1897] 2 Ch 48; *Exchange Telegraph Company v Howard* (1906) 22 TLR 375.
2. *Granard v Durkin* (1809) 1 Ball & B 207.
3. For copyright protection for works that pre-exist the 1963 Act see the Schedules to the 1963 Act for transitional provisions.

Part II Works

[10.04] 1. In the case of an unpublished but original literary, dramatic or musical work, protection became available once the work was either made, or substantially made. Copyright protection could, theoretically, be perpetual, the period of 50 years pma only beginning to run once the work, or an adaptation of the work, was published, performed in public, records of the work were offered for sale to the public, or broadcast, these terms being defined in ss 2 and 3 of the Act.[4] The author had to be a qualified person (defined below).

[10.05] 2. In the case of a published original literary, dramatic or musical work, the protection became immediately available upon publication, even if the work was incomplete or part of a larger work such as an episode in a serialised work or a single volume of a series of encyclopaedia. Conditions of entitlement, however, were that the work was first published within the State or that the author was an Irish citizen, or Irish domiciled or resident at the date of publication.[5]

[10.06] 3. By analogy with unpublished literary, dramatic and musical works, an unpublished original artistic work was protected once the work had been made or substantially made, as long as the author of the work was a qualified person. Copyright protection would be lost once the artistic work was published unless the publication met the conditions set out in the Act, namely, that the first publication took place in the State, or the author was a qualified person at the time of publication or, if the author had died prior to publication, the author was a qualified person immediately before the author's death.[6]

[10.07] 4. In the case of published artistic works, the protection was available as from publication, even if the work was incomplete as long as the first publication took place within the State or if the author was a qualified person as defined in the Act.[7]

[10.08] 5. However, although an engraving (or etching) is a work of an artistic nature, a specific rule was laid down for such works which were unpublished at the date of the death of the author. The period of protection for 50 years pma began to run as from the end of the year in which it was first published, thereby giving engravings a greater degree of protection than other posthumously published artistic works if the author of the engraving was not a qualified person, for example.[8]

---

4. CA 1963, ss 8(1) and (5).
5. CA 1963, s 8(2). Other persons were protected under Part VI of the Act.
6. CA 1963, s 9(2) and (4). Publication, as defined in s 3, did not include exhibiting the artistic work.
7. CA 1963, ss 9(3) and (5).
8. CA 1963, s 9(6). Compare s 9(4) on this point.

[10.09] 6. In the case of photographs, Article 7(4) of the Berne Convention permits countries of the Union to make specific provision for photographs, a desire being evinced to encourage the prompt exploitation of news photographs. Under the 1963 Act the period of protection is 50 years following from the end of the year in which the photograph is first published.[9]

[10.10] 7. In the case of works published anonymously or pseudonymously, the Berne Convention makes specific provision in Article 7 for a modification of the above rules. Statutory protection for all Part II works is to run for 50 years after the end of the year of first publication. This abridgement of the 50 year pma rule is not effective in cases where a person could, by reasonable inquiry, ascertain the identity of the author of the work.[10]

[10.11] 8. In the case of Part II works of joint authorship, that is, works of genuine collaboration by two or more authors, the period of protection is to run from the death of the last surviving author.[11] Where one or more of the joint authors of a work of joint authorship, which was published under two or more names is, or becomes, identifiable by reasonable inquiry, then the period of protection is to be 50 years after the death of the disclosed or identifiable author, or the death of the last surviving disclosed or identifiable author.[12]

[10.12] It is therefore evident that under these rules, some works could enjoy perpetual copyright. Other works could enjoy a copyright, the duration of which would be triggered by either the death of an author, or by first publication. Protection would depend upon the status of the author as a qualified person or upon the place of first publication. While on this latter point the Berne principles of national treatment, as implemented by Part VI of the 1963 Act and the 1978 Regulations[13] were less important in practice, these rules could operate arbitrarily, particularly where the work was an artistic work that existed in several derivative forms, eg protection for photographs or engravings of a painting or sculpture all made by the one artist would enjoy different periods of protection, depending upon the fact of publication, or not, and the medium in which the work was fixed.

Part III Works

[10.13] The historical, theoretical and practical aspects of Part III rights are considered elsewhere in this book. For the purposes of the present chapter, it is

---

9. CA 1963, s 9(7).
10. CA 1963, s 15.
11. CA 1963, s 16(3).
12. CA 1963, s 16(4).
13. Copyright (Foreign Countries) Order 1978 (SI 132/1978); Copyright (Foreign Countries (No 2) Order 1978 (SI 133/1978).

sufficient to note that Irish law provided a somewhat extensive kind of protection in respect of most Part III rights.

1. In the case of sound recordings, the Act provided a period of 50 years from the end of the year of first publication. Thus, an unpublished sound recording had perpetual copyright protection.[14]

2. In the case of cinematographic films, the Act provided a period of 50 years from the end of the year of first publication, thus, an unpublished film had perpetual copyright protection.[15]

3. Where a television broadcast or a sound broadcast is made by Radio Éireann, copyright is to subsist in that broadcast for a period of 50 years from the end of the year in which the broadcast is first made.[16]

4. In the case of the publication of editions of one or more literary, dramatic or musical works the publisher's copyright in the typographical arrangement of such a work is to subsist for 25 years from the end of the year in which the edition is first published.[17]

THE COPYRIGHT TERM AFTER 1 JULY 1995

[10.14] The Term Directive of 29 October 1993[18] was transposed into Irish law through the European Communities (Term of Protection of Copyright) Regulations 1995.[19] While these Regulations were signed by the Minister on 23 June 1995, they came into operation as from 1 July 1995, the deadline set by the Directive itself. The decision to implement the Directive by way of statutory order, rather than via primary legislation, was a pragmatic one. The fact that these measures directly affect individual property rights made it necessary to ensure that the legislative changes necessary were in place by 1 July 1995, there being a fear that the State could well have been exposed to liability under *Francovich*[20] if the State had been tardy in respect of the deadline.

[10.15] It is essential to note that there are no transitional measures in place under these Regulations. The effect of the Regulations is to extend, renew, or abridge certain copyrights as a measure of harmonisation which is thought necessary if the EU objective of creating a single market is to be achieved. The Regulations also change in several respects the triggering events which mark the

---

14. CA 1963, s 17(2).
15. CA 1963, s 18(2).
16. CA 1963, s 19(2). See also SI 101/1991.
17. CA 1963, s 20(4).
18. 93/98/EEC. OJ L 290.
19. SI 158/1995. Von Lewinski [1992] 23 IIC 785; Dworkin [1993] EIPR 151.
20. *Francovich and Boniface v Italy* [1992] IRLR 84; Syzszczak (1992) 55 MLR 690.

commencement of protection, and the Regulations also alter the identity of those persons whose lives measure the onset of the *post mortem* period for exploitation of several works. The Regulations also make provision for the resolution of difficulties that arise due to the exploitation of works that come back into copyright as the result of these provisions.

[10.16] Article 3 of the Regulations override ss 8(4) and (5), ss 9(5), (6) and (7), and ss 51(3) and (4) by providing that the copyright term for literary, dramatic, musical or artistic works shall be the lifetime of the author of the work and 70 years pma, irrespective of the date when the work is published or otherwise lawfully made available to the public. This effects a considerable change for it is no longer directly relevant to the issue of protection whether or not a work was published. Therefore, the deliberate withholding of works for posthumous publication, or the discovery of a new unpublished work, cannot, as such, facilitate the descendants of the author in exploiting such a work if the author died more than seventy years previously. In this respect the Regulations can be said to abridge the old statutory copyrights in unpublished works, a situation that is not totally remedied by Article 8 of the Regulations. This result, the loss of protection for unpublished works, is further underlined in Article 5 of the Regulations. Article 4(1) of the Regulations extends the protection available in respect of anonymous or pseudonymous literary, dramatic, musical or artistic works, by extending the protection to 70 years following the first publication of the work or the work being lawfully made available to the public. Article 4(2) also deals with instances where the pseudonym adopted leaves no doubt as to the author's identity, or the author discloses his or her identity during the 70 year period: in such cases the 70 year period pma provided in Article 4 is intended to act as updating s 15 of the 1963 Act. It is interesting to note that the Regulations, in Article 4(2) depart significantly from the language of s 15(2)(b), thereby ensuring that the Regulations are in conformity with Article 7(3) of the 1971 Paris revision of the Berne Convention.

[10.17] In regard to related rights under Part III of the 1963 Act, s 18 of the 1963 Act is significantly broadened for the 1963 Act gave a 50 year copyright in a cinematograph film to the maker of that film. The Directive, which selected a seventy year period is most effective in certain other EU States where the protection was for a lesser period (eg, Spain). However, there are other significant features to Regulation 6, which radically redefines the measuring standard *vis-à-vis* cinematographic works. Under the old law the older 50 year period was set off by first publication. Article 6 states that the copyright will subsist for 70 years after the death of the last of four categories of person to survive, namely, the principal director, the author of the screenplay, the author of the dialogue and the composer of music specifically created for use in the film.

This measure does not directly influence the issue of in whom copyright reposes, for the maker of a film is generally the producer of the film rather than one or more of the artistic talents behind the cinematographic work. This switch in emphasis can be seen as recognition that films represent a significant cultural as well as economic activity and that the artistically creative forces behind a film should be recognised as such. More pragmatically, once first publication was regarded as an unsuitable triggering event, some measuring lives had to be identified, for in practice the maker of a film may in many instances be a body corporate and therefore incapable of being a measuring life. The copyright afforded to the producer of a sound recording under s 17 is not expanded by Article 7 of the Regulations - a 50 year period in each case - but the triggering event is changed. The 1963 Act provided that first publication was to trigger the protection; under Article 7 it is to commence when the recording is made. However, if during this period the recording is published or communicated to the public, then a 50 year period of protection is to run from the date when the first of those two events occurs. Such an extension could prove a useful means of exploiting the forgotten or less meritorious recordings of artists by record companies. In relation to broadcasts and the copyright given to Radio Éireann by s 19 of the Act, it is not possible to interpret Regulation 7(3) as providing certain broadcasting organisations - local radio stations for example - with a copyright in their broadcasts. The statutory copyright in a broadcast is currently confined to radio and television broadcasts made by Radio Éireann, as defined in the Broadcasting Authority Act 1960, and local television and radio programmes made by bodies recognised[21] under the Radio and Television Act 1988. Article 7(3) of the Regulations, by providing that "the term of protection as respects the rights of a broadcasting organisation" shall expire 50 years after first transmission, does not extend the scope of copyright to all broadcasting organisations, a generic concept that goes further than Radio Éireann, a specific entity, for the Directive was not intended to give new rights to unrecognised broadcasting organisations.[22]

[10.18] Article 8 provides a *sui generis* exploitation right in respect of previously unpublished works, recordings, broadcasts or films. In cases where such protected works are within the public domain (eg, an unpublished sound recording is not lawfully communicated to the public within 50 years of its making) any subsequent lawful publication or lawful communication to the public is to give that person rights which are to be equivalent to the (expired) economic rights of the author, maker or broadcasting organisation (as the case

---

21. SI 101/1991.
22. The compelling argument against this is that the Directive was not intended to create new rights *per se*.

may be) for 25 years from the date of first publication or communication to the public. This new neighbouring right was proposed at a late stage in the legislative process in order to encourage the publication of previously unpublished works when copyright protection has expired. Presumably the exploitation of such works as between the rightholder and any successors in title will become a matter of contractual negotiation in some instances, thus indirectly strengthening the bargaining position of the author, *vis-à-vis* future exploitation of a work.

[10.19] Article 12 of the Regulations addresses the vexed question of revival of rights. Because two EU Member States provided more extensive periods of protection than the Berne 50 year pma minimum (eg, Spain provides 60 year pma protection while Germany provides for a 70 year period) the Harmonisation of Term Directive had to address the case of works within copyright in some Member States while being in the public domain elsewhere. Article 6 of the original proposal for a directive opted for the rule that legal certainty demanded, that is, that works that have fallen into the public domain would not become protected again, thereby envisaging that, for example, a work would be protected in Spain while being in the public domain elsewhere in the EU. The European Parliament proposed a different approach under which any work protected in at least one Member State on 1 July 1995 would be protected throughout the EU by way of a revival of rights. *Cohen Jehorem* has described the net effect thus, basing the argument on a combination of the Directive and the *Phil Collins*[23] decision:

> "One small concrete example may be useful here. The famous Dutch painter Piet Mondriaan died on 1 February 1944. The copyrights in his paintings are still very lucrative because of all sorts of merchandising activities. His highly abstract expressions are still widely used as patterns for designs of fashionable rugs, textiles, place-mats etc: a regular Mondriaan industry. Now the copyrights in these works will lapse in the Netherlands, and in nearly all countries of the world, 50 years pma, ie on 1 January 1995. Since the *Phil Collins* decision it is clear, however, that the successors in title of Piet Mondriaan will enjoy another 20 years of copyright protection in Germany, with its term of 70 years pma. This means that on 1 July 1995, half a year after the rights have lapsed in the rest of the world, they still subsist in one Member State of the community. Now through Article 10(2) this German copyright protection will trigger a revival of Mondriaan's rights in the rest of the Community, as of 1 July 1995, for another 19 the works will be in the public domain in the Netherlands and nearly everywhere in the Community. In that half year they can be freely exploited, as Article 10(3) provides, in order to protect acquired rights of third parties. The beauties of the EC directives are boundless."[24]

[23.] [1994] FSR 166. See Antill and Coles [1996] EIPR 379.
[24.] (1994) 25 IIC 821, at 835-6.

[10.20] However, the revival rule, favoured by the European Parliament, is balanced by a requirement that accrued rights, and lawful acts of exploitation, should be legally protected by Member States when these rights and acts conflict with the interests of the original, 'born again' copyright holder. In this regard, Article 14(1)(a) of the Regulations provides that a person who undertook the exploitation of a work before 29 October 1993 (the date of the adoption of the Draft Directive by the Council), that work then being in the public domain but subsequently revived by the Regulations, may avoid liability for copyright infringement and continue to exploit the work, notwithstanding the revival of copyright. Another situation covered by the Regulations is less clear for it deals with accrued rights in the period between adoption of the Directive and its transposition. First, if exploitation, or preparations of a substantial nature in regard to exploitation, have occurred between 29 October 1993 and 1 July 1995, those acts of reliance may be legally significant. However, these factors are ambiguous: are all acts, or preparatory acts, sufficient or must substantial expenditure or work be involved? Is it necessary for legally significant actions to occur, eg the purchase of related rights necessary to effect the exploitation? These qualitative issues can only be tested via litigation. The second requirement set under Article 14(1)(b) is also problematic: the exploiter must prove that he or she was not aware, or had no reasonable grounds for suspecting, that copyright would be revived by the Regulations or any other enactment. The exploiter will presumably discharge this onus of proof on a negative basis, eg no legal advice was sought on copyright matters during the period in question, or a belief that the original proposal which was not intended of effect on EU revival of rights, remained the legal position. In fact, a recent newspaper report indicates that the Kenneth Grahame book *The Wind in the Willows* is currently being adapted for a new cartoon film and that two other television productions of the work are at an advanced stage of production, the belief being that these acts of exploitation will be protected by the then forthcoming UK transposition provisions[25] which will have the effect of bringing the book back into copyright because Kenneth Grahame died 63 years ago. It is likely that similar acts of exploitation in Ireland, in relation to the works of James Joyce, for example, have taken place. Litigation is eagerly anticipated! Again, the effect of discharging the onus is to allow the exploiter to avoid liability to the copyright holder and allow exploitation to continue for the duration of the period of revival. It is by no means clear why the exploiter should have the right to continue to exploit the work for the entire period of the extension, and a fairer solution may well have been to permit exploitation only after a fair and

---

[25.] *The Observer*, 20 August 1995.

reasonable payment has been arranged with the holder of the revived copyright.[26]

THE 50 YEAR BERNE MINIMUM

[10.21] The period of protection set by the Berne Convention as a minimum requirement is the lifetime of the author and 50 years after the author's death. The special rules that Berne recognises for certain other works generally result in the abridgement of this period of protection, but the 50 year pma general term is capable of being extended by countries of the Berne Union. Within the context of the European Union however, Germany provides for a 70 year period of protection.

[10.22] Spain, since 1987, made provision for a 60 year period, while France provides a 70 year period of protection in regard to musical compositions with or without words. Some countries, namely Belgium, Italy and France, have provided periodic extensions of the copyright term in respect of works that had not been adequately exploited due to the substantial disruption effected by World Wars I and II.

[10.23] The selection of a 50 year minimum period of protection represents a balancing process between, on the one hand, civilian legal traditions and certain sectoral interests (eg publishers) who perhaps favour unlimited or extensive periods of protection, and on the other hand, more pragmatic schools of thought who espouse the notion that the economic or cultural monopoly that flows from copyright should only operate where some compelling public interest can be justified by the putative rightholder. The 50 year pma period is historically justified by claiming that the overriding concern that justifies such a period of protection is the safeguarding of the economic rights of the author and two generations of dependants that follow the author. The assumption is that the author's dependants must be protected for this later period although, as *Ricketson* has pointed out, the underlying assumption has never been challenged, save when there is agitation for an extension of copyright.[27] *Ricketson* concludes that the evidence in favour of selecting or continuing with a standard of protection that goes beyond even one generation of dependants is far from clear,[28] particularly when there is such a lack of clarity on whether we should be measuring the life of a dependant as being notional (eg, up to 60-70

[26.] This approach has been adopted elsewhere eg, the UK and Germany. See, 'Hardy Pensioner waits far from movie crowd', *Times* 28 May 1996, for an account of the windfall for certain Thomas Hardy heirs.

[27.] *The Berne Convention for the Protection of Literary and Artistic Works 1886-1986* (1987) (CCLS) para 7.5.

[28.] [1992] 23 IIC 751 at 762.

years) or simply a period of dependency (eg, birth to adulthood or 20-25 years). Rather, *Ricketson* and others tend to favour the view that the selection of a standard pma protection may not be justifiable economically or culturally. The only significant comment made in Ireland on this point occurred during the Committee Stage of the Bill that became the 1927 Act. A proposal to amend the 50 year pma period was made on the grounds that fixing a 30 year period instead would be "the time which would allow children of the author to come to manhood" and that "the monopoly rights of the writer ought to tend downwards rather than lengthen".[29] The proposal was lost on the basis that the Berne Convention should prevail. Nevertheless, the trend towards expansion of the Berne minimum period of protection has accelerated within the last three years in international copyright law. Further, the international community has tended to bring new objects of protection into the traditional copyright structure, the most striking example being the European Communities' decision to afford computer programs protection as a literary work (rather than *sui generis* protection) for 50 years pma and then 70 years pma.

THE TERM DIRECTIVE - WHY 70 YEARS PMA?

[10.24] The most important point to note about the Term Directive is that it is a measure intended to effect the overriding commercial goal of bringing about a European single market in goods and services. Information products such as video cassettes are clearly within the first category, while a film re-transmission organisation is clearly a service provider. However, in each of these cases, the rights of an importer to bring a product into a Member State,[30] or to re-transmit in one Member State a signal lawfully transmitted in another Member State,[31] could be truncated by national copyright laws. The power of community law to compel some kind of harmonisation of community copyright laws was finally shown to have no real muscle in *Patricia*:[32]

> "... that in the present state of Community law, which is characterised by a lack of harmonisation or approximation of legislation governing the protection of literary and artistic property, it is for the national legislatures to determine the conditions and detailed rules for such protection. Insofar as the disparity between national laws may give rise to restrictions on intra-community trade in sound recordings, such restrictions are justified under Article 36 of the Treaty if they are the result of differences between the rules governing the period of protection and this is inseparably linked to the very existence of the exclusive rights."[33]

[29.] *Per* Deputy Johnson, 17 *Dáil Debates* Col 593.

[30.] *Warner Bros v Christiensen* [1988] ECR 2605.

[31.] Coditel I [1980] ECR 881.

[32.] *EMI Electrola GmbH v Patricia* [1989] ECR 79.

[10.25] In the light of *Patricia* and the 1988 Copyright Green Paper[34] (which had alluded to the duration problem but had not emphasised this as a key topic for harmonisation) the 1991 Commission Action Plan[35] was able to compel a majority of Member States to agree to increase the standard copyright term by twenty years in those jurisdictions, even though there had been no significant debate on these issues in any Member State. The reasons advanced for this remarkable situation are set out in the explanatory memorandum accompanying the directive and the recitals to the Directive which, unfortunately are not transposed with the articles set out in the Directive.

[10.26] First, *Patricia* indicates that harmonisation of terms of copyright protection must occur, both in relation to the uniform periods of protection and standardisation of the events which trigger the protection, whether the events be the creation of the work, first publication, or the death of the author, as the case may be. The price to be paid for not harmonising these matters would be fragmented national markets and distortions and barriers to competition and free markets. A second justification for harmonisation was stated to be some desire on the part of 'interested circles' for greater uniformity and certainty, thus easing collective management of rights and in particular aiding Community action against third party piracy. Greater solidarity within the Community, so the argument ran, would heighten confidence within the European business community in relation to "future investment in the sector of (*sic*) creativity in the Community".[36]

[10.27] However, the real issue facing the Community was not whether to harmonise but, rather, how to harmonise? Should the term selected be in line with the term found in the majority of Member States, or some other term? Citing Community jurisprudence on accrued rights[37] and stressing that harmonisation downwards - to 50 years pma - was only superficially attractive because the observance of accrued rights would mean extraordinary transitional measures for Spanish and German rightholders, the result of which would be transitional periods that would "necessarily be long and would lead to a corresponding delay in the actual creation of the internal market".[38]

In such a context, the only realistic option was clearly to harmonise up to the highest standard set by German law.

[33.] *EMI Electrola GmbH v Patricia* [1989] ECR 79 at 96.
[34.] *Green Paper on Copyright and the Challenge of Technology* (88) 172 Final.
[35.] COM (90) 584 Final.
[36.] Explanatory Memorandum para 29.
[37.] *Verli-Wallace v Commission* [1983] ECR 2711; *Simmenthal v Commission* [1979] ECR 777.
[38.] Explanatory Memorandum para 33.

[10.28] However, the Commission advanced a number of ancillary points to justify this recommendation intellectually, although most commentators view these grounds as being spurious in the extreme. The first point is based upon the greater longevity of persons alive in the late twentieth century. If persons, including dependants, are living longer, then the period of protection should be extended. Critics of this argument point to the fact that automatic extension may not benefit the descendants of the author because rights may have been assigned previously, eg to a publisher, record company or film producer. Some limited support for this argument is to be found in the Irish implementing Regulations which give the benefit of any revival or extension to the author or the author's personal representatives unless there has been an express reference in any assignment to renewal or extension of copyrights. However, the Commission failed to meet *Ricketson's* arguments[39] that there is little evidence to support two later generations. Many commentators feel that the length of a copyright term is not likely to effect either the substantive bargaining position of an author vis-à-vis a publisher and other entrepreneurs, or the decision of such persons when a work is about to be exploited.[40] Short to medium term exploitation and income returns are the basis of investment decisions, rather than some hardly quantifiable estimate about the public's appetite for a work some thirty, fifty or seventy years after its creator has passed on.

[10.29] The decision to harmonise up, rather than down, while apparently justifiable in the view of EU Member States, has not however escaped criticism. One commentator has argued that the practice within the book trade has been to provide the public with new, cheaper editions of classical works only when copyright has expired and that the re-vesting of copyright in authors such as Yeats, Joyce, Hardy and DH Lawrence is unjustifiable and not in the public interest.[41] Other academic commentators have argued for a return to first principles, favouring the view that copyright term should be shorter and selectively conferred, but these arguments seem destined to fall on deaf ears.[42] We shall leave the last word on this question to *Laddie*:

"The question to be asked is: what justification is there for a period of monopoly of such proportions? It surely cannot be based on the principle of encouraging artistic creativity by increasing the size of the carrot. No one is going to be more inclined to write computer programs or speeches, compose

---

39. [1992] 23 ITC 753 at 761.
40. Cornish [1993[52 CLJ at 51; Landis & Posner [1989] 18 JLS 325; MacQueen [1994] 45 NILQ 30 at 43; Dawson [1994] 45 NILQ 193. See also the Preface to Laddie Prescott and Victoria, *The Modern Law of Copyright and Designs* Vol 2.
41. Parrinder [1993] EIPR 391.
42. See the compelling arguments put by a group of learned US academic lawyers in Karjala [1994] EIPR 531.

music or design buildings because 50, 60 and 70 years after his death a distant relative whom he has never met might still be getting royalties. It is noticeable that this expansion of term is not something which has only occurred in the last decade. On the contrary, it has been a trend which has been in evidence for the whole of this century. Before the 1911 Act, the term of copyright in artistic works extended to seven years after the author's death. In 1911 this was extended to 50 years after death. The growth of term is in fact greater than these figures suggest. Life expectancy in 1910 was far shorter than it is now. The result is that a monopoly which was expected to last about four decades in 1910 should be expected to last on average more than three times as long."[43]

---

43. 'Copyright: Over-Strength, Over-Regulated, Over-Rated?' [1996] EIPR 253, at 256.

Chapter 11

Protected Works - Literary and Artistic Works

INTRODUCTION

[11.01] The protection afforded to an original work through the law of copyright is entirely dependant upon the statutory provisions of the Copyright Acts, for common law copyright protection has been held to have been swept away by copyright legislation.[1] Copyright protection for an original literary work, for example, will only be available if the subject matter in question is capable of satisfying the cumulative notion of an original literary work. The Copyright Act 1963, however, does not provide any guidance on either the notion of originality or what may be considered to be a work. Section 2 of the Act provides that the phrase 'literary work' includes any written table or compilation. It is therefore necessary to scrutinise the cases in order to determine what the judges have considered to be an original literary work. Many of the older cases, however, must be viewed with some degree of caution because the earlier, pre-1911 legislative measures, did not, for example, in express terms, require a literary work to be original but this requirement was implicit in the older case law.

ORIGINAL

[11.02] The requirement that the work be original is intended to connect the work in question with the person responsible for this creation and its physical existence. In the leading case on originality, *University of London Press Ltd v University Tutorial Press Ltd*, Petersen J observed:

> "The word 'original' does not in this connection mean that the work must be the expression of original or inventive thought. Copyright Acts are not concerned with the originality of ideas, but with the expression of thought, and, in the case of 'literary work' with the expression of thought in print or writing. The originality which is required relates to the expression of the thought. But the Act does not require that the expression must be in an original or novel form but that the work must not be copied from another work - that it should originate from the author."[2]

[11.03] The limited scope of the concept of an original work can be illustrated by comparing the position of a person who creates a poem with that of a literary

---

1. *Donaldson v Beckett* (1774) 4 Burr 2408; *Rooney v Kelly* (1861) 14 Ir CL Rep 158.
2. [1916] 2 Ch 601 at 608-9.

editor who compiles an anthology of poems written and already published. In the former case copyright will be afforded to the poem if it has not been copied, or substantially copied, from the work of another person. It, as a piece of poetry, is original. However, in the latter case the anthology is derivative but may nevertheless be original, as an anthology, providing that such a compilation is not based upon some pre-existing work of compilation; some degree of skill, discretion or choice must have been exercised in selecting the items to be included in the anthology. The issue of originality, specifically whether there has been an exercise of labour, judgment or skill in the production of a work, arises most often in relation to compilations. In the leading case of *MacMillan & Co Ltd v K & J Cooper*,[3] the Privy Council observed that issues of this kind cannot be defined in precise terms and that the outcome in each case will depend largely on the facts of that case. However, the Privy Council there held that when the defendants edited or abridged the plaintiff's copyright work, North's translation of Plutarch's *Life of Alexander*, by leaving out the unimportant bits and deleting those parts of the work that were seen as verbiage, this was not of itself an act of creation. An original work, to exist, should demonstrate the exercise of skill or judgment; it should be an act of individuality. Even where a work is based upon a pre-existing literary work, the skill exercised in re-drafting, re-phrasing or reformatting the existing work may nevertheless involve sufficient skill or judgment so as to make the resulting work original.[4] The presentation of commonplace or prosaic kinds of factual material is sometimes denied copyright protection on the grounds of lack of originality, although these situations may just as conveniently be attributed to the non-literary quality of the work under review. The essential issue is whether the person who claims copyright has independently created the literary work or merely copied the efforts of others. A calligrapher who produces an ornamental piece of poetry by reference to a typed manuscript produced by a poet does not create an original literary work;[5] the only literary work in such a context remains the typed manuscript produced by the poet.

[11.04] The limited nature of the originality standard is in part due to the tendency of common law systems to provide copyright protection for creations which cannot be described as intellectually or culturally meritorious. The investment made in terms of time and effort is seen as worthy of protection because of the fact that the appropriation of another person's work cannot be satisfactorily addressed through traditional routes such as the criminal law[6] or

---

3. (1923) 93 LJPC 113.
4. *Express Newspapers v News UK* [1990] 3 All ER 376. There may still be an infringement of copyright in the original. *Ibid.*
5. Is it a work of artistic craftsmanship?
6. Intangibles cannot be stolen: See Clark, 'Computer Crime in Ireland' (1994) 2 Eur J Crime Cr L Cr J 252, at 257.

tort - Irish law does not recognise a tort of unfair competition,[7] for example. The minimalist nature of the originality test, however, does contrast with that standard found in civilian jurisdictions and it may be that, in the context of purely factual works, the originality standard in US law may be more demanding, but even in the English courts, the judges have stressed that it is not enough to confer the quality of originality on a work to show that labour and skill was expended in the process of copying or embellishing some pre-existing work.[8] Some independent product must be evident even if the source of the independent product is identifiable.[9]

LITERARY WORK

[11.05] Again the leading case is *University of London Press Ltd v University Tutorial Press Ltd* where Petersen J said:

> "In my view, the words 'literary work' cover work which is expressed in print or writing, irrespective of the question whether the quality or style is high. The word 'literary' seems to be used in a sense somewhat similar to the use of the word 'literature' in political or electioneering literature and refers to written or printed matter."[10]

This view of the meaning of 'literary' was gathered from the long line of cases under the 1842 Act. In Irish law the decision of Petersen J, while far from being binding upon Irish judges either before or after the foundation of the State, has been cited with approval in the few cases in which the interpretation of the phrase 'literary work' has arisen. In developing the concept of literary as distinct from non-literary works, the English judgments have stressed that a literary work should convey, in the words of the Court of Appeal in the *Exxon* case,[11] "information, instruction or pleasure."

[11.06] The broad view taken of the concept of a literary work is no doubt explained by the concern of the judiciary to protect the effort and investment made by the putative copyrightholder when others seek to take a free ride on the back of those efforts or investment. However is it not essential to show that the literary work has a commercial value. In a recent Canadian case the author of a learned treatise on the Old West successfully claimed for copyright infringement when parts of the thesis were used by the writer of a popular book

---

[7.] But see the Competition Act 1991.

[8.] *Per* Lord Oliver in *Interlego AG v Tyco Industries* [1988] 3 All ER 949, at 971.

[9.] *Ladbroke (Football) Ltd v William Hill (Football) Ltd* [1964] 1 WLR 273; *Fortuity Property Ltd v Barcza* (1995) 32 IPR 517. For a recent spirited defence of originality in copyright, see Lea [1996] Ent LR 21.

[10.] [1916] 2 Ch 601 at 608.

[11.] *Exxon Corp v Exxon Insurance Consultants International Ltd* [1981] 3 All ER 241; In Canada *British Columbia v Mihaljevic* (1991) 36 CPR (3d) 445.

on Canadian farming history. The fact that the thesis itself was not commercially exploitable did not preclude the plaintiff from asserting copyright in his work.[12] Other works that one would readily recognise as being literary efforts include the novels of Laurie Lee and the plays of Shaw, the letters of Swift and Pope, translated and annotated works of Plutarch, a John Osborne film script, and a learned scholar's annotation of an ancient Sanskrit text or the dead sea scrolls.[13] However, in the *University of London Press* case, Petersen J emphasised that the word literary was not to be interpreted "in the sense in which that phrase is applied, for instance, to Meredith's novels and the writings of Robert Louis Stevenson", and for this reason the efforts of newspaper reporters who file copy for an evening newspaper on the mundane proceedings of Dublin Criminal Courts,[14] the life of sporting celebrities,[15] or the British Royal family,[16] are considered to be literary works. The early Irish case of *Hodges v Walsh*[17] holds that law digests and reports are copyright protected[18] as literary works and a lawyer's precedents are also literary works.[19] Letters are literary works, regardless of the identity of the writer, and persons who write down a public speech or address, whether in long hand or shorthand, acquire a copyright in the document thus created, whether the speech is delivered in a perfect or garbled fashion, or the person taking down the speech demonstrates an ability to turn a halting or disjointed address into fluid prose or converts a flowing and coherent verbal presentation into a poorly constructed written format.[20]

[11.07] Judicial decisions have protected commercial documents that cannot be said to have any literary quality, in the popular sense of that phrase. Descriptive advertisements,[21] trade circulars and handbills,[22] consignment notes,[23] booksellers and pharmacists' catalogues,[24] have all been held to be literary works. Maps and charts,[25] telegraphic codes devised to assist in transmitting

---

12. *Breen v Hancock House Publishers Ltd* (1985) 6 CPR (3d) 433.
13. *Kimron v Herschel Shanks* [1993] EIPR D-151.
14. *Hall v Crosbie* (1931) 66 ICTR 22.
15. *Donoghue v Allied Newspapers* [1938] 1 Ch 106.
16. *Express Newspapers v News UK* [1990] 3 All ER 376.
17. (1840) 2 IR Eq R 266.
18. *Sweet v Benning* (1855) 16 CB 459; *Butterworth v Robinson* (1801) 5 Ves 709; *Saunders v Smith* (1838) 3 Myl & C 711.
19. *Co-Operative Union Ltd v Kilmore Dairy Society Ltd* (1912) 47 ILTR 7.
20. *Walter v Lane* [1900] AC 539.
21. *Maple v Junior Army and Navy Stores* (1882) 21 Ch D 369; *Slumber Magic Co v Sleep King Bed Co* (1984) 3 CPR (3d) 81.
22. *Native Guano Co Ltd v Sewage Manure Co* (1889) 8 RPC 125; *Lamb v Evans* [1893] 1 Ch 218; *Comyns v Hyde* [1895] 72 LT 250.
23. *Van Oppen & Co Ltd v Van Oppen* (1903) 20 RPC 617.
24. *Collis v Cater* (1898) 78 LT 613; *Andrew Cash & Co v Porter* (1996) 36 IPR 309 (pawnbroker's ticket).
25. *Stannard v Lee* (1870) 6 Ch App 346; *Carey v Fadin* (1799) 6 Ves 24.

telegraph messages,[26] railway guides and road guides,[27] football coupons,[28] lists of football fixtures and racing cards,[29] as well as radio and television listings,[30] are works which warrant copyright protection as long as an adequate level of skill or effort can be said to have gone into the production of that product.

[11.08] If there is insufficient skill or effort then the work will not be held to be literary. The unintelligible scribblings of a man executed whilst in a state of intoxication are not literary works, presumably because there was no information, entertainment or enjoyment conveyed by such a 'message'.[31] In the early case of *Bailey v Taylor*[32] copyright protection for annuity tables was denied on the ground that these tables could have been calculated by a competent person in a matter of hours. Similarly, in *Page v Wisden*[33] a scoring sheet drawn up to record the scores in cricket matches was denied copyright protection because the format employed was commonplace and merely mathematical in nature.

[11.09] Even when the work is of its nature derivative, there can be copyright protection for such compilations. Most maps, anthologies, annotations, abridgements, translations and written transcriptions of a verbal address are nevertheless the subject of copyright protection in appropriate instances.

[11.10] The necessary skill, labour and judgment will include both the skill, labour and judgment necessary to create the literary document but also the necessary skill, labour and judgment to create a document that has commercial value or integrity. In *RTE and Others v Magill TV Guide*[34] Lardner J said:

> "I am satisfied that each weekly schedule is the result of a great deal of preliminary consideration and work and of the exercise of skill and judgment. It is the creation of RTE ... the pattern and order in which the various programmes in each week are to be broadcast is determined by RTE - a determination which I am satisfied involves the exercise of skill and judgment."

[26.] *Ager v Peninsula & Oriental Steam Navigation Co* (1884) 26 Ch D 639; *Anderson & Co v Lieber Code Co* (1917) 33 TLR 420.

[27.] *Kelly v Byles* (1879) 13 Ch D 682; *Leslie v Young* [1894] AC 335.

[28.] *Ladbroke (Football) Ltd v William Hill (Football) Ltd* [1964] 1 WLR 273.

[29.] *Canterbury Park Race Course Co v Hopkins* (1932) 49 NSWWN 27; Selections or forecasts are not copyright protected: *Chilton v Progress Printing* (1894) 71 LT 664; *Bookmakers Afternoon Greyhound Services Ltd v Wilf Gilbert* [1994] FSR 723.

[30.] *RTE and Others v Magill TV Guide* [1990] ILRM 534.

[31.] *Fournet v Pearson Ltd* (1897) 14 TLR 82.

[32.] (1829) 3 LJ (OS) Ch 66. This seems to be wrongly decided.

[33.] (1869) 20 LT 435; *Kalamazoo (Aust) Ltd v Compact Business Systems Ltd* (1985) 5 IPR 213 suggests the test is one based upon whether the work is 'substantial'.

[34.] [1990] ILRM 534. Contrast facts *per se*: *Victoria Park Racing & Recreation Grounds Co v Taylor* (1937) 58 CLR 479.

[11.11] In *Football League Ltd v Littlewood Pools Ltd*,[35] Upjohn J considered that the considerable skill and judgment applied in ensuring that matches did not clash with local holidays, with other sporting events, and met the wishes of each Football League Club, whenever possible, meant that such skill and judgment, when coupled with the lesser task of transcribing the decision on when each match was to take place, was such as to satisfy the 'literary work' concept. More recently, the complex task of calculating betting odds, as part of a pools or computerised gaming activity,[36] has been held to satisfy the "skill, labour and judgment" requirement. Many of the cases in which the element of "skill, labour and judgment" has been missing involve the compilation of works from pre-existing sources, the works in question possessing a factual element. In *Leslie v Young*[37] the House of Lords held that the publication of railway timetables by the respondent, the timetables in question having been previously published by the appellant, was not an infringement of the appellant's copyright in these tables because the common source of each table was the railway company timetable - no independent work of significance had been done by either party. However, when the appellants had further processed information about railway journeys so as to compile a separate list of tours, this useful abridgement of information could be regarded as an independent literary work. The compilation of existing facts into a systematic course of instruction, for example, by adopting some kind of question and answer format, was held to be copyright protected, although the format is not the subject of a copyright in itself.[38] In the Canadian case of *Horn Abbot Ltd v WB Coulter Sales Ltd*[39] the plaintiffs sought to protect their board game, 'Trivial Pursuit' from being substantially reproduced. The court was at pains to point out that a question and answer board game could not be protected as such, but because the defendants had produced their own product in a short period of time and because there was a substantial similarity in relation to the nearly 5,000 questions and answers, an inference of copying could certainly be drawn.

[11.12] Sometimes copyright protection is denied on the ground that the plaintiff is seeking to protect information obtainable from common sources, the form in which the information is held by the plaintiff being of secondary importance. In *Odham's Press Ltd v London and Provincial Sporting News Agency (1929) Ltd*[40] the plaintiffs employed at race meetings two persons to transmit by

---

35. [1950] Ch 637.
36. *BC Jockey Club v Standen* (1985) 8 CPR (3d) 283.
37. [1894] AC 335.
38. *Jarrold v Houlston* (1857) 3 Kay & J 708.
39. (1984) 77 CPR (2d) 145.
40. [1939] 1 Ch 673. See also *Victoria Park Racing & Recreation Grounds Co v Taylor* (1937) 58 CLR 479.

telephone to the plaintiffs the starting prices of the three placed horses. Information was obtained from bookmakers, from 'tic tac' men and other trade sources. However, the only written account of this exercise was a notebook which was clearly not a detailed or systematic record of the research undertaken for the plaintiffs - Eve J clearly viewed the entry as a random jotting in the nature of an *aide memoir*. In *GA Cramp & Sons Ltd v Frank Smythson Ltd*[41] the plaintiffs' claimed that when the defendants reproduced in their 1942 diary some seven tables of factual material, taken from the plaintiffs' 1933 diary, there was an infringement of the plaintiffs' copyright. The House of Lords, overruling a majority judgment of the Court of Appeal held that there was no copyright held by the plaintiffs in these seven tables as a compilation. There was no proof that each table had been compiled by the plaintiff - indeed the tables were common place factual tables produced by organisations like the Post Office and the Automobile Association - and their lordships found that tables of this kind were commonplace in diaries of this kind. The selection of these seven timetables was said by Lord MacMillan to be a collection "of an obvious and commonplace character and I fail to detect any meritorious distinctness in it."

TITLES, SLOGANS AND WORDS AS LITERARY WORKS

[11.13] It is difficult to obtain copyright protection for the title of a book, a song, an advertising slogan or word. In certain instances, a word or phrase may be a registered trade mark and in such a case the use of the word or phrase may give rise to a remedy for the proprietor of the mark.[42] Similarly, the law of passing off may give protection when the name or phrase is used in connection with goods or services in a misleading manner.[43] In principle, however, a short poem or a part of a larger work, such as the title or chorus line of a song can be copyright protected as an original literary work if the work is original and has sufficient definition to be regarded as a work. In *Francis Day and Hunter Ltd v Twentieth Century Fox Corp Ltd*[44] the Privy Council held that the use of the phrase, "The man who broke the Bank at Monte Carlo" as the title of a feature film did not infringe the plaintiff's copyright in a song which bore that phrase as its title. The words of the song title were "too insubstantial" to attract copyright, *qua* title. In

---

41. [1944] AC 329.
42. "High Life", *Miller Brewing Co v The Controller* [1988] ILRM 259. "Bubble Up", *Seven Up Co v Bubble Up Co* [1990] ILRM 204.
43. *Valentine v Valentine* (1892) 31 LR Ir 488. The use of a title and other colourable imitations of another's work are protected under *Mack v Petter* (1872) LR 14 Eq 431; *Kelly v Byles* (1879) 13 Ch D 682, distinguishing *Metzler v Wood* (1878) 8 Ch 606 and *Croft v Day* (1843) 7 Beav 84. Stone [1996] 7 Ent LR 178, 263, in two interesting articles considers both the copyright and passing off reliefs available for titles character names and catch-phrases.
44. [1940] AC 112.

the recent case of *Canadian Olympic Association v Konica Canada Ltd*[45] the Canadian Federal Court of Appeal held that the phrase "Guinness Book of Olympic Records" was also not copyright protected and the infringement point was a *fortiori* within the "Man who broke the Bank at Monte Carlo" case.

[11.14] The balance of recent judicial authority in England favours the view that the selection of a title for a book from common phrases, or everyday words, cannot be regarded as exercising sufficient skill and judgment to warrant being held to be literary. In *Dicks v Yates*[46] the plaintiffs, assignees of copyright in a novel entitled 'Splendid Misery' which the plaintiff serialised in a weekly periodical. The defendant also published a serial entitled 'Splendid Misery'. Jessel MR held that these works are common English words and their combination produced was hackneyed, given that an earlier writer had used just this phrase in 1801 for the title of a novel. Nevertheless, should a combination of words be devised which is neither commonplace or hackneyed, it is in law still possible to argue that copyright in that title may subsist. A central issue is the skill and judgment exercised in selecting the title in question rather than the time skill or judgment exercised in reducing it into written form which will be minimal. *McIndoo v Musson Book Co*[47] a decision of the Ontario Court of Appeal leaves this point open for while the Court held that copyright cannot subsist for a book title *simpliciter*, it may be that if the author can demonstrate that the title amounts to a literary, scientific or artistic composition, protection will be available. It is conceivable therefore that if the author demonstrates originality, or skill, or effort, copyright protection may be available to a title.

[11.15] Where the claim is brought in respect of a short phrase, whether it be to convey information[48] or advertise some product[49] copyright protection is generally denied. In *Sinanide v La Maison Kosmeo*[50] the plaintiff, a beauty therapist, claimed copyright in a phrase, namely, that beauty was "a social necessity, not a luxury". The defendant later advertised his own beauty treatments with advertisements proclaiming that "a youthful appearance is a social necessity". While the case can be regarded as turning upon evidence that prior to the plaintiff's use of his phrase, a similar phrase had been constructed by

---

45. (1991) 24 IPR (3d) 216.
46. (1881) 18 Ch 76. See also *Licensed Victuallers Newspaper Co v Bingham* (1888) 38 Ch 139. The earlier case of *Weldon v Dicks* (1878) Ch 247 seems incompatible with these decisions.
47. (1916) 26 DLR 550. The point was also left open in the recent Scottish case involving reproduction of newspaper headlines on an Internet site: *Shetland Times v Jonathan Wills, The Times* 21 January 1997; Ward [1997] CLSR 123.
48. *Page v Wisden* (1869) 20 LT 435.
49. On what product is being advertised - see *Canadian Olympic Association v Konica Canadian Inc* (1991) 24 IPR 216.
50. (1928) 44 TLR 574; *Rose v Information Services* [1987] FSR 254.

yet another beautician (thus bringing the plaintiff's phrase within the notion of a commonplace or hackneyed expression and *Dicks v Yates*) Scrutton LJ went further and observed that in the absence of a passing off or trade mark action, the quotation of a bit of a sentence is too small a matter to afford a ground for a copyright infringement action; in other words, the basis of this part of the judgment is that quotation of a tiny portion of a literary work, here, the advertisement as a whole, is not substantial reproduction. The case is suspect, not least because Scrutton LJ regarded both the professional involved and the dispute as unmeritorious,[51] but because all the Court of Appeal decided was that this phrase was not original, nor had sufficient of the phrase been reproduced so as to constitute substantial reproduction of it, it clearly cannot be relied upon in an age when millions of pounds are apparently spent devising advertising slogans and phrases which cannot be considered to be hackneyed or commonplace, and which clearly serve to identify the advertiser's product or service.[52]

[11.16] Where the issue descends into the area of single words, whether they be ordinary words in English or some other language, or invented words, the balance of decided case law is against the word being copyright protected. In the *Wombles*[53] and *Kojak*[54] litigation the issue was regarded as being whether a proprietary right could exist in a word, whether actual or invented and in both instances the same judge answered the question in the negative. While it is understandable that the courts should be wary about extending property rights over parts of the language, this does not appear to be at all powerful when the word is invented, has been the subject of skill, judgment, investment or expertise in devising or selecting the word in circumstances where it can be concluded that an original literary work has been devised. Nevertheless, in *Exxon Corporation & Others v Exxon Insurance Consultants International Ltd*[55] the Court of Appeal regarded the word 'Exxon' as incapable of being itself an original literary work for, as an invented word, it by itself, divorced from the context of a supply of goods or services, did not convey information, instruction or pleasure.[56] While Stephenson LJ was not prepared to rule that an invented word could never of itself be an original literary work, Oliver LJ and Sir David Cairns expressed no opinion on this question. Elsewhere, the view in Canada seems to be that the words 'Expo' and 'Expo 86' whether they be regarded as a

---

[51.] See the opening passage of the Lord Justice's judgment at (1928) 44 TLR 574, 575.

[52.] *Cf Native Guano Co Ltd v Sewage Manure Co* (1889) 8 RPC 125.

[53.] *Wombles Ltd v Wombles Skips Ltd* [1975] FSR 488.

[54.] *Taverner Rutledge Ltd v Trexapalm Ltd* [1975] FSR 479.

[55.] [1981] 3 All ER 241.

[56.] Following Davey LJ in *Hollinrake v Truswell* [1894] 3 Ch 420 at 428; See Stephenson LJ at 248b, Oliver LJ at 249e.

single word, a name or a title of an event, are not copyright protected.[57] *Cullabine*, in his review of South African law noted that the scant case law in that jurisdiction meant the point was still open.[58] In England the recent decision of Laddie J in *In re Application by Elvis Presley Enterprises Inc*,[59] although essentially a trade mark apposition action, inclines towards rejecting the view that names are not in themselves distinctive or original.

[11.17] The only recent sign of the issue of whether an invented word may be able to obtain copyright protection comes as an *obiter dictum* in the *Ninja Turtles* case[60] where Browne-Wilkinson VC expressed the view that he saw no reason why such a word could not, in appropriate circumstances, be regarded as an original literary work. An Irish court has yet to address the point and the decision in *Reed v O'Meara*[61] which gave the plaintiffs a right to exclusivity in the use of the title 'The Grocer' would probably be regarded as a passing off rather than a purely copyright decision. The disgruntled novelist who finds that another writer has purloined a title must utilise passing off or rely instead on the substantive law of copyright infringement where the lifting of a plot or scenario constitutes copyright infringement in the work,[62] even if a different title is used. The use of a title to advertise a novel or play that does not bear any relationship with an earlier work - only the title, not the plot is copied - appears not to give the author of the first title any obvious remedy in copyright. If the word or phrase, however, appears in a distinctive form then protection of the stylised format may be available via artistic copyright.[63]

WHAT IS NOT AN ORIGINAL LITERARY WORK

[11.18] In the *Exxon* case[64] the Court of Appeal re-emphasised the notion that an original literary work must be able to convey information, instruction or pleasure. To this must be added the refinement that for the work to be literary it must be contained in print or writing.[65] The phrase must be regarded as

---

[57.] *British Columbia v Mihaljevic et al* (1991) 36 CPR (3d) 445.

[58.] [1992] 6 EIPR 205 at 210.

[59.] *The Times* 25 March 1997.

[60.] *Mirage Studios v Counter Feat Clothing* [1991] FSR 145.

[61.] (1888) 21 LR (Ir) 216; *Chappell v Sheard* (1855) 2 K & J 117.

[62.] *Correlli v Gray* (1913) 30 TLR 116; *Zeccola v Universal City Studios* (1982) 46 ALR 189.

[63.] *Paramount Pictures Corp v Howley* (1991) 39 CPR (3d) 419.

[64.] [1981] 3 All ER 241 at pp 248 and 249. *Kalamazoo (Aust) Ltd v Compact Business Systems Ltd* (1985) 5 IPR 213.

[65.] *Per* Petersen J in *University of London Press Ltd v University Tutorial Press* [1916] 2 Ch 601 at 608.

essentially composite in nature[66] but there are elements of the phrase that can be divided up.

[11.19] In *Hollinrake v Truswell*[67] copyright protection as a literary work was denied to a cardboard arm to be used as an aid to dressmaking. In *Libraco (Limited) v Shaw Walker (Limited)*[68] a system of colour coding a card index system was denied literary copyright on the ground that the cards merely gathered information under rubrics such as name and address. Copyright in a system of teaching by the use of sets of coloured rods was denied in the Canadian case of *Cuisenaire v South West Imports Ltd*,[69] a distinction being drawn between an explanatory book which could be copyright and the means of implementation which was in essence an idea. Shadow cards or silhouettes were denied literary copyright on the basis that such card was merely 'a child's toy',[70] while a Christmas card could be copyright protected via literary copyright in respect of the verse or sentiment therein.[71] The fact that a document contains or conveys information, instruction or pleasure does not guarantee the document the status of an original literary work if the document conveys such information or instruction in the only form in which that idea is capable of expression.[72] The requirement that a literary work must be held in the form of print or writing has caused difficulties for many judges when the issue of copying information held in electronic form has arisen. In the leading case of *Computer Edge Property v Apple Computer*[73] the majority of the High Court of Australia found that machine readable information held by a computer in object code could not be the subject of copyright protection because such information is not perceivable by human facilities - it conveys information to the machine when held in object code. However, the printed output of a computer program can be a literary work. In such a case the work is created by the computer programmer rather than the computer.[74] The status of a database compiled and held only in electronic from (CD-ROM) for example, is currently uncertain in Irish law for the same reason. These subjects, protection of computer programs and electronic databases, are treated separately in this work.

[66.] *Per* Oliver LJ in *Exxon, ibid.*
[67.] [1894] 3 Ch 420; *Davis v Comitti* (1885) 52 LT 539.
[68.] (1913) 30 TLR 22.
[69.] [1969] SCR 208; Contrast *Church v Linton* (1894) 25 OR 131.
[70.] *Cable v Marks* (1882) 47 LT 432.
[71.] *Hildesheimer & Faulkner v Dunn & Co* (1891) 64 LT 452.
[72.] *Kenrick v Lawrence* (1890) 25 QBD 93.
[73.] [1986] FSR 537.
[74.] *Express Newspapers v Liverpool Daily Post* [1985] FSR 306.

COMPILATIONS

[11.20] The otherwise unhelpful definition of literary work in s 2 of the 1963 Act declares that the concept 'includes any ... compilation'. The section therefore makes it clear that existing forms of literary work, when in printed or written form, may be selected or arranged in such a way as to obtain a separate copyright for the compiler or arranger if sufficient skill or judgment can be shown to exist in relation to the selection or presentation of the compilation. This is difficult to establish in relation to factual material such as tables of tides or postal charges[75] or railway timetables[76] gleaned from one central source which must be correct if they are to be of any value. The selection of factual information such as a person's name and address for inclusion in telephone, trade, professional or street directories has long been protected in the English courts, partly because these older cases tended to overlook the originality requirement which was an implicit requirement in the early statutory regimes. In contrast, however, the US Supreme Court[77] has recently ruled that purely factual data compiled by a telephone company about its subscribers and arranged in alphabetical form lacked the modicum of originality necessary to satisfy the US originality element. While the Supreme Court indicated that most compilations would easily pass such a test, there is some support for the view that the English courts may have to re-assess these directory decisions if skill and judgment, rather than the expenditure of money and effort in creating a compilation is to be the standard for copyright protection, particularly in a contemporary context where much of the labour and donkey work in producing such factual or data rich compilations can be organised by way of information technology.

[11.21] There is, of course, a requirement that any compilation of facts should pass an originality test because the idea/expression dichotomy would be nonsensical if one fact is not copyrightable but a grouping of 60 facts could be copyrightable. Predictable compilations, to be anticipated in the context in which the compilation is put, lack such originality.[78]

[11.22] Where the material selected or arranged is not overtly factual[79] then there will be greater room for the exercise of skill, judgment, taste or some subjective (and thus individualistic) criteria - eg the compiler's 50 favourite poems on the theme of love or beauty. So a compilation of tables of football matches, grouped in such a way as to allow punters to place bets on the outcome

---

75. *Cramp (GA) & Sons v Frank Smythson Ltd* [1944] AC 329.
76. *Leslie v Young* [1894] AC 335.
77. *Feist Publications v Rural Telephone Service* (1991) 20 IPR 129. See note by Ginsberg (1992) 92 Col LR 338. *Feist* has also been followed in Canada. This is fully discussed at para **[14.03]**.
78. *Cramp v Smythson, ibid.*
79. Eg *Slumber Magic Co v Sleep King Bed* (1984) 3 CPR (3d) 81.

of matches, was held to be an original work of compilation because the skill, judgment and labour exercised in selecting the bets could not be separated from the, admittedly, less meritorious, effort expended in putting this onto paper.[80]

[11.23] A similar procedure is found in relation to television programme listings. The argument that a television company that compiles a list of programmes to be shown cannot acquire a copyright in information or a mere listing, has been met by the argument that the skill and effort spent in devising a suitable schedule of programmes cannot be separated from the expression of that process of selection.[81] However, the compiler must of course obtain any copyright clearance necessary if the compiler is not also to be an infringer. An anthology of Elizabethan love poems will be a good deal easier to produce than a compilation of similar 20th century poems for obvious reasons.

[11.24] The fact that the English and Irish standard for originality is so low reflects the concern of the courts to prevent parasitic trading, which these jurisdictions find difficult to counteract for neither unfair competition nor passing off provide relief in such a context. The European Court of First Instance in *Magill*[82] clearly thought television listings to be inappropriate matters for copyright protection by indirectly criticising the Irish originality standard and it is noteworthy that the Database Directive selects a higher originality standard than that posited in Irish law, while providing a *sui generis* protection against unfair copying by competitors; most databases, electronic or otherwise, are compilations and this twin-track approach is to be commended as being in accordance with principle, while being economically effective.

LECTURES AND PUBLIC SPEECHES

[11.25] The distinction between a lecturer or speaker to control the right to publish or disseminate in literary form the contents of the lecture or speech, and the rights of others to record the lecture or speech is set out by Lord Halsbury in *Walter v Lane*.[83] The Lord Chancellor stressed the importance of maintaining the distinction:

> "... between two very different things; one, the proprietary right of every man in his own literary composition; and the other the copyright, that is to say, the exclusive privilege of making copies created by the Statute".[84]

[80.] *Ladbroke (Football) v William Hill (Football)* [1964] 1 All ER 465.
[81.] *Independent Television Publications v Time Out* [1984] FSR 64.
[82.] *RTE v Commission* [1991] 4 CMLR 586. For a broader European view, see Dreier & Karnell (1992) J Copyright Society of the USA 289.
[83.] [1900] AC 539.
[84.] [1900] AC 539 at 547.

[11.26] The proprietary right to control the public dissemination of one's own literary composition is generally controlled by common law principles.[85] The university professor who provides unpublished lectures to students gives the student the right to take notes of the lecture for study purposes, but in the absence of any implied contract, the student does not acquire a right to publish the lecture, whether the publication be a record of the lecture taken verbatim in perfect shorthand[86] or in garbled form.[87] In this context the right of the lecturer or speaker to exercise this proprietary right does not appear to depend on whether the lecture is delivered from notes or memory or extemporaneously.[88] However, when a lecture or speech is delivered any person who records the speech, regardless of the question of the accuracy of the record, acquires copyright in that report, so that if there should be a number of persons who take down an account of a speech in written form (eg journalists at a press conference) the journalist and not the speaker is the author of the written account even if it be a word for word transcription of the words spoken.[89] The skill, labour and expense incurred in transcribing the speech of another is sufficient to provide the writer with copyright in this work.[90] *Walter v Lane* was decided before UK copyright law contained an originality requirement and some doubt has been cast on the decision in *Walter v Lane* when the reporter transcribes an oral statement without embellishment or reorganisation of the speech,[91] and there is also some doubt about whether the decision in *Walter v Lane* would extend to a case where the speaker had written out the speech prior to it delivery and the speech was delivered from the written text or from memory.[92] The UK Copyright Designs and Patents Act 1988, s 3 now makes provision for copyright to subsist in spoken words, once those words have been recorded, this new copyright subsisting in the speaker, regardless of the question whether a separate copyright subsists in the written record itself. This represents an affirmation of *Walter v Lane* by the UK Parliament but still leaves open the relevance of the originality test in the context of written accounts of speeches.

[11.27] Where, however, a person is engaged to produce a written account of spoken words (eg an audio typist or stenographer) the copyright is held by the

---

85. *Abernethy v Hutchinson* (1825) 1 H & Tw 28.
86. *Nichols v Pitman* (1884) 24 Ch 274.
87. *Caird v Sime* (1887) 12 App Cas 327.
88. *Ibid*; *Gould Estate v Stoddart Publishing* (1996) 30 OR (3d) 520.
89. *Walter v Lane* [1900] AC 539.
90. *Per* Lord Davey [1900] AC 539 at 552.
91. *Robertson v Lewis* [1976] RPC 169.
92. *Ibid*.

speaker, the person transcribing this oral statement being regarded as an amanuensis.[93]

FORMATS

[11.28] The possibility that copyright may be used to protect ideas or the outlines that go into producing a literary or dramatic work - the formula or format for a show or entertainment - was addressed in *Green v Broadcasting Corporation of New Zealand*.[94] The broadcaster Hughie Green sued the defendants who replicated the *Opportunity Knocks* talent show. Evidence before the New Zealand courts and Privy Council established that, while a skeletal 'script' existed in the shape of the title, catch phrases and set methods of evaluating the performers, this structure for presenting a series of ever changing performance could both be described as either a literary or a dramatic work. This, however, is a matter of degree for once an idea finds a sufficient level of expression, the copying of that expression will infringe copyright but the degree of character development in a script is vital and if the program, or character, lacks distinctiveness[95] as in *Preston v 20th Century Fox Canada Ltd*[96] the claim will fail. Some show formats such as the radio programme *Desert Island Discs* clearly have sufficient originality and precision of form to merit copyright protection and show formats are franchised out, a practice which reflects the existence of rights in the devisor.[97]

DRAMATIC WORKS

[11.29] Again, the Copyright Act 1963 is somewhat unhelpful in terms of defining copyright works: s 2 provides that the phrase "includes a choreographic work or entertainment in dumb show if reduced to writing in the form in which the work or entertainment is to be presented"; film scripts and film scenarios are likewise included. Again, protection is based upon reducing the work into a protectable form; the introduction to a pantomime which was the only written part of the drama was protected as a dramatic work.[98] The question of distinguishing a dramatic work from a literary or musical work has arisen from time to time and the weight of precedent suggests that the presentation of a work with dramatic scenery or dramatic effect is an essential element: *Fuller v*

[93.] *Cummins v Bond* [1927] 1 Ch 167.

[94.] [1989] 2 All ER 1056.

[95.] *Hutton v CBC* (1992) 120 AR 291 (generic rock show; no copying); *Wilson v Broadcasting Corporation of New Zealand* [1990] 2 NZLR 565 shows each case turns on its own facts.

[96.] (1990) 33 CPR (3d) 242.

[97.] For recent UK debate, see McD Bridge & Lane [1996] Ent L Rev 212.

[98.] *Lee v Simpson* (1844) 3 CB 871.

Blackpool Winter Gardens.[99] More recently Lord Bridge in *Green v Broadcasting Corporation of New Zealand*[100] distinguished the literary nature of a script from its existence as a dramatic work. So the dramatic work must be capable of performance in the sense that elements such as music, movement, scenery, lighting and declaration *may* coalesce; of these elements movement seems to be the crucial element. So Beckett's *Waiting for Godot* is certainly a dramatic work while *Not I* may not be.[101]

[11.30] Problems of definition tend not to occupy the attention of the courts as distinct from the issue of authorship. The theatre owner or impresario that suggests a theme or plot to an author is not likely to be held to be an author or co-author of a dramatic work for the basic test is whether there is some pre-conceived plan to create joint work from separate contributions a 'joint' labouring under a common design".[102] The provision of some lines or scrutiny of the text written by an author following upon suggestions made will not suffice. It is essential that there be a substantial contribution to forming the written dialogue *qua* author, rather than *qua* muse,[103] critic[104] or editor.[105] Nor will the making of alterations to a settled text make the person making the alterations a joint author: *Shelley v Ross.*[106]

MUSICAL WORKS

[11.31] The Irish Act of 1963 does not define a musical work, although the 1988 UK legislation defines a musical work as "a work consisting of music, exclusive of any words or action intended to be sung, spoken or performed with the music".[107] Words are protected via literary copyright while the action or gestures which are to accompany the music are protected as dramatic works. Protection of musical works against reproduction under the Statute of Anne was established in 1777,[108] and works that consisted of music and lyrics written by two distinct persons involved two separate copyrights. The addition of lyrics to

---

99. [1895] 2 QB 429; Contrast *Russell v Smith* (1848) 12 QB 217.
100. [1989] 2 All ER 1056 at 1059.
101. 'The Complete Dramatic Works' (1986, Faber & Faber). There is some debate about whether Brian Friel's work, *Molly Sweeney* is a dramatic work at all (three characters on stools speaking with little or no movement).
102. Keating J in *Levy v Rutley* (1871) LR 6 CP 523; *Tate v Fulbrook* [1908] 1 KB 821; *Tate v Thomas* [1921] 1 Ch 503.
103. *Shepherd v Conquest* (1856) 17 CB 427.
104. *Wiseman v George Widenfield & Nicholson* [1985] FSR 525.
105. *Ashmore v Douglas Home* [1987] FSR 553.
106. (1871) LR 6 CP 53.
107. Copyright Designs and Patents Act 1988, s 3(1).
108. *Bach v Longman* (1777) Cowp 623. A performing right was added in the 1842 Act.

an old, public domain tune or air may create a copyright in the air and accompaniment.[109] The addition of new elements may create a copyright in the product[110] but it is necessary to note that many 'arrangement' or 'adaptation' copyrights claimed may lack the necessary originality element to sustain a copyright. Further, the unauthorised use of an existing musical work will constitute an infringement of the original[111] in practice digital sampling of existing works will be a copyright infringement as long as there is a sufficient amount of the original work used to amount to a substantial taking.[112] Short snatches of a tune or a musical jingle are capable of being copyright protected.[113]

ARTISTIC WORKS

[11.32] The boundary between copyright protection for artistic works, and the related protection for functional items that possess eye appeal, bedevils the law of copyright, particularly when we consider the fact that the Oireachtas has not addressed the policy issues raised herein except on an *ad hoc* basis in the 1987 Copyright Act. The legislation directs that in some instances, aesthetic qualities are irrelevant to the availability of protection and even where it is clear that aesthetic judgments are pertinent there are no compelling parliamentary or judicial statements that allow us to predict whether certain works are going to be protected or not.

[11.33] Protection for artistic works in s 9(2) of the Copyright Act 1963 is available only if it is an original artistic work; this means that the work must have been independently created and not copied from some pre-existing work.[114] The level of skill or artistry needed to execute the work is not uniformly drawn in the Act. Protection is available if the work falls into one of three categories as long as it possesses a physical form. In *Creation Records Ltd v Newsgroup Newspapers*[115] the arrangement of objects and members of the group *Oasis* in order to produce an album cover were denied the status of an artistic physical work, the Court drawing a distinction between the physical thing photographed and the photograph of that physical subject itself.

[109.] *Leader v Purday* (1849) 7 CB 4.

[110.] *Wood v Boosey* (1868) LR 3 QB 223; *CBS Records v Gross* (1989) 15 IPR 385.

[111.] *ZYX Music v King* [1995] 3 All ER 1; *CBS Records v Gross* (1989) 15 IPR 385.

[112.] *Redwood Music v Chappell* [1982] RPC 109.

[113.] *Lawson v Dundas* Times 13 June 1985.

[114.] Lord Oliver in *Interlego v Tyco Industries* [1988] 3 All ER 949 at 976; merely mechanical efforts at creating an artistic work may not suffice: see *The Reject Shop plc v Robert Manners* [1995] FSR 870; *Alwest Neon Signs v 464460 Alberta* (1994) 58 CPR (3d) 176.

[115.] *The Times* 29 April 1997.

(a) Paintings,[116] sculptures,[117] drawings,[118] engravings[119] and photographs[120]irrespective of their artistic quality

[11.34] The fact that the level of artistic skill is not significant is illustrated from the old Irish case of *Green v Independent Newspapers and Freeman's Journal*.[121] In that case an artist named Bownass produced a 'common place' drawing of Santa Claus on a poster which was reproduced without permission in an advertisement. Walker LJ[122] said that Bownass's drawing, reproduced in an evening newspaper without consent, must be given the same treatment "as if the original drawing was by Millais and its copying by an engraving in the Art Journal".

[11.35] However, there must be an act of independent creation and the reproduction of an existing work will not suffice[123] to create an independent work, unless the transposition of the work into another form constitutes independent skill and judgment.[124] So my hastily taken wedding snaps are to be viewed as copyright protected, no matter how much red eye there is, and an unauthorised reproduction will be an infringement of my copyright.[125]

[11.36] However, the protection of functional drawings as artistic works had a deleterious effect on the structural balance of intellectual property law when it

---

116. *Hanfstaengl v Empire Palace* [1894] 2 Ch 1; but not make-up on a human face: *Merchandising Corporation of America v Harpbond* [1983] FSR 32.

117. "includes any cast or model made for purposes of sculptures": s 2. *Martin v Polyplas Manufacturers Ltd* [1969] NZLR 1046 (three dimensional engravings used to make moulds for producing plastic coins). *Wham-O-Manufacturing v Lincoln Industries* [1984] 1 NZLR 641 (moulds to make frisbees); *Breville Europe v Thorn EMI Domestic* [1995] FSR 77 (plaster casts of sandwiches).

118. "includes any diagram, map, chart or plan"; s 2. Architect's drawings; *Burke v Earlsfort Centre* HC 24 February 1981; *Meikle v Maufe* [1941] 3 All ER 144. Engineering drawings; *Purefoy Engineering Ltd v Sykes Boxall* (1955) 71 RPC 227. House design and drawings; *Beazley Homes v Arrowsmith* [1978] 1 NZLR 394.

119. "includes any etching, lithograph, woodcut, print or similar work not being a photograph". Apart from fine art works this word covers items such as frisbee moulds; *Wham-O-Manufacturing Ltd v Lincoln Industries Ltd* [1984] 1 NZLR 641.

120. Defined in s 2. A single frame taken from a cinematographic film can be a photograph; *Spelling Goldberg v BPC Publishing* [1979] FSR 494. An unauthorised photograph of a physical subject is not however a reproduction of an authorised photograph: *Creation Records Ltd v News Group Newspapers*, The Times, 29 April 1997.

121. [1899] 1 IR 386.

122. *Ibid* at 396.

123. *Anvil Jewellery Ltd v Riva Ridge Holdings Ltd* [1987] 1 NZLR 35; *Krisarts v Briarfine* [1977] FSR 577.

124. *Martin v Polyplas Manufacturers Ltd* [1969] NZLR 1046.

125. See *Bauman v Fussell* (1953) [1978] RPC 485; *Warne v Genex Corp Pty Ltd* (1996) 35 IPR 284; Lupton [1988] EIPR 257.

came to be realised that items that could not be regarded as protectable *via* registered design legislation could be capable of being copyright protected, no matter how prosaic or unattractive the item was. English cases that produced such a scenario[126] were to prove influential in Ireland. In *Allibert SA v O'Connor*[127] the plaintiffs established that the defendants had infringed the plaintiff's copyright in stackable fish boxes when they imported into Ireland a product that had been copied from the plaintiff's own product. Such a legal position had deleterious effects on the right of persons to repair their own property and gave industrialists excessive protection; indeed the House of Lords was constrained to cut this gordian knot by refusing to allow a rightholder to enforce a statutory copyright on public policy grounds.[128] The Oireachtas, in s 1 of the Copyright (Amendment) Act 1987, has provided that where a design is wholly or substantially functional in nature and that design has led to the production of more than 50 identical objects, the artistic copyright protection is not to be available. This provision does not apply to architectural drawings.

(b) Works of architecture being either buildings or models for buildings

[11.37] The unauthorised construction of a facsimile of a building which is of recent construction or the use of a design model to produce a building will infringe copyright in the original building or model for as long as the building or model is within copyright. While many cases involve copying from plans, taking the main features of a building which is itself innovative in design terms may infringe copyright as long as there is a 'substantial taking' of the original building.[129] In this context the moot issue will sometimes be who is the copyright holder - it may not be the owner of the building because the commissioned work exception in s 10(3) does not cover architectural works - and it can transpire that substantial taking of design features in order to enhance an extension or addition to the original building may infringe the architect's copyright.[130]

(c) Works of artistic craftsmanship not within the preceding forms of artistic work

[11.38] This distinct category of copyright law developed from the protection afforded to fine arts works, which are protected under (a) above, when the Art

---

[126.] *Dorling v Honnor Marine* [1965] Ch 1; *LB (Plastics) Ltd v Swish Products* [1979] FSR 145.

[127.] [1981] FSR 613.

[128.] *British Leyland v Armstrong Patents* [1986] AC 577: this was done through the 'repairer' defence which is still useful: see *Green Cartridge Co (Hong Kong) Ltd v Canon* (1996) 34 IPR 614.

[129.] Eg *Beazley Homes Ltd v Arrowsmith* [1978] 1 NZLR 394; *LED Builders Ltd v Eagle Homes Pty* (1996) 35 IPR 215.

[130.] *Meikle v Maufe* [1941] 3 All ER 144.

and Crafts movement in the Nineteenth Century made it clear that items that have decorative practical or aesthetic qualities, produced by artists and craftsmen, were worthy of protection from unauthorised imitation. However, a definition of artistic craftsmanship is absent from the Act and in this context the courts have been engaged in addressing a number of complex issues. Firstly, who is to determine whether an object is a work of artistic craftsmanship? One Canadian judge has spoken for the judiciary generally when he observed that:

> "Artistic values cannot be weighted, for no universally acceptable unit or artistic weight has ever been agreed upon, nor have any so called artistic laws retained their sanctity for a protracted period of time. I think it unlikely that any legislature would be so addle-pated as to appoint the judiciary to decide whether Frank Lloyd Wright's Palladio, Pheidias, Corbusier or the plaintiff had produced buildings of artistic character or design in the sense that they are artistically good or artistically bad."[131]

[11.39] Nevertheless, it will be for the court to decide what credibility is to be given to expert testimony, public reaction to the work as well as the intention and skill of the artist in creating the work. In *George Hensher Ltd v Restawile Ltd*[132] the House of Lords indicated that the court is not to hold the plaintiff's claim to protection to be bad if a predominantly utilitarian reason is shown to explain the appeal of the item - the fusion of aesthetic beauty or 'delight'[133] in an item with its functionality is the very basis of the concept of artistic craftsmanship. Lord Simon in *Restawile* considered the protection of copyright should be established by reference to the craftsman's artistic skill and evidence on his intention; was it the craftsman's view that he was creating a work of art? While Lord Simon was later followed on this point in *Merlet v Mothercare*[134] by Walton J, one other member of the House of Lords in *Restawile* emphasised that if public opinion viewed the work as pleasing in its appearance then artistic craftsmanship can be made out.[135] This resort to popular opinion "by a show of hands or a card vote"[136] is not, it is submitted, very satisfactory and it is submitted that the 'vocational' test is a better one, even if it results in the works of Koons being afforded the same status as a Faberge egg. Stewart J in *Hay Construction Ltd v Sloan* gave the following illustration:

> "to interpret the Act properly, the tribunal should not attempt to exercise a personal aesthetic judgment but to consider the intent of the creator and its result. Suppose a man were to build himself a pig-pen garnished with fretted

---

[131] Stewart J in *Hay and Hay Construction Ltd v Sloan* (1957) 27 CPR 132.
[132] [1974] 2 All ER 248.
[133] See (1957) 47 CPR 132, at 136.
[134] [1986] RPC 115.
[135] Lord Reid in *George Hensher Ltd v Restawile Ltd, ibid.*
[136] *Per* Lord Simon *ibid* at 435.

gingerbread and with four lovely turrets, yet firm and commodious. Let it stand in its multicoloured horror a mid-Victorian blot upon the landscape. Let us assume that no contemporary could accept this edifice as anything but an architectural excrescence of the most loathsome kind, yet to its creator it would well be a thing of beauty and to its inhabitants a porcine paradise. An attempt has been made to produce *vensutas* and some originality displayed. This, in my view, is sufficient to render such building the subject matter of copyright."[137]

[11.40] The imprecision of the artistic craftsmanship notion makes it difficult to predict how an item will be judged; handprinted wallpapers, jewellery, stained glass windows will have little difficulty but items of clothing or furniture will be marginal. The *Restawile* case makes it very clear that functional items may attract registered design and artistic copyright, but when an item is mass produced or machine produced, there will be some difficulty in making out an artistic copyright claim, especially if the item is functional. While Chanel designed and produced dresses and Clarice Cliff tableware are in their finished form potential works of artistic craftsmanship, most means of production involved automation in terms of production of the work, but this should not invalidate an artistic craftsmanship copyright claim.

[11.41] This leads on to another point. If an item is produced via collaboration between two or more persons (eg a dress designer may produce the design but the finished product will only result from the work if skilled cutters and tailors are involved) can the designer still claim artistic copyright? Despite the decision in *Burke and Margot Burke Ltd v Spicers Dress Designs*[138] most of the more recent authorities answer this in the affirmative if the designer is the employer of these persons[139] and the item so produced is original.

---

137. (1957) 47 CPR 132 at 137.

138. [1936] Ch 400, doubted in *Cuisenaire v Reed* [1963] VR 719.

139. *Spyrou v Radley Gowns* [1975] FSR 455; *J Bernstein Ltd v Sidney Murray Ltd* [1981] RPC 303. *Merlet v Mothercare* [1986] RPC 115; *Thornton Hall Manufacturing v Shanton Apparel Ltd* [1989] 1 NZLR 239.

Chapter 12

Protected Works - Neighbouring Rights, State Copyright, Performers' Rights

[12.01] In theoretical terms, there is a substantial difference between Part II works and Part III works, despite the fact that the 1963 Act gives both categories of work the same status - a copyright rather than a *sui generis* civil right to sue infringers, for example. In Part III works the rightholder does not acquire the right in question by virtue of an act of authorship, unlike a novelist, dramatist, composer or artist. The Part III right will frequently arise in relation to such original works and such rights will interact with traditional Berne Convention copyrights, but Part III rights are entrepreneurial or exploitative in nature. For this reason they are often described as related rights or neighbouring rights - '*droit voisin*' in the civil law tradition. Because such rights do not exist by virtue of authorship and do not seek to ensure adequate remuneration to an author and the author's descendants, the period of protection is for a fixed period - no life of the author rule exists in relation thereto. Protection is granted to facilitate the distribution of works and ensure a reasonable prospect of remuncration to the entrepreneur.

SOUND RECORDINGS

[12.02] Copyright subsists in a sound recording[1] if the maker was a qualified person at the time the recording was made or if the sound recording was first published within the State, 'publication' in this context meaning the issuing of records embodying the recording or part thereof.[2] While a sound recording is defined as being the aggregate of sounds embodied in, and capable of being reproduced in, a record the definition excludes the soundtrack of a film. Sound recordings of music, speech, birdsong or the elements create a copyright that can be exploited by the maker - normally the producer in the form of a sound engineer employed by a recording company, due to either the commissioned work provision in s 17(3) or an assignment of rights.

---

1. See Boytha (1993) 24 IIC 295. This right is found in CA 1963, s 17. For a discussion of the nature of this right see *PPI v Somers* [1993] 1 IR 202.
2. CA 1963, s 17(4). Note that under the 1927 legislation copyright in mechanical contrivances was available: see 198 *Dáil Debates* Col 242 and 199 *Dáil Debates* Cols 1430-3.

[12.03] The definitions of 'record' and 'reproduction' in s 2 refer to old analogue technology, and doubts exist about whether a digital representation of sound, as distinct from an automatic reproduction of sound[3] is within these provisions. It is submitted that objections of this kind are unlikely to persuade a court to hold digital recordings to be outside s 17 but this point will be resolved in the forthcoming legislation.

FILMS

[12.04] Section 18 gives the maker of a cinematographic film a copyright, if the maker is a qualified person, or the work is first published[4] within the State. The definition of a film - a cinematographic film in the technical words used in sub-s 18(10) - is any sequence of visual images recorded on material of any description (whether translucent or not) so as to be capable, through use, of being recorded on other material so that it can be shown. This definition is very broad and raises the question whether any sequence of visual images in any medium is within the definition (eg the running of computer game).[5] A film soundtrack is outside this definition but sub-s (8) includes the sounds embodied in any soundtrack[6] associated with the film within the concept of a film. The copyright in the film is vested in the person responsible for arranging for the film to be made - the film producer and, save for rights given by the Rental and Lending Rights Directive, when implemented, the principal director of a film is not given any copyrights by Irish copyright law. The commissioned work provisions in s 18(3) allows copyright to vest in the person, legal or natural, who finances the work, unless contract resolves the issue of ownership. Protection under the Act exists for films made on or after 1 October 1964.[7] Works made before that time may be protected as dramatic works.[8]

BROADCASTS

[12.05] Copyright in any television broadcast or radio broadcast made by Radio Éireann[9] (now RTE) from within the State is to subsist as from the first making or transmission of the broadcast and copyright is vested in RTE.[10] Copyright is

---

3. See Drier (1993) 24 IIC 481.
4. See CA 1963, s 18(10).
5. *Nintendo Co Ltd v Golden China TV Game Centre* (1993) 28 IPR 313. In *Sega Enterprises v Galaxy Electronics Ltd* (1996) 35 IPR 161 an Australian court has held that computer games embodied in a semi-conductor chip can be a cinematographic film.
6. As defined in CA 1963, ss 18(11).
7. Copyright Act 1963 (Commencement) Order 1964 (SI 177/1964).
8. CA 1963, First Schedule Part II. *DPP v Irwin* High Court, unrep, 25 October 1984.
9. See Broadcasting Authority Act 1960, s 2.
10. CA 1963, ss 19(1) and (3).

not to be renewed by virtue of a repetition of a broadcast in the form of a new release of material (eg highlights of old GAA matches on video cassette).[11] The definitions of 'television broadcast' and 'sound broadcast' are extremely wide and cover satellite and terrestrial broadcasting made by RTE. Despite the liberalisation of broadcasting and the ending of the RTE monopoly in 1988 under the Radio and Television Act 1988, Irish law did not provide Irish independent broadcasters with a statutory copyright until 1991.[12] The recently implemented Term Directive serves only to extend existing copyrights rather than provide new rights where none existed before.[13] In relation to broadcasts made before 1 October 1964 no broadcast copyright exists.[14]

TYPOGRAPHICAL ARRANGEMENTS

[12.06] In relation to a published edition[15] of a literary, dramatic or musical work, which was either first published in that edition within the State, or was first published by an editor who was a qualified person at that time, a copyright exists to protect the typographical arrangement of that edition.[16] The typographical arrangement of the work relates to print type, print size, layout of a page and the placement of illustrations, for example, and the protection requires originality because no copyright exists if the edition in question reproaches the typographical arrangement of a previous edition of the same work or works.[17] The right is ceded to the publisher of that edition for 25 years for the end of the year of first publication.[18]

MISCELLANEOUS STATUTORY COPYRIGHTS

[12.07] Section 51 gives to the Government certain statutory rights in relation to literary, dramatic, musical or artistic works, sound recordings or cinematographic films which have been made by or under the control of the Government or a Minister of State. The section provides that if no copyright otherwise would exist then a copyright will exist, and in any case the Government shall be entitled to the copyright in the work.[19]

---

11. CA 1963, s 19(4) and First Schedule, Part II.
12. SI 101/1991.
13. SI 158/1995.
14. CA 1963, First Schedule, Part II. SI 177/1964.
15. See CA 1963, s 3(3) on the concept of first publication.
16. CA 1963, s 20. See *Machinery Market Ltd v Sheen Publishing Ltd* [1983] FSR 431; *Nationwide News Ltd v Copyright Agency Ltd* (1996) 34 IPR 53.
17. CA 1963, s 20(2).
18. CA 1963, ss 20(3) and (4).
19. CA 1963, s 51(1).

[12.08] The duration of copyright under this provision is fixed by the Term Directive, as implemented by SI 158/1995. So at least in relation to literary, dramatic, musical and artistic works the applicable term is fixed at the lifetime of the author and seventy years pma.[20] The sound recording and cinematographic film copyrights are similarly subject to the Term Directive for s 51(5)(b) has the effect of deeming these rights to be s 17 or 18 copyrights which are in turn amended by Articles 6 and 7 of SI 158/1995. While the statutory Government copyright can be displaced by contrary agreement[21] and while other parts of the Act apply - (eg the fair dealing defences) this section, while it has not been tested in the courts, is controversial. First, its scope is uncertain. The Government claim copyright under s 51 in a diverse range of materials including High Court judgments and Statutes, but can it truly be said that judgments and laws are prepared by or under the direction of the Government? Secondly, is it Constitutional for the State to deprive citizens of the right to access materials created from resources released by general taxation? Licensing requirements are insisted upon by the Department of Public Works if publishers seek to reproduce a wide range of Government sponsored materials but doubts must remain about this attempt by the Irish State to hang onto the last vestiges of a Crown copyright, which is under substantial attack in the United Kingdom also at the present time.[22]

PERFORMER'S RIGHTS

[12.09] The traditional copyrights given in respect of original literary, dramatic and musical works attach to the author of the work, and IMRO, the collecting society that administers the performing rights to those works, does so in favour of the author or publisher of the work. Furthermore, the Part III rights that arise in favour of the makers of a sound recording, for example, typically a recording company, are the result of economic investment or entrepeneurship. The artist responsible for interpreting and shaping the work, in terms of giving a work some kind of unique form of expression does not, as Irish law currently stands, possess any right that is an any way analogous to a statutory copyright.

[12.10] Ireland has ratified the primary International Treaty protecting performers, the Rome Convention for the Protection of Performers, Producers of Phonograms and Broadcasting Organisations of 1961, but while the two latter entities described in the title in this Convention have been afforded copyrights

---

[20.] SI 158/1995, Article 3, replacing CA 1963, ss 51(3) and (4).

[21.] CA 1963, s 51(6).

[22.] Note that while the Berne Convention, Article 2(4) gives Member States a right to regulate availability of public documents, Ireland and the UK are isolated in the EU on the extent to which State copyrights are insisted upon.

under Part III of the Copyright Act 1963, performers have been treated differently by giving them rights which allow them the possibility of preventing unauthorised fixation and broadcasting of performance rather than exclusive rights to authorise and permit such actions by others. The Performers Protection Act 1968 allows persons engaged in performance - defined as:

> "a performance of any actors, singers, musicians, dancers or other persons who act, sing, deliver, declaim, play in or otherwise perform literary, dramatic, musical or artistic works"

Some form of right other than a copyright. The Act provides that the gardaí may proceed against persons who make, deal in or use unauthorised recordings of performances[23] or films,[24] or who broadcast a performance without the consent of the performer,[25] who are deemed guilty of a criminal offence.[26] The penalties for infringement are modest and there are a substantial range of defences such as private use in the case of unauthorised recordings. The reasons for this limited protection are in part due to the often unorganised nature of performers and their limited bargaining power in crafts or professions where supply often exceeds demand, a reluctance by rightholders to benefit performers because of the supposed complexity that could result if performers obtained exclusive rights that could impede exploitation of copyright works, and a view that efficient protection and recognition can best be afforded by way of contractual arrangements for remuneration between broadcasters and actor and musician unions, for example. The fact that US law affords performers few rights is often cited as a reason for continuing with this approach, and US opposition to the broadening of performers' rights (eg in the GATT/TRIPs Agreement) has long been an impediment to a broader International Instrument than the Rome Convention. However, it should be noted that US domestic law does provide some measure of protection for celebrity performers who have their performances recorded via the law of publicity, for example,[27] and it is certainly true to say that the time is ripe for a thorough revision of Irish law, for a number of reasons.

[12.11] First, even within the confines of the 1968 Act, it is possible for a performer to seek to use the civil courts to prevent the unauthorised recording of

---

23. CA 1963, s 2.
24. CA 1963, s 3.
25. CA 1963, s 5.
26. See Cohen Jehoram, 15 Col VLA Journal of Law and Arts 75 (1990) for a discussion of the performer as a special case.
27. *Zacchini v Scripps Howard Broadcasting* (1976) 433 US 562 (unauthorised filming of human cannonball: see generally, Gordon (1960) 55 NUL Rev 553; Frazer [1983] EIPR 139 and (1983) 99 LQR 281.

a performance (bootlegging) and, more realistically, the distribution of copies of the recording. The precise judicial basis of this right has been explored in a series of English cases. The net result of these cases[28] indicates that the right is available to the performer and that the recording company has no *locus standi* to seek to enforce the performer's right, which exists by virtue of Performers Protection legislation and is thus personal to the performer. In the leading case of *Rickless v United Artists*[29] the estate of Peter Sellers obtained relief in the civil courts against the use of out-takes from the 'Pink Panther' series in order to produce a new film, action which Peter Sellers actually opposed during his lifetime. The Court of Appeal followed the earlier cases and found that because the intention behind the UK legislation was to give effect to the Rome Convention, the legislation had to be viewed as granting civil relief to the performer. While the Court of Appeal conceded that the result was somewhat anomalous - it was not clear when the performer or the performer's estate would lose such rights to object because the right is not defined in such terms in the legislation - this strengthening of the performer's right is certainly sympathetic with the wider objectives of the Rome Convention.

[12.12] It remains to be seen just how an Irish court would respond to a similar action brought by or on behalf of a performer. *Mannion* has argued[30] that while the legislative history of the 1968 legislation indicates that there was no Government intention to give performers a property right enforceable in the civil courts, the Rome Convention and the constitutional right of a citizen to earn a livelihood in the face of illegal conduct together would compel a court to follow *Rickless* in some shape or form.

[12.13] A second, but more indirect route for the performer would be to utilise some other cause of action, such as wrongful intervention in business relations. A copyright holder[31] or even a collecting society acting on behalf of a copyright owner[32] could proceed against pirates and bootleggers. In some cases unauthorised use of the performer's image (eg on labelling) might ground a passing off action, but the best form of reply to the bootlegger is to grant concurrent rights of enforcement to performers and recording companies via exclusive and separate statutory rights.

---

28. *Island Records v Corkindale* [1978] FSR 505; *Lonrho v Shell* [1982] AC 173; *RCA v Pollard* [1983] Ch 135.
29. [1987] FSR 362.
30. (1992) 10 ILT (ns) 276.
31. Despite *Lonrho* the performer will presumably often perform the works of an author or composer, unauthorised recording of which will breach CA 1963, s 8(6).
32. *Carlin v Collins* [1979] FSR 548.

RECENT DEVELOPMENTS

[12.14] The *Rickless* case in the United Kingdom had the effect of making the law so confused that some legislative response was inevitable. Accordingly, the 1988 Act in the UK gave performers[33] (defined more broadly than before by including performers of variety acts or similar presentations) an exclusive, non-assignable right which requires the performer to give his consent to the exploitation of his performances.[34] These rights are exercisable, broadly, by all EU citizens in respect of EU performances[35] and operate for 50 years following the end of the year of the performance. These provisions will not, however, provide the basis for future Irish reform because the provisions of Chapter II of the Rental and Lending Right Directive largely supersede and strengthen the Rome Convention.

[12.15] While implementation of the Directive should have occurred before 31 July 1994, no legislation has yet been drafted in Ireland. The Directive gives performers the exclusive right to authorise fixations of performances and the exclusive right to authorise the issuing of copies of such fixations to the public. The Directive also permits performers an exclusive right to authorise the broadcasting of a performance. UK implementing legislation also gives performers a right to share in payments made in respect of the use of sound recordings in broadcasts, cable diffusion or by way of public performance, a provision that strictly speaking goes beyond the essential requirements of the Directive but it is nevertheless to be welcomed.

[12.16] It should also be noted that the International Community has gone some way towards providing performers with substantial rights in the form of provisions set out in the Geneva (1996) Treaty on Performer's Rights and Phonograms[36] by granting exclusive rights to authorise the fixation, reproduction, distribution and communication to the public of aural performances - thus giving musical performers rights analogous to copyright. This Treaty broadens the concept of performer, so as to include performers of folklore, for example, and the Treaty also clearly covers digital fixations of performances. At the moment, however, performers are not given the recognition or respect that original artistic performances deserve and it is still going to be essential for performers to rely on agreements negotiated by bodies such as Irish Actor's Equity or the Musicians Union.[37] These agreements are

---

[33.] Copyright Designs and Patents Act 1988, s 180(2).

[34.] Copyright Designs and Patents Act 1988, s 180(1).

[35.] See technical definitions of qualifying person and qualifying country; Copyright Designs and Patents Act 1988, s 206(1).

[36.] Agreed at a Diplomatic Conference by convened WIPO on 2-20 December 1996.

[37.] See Profile of Dick Doyle, *Sunday Tribune* 12 January 1997.

important. For example, the sound recording industry provides *ex gratia* payments to Irish musicians in the form of PPI disbursements that totalled £0.50 million in 1995. Those payments are made by PPI who recognise both the need to remunerate performers and provide rights that create an incentive for performers to counteract piracy of sound recordings. It seems that the only reason why performers are not protected through copyright is legislative indolence.[38]

[38.] Many musicians and film actors benefit from contractual agreements of this kind indicating a broad consensus that rights should be ceded: debate concerns the extent to which contract may qualify these rights.

Chapter 13

The Protection of Computer Programs as Copyright Works

INTRODUCTION

[13.01] Computer programs have been the subject of express legal protection as a result of the transposition of the Computer Programs Directive[1] into Irish law by way of statutory instrument.[2] The Directive, however, does not answer all of the issues that copyright protection raises in such a context, and it is both necessary and desirable to consider many of the problems that this collision between legal regulation and new technology produce if a satisfactory grasp of the law is to be acquired.

[13.02] Under the terms of Part II of the Copyright Act 1963, a copyright work could be protected as a literary work, a dramatic work, or an artistic work. The most obvious possibility in such a context is that the concept of an original literary work would be applicable to software. The Copyright Act 1963 does not provide an extensive definition of literary work for all that s 2 states is that the definition includes a written table or compilation. In the High Court decision in *RTE and Others v Magill TV Guide*[3] a decision on the availability of interlocutory relief, Lardner J affirmed the traditional view that a literary work must be "a printed or written work", thus echoing the leading English decision on this particular point.[4] This requirement will of course be difficult to comply with when the program exists in a form which does not communicate with human beings via print or writing but rather provides instructions to a machine - typically when the program exists in machine code and is provided to the consumer in that 'perfected', ready to use form.

[13.03] This central issue, can existing copyright regimes protect computer programs in the many forms in which such programs exist, has been a controversial one. Certain academic commentators have taken the view that the concept of a literary work can accommodate all computer programs[5] although

---

[1.] Council Directive 91/250/EEC; OJ L 122/42.
[2.] SI 26/1993.
[3.] [1990] ILRM 534.
[4.] *University of London Press Ltd v University of Tutorial Press Ltd* [1916] 2 Ch 601 at 608-9.
[5.] Eg Kindermann [1981] EIPR 6; Keplinger [1985] Copyright 119;

many others take the view that this approach is too simplistic, for when a program exists in object code it cannot be said to be literary in any real sense[6] and if anything the program comes closer to a work that more properly answers the description of an audio-visual work or an industrial design. The Whitford Committee in 1977[7] examined this issue and reached a similarly ambivalent conclusion on the state of legal protection, noting that English law probably protected a programmer's original written work from direct copying but that, in the absence of case law, other possible abuses by unauthorised copying were only capable of redress via licensing conditions and the law of confidence, remedies that could not affect an innocent use of an unauthorised copy.[8] At the level of International Treaties, both the Berne Convention and the Universal Copyright Convention fail to address the question of protecting computer programs. *Cornish* argues that the central issue surrounding the implied protection afforded to computer programs turns on the scope of the Paris Act version of Article 9(1), the reproduction right,[9] but he notes that even if all unauthorised uses infringe the reproduction right this will not be of much use to the rightholder if the program, in the relevant form, is not literary. However, the climate of opinion has been significantly changed by the TRIPS Agreement, Article 10(1) of which obliges States which are party to the agreement to protect computer programs in both source code or object code, as literary works under the Berne Convention. This has led WIPO experts looking at the possible protocol to the Berne Convention to reach "practically unanimous agreement that computer programs, and in both source and object codes, were protected by copyright, and further, that the obligation to protect such programs at the same level as literary works could be deduced from the present text of the Berne Convention."[10]

[13.04] Leaving the issue of interpretation of the Paris Act of the Berne Convention to one side, the debate in the national courts has tended to be somewhat inconclusive when the judges have been presented with national legislation that fails to expressly declare that computer programs are either literary works or are to be regarded as if they were literary works. Indeed, the pattern of judicial decisions in common law jurisdictions has tended to come out

---

6.   Vaver (1986) 17 IIC 557; Cornish [1990] EIPR 131; Soltysinski (1990) 21 IIC 1.
7.   Cmnd 6732.
8.   *Ibid*, paras 479-482.
9.   Cornish, *Computer Program Copyright and the Berne Convention* in Lehmann and Tapper, *A handbook of European Software Law* (Claredon, 1995); Cornish [1990] EIPR 131. It should be recalled that Ireland is party to the 1948 Brussels version.
10. WIPO, *Committee of Experts on a Possible Protocol to the Berne Convention*, Fourth Session, Memorandum para 8. Nevertheless, the Protocol or First Treaty agreed in Geneva in December 1996 provides that computer programs in whatever form are literary works.

against an inclusive view of the protectability of computer programs when the judges have attempted to apply the words of the legislation to the technology before them.

PROTECTION OF COMPUTER PROGRAMS UNDER THE 1963 ACT

Source Code[11]

[13.05] This raises the question whether preparatory printed or written material is capable of being protected as an original literary work. Where a program is in written format in the sense that the operations the computer is required to perform is written in ordinary language, that language being accompanied by labels, mathematical symbols and/or flow-charts, it is clear that such high level language, preparatory material will be copyright protected. Such preparatory material is literary in the sense that it communicates information or instruction from one person in a way that another person can make sense of it.

[13.06] In the Australian case of *Computer Edge Property Ltd v Apple Computer Inc*[12] it was not contested, and indeed it was largely assumed, that such preparatory written material is capable of attracting copyright, as long as it is an original literary work.

[13.07] Whether the written statements are used to develop a source code, or whether the creation of a source code is the first step taken to develop a program, leads us on to the question as to whether source code is copyright protected. In *Computer Edge Property Ltd v Apple Computer Inc* the defendants contended that a source code written in an assembly code could not itself be capable of copyright protection. All members of the High Court of Australia rejected this submission. Citing the test of Davey LJ in *Hollinrake v Truswell*[13] that is, a "literary work is intended to afford either information and instruction, or pleasure, in the form of literary enjoyment", Gibbs CJ indicated that the test was satisfied on the facts of *Computer Edge Property Ltd v Apple Computer Inc*: the source code "afford instruction to the operator keying in the machine that will convert the source code to object code".[14] Opinion in other jurisdictions supports the view that source code can be the subject of copyright protection. In *Apple Computer Inc v Mackintosh Computers Ltd*[15] the alleged infringers

---

[11.] See the author's report in *Copyright Software Protection in the EC*, eds Jongen & Meijboom (Kluwer) (1994).

[12.] (1986) 60 ALJR 313.

[13.] [1894] 3 Ch 420, at 428.

[14.] (1986) 60 ALJR 313, at 315; Mason and Wilson JJ in a joint judgment agreed; *Ibid* at 320; see also Brennan J at 324. Deane J at 329 did not find it necessary to decide this point.

[15.] (1987) 44 DLR (4th) 74, reasoning of both Courts below affirmed by the Supreme Court of Canada at (1990) 71 DLR (4th) 95 in a short judgment.

conceded before the Federal Court of Appeal that original computer programs written in assembly language were literary works within the meaning of the Federal Copyright Law.[16] Similarly, the English judiciary addressed this question during proceedings in which an interlocutory injunction was sought and the issue of whether copyright could subsist in a source code was held to be established, at least provisionally.[17] The most emphatic statement on which to base an assertion that source code is copyright protected appears in the New Zealand case of *IBM v Computer Imports Ltd*[18] where Smellie J concluded that, whether source code be written down as a list of instructions, or keyed directly onto a computer and displayed onto a screen, it is an original literary work:

> "Source programs are the product of substantial originality and skill, they are expressed in writing, they are intended to convey and do convey information to human beings and they are expressed in a comprehensible form."[19]

Object Code

[13.08] When source code is converted into machine readable language, the form in which the code is converted in order to make the computer read the source code, this has the effect of making the computer program, in this form, a program that is not in print or writing. The computer program, when it exists in object code, or machine code, does not subsist in a form of notation. When the Irish Copyright Act 1963 states that the definition of 'writing' includes any form of notation, it is clear that the statutory definition is not exhaustive, but, it is submitted, it is essential that the work exist in some tangible or perceptible form at least. Whether a work which exists only in the sense of subsisting in a series of electrical impulses which exist independently from the binary or hexadecimal notation which represents the impulses, or whether the static circuitry that contains the program in a ROM chip, are very distinct issues. The first way in which protection may be sought is to argue that copyright may subsist in a series of impulses or in chip circuitry, as literary works. This first argument was decisively rejected in *Computer Edge Property Ltd v Apple Computer Inc*[20] by way of unanimous decision on this point. Gibbs CJ in the leading judgment rejected the view that a literary work itself need not be expressed in writing.

---

16. See judgment of Mahoney J at p 78.
17. Goulding J in *Sega Enterprises v Richards* [1983] FSR 73. In *Thrustcode Ltd v WW Computing Ltd* [1983] FSR 502 a motion seeking an interlocutory injunction was heard on the assumption that copyright in a program could subsist; the only copyright material before the court was source code; *Ibid* 506.
18. [1989] 2 NZLR 395.
19. *Ibid* at 409.
20. (1986) 60 ALJR 313.

Pointing out that a literary work is protected from the time it is reduced into writing or some other material form, the Chief Justice stated:

> "It seems to me a complete distortion of meaning to describe electrical impulses in a silicone chip, which cannot be perceived by the senses and are to intended to convey any message to a human being and which do not represent words, letters, figures, or symbols as a literary work; still less can a pattern of circuits be so described."[21]

[13.09] This approach was supported by Smellie J in *IBM v Computer Imports Ltd*.[22] In the Canadian Case of *Apple Computer Inc v Mackintosh Computers Ltd*,[23] it was contended that the circuitry of a ROM chip could be a literary work but, as Gibbs CJ points out in the above extract from his judgment in the *Computer Edge* case, information held in electronic circuitry is *a fortiori* not covered by copyright. It is a 'form' which does not contain a 'work'. A further argument that may be advanced in order to obtain protection is based upon the argument that if copyright protection is afforded to source code, then the object code version of the source code - assuming the program has not been written directly into a machine readable format - represents an adaptation of the original and is thus a restricted act. The relevant restricted acts in s 8(6) of the 1963 Act are as follows:

(a) reproducing the work in any material form;

(b) performing the work in public;

(c) making any adaptation of the work.

Again there is scant direct Irish case law on the meaning of these terms and there is no Irish case law on infringement of computer programs. Let us look at these three possible arguments in the light of case law from other common law jurisdictions.

REPRODUCTION UNDER THE 1963 ACT

[13.10] Proponents of the view that the words 'any material form' are to be given an extended definition use this argument to make the further point that if the infringing work is a reproduction of a literary work, then as long as it subsists in 'any material form', it does not matter that the reproduction itself is not a literary work. This argument was rejected in *Computer Edge Property Ltd v Apple Computer Inc* by Gibbs CJ, Deane J and by Brennan J on the ground that there was no similarity between the copyright work, the source program, and the alleged reproduction, the ROMs and EPROM. These judges also resisted the

---

[21.] *Ibid* p 316.
[22.] [1989] 2 NZLR 395.
[23.] (1987) 44 DLR (4th) 74.

argument that copyright could subsist in the collocation of ideas represented in the written original which was reproduced in ROMs/EPROM. In Brennan J's view:

> "there is no resemblance between the Wombat ROMs and EPROM and the written compilations of the source programs. It is immaterial that the former were divided from the latter when there is no resemblance between them, for both resemblance and derivation are essential to reproduction."

Carrying out instructions in order to produce something in another material form is not a reproduction.[24]

[13.11] However, in the Canadian Federal Court of Appeal, a different approach was taken on the question of reproduction. The Federal Court of Appeal asked itself whether the chips, and in particular the programs, as embodied in ROM chips, were reproductions in material form of the source code. Mahoney J, Hugesson J and MacGuigan J took the robust view that reproduction in any material form meant not only that the reproduction did not have to be humanly readable (ie itself a literary work) but the Federal Court of Appeal also implicitly rejected the view that reproduction involves similarity and a causal link. The Federal Court of Appeal also failed to address the question of whether references to reproduction in any material form also distinguish between literary 'dramatic or musical works' on the ground that dramatic or musical works are protected, even if a written form is not needed, unlike for literary works; see *Computer Edge Property Ltd v Apple Computer Inc.*[25] Both the Canadian Federal Court of Appeal and Smellie J in the New Zealand case of *IBM v Computer Imports Ltd*[26] explained that the substantial objective similarity criteria, relied upon by the majority in the High Court of Australia, was purely evidentiary; once it could be established that there existed a causal link between an original literary work and an alleged unauthorised reproduction - eg running an object code through a dissembler program to produce source code, or by obtaining a print out etc - then the comparison necessary in order to establish infringement by reproduction can be made.

[13.12] The temptation to find an infringement by way of unauthorised reproduction would be very hard to resist for an Irish judge. However, the definition of reproduction in the Irish Copyright Act 1963 may make this an impossible interpretation to put upon the 1963 Act. Reproduction is defined so as to include, in the case of a literary, dramatic or musical work, "a reproduction in the form of a record or of a cinematograph film"; record is defined as

---

24. *Ibid.*
25. (1986) 60 ALJR 313.
26. [1989] 2 NZLR 395.

meaning "any disc, tape, perforated roll or other device in which sounds are embodied so as to be capable of being automatically reproduced therefrom."

[13.13] It is arguable that despite the fact that the definition of reproduction is not exhaustive, the notion of reproduction in any material form depends on whether the material form in question refers to a literary, dramatic or musical work. Fixation of any of these works in a mechanical way depends on the medium of fixation. The Irish Act is directed at fixation in either a recording format (in which case it excludes visual), fixation for record means a method of embodying sounds or by way of cinematograph fixation of literary, dramatic or musical works. The idea that a traditional copyright statute should be interpreted so as to include technological advances when the legislation is technology specific (even if it is late nineteenth century technology) seems to this writer to be unlikely. It is this writer's view that an Irish court, on the issue of reproduction, would be likely to following the majority of the High Court of Australia in *Computer Edge Property v Apple Computer Inc.*

[13.14] It is, however, possible to argue that the decision of the High Court of Australia has, on this point, been weakened by the decision of a later court in *Autodesk Inc and Another v Dyason and Others*[27] for in that case the High Court of Australia held that for infringement to occur by way of unauthorised reproduction of a substantial part of a computer program, it was not necessary that the reproduction itself should be a computer program, as defined in Federal copyright law by way of statutory amendment in 1984.

PUBLIC PERFORMANCE

[13.15] In the Canadian case of *Apple Computer Inc v Mackintosh Computers Ltd*[28] the trial judge, Reed J, observed that she thought there was merit in the argument that the chips into which object code had been incorporated was a contrivance whereby the source code could be, as a work, 'delivered' to others, an infringement under the Canadian Copyright Act. This argument was doubted by Hugessen J in the Federal Court of Appeal on the ground that delivery was used in the legislation in the sense of communication by audible means.

[13.16] Under the Irish Act it is possible to advance the argument that the public display of a program which is embodied in object code, by way of display or delivery may, in appropriate factual circumstances be an infringement. The definition of 'performance' in s 2 of the Copyright Act 1963 is very broad:

[27.] (1992) 173 CLR 330. Prescott [1992] I EIPR 211, is extremely critical of this decision.
[28.] (1987) 44 DLR (4th) 74.

performance includes delivery, in relation to lectures, addresses, speeches or sermons, and in general, subject to the provisions, visual or acoustic presentation, including any such presentation by the operation of wireless, telegraph apparatus, or by the exhibition of a cinematograph film, or by the use of a record, or by any other means ...

The argument here in favour of protection is to the effect that the public display of source code, by visual presentation, through object code produced by another person who copies the source code, may be a performance in public.[29] The issue is whether the act of visual presentation is proximate enough to the copyright work. The point is open, for in the Federal Court of Appeal in the Canadian *Apple Computer* case, both Mahony J and MacGuigan J expressed no opinion on this point. Hugessen J's view of the meaning of 'delivery' under the Canadian Act is not dispositive of the meaning of performance under the Irish Act.

ADAPTING THE WORK

[13.17] The possibility that copyright in source code may be infringed by utilising the source code by reproducing in object code, has been canvassed on the basis that any object code representation of the source code as a derivative of that source code may be an adaptation of the work. The definition of any adaptation in s 8(7) includes 'a translation of the work'.

[13.18] This argument has been exhaustively reviewed in Australian, Canadian and New Zealand case-law. The weight of judicial opinion is against the argument being successful. In the Australian case of *Computer Edge Property Ltd v Apple Computer Inc* the High Court of Australia by a majority of 3:2 held that an object program, if derived from a source program, is not a translation of the source program. The word 'translation' was given the meaning "the expression or rendering of something in another medium or form". Gibbs CJ held that the definition required that the translated work must refer to the portrayal, utterance, representation, reproduction or depiction of the thing in a different form. The source code was a set of instructions effectuated by the electrical impulses in object code which causes a computer to function. Brennan J agreed in the sense that, while he held it was arguable that object code was a translation of source code, the argument failed because the adaptation itself had to be a work. A set of electrical impulses could not be a work. Deane J agreed that electrical impulses could not be held to be a translation or adaptation of a written source code.

[29.] See, by analogy, *Bookmakers Afternoon Greyhound Services Ltd v Wilf Gilbert (Staffordshire) Ltd* [1994] FSR 723.

[13.19] In the Canadian Federal Court of Appeal's decision in *Apple Computer Inc v Mackintosh Computers Ltd* the Court emphatically rejected the argument, agreeing with Reed J at first instance that the conversion of source code into object code does not result in the creation of a new literary work, while disagreeing with Reed J's conclusion that such a conversion is a translation. Reed J advanced the analogy that a written message, when converted into Morse Code by a telegraph operator is a translation of the written message. The Federal Court of Appeal concluded, however, that such a process is not one of translation but is reproduction of the written message in a material form, namely, the dots and dashes that make up Morse Code.

[13.20] The only decision which goes the other way is that of Smellie J in the New Zealand case of *IBM v Computer Imports Ltd* but it is submitted that the reasoning advanced by the judge is at odds with the Australian and Canadian appellate decisions and, further, is based upon principles of statutory interpretation that depend heavily on New Zealand statute law.

[13.21] It should be noted in passing that recent United Kingdom case law has acknowledged that the conversion of a computer program from one language or code into another language or code is to be treated as an adaptation[30] but this conclusion is reached as the result of the direct effect of the 1985 and 1988 legislation.[31] It is also hardly surprising to note that computer program protection in those common law jurisdictions that addressed the issue via the courts has been introduced by specific statutory amendment to these 'traditional' copyright legislative models. This conclusion forces us to conclude that prior to the transposition of the analysis Directive, Irish copyright law probably afforded copyright protection to source code, but other forms in which a program was expressed was in all probability unprotected under the 1963 Act.

TRANSPOSITION OF THE DIRECTIVE INTO IRISH LAW

Introduction

[13.22] Council Directive 91/250/EEC on the Legal Protection of Computer Programs was transposed into Irish law by the European Communities (Legal Protection of Computer Programs) Regulations 1993[32] made on the basis of the European Communities Act 1972 because Irish copyright legislation does not

---

[30.] *John Richardson Computers Ltd v Flanders* [1993] FSR 497.

[31.] Copyright (Computer Software) Amendment Act 1985, s 1(2); Copyright, Designs and Patents Act 1988, s 21(4). On the UK position see Bainbridge (1991) 54 MLR 643; (1993) 56 MLR 591; Chalton [1993] EIPR 138.

[32.] SI 26/1993. see 'Copyright Software Protection in the EC' (1993) eds Jongen & Meijboom *supra*; Tapper and Lehman, *A Handbook of European Software Law* (1995, Clarendon).

authorise substantive law making in the form of Ministerial delegated legislation. The validity or interpretation of these regulations has not been tested by litigation although the regulations were directly referred to in *News Datacom Ltd v Lyons*.[33] The Statutory Instrument was signed by the Minister for Enterprise and Employment on 2 February 1993, thus missing the implementation deadline. However, the regulations were expressed to be retrospective to come into operation on 31 December 1992, although the implementation was not to result in making or declaring any acts to be unlawful if the act in question was lawful at the date of its commission. This provision against retrospective legislation and prejudice to accrued rights is a Constitutional imperative in both national and European Community law.

COMPUTER PROGRAMS AS A LITERARY WORK UNDER THE 1963 ACT

[13.23] Although the entire scheme behind the Directive is based upon the view that copyright protection, rather than any form of *sui generis* right or even an industrial design protection, is the preferred option because of the prospect of greater international acceptance, the Irish mode of implementation is half-hearted on this central issue. The key regulation does not provide that a computer program is a literary work, but rather, that the Acts of 1963-87 "shall apply ... as if it were a literary work".[34] Nevertheless, the likely effect of the Article is to make several of the key provisions found in the Copyright Acts applicable to computer programs. Therefore, the provisions of those Acts which directly relate to literary works seem to apply to computer programs, even if this results in overlapping protection for computer programs under the Acts and the Regulations. For example, the Copyright Act 1963, s 12 sets out a number of 'fair dealing' provisions which, arguably, authorise certain acts which would otherwise be copyright infringements (or restricted acts under s 8(6) of the Act). These 'fair dealing' defences can be seen as covering much of the same territory as Articles 5 and 6 of the Directive, those articles being incorporated into Irish law by the 1993 Regulations.[35] Thus, in a copyright infringement action involving computer software, the defendant may invoke both s 12 of the Copyright Act 1963 and the customised defences found in the 1993 Regulations which are based on the Directive, Articles 5 and 6. Similarly, the restricted acts set out in s 8(6) of the Copyright Act 1963 may be seen as similar in nature to the exclusive rights given to a rightholder under Article 4 of the Directive but the regulations are clearly much broader in scope and the restricted acts are tailored to the needs of the industry. It is doubtful, for example, whether the 1963 Act made the "loading, displaying, running, transmission or storage" of a

---

[33.] [1994] 1 ILRM 450; see [1995] EIPR D-70 (Hann).
[34.] Reg 3.
[35.] Reg 6.

literary work a restricted act while the 1993 Regulations clearly give the rightholder authorisation rights to such acts in certain instances. However, the 1993 Regulations do not attempt to enhance the range of remedies available to a rightholder, at least in procedural terms. The rightholder who reasonably anticipates or fears that software has been unlawfully copied or pirated must, in procedural terms, rely on Anton Piller relief or on the search and seizure remedy given under s 27 of the Copyright Act 1963, as amended by s 2 of the Copyright (Amendment) Act 1987. Indeed, it is understood that in the case of *News Datacom Ltd v Lyons*[36] such reliefs were made available to the rightholder prior to the hearing of the application for interlocutory relief.

THE ORIGINALITY STANDARD

[13.24] The standard set by both the Directive and the regulations are that the work must be the author's own intellectual creation. The regulations do not go further by insisting that "no other criteria shall be applied to determine [the programs] eligibility for protection".[37] While the view in the United Kingdom appears to be that the test simply reflects the lower common law threshold of originality,[38] the reference to 'intellectual effort' rather than 'original effort' *per se* can arguably posit an intermediate standard that is above the Irish and UK standard but considerably lower than in other EU States. Litigation is eagerly awaited.

OWNERSHIP OF RIGHTS

[13.25] One of the most controversial aspects of the Directive is the issue of authorship and ownership of rights. On the question of who may be an author, the Directive follows the civilian tradition in insisting that authors are human persons; the Directive provides that natural persons or groups of natural persons are authors unless a national law allows for designation of a legal person in such cases - which Irish law does not, in a direct sense. The central point here is that works created by computer programs - and programs can and do create other programs - cannot under the Directive benefit from the 'deemed authorship' provisions, such as are contained in the 1988 UK Act, which gave copyright in such works to the person responsible for making the arrangements necessary to create the program (as distinct from other potential authors such as the employee programmer/consultancy software house actually responsible for creation of the program). The 1963 Act already gives effect to this provision[39] while also implementing the common law 'work for hire' doctrine that directs that the

---

[36.] [1994] 1 ILRM 450.

[37.] Article 2.1 of the Directive.

[38.] Eg *Tapper* in 'A Handbook of European Software Law', p 6 of the UK Report.

[39.] Article 2 of the Directive; Regulation 4 of the Statutory Instrument excludes the operation of CA 1963, s 10(4) (copyright in employment by a newspaper or similar publisher).

employer acquires copyright in computer programs created by an employee during the course of the employee's duties, subject to contrary provision by way of contract.[40] Even if the creator of the program is an independent contractor, recent case law suggests the courts will readily infer an equitable trust that will give the employer, not the independent contractor, equitable title to the program created under contract.[41] The issue of residual moral rights mentioned in Article 3.3 of the Directive by implication, are not examined at all by the regulations, because Irish law has not yet legislated for authors' moral rights.

[13.26] Of course, once the works are created ownership of those rights can be transmitted in the usual way, by assignment under s 47 of the 1963 Act or by way of an equitable assignment. Legal persons may thus become rightholders.[42]

RESTRICTED ACTS AND EXCEPTIONS THERETO

[13.27] We have already seen that under s 8(6), several of the acts of reproduction and use of a computer program would infringe copyright, as long as the program in question was a protected work under s 8 (ie a literary, dramatic or musical work). In order to address certain doubts about whether all prejudicial acts of exploitation would be caught by copyright law, the Directive provides an extensive definition of the acts which the rightholder is entitled to do, or authorise others to do; Regulation 5 thus provides that these exclusive rights include:

    (a)   the permanent or temporary reproduction of a computer program by any means and in any form, in part or in whole. Insofar as loading, displaying, running transmission or storage of the computer program necessitate such reproduction, such acts shall be subject to authorisation by the rightholder;

    (b)   the translation, adaptation, arrangement and any other alteration of a computer program and the reproduction of the results thereof, without prejudice to the rights of the person who alters the program;

    (c)   any form of distribution to the public, and including the rental, of the original computer program or of copies thereof. The first sale in the community of a copy of a program by the rightholder or with his consent shall exhaust the distribution right within the community of that copy, with the exception of the right to control further rental of the program or a copy thereof.

[13.28] While these word-for-word measures of implementation cannot lead to any real controversy in relation to the restricted acts, the same cannot be said of the way in which implementation of the lawful acquirer/user exceptions in

---

[40.] See CA 1963, s 10(3).

[41.] *John Richardson Computers Ltd v Flanders* [1993] FSR 497.

[42.] See Article 3 of the Directive.

Article 5 of the Directive has been made. Under the Directive a distinction is drawn between these acts of reproduction that constitute acts of loading and running necessary for lawful use by a lawful acquirer, and acts of error correction, cannot be displaced by contract, for Recital 17 in the Directive expressly so provides. However, while Articles 5.1 and 9.1 generally provide that lawful acquirers do not need authorisation to do those things listed in Article 4(a) and (b), specific contractual provisions may otherwise so direct. The implementing provision in Regulation 6 does not take account of the ambiguity in Recital 17 and Article 5.1 of the Directive although Ireland is not alone in this.[43] This is in contrast to the rights to make a back up copy and the right to run a program so as to observe, study or test a program which cannot be excluded.[44]

DECOMPILATION

[13.29] The decompilation provisions of the Directive are transposed almost word for word, by the Regulations.[45] It is worth noting that the fair dealing defences are still available to these acts of creation (as well as the observe, study and test rights expressly provided in Regulation 6.3). The UK Regulations in contrast, exclude fair dealing defences in general copyright law from the UK measures implementing the Directive, despite the permissive nature of Article 9.1 of the Directive itself.

THE LIMITS OF THE DIRECTIVE

Proof of Infringement

[13.30] In cases where the plaintiff alleges literal copying of a computer program, in the form of making another physical copy of the program by way of unauthorised reproduction of a tangible copy of that program, or through utilisation of knowledge or information previously acquired about the plaintiff's copyright work, the task facing the court will be to decide if copying has taken place. The fact that the defendant's program achieves the same results as the plaintiff's work, or that it supplants the plaintiff's product, does not signify copyright infringement, for first principles direct that the simultaneous or independent creation of works do not infringe any copyright. The issue of whether independent effort to create a derivative but superior competing product involves several complex legal and policy issues that the courts in many countries are grappling with. It is submitted that efforts towards the resolution of these difficulties have not been assisted by affording to computer programs the

---

[43] See *Meijboom*, in 'Copyright Software Protection in the EC', p 12-13. Chalton [1993] EIPR 138 at 141.
[44] Article 9.1 of the Directive.
[45] Article 6 of the Directive, Reg 7 of the Regulations.

full blown status of literary copyright and that the resolution of these difficulties may best be achieved by qualifying the reproduction right afforded under the Berne Convention - something national laws may well do under Article 9(2) of the Convention.[46]

[13.31] English case-law has tended to focus attention on the objective similarities between the programs in question, and these decisions will clearly be influential in an Irish court.[47] However, the cases have not been free from difficulty and some decisions are clearly unreliable[48] as propositions of general principle. For example, it is clear that many computer programs are in fact made of a combination of existing code, routines and sub-routines. Despite doubts expressed in one English case,[49] the linking together of several distinct programs is clearly copyright protected as a compilation of works.[50] So, if copying is admitted but the issue before the court is whether the dependent has copied a work, an affirmative answer to this will normally be dispositive. It may be that the court may hold that the work was copyright and copying took place, but the defendant may avoid liability on the ground that no *substantial* copying took place. So in one case, *Data Access Corporation v Powerflex Services Pty Ltd*[51] the reproduction of an error text program in the plaintiff's 'Data Flex' applications organisation program was not substantial infringement of the 'Data Flex' program because 'Data Flex' could function adequately without the error text program.

[13.32] Where such concessions are not made, the court will have to establish copying as a fact. The original work can be either reproduced substantially by the infringer, or rewritten into another programming language by the infringer, and in either case the infringement will be made out if the usual defence of independent creation does not prevail.

[13.33] The decision of Jacob J in *Ibcos Computers Ltd v Barclays Mercantile Finance Ltd*,[52] although a first instance decision, represents the most thorough English analysis of a software infringement claim. However, it is submitted the fact that the court concluded that there had been disk to disk copying by the

---

46. Cornish [1990] EIPR 129.
47. The only Irish decision to date is *News Datacom Ltd v Lyons* [1994] ILRM 450: Murray [1996] CLSR 157.
48. *Total Information Processing Systems Ltd v Daman Ltd* [1992] FSR 171.
49. *Ibid.*
50. *Accounting Systems 2000 (Developments) Pty Ltd v CCH (Australia) Ltd* (1993) 27 IPR 133; *Ibcos Computers Ltd v Barclays Mercantile Highland Finance Ltd* [1994] FSR 275; *Trumpet Software Pty Ltd v Ozemail Pty Ltd (1996)* 34 IPR 481.
51. (1996) 33 IPR 194: A careful study of the *Ibcos* case also throws up instances of insubstantial copying.
52. [1994] FSR 275.

defendant of the plaintiff's programs[53] make many of the learned judge's observations strictly *obiter*, and in this area many doubts can only be resolved following clear decisions of the highest appellate tribunals. *Ibcos* complained that the defendant had copied their ADS accountancy workpackage. The defendant was responsible for developing ADS when engaged by *Ibcos's* predecessor in title. On leaving that employment he developed a rival Unicorn package that competed with ADS. Jacob J rejected the blanket proposition that there could not 'be copyright in an idea', remarking that, if the 'idea' is applied to an 'original work', the inquiry goes beyond the general into the specific issue: he confined the utility of the proposition to certain situations:

> "For instance if all a defendant has done is to copy a general idea then it does not matter whether there is copyright in the plaintiff's work or whether the plaintiff owns that copyright."[54]

[13.34] However, in *Ibcos* there was no mere taking of a general idea (ie compile an accounting package to be used in the financial workings of an agricultural dealership). Proof of copying by the defendant in creating Unicorn was established by pointing to the resemblance between the two programs in both essential and inessential matters. These similarities included common spelling mistakes, headings, the presence of otiose references to ADS programs in the Unicorn source code, use of ADS file records in Unicorn, as well as the presence of redundant or unexplained code in each program: from these factors the court deduced that acts of file to file, disk to disk copying, had taken place. This comparative analysis was also utilised in *Prism Hospital Software Inc v Hospital Medical Records Institute*,[55] where a comparison of the original program, rewritten by the defendant in a more stable programming language than the original, was held to infringe as being both a reproduction and an adaptation of the original program. Unauthorised reproduction of a program by loading it onto a File Transfer Protocol site for downloading by others, or by distribution on diskette, either in original or adapted form, without consent, is a clear infringement.[56]

Proof of Infringement in Interlocutory Proceedings

[13.35] Within the context of a dispute involving computer software the principles which govern the decision to grant relief by way of an interlocutory injunction have been recently clarified by Laddie J in *Series A Software v Clarke*.[57] In essence, Laddie J emphasised that *American Cyanamid*[58] principles

---

53. [1994] FSR 275, at 303.
54. *Ibid* at 292.
55. (1994) 57 CPR (3d) 129: *Honda* (1995) 26 IIC 527.
56. *Trumpet Software Pty Ltd v Ozemail Pty Ltd* (1996) 34 IPR 481.
57. [1996] 1 All ER 853.
58. *American Cyanamid v Ethicon Ltd* [1975] 1 All ER 504.

are to govern but the learned judge made it clear that a court should have regard to the strength of each party's case but that the court should refrain from resolving difficult areas of fact or law. In this context, the strength of the case of each side will need to be resolutely set out in affidavit form and the court will have to assess the weight of such evidence in the usual way.[59] A failure to address specific allegations in the form of rebuttal statements in evidence will clearly be damaging. Affidavit evidence on similarity between the two programs can be provided by expert testimony that draws up conclusions reached as a result of the running of the two programs but such testimony will presumably be treated with caution if that expert has not had access to computer code, for example.

[13.36] If the program does not, objectively speaking, reveal any evidence of copying, and this can often only be achieved by submitting to the court evidence in the form of screen displays, print-outs, material that is the product of the program rather than the program itself, it may be very difficult to persuade a court that there is any evidence of copying. In the leading English case of *Thrustcode Ltd v WW Computing Ltd*.[60] Megarry VC said:

> "In the normal case in which an infringement of literary copyright is alleged, it is possible to put side by side the written, typed or printed words in which the plaintiff claims copyright and the corresponding words which are said to infringe that copyright. The words can be seen and compared and discussed. In the case of computer programs, the software appears to consist of articles which by magnetic or electrical means will make the hardware do certain things, together with what is recorded on various tapes and discs. By means of this, the letters, signs and numbers of the program may be made to appear on a screen or on a print-out; and if this is done, then the familiar process of comparison is made possible. Yet where, as here, the claim is to copyright in the program itself, the results produced by operating the program must not be confused with the program in which copyright is claimed. If I may take an absurdly simple example, 2 and 2 make 4. But so does 2 times 2, or 6 minus 2, or 2 per cent of 200, or 6 squared divided by 9, or many other things. Many different processes may produce the same answer and yet remain different processes that have not been copied one from another. For computers, as for other things, what must be compared are the thing said to have been copied and the thing said to be an infringing copy. If these two things are invisible, then normally they must be reproduced in visible form, or in a form that is some way is perceptible, before it can be determined whether one infringes the other.
>
> In some cases, no doubt, it may be possible in some other way to demonstrate that one is a copy of the other, as where there is some evidence or some admission that when one computer was being programmed, someone was

---

[59.] *Eg Carolian Systems International Inc v Triolet Systems Inc* (1989) 25 CPR (3d) 87.
[60.] [1983] FSR 502, followed in *John Richardson Computers Ltd v Flanders* [1993] FSR 497.

watching and was programming a rival computer in the same or a similar way. Normally, however, what will be needed is a print-out or other documentary evidence of the program alleged to have been copied, and of the alleged infringing program, or sufficient parts of each. You must look at what the programs are, and not only at what they do or can do."[61]

[13.37] In *News Datacom Ltd v Lyons*[62] Flood J faced an even more difficult problem. The plaintiff produced a card which unscrambled an encrypted broadcast signal. The defendant produced a card that did the same thing but the defendant denied any copying of the plaintiff's program. All each card did was to cause the same screen display (ie, Sky TV programmes) to appear. Asking whether there was a similarity in the screen display here was irrelevant, and in the absence of any procedure which would allow the court to appoint an expert to decompile each program for the purposes of independent analysis, the court was unable to grant the relief sought. After citing the *Thrustcode* case Flood J examined the merits of the claim to injunction relief:

"It is the plaintiffs' case that a card could be analysed by an electron microscope or similar device but no such examination has been carried out by the plaintiffs to thereby obtain a basis of comparison. Further the plaintiffs say in evidence that they changed the algorithm every few months to increase the security of their operation and in such an event according to the same affidavit the scrambling seeds will have been replaced by scrambling seeds based on a different algorithm and yet the plaintiffs admit that the defendants have produced within relatively short periods of time after such change a smart card which could operate to descramble the amended encrypted system. This to me seems to render even more unlikely - in fact highly improbable - the plaintiffs' only explanation for the functional similarity of the two cards namely, copying and to render highly probable the defendants' claim that they have in no way infringed or copied the plaintiffs' software.

In my opinion the plaintiffs in the evidence tendered to the court at this stage have failed to show that they have sown the seed which could fructify at the hearing into a stateable case of infringement by copying of a copyright. At most they have merely shown the fruits of the software and not direct evidence of any similarities in the software itself or, if it had been more accurate to say so, they have simply shown the fruits of the respective algorithms used by the respective parties but have not shown direct evidence of any similarities between the algorithms."[63]

---

61. At pp 505-506.
62. [1994] 1 ILRM 450.
63. *Ibid* at 456-457.

Non-Literal Infringement

[13.38] Where direct copying or direct adaptation of an original program has not be conceded, or shown to exist, the courts will have to consider whether non-literal copying of a program may be an infringement of copyright in some pre-existing work. Here it is not thought that the defendant has use of the source code in the original work but that the defendant has replicated either *the structure of the program* - sometimes expressed as being the structure, sequence and organisation of the program, or the *user interface* - the look and feel,[64] made up of the screen displays and menu hierarchy or menu sequence.

Structure of the program

[13.39] In the leading English structure and sequence case of *John Richardson Computers Ltd v Flanders*[65] the defendant was an independent consultant who was engaged by the plaintiff to develop a program for the labelling of medicines that could run on a BBC computer (at the time a popular model) and be used by both Irish and UK pharmacists. The defendant ceased to work for the plaintiff and independently sought to produce a better program that would serve the Irish market and also function on IBM machines. These programs were written in different languages but when the plaintiff discovered that the defendant intended to distribute the new program in the UK, litigation ensued. After finding that the defendant's work was to be the property of the plaintiff *via* the law of trusts,[66] Ferris J outlined the nature of the plaintiff's complaint thus:

> "What is said is that the defendants have taken the general scheme of the BBC program, including the detail of certain routines of an idiosyncratic nature. The case was likened by (counsel for the plaintiff) to one in which the plot of a book or other literary work has been taken."

[13.40] Apart from the cases cited[67] by counsel for the plaintiff, the concept of non-literal copying of a work being held to be an infringement is often illustrated by the case of *Correlli v Gray*.[68] Miss Corelli wrote a novel called 'Temporal Power'. She claimed that the defendant's play or dramatic sketch, entitled 'The People's King' infringed copyright. The trial judge concentrated on six incidents in the play that bore such a strong resemblance to the incidents in the plaintiff's work in terms of the identity or language of the work and he

---

64. *Francis* (1992) 18 MULR.584; *Valsco* (1994) 94 Col L Rev 242.
65. [1993] FSR 497. See also *Computer Aided Design v Bolwell* High Court, unrep, 23 August 1989, Hoffman J; *Sykes* [1990] CLSR 30
66. Following *Massine v de Basil* [1936-45] Mac CC 223.
67. *Rees v Melville* [1936] Mac CC 107; *Harman Pictures v Osborne* [1967] 1 WLR 723; *Nichols v Universal Pictures Corporation* 45 F (2d) 119 (1930).
68. (1913) 30 TLR 116.

was unable to find any real prospect of coincidental creation. Although not one sentence in the plaintiff's novel had been reproduced by the defendant, both the trial judge and the Court of Appeal agreed that when the defendant wrote his work, the work of the plaintiff must have been present before him, either physically or in his memory.

[13.41] A more recent illustration of this can be found in the Australian case of *Peter v Coulter*.[69] The applicant wrote a novel, 'Monument of Stone'. He sought to establish a copyright infringement by the respondent when he wrote and produced a play 'Stretchmarks', citing some 25 instances of acts of reproduction of plot, character and events. The respondent sought to dismiss the applicant's statement of claim on the ground that it disclosed no cause of action. The motion to dismiss failed, Branson J agreeing with Jacob J in *Ibcos*[70] that in cases of this kind: "[i]n the end the matter must be left to the value judgment of the court".[71]

[13.42] To return to the decision in *John Richardson Computers* itself, Ferris J, in examining this issue of non-literal copying of work, managed to combine the traditional English approach with the perspective given by several recent American cases in which the judges have sought to provide a means of drawing the line between non-copyright protected ideas and copyright protected expression. In essence, the issue is one of impression: at which stage do the plaintiff's efforts at fixing the idea into a work transform the idea into a stable and identifiable format that is original and distinctive enough to warrant protection via copyright? The approach favoured by Ferris J was that of the US Court of Appeals for the Second Circuit in *Computer Associates International Inc v Altai*.[72] In that case a programmer, previously employed by the plaintiff, wrote a rival program which not only produced the same kind of result, it allegedly replicated the appearance to the user of the plaintiff's program. In that case the court developed an 'abstractions' test which allowed it to side-step the defence argument that, because there was no evidence of direct copying, and because the defendant had written their program in a different language, there could be no copying in that instance. The Court took the view that if non-literal copying could be established then a infringement would follow. This turned upon the abstractions test. The abstractions test, in essence, requires the Court to engage in the following analysis. The extract reproduced below involves a discussion, by Ferris J, of the background to the decision of the Second Circuit Court of Appeals in *Altai*. After noting that the Court in *Altai* had declined to

---

69. (1995) 33 IPR 450. See Jacobs [1994] EIPR 206.
70. Citing (1994) 24 IPR 250, at 49.
71. (1995) 33 IPR 50 at 52.
72. (1992) 23 IPR 385.

follow *Whelan Associates Inc v Jaslow Dental Laboratory Inc*,[73] Ferris J continued:

"The Court of Appeals agreed with the District Judge's decision not to follow *Whelan*. It then became necessary for the Court of Appeals to formulate an alternative test. This it did by going back to what Judge Learned Hand had said in the *Nichols* case. It described this as the 'abstractions test'. In order to understand this label and the test itself it is necessary to read again part of the passage from *Nichols* which I have already read. As cited by the Court of Appeals in *Consumer Associates* it is as follows:

'Upon any work ... a great number of patterns of increasing generality will fit equally well, as more and more of the incident is left out. The last may perhaps be no more than the most general statement of what the (work) is about, and at times might consist only of its title; but there is a point in this series of abstractions where they are no longer protected, since otherwise the (author) could prevent the use of his 'ideas', to which, apart from their expression, his property never extended.'

The Court of Appeals elaborated upon this process by saying that:

"Initially, in a manner that resembles reverse engineering on a theoretical plane, a court should dissect the allegedly copied program's structure and isolate each level of abstraction contained within it. This process begins with the code and ends with an articulation of the program's ultimate function. Along the way, it is necessary essentially to retrace and map each of the designer's steps - in the opposite order to that in which they were taken during the program's creation.

As an anatomical guide to this procedure, the following description is helpful:

'At the lowest level of abstraction, a computer program may be thought of in its entirety as a set of individual instructions organised into a hierarchy of modules. At a higher level of abstraction, the instructions in the lowest level modules may be replaced conceptually by the functions of those modules. At progressively higher levels of abstraction, the functions of the higher-level modules conceptually replaces the implementations of those modules until, finally, one is left with nothing but the ultimate function of the program ... A program has structure at every level of abstraction at which it is viewed. At low levels of abstraction, a program's structure may be quite complex; at the highest level it is trivial.'

That description is, I think, taken from a text book which had been cited to the Court of Appeals.[74]

---

73. [1987] FSR 1.
74. This is in fact David Nimmer, *Nimmer on Copyright* (Matthew Bender, 1989).

In the test propounded in *Consumer Associates* the discovery of a program's abstraction levels is the first step. The second step is to filter these abstractions in order to discover a 'core of protectable material'. In the process of filtration there are to be excluded from consideration (a) elements dictated by efficiency; (b) elements dictated by external factors and (c) elements taken from the public domain. Each of these categories is explained at some length. The essence of the 'elements dictated by efficiency' is that if there is only one way to express an idea the idea and its expression are inseparable and copyright does not prevent the copying of the expression. The exclusion of "elements dictated by external factors" arises from the fact that if two persons set about the description of the same event there may be a number of particular facts which can only be described in a particular way. The Court of Appeals cited with evident approval the observation of Professor Nimmer (a well-known academic commentator on US copyright law) that:

'in many instances it is impossible to write a program to perform particular functions in a specific computing environment without employing standard techniques.'

As to "elements in the public domain":

'plaintiffs may not claim copyright of an expression that is, if not standard, then commonplace in the computer software industry.'

The third step in the process suggested in the *Computer Associates* case is to compare what is left of the 'abstractions' made from the plaintiff's program after filtering out these elements with the program which is said to be an infringement of that program."[75]

[13.43] This ringing endorsement of the *Altai* decision by Ferris J[76] has, of course, not been by any means representative of all reactions to the judgment, either by judges or academic commentators. Some academics see the second stage to be too rigorous insofar as it can filter out too much[77] and within the context of programs that are other compilations of existing code this comment has much force. Other commentators generally support the *Altai* decision,[78] often with reservations.[79] Later US judicial decisions, however, have divided on the utility of abstraction, filtration and comparison approach. Some courts have followed *Altai*[80] while in other cases, such as *Lotus Development Corp v Borland International*[81] the Court of Appeal for the First Circuit observed that

---

[75] [1993] FSR 497 at 525-6

[76] It has been pointed out that Ferris J concentrated more on the output of the program in order to test similarity and in this may have fallen into error: eg Grewal [1996] EIPR 454.

[77] 106 Harv L Rev 1061, at 1084 (1992).

[78] Eg *McCarthy* (1993) 66 Temp L Rev 273.

[79] Eg, *Valasco* (1994) 94 Col L Rev 242.

[80] Eg, *Gates Rubber Co v Banab Chemical Industries* (1993) 9 F (3d) 823; *Apple Computer Inc v Microsoft Corp* (1994) 35 F (3d) 1435.

[81] (1995) 33 IPR 233.

the *Altai* test has no real relevance to the basic issue of whether a work should be copyright protected at all.[82] While the *Altai* approach has been cited with approval in Canada,[83] the real support for this or any American tests in the English courts has come from Ferris J in *John Richardson Computers Ltd v Flanders*. It must be noted however that while Ferris J supported *Altai* he did not really attempt to operate abstraction/filtration comparison himself, and as a general criticism of this entire USA approach one must doubt whether tests that are so opaque that they cannot be operated by the judges are really worth persevering with at all. In any event, Jacob J in *Ibcos* took the view that these US tests are unsuitable in an English context, basically because both the US copyright legalisation and US judicial attitudes towards functional works and compilations have tended to differ from approaches and attitudes to such matters in English law. In this Jacob J is clearly correct. However, the filtration stage does at least allow the court to concentrate aspects of the program that, seen individually, would not be seen as original works, thus facilitating clarification of the question whether the programs, on the whole, are works and infringing works respectively. It is submitted, therefore, that an Irish court should engage in the broad impressionistic approach canvassed by Jacob J but should still consider the relevance of looking at the program in a fragmented sense: how much code is conventional or standard 'boilerplate'?[84] Are symbols or words or 'macros' commonplace - '*scenes a faire*'.[85] Is there some common origin that does not involve an infringement of rights?[86] Is the expression of the idea only possible in one form, in which case the idea merges with the expression and no infringement can be established unless there is exact copying of the form in which that idea is expressed?[87] Merger is certainly an important part of the approach adopted by Ferris J in *John Richardson*[88] and it must be seen as a very relevant element in any 'filtering' process. The question of whether similarities can be put down to individual skills or techniques rather than copying is the most significant feature of the filtering process, at least in regard to instances where the defendant has not been shown to have resorted to direct copying but rather is alleged to have reconstructed the look and feel of the sequence or structure of a program. The Canadian case of *Carolian Systems Inc v Triolet*

[82.] *Ibid* at 241-242.

[83.] *Carolian Systems Inc v Triolet Systems Inc* (1992) 47 CPR (3d) 1.

[84.] *Total Information Processing Systems Ltd v Daman Ltd* [1992] FSR 171. However, if the compilation of code is original protection should be available, and on this point the *Daman* case has not been followed: see *Ibcos op cit* p 290.

[85.] For original macros, see *Data Access Corporation v Powerflex Services Pty* (1996) 33 IPR 194.

[86.] Eg, so-called 'Freeware': See *Trumpet Software Pty Ltd v Ozemail Pty* (1996) 34 IPR 481 at 485. See *Richardson* [1996] EIPR 669.

[87.] The merger doctrine, which in England was accepted in *Kendrick v Lawrence* (1890) 25 QBD 99 but explained with greater clarity by Jacob J in *Ibcos, op cit*, p 290-291.

[88.] [1993] FSR 497 especially in relation to the stock control features of each program at 555.

Systems Inc[89] holds out some hope for a programmer who used individual skills, know-how, background knowledge on the features of the hardware, in order to create an independent but competing program. The English decisions however show that pleas of independent effort and skill by a defendant will be taken with some scepticism, and once sufficient evidence of objective similarity and opportunity are put before the Court, the onus of proof will shift to the defendant.[90]

Copyright Protection for Screen Displays

[13.44] In this context the most obvious scenario is as follows: the defendant takes the features of the plaintiff's work as set out in the screen display and reproduces these features so as to induce buyers and others to use the program. Ingenuity, investment and design skills go into creating a user interface and if competitors can replicate the screen display, which is an output from the program and not a program in itself, the plaintiff would face an element of unfair competition. For this reason copyright in the user interface is asserted but the display itself is not to be confused with the copyright in the underlying program; it may however provide proof of copying in the underlying code. In *John Richardson Computers Ltd v Flanders* Ferris J put this issue very succinctly:

> "The two main ways, perhaps the only ways, in which a computer program can be made visible are by printing out the code on paper or by displaying on screen the prompts, entries, reports and other material which the program presents invisible form to the user. The latter is not, however, itself the program. It is a product of the program. The fact that two programs may produce a similar screen display may or may not be indicative of a similarity in the programs. The screen display is not itself the literary work which is entitled to copyright protection. A particular display may enjoy a separate copyright protection as an artistic work in the form of a photograph, or as a film, or as being a reproduction of an artistic work in the form of a drawing the copying of which will be, for copyright purposes the copying of the drawing. But no such copyright is relied on in this case. It appears to me, therefore that screen displays are only to be relied upon in this case to the extent that they demonstrate the contents of the underlying program in which the relevant copyright subsists."[91]

[13.45] The question whether a screen display can be reproduced by a competitor without permission has raised directly the issue of whether a screen display is copyright protected as a literary work. In the US the decision in *Lotus*

[89.] (1992) 47 CPR (3d) 1.

[90.] *John Richardson Computers Ltd v Flanders* [1993] FSR 497 at 543; *Ibcos Computers Ltd v Barclays Mercantile Highland Finance Ltd* [1994] FSR 275, at 302-4.

[91.] [1993] FSR 497 at 527

Development Corporation v Borland International[92] favours a negative answer to this question on the basis that a screen display, in the form of a menu hierarchy to guide the user through the software package, is a 'method of operation' which is not copyright protected under US law.[93] No such express exclusion to instructions of this kind are found in English or Irish law so *Borland* has no real application.

[13.46] Where a screen display is reproduced (eg, by running the program and causing moving images to be shown) a recent Australian case suggests that the person responsible for making the infringing program may be held to have infringed a separate copyright in a cinematographic film. In *Sega Enterprises Ltd v Galaxy Electronics Pty*[94] the defendants were held to have infringed copyright in a cinematographic film when they reproduced two computer games by importing into Australia integrated circuits which 'housed' those games. The interactive nature of the video game was not an obstacle to giving the concept of a film a very broad meaning.[95]

Copyright protection and computer produced 'works'

[13.47] If something is produced by a natural force by non-human intervention then that product cannot be a 'work' for a work requires the presence of an author. A work that is produced by a human being who produces that work by using a typewriter or work processor is clearly not deprived of protection because of the mechanical means used to fix the work, but problems arise where the work is created after a computer produces that work following upon a program being written and used in order to generate the work. In *Express Newspapers Plc v Liverpool Daily Post and Echo*[96] Whitford J regarded a group of numbers produced by way of a computer program to be a work, the computer as a machine being merely a tool by which the literary work could be produced *via* the operation of the computer program. However, where the work is produced by a machine - a satellite photograph or even some computer code generated by that machine with minimal human input - some difficulties will

---

92. (1995) 33 IPR 233: Schwarz [1995] EIPR 337.

93. US Copyright Act 1976, s 102(b).

94. (1996) 35 IPR 161; *Avel Pty Ltd v Wells* (1992) 23 IPR 353.

95. The Court cited para 93 of the Gregory Report:

"Further, it can no longer be assumed that the reproduction of visual effects must be preceded by photographs, and we are given to understand that even now it is possible to record on a magnetic tape a spectacle which can be reproduced visually as a television program. Accordingly, in drafting provisions relating to records, cinematograph films and such matters, we consider that the wording adopted should have regard to the end-product (eg, sound or visual representation) rather than to the means whereby the effects are produced."

96. [1985] 1 WLR 1059.

arise. A distinction between computer aided (eg computer aided designs) and computer generated works is found in the literature and the distinction was approved in the recent South African case of *Payer Components South Africa Ltd v Bovic Gaskets*.[97] The importance of such a distinction is that works within the first category will be protected as original works while those in the second category will not, unless individual jurisdictions amend copyright law to afford protection to those works and identify who the rightholder is to be and for how long the right is to last. The 1988 UK Act, in s 12(3)[98] states that protection for computer generated works is taken for 70 years from the end of the calendar year in which to work is made. The rightholder is identified in s 9(3) as "the person by whom the arrangements necessary for the creation of the work are undertaken". In deeming this person to be the author, the Act makes it clear that authorship is entrepreneurial rather than being creative in nature: a more neutral meaning of author would be the technical staff who collectively or alone enabled the computer to generate the work.

[13.48] No solution to this problem of computer generated works is presented by the Irish Act. While the Software Directive initially attempted to address this issue a provision which mirrored the UK approaches was dropped from the Directive.

[97.] (1995) 33 IPR 407.

[98.] As amended to take account of the Term Directive; see Ch 10 *ante*.

Chapter 14

Databases

INTRODUCTION

[14.01] The very term 'database' is somewhat ambiguous. Data, as a word, refers to the raw material that can be gathered or held by any person or organisation, regardless of its nature or content, and implicit in this term is the idea that some further refinement, processing or extraction will need to take place before information or knowledge can be obtained by a user. The database, in contrast, conjures up an image of a place, machine or material entity that holds or maintains data, whether it be a filing cabinet, a personal or mainframe computer, or a series of printed volumes, for example. In our contemporary information technology-driven world, a database most typically evokes the picture of a computerised information system, operated by way of a computer program, which can process, arrange or select words, sounds and images and project them onto a screen or print-out. Nevertheless, the older notion of a database still endures and newspapers, encyclopaedia and other journals are essentially databases in the sense that these information products have generally been created by a process of selecting existing works (whether copyright protected or not), by collecting facts and figures and commentary from other persons, and partly by independently commissioning contributions to the database. One need only think of a newspaper that serialises a politician's recently published memoirs, reprints a sonnet by Shakespeare, that invites and publishes letters from readers to the editor, or carries cartoons by its resident cartoonist, for examples of these quite commonplace elements. It is the decision to select or not and the fact that these selected items are put before the public in such a format that makes the database a potential subject for copyright protection, regardless of the material form or support on which the database is held (paper/print or electronically). However, for protection to be available for a database as a literary work, for example, the database must satisfy the originality criteria found in the Copyright Act 1963.

[14.02] It should be noted that copyright protection is avoidable for works which are secondary in the sense that the constituent parts of the work already exist and s 2(1) provides a non-exhaustive definition of literary work as including "any written table or compilation". Thus, an anthology of poetry, or a selection of television programmes to be broadcast at a later date will attract literary copyright as long as the necessary element of skill or judgment is present in regard to the process of selection, arrangement, or both.[1] While the originality issue is addressed extensively in this work, it is sufficient for present purposes to note, firstly, that a compilation of factual material from some pre-existing source is less likely to attract copyright for the compilation. The aesthetic judgment or subjective elements in a process of selecting 50 love poems produces more latitude than the selection tables setting out the movements of the tides: a table will be right or wrong and little or no skill or judgment arises in such a selection.[2] Secondly, a factual compilation (eg of names and addresses in a trade street directory, even if created by the person claiming copyright, may not be copyright protected. There are no Irish cases on the point, but the balance of earlier[3] and more recent[4] English cases is to hold that if a body of factual material of this kind has been created by loading information into a compilation, the skill and effort involved will merit copyright protection. It has to be said in both these later English cases, the analysis of each court was concerned not so much with the issue of originality but rather with issues of unfair utilisation by a trade competitor of the contents of a database. The leading modern US case of *Feist Publications Inc v Rural Telephone Service*[5] suggests that the American courts at least will not allow works that are compiled by reference to obvious criteria such as the alphabetical listing of surnames, without further refinement or selection criteria, from passing the selection and arrangement test necessary for purely factual compilations. While this approach has caused considerable alarm amongst many in the information industry, it must nevertheless be said that the *Feist* result has possibly been overstated for O'Connor J remarked that even for factual databases, some limited modicum of selection, arrangement or classification would suffice to satisfy the originality requirement: mere alphabetical listing, which requires no skill or judgment but observance of an inflexible standard, will not be enough.[6]

[14.03] Recent case-law suggests that the *Feist* reasoning may be applicable outside the USA, in other common law jurisdictions. In *Tele-Direct (Publications) v American Business Information*[7] the Federal Court of Canada denied copyright status to a yellow pages directory which the defendants downloaded onto an electronic database and then used as the basis for their own,

---

[1.] *RTE and Others v Magill TV Guide* [1990] ILRM 534.

[2.] *Cramp (GA) & Sons v Frank Smythson Ltd* [1944] AC 329.

[3.] *Morris v Wright* (1869) 5 Ch 279, see also *Morris v Ashbee* (1868) 7 Eq 34 and *Lamb v Evans* [1893] 1 Ch 218.

[4.] *Rose v Information Services* [1987] FSR 254; *Waterlow Directories Ltd v Reed Information Services Ltd* [1992] FSR 409.

[5.] [1991] 20 IPR 129; *Geller* (1991) 21 IIC 802; *Schwarz* [1991] EIPR 178.

[6.] See *Bellsouth Advertising v Donnelley Information Publishing* (1991) 933 F (2d) 952.

[7.] (1996) 35 IPR 121.

much enhanced database which they marketed in parallel with the plaintiff's product. While McGillis J decided that there was no substantial infringement because the two works were not competing, or substantially similar, the basic reason why copyright protection was denied centred on the lack of originality of the plaintiff's directory: even the usual presumption of copyright protection was to no avail, the Court choosing to follow the *Feist* reasoning, even in relation to a commercial, Yellow Pages directory as distinct from a standard White Pages directory.

> "In conclusion, Tele-Direct arranged its information, the vast majority of which is not subject to copyright, according to accepted, commonplace standards of selection in the industry. In doing so, it exercised only a minimal degree of skill, judgment or labour in its overall arrangement which is insufficient to support a claim of originality in the compilation so as to warrant copyright protection. In my opinion, the defendant has successfully displaced the presumption in favour of copyright created by ... the Act."[8]

[14.04] Nevertheless the absence of copyright protection *pace Feist*, and the effect the case has had on parasitic trading practices, has been recently noted in the international press,[9] where a number of US companies have used established print directories in order to produce electronic database products (eg on CD-ROM) from low labour cost countries, thus providing direct evidence of the importance of both Community harmonisation and the evolution of world-wide standards of protection through international treaties.

[14.05] The protection of compilations of works that of themselves are not literary is also not directly addressed by existing Irish law. If the works are, or include, artistic works, for example, case-law suggests that the compilation as a whole is to be regarded as literary[10] and it should be noted that the Paris Act of Berne, in Article 2(5), sets out that "collections of literary or artistic works such as encyclopaedias and anthologies which, by reason of the selection and arrangement of their contents, constitute intellectual creations shall be protected as such". At the level of International Treaty Law the protection available to database compilers has been broadened by the TRIPs and the recent Geneva Protocol to the Berne Convention, which documents are both intended to have the same result. These two provisions are set out towards the end of this chapter but they are seen as being of cardinal importance. Commercial interests in

---

[8.] *Ibid* at 136. Contrast a short report of British Telecom obtaining an injunction to prevent a German company from distributing a CD-ROM directory: 'BT Blocks Rivals Computer Phone List' *Times* 21 September 1996.

[9.] *The Economist*, 15 August 1994.

[10.] *Davis v Benjamin* [1906] 2 Ch 491; *Kalamazoo (Aust) Pty v Compact Business Systems* (1985) 5 IPR 213.

Ireland are anxious that these provisions should be implemented into law, for the avoidance of doubt, at the earliest opportunity.

[14.06] The issue of creativity has proved to be a sensitive one in the United Kingdom. As the European industry leader, particularly in relation to on-line databases, the United Kingdom Government has been extremely proactive in protecting electronic databases, the 1988 legislation being specifically drawn up so as to protect electronic databases as compilations,[11] and there is little doubt that the limited nature of the UK and Irish originality test, embracing as it does a 'sweat of the brow' element, gives copyright protection to data sets that represent a minimal amount of independent skill and labour. The European Commission's insistence upon retention[12] of an originality test that requires the database to "constitute the author's own intellectual creation" pitches the originality standard above the UK/Irish threshold and somewhat below most European standards, representing a classical compromise but one that has been criticised nevertheless.[13]

CAN A DATABASE BE A WORK?

[14.07] Even if the originality standard can be overcome, the compiler of a database still faces other difficulties. If the material to be included within the compilation is copyright material, then reproduction without the consent of the author may be an infringement of copyright, certainly when the work is reproduced in a printed format. However, the situation is less certain if a database exists in an electronic form (eg on-line) and a user downloads the contents of the database onto another electronic format (eg the hard disk of a personal computer). It is by no means clear, under existing Irish law, that the original database is itself copyright protected in that form because case law requires a literary work to exist "in print or in writing"[14] and that it shall exist in a form that is perceptible to the human senses.[15] Further, an unauthorised act of downloading material into a digital format may not be an act of reproduction under the 1963 Act, for, while the definition of 'reproduction' in s 2(1) is not exhaustive, the reference therein to 'records' which encapsulate sounds and 'cinematographic film' speak only to earlier technologies only.

---

11. Copyright Designs and Patents Act 1988, ss 1(1)(a), 3(1)(c) and 178: see *Frome and Rowe* [1990-91] CLSR 117.
12. Article 3.1.
13. Eg [1993] CLSR 4. For the pre-directive view on German law, see Katzenberger (1990) 21 IIC 310.
14. Petersen J in *University of London Press Ltd v University Tutorial Press* [1916] 2 Ch 601, at 609.
15. *Computer Edge Property v Apple Computer Inc* [1986] FSR 537.

[14.08] The uncertainty surrounding both the originality standard and the applicability of old concepts to these new methods of holding and distributing information were readily appreciated by the information industry. The UK legislated to bring electronic databases into copyright in 1988 and in the same year the European Commission Green Paper canvassed European Community action in order to protect this significant, but underdeveloped sector of European industry by creating a stable and secure legal environment for the information industry to develop within.[16]

COMMUNITY ACTION

[14.09] The 1988 Green Paper[17] was followed by a Commission hearing held in April 1990 in order to gather opinion on the need for harmonising legislation, and in the 1991 follow-up document,[18] Community legislation on databases was promised. Three major versions of the proposed Directive have appeared, namely the initial 13 May 1992[19] proposal,[20] the Amended Proposal of 4 October 1993,[21] and the Common Position adopted by the Council of Ministers on 10 July 1995. This illustrates that there have been significant shifts of perspective in the tortuous process of obtaining the agreement of Member States, and further adjustments by the Parliament have prolonged the process of getting agreement on this important document. The Directive was finally agreed however on 11 March 1996.[22]

[14.10] The motives behind the drafting of the Directive were clearly based upon internal market objectives and a desire to ensure that the European Industry was not at a disadvantage *vis-à-vis* third countries such as the USA and Japan. The Directive noted that the levels of protection were not clearly stated in all EU States at present and that such uncertainty could act as a brake upon the freedom to provide goods and services within the European Union. Further, where protection existed the protection took different forms (particularly in relation to the originality threshold) and for these reasons a harmonisation measure was seen as essential. The Directive also recognised the importance of providing a stable and uniform legal environment for the European information industry, acknowledging that levels of investment in the European Union Member States were significantly lower than those in major competing States. The interests of both European industrial users of information products, and

---

16. See Huber [1993] CLSR 2.
17. Com (88) 172 Final.
18. Com (90) 584 Final.
19. Common Position (EC) No 20/95.
20. Com (92) 24 Final Syn 393.
21. Com (93) 464 Final Syn 393.
22. Directive 96/9/EC. OJ L 77/20.

those seeking access to the Community's cultural heritage, necessitated legal measures to protect databases in the form of copyright protection and measures to counteract unfair competition. While there have been significant changes in the Directive during its path towards adoption, the main features are set out below.

SCOPE OF PROTECTION

[14.11] Article 1.2 defines a database as "a collection of independent works, data or other materials arranged in a systematic or methodical way and individually accessible by electronic or other means". This broadening of the definition thus brings in raw data specifically - the original definition spoke only of 'materials' - and, significantly, brings in manually compiled databases which are to be individually accessed by using the human eye and intellect. The materials must be a collection of works, data or other independent materials so one act of downloading of a film or scanning today's newspaper onto hard disk would not create a database. However, the selection and arrangement of materials - print, sound, graphics to create an electronic journal or newspaper, would be a collection of materials protected under the Directive as a compilation. The criteria of selection or arrangement may have the effect of excluding compilations that are created by reference to no real selection criteria, eg the mere downloading of printed matter perhaps to be selected and accessed by using software at a later date. In such a case the software may allow the database to meet the accessing criteria but the database itself will remain unstructured and possibly unprotected. Computer programs are not covered unless they are collections of independent materials, eg my 50 favourite Sega mega drive games.[23]

WHO IS PROTECTED?

[14.12] The Directive refers to the author of the database: the author in this context is the natural person or group of natural persons who create the database.[24] Thus, authorship can arise in a collective group, which of course is the current position under s 16 of the Copyright Act 1963. While the Directive allows Member States to nominate a legal person to be the rightholder, this kind of provision does not appear in Irish legislation and may not be utilised in drafting the Irish transposition measure. On other matters of ownership the Directive is silent. So, if the author is an employee then the owner will be the employer of the author under s 10(4) of the 1963 Act. The most significant omission on the issue of ownership is the failure of the Directive to deal with the

---

[23.] CD compilations of musical performances are also not covered - Recital 19 - "as a rule".
[24.] Article 4.

ownership of computer generated works, eg databases compiled by way of a computer program. While UK legislation currently provides that ownership vests in the person who makes the arrangements necessary to create the work, agreement could not be reached on this kind of problem in relation to the 1991 Computer Programs Directive so the issue was not pushed by the Commission.[25] Doubts exist about whether copyright provisions such as the aforementioned computer generated work UK provision are permissible under the Directive,[26] the view being that such investment is protected under the *sui generis* right.

WHAT RIGHTS ARE GIVEN OR NOT GIVEN?

[14.13] The restricted acts in relation to the Directive are based upon traditional copyrights and employ also the broader rights found in the Software Directive which is already in force in Ireland.[27] Thus, temporary or permanent reproduction, in whole or in part, by any means, is a restricted act, as is the translation, adaptation, arrangement or other alteration of the database, public distribution (subject to a first sale of a tangible database within the Community exception), public communication, display or performance. These rights also apply in relation to translations and adaptations of the database.[28] These rights apply in relation to the database as a compilation of materials so reproduction of the database, for example, infringes copyright in the compilation and not necessarily the individual works that form part of the database. Reproduction of individual works or data may constitute a breach of the *sui generis* right but not the copyright afforded to the author of the database under the Directive. As in the Software Directive, the expansion of the author's rights into acts such as viewing a database or temporary reproduction may seem extreme[29] but they are necessary to protect the author's rights and subject to qualification by the Directive in relation to lawful users of the database.

THE LAWFUL USER'S RIGHTS

[14.14] The provisions setting out the restricted acts would prevent any use at all if they were insisted upon, so there is an exception in the case of lawful users[30] who are able to do all or any of the otherwise restricted acts which are necessary to access the contents of the database and which are a normal use of those contents. This right only applies to those parts of the database that are

---

[25.] Copyright, Designs and Patents Act 1988, s 9(3).

[26.] See Kaye [1995] EIPR 583; Chalton [1995] CLSR 295.

[27.] SI 26/1993.

[28.] Article 5.

[29.] It is this issue that was to cause substantial problems in the Geneva 1996 Conference on the scope of the reproduction right, and exceptions thereto. See para **[20.35]**.

[30.] Article 6.

compatible with lawful use (ie parts publicly available or parts for which the user has been permitted to use, by paying a subscription for example). Apart from this mandatory provision, Member States can go further by broadening the rights of individual users by taking advantage of certain permissive provisions in the Directive. Member States may extend existing natural laws on fair dealing[31] to the use of databases. Alternatively, there are tailormade fair use provisions that an be utilised which are instances of reproduction for private purposes of non-electronic databases, use for the sole purposes of teaching or scientific research[32] where such use is justifiable by non commercial purposes,[33] or use for public security or the proper performance of administrative or judicial procedures.[34] These fair dealing exceptions, however, are themselves conditioned by the overriding criteria that the use permitted by these provisions are not to allow a use that unreasonably prejudices the rightholder's legitimate interests or conflict with normal exploitation of the database[35] (eg lead to the parasitic and direct production of rival goods or services).

THE *SUI GENERIS* RIGHT

[14.15] The Directive contains a further mechanism which permits the database creator to protect the contents of the database from being substantially used or re-utilised by others. As long as the maker of the database can show that the creation of the database involved a substantial investment in terms of obtaining, verifying or presenting the contents of the database, any permanent or temporary extraction and/or re-utilisation of the contents by making those contents available to the public will be held to constitute an infringement of the database creator's right.[36] This form of right to control copying or public distribution of contents is necessary because the raising of the originality threshold for some Member States, the fact that the copyrights afforded by the Directive apply to an author, and that those rights apply to the compilation, *qua* compilation rather than elements within the database, made some kind of entrepreneurial right to protect investment in otherwise unprotected compilations a necessary corollary to copyright protection. This right provides an unfair competition right which is otherwise not available under Irish law and the measure is to be welcomed. The model for this provision comes from Scandinavian legislation that has apparently worked well although not a substantial volume of case law has emerged from such provisions. The right is to operate for fifteen years and an

---

31. Ie CA 1963, ss 12 and 14.
32. Defined so as to cover both natural and human sciences (Recital 36).
33. See for example, *American Geophysical Union v Texaco* (1994) 29 IPR 381.
34. Article 6(c).
35. Article 6(3).
36. Article 7.

extension of the right can be obtained if the contents of the database are substantially changed during the period of protection. Again, in considering whether a substantial change has taken place which will justify a further 15 year extension, the core issue is whether there has been a substantial new investment. Thus, the relative shortness of the right is counterbalanced by the likelihood that changes to the contents and structure of a data base are likely to satisfy the substantial change test and result in a further extension of rights.[37] While there are legitimate user exceptions[38] and fair dealing provisions[39] in the Directive, this twin track approach represents an ingenious approach to reconciling users and producers as well as diverse legal traditions in the European Union.[40]

THE WIPO TREATIES/GATT TRIPS

[14.16] At the level of International Agreement, the climate is very much in favour of protecting compilations of works, or other material held electronically or in traditional formats as being copyright protected as compilations. Article 10.2 of GATT/TRIPS[41] provides:

> Compilations of data or other material, whether in machine readable or other form, which by reason of the selection or arrangement of their contents constitute intellectual creations, shall be protected as such. Such protection which shall not extend to the data or material itself, shall be without prejudice to any copyright in the data or material itself.

[14.17] This approach to the compilation of both 'works' (whether in the public domain or copyright protected) and to non-copyrightable data (such as personal names, addresses and telephone numbers for example), has been further emphasised in recent work by WIPO on the possible Protocol to the Berne Convention. The Committee of Experts, by the end of 1994[42] had concluded that compilations of works and data should be regarded as copyright protected as compilations when the necessary originality standard is satisfied and that statements to this effect in the proposed protocol should be regarded as declaratory in nature. The problem of protecting the database industry where the contents or criteria for selection fail to pass an originality test were also reviewed and the Committee considered the question whether such databases

---

[37.] Article 10(3).

[38.] Article 9.

[39.] *Ibid.*

[40.] See Huber [1993] CLSR 2. However, one commentator has doubted whether the Database Directive will alone provide the necessary protection available in relation to multimedia products: see Beutler [1996] Ent LR 317 for a critical look at the Directive in this context.

[41.] Agreements on Trade Related Aspects of Intellectual Property Rights including Trade in Counterfeit Goods.

[42.] WIPO, Fourth Session, 5 to 9 December 1994 BCP/CE/IV/2.

should be included in the provisions of the Protocol and what should be the nature and contents of those provisions. Those deliberations led to the evaluation of a database provision in the Protocol document, or First Treaty, which recognised that "compilations of data or other material, in any form, which by reason of the selection and arrangement of their contents constitute intellectual creations are protected as such" (without prejudice to copyright protection of the contents, as such). No agreement was reached on a Third Treaty, put before the Conference and modelled on the EU Directive, conferring *sui generis* rights, but efforts are to be made in the months ahead to agree such a Treaty.

DATABASES - OTHER MEASURES

[14.18] Other means of protecting the investment and effort involved in compiling and marketing a database may be found in recent Irish legislation that only indirectly addresses issues of ownership in information and information systems.

[14.19] Under the Data Protection Act 1988,[43] personal data, that is, data concerning a human person that is capable of being automatically processed (eg retrieved by way of a computer) must be protected by data controllers from unauthorised use or disclosure, and there is no doubt that certain kinds of data misuse could well lead to criminal or civil liability in certain situations. Indeed, unauthorised disclosures of personal data can breach the criminal law and personal data misuse that constitutes a breach of duty under s 7 of the Act may be actionable as a statutory tort. In seeking to maintain the integrity of information and the privacy of human persons, the Data Protection Act 1988 provides additional protection for computerised databases. The current explosion of interest in counteracting computer fraud and hacking in most countries has been acted upon by the Oireachtas in the form of the Criminal Damage Act 1991.[44] Specific attention should be paid to the provisions of s 5 which make it an offence to operate a computer, without lawful excuse, with the intention to access any data. This offence is a broad one for it is committed even if access is not obtained and data is defined so as to cover "information in a form in which it can be accessed by means of a computer and includes a program". Where some kind of commercial or professional relationship exists, it may be possible to invoke the law of passing off or the law of confidence in certain instances.[45]

---

43. See generally Clark, *Data Protection Law in Ireland* (1990, Round Hall Press).
44. See Clark, [1994] Eur J Crime Cr L Cr J 252.
45. Wadlow, *Passing off* (2nd ed, 1995, Sweet & Maxwell): Lavery, *Commercial Secrets* (1997, Round Hall Sweet & Maxwell).

Chapter 15

Ownership and Dealings in Copyright Works

INTRODUCTION

[15.01] The starting point in any examination of how a work may become the subject of subsequent transfers and dealings is of course the act of authorship, or making a correct attribution of authorship. The work must be literary, dramatic, musical or artistic, it must be original and it must be created by a human person; the products of natural forces such as water and sand cannot as such be protected works[1] and computer generated works are not protected under Irish law,[2] as it presently stands. While copyright in such works can vest in a company through a number of legal concepts and devices, a human person (or persons) must create the work, not least because identification of the author or authors assists in measuring the duration of copyright in most situations.

THE ORIGINAL VESTING OF COPYRIGHT

[15.02] We start from the proposition that ownership of copyright subsists in the author or co-author of a work.[3] Authorship is not defined in the 1963 Act but this question has been teased out in many cases. In relation to musical works the composer of the piece as a matter of statute has copyright and the right is not lost by performance or use of that piece.[4] Where, however, a piece has been produced as a result of interaction between an author, impresario and others, nice questions of judgment can arise. In *Tate v Thomas*,[5] Petersman suggested the title of a play to composers who he engaged to write music for the play. Petersman also engaged two others to write the libretto and during the writing of these pieces he suggested the names of the leading characters and some details of plot and incidental dialogue. On these facts the court found that Petersman was not the author, or even a co-author of either element in the work. Persons who simply transpose speech into some other format, do not, unless there is sufficient skill or effort used to put the speech into a presentable form, thereby

---

1. *Komesaroff v Mickle* (1986) 77 ALR 502.
2. See the distinction between computer aid and computer generated works in *Payen Components South Africa Ltd v Bovic Gaskets* (1995) 33 IPR 407.
3. CA 1963, ss 8(1) and 9(2).
4. *Storace v Longman* (1788) 2 Camp. 27n; *Chappell v Boosey* (1882) 21 Ch D 232.
5. [1921] 1 Ch 503.

acquire a copyright in the work thus generated.[6] If, however, a work exists which is then reworked or reformatted in such a way as to produce a derivative piece it may be possible to identify a separate copyright in the later piece[7] although any such piece may be itself an infringement of copyright in the original work.[8] In *Donoghue v Allied Newspapers Ltd*[9] a successful jockey was contracted to produce a number of newspaper articles about his 'racing secrets'. The defendant engaged a journalist to convert Mr Donoghue's racing anecdotes into literary form, often in the shape of conversations and dialogues. While the contract was silent on copyright, and it is clear that Donoghue supplied the content of each article, the journalist engaged by the newspaper gave the stories much of their shape and style. In this case the court held that Mr Donoghue was not the owner or even part owner of the stories and could not therefore prevent the defendant from using the stories again.

[15.03] While there are situations where joint copyright may be held to exist,[10] the input of ghost-writers is normally addressed by contract. Where the work is subsequently altered by an editor or through editorial processes, express contractual provisions should be used to regulate both ownership and issues concerning editorial powers and subsequent utilisation.[11] Mere editorial input or critical advice in shaping the work will not allow that person to claim even a share in copyright.[12] However, in the case of artistic works the draftsman engaged to give artistic expression to the thoughts and ideas of a client may more readily be forced to yield any claim to sole copyright. In *Kendrick v Lawrence*[13] emphasis was placed on the need for the person giving instructions to the artist to in some way share in putting the work onto the paper: this seems to require an element of interaction and review of work in progress rather than physically executing the drawing or artwork. In *Cala Homes (South) Ltd v Alfred McAlpine Homes East Ltd*,[14] the plaintiffs, who had engaged a firm of technical draughtsmen to assist in executing design drawings, were able to successfully assert than when the draughtsmen utilised those drawings to assist the defendant, they infringed copyright in the original drawings which were acts

---

6. *Walter v Lane* [1900] AC 539. Irish law does not recognise a copyright in speech; for a recent Canadian case in point see *Gould Estate v Stoddart Publishing* (1996) 30 OR (3d) 520 - contrast s 3(1) of the 1988 UK legislation.
7. *Springfield v Thaine* (1903) 19 TLR 650.
8. *Express Newspapers plc v News UK Ltd* [1990] 3 All ER 376.
9. [1937] 3 All ER 503; *Evans v Hutton (E) & Co* (1924) 131 LT 534.
10. *Heptulla v Orient Longman* [1989] FSR 598.
11. *Samuelson v Producers Distributing* [1932] 1 Ch 201.
12. *Wiseman v Weidenfeld & Nicholson Ltd* [1985] FSR 525; *Ashmore v Douglas-Home* [1987] FSR 553.
13. (1890) 25 QBD 99.
14. [1995] FSR 818; *Antill & Gourgey* [1996] EIPR 49.

of joint ownership. While the draughtsmen were solely involved in creating the drawings, the high degree of consultation and supervision undertaken by the plaintiff's employee in the process of creating the drawings made the work a work of joint authorship.

[15.04] In relation to works of compilation[15] such as a newspaper or encyclopaedia, persons who write the individual entries will generally be regarded as the author of the work, but the issue of ownership of copyright may be resolved by express terms or through an implied transfer of copyright due to the fact of commissioning and payment to the contributor.[16] Ownership of individual elements that form part of the collection should also be distinguished from the issue of ownership in the compilation. Even if the work of compilation consists of pre-existing material, the persons responsible for that work of compilation are the first owners of copyright.[17]

Employees

[15.05] The relationship of employer and employee or master and servant gives rise to a number of common law duties and implied contractual rights, which in the field of intellectual property may be said to favour the employer. When an employee makes a discovery or creates something of value in the course of doing that which the employer has engaged him to do, the fruits of that employment will generally be the property of the employer and not the employee[18] save where it can be said that the discovery or product did not involve the use of the employer's time, information, trade secrets, or overlap with the contractual obligations or job description of the employed person.[19] In the area of copyright, s 10(4) of the 1963 Act provides that where a work is made in the course of the author's employment by another person under a contract of service or apprenticeship, the employer is to be entitled to any copyright subsisting in that work.[20] It may be difficult at times to determine what kind of employment is involved and the courts may have to distinguish between employee, independent contractor or even agent status in an extreme case.[21] The leading English case is *Stevenson Jordan and Harrison Ltd v MacDonald &*

---

15. The definition of literary work 'includes' a compilation: CA 1963, s 2.
16. *Lawrence & Bullen Ltd v Aflalo* [1904] AC 17.
17. *A-One Accessory Imports Pty Ltd v Off Road Imports Pty* (1996) 34 IPR 306.
18. *British Reinforced Concrete Co v Lind* (1917) 116 LT 243; *Sterling Engineering Co v Patchett* [1955] AC 534; *British Syphon Co v Homewood* [1956] 1 WLR 1190. See *Accountancy & Business College (Ireland) Ltd v Ahern & Plant* (HC) *Irish Times*, 4 February 1995.
19. *Re Selz Ltd* (1953) 71 RPC 158.
20. Subject to certain exceptions vis-à-vis journalistic employment and certain artistic works, mentioned below.
21. *Community for Creative Non-Violence v Reid* (1989) 17 IPR 367.

Evans.[22] In that case an accountant had written a number of public lectures and he had prepared the text of a study, while employed by the plaintiffs. The plaintiffs sought to prevent posthumous publication of these lectures, and the study, on the ground, *inter alia*, that copyright vested in the plaintiffs.

[15.06] In *Stevenson Jordan* the Court of Appeal took the view that the accountant was not employed as a lecturer but, rather, was willing to give lectures outside the course of his employment to enhance his own position within the firm and provide positive publicity for the firm; the lectures and the text thereof were not caught by the statutory provision[23] although the separate item of text compiled as a consequence of a specific task undertaken for the employer, was so caught. Indeed, even if a university teacher or professor is employed to give lectures, copyright in the text does not attach to the university that employs that person, according to *dicta* in *Stephenson Jordan*. The position of research students and teaching assistants is probably within this *dicta* also, unless the contract of employment specifically directs that the creation of literary texts is an element in the contractual duties of the employee. Some universities seek to claim ownership of research work *via* the regulations governing entry on a course of study, although it is submitted that these could be challenged *via* unconscionability concepts. The course of employment exception applies also to many forms of artistic work and s 10(4) will operate so as to transfer copyright to an employer in appropriate cases. In *Danowski v Henry Moore Foundation*[24] the artist Henry Moore entered into a contractual arrangement with a limited company and registered charity to preserve his work. Sale and service agreements were struck under which Moore agreed not to carry on the business of sculptor for anyone other than the company, and further, vesting copyright in his works in the company. It was held that the company was entitled to ownership in all Moore's works, including a number of 'artist's copies', for these were made in the course of his employment.

[15.07] Most disputes in relation to the employment exception tend to centre on whether the person creating the work is an employee. These disputes involve a fastidious scrutiny of the contract and the incidental aspects of the relationship between the parties.[25]

---

22. [1952] 1 TLR 101.
23. See also *Byrne v Statist Co* [1914] 1 KB 628.
24. *The Times*, 19 March 1996. *Greenfield Products v Rover-Scott Bonnar* (1990) 17 IPR 417.
25. *Beloff v Pressdram Ltd* [1973] 1 All ER 241. Many of these cases are tax and social welfare cases eg *Graham v Minister for Industry & Commerce* [1933] IR 156; *Minister for Social Welfare v Griffiths* [1992] ILRM 667.

[15.08] The fact that a person is an officer of a company will not prevent that person from also functioning as an employee.[26] Issues of this kind may be side-stepped by joining the author as a co-litigant.[27]

Contributions to Newspapers, Magazines and similar Periodicals

[15.09] Section 10(2) of the 1963 Act[28] makes provision for the sharing of a copyright when a literary, dramatic or artistic work is made in the course of employment and the author of that work is an employee or apprentice. The employer, as proprietor of a newspaper, magazine or similar periodical is to have copyright in that work, when made for those purposes but the copyright so obtained is limited to republication in some other newspaper, magazine or similar periodical. Thus, the pirating of an article by some other proprietor will infringe the employer's copyright, and it is likely that if the employee or apprentice author sold that story for publication in another newspaper, magazine or similar periodical this would infringe the proprietor's copyright and possibly breach an implied term in the contract of employment or apprenticeship. However, the proprietor's copyright is limited, for the closing words of s 10(2) make it clear that, in all other respects, copyright is with the author. The requirement that the proprietor is entitled to assert copyright *vis-à-vis* a periodical is a limitation; the journalist may assert republication rights in an anthology, for example, but the notion of a periodical should also extend to publication in some form other than print medium; although there is no case in point, the unauthorised use of copy by electronic republication on a bulletin board should infringe the publisher's copyright. The copyright is not shared if the journalist/contributor is a freelance or non-employed person and again the cases are of importance[29] in identifying employees and independent contractors. Section 10(2) does not apply to musical works here so the proprietor obtains copyright under the s 10(4) presumption. The effect of the s 10(4) provision is that where there is subsequent use of a newspaper article, by a clipping service, or in relation to photocopying of that work, the journalist owns copyright. It is also arguable that in relation to other types of electronic reproduction, except in an electronic version of the newspaper in which the work appeared, which is published contemporaneously, it is the journalist not the proprietor who is the rightholder.[30]

---

26. *Re Beeton* [1913] 2 Ch 279; *Wilder Pump v Fusfield* (1985) 8 IPR 250.
27. *University of London Press v University Tutorial Press* [1916] 2 Ch 601; *House of Spring Gardens v Point Blank Ltd* [1984] IR 611.
28. The predecessor of s 10(2) was considered in *Hall v Crosbie & Co* (1931) 66 ILTR 22.
29. *Re Sunday Tribune* [1984] IR 505; *O'Riain v Independent Newspapers* UD 134/1978; *Kelly v Irish Press* (1986) 5 JISLL 170; *Allen v Toronto Star* (1995) 129 DLR (4th) 171.
30. *De Garis v Neville Jeffress Pidler Pty* (1990) 18 IPR 292; *Nationwide News Pty v Copyright Agency* (1996) 34 IPR 53.

[15.10] Section 10(2) can be displaced by contractual provisions to the contrary.

Commissioned Photographs and certain other Commissioned Works

[15.11] Save in cases where the work is covered by s 10(2), the sharing of copyright provision as between an employed journalist and the proprietor, the 1963 Act provides that where a person commissions the taking of a photograph, a portrait[31] or the making of an engraving,[32] and the commissioner pays or agrees to pay for it in money or money's worth, the work so created is to be copyright of the commissioner. If a photographer invites persons to visit his studio in order to have portraits taken, a conclusion that the commissioner is bound to pay for the work done will lead to copyright being vested in the commissioner.[33] There are cases where the photographer has been successful even if the subject of the photograph obtains free copies of the work and later pays for copies of the work. In *Davis v Baird*[34] the plaintiff photographed a professional wrestler in his studio at a free sitting. Complimentary copies were given and the wrestler later ordered fifty copies of the portrait. In giving judgment for the plaintiff, Porter MR said that the circumstances surrounding the transaction pointed away from the portrait being the property of the subject. Should the contract stipulate that copyright is to vest in the author, notwithstanding the fact that it has been commissioned for money, s 10(3) will not prevent first copyright vesting in the photographer.[35]

Commissioned Works Generally

[15.12] The commissioned artistic works provision, which has just been considered, is the exception that proves the rule; first ownership in a work that has been specifically ordered or commissioned vests in the author. There are, however, a number of situations where this conclusion may not be reached. An entrepreneur who plants the seed of an idea does not *per se* acquire copyright[36] but it may be that where an entrepreneur commissions others to produce works, for a fee, and the circumstances do not point towards any attempt on the part of the authors to reserve copyright, then copyright as a matter of implied contract may subsist in the entrepreneur. The leading case is *Sweet v Benning*[37] and, although the decision did not involve a dispute between an entrepreneur and a contributor but an entrepreneur and a pirate, it has passed into the literature as

---

31. See *Leah v Two Worlds Publishing* [1951] Ch 393.
32. *Con Planck Ltd v Kolynos* [1925] 2 KB 804.
33. *Boucas v Cooke* [1903] 2 KB 227; *Sasha v Stoenesco* (1929) 4 TLR 350.
34. (1903) 38 ILTR 23.
35. CA 1963, s 10(5); *Christopher Bede Studios Ltd v United Portraits Ltd* [1958] NZLR 250.
36. *Tate v Thomas* [1921] 1 Ch 503.
37. (1855) 16 CB 459; *Lamb v Evans* [1893] 1 Ch 218. For musical works see *Wallerstein v Herbert* (1867) 16 LT 453.

turning on drawing certain inferences of fact from the conduct of the parties in each case. In *Lawrence & Billen v Aflalo*,[38] the House of Lords affirmed that for copyright to vest in the commissioner, no written contract is needed and that express words are not needed to constitute such a bargain. The language of the House of Lords reflects a business efficacy, implied term, approach: the author must be taken to have intended to give copyright to the commissioner, as a reasonable person, for the author has been paid for creating the work on a bespoke basis,[39] and to allow the author to use the work again, to the prejudice of the commissioner's interests, would clearly not be reasonable. Advertisers[40] and certain clients of professional persons[41] have also benefited from this implied contract, particularly in relation to artistic copyright and design prototypes.[42]

[15.13] Apart from an implied contract argument, there are also equitable rules that may allow a person other than the author to claim that copyright in the work should be held, in equity, by the author in trust for that other party who may be entitled to call for copyright to be assigned to him. The leading case is *Massine v de Basil*.[43] In that case a choreographer was engaged to produce ballets at Covent Garden and was held to be liable in equity to transfer any copyright to the director of the ballet. This equitable ownership has been held to apply to computer programmers engaged as independent contractors to work on specific projects,[44] to members of a partnership[45] and company officers in appropriate cases.[46] In *A-One Accessory Imports Pty Ltd v Off Road Imports Property Ltd*[47] two persons began work on a sales brochure intending to trade through the plaintiff company which they were in the process of setting up. However, while this meant the plaintiff company was not first owner of copyright, the two founders of the plaintiff company had beneficial ownership of the works, which they held in trust for the plaintiff company.

[38.] [1904] AC 17.

[39.] On which see *PS Johnson v Bucko Enterprises* [1975] NZLR 311.

[40.] *Harold Drabble Ltd v Hycolite Manufacturing Co* (1928) 44 TLR 264.

[41.] *Chantrey, Chantrey & Co v Dey* (1912) 28 TLR 499; Contrast *Meikle v Maufe* [1941] 3 All ER 144.

[42.] *PS Johnson v Bucko Enterprises* [1975] NZLR 311; *Cope Allman v Farrow* (1984) 3 IPR 567; *Enzed Holdings v Wythnia Pty* (1984) 3 IPR 619.

[43.] [1936-45] Mag CC 223. A contract of service was held to exist in any event; see *Missing Link Software v Magee* [1989] FSR 361.

[44.] *John Richardson Computers Ltd v Flanders* [1993] FSR 497.

[45.] *Roban Jig and Tool Co v Taylor* [1979] FSR 130; *Robert J Zupanovich Pty v B & N Beale Nominees Pty* (1995) 32 IPR 339.

[46.] *Wilden Pump v Fusfield* (1985) 8 IPR 250.

[47.] (1996) 34 IPR 306.

Beneficial Ownership and Wrongdoing

[15.14] English case law establishes that where a Crown servant owes a duty not to disclose information that is secret and confidential, and that duty is breached by publication in a literary work, equity may impose a duty upon that person to hold the fruits of the wrongdoing for the person to whom the duty was owed, namely the Crown.[48] The enforcement of statutory copyright ownership rights may be denied on public policy grounds if some wrongdoing such as an actionable conspiracy is disclosed in pleading infringement of copyright[49] and even where some superior private law right requires the subordination of copyright.[50]

Ownership of Copyright in Part III Works

[15.15] The copyrights available in respect of sound recordings, films, broadcasts and typography of published editions of books, may vest in the maker of the recording or film, the broadcaster and the publisher, as the case may be. These rights can vest in corporate bodies directly and this will be the general rule, as distinct from vesting in the human persons who made the recording or pointed the camera, as the case may be.[51] Note, however, that the measuring of duration of copyright can require the rightholder to track the lifetime of persons active in creation of the work eg, in relation to films under the new rules implemented by the Duration Directive.[52]

ASSIGNMENT AND LICENSING

[15.16] It is important to distinguish between the concept of an assignment and a licence agreement. The assignment of rights will transfer ownership of rights and is itself further transferable, while a licence may be personal to the licensee and prevent the licensee from altering the work (eg, editing parts of the work[53]). A transfer may be held to be in law an assignment of rights, although it is described as being a licence.[54] Requirements of legal form attach to assignments while licence agreements do not in themselves so require.[55]

---

48. These observations are found by several judges in the *Spycatcher* litigation (*AG v Guardian Newspapers (No 2)* [1988] 3 All ER 545) and most recently reformulated in *AG v Blake* [1996] 3 All ER 903. These observations are *obiter*.
49. *Massie v Renwick Ltd v Underwriters Survey Bureau* [1940] 1 DLR 625.
50. *British Leyland v Armstrong Patents* [1986] AC 577.
51. *Country Communications Ltd v Mayfair Entertainment* [1993] EMLR 335; *A & M Records v Video Collection* [1995] EMLR 25 sets out a test of entrepreneurial risk.
52. 92/100/EEC.
53. *Frisby v BBC* [1967] Ch 932.
54. *Messager v BBC* [1929] AC 151.
55. Agreements not to be performed within one year under the Statute of Frauds 1695 could be a barrier in certain instances.

Assignments - Total and Partial

[15.17] As s 47(2) declares, an assignment may be limited by restricting the activity of the assignee to one or more, but not all the rights afforded by the Act to the assignor. The assignment may also limit the assignment geographically, restricting the right to one or more countries in relation to which the assignor has those rights and the assignment may be limited in terms of the duration of the assignment, giving the assignee rights in relation only to part of the period in which statutory copyright subsists.

[15.18] In the area of musical copyright, for example, the performing rights in Ireland are normally assigned by PRS members to the Irish Music Rights Organisation, while certain reproduction rights may be assigned by the same rightholder to the Mechanical Copyright Protection Society. In one recent Canadian case it has been held that a composer who assigns performance and broadcasting rights to a company does not thereby assign reproduction rights.[56] In *Jonathan Cape Ltd v Consolidated Press Ltd*,[57] the plaintiff obtained an assignment of volume publication rights to cover a number of countries, including Australia, and was able to bring infringement proceedings against the defendant who reproduced the story without the plaintiff's permission.

[15.19] The question whether an assignment has been granted depends on the intention of the parties gathered from the words used. In *EW Savory Ltd v World of Golf*[58] a document referred to the sale of "five original card designs inclusive of copyrights" and went on to state the subject of the cards. Proof by parole identifying the cards was possible. It was held that there was an assignment. Similarly, in *London Printing and Publishing Alliance Ltd v Cox*[59] sale of a picture for a stated price which "includes sole and entire copyright nett" was held to assign total copyright to the buyer. In contrast, the sale of electro blocks to a buyer who used them to print advertising posters was not an assignment but a mere personal licence to that buyer who could not validly allow others to reproduce posters from those blocks.[60]

[15.20] In the context of publishing agreements the separation of rights can be quite bewildering; in relation to reproduction alone, the rightholder may carve up foreign language rights, serialisation rights, electronic publishing rights, talking book rights, film or adaptation rights, etc. Sometimes the act of

---

56. *Tele Metropole v Bishop* (1990) 20 IPR 318.
57. [1954] 3 All ER 253.
58. [1914] 2 Ch 566.
59. [1891] 3 Ch 291; *Lacy v Toole* (1867) 15 LT 512.
60. *Cooper v Stephens* [1895] 1 Ch 567; *Tuck v Canton* (1882) 51 LJQB 363; *Marshall v Bull* (1901) 85 LT 77; *Hutchison Personal Communications Ltd v Hook Advertising Ltd* [1996] FSR 549.

reproduction may require a publisher and others to undertake certain specific tasks in relation to that work and in such a context a claim of joint ownership may emerge. An agreement as between an author and a publisher to publish a work on a profit sharing basis does not assign copyright[61] unless the terms are clear, even if the word assignment is not used.[62] If, however, a work is published on terms whereby copyright is vested in two parties there can be certain difficulties. With one exception[63] which relates to co-authors, the weight of opinion favours the view that co-ownership involves a joint tenancy in the copyright and that where a right is so shared the consent of each holder of a right must be obtained before any dealing in the work is lawful.[64] So in *Cescinsky v Routledge & Sons*[65] the plaintiff had published literary works on antique furniture with the defendant on the basis of equal copyright in the work by both parties. It was held that reproduction of part of that work by the defendant in another book, without the permission of the plaintiff, infringed the reproduction right of the plaintiff. No implied licence is possible in such a case. While these cases indicate that one co-owner cannot create a licence or assignment without the consent of the other co-owner, the cases hold that one co-owner can bring an infringement action without joining the other co-owner.[66] It is possible that an owner or a co-owner may lose rights to object to another's title through estoppel, as in the old Irish case of *In re Curry*.[67] Here a publisher's assertion of copyright on the title covers was not objected to by an author. Of course, these problems will not arise if the work is in reality a bundle of separate copyrights and these rights are identifiably the works of separate authors[68] (eg, a film with dialogue, music, screenplay etc). However, proof of separate creation should be before the court and if it is not then the total output of the authors may be held to be works of joint authorship.[69]

Formal Requirements for an Assignment

[15.21] Section 47(3) provides that no assignment of copyright, whether total or partial, shall have effect unless it is in writing, signed by or on behalf of the

---

61. *Stevens v Benning* (1855) 6 DeGM & G 223; *Lucas v Moncrieff* (1905) 21 TLR 683; *Re Jude's Musical Compositions* [1906] 2 Ch 595.
62. *Ward Lock & Co v Long* (1906) 22 TLR 798; *Coleridge-Taylor v Novello & Co* [1938] 1 Ch 608.
63. Said to be tenants in common in *Acorn Computers v MLS Microcomputer Systems* [1984-5] ALR 389; *Dixon Projects Pty Ltd v Masterton Homes* (1996) 36 IPR 136.
64. *Powell v Head* (1879) 12 Ch D 686; *Lauri v Renad* [1892] 3 Ch 402.
65. [1916] 2 KB 325; *Spiroflex Industries v Progressive Sealing* (1986) 34 DLR (4th) 201.
66. *Mail Newspapers plc v Express Newspapers plc* [1987] FSR 90.
67. (1848) 12 Ir Eq R 382.
68. *Thibault v Turcot* (1926) 34 RNLS 415.
69. *ATV Music Publishing of Canada v Rogers Radio Broadcasting Ltd* (1982) 134 DLR (3rd) 487.

assignor. An assignment may be held to exist even if the issue of copyright does not appear to have arisen in the negotiations or in the instrument which sets out the transfer, as in a declaration that the parties intend to transfer "all the right, title and interest", plus the goodwill of a publishing business[70] but a mere sale of business equipment - moulds and master patterns for use in jewellery manufacturing - will not create an exclusive licence, much less a copyright assignment, without more.[71]

[15.22] If there is no written instrument of assignment the assignor will have to seek to enforce the assignment through a more circuitous route.

The Assignment of Future Copyright[72]

[15.23] Section 49 of the 1963 Act makes it possible for a person, who is the prospective owner of a copyright work in the sense that the work has yet to be created, to vest copyright in that putative work in another person.[73] Section 49(1) provides that where a contract to this effect is signed by or on behalf of the prospective owner and the agreement purports to assign copyright (wholly or partially in another) then on the coming into existence of copyright that copyright will vest in the assignee or his successor in title without further assurance.

[15.24] The key element in this sub-section is that the vesting will only take place if the assignee would, without this sub-section, be entitled to call for specific performance of the agreement. The assignee should be entitled to specific performance and thus an agreement made gratuitously (ie without consideration) or with an infant, or in restraint of trade (all circumstances where specific performance will be denied) will not satisfy s 49(1).

Equitable Assignments

[15.25] The writing requirements set out in relation to assignments of existing or future copyrights in ss 47 and 49 would appear to suggest that where these statutory provisions are not complied with there can be no other effective transfer of title, but there is judicial support for the view that equity will allow transactions of substance to be effective even if writing requirements in a statute are not satisfied.[74] Equitable assignments may be created when, for example, an independent contractor is engaged to create design drawings, verbally agreeing

---

[70] *Murray v King* (1985) 3 IPR 525; Contrast *Greenfield Products v Rover-Scott Bonnar* (1990) 17 IPR 417.

[71] *Anvil Jewellery Ltd v Riva Ridge Holdings Ltd* [1987] 1 NZLR 35.

[72] For a definition see s 49(4).

[73] The section is intended to remove the effect of *PRS Ltd v London Theatre of Varieties* [1924] AC 1.

[74] *Brooker v John Friend Ltd* [1936] NZLR 743.

that copyright in those works will, upon their creation, be vested in the commissioner. If such an agreement can be made out then the artist will hold legal title for the assignee, who will have beneficial ownership, and the beneficial owner may call upon the legal owner to execute a written assignment to perfect legal and equitable title. In practice, there should be a written assignment in favour of the beneficial owner at some stage if the beneficial owner is to be able to not only seek interim relief[75] but get final judgment against an infringer. While one English case suggests that the assignment of the legal title should take place prior to the issuing of a writ,[76] *Wah Sang Industrial Co v Takmay Industrial Co*,[77] a Hong Kong case, decides that if the assignment takes place after the writ has been issued, the assignee should either join the legal owners or commence a new action. Notwithstanding *Wah Sang Industrial Co v Takmay Industrial Co*, an equitable owner at the time of issue of the writ has been held to be capable of obtaining final judgment if before judgment in the action he becomes the legal owner, by assignment, of that copyright: *Batjak Production Inc v Simitar Entertainment (UK)*.[78]

[15.26] If the work is in existence and this is not a future work but the author agrees to assign copyright in the future, then *a fortiori* there will be an equitable assignment[79] and confirmation in the form of an assignment instrument may be expected[80] but, if no such instrument is ever created, will the assignment be invalid? It appears that Irish law does not have a provision that corresponds with s 53(i)(c) of the English Law of Property Act 1925 which requires a disposition of an equitable interest or trust to be in writing signed by the person disposing of this interest, a provision that had been held to make verbal agreements to transfer equitable ownership ineffective.[81] However, *Wah Sang Industrial Co v Takmay Industrial Co*[82] makes it clear that an equitable interest of this kind can subsist without a writing being required and that as long as the equitable owner's title is perfected in accordance with statutory requirements relating to proof of legal title an equitable assignment for value will be recognised in law. *Batjak Production Inc v Simitar Entertainment (UK)* suggests that title can be perfected at any time up to final judgment.[83]

---

75. *PRS Ltd v London Theatre of Varieties* [1924] AC 1; *Merchant Adventurers v Grew* [1972] 1 Ch 242.
76. *Roban Jig & Tool Co v Taylor* [1979] FSR 130, applying *Creed v Creed* [1913] 1 IR 48.
77. [1980] FSR 303.
78. [1996] FSR 139.
79. *Western Front Ltd v Vestron* [1987] FSR 66.
80. *Kambrook Distributing Pty v Delaney* (1984) 4 IPR 79.
81. *Roban Jig & Tool Co v Taylor* [1979] FSR 130.
82. [1980] FSR 303.
83. [1996] FSR 139.

Licences

[15.27] In general, a licence to use or reproduce a copyright work can be created by way of express or implied contract. It may be, however, that the licence is granted gratuitously. In *Trumpet Software Property Ltd v Ozemail Pty Ltd*,[84] the plaintiff company produced an Internet navigation software package which it agreed to allow the defendant to distribute with its magazine as shareware to allow consumers to consider taking the program. The defendant modified the program and distributed it in that form. It was held that as the permission to distribute was given without consideration moving from the defendant, the licence was bare and revocable at will. Even if the licence had not been revoked, distribution in a modified form constituted breach of the licence agreement.

[15.28] If the licence is contractual, the contract itself will determine its incidents, supplemented by any implied terms the court regards as being necessary to give the agreement business efficacy.[85] If the licence is express then it may not be revocable unless revocation is expressly or impliedly afforded to the licensor[86] and it is difficult to persuade a court that a contractual licence can be impliedly revoked when the agreement is an exclusive licence.[87]

[15.29] An implied licence may be inferred from either the dealings that have taken place as between the parties or through some trade custom that operates within a particular industry. For example, is there a custom in the newspaper industry that allows one newspaper to reproduce, in substance, copy lifted from another publication?[88] It has certainly been held that submitting an article to the editor of a periodical with a view to it being adopted and paid for by the editor may give the editor an implied right to publish that piece without the need to revert to the author for any express permission.[89]

[15.30] It may be possible to infer a licence in cases where the rightholder and the putative licensee have previously contracted to allow the licensee or his predecessors in title to use that work.[90] In one case,[91] the plaintiff produced

---

84. (1996) 34 IPR 481. *McGill v S* [1979] IR 283. Reasonable notice, however, must be given to the bare licensee.
85. *Ibid.*
86. *Winter Garden Theatre (London) Ltd v Millenium Productions Ltd* [1948] AC 173; *Whipp v Mackey* [1927] IR 372.
87. *Crown Industrial Products Co v IDI Electric (Can) Ltd* (1971) 2 CPR (2d) 1.
88. *Walter v Steinkopff* [1892] 3 Ch 489; *Express Newspapers v News (UK) Ltd* [1990] 3 All ER 376.
89. *Hall Brown v Illiff & Sons* [1928-35] Mag CC 88. Copyright of course remains in the author; *Knaplock v Curl* (1722) 4 Vin Abr 278 pl 3.
90. Use is not unlimited; *Roberts v Candiware Ltd* [1980] FSR 352.
91. *Silverson v Neon Products Ltd* [1978] 6 WWR 512.

artwork for a motel proprietor who had developed a distinctive sign to advertise the motel. The plaintiff registered his copyright (probably unlawfully for the plaintiff was an employee) in the design. It was held that the dealings between the parties gave the motel proprietor, and the sign manufacturer engaged by the proprietor, irrevocable licences to use and reproduce the design. Third parties, however, may not acquire such rights as readily as persons who have commissioned or purchased that licence, thus leading to the conclusion that most licences are personal and non-transferable.[92]

[15.31] The implied licence argument has surfaced in several cases where architects have been engaged to prepare plans to be used in order to secure planning permission. In the event that these plans are completed and paid for, is there an implied licence that the person who ordered and paid for these plans can use them for any purpose they wish, including the construction of a building without necessarily engaging the architect to complete the work? Despite the breadth of the judgment in *Blair v Osborne and Tompkins*[93] the Court of Appeal in *Stovin Bradford v Volpoint Properties*[94] suggests that this licence will not be implied if the fee paid to the architect is not a full scale fee and, even if it is, such an implication will only be made if it is fair to both parties.[95] The same approach is sometimes adopted in relation to designs and plans completed by structural engineers.[96]

[15.32] A licence may be created by way of laches or acquiescence. Certain acts of infringement may occur and if the rightholder does not act promptly to obtain relief the rightholder may be denied protection because of the plaintiff's delay in seeking equitable relief. It may be that the plaintiff's failure to pursue the infringer may be due to market circumstances - the *de facto* licensee may be acting in a way which is to the advantage of the rightholder.[97] In the context of copyright infringement, a recent English case provides a very broad basis upon which an apparent infringer may avoid liability. In *Film Investors Overseas Services SA v Home Video Channel Ltd*,[98] the licensee infringed the scope of a licence by showing films on a satellite channel over areas that the licence did not cover. The defendant sold decoders in areas outside the licence area, in breach of an implied term in the licence agreement. Nevertheless, Carnwath J held that the plaintiff could not complain because it suited the plaintiff to ensure that his

---

92. *Mateffy Perl Nagy Pty Ltd v Devefi Pty* (1992) 23 IPR 505.
93. [1971] 1 All ER 468.
94. [1971] 3 All ER 570.
95. *Per* Salmon LJ *Ibid* at p 578.
96. *Netupsky v Dominion Bridge Co* (1971) 24 DLR (3d) 484.
97. *Dominion Rent a Car Ltd v Budget Rent a Car Systems* (1970) Ltd [1987] 2 NZLR 395.
98. *The Times* 2 December 1996; *Masterton Homes Pty v LED Builders Pty* (1996) 33 IPR 417.

films received broader distribution and exposure and that his delay in seeking relief was an acquiescence on the principle that "it would be unconscionable for a party to be permitted to deny that which, knowingly or unknowingly, he has allowed or encouraged another to assume to his detriment".[99]

[15.33] Licences granted by the owner of copyright are binding on every successor in title except a purchaser in good faith for valuable consideration and without notice, actual or constructive.[100] This provision also extends to licences of future copyrights.[101]

The Licensing of Use in Copyright Works

[15.34] Authorising persons to use a copyright work is of substantial benefit to the rightholder and different methods of granting licences exist. At one extreme stands the practice of employing individuals to maximise the income that a work may generate. For example, the author of a literary work may engage a literary agent to negotiate the sale of publication rights with a publisher even before the work has been created and even persons of limited literary expertise - celebrities, politicians etc - engage in the business of touting memoirs and the like via an agent. The sale of future works to a publisher via a literary agent, even in the case of celebrated and talented authors, and the level of advance obtained, is viewed with great interest.[102] Sale and distribution practices in the fine arts field also can involve an artist agreeing to distribute works either via a dealer or some foundation, for a variety of motives. In some instances the rightholder may engage an agent to control certain rights while employing others to deal with other rights. For example, in the area of dramatic works, the major British publishers such as Samuel French Ltd and Warner Chapell Ltd have distributed play texts and performance licences to Irish drama societies through agents in Ireland.[103] These arrangements, which involve close personal contact between the rightholder's agent and the user, often represent the only practical means of ensuring that certain acts of exploitation by users lead to an income for the rightholder but it must be pointed out that the market is somewhat haphazard and levels of income and efficiency in collection of revenues differ markedly from sector to sector.

[99.] Oliver J in *Taylor Fashions Ltd v Liverpool Victoria Friendly Society* [1982] 1 QB 133, at 151.

[100.] CA 1963 s 47(4).

[101.] CA 1963 s 49(3).

[102.] Note the controversy surrounding Martin Amis and his £500,000 1996 two book deal with Harper Collins, recently topped by a £1 million four book deal with Random House; *Times* 17 December 1996.

[103.] See 'Mister Copyright' *The Irish Times* 7 September 1994.

IMRO

[15.35] The most high profile area of third party licensing is in the music sector. The right to authorise the public performance of a musical work - the performing rights - have traditionally been administered collectively, on behalf of composers and music publishers, by the Performing Rights Society (PRS), a body established in 1914[104] to administer performing rights on behalf of the PRS membership. In 1988 PRS established the Irish Music Rights Organisation (IMRO) to act as the collecting body for the Republic of Ireland. The link between PRS and IMRO was broken in 1995 when the IMRO membership balloted to become independent of PRS, a move further enhanced by the resignation of PRS members from the Board of IMRO during 1995. In essence, IMRO has the legally butressed right to collect on behalf of its members as the result of an assignment of the performing rights by members to IMRO. In the year ended 1995, IMRO had a total membership of 1,139. Total licensing revenue for 1995 was £8,271,974, the main sources of which are represented in the following table taken from the IMRO Annual Report.[105]

	1995
REVENUE	£IR
Broadcasting	
Radio Telefís Éireann	1,975, 000
Cable television	3,107, 937
Satellite TV	128, 715
Independent radio	868, 165
Total broadcasting	6,079, 817
Public performance	4,639, 847
Overseas income	342, 978
	11, 062, 642
Cable rightholders	(2,790, 668)
Total Licence Revenue	8,271,974

[15.36] It should be noted that IMRO has concluded licensing agreements with RTE for the period 1995-98 and has thus managed to settle one of the key issues

---

104. By several composers including Sir Edward Elgar.
105. *Directors' Report and Financial Statements 31 December 1995.* IMRO does not licence performing rights for entire works with some dramatic content eg, public performance of an opera or musical. These rights, 'grand rights' are administered by or through the rightholder.

that has caused the collecting societies generally to be concerned about the public perception of music collecting in Ireland. Other high profile disputes, however, are still simmering, in particular, the whole philosophy behind public performance and copyright has been challenged by bodies like the Vintners Federation of Ireland, who suggest that collecting societies hold and abuse a monopoly - assertions that we will look at later in the context of competition law.

[15.37] IMRO, as a company limited by guarantee, does not make a profit and it is committed to distributing all income to its members and to overseas affiliated bodies, after making deductions for administration costs. Distributions are periodic although concert promotion income is now distributed one month after the concert has been held. IMRO is currently engaged in developing a more aggressive approach to the relatively low level of membership income from certain other jurisdictions, particularly the USA, and is threatening to use GATT dispute mechanisms if these issues cannot be resolved satisfactorily.[106] IMRO has also been a very vocal organisation in emphasising the importance of a stable and contemporary legal environment, especially in copyright matters, if the economic and employment potential of the Irish music industry is to be realised.[107]

[15.38] The fact that IMRO regulates performing rights only on behalf of composers and publishers raises the issue of who regulates the right to reproduce the work, particularly the right to make recordings of a work. It should be recalled that under s 13 of the Act, the right to make a recording of a published musical work is given to anyone who is prepared to pay equitable remuneration to the rightholder.[108] The right to reproduce either the musical work itself on a record, or reproduce the author's copyright in a sound recording, are known as mechanical rights and these are administered in Ireland by the Mechanical Copyright Protection Society. In essence, the members of MCPS are music publishers and composers and under contract, not assignment, these members deal with major commercial interests who seek to make recordings of copyright works. MCPS therefore deals with record companies, broadcasting organisations, video companies, film and advertising companies and agencies, record importers, indeed any person or body that wishes to reproduce a copyright musical work; even the reproduction of a musical work through door bell chimes or in a child's toy involve mechanical copyright.

[106.] *Ibid*; See also IMRO, *International Licensing Survey 1992-4* (Nov 1996).

[107.] See *A Strategic Vision for the Irish Music Industry* (Simpson Xavier Horwath Consulting); *Striking the Right Note* (IBEC).

[108.] This right is thought likely to disappear in the forthcoming Act. If so, the reproduction right however will, in practice, continue to be administered by MCPS on a licensing basis.

MCPS also has a substantial role to play in relation to mechanical reproduction abroad and arrangements with affiliated societies in other countries are in place to allow collection and distribution to Irish members through mechanical reproduction that takes place abroad. Although MCPS, as a body, does not feature as a significant player *vis-à-vis* the Irish consumer, it is likely that because digital distribution of works may give Irish consumers the chance to make digital copies of works (eg downloading onto a personal computer) MCPS may actually have a larger role to play in the years ahead. MCPS has taken a significant role in encouraging domestic law reform to counteract piracy.[109]

PPI

[15.39] The third significant collecting society is Phonographic Performance Ireland, or PPI. This company was established in 1968 by the leading UK and Irish recording companies and in effect represents all the leading multinational labels. This society administers the s 17 sound recording copyright vis-à-vis all kinds of format - disk, tape, CD - in relation to both public performance and broadcasting rights only; the reproduction rights are administered by the rightholder directly via licensing agreements which allow the sound recording to be used in advertisements, etc. These public performance and broadcasting rights are quite distinct from the activities of IMRO and this fact can be a source of confusion to the users of recorded music. The fact that two kinds of licence are needed if a restauranteur or publican is to play recorded music on premises, allied to the relatively higher tariff rate charged by PPI, makes collective licensing of music the most controversial aspect of copyright law in Ireland today. In the PPI case, however, the distribution of revenue amongst the companies that make up the PPI membership represents the scope of the right, for equitable remuneration is all the rightholder may insist upon for s 17 does not permit the rightholder to refuse permission for public performance of a sound recording. PPI also serves to provide income for Irish artists and musicians and collective agreements between PPI and the Musicians Union, for example, assist session musicians and other performers, *via ex gratia* payments or contract law, with a vital level of remuneration. It is understood that PPI, as a collecting society, may wish to broaden its activities in the future so as to act on behalf of musical performers in relation to the unwaivable right to equitable remuneration in relation to the Rental and Lending Directive.[110]

[15.40] In the area of film rights, which are normally held by film corporations, the statutory copyrights, at least in relation to reproduction and adaptation, are

---

[109.] *Striking the Right Note* (IBEC) Chs 3 and 4. One instance of this is the widely reported loading of pirated U2 unpublished recordings onto various Internet sites (November 1996).
[110.] 92/100/EEC.

administered by the rightholder directly. Public performance in the form of film distribution are also administered by the film company while private rental in the form of video is administered by specialist branches of these corporate bodies. In Ireland, many of these rights are protected in the form of an Industry Organisation, INFACT (Irish National Federation Against Copyright Theft) which is active in the area of counteracting video piracy in the form of importation and distribution of pirated copies, as well as domestic pirating of video products. INFACT also operate against those in the rental sector who distribute illegal products to the public. This policing role, carried out with the assistance of the gardaí and the Revenue Commissioners by using a number of legislative supports,[111] is generally regarded as being an area where new legislative measures are urgently required in order to strengthen the effectiveness of the law in relation to piracy.

[15.41] In contrast to the music industry, the traditional print media has not until recently been at the forefront of collective licensing in Ireland. Permission to reproduce substantial extracts from books, journals and other literature (when not covered by a fair dealing defence or one of the educational use exceptions) had to be obtained from the publisher who often charged a tariff and imposed limiting conditions in relation to use. However, levels of compliance with copyright law in this sector have not been high and the use of photocopiers to reproduce both literary copyright works as well as published edition typography has heightened concern about the extent to which these practices may prejudice rightholders. The industry, through the Irish Book Publishers Association,[112] has established a licensing body that licences the use of portions of a copyright work on terms. The Association has standard tariffs and standard licensing conditions that are to be observed. The authority has been very successful in generating and distributing income that previously did not enure to either publisher or author, although as a body that operates on the cusp of fair dealing, exclusive rights and educational or public interest use of copyright works, there has been substantial concern[113] over some of the activities of this body, the Irish Copyright Licensing Agency (ICLA). The newspaper industry has also realised that the unregulated use of newspaper copy, through clippings services and others, as well as digital reproduction and electronic distribution, represents a substantial loss of revenue and, more broadly, a threat to its vital interests, and the Irish National Newspaper Industry has decided to consider establishing a licensing body that would licence reproduction of newspaper materials.[114]

[111.] Eg Video Recordings Act 1989 as well as the Copyright Acts 1963 to 1987.

[112.] CLÉ.

[113.] See *Irish Times*, 10 October, 1996 and 15 October 1996.

[114.] In the UK, this is done by the Newspaper Licensing Agency which charges colleges, schools, press offices and businesses for the right to reproduce press clippings.

[15.42] The realisation that many rightholders have not been able to obtain a full economic return for their copyright works, and the possibility that new forms of reproduction and distribution will not only create new markets for works, allied to the considerable benefits and economies that collective management of rights can produce, means that collective licensing of works will become more and not less important in the future. Further, the broadening of categories of rightholders, particularly performers and film directors, will increase the prospect of concerted action by new rightholders and this will no doubt lead to new forms of collective agreement or industry-wide negotiating practices which will probably spawn renewed interest in collective management of rights. However, conflicts will also come into play and new mechanisms and compromises will have to be produced if past experiences are anything to go by.

DISPUTE RESOLUTION

[15.43] The fact that most dealings in copyright works are the creature of contract law means that dispute resolution is often centred on the traditional court structure and that attempts to resile from agreements have relied on contract or contract-related doctrines. There have been a number of highly publicised cases in England where songwriters and composers of popular music have successfully challenged the effectiveness of certain management contracts, a prominent feature of which has often been the assignment of copyright in compositions to either a music publisher, a manager or management company, or a recording company. The legal basis for disturbing these contracts has differed somewhat, spanning the recognised concepts of restraint of trade, undue influence, as well as less firmly rooted notions such as inequality of bargaining power.[115]

[15.44] In some of these cases the plaintiff has sought to be relieved from the consequences of entering into one-side publishing or recording contracts, in the form of a declaration that the contract is unenforceable[116] but it is likely that where such a declaration has been obtained, any copyright already transferred will not revest in the original author unless specific relief is sought along those lines. Even if copyright is revested in the composer the court may, as part of its equitable jurisdiction in relation to restitution, allow the defendant some reasonable remuneration for work undertaken during the currency of the agreement.[117] It should be noted that while such agreements have been held to be

---

[115]. Eg *Zang Tumb Tuum Records Ltd v Johnson* [1993] EMLR 61 (Holly Johnson); *Silvertone Records Ltd v Mountfield* [1993] EMLR 152 (Stone Roses).

[116]. *Ibid.*

[117]. *O'Sullivan v Management Agency & Music* [1985] 3 All ER 351.

in restraint of trade, in appropriate cases,[118] one older Irish case holds the restraint of trade to be inapplicable to authors' contractual assignments but this case is clearly too wide.[119] Other traditional concepts that have been successfully invoked have included undue influence[120] and breach of fiduciary duty.[121] Assignments made by persons labouring under the disability of infancy (in Ireland under 18 years of age) do not suffer the same degree of vulnerability[122] but the post-*Schroeder v Macaulay* developments make this case, without more, somewhat unreliable.

Performing Rights and Dispute Resolution

[15.45] However, these cases and their complexity, as well as the expense involved in mounting litigation of this kind, help in some ways to point out the need for special methods of resolving disputes between rightholders and others who deal in, or use, copyright materials. In the United Kingdom the 1956 Act set in train a tribunal system, the Performing Rights Tribunal, which was authorised to investigate complaints into the music industry and possible abuse of the power of collecting societies to seek payments in return for performing rights. The Copyright Act 1963 adopted this initiative and, in introducing the Copyright Bill 1962 to the Seanad, the Minister for Industry and Commerce, Mr Lynch, had this to say of the need to provide control over copyright in musical works:

> "It is well known that the performing right in musical works is exercised by composers by means of an organisation set up for that purpose. This was probably inevitable, as it would be extremely difficult for an individual composer to keep track of all the various public performances that might be given of a work which he had published, and of which a copy could be bought in a shop. But the fact that the great bulk of what may be called popular music is within the control of one organisation, and that this music must be used by classes of persons such as cinema proprietors, dance promoters and entertainment organisers of various descriptions, has given rise to suggestions that there should be some means by which disputes between such an organisation of copyright owners and users of copyright works could be resolved. I may say that the use of gramophone records for playing in public is a similar case.
>
> The Bill, therefore, in Part V, proposes to set up an appeal body, consisting of the Controller of Industrial and Commercial Property, before whom cases of

---

118. Eg *Schroeder v Macaulay* [1974] 3 All ER 616 (songwriter Tony Macaulay); *Clifford Davis v WEA Records* [1975] 1 All ER 237 (Fleetwood Mac). Contrast *Panayiotou v Sony* [1994] EMLR 229 (George Michael).

119. *Educational Company of Ireland v Fallon Bros* [1919] 1 IR 62.

120. *Elton John & Others v James and Others* [1991] FSR 397.

121. *O'Sullivan v Management Agency & Music* [1985] 3 All ER 351.

122. *Chaplin v Leslie Frewin Publishers (Ltd)* [1966] Ch 71.

dispute may be brought. Royalties charged by an individual author for the use of his works will not be a matter that could be brought before the Controller but licensing schemes operated by an organisation of copyright owners can be reviewed at the instance of an organisation of persons requiring such licences."[123]

[15.46] This appointment of the Controller, however, was not universally welcomed and Declan Costello TD (now the President of the High Court) was of the view that a tribunal of three persons would have been a better board to determine these important issues of property rights.[124]

[15.47] The limits of the Part V procedure should be noted. Section 31(1) gives jurisdiction as between a composer and the manufacturer of a recording under s 13(1). Section 31(2) deals with the apportionment of royalties due vis-à-vis public performance or broadcasting of a musical work. Section 31(3) provides jurisdiction to fix equitable remuneration under s 17(4) in favour of the sound recording copyright. Section 31(4) gives the Controller jurisdiction in relation to disputes when RTE use music in a film; in fact, the Bill as originally introduced, gave the Controller a wider jurisdiction than this, allowing the Controller to resolve disputes between persons who showed or performed musical works which were then incorporated in films and the musical copyright holders themselves. This provision was modified at Committee stage in the Dáil[125] because of fears that such a jurisdiction conflicted with the Berne Convention for it is not possible to place individually held rights within the remit of public control.

[15.48] Section 32 takes this situation a step further by giving the Controller jurisdiction in relation to licensing schemes, when there is a dispute between users of a work, or an organisation representing such persons, and collecting societies that are representative of rightholders. Section 32 is much broader for it allows jurisdiction in relation to licensing practices that are outside the specific provisions of s 13(1) and 17(4) and it is clear that the intention was to allow the Controller to rule on disputes between the PRS and concert promoters, ballroom dance promoters and the like. There has, however, been important litigation on the link between ss 31 and 32. In *Phonographic Performance (Ireland) Ltd v Controller of Industrial and Commercial Property and Radio Telefís Éireann*[126] the Supreme Court held that a dispute between PPI and RTE about the rate of equitable remuneration payable in relation to s 17(4) was properly referred to

---

123. Seanad Debates Cols 389-90
124. 200 Dáil Debates Col 424, rejected because of the expense; Col 1460.
125. 201 Dáil Debates Col. 475.
126. [1996] 1 ILRM 1.

the Controller under s 31(3) and that the Controller had jurisdiction under s 31(3), rejecting PPI's submission that, where a licence system was in place any disputes in relation thereto had to be submitted under s 32(1)(b). The Supreme Court held that s 17(4) rights operated when a sound recording had been used and that s 31(3) jurisdiction could not be invoked in relation to disputes about the level of equitable remuneration that may be charged in relation to future use of sound recordings. However, because of the passing of time, the Supreme Court held that, while the Controller had been incorrect in accepting that, in 1990, he could, under s 31(3) determine equitable remuneration for the period 1986 to 1994, he could in 1995 now so act. The decision of the Supreme Court left open the question of the relevance of s 32(2)(b) but it seems clear that where PPI or IMRO present a music user with a licence agreement as to future public use of sound recordings or copyright music, s 32 is the relevant statutory provision. The net effect of this decision, where a person has used sound recordings but disputes the equitable nature of licence fees levied by PPI, is to make injunctive relief unlikely for at least in relation to s 17(4) the person who accepts that some equitable remuneration is payable but disputes the rate, does not infringe copyright.[127] In related litigation[128] involving disco owners, the Supreme Court, in the same judgment, observed that s 31(3) is also a valid basis for the Controller to act. It is a point of importance because High Court practice had been to grant injunctions in appropriate cases which had the effect of closing down hotel and other premises unless PPI's licence conditions were fulfilled. This powerful lever no longer appears to be available to PPI as a result of this decision.

Disputes in Ireland

[15.49] Despite the jurisdiction given to the Controller and the fact that several references have been made, the Controller has not, to date, ruled on any of the matters given to him under Part V of the Copyright Act 1963, so there is no body of custom or practice on issues such as the level of equitable remuneration.[129] However, we know that several areas of conflict do exist in Ireland, but resolution of these disputes seem to take place in the courts or through other channels. The use of collective licensing by music rightholders through IMRO, and the level of charge, has been a constant source of controversy, and

---

[127.] Section 17(5).

[128.] *Phonographic Performance (Ireland) Ltd v Controller of Industrial and Commercial Property, John Ryan, White Sands Hotel Ltd and Hotel Imperial Dundalk Ltd* [1996] 1 ILRM 1, at 12.

[129.] For an interesting Australian case see *APRA Reference* (1992) 25 IPR 257. It is understood that the Controller has appointed an arbitrator to rule on the PPI/Discotheque owners' dispute on equitable remuneration; no arbitrator has been appointed in relation to the PPI/RTE dispute: *Sunday Tribune* 12 January 1997.

parliamentary questions and comments pre-date the 1963 Act.[130] The 1963 Act has so far proved to be ineffective and the Irish Vintners Federation and others have challenged the collecting societies to justify the level of tariff charged for the public use of recorded music. Allegations that charges are arbitrary and imposed retrospectively by bodies that enjoy a monopoly have been repeatedly made[131] and although the facts do not bear out assertions that charges are imposed without reference to the ability to pay, allegations of intimidation by "a legalised Mafia operation",[132] no matter how misplaced, do put the collecting societies on the defensive. More recently, the announcement that IMRO would seek to levy royalty charges for musical performances at school concerts led the Government to hint at legislative changes[133] but these matters have been resolved by agreement between IMRO and the Department of Education. While the courts continue to defend the rights of composers to their due in terms of public performance rights[134] there is some discussion in certain Government circles about some kind of pricing mechanism through the Department of Enterprise and Employment or the Controller.[135] In the area of the print media a similar controversy has broke out in relation to the Irish Copyright Licensing Agency, and demands for universities and colleges to pay a fee in order to engage in multiple copying of texts for distribution to students[136] could well spark off a reference under s 32 of the Act. In the area of television distribution of musical and dramatic works these issues are currently being resolved by agreement but the distribution of broadcasts themselves when the broadcast originates in the United Kingdom is not fully resolved in relation to redistribution of the signals by Community Distribution Companies without a wireless telegraphy licence. Major litigation is taking place[137] in which the legality of the refusal to licence programme retransmissions operators is being challenged.[138] This has caused UK broadcasters and other rightholders to feel

---

130. Eg 199 *Dáil Debates* Col 1120 (Parliamentary Question on Copyright Fees by Mr Tierney).

131. Eg in the Seanad: see 136 Seanad Debates Cols 1090 *et seq.*

132. Senator Maloney at 136 Seanad Debates Col 1098.

133. 464 *Dáil Debates* Cols 806-812.

134. See IMRO, *Copyright News* January 1996, for a report on a District Court case in which the validity of the IMRO contractual license with the defendant, a Kerry publican, was upheld. See also 'Debts Delay held to be Unjust', *Irish Times*, 20 March 1996.

135. See the then Minister of State, Mr S Brennan, at 136 Seanad Debates Col 1104.

136. See the *Irish Times* 10 October 1996 and 15 October 1996. A £1 fee per student is being sought. In the UK a £4 fee is paid.

137. *Carrigaline Community Television Broadcasting Co Ltd and others v The Minister for Transport, Energy and Communications and Others* High Court, unrep, 10 November 1995, Keane J.

138. See 'British broadcasters seek crackdown on Irish who tune in free', *The Times* 3 December 1996.

that unlicensed operators are being able to pirate broadcasts without being liable to pay remuneration.

[15.50] These situations point up the need for immediate reform. One must venture the opinion that dispute resolution mechanisms in Ireland are so ineffective that the forthcoming legislation should make an entirely new start on this crucial area, and that the mistake made in 1963, to devise a cheap but ineffective system of dispute resolution, must not be repeated.

Competition Law

[15.51] Part of the controversy over music collecting societies is fuelled by allegations that these societies have monopoly powers that are being abused. Indeed, a suggested pro-competition law amendment to s 32(5) of the 1963 Act was unsuccessful. It sought to give the Controller power to have regard to whether monopoly powers existed which were being abused even though the Minister of the day was clearly sympathetic to the amendment.[139] More recently, however, the Competition Act 1991 has transformed the legal climate significantly.

[15.52] Section 4(1) of the Competition Act 1991 prohibits and declares to be void all agreements between undertakings, decisions by associations of undertakings and concerned practices which have as their object or effect the prevention, restriction or distortion of competition in trade in any goods or services in the Irish State or in any part of the Irish State.

[15.53] Section 4(2) provides that a licence may be granted by the Competition Authority where the Authority considers that an agreement contributes to the production of goods or provision of services, or it is promoting technical or economic progress, while allowing consumers a fair share of the resulting benefit, as long as the agreement does not impose on the undertakings concerned terms which are not indispensable to the attainment of those objectives, and do not afford to the undertaking the possibility of eliminating competition in respect of a substantial part of the products or services in question.

[15.54] Section 4(4) empowers the Authority to declare that a notified agreement does not offend s 4(4) at all.

[15.55] The Competition Act 1991 has been modelled on European Community law, particularly Articles 85 and 86 of the Treaty of Rome, and the impact that Community law has had on the interpretation of the Competition Act should not be underestimated. The Authority has given definitive rulings on a number of agreements notified to the Authority by the Performing Rights Society (PRS)

[139.] *Per* Declan Costello TD at 199 Dáil Debates Col 1463.

and the Irish Music Rights Organisation (IMRO), and while Phonographic Performance Ireland (PPI) have notified a number of agreements, no outcome to these notifications exists as yet.

[15.56] PRS/IMRO sought to challenge the jurisdiction of the Authority in a number of ways. Firstly, agreements between PRS members and PRS were claimed not to be agreements between undertakings.[140] This has been roundly rejected on the basis that individual composers, lyricists and publishers (whether corporate or non-corporate) operate for gain and, as such, are undertakings and that resultant agreements on collective licensing represent agreements between undertakings. The Authority has also rejected the view that because Part V of the Copyright Act 1963 sets out a mechanism for resolving disputes, the Competition Authority has no jurisdiction. Notwithstanding these preliminary points, the Competition Authority has ultimately resolved the substantive notification issues in favour of IMRO.

[15.57] In relation to the PRS Standard Assignment of Copyright between individual creators and publishers, under which PRS members assign performing rights and film synchronisation rights, the Competition Authority, in Decision No 326,[141] found against PRS on the ground that s 4(1) was infringed. The market for musical works and the performing right therein was being restricted, distorted or inhibited by terms in the assignment, and related PRS rules and practices, particularly rules that prevented members from administering all or part of these rights themselves. Furthermore, the Authority impugned rules that prevented members from allowing organisations other than PRS to administer these rights, as well as deprecating the fact that standard licensing tariffs eliminated price competition for consumers. The fact that members could only be terminated at three yearly intervals was also contrary to s 4(1). The Authority, while holding that collective licensing of copyright works has substantial benefits for both to the rightholder and the public at large, could not bring these agreements into the licensing provisions in s 4(2). On this first point the Authority addressed the issue of whether collective licensing was the only way in which creators could ensure effective protection for their works, and while the Authority held that collective licensing was both efficient and beneficial to consumers, particularly smaller users who are thus able to avoid the substantial costs that would arise in negotiating separate licences, these assignments and related rules did not satisfy s 4(2). In particular, it could not be shown that the exclusivity provisions were indispensable to the effectiveness of PRS, the Authority noting that within the USA, for example, licences could be

---

[140.] As defined in s 3(1) of the Competition Act 1991; see Decision No 5 of 30 June 1992 - PRS/IMRO Transfer of Function Agreement.

[141.] 18 May 1994.

obtained by members to administer part of their performing rights, on their own behalf, vis-à-vis individual users.[142] The Authority also ruled that the three year membership tie was also not indispensable to the securing of the advantages offered by collective licensing.

[15.58] Following on Decision No 326, a number of structural and organisational changes took place as between PRS and IMRO. In December 1994, IMRO separated from PRS and began to function independently as from January 1995.[143] In the wake of the decision to refuse to licence the PRS assignments, IMRO notified three assignments of copyright standard agreements in January 1995 between IMRO and writers, non-corporate publishers, and corporate publishers, respectively. These notified agreements, as well as the IMRO Memorandum of Association, Articles of Association and IMRO Rules, were substantially different to those before the Authority in Decision No 326 and significant amendments were made to these documents even after they had been lodged in January 1995. The Authority noted a number of significant differences between these documents and the earlier PRS documents. Under these rules, the member could apply to obtain a non-exclusive licence allowing that member to administer all or any of the member's performing rights. The member may also resign membership after one year rather than at three year intervals, and finally, the elimination of PRS nominees from the Board of IMRO was held to bring these provisions into the 'indispensable' criteria set by s 4(2) of the Act. The licence thus granted[144] to run from 31 October 1995 for a period of 15 years, was to set clear the path for a number of separate but related agreements. However, proceedings in the High Court to challenge these decisions have been started.[145]

[15.59] While the PRS decision and the later IMRO assignment notifications reflect a tension between IMRO and some of the Pop Supergroups who have pressed for the right to administer their own performing rights in relation to live concerts, the most political conflict in this area is between the collecting societies and commercial users of recorded music. This conflict formed the backdrop against which the IMRO Standard Public Performance Licence was tested by the Competition Authority. The IMRO Public Performance Licence was attacked by bodies such as the Vintners Federation of Ireland through a

---

[142] Eg concert promoters in relation to live performances, by performer/composers of their own works.
[143] Two PRS representatives sat on the IMRO Board but this situation was changed on 31 October 1995 when PRS nominees were removed from the IMRO Board.
[144] Decision No 445 - 15 December 1995.
[145] By members of the Vintners Federation of Ireland. See *Publicans in Dispute over Music Rights, Irish Times*, 25 February 1997.

representative body called IMUC.[146] IMUC and others allege that a monopoly exists on the part of IMRO, that no effective appeal or review mechanism exits, that IMRO refuses to negotiate individual agreements with most users and that charges are levied and raised unilaterally at excessive levels which do not take account of the user's ability to pay such charges. In the light of the changes made to IMRO's rules,[147] the fact that the user could play non-copyright music, the possibility of a non-Irish society granting a licence to a user, as well as the possibility that a competing society to IMRO could theoretically emerge, the Competition Authority granted a licence to IMRO in respect of their Public Performance Licence.[148] One very significant feature of the decision, however, is the position taken by the Competition Authority on the main substantive objection to the licence provisions used by IMRO, namely, that licence charges were excessive, unreasonable and placed a large financial burden on the business community. The Competition Authority, in effect, took the view that it did not have a broad consumer protection role to play:

> "the Authority's functions under s 4 of the Competition Act are confined to considering whether or not an agreement 'prevents, restricts or distorts competition'. By and large, therefore, it is not the function of the Authority to adjudicate on the fairness of the terms of an agreement as between the parties, and, in particular, to arbitrate on matters such as prices. IMUC in its submissions also alleged abuses by IMRO of its dominant position. Such behaviour is prohibited under s 5 of the Competition Act. It is not the function of the Authority to take a view on any s 5 issues that might arise out of the notified arrangements."[149]

[15.60] While not all the IMRO notified agreements were dependant upon the success of the notification of the standard assignment agreements,[150] Decision 445 cleared the way for the Authority to grant licences under s 4(2) of the Competition Act 1991 for the IMRO Broadcast Music Licence with Independent Radio Stations[151] and with RTE.[152]

---

146. Irish Music Users Council.
147. EG The possibility of individual rightholders granting licences under the rules discussed in Decision No 445.
148. Decision No 447 of 21 December 1995.
149. Decision No 451 para 28.
150. Decision No 383 - IMRO and UK television companies and other copyright holders and Cable Relay and MMDS operators; Decision No. 384 - IMRO and UK television companies/copyright holders.
151. Decision No 449 of 18 December 1995.
152. Decision No 456 of 21 December 1995.

COMMUNITY LAW AND NATIONAL COPYRIGHT LEGISLATION

[15.61] The provisions of Community Law apply to all intellectual property laws and although it is widely accepted that national laws granting and regulating intellectual property remain valid and dispositive in most areas, the growing incidence of Community sponsored legislation across the entire field of intellectual property, in the form of Council Regulations and Council Directives hold out the prospect of a greater degree of legislative harmonisation than would have appeared possible a decade ago. The relevance of the Treaty of Rome to the exercise of national copyright is best understood within the broad context of Community law and industrial and commercial property rights - typically, patent, trade mark and industrial design law. The most obvious Treaty provisions that could operate against national legislation conferring intellectual property rights are Articles 85 and 86 of the Treaty of Rome. Article 85 invalidates agreements and concerted practices that distort or restrict competition with the Community; Article 86 operates against rules and practices which allow an undertaking to abuse a dominant position.[153] Early decisions in the area of patent law[154] indicated that the mere exercise of statutory patent rights, in the absence of any evidence of an agreement or concerned practice (Article 85) or an abuse of a dominant position (Article 86) could not result in conflict with either of those provisions.

Exhaustion of Rights

[15.62] However, in drawing the distinction between the existence of an intellectual property right and the exercise of that right, the ECJ indicated that it would be vigilant to ensure that rights were not abused by their exercise, but Articles 85 and 86 themselves provide only a limited power to control the fragmentation of markets, through the combined operation of national laws and contractual practices aimed at dividing up markets.

[15.63] In relation to the free movement of goods, however, Article 30 of the Treaty provided a much more interesting opportunity to counteract restrictions on the free flow of goods throughout the Community. Any quantitative restrictions on the importation of goods, and any measures having equivalent effect, are prohibited, and it is clear that national laws come within the Article 30 prohibition. Article 36, which provides an exception in the case of restrictions based on industrial and commercial property rights (*inter alia*) is a derogation principle which is strictly policed through the application of a proportionality test[155] which allows a relaxation of the free movement of goods

---

[153.] In national law the Competition Act 1991, ss 4 and 5 are counterparts to Articles 85 and 86.
[154.] Eg *Parke, Davis v Centrafarm* [1968] ECR 55.
[155.] *Simminthal SpA v Italian Minister for Finance* [1976] ECR 1871; *Bristol-Myers Squibb v Paranova CH* and *Boehringer Sohn v Paranova* (joined cases C-427/93, C-429/93 and C-436/93, judgment delivered 11 July 1996); *Merk & C v Primecrown Ltd* and *Beecham Group plc v Europharm of Worthing Ltd* [1997] 1 CMLR 83.

principle only insofar as it is justified for the purpose of safeguarding rights constituting the specific subject matter of that property. The case that establishes the relevance of this approach in the area of copyright is *Deutsche Grammophon Gessellschaft mbH v Metro*[156] (hereafter *Deutsche Grammophon*). In this case the plaintiff manufacturer of gramophone records in Germany sold copies of them to a French subsidiary company, who then passed them on to the defendant who proposed to sell them in Germany. German law gave the plaintiff a neighbouring right which the plaintiff sought to exercise by obtaining an injunction restraining the resale, or reimportation, into Germany, but the action failed on the ground that such a right could not be used to prevent the marketing, in a Member State, of products distributed by the rightholder or under the consent of the rightholder in another Member State, on the sole ground that the distribution did not take place on the national territory. A contrary conclusion would have defeated a central object of the Treaty, that is, the unification of national markets into a single market.

[15.64] This principle, therefore, will focus attention on the exercise of a right against the lawful marketing of goods within the Community rather than on the presence of restrictive contractual practices. First marketing of goods by the rightholder, the rightholder's agent or licensee, will exhaust, within the Community, any industrial property rights vested in the rightholder.

[15.65] The *Deutsche Grammophon* case was applied directly to copyright in *Musik Vertrieb Membran v GEMA*.[157] Here an attempt by the German collecting society GEMA to levy a charge of 8% in the form of a mechanical right royalty on recordings made under a voluntary licence in the UK, where a lower royalty charge of 6¼% was imposed, was held to be unlawful. GEMA could not collect the difference between these two rates; when the rightholder authorised the UK manufacturer in return for the lower rate of royalty, the rightholder there and then consented to the Community wide distribution of that product on those terms. The notion of consent can become complicated where substantive rights differ from Member State to Member State. In *Warner Brothers v Christiansen*[158] Danish law gave the author or producer of a cinematographic work the right to regulate the commercial hiring out of that work. Christiansen purchased in London video-cassette copies of the film "Never Say Never Again" and imported them into Denmark. The Danish rightholder sought to restrain the commercial hiring out of the film in that video-cassette format. The Danish High Court asked whether Articles 30 and 36 applied *vis-à-vis* Danish

---

156. [1971] ECR 487.
157. [1981] ECR 147; *Merck v Stephar* [1981] ECR 2063; *Merk & Co v Primecrown Ltd.* Joined cases C-267/95 and C-268/95, judgment 5 December 1996.
158. [1988] ECR 2605.

national legislation which gave the rightholder the right to prevent hiring out of the works when they have been put onto the market in another Member State through first sale. The ECJ held that commercial rental was a significant commercial activity and that national laws regulating rental were not quantitative restrictions but measures having equivalent effect under Article 30. However, the measure was justified under Article 36 on the basis that if there was no method of regulating commercial rental, there was no certainty that authors and investors in films would secure an adequate return for work and investment. National laws which give collecting societies rights to collect supplementary reproduction fees, even if similar fees are not available under the law of the Member State where the work was first marketed are also within the Treaty.[159]

[15.66] The exhaustion principle does not apply to copies of works that are placed upon the market of a Member State because copyright has expired; in such a case the placement is clearly not consented to by the rightholder, so, where goods were marketed in Denmark, copyright having expired, the importation into Germany of those works, copyright continuing to subsist there, could be prevented by the German rightholder.[160] Cases of this kind served to persuade Member States to harmonise the duration of copyright but such problems will not automatically disappear[161] unless some other provision, such as the prohibition of discrimination on grounds of nationality, operate.

[15.67] In cases where the copyright is in the nature of a performing right the exhaustion rule does not apply. In *Coditel v Ciné Vog*[162] Ciné Vog had a seven year exclusive licence to show the film, "Le Boucher" in Belgium. The licence agreement also covered television transmission rights. The copyright holder granted the German television company, ARD, television performance rights in Germany. Coditel picked up the German signal and transmitted it via cable to its subscribers in Belgium. Ciné Vog sued Coditel for damages. Coditel pleaded that liability would conflict with Article 59 of the Treaty guaranteeing free movement of services. The ECJ drew a distinction between the placing of copies of literary and artistic works onto a market and making a cinematographic film available to the public in the form of "performances which may be infinitely repeated". The Court reasoned that part of the essential function of copyright in a cinematographic work is to provide an income in the form of fees for the public performance of that work and Article 59 did not therefore prevent the

---

[159.] *Basset v Salem* [1987] ECR 1747.
[160.] *EMI Electrola GmbH v Patricia* [1989] ECR 79.
[161.] *Phil Collins v IMTRAT* [1993] ECR 545; *Dworkin and Sterling* [1994] EIPR 187.
[162.] [1980] ECR 881 (Coditel I).

assignee from relying on copyright to regulate exhibition of that film. A similar position applies to the public performance of sound recordings.[163]

[15.68] While *Coditel I* and *Christiansen* lead to narrow distinctions in the form of different definitions of the specific subject matter of a film being exploited by performance (as opposed to commercial hiring of tangible copies) the exhaustion principle is very much confined to first sale of goods. In the recent follow up[164] to the Green Paper of July 1995[165] the European Commission has this to say about future legislative plans *vis-à-vis* distribution rights:

> "The distribution right for authors should be harmonised with respect to *all* categories of works. Such harmonisation should provide that only the first sale in the Community by or with the consent of the rightholder exhausts the distribution right.
>
> Furthermore, harmonised legislation should affirm that the principle of exhaustion applies to the distribution of goods only and not to the right applicable to the provision of services, notably not of on-line services. Such a measure, which would reflect the existing case law of the Court of Justice on the non-applicability of exhaustion to the provision of service, would enhance legal certainty across Member States."

[15.69] The geographical scope of the exhaustion principle is also important to note. Parallel imports[166] from non-EC countries are still capable of being excluded even if the Community has free trade agreements with other countries.[167] The rules on national or international exhaustion of rights differ within the various Community Member States, and this issue, while not dealt with in the GATT/TRIPS, is still a controversial one which surfaced in the December 1996 Diplomatic Conference on Certain Copyright and Neighbouring Rights Questions, in the form of draft Article 8, which set out options for both national and international exhaustion rules. No agreement was reached on this matter. Irish law certainly applies a national exhaustion principle in cases where the goods are not first marketed within either the Community or the European Economic Area.[168] This is illustrated by case law in 1992 when a Dublin bookseller imported from the USA hardback copies of novels by best-selling authors which had been published and sold in the USA at heavily discounted

---

[163.] *Ministere Public v Tournier* [1989] ECR 252.

[164.] Com (96) 568 Final (November 1996), at p 19.

[165.] Com (95) 382 Final (July 1995).

[166.] Oliver *Free Movement of Goods in the EEC* (3rd ed) (Sweet & Maxwell, 1995); Rothnie *Parallel Imports* (Sweet & Maxwell, 1993).

[167.] Abbey [1992] ECLR 231.

[168.] Apart from the 15 Member States of the Union, the Area includes Iceland, Liechtenstein and Norway.

rates, and were thus much cheaper than copies produced by the UK and Irish rightholder. Injunctive relief was given against importation and sale.[169]

Competition Law

[15.70] Article 85 of the Treaty provides a mechanism whereby a person affected by agreements and concerted practices that restrict competition in internal community trade may seek to have such agreements or practices invalidated. The European Court of Justice, building on the distinction between the existence of a right and the exercise of that right, observed in *Coditel II*[170] that while a contract giving one party an exclusive right to exhibit a film may not itself infringe Article 85, the exercise of that right may, in the context of the accompanying economic and legal circumstances, result in the restriction of competition. In consequence that national courts must police licence agreements of this kind to prevent the creation of:

> "barriers which are artificial and unjustifiable in terms of the needs of the cinematographic industry, or the possibility of charging fees which exceed a fair return on investment, or an exclusivity the duration of which is disproportionate to those requirements, and whether or not, from a general point of view, such exercise within a given geographic area is such as to prevent, restrict or distort competition within the common market."

[15.71] It should be noted that national courts in the United Kingdom and Ireland have been somewhat reluctant to find a breach of Article 85 although the point has been pleaded in a number of cases involving exclusivity agreements in the copyright field.[171] The European Commission, via its powers under Article 85 in the form of a licensing authority, has endorsed the view that certain types of provision such as no challenge clauses, non-competition clauses, royalty charges on products not protected by copyright, and certain kinds of title transfer clauses, may infringe Article 85.[172]

[15.72] Article 86 on the other hand has been extremely effective in judicial proceedings before the ECJ. The activities of collecting societies have been carefully scrutinised by the ECJ on a number of occasions in order to test whether the societies abuse any dominant position they may occupy by reason of any *de facto* monopoly they may enjoy in a given Member State. Membership rules and distribution rules that may be arbitrary or oppressive may be open to

---

[169.] *Irish Times*, 25 September 1992 and 29 September 1992.

[170.] *Coditel v Ciné-Vog Films* [1982] ECR 3381.

[171.] *British Leyland v Armstrong Patents* [1986] AC 577; *Panayiotou v Sony Music* [1994] EMLR 229.

[172.] Neilson-Hordell/Richmark - *12th Annual Report on Competition Policy 88;* See generally Van Bael and Bellis, *Competition Law of the European Community* paras 454-56 (CCH, 1994).

challenge,[173] as may assignment provisions or provisions which restrict a member's right to choose another collecting society to represent that member outside the Community. Broader issues have also arisen in relation to third party complaints that a collecting society has abused its dominant position by virtue of the levels of fee charged by it within a Member State. In the leading case of *Ministére Public v Tournier*[174] the Court held that a national collecting society which stood in a dominant position would be in breach of Article 86 when it imposed public performance tariffs on discotheques in one Member State which are significantly higher than those that would be charged by a similar collecting society in another Member State. Such differences could be justified if it could be shown that the society in question could point to objective qualitative differences in the level of service it provided to its members, as against the comparator societies in other Member States.

[15.73] The role of collecting societies[175] in the area of copyright is likely to expand and increase in the years ahead; it is a mistake to characterise these societies as anachronistic for new kinds of right and rightholder - performers rights, rental rights for performers and directors of cinematographic films, for example, will require collective licensing or exercise of these rights. Mechanical reproduction of musical works will survive the abolition of non-voluntary licences under s 13 of the 1963 Act. However, collecting societies will continue to be scrutinised by European Community Institutions. In the most recent statements of European Commission policy on collecting societies,[176] the Commission has stressed the need to re-assess the management of copyrights in the light of digitisation and multimedia markets. Indeed, the Commission predict that individual management of rights will become even less practicable in the future and that new central management or collective management structures may need to evolve. The fact that similar rights in Member States may be administered in different ways - some rights may be administered collectively in certain States but individually in others - will require the Commission to consider whether these differences create barriers to trade which would impede the effective exploitation of rights across Member States. While the Commission have decided that the evolution of licensing schemes should be

---

173. The Leading Commission Investigation in GEMA [1971] CMLR D35.

174. [1989] ECR 2521. See also *Lucazeau v SACEM* [1989] ECR 2811.

175. See generally, Cohen Jehoram and others, *Collective Administration of Copyrights in Europe* (Kluwer 1995); Van Bael and Bellis, *Competition Law of the European Community* (3rd ed) Ch 9; Bellis, *Collecting Societies and EEC Law* in Peeperhorn and C. Van Riji, *Collecting Societies in the Music Business.*

176. Copyright and Related Rights in the Information Society COM (95) 382 Final: Follow-Up to the Green Paper on Copyright and Related Rights in the Information Society, COM (96) 568 Final.

left for the market to develop, rather than insist on a legislative movement towards compulsory licensing or one-stop shop solutions, the Commission do not rule out Commission moves on regulating societies in Europe; "As far as collective management is concerned, there are already indications for the need to define, both under the Single Market and the Competition Rules of the EC Treaty, at community level the rights and obligations of collecting societies, in particular, with respect to the methods of collection, to the calculation for tariffs, to the supervision mechanisms and to the application of the rules on competition to collecting societies and collective management".[177]

Article 86 and Licensing Obligations

[15.74] It is established that Article 86 can operate so as to render the acquisition of an exclusive licence an abuse of an already dominant position.[178] In the area of registered designs the court has ruled that a refusal[179] to grant a licence to manufacture goods in accordance with a registered design is not *per se* an abuse of dominant position. The basic principles that operate in this area were stated in *Volvo v Veng* to be that a motor vehicle manufacturer who refuses to licence others to manufacture spare parts does not as such abuse his dominant position and that a manufacturer may assert a right to prevent third parties from creating products that incorporate the design without consent constitutes the very subject matter of his exclusive right. If that manufacturer was obliged to grant licences even for a reasonable royalty, this would deprive the manufacturer of his exclusive right. The court went on to state, however, that:

> "the exercise of an exclusive right by the proprietor of a registered design in respect of car body panels may be prohibited by Article 86 if it involves, on the part of an undertaking holding a dominant position, certain abusive conduct such as the arbitrary refusal to supply spare parts to independent repairers, the fixing of prices for spare parts for a particular model even though many cars of that model are still in circulation, provided that such conduct is liable to affect trade between Member States."

Despite this balanced approach to the issue of Article 86 and the emphasis placed by the court on the need to establish abusive or arbitrary conduct, the decision of the Commission and both European Courts in the *Magill TV Guide* litigation[180] has resulted in uncertainty about the scope of Article 86 and the possibility that copyright holders may be prevented from exercising traditional

---

177. COM (96) 568 Final, pp 26 and 27.
178. *Europemballage Corp & Continental Can Co v Commission* [1973] ECR 215; *Tetra Pak I* OJ 1988 L272/27.
179. *Volvo v Veng* [1988] ECR 621; *Maxicar v Renault* [1988] ECR 6039; Korah [1988] EIPR 381.
180. *RTE and ITP v EC Commission* [1995] FSR 530. See Walker [1996] IJEL 173.

copyrights such as the reproduction right, even where abusive conduct within *Volvo v Veng*, does not appear to be present.

Chapter 16

Infringement of Copyright

INTRODUCTION

[16.01] As a creature of statute, copyright infringement occurs whenever a person does something in relation to a copyright work that the Copyright Acts forbid. Rightholders may seek to use some related cause of action, such as the law of contract, passing off, or a trade mark infringement, and a successful plaintiff may be able to establish liability under a number of different heads.[1] However, in this chapter we are only concerned with copyright infringement: separate attention is paid to these issues in other parts of this book.

INFRINGEMENT OF PART II WORKS

[16.02] Copyright infringement occurs in relation to literary, dramatic or musical works if a person does any of the following things without the consent of the rightholder:

    (a) reproducing the work in any material form;

    (b) publishing the work;

    (c) performing the work in public;

    (d) broadcasting the work;

    (e) transmitting the work via a diffusion service;

    (f) making any adaptation of the work;

    (g) doing anything listed in (a) to (e) to an adaptation of the work.[2]

[16.03] The 1963 Act describes these rights negatively as restricted acts. It should be noted that certain types of commercial activity are not currently regulated under Irish copyright law (eg the rental or lending of a copyright work) and attempts are made by rightholders to regulate these dealings by way of contractual provisions, with limited success. One of the more obvious aspects of copyright law is the extent to which technological developments may force legislators to broaden the nature and scope of rights and infringing acts.

[16.04] In relation to artistic works the restricted acts are:[3]

[1.] Eg *House of Spring Gardens Ltd v Point Blank Ltd* [1984] IR 611.
[2.] CA 1963, s 8(6).
[3.] CA 1963, s 9(8).

(a) reproducing[4] the work in any material form;

(b) publishing the work;

(c) including the work in a television broadcast;

(d) including the work in a programme transmitted by a diffusion service.

Many of these concepts are in part defined in the Copyright Acts but they can still cause substantial difficulties.

'Reproducing ... in any material form'

[16.05] In relation to literary, dramatic or musical works, the Act defines reproduction as including making a record or cinematographic film. It is generally agreed that the reproduction should produce something which can be discerned by the human senses, so prior to the implementation of the Software Directive, it is likely that computer programs intelligible only to a machine were outside the concept of a reproduction.[5] Reproduction or copying, extends to expression of the work in other forms such as turning a novel into a ballet,[6] putting printed pages onto a word processor or computer,[7] using a photographic portrait in a newspaper,[8] or reworking newspaper articles into magazine articles.[9] The same is true of artistic works. So, using one artist's paintings in order to induce another artist to paint similar street scenes is, arguably, reproduction of the original work,[10] if the objective is to take the feeling and artistic character of the original. Infringement by copying of an artistic work, however, is much broader because the Act specifically provides that the two dimensional reproduction of an artistic work which exists in three dimensions (eg drawing a sculpture) and vice versa, are acts of reproduction. So, taking an artistic drawing such as a cartoon character and using the drawing to manufacture dolls and brooches of the character is an act of reproduction.[11] Furthermore, the taking of a three dimensional object and the reproduction of that object (eg taking a sailing dinghy and copying its features) represents an indirect infringement of the original design drawings and is a reproduction[12] within the Act, even if the original drawings have not been used or seen by the

---

4. See 'Zig and Zag Creators get Injunctions on Reproductions', *Irish Times* 12 May 1989.
5. *Computer Edge Property Ltd v Apple Computer* (1986) 161 CLR 171; *International Writing Institute v Rimila Property* (1993) 27 IPR 546.
6. *Holland v Van Damm* [1936-45] Mar CC 69.
7. *Waterlow Directories Ltd v Reed Information Services Ltd* [1992] FSR 409.
8. *Davis v Baird* (1903) 38 ILTR 23.
9. *Donoghue v Allied Newspapers Ltd* [1937] 3 All ER 503.
10. *Krisants v Briarfine* [1977] FSR 577. See also *Bauman v Fussell* [1978] RPC 485.
11. *King Features Syndicate Inc v Kleeman* [1941] AC 417.
12. *Dorling v Honnor Marine* [1964] 1 All ER 241; *Allibert SA v O'Connor* [1981] FSR 613; *Plix Products v Frank M Winstone* [1986] FSR 63.

copyist. In *Bookmaker's Afternoon Greyhound Services Ltd v Wilf Gilbert (Staffordshire) Ltd*[13] it was held that the display of a literary work, a greyhound race card, on a television monitor constituted a reproduction under the UK 1956 Act, there being no need for the concept of material form to be given a restricted meaning. However, it is by no means clear that a digital representation of a work is necessarily within the existing definition of 'reproduction' and 'record' and although one recent Australian case decides that a CD is a record,[14] the Court did not address the technological issues involved.[15]

'Publishing the work'

[16.06] This act of distribution, which in the recent UK legislation is perhaps more vividly described as issuing copies to the public, must be carefully regulated by the rightholder, for once a copy of the work has been lawfully published, the rightholder may find that the power to regulate further acts of distribution will be prejudiced[16] (eg in relation to musical works under s 13 and through the exhaustion of rights doctrine in EU law). The 1963 Act directs that for the purpose of determining whether a work was published, no account is to be taken of any unauthorised act or unauthorised publication. The Act goes on to state that the copyright owner's conduct or licence is to be the sole reference whereby publication is to be tested.[17] The place of publication will be regarded as the place where the publisher invites the public to seek to acquire copies rather than the place where copies are received, otherwise there would be a multiplicity of places of publication[18] or the courts would have to ascertain where the first copy was received. A clandestine distribution to political sympathisers or friends is not intended to satisfy 'the public' and is thus not a publication,[19] even if the author's wishes are met by this kind of distribution.

'Performing the work in public'

[16.07] This has been one of the most frequently litigated points of copyright law. Performing rights societies throughout the world seek to collect royalties in relation to the public performance of musical and dramatic works, in particular, because the performance of a literary work (eg reading parts of a novel to an audience) is a restricted act.[20] In determining whether infringement has

---

[13.] [1994] FSR 723.

[14.] *Polygram Records Inc v Raben Footwear Pty Ltd* (1996) 35 IPR 426.

[15.] Works are 'represented' digitally: Negroponte, *Being Digital* pp 14-17.

[16.] *Turner v Robinson* (1860) 10 IR Ch R 510.

[17.] Section 3(3).

[18.] *Francis Day v Feldman* [1914] 2 Ch 728; *British Northrop v Texteam Blackburn* [1974] RPC 57.

[19.] *Bodley Head v Flegon* [1972] 1 WLR 680.

[20.] But see CA 1963, s 12(4).

occurred, the courts stress that the vital distinction is between performances to a domestic or quasi-domestic audience, which do not infringe as distinct from other kinds of performance, which do generally infringe. The basic issue is whether the audience come together as a result of some domestic or quasi-domestic tie. Even if this is so, as in *Duck v Bates*[21] a case in which a play performed by amateurs to an audience of doctors, nurses, students and patients was held not to be in a place of public entertainment, the courts view the notion of a common tie as being somewhat restrictive. Membership of a club or institute and closed meetings of societies do not suffice[22] to make use of the work lawful. So musical performances by a band to members of a club[23] or to patrons of a hotel[24] are infringements and it does not make any difference whether a fee is paid for admission or not.

[16.08] The performance of recorded music to a captive audience of factory workers, even those engaged in vital assembly work in time of war will still constitute an infringement of copyright, the courts emphasising that while the audience was gathered together for purposes other than entertainment this fact could not bring these performances into the domestic sphere.[25] Similarly, in *APRA v Commonwealth Bank*[26] the Federal Court of Australia held that the performance of recorded music on a training video, shown to a group of eleven employees outside of banking hours, was an infringing act. Gummow J held that the fact that the performance occurred as an adjunct to a commercial activity made such a performance likely to be regarded as a public performance.

[16.09] The courts here often emphasise that they are concerned to protect the statutory monopoly given to the rightholder because of the diluting effect such performances have on other acts of distribution, particularly sales. It is no argument for the infringer to say that performance in public may boost sales by increasing exposure of the work to the buying public.[27] Limited statutory exceptions are found in relation to the sound recording copyright.[28]

---

21. (1884) 13 QBD 843.
22. *Jennings v Stephens* [1936] Ch 469.
23. *Harms (Incorporated) Ltd v Martans Club Ltd* [1927] 1 Ch 526.
24. *PRS Ltd v Hawthorns Hotel* [1933] Ch 855.
25. *Turner v PRS* [1943] Ch 167; *PRS v Rangers* [1975] RPC 626.
26. (1992) 25 IPR 157. For performance in public of a literary work by display see *Bookmaker's Afternoon Greyhound Services Ltd v Wilf Gilbert (Staffordshire) Ltd* [1994] FSR 723. The Premier League also charges UK bookmakers for using fixture lists for fixed odds betting (see IMRO News, March 1996).
27. *PRS v Harlequin Record Shops* [1979] FSR 233.
28. Section 17(8): *Phonographic Performance v Pontins Ltd* [1967] 3 All ER 736. See also s 52(1) on RTE broadcasts and sound recordings.

'Broadcasting the Work'

[16.10] The broadcast must be an RTE broadcast or a broadcast authorised under the Radio and Television Act 1988[29] if it is to be a protected broadcast under the Copyright Acts. The notion of a broadcast, of sound or television, is based upon the Wireless Telegraphy Acts 1926 to 1988.[30] Broadcasting of a work is deemed not to be a performance of that work, nor an act of causing visual images or sounds to be seen or heard.[31]

'Transmitting the work via a diffusion service'

[16.11] The distributing of broadcasts via a cable service in the form of Cablelink Ltd subscription services require the operator - Cablelink Ltd, for example, or its licensees - to obtain licences when copyright works are incorporated into broadcast. The 1963 Act specifically requires the use of 'material substances'- copper wire or optical fibre, for example, and for the works to be comprised in the form of broadcast programmes or other programmes. Irish law does not appear to catch services such as 'dial a disc' or 'music on hold' provided by Telecom Éireann,[32] for the distribution of music via a telephone system is not likely to be caught by the diffusion service right. 'Music on hold' is, however, a performance making the telephone subscriber, as distinct from the network operator, liable to get a licence from the relevant bodies.

'Acts of adaptation'

[16.12] Acts of adaptation - turning an artistic work into a literary work, a musical work into a dramatic work, for example, overlap substantially with the concept of reproduction in any material form. Section 8(7) defines an adaptation as follows:

> (a) in relation to a literary or dramatic work, means any of the following:
>
> > (i)   in the case of a non-dramatic work, a version of the work, whether in its original language or a different language, in which it is converted into a dramatic work;
> >
> > (ii) in the case of a dramatic work, a version of the work, whether in its original language or a different language, in which it is converted into a non-dramatic work;

[29.]   SI 101/1991.

[30.]   See generally, Hall; *The Electronic Age: Telecommunications in Ireland* (Oak Tree Press, 1993).

[31.]   CA 1963, s 2(2) and 2(5).

[32.]   For a recent Australian case in which an Australian telephone company were held liable, see *APRA v Telstra* (1995) 31 IPR 289. The leading Irish case is *PRS Ltd v Marlin Communal Aerials Ltd* [1977] FSR 51.

(iii) a translation of the work;

(iv) a version of the work in which the story or action is conveyed wholly or mainly by means of pictures in a form suitable for reproduction in a book or in a newspaper, magazine or similar periodical; and

(b) in relation to a musical work, means of an arrangement or transcription of the work.

[16.13] The notion of a translation does not extend to conversion of a printed work into an electronic format.[33] However, despite the early Irish case of *Turner v Robinson*[34] the performance or reproduction of an artistic work by way of a *tableau vivant* is not an infringement.

INFRINGEMENT OF PART III WORKS

[16.14] The s 17 sound recording copyrights, s 18 cinematographic film copyright, the s 19 broadcast copyright and the typographical copyright in published editions of works provided by s 20, are the Part III works in question. As such, many of the concepts found in relation to Part II infringements are applicable to Part III infringements. However, it should be noted that restricted acts in relation to sound recordings include making a record embodying the sound recording, which is not to be confused with the author's mechanical right in s 13. The public performance infringement in relation to published sound recordings in s 17(4)(b) is only committed where the s 17 rightholder refuses to pay, or undertake to pay, equitable remuneration.[35] There is no Irish decision on the question of whether a digital recording or remastering constitutes a sound recording. It should also be noted that the infringement by copying of a broadcast includes a private copying exception[36] and that the public performance infringement provision requires the infringer to charge for admission,[37] which is hardly likely in the context of existing domestic Irish broadcasts at the time of writing.

Secondary Infringement

[16.15] The expression 'secondary infringement' is used to describe situations where the infringer handles infringing copies by way of importation, sale or letting, or by way of trade offers, exposes for sale, or exhibits, infringing copies.[38] The infringement covers not only copies that are counterfeit but copies

---

33. *Computer Edge Property Ltd v Apple Computer* (1986) 161 CLR 171.
34. (1860) 10 IR Ch R 510.
35. *Phonographic Performance (Ireland) v Controller* [1996] 1 ILRM 1.
36. CA 1963, s 19(5)(a) and (b).
37. 'Broadcast ... by a paying audience': see ss 19(5)(c) and (q).
38. CA 1963, s 11.

that are legitimate but in the hands of the infringer in breach of the rights of the plaintiff. It thus applies to parallel imports that do not benefit from EU exhaustion rules, such as US published books imported into Ireland without the permission of the Irish rightholder.[39] The secondary infringer must, on an objective basis, know that the articles must be infringing copies[40] and in practice those problems of proof can be sidestepped by putting the person trading in the goods on notice that the goods or packaging infringes copyright.[41] Secondary infringement also consists in permitting a place of public entertainment to be used to mount a performance in public of a Part II work, subject to certain exceptions as found in s 11(4) and (5) of the 1963 Act. It should also be noted that several of the provisions in s 54 of the 1963 Act, which concern dealing in works that have been altered to mistate the identity of the author, have direct relevance to secondary infringers all well as persons responsible for making the alterations in question.

THE BOUNDARIES OF INFRINGEMENT

[16.16] If a competitor does not copy from the work of a rival no copyright infringement occurs. Problems, however, arise when a rightholder asserts that there has been a substantial taking, a claim denied by the defendant who must attribute any objective similarity between the works to coincidence. A defence of coincidental creation is effective where it can be made out, but it can be difficult to sustain. Witness the action in the courts of the United States[42] where George Harrison was held to have infringed copyright when his song, 'My Sweet Lord' involved a substantial taking from the Chiffon's earlier hit, 'He's So Fine'. More recently a controversy broke out[43] over the Irish 1995 Eurovision entry 'Dreamin', when substantial similarities were detected with the Julie Felix seventies hit, 'Moonlighting'. The same scenario reappeared in 1996 with allegations that the British Eurovision song has plagiarised an earlier work[44] and much publicity was given in December 1996 to allegations that the Spice Girls had stolen a hit tune from an Israeli composer. Such allegations can be dangerous however, leading to countersuits.[45] Literary figures such as the Duchess of York and Ian McEwan have also produced works that have been thought to bear similarities with earlier works in relation to plot structure, but plot structure in a literary work is eminently open to coincidental creation.

[39.] See 'Man Agrees not to sell US books' *Irish Times* 29 February 1992.
[40.] *Infabrics v Jaytex* [1978] FSR 451.
[41.] *Frank v Hirsch (Pty) v A Roopanand Bros* [1994] IPR 465.
[42.] *ABKCO Music Inc v Harrisongs Music* (1983) 722 F (2d) 988.
[43.] See *Irish Times*, 6 May 1995.
[44.] 'Dispute over British Eurovision Song', *Irish Times*, 8 March 1996.
[45.] See 'Lloyd-Webber Sues Songwriter for $78' *The Times* 5 June 1996.

[16.17] The leading English case dealing with this issue is the Court of Appeal decision in *Francis Day & Hunter Ltd v Bron*.[46] The plaintiff alleged infringement of a musical copyright by the defendant who wrote another song which, the defendant conceded, had similarities with the plaintiff's song. In considering whether infringement has occurred in a literary, dramatic or musical work the Court of Appeal held that two elements must be present: sufficient objective similarity between the copyright work and the later 'infringing' work or a substantial portion thereof, and evidence that the copyright work is the source from which the infringing work is derived - a causal link. Intention, or knowledge, is not relevant to the issue of infringement although these factors may be considered later in relation to the award of damages. The Court of Appeal endorsed Wilberforce J's assessment of the three principal conclusions a court may reach in an infringement action, namely, conscious copying, unconscious copying, and coincidence. The first two conclusions represent infringement while the third does not. After eliminating conscious copying in the case at bar the Court of Appeal endorsed Wilberforce J's assessment of the factors that are relevant to the enquiry into unconscious copying: these are the degree of familiarity with the plaintiff's work, the character of the work and its qualities in impressing on the mind of the listener, objective similarity, the inherent probability of coincidence, ie, the influence of other factors on the mind of the defendant, and the defendant's evidence on influences upon the defendant's work.[47]

[16.18] Many of the factors are also relevant to an enquiry into the likelihood that the defendant consciously copied the plaintiff's work. However, unless there has been a substantial taking from the original work, no infringement can be made out. If the element of the work taken is commonplace or itself derivative then infringement will not occur, while if the plaintiff's work is original a small percentage of the total work will be a substantial taking, particularly if memorable or distinctive.[48]

COPYRIGHT INFRINGEMENT - THE NATURE OF THE RESTRICTED ACT

[16.19] For an infringement to be made out by a rightholder, it will be necessary to establish that the infringer has committed the infringing act - it is not enough to show that the defendant has acted in a way that strikes at the economic

---

[46.] [1963] Ch 587.

[47.] *Per* Willmer LJ in *Bron* [1963] Ch 587 at 614.

[48.] *Hawkes & Sons v Paramount Film Service* [1934] Ch 593. In the *Acuff Rose* case (Pretty Woman) only the title and opening bass riff were taken but this was clearly a substantial taking. Other examples come to mind. The opening chords of Eric Clapton's 'Layla' are really the only memorable part of the composition.

integrity of the rightholder's investment. In *News Datacom Ltd v Lyons*[49] the defendant manufactured computer smart cards that decoded the plaintiff's encoded broadcast signal of SKY television subscription channels. In an infringement action seeking interlocutory relief, the plaintiff asserted that in order to achieve this result the defendant must have reproduced the algorithm, in whole or in part, that was contained in the smart card. Flood J, however, was faced with evidence only that the defendant's card could achieve the same result as the plaintiff's and, on this basis, functional similarity was not enough to establish the probable 'fact' of copying. Copyright law is not intended to deter competition but, rather, it is intended to prevent others from taking a competitive advantage from the efforts and talents of others by copying the tangible products of original skill, talent or innovation. If parasitic copying were facilitated the law would be tolerating anti-competitive practices. The defendant, in *News Datacom*, may not have copied the algorithm but he certainly embarked upon a trading practice that was regarded by the plaintiffs as unfair competition, which is not an independently actionable common law tort in Ireland.

[16.20] Volume is not a determining factor: small snatches of a song or novel - even one line from a poem may be protectable while titles no matter how distinctive are not protected.[50]

[16.21] The case of *Ravenscroft v Herbert*[51] has proved influential in filtering some of the factors necessary to examine substantial infringement. Whitford J approved counsel, Mr Laddie's observations on the principal factors which are relevant:

> "First the volume of the material taken, bearing in mind that quality is more important than quantity; secondly, how much of such material is the subject matter of copyright and how much is not; thirdly, whether there has been an *animus furandi* on the part of the defendant; this was treated by Page Wood VC in *Jarrold v Houlston* (1857) 3 K & J 708 as equivalent to an intention on the part of the defendant to take for the purpose of saving himself labour; fourthly, the extent to which the plaintiff's and the defendant's book are competing works."[52]

[49.] [1994] 1 ILRM 450; see *British Sky Broadcasting Group Ltd v Lyons* [1995] FSR 357 for a follow up case in the UK.

[50.] *Francis Day & Hunter Ltd v Twentieth Century Fox* [1939] 4 All ER 192.

[51.] [1980] RPC 193.

[52.] *Ibid*, p 201.

Volume of Work Taken

[16.22] This is always a question of fact and although both quality and quantity are relevant, the quality of the taking seems more important. In the case of literary works in particular it is often possible for the parties to rely on expert testimony from academic[53] or publishing[54] specialists. Expert testimony will be particularly important in infringement actions involving computer programs but the cases tend to reveal there is ample room for fundamental disagreement between expert testimony on this point in particular.[55] However, the most significant problem in this field is raised by one of definition. Copyright protects the creator of forms of expression or articulation. Copyright does not protect ideas *per se*; such as ideas that have not been expressed in a protectable form previously, or ideas that by their nature are limited to one form of articulation. The judges however echo academic commentators by saying that while this is a truism, the boundary between protectable expression and a non-protectable idea depends on what is meant by an idea. The level of abstraction at which the idea is pitched is of particular significance here. If an idea is capable only of one form of expression then actual copying of that form of expression will need to be shown.[56] The leading case on this point involved an artistic copyright infringement whereby a hand pointed to a square on an electoral ballot paper indicating how to cast a vote. Wills J said that such an idea is the common property of the world:

> "the mere choice of subject can rarely, if ever, confer upon the author of the drawing an exclusive right to represent the subject ... something special in the way of artistic treatment even of this simple operation, if it existed, might be the subject of copyright but nothing of the kind has been suggested."[57]

[16.23] In the field of artistic copyright the essence of such a work is said to be that which is 'visually significant'.[58] Where the work is literary the quality of the work may be thematic and several older cases make it clear that taking the plot of a story so as to serve as the outline of a play or film could be a substantial taking, even though there is no copying or reproduction of the original script, or even if shifts in time, place or theme occur. These cases will, of course, need to

---

53. *International Writing Institute v Rimila Property Ltd* (1993) 27 IPR 546; *House of Spring Gardens Ltd v Point Blank Ltd* [1984] IR 611.
54. *Silletoe v McGraw Hill Book Co* [1983] FSR 545.
55. See *John Richardson Computers Ltd v Flanders* [1993] FSR 497 and *Ibcos Computers Ltd v Barclays Finance Ltd* [1994] FSR 275.
56. *Kendrick v Lawrence* (1890) 25 QBD 93, criticised in *Ibcos Computers Ltd v Barclays Finance Ltd* [1994] FSR 275.
57. *Ibid* at p 102.
58. *Rose Plastics GmbH v William Beckett & Co* [1989] FSR 113 cited with approval in *Interlego AG v Tyco Industries* [1988] 3 All ER 949.

address the issue of coincidental creation[59] but they suggest that the idea/expression dichotomy can be difficult to draw in the context of dramatic works at least. Protection tends to be extensive when a court opts to protect an investment from unfair copying, as distinct from looking to the level of reproduction by the infringer, and, despite dicta to the contrary, there are a number of cases which allow the protection of literary works because of the level of investment made in creating a work even if this results in protection of information *per se*.[60]

How much is copyright protected?

[16.24] Apart from the idea/expression dichotomy, considered above, the courts must distinguish between the defendant's use of non-copyright information from the defendant's reliance upon the plaintiff's work, which is not always the same thing. While an edited or annotated edition of a literary work that itself is copyright protected will create a copyright in that edited or annotated edition, the use of parts of the 'public domain' element of the work will not infringe copyright in the edition. In *Warwick Film v Eisinger*[61] the plaintiff's copyright in an edited version of the trial of Oscar Wilde was not infringed when the defendant was shown to have used the trial transcript as distinct from the plaintiff's edited work.

[16.25] There may be some reliance by a defendant on the plaintiff's work without a copyright infringement being shown. If the plaintiff's work is factual then a plaintiff may not complain if the defendant uses the historical facts to assist in creating an independent work of fiction - knowledge is meant to be built upon - but the plaintiff can complain if the structure of such a work, and theories and speculations of the author are lifted by a novelist.[62] Use by the defendant of a common source is not an infringement.[63] In the case of factual works like maps or television listings, the external similarities will be excused upon proof of independent work or common sources.[64]

The intention to take the plaintiff's work

[16.26] Once it has been shown by the plaintiff that the defendant intended to use the plaintiff's work it may be difficult for the defendant to argue that the use was not an infringement, certainly in cases where the use is not transformative in

---

[59.] *Corelli v Gray* (1913) 30 TLR 116; *Vane v Famous Players* [1928-35] Mac CC 6.

[60.] Eg are these ideas hackneyed, *scenes a faire* etc? *Elanco v Lindops* [1979] FSR 46. See also the TV listings cases.

[61.] [1969] 1 Ch 508.

[62.] *Ravenscroft v Herbert* [1980] RPC 193; *Harman Pictures NV v Osborne* [1967] 1 WLR 723.

[63.] *Geographia Ltd v Penguin Books Ltd* [1985] FSR 208.

[64.] *TV Guide Inc v Publications La Semaine Inc* (1984) 9 CPR (3d) 368.

nature. If little or nothing remains of the original then the defendant may be held to have created a separate and independent work that not only attracts a separate copyright but is also a new work that does not infringe earlier works, even if the earlier work was inspirational.[65] Where the defendant has merely taken the plaintiff's work without alteration in order to save time and effort, this will not free the defendant from liability, even if the information set out in the plaintiff's work, eg a trade directory[66] or advertising material,[67] refers to individuals who have in some way consented to personal details of this kind being reproduced. Substantial problems may arise where the defendant is actually the person who created or contributed towards the plaintiff's copyright work (eg an employee or assignor) who subsequently uses his expertise or skill to create a similar work. In the software engineering industry or in technical areas such as cartography, liability has been negatived when the similarities have been ascribed to the personal qualities or conventions found in the relevant sector.[68] Wholesale reliance on other works, however, will not be excused.[69] An author, even one who has assigned copyright, is free to create an independent work but it is common for many contracts to provide anti-competition clauses which prevent an author from creating a competing work. These clauses are seen to be of doubtful constitutional validity and arguably are not likely to be enforceable under domestic competition law, so the earlier Irish case of *Educational Company of Ireland v Fallon*[70] in which a restraint clause of this kind was upheld, may no longer be reliable.

[16.27] The courts will be hostile to attempts to use the plaintiff's work while modifying its literal features by colourable alterations.[71] The leading case in Ireland is *House of Spring Gardens Ltd v Point Blank Ltd*.[72] In that case, the defendants sought to avoid liability for copyright infringement by re-designing a bullet-proof vest that the plaintiffs had sold to the Libyan government, the re-designing exercise being undertaken following settlement of earlier litigation. The re-design exercise took place in consultation with lawyers and accountants acting for the defendants but the product that emerged was held to have been a

---

65. *Williamson Music v Pearson* [1987] FSR 97.
66. *Morris v Ashbee* (1868) LR 7 Eq 34.
67. *Allied Discount Card v Bord Failte* [1990] ILRM 534. In relation to the published edition copyright issues of intention raise different concerns: see *Nationwide News Pty Ltd v Copyright Agency* (1996) 34 IPR 53.
68. *Delrina Corp v Triolet Systems* (1993) 47 CPR (3d) 1. *Geographia Ltd v Penguin Books Ltd* [1985] FSR 208.
69. *Sands & McDougall v Robinson* (1917) 23 CLR 49.
70. [1919] 1 IR 62.
71. *Elanco v Lindops* [1979] FSR 46.
72. [1984] IR 611.

substantial reproduction of the original work. McCarthy J in the Supreme Court viewed the re-design exercise with:

> "dismay that solicitors and counsel should consider it proper to be so personally involved with such a matter. I assume that neither the Law Society of England nor the Inns of Court in London provide tuition or require any aptitude in tailoring or cognate disciplines".[73]

Competition between two works

[16.28] This factor remains significant, particularly in the areas of professional or trade directories,[74] television listings cases,[75] the computer programs sector[76] and the newspaper industry where a recent case law[77] suggests that the plaintiffs have sought to enforce copyright in order to protect market position or repulse 'literary larceny'.[78] The decision of the European Court of Justice in *McGill*,[79] however, suggests that this desire to avoid 'undesirable' monopolies may take on a rather more active role where copyright is used to protect the rightholders market position, at a cost to the consumer in terms of quality of product. In a recent Canadian case[80] the defendant was held to have infringed the plaintiff's copyright in his doctoral thesis on the history of the Canadian West when parts were used by the defendant in a book on ranching; the non-commercial nature of the thesis was a factor in the court's decision not to award damages.

---

73. [1984] IR 611 at 708.
74. *Kelly v Morris* (1866) 1 Eq 697; *Morris v Ashbee* (1868) LR 7 Eq 34; *Rose v Information Services* [1987] FSR 254; *Waterlow Directories v Reed* [1992] FSR 409. *Waterlow v Rose* [1995] FSR 207; *Tele-Direct (Publications) Inc v American Business Information* (1996) 35 IPR 121.
75. *BBC v Wireless League* [1926] 1 Ch 433; *Independent Television v Time Out Ltd* [1984] FSR 64; *RTE v Magill TV Guide* [1990] ILRM 534.
76. See generally Chapter 13.
77. *Express Newspapers v News (UK)* [1990] 3 All ER 376.
78. Per North J in *Walter v Steinkopff* [1892] 3 Ch 489, at 496.
79. [1995] FSR 530.
80. *Breen v Hancock House Publishers Ltd* (1985) 6 CPR (3d) 433.

Chapter 17

Defences to Copyright Infringement

INTRODUCTION

[17.01] The Copyright Acts provide a range of circumstances and situations in which certain dealings in, or use made, of a copyright work will not be actionable by the rightholder. Many of these provisions are based upon the traditions that can be traced back to the Berne Convention which attempts to strike a balance between the interests of rightholders and users, particularly when the user is for certain special circumstance defined by national law which does not unreasonably prejudice the rightholder,[1] or where use is in the public interest or has an educational purpose.[2] However, the introduction of new technology, particularly the photocopier and the digitisation of information, which allow for perfect copies to be taken from all kinds of works, require a re-assessment of international and national law provisions on these various 'fair use' defences.

(I) EXPRESS OR IMPLIED AUTHORISATION BY THE RIGHTHOLDER

[17.02] Because copyright normally consists of an exclusive right to do or authorise others to do certain things in relation to a work,[3] it follows that where the rightholder has authorised such user there can be no infringement. The onus of showing that permission or consent has been given rests on the person alleging the agreement.[4] A recent Australian case in which an alleged oral licence was pleaded by way of defence, held that the court should enquire about whether consent was given rather than embark upon a contractual analysis of the case.[5]

(II) FAIR DEALING

[17.03] This is the broadest exception to the rightholder's exclusive rights in literary, dramatic or musical works. The user must bring the use, or intended

---

1. Article 9 of the Berne Convention.
2. Articles 10 and 10 *bis* of the Berne Convention.
3. CA 1963, ss 7(1) and 11(2).
4. *Blair v Osborne & Tompkins* [1971] 1 All ER 468; *Computermate Products v Ozi-Soft Property* (1988) 12 IPR 487. See Ch 15.
5. *Clune v Collins, Argus & Robertson Publishers Property Ltd* (1992) 25 IPR 246.

use, within one of the excepted activities, and the court must determine whether on the facts the use was a fair dealing. If, for example, the fair dealing is for the purpose of research or private study or criticism or review then no infringement takes place.

'Research or private study'[6]

[17.04] The making of one copy of a copyright work for research or private study, a broadly educational use, has been upheld as a fair dealing, but the statutory defence is narrowly construed. The making of several copies for distribution within a school or business is not within this defence when the school or business operates as a commercial entity.[7] The provision of extracts from news broadcasts by a commercial news monitoring entity to commercial customers who in turn use the material for their own commercial purposes is also not within the defence, for here there is a simple appropriation of another's work for a commercial profit.[8] Similarly, the substantial taking of extracts from novels or plays for incorporation in 'cramming' guides sold to students cannot be within the defence for these activities clearly prejudice the legitimate interests of the rightholder - the use diminishes the market for the original.

[17.05] One significant factor that will be of great practical importance for this defence is the availability of contractual licences from publishers; since 1992 the Irish Copyright Licensing Agency has sought to regulate unauthorised reproduction of printed materials on behalf of Irish publishers. While the Agency has been anxious to deal with mass photocopying by schools, universities and other institutions, it is certainly arguable that individual users may find that the availability of permission upon payment of a fee may well make unauthorised private copying of printed material something other than a fair dealing.[9] There are other specific educational copying defences considered below.

'Criticism or Review'

[17.06] The use of substantial extracts from a literary, dramatic or musical work for the purpose of criticism or review of the work is permitted.[10] One early case indicated that where a work is unpublished, that is, the author has not put the

---

6. CA 1963, s 12(1)(a).
7. *American Geophysical Union v Texaco* (1994) 29 IPR 381.
8. *TVNZ v Newsmonitor* (1993) 27 IPR 441; *Basic Books Inc v Kinko's Graphics* (1991) 23 IPR 565.
9. See *American Geophysical Union v Texaco* (1994) 29 IPR 381 where the licensing terms were described as fair, hence a refusal to comply with them made unauthorised copying unlawful.
10. CA 1963, s 12(1)(b). *Wigginton v Brisbane TV* (1992) 25 IPR 58.

work before the public, the defence should not be available[11] but this view has not prevailed in recent cases[12] which hold that the publication status of the original work is only a factor in the fair dealing issue.

[17.07] If the 'critical' work makes use of the original text so as to compete with the original work this will prevent the defence from being available[13] but reproduction of an entire work may still be within the defence.[14] It is clear that the concept of 'criticism or review' is not to be confined to criticism or review of the work as a work; in *Hubbard v Vosper*[15] the defence was available to a critic of the Church of Scientology who used the works of the founder of the Church to criticise the ideas and philosophy behind the Church. Similarly, in *Time Warner v Channel 4 Television Corporation*[16] a television documentary that was in part critical of the sociological thesis behind Kubrick's *Clockwork Orange* was held to be within this defence, even if the critique ran the risk of misrepresenting or possibly giving a distorted view of the original film.

There must be a sufficient acknowledgement of not only the source of the work but the author of the work.[17]

'For the purpose of reporting current events'[18]

[17.08] Under the 1963 Act, the public are entitled to be informed about matters of controversy or contemporaneous events such as political stories, celebrity life-styles or sporting or cultural features, and the use of literary, dramatic or musical works which have appeared in a newspaper or similar periodical, with sufficient acknowledgements, or in a broadcast or film is not an infringement if the use is within the fair dealing context. However, if there is no real contemporaneous event, such as the death of a celebrated actor or the opening of a new play, the section may not be satisfied. So in *Associated Newspapers Group plc v News Group Newspapers*[19] the death of the Duchess of Windsor was not an event which justified the unauthorised publication of correspondence written many years before between herself and her husband. The courts are suspicious of this defence, on the ground that sensational stories puffed up by way of copyright material used without permission to sell newspapers is

---

[11] *British Oxygen v Liquid Air* [1925] Ch 383.
[12] *Beloff v Pressdram Ltd* [1973] 1 All ER 241.
[13] *Silletoe v McGraw Hill Book Co* [1983] FSR 545.
[14] *Per* Megaw LJ in *Hubbard v Vosper* [1972] 1 All ER 1023.
[15] [1972] 1 All ER 1023.
[16] [1993] 28 IPR 454.
[17] *Express Newspapers plc v News UK* [1990] 3 All ER 376. In Ireland see interlocutory proceedings arising from the Bishop Casey controversy: *Irish Times* 20 and 23 March 1993.
[18] CA 1963, s 12(12).
[19] [1986] RPC 515.

unmeritorious. However, in relation to injunction proceedings arising out of the unauthorised use of extracts from Annie Murphy's book on her relationship with the former Bishop of Galway, Dr Casey, a fair dealing defence under s 12 was used, with some success.[20] The defence is used to protect journalists who 'lift' stories from rival newspapers but no definitive decision on the lawfulness of this practice has been given.[21] The defence in relation to broadcast use only covers broadcasts of copyright literary, dramatic or musical works; the defence does not yet extend to broadcasters using broadcast material such as unscripted sporting contests.[22]

'Fair Dealing'

[17.09] In *TVNZ v Newsmonitor*[23] Blanchard J commented that fair dealing is simply reasonable use. Echoing the words of Denning MR in *Hubbard v Vosper*[24] Blanchard J indicated that the important issues are an examination of the nature of the work, the purpose for which the defendant has used them, the quantity of the material taken, and the effect that the defendant's activity has on the plaintiff's work; in particular does the defendant's use have a depreciating effect? A substantial use of some 10% of the original may be upheld as in the *Clockwork Orange* case,[25] and the use of the most important elements (such as film of the goals in a soccer match) may be within the defence.[26] It will be extremely difficult to make out the defence in cases where the defendant intends some 'parasitic'[27] or competing user with the plaintiff.

Fair dealing and artistic works

[17.10] The fair dealing exceptions discussed above in relation to literary, dramatic or musical works also apply in relation to artistic works.[28]

(III) REPRODUCTION FOR THE PURPOSE OF JUDICIAL PROCEEDINGS

[17.11] In the case of literary, dramatic and musical works, the reproduction of such works for the purpose of judicial proceedings[29] is not an infringement. This

---

20. *Irish Times* 20 and 23 March 1993.
21. *Express Newspapers plc v News UK* [1990] 3 All ER 376.
22. In the UK see *BBC v BSB* [1991] 3 All ER 833.
23. (1993) 27 IPR 441.
24. [1972] 1 All ER 1023.
25. (1993) 28 IPR 454.
26. *BBC v British Satellite Broadcasting* [1991] 3 All ER 833. (Irish law does not, unlike UK law, apply the defence to broadcasts).
27. *TVNZ v Newsmonitor* (1993) 27 IPR 441.
28. CA 1963, ss 14(1) and (2).
29. CA 1963, s 12(3); this also applies to reports of such proceedings.

exception also apples to artistic works,[30] cinematographic films[31] and sound and television broadcasts.[32]

(IV) EDUCATIONAL USAGE

[17.12] The fair dealing exceptions in ss 12 and 14 address the issue of individual fair dealings in works. There are other provisions that can be broadly described as educational use exceptions. The use of short passages from a copyright Part II work is permitted if the passages are included in a compilation intended for use in schools under stringent conditions laid down in the Act.[33] This exception is available to publishers of school texts. The Act also allows for reproduction of Part II works by teachers or pupils in the course of instruction as long as the reproduction does not take place by a duplicating process - a photocopier, for example. Reproduction for examination purposes is also permitted.[34] These provisions are limited; other educational use or reproduction will require the consent or licence of the rightholder.

(V) PUBLIC PERFORMANCE EXCEPTIONS

[17.13] A number of somewhat diverse infringement exceptions and defences can be found in the 1963 Act. For the sake of ease of analysis, these are being grouped together. The reading or recitation of reasonable extracts from a published literary or dramatic work, when sufficiently acknowledged, is not an infringement.[35] In the case of sound recordings, persons who cause the recording to be heard in public, broadcast, or communicated on a diffusion service do not infringe copyright if that person undertakes to refer the dispute about payment of equitable remuneration to the Controller under s 31 of the Act.[36] A person who causes a sound recording to be heard in public by hotel guests, and the like, or in clubs or associations that are charitable in nature[37] likewise does not infringe copyright if strict conditions are met.[38] In the cases of films that are newsreels, infringement does not occur if the newsreel is seen or heard in public, or broadcast after the end of 50 years in which the events depicted occurred.[39] Where a sound or television broadcast is heard in public, the person so causing

---

[30.] CA 1963, s 14(6).

[31.] CA 1963, s 18(5).

[32.] CA 1963, s 19(11).

[33.] CA 1963, s 12(5).

[34.] CA 1963, s 53.

[35.] CA 1963, ss 12(4) and (12). See 199 Dáil Debates Cols 1420-1422.

[36.] CA 1963, s 17(5).

[37.] CA 1963, s 17(8); see *Phonographic Performance Ltd v Pontins Ltd* [1968] Ch 290. See, however, 'Hotels complain at levy for music on bedroom TVs: *Times* 28 March 1995.

[38.] CA 1963, s 17(9).

the broadcast to be heard in public does not infringe copyright in the sound recording[40] and a similar exception is provided for persons who by receiving a broadcast cause a film to be seen or heard in public.[41] An even broader exception, covering Part II copyrights, as well as a cinematographic film copyright, operates *vis-à-vis* authorised broadcasts distributed by way of a diffusion service.[42] However, s 19(5) still gives RTE an exclusive broadcasting right *vis-à-vis* causing the broadcast to be seen or heard in public.

(VI) REPRODUCTION EXCEPTIONS

[17.14] Exceptions to an author's right to authorise reproduction of Part II works are again somewhat diverse. In the case of publicly available manuscripts unpublished but made 100 years previously, the author having died 50 years previously, copyright is not infringed by publishing the work in accordance with directions made by the Minister.[43] The reproduction of a literary, dramatic or musical work which RTE have been authorised to broadcast by way of an ephemeral recording, made entirely for broadcast purposes, does not infringe copyright if RTE comply with the requirements of the Act.[44] There is, however, a further archival exemption, discussed below. A similar exemption operates in relation to the sound recording copyright.[45] The most significant reproduction right exception in relation to sound and television broadcasts is the right of persons to make a recording for private purposes, whether this be by way of a film[46] or a television broadcast (eg a video recording) or a sound recording[47] of a sound broadcast (eg cassette taping of a radio broadcast). Again, this does not authorise an infringement of any Part II rights held by others (eg the composer of music used in the broadcast) or infringement of the s 17 sound recording copyright. Finally, in relation to the s 20 copyright in the typographical arrangement of a published edition, reproduction in the form of a photographic reproduction (photocopy) does not infringe that copyright if undertaken for private research or study purposes.[48]

[39.] CA 1963, s 18(7). Where a film incorporates Part II material but copyright in the film expires, public performance of the film does not infringe the underlying copyrights; CA 1963, s 18(6).

[40.] CA 1963, s 52(1); the author's copyright as distinct from the phonogram producer's copyright is, however, so infringed; *PRS v Rosses Point Hotel Co* High Court, unrep 20 February 1967.

[41.] CA 1963, s 52(2).

[42.] CA 1963, s 52(3). See *PRS v Marlin Communal Aerials* [1982] ILRM 269.

[43.] CA 1963, s 12(6); see now SI 158/1995 which is subject to s 12(6); For national archives see National Archives Act 1986, s 17.

[44.] CA 1963, s 12(7) and (8).

[45.] CA 1963, ss 17(11) and (12).

[46.] CA 1963, s 19(5)(a).

[47.] CA 1963, s 19(5)(b).

[48.] CA 1963, s 20(6).

(VII) ARCHIVAL EXCEPTIONS

[17.15] In relation to the ephemeral recording exceptions given to RTE in relation to the authorised use of literary, dramatic and musical works in s 12, and the similar exception in relation to RTE's use of sound recordings in s 17, the obligation to destroy such recordings within six months is not to apply if the recording is stored as being one of exceptional documentary character.[49]

(VIII) ARTISTIC WORKS

[17.16] The fair dealing exceptions discussed above also apply in relation to artistic works where the purpose is research or private study or criticism or review. The inclusion of an artistic work in a broadcast or film is also permitted on a fair dealing basis.[50] A specific exception to the reproduction right is also expressly provided for where a sculpture or a work of artistic craftsmanship is permanently situated in a public place or public venue; the work may be photographed, painted, drawn or an engraving of it made. Such a work may also be included in a broadcast or a film. The same freedoms exist in relation to architectural works. Publication of the result is also not an infringement of copyright.[51]

[17.17] A broader exception, applicable to all artistic works included in a film or television broadcast exists where inclusion is for background purposes or is incidental to the main purposes behind the film.[52] An artist who uses a drawing or a model, for example, in creating a work, who later uses the same drawing or model to create a subsequent work does not infringe copyright in the first work unless the subsequent work repeats or imitates the main design in the earlier work.[53] In relation to architectural works, reconstruction of a building in accordance with the original or with drawings of the original building does not infringe copyright.[54] The ephemeral reproduction right given to RTE is also applicable to artistic works, as is the archival exception for works, having exceptional documentary character.[55]

(IX) NON-VOLUNTARY LICENCES FOR RECORDINGS OF MUSICAL WORKS

[17.18] A very substantial exception to a composer's right to authorise the reproduction of a musical work is found in s 13 of the 1963 Act. Under this

---

[49.] CA 1963, s 12(9) and 17(13).
[50.] CA 1963, s 14(1) and (2).
[51.] CA 1963, ss 14(3) and (5).
[52.] CA 1963, s 14(4).
[53.] CA 1963, s 14(8).
[54.] CA 1963, ss 14(9) and (10).
[55.] CA 1963, ss 14(11) to (14).

section any person may manufacture a record of a musical work, or an adaptation of that work in the State as long as that musical work has previously been made or imported into the State for retail sale by the rightholder or with the rightholder's licence. This exception was developed in order to allow the public to gain access to recordings of musical works while providing the composer with a right to equitable remuneration. There are a number of procedural requirements laid down in the Act - notice must be given to the rightholder prior to manufacture and the manufacturer must intend to work for retail sale - and an agreed royalty (normally around 6% of the ordinary retail selling price of the record) should be paid to the rightholder. The right to manufacture reproductions of a musical work is generally known as the mechanical right and the licensing of this right is exercised by the Mechanical Copyright Protection Society (MCPS) on behalf of rightholders. The Act contains a dispute resolution procedure[56] and envisages that where copyright in the musical work and any literary work (ie the lyrics of a recorded song) are held by different persons, apportionment of the royalty paid by the manufacturer should be agreed as between these rightholders.[57] A manufacturer does not infringe copyright in either the musical work or any literary copyright if the manufacturer complies with s 13.

[17.19] The trend, in an international context, is against the non-voluntary licence system and it was abolished in the UK in 1988. This practice will probably not survive the next revision of Irish copyright law.

(X) PUBLIC POLICY

[17.20] Although copyright is an exclusively statutory regime, there are a number of situations in which a rightholder may find that the courts are not prepared to uphold a copyright when this would conflict with some compelling or competing policy objective.[58] Firstly, the courts have declined to allow rightholders to proceed against infringers in equity when the work in question, which has undoubtedly been pirated, is itself regarded as obscene, or a work calculated to injure the public.[59] Even at common law, a scandalous work which had been pirated by another could be outside the protection of the courts[60] and in the leading modern English case of *Glyn v Weston*[61] the novel *Three Weeks* by Elinor Glyn which had been denounced as encouraging free love and adultery,

---

[56.] CA 1963, s 13(2). For legislative history, see 199 *Dáil Debates* Cols 1425-1429.

[57.] CA 1963, s 13(5).

[58.] For an unsuccessful Irish attempt see *Hodges & Smith v Welsh* (1840) 2 IR Eq R 266.

[59.] *Southey v Sherwood* (1817) 2 Mer 435; *Lord Byron v Dugdale* (1823) LJ OS Ch 239; *Baschet v London Illustrated* [1990] 1 Ch 73.

[60.] *Stockdale v Onwhyn* (1826) 5 B & C 173.

[61.] [1916] 1 Ch 261; See Phillips (1977) 6 Anglo Am L Rev 138.

in cases where the marriage tie had merely been made irksome, was not protected from an act of infringement by the defendant. More recently, however, the American courts have departed from this kind of position, describing these defences as the vestiges of a bygone era.[62] In the Canadian case of *Aldrich v One Stop Video*[63] the view was expressed that only in clear cases should a court opt to use this residual jurisdiction to protect the social or economic well-being of the public, observing that the Berne Convention does not support content-based denials of copyright in works. The court indicated that unlawful distribution of a work rather than obscenity should be the central issue when a court declines to allow copyright to be enforced against an infringer by refusing to award damages to the rightholder. The use of the 'clean hands' doctrine to deny an injunction to restrain unauthorised distribution of the work by a pirate may, in any event, be a somewhat short-sighted response; the infringer or pirate can continue to distribute the work to a wider audience with relative impunity!

[17.21] Public policy also intervenes when a rightholder seeks to use the monopoly powers given by the Copyright Acts to protect his own market interests while at the same time harming the community as a whole. For this reason the House of Lords in *British Leyland v Armstrong Patents*[64] prevented British Leyland from enforcing artistic copyright in parts used in constructing motor vehicles, on the ground that the sale of vehicles by British Leyland ceded to a purchaser the inherent right to have the vehicle maintained and repaired in the most economical way possible, even if the purchaser and subsequent owners resorted to persons such as the defendant who have manufactured identical replacement parts which competed with the plaintiff's own spare parts. The House of Lords noted that while it was novel to apply the principle that a grantor should not derogate from his grant so as to preclude the enforcement of a statutory right to which the grantor was *prima facie* entitled, the principle could apply to this novel set of circumstances. The Hong Kong Court of Appeal, in *Green Cartridge Co (Hong Kong) Ltd v Canon*[65] has applied the repairer principle to a case where the plaintiffs sought to prevent the defendant from reverse engineering the replaceable toner cartridges provided by the plaintiffs in their printers and photocopiers in order for the defendants to produce a cheaper rival product. Because the owner of a computer printer is entitled to repair that

---

[62.] *Mitchell Bros Film Group v Cinema Adult Theatre* 604 F 2nd 852 (1979). Contrast the South African case of *Goeie Hoop Uitgewer S(Eindoms) Beperk v Central News Agency* [1953] 2 SA 843.

[63.] (1987) 39 DLR (3d) 362.

[64.] [1986] FSR 221. For copyright misuse defences in the USA see *Hanna* (1994) 46 Stanford LR 401. So far these defences have not prevailed in UK computer cases; *Ibcos Computers Ltd v Barclays Finance Ltd* [1994] FSR 275.

[65.] (1996) 34 IPR 614.

printer, the majority of the Court reasoned that this gave a right to repair the printer in the most convenient manner, which in this case involved the right to select a replacement cartridge.

[17.22] Public policy, however, is not to be taken too far in this regard. The fact that a rightholder may have himself infringed copyright in producing the work that the rightholder is seeking to protect is not in itself a basis for denying to protect the work.[66]

(XI) PARODY

[17.23] The fact that an existing work has been used to create a separate work which is intended to parody that work is regarded in the United States as within the 'fair use' doctrine.[67] English case law does not recognise parody as a legitimate defence[68] but approaches the issue by considering whether the use of the original work is such as to create a new, separate work, little or nothing of the original remaining. This seems to ignore the fact that a parody can only be effective if the parody mirrors the original. This factor, and the moral rights implications of treating the original work to derogatory treatment will have to be considered in future cases.

[66.] *ZYX Music v King* [1995] 3 All ER 1; affirmed [1997] 2 All ER 129; *A-One Accessory Imports Pty v Off-Road Imports Pty* (1996) 34 IPR 306. But contrast *Wright v Tallis* (1845) 1 CB 863.
[67.] *Acuff Rose Music v Campbell* (1994) 114 SC 1164; *Depel* [1994] EIPR 358.
[68.] *Joy Music Ltd v Sunday Pictorial* [1960] 1 All ER 703; *Williamson Music v Pearson* [1987] FSR 97.

Chapter 18

Remedies for Copyright Infringement

INTRODUCTION

[18.01] In general terms, the Copyright Acts provide the rightholder with a number of specific remedies, while emphasising that the primary reliefs are the same as those available to a person who issues proceedings in respect of an infringement of other proprietary rights - breach of confidence, passing-off, and trade mark infringement, for example; this is hardly surprising given the overlap between copyright and these related causes of action. The range of remedies and the methods of enforcing these remedies can be somewhat complex, representing as they do a curious amalgam of self help remedies, civil enforcement procedures and reliefs, and criminal and customs law. The recent emphasis on effective enforcement measures, as outlined in the 1988 European Commission Green Paper[1] and the GATT[2] require the drafters of the forthcoming legislation to pay particular attention to the enhancement of substantive reliefs and enforcement procedures.

COMMENCEMENT OF PROCEEDINGS

[18.02] The 1963 Act specifically states[3] that infringements of copyright are to be actionable at the suit of the owner of the copyright. Transfer of ownership from the original creator should take place on the foot of a written assignment and where the assignment is a partial assignment of rights, eg by a composer of the performing rights in a musical work to IMRO, then only the owner, in this case, IMRO, may sue and obtain the full reliefs. In cases where the owner has granted an exclusive licence which is currently in force then the exclusive licensee can enforce the same rights of action as the owner (save against the owner) and these rights in respect of most reliefs[4] are concurrent with those of the owner. Except where the court directs otherwise, the owner or exclusive licensee who issues proceedings cannot proceed with the action unless the other party is joined as a plaintiff in the action or added as a defendant.[5] If however

---

[1.] Copyright and the Challenge of Technology (1988) COM (88) 172 Final.

[2.] *Agreement on Trade Related Aspects of Intellectual Property Rights.* See Blakeney, *Trade Related Aspects of Intellectual Property Rights* (Sweet & Maxwell, 1996)

[3.] CA 1963, s 22(1).

[4.] CA 1963, s 25(2). 'Most reliefs' are those in s 22.

[5.] CA 1963, s 25(3). For a recent illustration, see *Dixon Projects Pty v Masterton Homes Pty* (1996) 36 IPR 136.

the relief sought is an interlocutory injunction then either the owner or the exclusive licensee may proceed with such an action.[6] Should the action be proceeded with by one party only, then damages are to be assessed by reference to liabilities that the plaintiff (if the exclusive licensee) may be subject to (in the form of royalties or otherwise) or any other pecuniary remedy already awarded under s 22 or any remedy that the other party may have against the defendant.[7] Where the relief sought is an account of profits then such apportionment as between owner and exclusive licensee as the court thinks just may be ordered (subject to any arrangement made by those parties of which the court is aware).[8] Where an owner or exclusive licensee has already obtained judgment under s 22 in respect of the same infringement, no subsequent order in favour of the other party may be made where the orders sought or already obtained relate to damages or an account of profits.[9] These provisions are clearly intended to prevent the defendant from being exposed to double jeopardy and to encourage all the parties to be before the courts and shorten litigation. For example, the defendant is to have as against the exclusive licensee any defence that could be validly asserted against the owner (such as consent).[10] Where the owner or exclusive licensee is not joined as a plaintiff but is added as a defendant that joined defendant is not to be liable for any costs in the action unless he enters an appearance and takes part in the action.[11] Save in these cases of exclusive licensing, the Act does not prevent a work that is jointly owned by two or more persons from being protected by way of legal action by one of them acting without the other owner or owners.[12] In cases of equitable interests or equitable titles, proceedings may be commenced by such a person in order to obtain an interlocutory injunction[13] but that final reliefs will not be made until the equitable title has been perfected or the legal owner joined as co-plaintiff (or possibly co-defendant).[14]

Identifying the Correct Defendant

[18.03] Persons who, without the consent of the owner, do or authorise others to do restricted acts, are the correct defendants.[15] In cases of primary infringement

---

6. CA 1963, s 25(4). For definitions see s 25(10).

7. CA 1963, s 25(6).

8. CA 1963, s 25(7).

9. CA 1963, s 25(8).

10. CA 1963, s 25(5).

11. CA 1963, s 25(9).

12. *Lauri v Renad* [1892] 3 Ch 402; *Dixon Projects Pty v Masterton Homes Pty* (1996) 36 IPR 136.

13. *Merchant Adventurers Ltd v Grew* [1971] 1 Ch 24; *John Richardson Computers Ltd v Flanders* [1993] FSR 497.

14. *PRS v London Theatre of Varieties* [1924] AC 1. *Batjak Productions Inc v Simitar Entertainment (UK)* [1996] FSR 139.

15. For music performance problems see *Phonographic Performance NZ v Lion Breweries* [1980] FSR 1; *Warne v Genex Corp* (1996) 35 IPR 284 illustrates that a wrong choice can be made.

it is possible for a number of joint tortfeasors to be sued and rendered liable under the Civil Liability Acts.[16] Most of the pending actions brought by music rights collection societies are representative in the sense that individual publicans and discotheque owners may be members of a trade association, individual members of which may be acting in concert, the choice of defendant being thus a matter for IMRO or PPI. It may be that a company officer such as an executive director may be personally liable for instructing or requiring other company personnel to infringe copyright,[17] thus making the company and that director each separately liable. However, the precise test in establishing liability remains uncertain for recent lines of authority in both Canada and Australia tend to favour a test which is higher than that set in the traditional English cases, a test which requires the Court to decide not simply whether the director has committed or directed the tort so deliberately or recklessly that he has made the tort his own.[18]

Presumptions of Title

[18.04] The rightholder obtains the benefit of a number of presumptions under s 26 of the 1963 Act. Copyright is presumed to exist both in a work and it is to be vested in the plaintiff if the defendant does not put these matters in issue.[19] This raises the question of what consequences follow if the defendant makes ownership of copyright an issue. In *PPI v Cody and Princes Investments Ltd*[20] Keane J held that ownership does not always have to be proved by direct oral evidence of witnesses which is then subject to cross-examination. Keane J held that the High Court can allow proof of any facts by way of affidavit under Order 39 Rule 1 of the Rules of the Superior Courts. As a matter of judicial discretion, Keane J was prepared to allow proof of title to be established by way of affidavit when the putative owners of copyright were predominantly foreign record companies. However, the judgment makes it clear that the defendants were still free to challenge the issue of title or ownership at the trial of the action.

[18.05] A presumption of authorship is also available where the name of a person appears as author on a literary dramatic, musical or artistic work and this

---

[16.] *Ravenscroft v Herbert* [1980] RPC 193; *House of Spring Gardens Ltd v Point Blank Ltd* [1984] IR 611.

[17.] *C Evans v Spritebrand* [1985] 1 WLR 317; *APRA v Valamo Property Ltd* (1990) 18 IPR 216.

[18.] *Mentmore Manufacturing Co v National Merchandising Manufacturing Co* (1978) 89 DLR (3d) 195; *Apple Computer Inc v Mackinsosh Computer Inc* (1986) 8 CIPR 153; *King v Milpurrurru* (1996) 34 IPR 11. *Mentmore* was cited by Costello J with approval in *House of Spring Gardens*.

[19.] CA 1963, s 26(1)(a) and (b).

[20.] [1994] 2 ILRM 241.

shall be effective unless the contrary is proved[21] and this is also to be so where the work which purports to be a work of joint authorship.[22]

[18.06] A similar presumption arises in favour of publishers.[23] Deceased authors benefit from presumptions that the work was original and first published in the place where the plaintiff alleged it to have been so published,[24] and these presumptions are to apply to actions brought by a plaintiff in respect of anonymous or pseudonymous works, even if the author is living.[25] In respect of the sound recording copyright, labels on records or containers stating a named person to be the maker of the recording, the first publication date, and country of first publication are to be sufficient evidence of those facts unless the contrary is proved.[26]

Authorising Infringement

[18.07] In the leading case[27] the concept of authorising an infringement has been summarised as granting or purporting to grant, expressly or by implication, the act of infringement which is complained of. An implied grant will occur when the defendant cedes to the user the apparent right to do the thing complained of when that usage is the only real use contemplated, eg renting a film to a cinema owner who shows it to be public.[28] Some element of active participation or failure to control the boundary between lawful and unlawful use of the work should be shown, such as indifference to controlling photocopying machines[29] where these are within the power of the defendant. Hiring out records or machines while being indifferent as to whether someone else infringes, is not to authorise, for the hirer cannot exercise control over the record or machine.[30] Cynical advertising of the infringement potential of a machine in order to encourage sales will not 'authorise' infringement.[31] On this point the law appears somewhat irrational for a person who blatantly flouts the rightholder's interests may avoid liability while innocence, or reasonable belief, may not be a defence.[32]

---

21. CA 1963, s 26(2).
22. CA 1963, s 26(3).
23. CA 1963, s 26(4).
24. CA 1963, s 26(6).
25. CA 1963, s 26(7).
26. CA 1963, s 26(8).
27. Atkin LJ in *Falcon v Famous Players* [1926] 2 KB 474 at 499, approved in *CBS Songs v Amstrad* [1988] 2 All ER 484.
28. *Falcon v Famous Players* [1926] 2 KB 474.
29. *Moorehouse v University of NSW* [1976] RPC 151; *APRA Ltd v Jain* (1990) 18 APR 663.
30. *CBS Inc v Ames Records and Tapes* [1981] 2 All ER 812; *Vigneux v CPRT* [1945] AC 108.
31. *A & M Records v Audio Magnetics* [1979] FSR 1; *CBS Songs v Amstrad* [1988] 2 All ER 484.

SEARCH AND SEIZURE REMEDIES

[18.08] There are a number of procedures which can be sued to limit or control the distribution of infringing copies of copyright material, and although these powers mostly have a statutory basis, the provisions of the Irish Constitution require that these powers be exercised in accordance with constitutionally mandated norms and values.

[18.09] Section 27(1) of the 1963 Act sets out a number of specific offences which relate to the manufacture, sale, exhibition or importation of infringing copies of a work. Section 27(2) sets out offences in relation to the distribution of infringing copies while s 27(3) makes possession of a plate an offence. In such a context the 1963 Act, as amended in 1987, sets out a procedure whereby the owner of a work may apply to the District Court for an order authorising a member of the Garda Siochána to seize copies without warrant and bring these copies before the court. This power to authorise without warrant is to be exercised where there is reasonable ground for believing that infringing copies are being hawked, carried about, sold or offered or exposed for sale, let for hire or offered or exposed for hire, and following upon the delivery up to the court of any infringing copies seized, the District Justice may either order the destruction of these infringing copies or otherwise deal with them as the court sees fit.[33] These provisions really deal with retail, sale or distribution on the street and are to be so construed. Subsection (5) however, goes further by allowing the District Court in cases where there is reasonable ground for believing that offences under sub-ss 27(1), (2), (3) or (8) have been committed on premises to authorise a search warrant to a named garda to enter those premises, seize infringing copies and deliver them up to be dealt with by the District Justice in the manner already outlined[34] under sub-s (4). These powers are not to be exercised against persons or vehicles.[35] In relation to copyright in films where video piracy is involved, the copyrightholder is likely to be represented by INFACT (Irish National Federation Against Copyright Theft) and the courts have accepted proofs of ownership and capacity to act on the part of rightholders.[36]

[18.10] While the provisions in s 27 were amended in 1987 to clarify and enhance the effectiveness of these procedures, the individual rightholder is still free to pursue delivery up remedies through the civil law, for example, by seeking discovery of documents and infringing copies. The likelihood of

---

[32.] *PRS v Bray UDC* [1930] IR 509; no mental element is needed in authorising infringement: *King v Milpurrurru* (1996) 34 IPR 11.

[33.] CA 1963, s 27(4) as amended by Copyright (Amendment) Act 1987, s 2.

[34.] CA 1963, ss 25(5) and (6).

[35.] *Roche v District Justice Martin and the DPP* [1993] ILRM 651.

[36.] *Ibid.*

destruction of evidence led the English courts to evolve specific procedural devices allowing entry and search of premises to preserve evidence - Anton Piller Orders.[37] Such orders have been granted in the Irish courts, specifically in *House of Spring Gardens Ltd v Point Blank Ltd*[38] and *News Datacom Ltd v Lyons*[39] but there are no Irish cases which directly state the criteria to be met in obtaining such an order, nor has the constitutionality of such a procedure been specifically tested.

[18.11] The importation of infringing copies of published literary, dramatic or musical works, or sound recordings, may be controlled by a rightholder by giving notice to the Revenue Commissioners requesting them to treat copies of the work to be prohibited goods.[40] The notice is to be in prescribed form[41] and should not last for more than five years or the length of the period of copyright. The prohibition does not apply to copies imported by a person for private or domestic use. Such importation, however, does not create a criminal offence, nor is the importer liable to any penalty under the Customs Acts other than seizure. However, acts of importation, sale or exhibition may be infringements under s 11 of the 1963 Act and thus lead to liability thereunder.[42]

DAMAGES

[18.12] The principles which underlie the award of damages following upon a copyright infringement are based upon the principle of compensation, although there are other possibilities, as we shall see. This is an area of law in which the 1988 UK legislation has been reshaped and the forthcoming Irish Act may be influenced accordingly. At a later stage in this work we will consider the extent to which copyright damages and an award for breach of confidence may overlap. It sometimes occurs that the issue of damages is not central to the litigation - the establishment of infringement of right may be more important to a plaintiff and some judges may simply award a figure without any enquiry into loss.[43]

Measure of Loss

[18.13] The measure of damages following on from an infringement of copyright is sometimes said to be a matter which is left 'at large' - that the award

---

[37.] *Anton Piller KG v Manufacturing Processes Ltd* [1976] Ch 55.
[38.] [1984] IR 611.
[39.] [1994] 1 ILRM 450.
[40.] CA 1963, s 28.
[41.] SI 231/1964.
[42.] See the importation of brochures point in *House of Spring Gardens*.
[43.] *H Blacklock & Co v Pearson* [1915] 2 Ch 376.

is a matter for the court's judgment and discretion.[44] However, it is accepted that the plaintiff will normally seek to obtain the amount by which the value of the copyright of the plaintiff has been diminished as a chose in action; this is often calculated by looking at the volume of sales made by the defendant of the pirated work and deducting the cost of production from the income made by the defendant by way of the unauthorised reproduction and sale.[45] This approach, however, does not always provide adequate compensation to the plaintiff, even if it has the merit of being simple and compatible with the principles of unjust enrichment. The plaintiff may be able to show that his product was more expensive and had a higher profit margin that the pirated work, so merely giving the plaintiff the defendant's profit may not compensate the plaintiff for lost volume of sales. This is particularly important and some cases hold that where the defendant's product undercuts the plaintiff's product, this should be reflected in the compensation award.[46]

[18.14] The leading case dealing with the evidentiary problems that confront a plaintiff who is seeking damage for lost volume sales is *Columbia Pictures v Robinson*.[47] The plaintiffs sought to obtain damages based upon the lost profits which they claimed was the result of the defendant's release onto the market of cheaper, inferior versions of their video cassette product. Disputed figures on how the film cassette would have sold but for the pirated version, led Scott J to direct that the normal measure of damages will be pitched between the minimum number of pirated copies sold and a maximum of the number of legitimate copies that could have been anticipated to have been sold in order to meet commercial expectations of the film. Further, the pirate cannot expect to put the plaintiff to precise proof of normal or reasonable commercial expectations, and upon proof of the existence of pirated copies, and in the absence of another explanation for the diminished success of the film, the rightholder is entitled to attribute the shortfall in sales to the activity of the pirate.

Aggravated, Exemplary or Punitive Damages

[18.15] Apart from the normal compensatory principle based upon lost volume of sales, general principles of compensation permit a court to take cognisance of any aggravated damage that the plaintiff has suffered, such as loss of

---

[44.] Particularly where estimates are approximate: *Schindler Lifts v Milan Debalak* (1989) 15 IPR 129.

[45.] As in *Allied Discount Card Ltd v Bord Failte* [1990] ILRM 811. *Star Micronics Property Ltd v Five Star Computers Property* (1991) 22 IPR 473.

[46.] *Birne v Keen* [1918] 2 Ch 281; *International Writing Institute Inc v Rimila Pty* (1994) 30 IPR 250, at 254; *Polygram Records Inc v Raben Footwear Pty* (1996) 35 IPR 426, at 444.

[47.] [1988] FSR 531.

reputation,[48] mental stress or emotional injury that the defendant's conduct has produced.[49] The important Australian decision in *Milpurrurru v Indofern Pty*[50] holds that ordinary damages awards under the Australian equivalent of s 22 make it possible to compensate the plaintiff for suffering and humiliation experienced within a particular artistic community, on basic compensatory principles.

[18.16] Apart from aggravated damages which are broadly compensatory anyway, there is also some scope for the award of exemplary or punitive damages where the plaintiff's award will provide compensation but still leave the defendant with a sizeable profit.[51] Under Irish law a similar rule has been used in defamation cases[52] and a general principle, intended to prevent unjust enrichment has been canvassed.[53] It is essential to point out that these residual powers exist because of the uncertainty that surrounds the scope of s 22(4) of the 1963 Act. While the Gregory Committee regarded the provision as a form of exemplary damages, *Beloff v Pressdram*[54] *obiter*, states that this provision constitutes a basis for aggravated damages rather than exemplary damages, but the terminology is unhelpful. Note that the section uses the word 'additional' rather than 'aggravated' or 'punitive' or some other descriptive term. The leading Irish case on this provision is *Folens v O'Dubhghaill*[55] where the defendant infringed the plaintiff's copyright into two schoolbooks by using part of the text to produce another book when the school course syllabus changed. The High Court awarded £1 in damages, saying that the change in syllabus has made the breach a technical one but awarded £250 in punitive damages under s 22(4). The Supreme Court rejected this approach on the grounds that the High Court was erroneous in not deciding whether an injunction could have been an adequate remedy. The basic fact is that s 22(4) is badly drafted and limits the court's power to award punitive damages, a point made in Dáil Éireann by Deputy Costello, now President of the High Court. Deputy Costello remarked that in his experience Irish courts were slow to give exemplary damages and that the use of words like 'flagrancy' in the section did not improve matters.[56] The

---

48. *Star Micronics Property Ltd v Five Star Computers Property* (1991) 22 IPR 473.
49. See *Flamingo Park Property Ltd v Dolly Dolly Creations* (1986) 6 IPR 431; *Amalgamated Mining Services v Warman Int* (1992) 24 IPR 461.
50. (1994) 30 IPR 209.
51. *Cassell v Broome* [1972] AC 1027; *Herbert v Ravenscroft* [1980] RPC 193. See generally O'Dell [1993] DULJ 27.
52. *Cassell v Broome* [1972] AC 1027 was followed in *Garvey v Ireland* [1981] IR 75 which was not a defamation case, but a wrongful dismissal case.
53. *Hickey v Roches Stores* High Court, unrep, 14 July 1976.
54. [1973] 1 All ER 241.
55. [1973] IR 255.
56. 200 *Dáil Debates* Cols 421-427.

Australian courts have consistently used their provision, s 115(4) of the Copyright Act 1968, to award punitive damages.[57] The fact that the English equivalent of s 22(4) of the Irish Act was so curiously worded inhibited judicial behaviour in England and it is no surprise to discover that when the UK Copyright Act 1956 was revised, a new statutory power to give additional damages "as the justice of the case may require" in s 97(2) of the Copyright, Designs and Patents Act 1988. In *Cala Homes (No 2)*[58] this statutory provision was likened to a power to give exemplary damages. Indeed, this broad provision is one of the basic reasons why the UK Parliament did not renew the conversion damages provisions in 1988.

The Licensing Measure

[18.17] An alternative measure of compensation that is sometimes used is the licensing measure. Under this approach the court considers what figure would have been an appropriate amount had the reproduction taken place on foot of a licensing agreement between the parties. This measure of compensation is frequently used where copyright in architectural drawings is infringed. The measure is not the profit the plaintiff would have made on the commission but the reasonable fee the rightholder could have charged if he had licensed the architect to do the work using the rightholder's design.[59] Where the work has been licensed to others then the fee thus charged is normally the measure against an infringer[60] although in cases where the infringement is heavy handed the courts' discretion can come into play. In *Hay and Hay Construction v Sloan*[61] reproduction of design drawings was expressly forbidden by the plaintiff although isolated permissions to reproduce at a small fee of £60 were allowed. Damages were assessed at £650 in excess of the fee permitted, because of the surrounding circumstances, particularly the flagrant disregard of the plaintiff's wishes and profits made by the defendants and additional damages because of the flagrant nature of the infringement. This approach has been endorsed in *Columbia Pictures Industries v Luckins*[62] a secondary infringement by

---

[57.] *Concrete Systems Pty v Devon Symonds Holdings* (1978) 20 ALR 677; *Autodesk Australia Pty v Cheung* (1990) 17 IPR 69; *Bailey v Namol Pty* (1994) 30 IPR 147; *Milpurrurru v Indofern Pty Ltd* (1994) 30 IPR 209; *Columbia Pictures v Luckins* (1996) 34 IPR 504; *Polygram Records Inc v Raben Footwear* (1996) 35 IPR 426.

[58.] [1996] FSR 36. *Cala Homes (South) Ltd v Alfred McAlpine Homes East Ltd (No 2)* suggests that punitive damages under s 97 may be added onto an account of profits but this decision has been disapproved by the Inner House of the Court of Session in *Redrow Homes Ltd v Bett Bros*, *Times*, 2 May 1997. See also *ICC Ltd v Axelsen* [1974] 1 NZLR 695.

[59.] *Stovin Bradford v Volpoint* [1971] Ch 1007, applying *Chabot v Davies* (1936) 53 TLR 60; *Dixon Investments Property Ltd v Hall* (1990) 18 IPR 490.

[60.] *PRS v Bradford Corporation* (1921) Mac GC 309.

[61.] (1957) 27 CPR 132.

[62.] (1996) 34 IPR 504.

importation case, where the Federal Court of Australia held the licensing measure to be inappropriate where it was clear that a licence would never be granted and where the infringer acted in direct competition with the plaintiff.

Conversion Damages

[18.18] While the Irish courts seem anxious not to overcompensate a plaintiff by viewing s 22(4) as giving approval for the award of punitive damages, case law has, however, led to the development of a broad, overcompensating approach to infringement, particularly in relation to artistic copyright. Section 24(1) provides that, subject to the Act:

> the owner of any copyright shall be entitled to all such rights and remedies in respect of the conversion or detention by any person of an infringing copy, or of any plate used or intended to be used for making infringing copies as he would be entitled to do if he were the owner of every such copy or plate and had been the owner thereof since the time when it was made.

Some judges have drawn a distinction between cumulative and overlapping awards,[63] which is an important reference point in this process. According to the English leading cases,[64] the deemed ownership of the original pattern or model (the plate) and the copies thus manufactured, will provide the rightholder with damages based upon the value of the infringing copies thus sold and not merely the profit margin recovered by the pirate after allowing for production costs. The fact that the infringement does not cause market confusion - the infringing product and copy do not compete or diminish the reputation of the plaintiff - cannot influence such an award and the courts will resist a plea for the court to impose the reasonable licensing measure as an alternative,[65] because the s 22 general damages provision is subordinate to the s 24(1) conversion measure, although the standard of proof needed to establish conversion damages is higher[66] and where s 22 and s 24 damages overlap, the conversion damages should be reduced.[67] Conversion damages have been abolished in the United Kingdom following adverse comments, by both Whitford and senior judicial figures, but, in the absence of reform, an Irish plaintiff may select the s 24 measure along with ordinary damages in s 22, leaving it to the court to limit the award to avoid overcompensation. Australian courts have shown a reluctance to permit conversion damages in cases where the effect would be ludicrous or

---

63. *Graves v Pocket Publications Ltd* (1938) 54 TLR 952.
64. *Caxton Publishing Co v Sutherland Publishing Co* [1939] AC 178; *Infabrics v Jaytex* [1982] AC 1.
65. *Lewis Trusts v Bamber Stores* [1983] FSR 453. See, however, *Alwinco Products Ltd v Crystal Glass Industries* [1985] 1 NZLR 716.
66. *Columbia Pictures v Robinson* [1988] FSR 531.
67. *Lewis Trusts v Bamber Stores* [1983] FSR 453.

disproportionate, arguing that for conversion damages to apply the plaintiff must establish a realistic value for the converted goods, which will probably be the price for which the goods have been sold.[68]

THE INNOCENT INFRINGER DEFENCE

[18.19] Section 22(3) provides that where it is proved or admitted that the defendant infringer, at the time of the infringement, was not aware and had no reasonable grounds for suspecting that copyright existed in the work, then damages shall not be awarded.[69] The plaintiff is, however, to be entitled to an account of profits, notwithstanding the success of the innocent infringer defence.

[18.20] The defence does not apply where the defendant mistakenly believes that copyright is held by X who has apparently consented to the defendant's use of the work. In *PRS v Bray UDC*[70] the honest belief that a band had been given permission to perform works to the Bray public from PRS was not within the similar defence set by the 1911 Act.

[18.21] Similarly in *Byrne v Statist Co*[71] the defendants reproduced verbatim the text of an advertisement which the plaintiff had independently translated for reproduction in a newspaper. The original advertisement had appeared in a Brazilian newspaper and it had been translated by Byrne for publication in the Financial Times with a translation by-line of F Byrne. The defendants who 'lifted' the Financial Times advertisement pleaded the defence, based upon an alleged lack of copyright in an advertisement and the fact that the Brazilian authorities who placed the Portuguese original had apparently consented. Bailhache J said the section:

> "... is no protection to a person who, knowing or suspecting that copyright exists, makes a mistake as to the owner of copyright and under that mistake obtains authority to publish from a person who is not in fact the owner."

[18.22] The defence has been made out successfully where a rightowner could be said to have intimated by way of a licensing tariff that consent had been given.[72] It is sometimes possible for the defendant to consider that the length of time a work has been published, the fact that it may be of foreign origin or difficult to trace the rightholder, if any, may be factors that could assist in

---

68. *WH Brine Co v Whitton* (1981) 37 ALR 190; *Autodesk Inc v Yee* (1996) 35 IPR 415.

69. See also CA 1963, s 24(3) *vis-à-vis* conversion damages.

70. [1930] IR 509.

71. [1914] 1 KB 628: *John Lane, The Bodley Head Ltd v Associated Newspapers* [1936] 1 All ER 379. Contrast the broader Australian defence, discussed in *Golden Editions Pty v Polygram* (1996) 334 IPR 84.

72. *Spelling Goldberg Productions v BPC Publishing* [1981] RPC 283.

establishing the defence. However, the recent Term Directive, as implemented into Irish law,[73] gives an innocent infringer a separate defence when a work is out of copyright when exploitation has taken place, or such exploitation has commenced, prior to implementation of the expansion of protection.

[18.23] The innocent infringer defence is also available in relation to conversion damages under s 24. So in *Allibert SA v O'Connor*[74] an innocent importer of items that infringed artistic copyright was held to be able to shelter behind s 24(3)(a) but the supplier from abroad was not.

ACCOUNT OF PROFITS

[18.24] The Act acknowledges that where an infringement of copyright has occurred, the rightholder has a right to seek an account of profits on the same basis as any infringement of other proprietary rights.[75] Further, where an innocent infringer defence has been made out the only realistic financial remedy may be an account of profits.[76] As an equitable remedy, however, there is no *per se* entitlement to an account of profits and it is within the discretion of the court to order the account or decline to do so. An account is ordered on the basis that the infringer's misuse of copyright material renders the infringer liable to disgorge the profits made. The leading Irish case is *House of Spring Gardens Ltd v Point Blank Ltd*.[77] In that case Griffin J in the Supreme Court observed that the basic principle upon which an account should be ordered is the prevention of unjust enrichment, affirming the prevailing English view that:

> "the object of ordering an account ... is to deprive the defendants of the profits which they have improperly made by wrongful acts committed in breach of the plaintiff's rights and to transfer such profits to the plaintiffs".[78]

[18.25] The order made should enable the court to compel the surrender of profits made in breach of the plaintiff's rights, and in *My Kinda Town Ltd v Soll* Slade J, *obiter*, indicated that where part of the profit is unlawfully made, a proportion thereof can be transferred to the rightholder. Normally the process of ordering an enquiry into profits is a complex and expensive one. However, in exceptional circumstances the court, where accounts are already in evidence before the court, may order the payment over of the difference between the price of the infringing goods sold, minus manufacturing and transportation costs.[79] Some allowances for the benefits, talents and skills of the infringer in providing

---

73. SI 158/1995 discussed above in Ch 10.
74. [1982] ILRM 40.
75. CA 1963, s 22(2).
76. CA 1963, s 22(3).
77. [1984] IR 611.
78. Slade J in *My Kinda Town Ltd v Soll* [1983] RPC 15, at 49.

services may be permitted.[80] An account may be declined in the event of delay, because of the trivial nature of the breach of right, or condonation of the infringement.[81]

[18.26] The decision whether to seek to obtain an account or damages is a somewhat difficult one, for in the leading case of *Caxton Publishing v Sutherland Publishing*[82] Lord Porter indicated that once the election is made and ordered the plaintiff loses any right to seek damages, whether general damages or conversion damages. In the recent English case of *Island Records v Tring International plc*[83] Lightman J had to consider the general question of when a plaintiff had to elect as between these remedies. The plaintiff was seeking summary judgment under Order 14 in respect of the defendant's uncontested infringement in sound recordings. Lightman J, starting from the position that the plaintiff could not obtain damages for infringement and an account for profits and that the plaintiff should not be required to exercise the election until he was in a position to make an informed choice, was of the view that the judiciary should develop flexible procedures to facilitate the reconciliation of these two principles. In rejecting the defendant's view that the election should take place at the hearing of the motion for summary judgment, Lightman J ordered the defendant to provide an audited schedule of sums received and sales figures within two months. Such a procedure should greatly enhance the use of the election procedure in cases of volume piracy infringements.[84]

INJUNCTIVE RELIEF

[18.27] An extensive review of the principles governing the granting of injunctive relief is inappropriate to a work of this kind but the main features of the exercise of the equitable discretion to award an injunction can be briefly described at this point.

There are several different kinds of injunction:

[79.] *House of Spring Gardens Ltd v Point Blank Ltd* [1984] IR 611; *Zupanovich Pty Ltd v B & N Beale Nominees Pty* (1995) 32 IPR 339 contains a very scholarly analysis of the remedy by Carr J in the Federal Court of Australia in which he stresses the restitutionary and equitable characteristics of the remedy, citing extensively from Bently [1991] EIPR 5.

[80.] *Redwood Music v Chappell & Co* [1982] RPC 109; *O'Sullivan v Management Agency v Music Ltd* [1985] 3 All ER 351.

[81.] *Ivan Camp Chocolates v Aulse Brooks Ltd* [1984] 1 NZLR 354.

[82.] [1939] AC 178.

[83.] [1995] 2 All ER 444.

[84.] Lightman J relied heavily on *Minnesota Mining and Manufacturing Co v C Jeffries Property Ltd* [1993] FSR 189.

(1) Perpetual Injunction

[18.28] A perpetual injunction is considered at the close of the actual hearing of the merits of the dispute between the parties. The injunction is given to finally resolve the issues before the court and it may be awarded even if there is little or no prospect that infringement will occur again. All that is needed is a judicial apprehension that the defendant has infringed the plaintiff's rights previously; what is at issue is the resolution of the dispute on a permanent basis so an injunction may be appropriate because the final resolution of the conflict makes this a prudent if somewhat empty relief. The relief will be given if the injury is continuous and recurring and damages will not be an adequate remedy.[85] Delay does not generally preclude the award of a perpetual injunction.

(2) Interlocutory Injunction

[18.29] This kind of injunction is, in practice, the most important relief for not only are the parties free to treat the injunction application at interlocutory stage to be the hearing of the action, the successful award of an injunction may, in practice, resolve the matter because the defendant's commercial activities will be stopped or abridged by the grant of the injunction. The injunction is sought by an applicant who will assert that irreparable damage to the applicant before the trial of the action will result from the activities of another and that surrounding circumstances make the award of an injunction necessary to preserve the status quo until the hearing of the action. Normally, service of the proceedings will be necessary four days before the hearing of the application, although in extreme cases where damage is immediate an *ex parte* application can be made and an interim injunction can be given until the hearing of the application for interlocutory relief or some other date or event. The application will be made on affidavit and the court will have to decide whether facts disclosed in the affidavit indicate to the court that there is a serious issue to be tried;[86] the claim must not be frivolous or vexatious and unless the material before the court discloses that at the hearing of the action the plaintiff has no real prospect of obtaining a perpetual injunction the court will, after concluding that damages will not be an adequate remedy for either party, go on to consider the issue of where the balance of convenience lies.

[18.30] The governing principle here is whether the plaintiff in succeeding in establishing an infringement in the main action is capable of being adequately compensated in damages. The applicant must give an undertaking that he will compensate the defendant should the defendant succeed, while the defendant

---

85. *Evans Marshall & Co v Bertolla* [1973] 1 All ER 992.
86. *American Cyanamide v Ethicon* [1975] AC 396; *News Datacom Ltd v Lyons* [1994] 1 ILRM 450; *Series A Software Ltd v Clarke* [1996] 1 All ER 853.

may of course assert that either the plaintiff will not be able to compensate the defendant adequately or that the defendant's loss will be irreparable, which is much the same kind of issue. In *PPI Ltd v Chariot Inns Ltd*[87] interlocutory relief was awarded in the form of an order closing down a discotheque for non-payment of licensing fees because at the hearing of the action the various discotheque proprietors involved in the representative action may have transferred ownership to other entities to avoid making the payment. Damages may be an inadequate remedy for either party, in which case an injunction will issue.[88] Sometimes the parties may avoid the grant of an injunction pending trial by giving an undertaking not to use the infringing materials but this may not be successful if the undertaking offered is not acceptable.[89] Apart from factors such as delay which may lead the court to decline to exercise its discretion,[90] the courts do consider factors such as a citizen's freedom to communicate information and other constitutionally mandated factors within this balancing process.[91] The English courts have similarly prevented gagging a defendant through the award of an interlocutory injunction when the public interest so requires.[92] Where the plaintiff is a large industrial entity with the largest market share there may be a trend towards allowing competitors to enter the market by refusing to grant interlocutory relief although the adequacy of the defendant's ability to meet a claim in damages if unsuccessful will of course be crucial here.[93] Threatened or apprehended infringements of rights are remediable via an interim or interlocutory injunction or a *quia timet* (because he fears) basis. This relief may be very important in counteracting unspecified or prospective infringements particularly if the work in question does not yet exist. The courts in Ireland have been active in protecting the future repertoires of collecting societies when broadcasters may appear to intend broadcasting works to the public in the short to medium term - an important factor in the ephemeral world of popular music. Damage will be inferred where a breach of right is reasonably apprehended.[94]

[18.31] The mixture of search and seizure provisions under the Copyright Acts and civil proceedings is sometimes evident in the case law. In *Orion Pictures*

[87.] High Court, unrep, 8 October 1992. The fact that the defendant is not a mark was important in *Mirage Studios v Counter Feat Ltd* [1991] FSR 145.

[88.] *Elanco v Lindops* [1979] FSR 46; *Waterlow Directories Ltd v Reed Information Services Ltd* [1992] FSR 409.

[89.] *Ibid.*

[90.] *Lennon v Ganley* [1981] ILRM 84.

[91.] *AG for England and Wales v Brandon Brooks* [1987] ILRM 135.

[92.] *Fraser v Evans* [1969] 1 QB 349; *Woodward v Hutchins* [1977] 2 All ER 751; *Lion Laboratories v Evans* [1984] WLR 539.

[93.] *Kelloggs Ltd v Dunnes Stores* Irish Times, 12 April 1995.

[94.] *C & A Modes and C & A (Ireland) v C & A (Waterford) Ltd* [1976] IR 198.

Corp v Hickey[95] the defendant was suspected of distributing pirate videos through his shop. The rightholder obtained interim and interlocutory injunctions preventing the defendant from infringing the rights of the rightholder but following on a later search on the foot of s 27(5) order, the defendant was found to be still distributing pirated copies. Costello J viewed this as a serious civil contempt of the injunctions and imposed concurrent sentences of one month on the defendant.

CRIMINAL OFFENCES UNDER THE COPYRIGHT ACTS

[18.32] Apart from the remedies available to a rightholder by way of the ordinary civil law in respect of infringement of proprietary rights, there are specific criminal offences prescribed under the Copyright Acts.[96]

[18.33] Section 27(1) provides that a person who knows that articles he makes for sale or hire, sells, lets, offers for sale or exposes for sale or hire, exhibits in public or imports, are infringing copies of work, commits a criminal offence. Section 27(2) also makes distribution of copies of a work known to be infringing copies a criminal offence. Possession of a plate known to be used in making infringing copies is also an offence under s 28(3). These provisions are used to counteract the wholesale commercial reproduction for works or their importation into the State.[97] Essential proofs include that the defendant know that the copy be an infringing copy and for most works in the audio-visual sector it will be necessary to show that the work was made before 9 May 1978, the date the Copyright (Foreign Countries) Order 1978 came into force.[98] The courts have tended to be sceptical of a defendant's bare assertion that he had no knowledge that the copy was an infringing copy, certainly in relation to defendants who operate in the industry, at least where INFACT inspectors provide evidence that the copy was an infringing copy and was evidently so.[99] It should be noted that proceedings may also be brought in respect of video recordings which have not been lawfully imported or licensed under the Video Recordings Act 1989.[100]

[18.34] Proceedings under the Copyright Acts in respect of s 27(1) and (2) are proceeded with summarily and the penalties prescribed are regarded in the industry as derisory in the extreme, despite the 1987 Act which upgraded the

---

[95.] High Court, unrep, 18 January 1991. See also *Microsoft Corp v Monks* (1995) 33 IPR 15.

[96.] See 'Court fines Garda over pirate videotapes' *Irish Times* 3 June 1993.

[97.] Other than for private and domestic use, CA 1963, s 27(i)(d).

[98.] SI 134/1978; See *DPP v Irwin* High Court, unrep, 25 October 1984.

[99.] *Orion Pictures v Hickey* High Court, unrep 18 January 1991; *Roche v District Judge Martin and the DPP* [1993] ILR 651.

[100.] See Bridgeman [1995] CLP 251.

fines to £100 for each item up to a maximum of £1,000 for each occasion with a similar fine, or six months imprisonment or both for subsequent offences.[101]

[18.35] The s 27(3) and s 27(8) offence of knowingly permitting public performance of an infringing work has also been upgraded by a maximum fine of £1,000 for a first offence, or in any other case to a fine of £1,000 or six months imprisonment or both. Infringement by showing a film on a television broadcast attracts a maximum fine of £100.[102] The software industry has been active in lobbying the Director of Public Prosecutions to proceed against infringers by way of indictment, presumably for conspiracy and other dishonesty offences, but to date, no such proceedings have been commenced.

[101.] In the UK video pirates are often sent to prison in situations where the pirate runs a substantial business: see 'Film Copier jailed for ten weeks' *Times* 14 March 1996.
[102.] CA 1963, ss 27(10) and (10A).

Chapter 19

Moral Rights and the Droit de Suite

MORAL RIGHTS

Introduction to Moral Rights

[19.01] The historical development of copyright within the book publishing industry in England during the eighteenth century[1] saw the notion of copyright as a publishing right that was vested initially in the author under the Statute of Anne. Dealings in copyright works, particularly as between the author and the publisher, both then and now, frequently involve the transfer or assignment of many, if not all, of the author's statutory rights. If copyrights are seen as being personal property[2] which can be totally transferred to others, then it follows that upon the total assignment of copyright the author/transferor cannot enjoy any remaining copyrights: the transferee holds any or all such rights and is free to deal in the work in any way the transferee sees fit within the English common law tradition. Certainly after the Statute of Anne, copyrights are seen as exclusively statutory when the work in question is a published work: the common law gives no additional rights and it is the role of the courts to provide remedies where statutory rights are infringed. Thus, copyrights are economic rights that are, in general, freely transmissible. In contrast however, the civilian tradition, particularly in French legal theory, copyright, or the *droit d'auteur*, is seen as an author's right, based upon an act of creation by the author or artist. The work thus produced is seen as a part of the identity, personality or integrity of the author or artist and, as such, subject to economic *and* moral laws.[3] Thus, the civilian tradition recognises a *droit moral*. Article 6 *bis* of the Berne Convention makes due provision for the balancing of economic rights by reference to certain essential interests of the author of the literary or artistic work in question:

Article 6 *bis*

(1) Independently of the author's economic rights, and even after the transfer of the said rights, the author shall have the right to claim

---

[1.] Feather [1988] EIPR 377.

[2.] CA 1963, s 47(1).

[3.] Roeder (1940) 53 Harv L Rev 554; Dworkin (1981) 14 IIC 476; Chang [1995] CLP 243; Dietz (1994) 25 IIC 177. Deitz (1995) 19 Colum VLA JL & Arts 199 and Dworkin (1995) 19 Colum VLA JL & Arts 229 provide contrasting looks at civil law and common law systems.

authorship of the work and to object to any distortion, mutilation or other modification of, or other derogatory action in relation to, the said work, which would be prejudicial to his honour or reputation.

(2) The rights granted to the author in accordance with the preceding paragraph shall, after his death, be maintained, at least until the expiry of the economic rights, and shall be exercisable by the persons or institutions authorised by the legislation of the country where protection is claimed. However, those countries whose legislation, at the moment of their ratification of or accession to this Act, does not provide for the protection after the death of the author of all the rights set out in the preceding paragraph may provide that some of these rights may, after his death, cease to be maintained.

(3) The means of redress for safeguarding the rights granted by this Article shall be governed by the legislation of the country where protection is claimed.[4]

Moral Rights for Authors and Artists

[19.02] It must be said at the outset that the existence of moral rights within certain legal traditions are hotly debated subjects of controversy which cause opponents of these rights to argue that the mere existence of residual moral rights, which are essentially uncertain and subjective in nature, represent a substantial barrier to the 'sensible' exploitation of a work, which is not in the interest of rightholders or authors. However, it is certainly impossible to point to any substantial body of case law that supports such a view: French case law, for example, is not voluminous and one recent French decision indicates that moral rights are far from absolute and must, in certain instances, be subject to a judicial balancing exercise in which the broadest public interest may be a dispositive factor.[5]

[19.03] The debate on moral rights in some countries that share the traditional English approach to such rights, namely Canada[6] and Australia[7] has moved the position in those countries towards some form of *droit moral*, based in the main on an appreciation that authors and creators do need some additional measures of protection: the position taken by the UK Gregory Committee in 1952[8] is no

---

4. See Ricketson, *The Berne Convention for the Protection of Literary and Artistic Works 1886-1986*, (Centre for Commercial Law Studies QMC London 1987).

5. *Foujita v Sarl Art Conception Realisation ACR* [1988] FSR 523. See generally Sarraute (1986) Am JCP 465.

6. Keyes and Brunst, *Copyright in Canada: Proposals for a Revision of the Law* (1977).

7. Ricketson [1990] 17 MULR 463; Strauss (1995) 4 AJCL 506. The Pearce Committee, due to report in 1998, will re-examine this topic.

8. Report of the Copyright Committee, para 219-226 (Cmnd 8662).

longer shared in those countries and the 1977 Whitford Report[9] came out in favour of legislation to implement the Berne minima.[10]

[19.04] While there is no existing Irish *droit moral*, there is a significant body of case law which supports the general thrust of the Gregory Committee's conclusion that existing protections are significant. However, the scope of these rights are either uncertain or limited in scope.

(i) Constitutional Protection and the 1963 Act

[19.05] It is quite difficult to identify those aspects of Irish constitutional law that may be pertinent to this enquiry. However, a few may be advanced as relevant.

(a) The right to privacy

[19.06] It is sometimes speculated that the right to paternity, implicitly raises the issue of a right to anonymity or a right to disclaim authorship.[11] Irish case law has recognised that the Irish Constitution contains an implicit right of privacy, and it may be suggested that this right could be utilised by an author in appropriate circumstances. However, the case law that exists and explores this right to privacy does so in the context of communications between citizens (*Kennedy & Arnold v Ireland and the Attorney General*),[12] in matters of sexual freedom (*McGee v AG, Norris v AG*),[13] and most recently in relation to abortion services (*AG v X*),[14] where a State law, a State agency or a Minister of Government purports to impinge upon the affairs of citizens. It is by no means clear that this unenumerated personal right may be utilised, for example, in contractual relations between citizens. Nevertheless, it is possible to foresee situations where an author's privacy interest could be infringed by publication or treatment of works that could perhaps prove to be an embarrassment to the author.[15]

(b) Good name and property rights of a citizen

[19.07] Article 40.3.2° of the Irish Constitution provides that "the State shall, in particular, by its laws protect ... and vindicate the ... good name and property rights of the citizen". This Article, and Article 43, control the extent to which

---

9. Copyright and Designs Law 1977 para 51-7 (Cmnd 6732).
10. See generally Dworkin (1981) 4 IIC 476, at 490-2.
11. For privacy in making broadcasts see Broadcasting Authority Act 1960, s 19 and the Radio and Television Act 1988, s 9.
12. [1987] IR 587.
13. [1984] IR 36.
14. [1992] ILRM 401.
15. *Chaplin v Leslie Frewin Ltd* [1966] Ch 71. For cases involving constitutional rights in relation to the privacy of a person who is the subject of a literary work, see *MM v Drury* [1994] 2 IR 8.

personal rights to property can be affected by legislation. Property will clearly include intellectual property rights. In *PPI v Cody and Princes Investments Ltd*[16] Keane J characterised the rights of an author not to have a work stolen or plagiarised as being rights which could be protected under the Constitution, independent of any statutory right. While this is an *obiter* statement, it presents a tantalising scenario within the context of future constitutional litigation: does the notion of plagiarism extend to unfair appropriation, eg by parody?

[19.08] If and when moral rights are passed into law it could conceivably lead to circumstances in which a rightholder, eg a publisher who has obtained copyright, could challenge an exercise of a moral right by an author on the ground that the legislation inhibits the exercise of property rights and as such moral rights represent an unjust attack on his property rights. On the other hand, the Constitution may also operate within the existing moral rights vacuum, notwithstanding the generally accepted view that if statutory copyright does not afford the author specific protections there are no residual rights at common law that can be invoked.

So in relation to an artistic work which has been altered since the author parted with possession of the work, s 54(4) of the Copyright Act 1963 makes it a contravention of the Act to publish, sell, let for hire, or by way of making a trade offer or expose for sale or hire of the work, as altered, as being the unaltered work of another, or do any of these in relation to a reproduction, when it is known by that person not to be so unaltered. Section 54(6) creates a similar contravention in relation to artistic works which are published, sold, let for hire, trade offer or trade exhibit as being reproductions made by the author when the reproductions were not reproductions of the author.[17] When the Gregory Committee reviewed[18] the area of moral rights in 1952 the specific protection afforded to artistic works was cited with approval but it was not built upon by the UK Parliament in the 1956 Act. Instead, the UK Parliament passed a rather curious provision which makes it actionable for a person to do any of the following things to a literary, dramatic, musical or artistic work:

(a) fixing the name of that person to the work in a way which implies that that person, not the author, is the author of that work;

(b) publication, sale, letting for hire, the making of trade offers, exposure for sale or hire, or trade exhibit, a work on which another person's name appears if to the knowledge of the offender that other person is not the author of the work;

---

[16]. [1994] 2 ILRM 241.
[17]. *Carlton Illustrators v Coleman* [1911] 1 KB 771.
[18]. *Supra.*

(c) doing any of the above in relation to a reproduction of the work;

(d) public performance or broadcasting of a work when aware that the work as represented is the work of another author.

[19.09] The Irish draftsman lifted this provision from the UK 1956 legislation[19] and imported it into the Irish 1963 Act.[20] The precise effect of this provision was not readily understood as the following parliamentary exchange indicates:

"Mr. Cosgrave: There is another matter referred to in the Minister's speech in relation to s 53 of the Bill. He says the Bill provides that offences under the section will be prosecuted, not by the Minister as at present but by the person to whom the work has been falsely attributed or, if he is dead, by his personal representative. Take a person who has a large number of literary or artistic productions to his credit, say a well-known author like the late Bernard Shaw, who wrote over a long period and who has now been dead for some years. Is it his personal representative who has the right to take action? Is there any reason why under this proposed Act the change is being made under which this right is vested in the person or his personal representative rather than in the Minister?

Mr. A Barry: I am not clear about the third point Deputy Cosgrave raised. Why should a person to whom work has been falsely attributed initiate a prosecution? Surely it would be the person who wrote the work. I am not clear why the Minister should use those words.

Mr. J Lynch: If Deputy Barry were a composer of a note, composing works of high musical content and somebody composed what might be called a Tin Pan Alley ditty and put Deputy Barry's name under it, Deputy Barry in those circumstances would be an aggrieved party and would have the right to prosecute the person who composed this Tin Pan Alley ditty.

Mr. A Barry: It does not relate to the pirating of my works?

Mr. J Lynch: No, on the contrary.

Mr. A Barry: I thought it was protection against the pirating of works.

Mr. J Lynch: No, it is false attribution, that is, having the work falsely attributed to somebody other than the real author."[21]

[19.10] It is important to note that s 54 is actionable as a breach of statutory duty at the suit of the person named, or if deceased, his personal representatives. In this latter situation damages recoverable devolve as part of the estate: ss 54(8) and (9). This section may prove to be a most useful support to the common law actions for breach of contract and misrepresentation but they are very limited. Neither the section nor these common law causes of action respond to a right of paternity: these remedies simply provide that another person cannot seek to affix that person's name to the copyright work of an author in circumstances where

---

[19.] CA 1956, s 43.
[20.] CA 1963, s 54(2).
[21.] 198 Dáil Debates Cols 246-7.

third parties would believe that other person to be the author - a kind of passing off in reverse.[22]

(ii) Statutory protection for works outside the field of copyright

[19.11] Consumer protection legislation affords indirect protection for works if, for example, the work is incorrectly described, marked or labelled. The Consumer Information Act 1978 creates several criminal offences relating to false or misleading descriptions so it is possible to invoke the criminal law if works are misdescribed: indeed conspiracy charges may be possible in cases of serious racketeering in pirated goods.

(iii) Statutory protection in the Copyright Act 1963

[19.12] Section 54 of the 1963 Act does make provision for protecting artistic works from being falsely described as being the work of a particular person. Section 54 was based upon the protection found in the Fine Arts Copyright Act 1862[23] and is the only provision in the Copyright Acts that allows the artist to proceed against another person who misdescribes an artistic work as being unaltered. This provision is therefore a hybrid right that comes somewhere between a right of integrity and a right of paternity.

(iv) Miscellaneous Causes of Action

[19.13] Opponents of moral rights legislation point to the availability of other causes of action which go some way towards achieving the primary object of *droit moral* - the preservation of the reputation and honour of the creator of a work. While these causes of action do not answer every situation, the common law system does provide various means of redress to an author who finds that the activities of others threaten to diminish the author's standing or reputation within the community:

> (a) *Defamation*: The wrongful publication of a false statement about a person, which tends to lower that person in the eyes of right thinking members of society, or causes that person to be held up to ridicule or contempt, or causes that person to be shunned and avoided by right thinking members of society, is actionable through the tort of defamation.[24] In some cases the publication of works protected by copyright may take place in circumstances where publication is defamatory. To wrongfully attribute authorship to a person when the work in question is a scandalous or obscene publication, for example,

---

[22.] See *Moore v News of the World* [1972] 1 QB 441.

[23.] Finally repealed by the Industrial and Commercial Property (Protection) Act 1927: see, however, s 186 of that Act.

[24.] See generally, McMahon and Binchy, *Irish Law of Torts* (2nd ed) (Butterworths, 1990).

may be defamatory.[25] Similarly, to publish a work written by an author in a format which does not advance the reputation of the author but rather threatens to injure the reputation of the author is actionable.[26]

(b) To pass off a book as being the work of another, a celebrated author, for example, is clearly a misrepresentation which can be actionable by the person misrepresented as the author.[27]

(c) It may be an injurious falsehood to claim that a particular work is the work of another person.[28]

(v) The Law of Contract

[19.14] If we start from the position that is sketched by the Copyright Act 1963, namely, that copyright vests in the author of a work following upon the creation of that work, it is arguable that the author should be able to protect that work by using the methodology of contractual protection against prejudicial treatment of that work by a publisher, broadcaster, or other persons. While in theory this may be so, there are practical reasons why the law of contract may not be operative. Firstly, an assignment may have already taken place of the copyright even in a future work. Secondly, some editorial work may be an implicit right for a publisher to assert in relation to a manuscript and, finally, to claim that authors and artists are financially or legally able to address problems of great technical complexity, is disingenuous.[29] While the courts[30] have recently overturned a number of copyright assignments and contractual arrangements by using concepts such as breach of fiduciary duty, undue influence and restraint of trade, the balance of power and expertise will still tend to rest upon the entrepreneur rather than the creator of a work. There are some examples of contractual arrangements being struck which enable the author to protect the integrity of a work against unauthorised structural alterations of a text, but such clauses must be specifically included in a contract.[31] There is little or no room for implied terms in such a context.[32]

---

25. *Ridge v English Illustrated Magazine* [1911-16] MCC 91.

26. *Archbold v Sweet* (1832) 1 Mood & Rob 162; *Lee v Gibbings* (1892) 67 LT 263.

27. *Wood v Butterworth* (1901-4) Macg Cop C 16; *Samuelson v Producers Distributing* [1932] 1 Ch 201.

28. *Per Archbold v Sweet* (1832) 1 Mood & Rob 162.

29. Exceptionally, some writers are fastidious and learned on copyright matters, eg, Anthony Trollope, J P Donleavy.

30. *Schroeder v Macauley* [1974] 3 All ER 616; *O'Sullivan v Management Agency Ltd* [1985] QB 428; *John v James* [1991] FSR 397. Contrast *Panayiotou v Sony Music Ent* [1994] EMLR 229.

31. *Joseph v National Magazine* [1959] 1 Ch 14; *Frisby v BBC* [1967] Ch 932.

32. See the recent controversy on the publication of the book, *Cré na Cille* in an edition of which the author's surviving relatives did not approve: *Irish Times* 19 September 1996.

THE LIMITS OF EXISTING PROTECTION IN IRISH LAW

[19.15] While there are no compelling Irish cases on moral rights related issues, other common law jurisdictions show that authors, artists and performers do not enjoy personality based rights to privacy. The integrity of their work[33] or any right to disown or disclaim a work which the author now wishes to distance himself from.[34] Constitutional protection is speculative at best. Ireland's failure to at least implement Article 6 *bis* of the Berne Convention constitutes a breach of international obligations[35] and for all of these reasons, legislation is needed on the issue of the *droit moral*. The crucial issue, however, concerns the scope of any future legislation, for, despite the provisions of the Berne Convention, substantial areas of divergence currently exist on a number of matters such as the nature of the rights themselves, their duration, the categories of person who may claim moral rights, and the waiver or modification of these rights. It must be noted that the future shape of Irish moral rights legislation is likely to be heavily influenced by the United Kingdom 1988 statutory provisions and while this is hardly a new or unexpected development, it would be unfortunate if the somewhat curmudgeonly approach by the Westminster Parliament was adopted in Ireland, not least because the letter and spirit of the UK provisions may not satisfy either the Berne Convention or the standards set by Articles 40 and 43 of the Irish Constitution.

(1) The right to claim authorship of the work

[19.16] While this right is one of the two Berne Convention moral rights, it is not always a right that arises automatically following upon the creation of the work. The UK legislation[36] complies with Berne by giving the author of a copyright work the right to be identified as the author of the work, but the right must be positively asserted by the author (eg at the time of assignment of copyright if any) and the right to claim paternity may be waived, for example, by signing a publishing contract that precludes any right to be identified as an author when the work subsequently appears before the public. Waiver of contractual or even constitutional rights, expressly or by implication, are familiar topics to Irish lawyers, but the Berne Convention arguably does not recognise this kind of standard form waiver, the net effect of which is likely to be the emasculation of the paternity right. Aside from this general power to displace the right, there are a number of situations in which the right does not arise under the UK Act. The authors of computer programs and computer

---

33. *Kaye v Robertson* [1991] FSR 62.
34. *Harris v Warren & Phillip* [1918] WN 173; *Chaplin v Leslie Frewin* [1966] Ch 71; *Harrison & Starkey v Polydor* [1977] FSR 1.
35. See Chang [1995] CLP 243.
36. Copyright Designs and Patents Act 1988, s 77.

generated works, employee authors or employee film directors, works appearing in newspapers, magazines, encyclopaedia or similar works, do not attract paternity rights and there are substantial fair dealing defences attached to use of works without recognising the identity of the author. While the UK legislation characterises the paternity right as being quasi-copyright by giving film directors a general paternity right (save for rental and lending rights, film directors are not considered authors) and by allowing paternity rights for artistic works that are being publicly exhibited, these rights are broadly in line with civil law moral rights, no matter how uneasily they sit with Anglo-Saxon legal traditions.[37] It should be noted that even if in the UK the author is lucky enough to escape the exclusions, has had the wit not to waive the right, and has taken steps to positively assert that right, the right is a right to be identified as author of the work in a way that is prominent: this essentially means that the name should appear on each copy, or if not practical, in any that brings the author's identity to the attention of others. Great uncertainty surrounds the meaning to be attached to this requirement of notice of authorship being prominent.

(2) The right to integrity

[19.17] The other element in the Berne Convention schemes for protecting moral rights is the right to object to derogatory treatment of a work and the UK Act follows the language of the Berne Convention quite closely, although the possibility of waiver, and the quite sweeping powers of amendment for broadcasters in relation to good taste and decency,[38] as well as the substantial exclusions[39] make this a somewhat pale shadow of the Berne Convention provisions. The rights of an author to protect the author's work are far from absolute even under the Berne Convention for a number of extremely loose concepts are set out in Article 6 *bis*.

The author has the right to object to the following:

'Distortion' of the work

[19.18] Suppose a work is distorted? What constitutes distortion? Casting female actors in a play that was expressly stated to be performed by male actors (eg the two tramps in *Waiting for Godot*: this has been held to infringe Beckett's moral rights in a French court but not in a Dutch court.[40] Problems of distortion may arise when part of a musical work is lifted from the original and then superimposed onto another work (described as sampling) in order to produce a

---

37. It should be noted that statute law even in the USA gives some paternity rights to visual artists, but significantly, these rights are waivable and cannot be equated to copyright moral rights.
38. Copyright Designs and Patents Act 1988, s 103(2).
39. Eg Copyright Designs and Patents Act 1988, s 81.
40. See recently *SA Argos Films v Ivers* [1992] FSR 547.

new music genre. This right may be important if, for example, the composer has assigned copyrights to a recording company that has licensed the use of the recording in this way.

'Mutilation' of the work

[19.19] Suppose a work is mutilated, eg by turning a classical composition into some kind of synthesised or electronic dance number[41] or extracting snatches of the work and incorporating them into a new composition or compilation.[42] Is this an infringement of the right to integrity or can it be defended as a transformative use of the work? In the area of parody there are American decisions which support the view that transformative use of original works may be defended as fair dealings in a work, although it has to be said that the American case law on fair dealing does not afford to the integrity of the original work or the sensitivities of the original author the kind of determining role that a moral rights analysis would appear to require.[43]

'Or other modification of' a work

[19.20] Suppose a work is translated from one language into another but the result is, in the view of the author, horrendous. Surely the author should be able to object to this kind of butchery; however, the UK Act excludes translations for no apparent reason,[44] from the concept of treatment of a work but it is submitted that any form of unacceptable or prejudicial adaptation should be caught by the notion of a modification of the work.

'Derogatory action in relation to the said work'

[19.21] It is by no means clear that the UK legislation is at all relevant to cases where the work itself is not in any way tampered with or utilised by another person; if a work is juxtaposed with some other medium or work (eg a painting is exhibited next to another painting in order to show up the lack of skill or vision by one of the artists) there may be no derogatory treatment according to a leading authority.[45] However, the physical destruction of a work, eg the pulping of copies of an unsuccessful novel or guide or the obliteration of an artistic work by painting over a screen or canvass is clearly a derogatory action but the Berne

---

41. *Holst v RCA Times* 18 May 1977. For discussion on the concept of 'debasing' a work in a compulsory licensing context see the Australian case *Schott Music Int GmbH v Colossal Records* (1996) 36 IPR 267 (techno-dance version of 'O Fortuna' chorus from *Carmina Burana* not debasing).
42. *Morrison Leahy Music Ltd v Lightbond* [1993] EMLR 144.
43. Particularly *Acuff Rose Music v Campbell* (1994) 114 SC 1164.
44. Copyright Designs and Patents Act 1988, s 80(2)(a). The colourisation of old black and white films is further example: see Beyer [1988] North-Western UL Rev 1011.
45. See Cornish, *Intellectual Property* (Sweet & Maxwell, 1996), p 393.

Convention does not require members of the Union to proscribe such acts under the guise of the integrity right. However, it is submitted that deliberate and public acts of destruction which are intended to ridicule the author (rather than redistribute warehouse space, recycle materials or 'tidy up' some unappreciated functional item) should be within any Irish legislation on derogatory action: this can be achieved by giving due emphasis to the final element on this notion of the integrity right, that the action be prejudicial to the author's honour or reputation.

'Prejudicial to his honour or reputation'

[19.22] The key element in the integrity right is that treatment afforded to the work must be prejudicial to the author's honour or reputation. Thus hanging streamers from a piece of sculpture exhibited in a Toronto shopping mall was held prejudicial to the honour and integrity of a sculptor in *Snow v Eaton Centre Ltd*.[46] The removal of an artistic work from public display is hardly prejudicial, and if the work is a piece of political art, such as a statue of some head of a discredited political dynasty[47] the removal of such a piece may be a political inevitability, even if the statue is buried deep in the earth.[48] In the area of parody where in many instances impersonation is a form of flattery, the moral right of an author is not going to be infringed if there is some use made of a painting or musical composition for advertising purposes - depending on what is being advertised perhaps. Use of an original with a view to lampooning the supposed banality of the original, however, may not be readily excused if it is clearly the parodist's intention to damage or destroy the reputation of the original author, as was the case in the *Pretty Woman* case.[49] The failure to complete work on a piece of sculpture or a building has been held to infringe the right of integrity before the French courts[50] and an interesting UK parallel has already been sketched[51] in relation to modes of exhibiting artistic works.

Other moral rights issues for artists and authors

[19.23] Apart from the Berne Convention minima, some civilian jurisdictions have additional moral rights. The two most frequently cited examples are the right to recall a work on the basis that the work no longer reflects the view or artistic aspirations of the author, a right unknown as a cause of action before the English and probably the Irish courts,[52] and the basic right to determine details

---

[46.] (1982) 70 CPR (2d) 105.

[47.] *Re Lenin's Monument* [1992] FSR 265.

[48.] Recall also the fate of the statue of Queen Victoria, visibly on campus at University College Cork until the 1930s.

[49.] *Acuff Rose Music v Campbell* (1994) 114 SC 1164.

[50.] *La Regie Nationale des Usines Renault v Dubuffet* [1982] ECC 7.

[51.] Solomon and Mitchell (1991) 141 NLJ 1654.

[52.] *Harrison and Starkey v Polydor Ltd* [1977] FSR 1.

concerning publication of a work.[53] Ironically, the recent Term Directive has actually reduced the author's right to regulate publication following upon the death of the author because under the 1963 Act the copyright period did not run until publication pma. The new legislation provides that unless publication occurs within 70 of the author's death, the author's rights are lost and supplanted by the new entrepreneurial right.[54] The moral rights reforms made in the UK did not embrace these two principles and it is thus unlikely that forthcoming Irish legislation will address them. In the international context, the hostility in many common law jurisdictions, based upon the fear that these rights may render exploitation of works burdensome or impossible, will probably prevent any further movement in either WIPO or even at EU level. In 1992 the European Commission held a public hearing to consider whether further harmonisation measures, this time in the moral rights arena, were necessary and possible. The hearing produced a division very much on foreseeable lines, with the representatives of authors, performers, libraries and UNESCO favouring harmonisation, while publishers, producers, broadcasters and employers were generally against or in favour only of the Berne minimum harmonisation measures. While moral rights issues were seen by some interest groups as causing problems in relation to digitised use in software or database problems in particular, no consensus emerged about the possible way ahead and it is unlikely that any EU initiative will emerge in the very near future[55] even though the 1995 Green Paper raises moral rights as a matter for discussion and future monitoring.

Moral Rights in the Neighbouring Rights Arena

[19.24] Since moral rights are seen as being essentially based on human personality or integrity the issue of whether corporate rightholders should be given non-economic rights hardly arises. So moral rights for phonogram producers, film producers, and broadcast organisations are simply not on the agenda. However, in the field of performer's rights the December 1996 Second WIPO Treaty provides in Article 5:

Moral Rights of Performers

(1) Independently of a performer's economic rights, and even after the transfer of those rights, the performer shall, as regards his live aural performances or performances fixed in phonograms, have the right to claim to be identified as the performer of his performances, and to object to any distortion, mutilation or other modification of his performances that would be prejudicial to his reputation.

[53.] See Lord Mansfield's early efforts in this regard in *Millar v Taylor* (1769) 4 Burt 2303, 2398-9.

[54.] SI 158/1995: see Ch 11.

[55.] Conclusions of the hearing on moral rights, Brussels 30 November/1 December 1992 - see the 1995 Commission Green Paper, *Copyright in the Information Society.*

(2) The rights granted to a performer in accordance with paragraph (1) shall, after his death, be maintained, at least until the expiry of the economic rights, and shall be exercisable by the persons or institutions authorised by the Contracting Party where protection is claimed. However, those Contracting Parties whose legislation, at the moment of their ratification of or accession to this Treaty, does not provide for the protection after the death of the performer of all the rights set out in the preceding paragraph may provide that some of these rights may, after his death, cease to be maintained.

(3) The means of redress for safeguarding the rights granted by this Article shall be governed by the legislation of the Contracting Party where protection is claimed.

In confining this right to aural performances, the International Community has bowed to the wishes of the film industry. It remains possible that the September 1997 conference may resolve to extend those rights to audio-visual performers also but the prospects of this happening are not thought to be very bright.

DROIT DE SUITE[56]

[19.25] The Berne Convention, specifically Article 14 *bis* in the 1948 Brussels Revision, permits members of the Berne Union to enact legislation which allows artists to share in the profits made upon subsequent sales of artistic works; artistic works are generally unique - many are not reproduced or capable of mass reproduction so when the work is sold on it may normally be expected to increase in value. In such circumstances, if the artist has originally sold the work to a dealer who then profits from the fame or investment potential of an artistic work it is thought only right that a percentage of the resale profits should enure to the benefit of the artist or the artist's estate. While the identity and traditions of the first jurisdictions to enact the resale right, France and Belgium,[57] tend to suggest that the right is historically civilian in tone, recent developments in the EU and the United States suggest that while only a minority of Berne Union States have enacted resale rights, there is the prospect of renewed interest in the *droit de suite*. In France, the *droit de suite* consists of a fixed tariff of 3% of the sale price when the price exceeds 100 Francs. The tariff is collected by an art auctioneer, who is in fact a public official, who pays over the sum collected to the artist or the heirs of the artist if the artist is deceased; if the payee cannot be traced, as is sometimes the case, the sums are repaid to the seller of the work. While non-French nationals are entitled to claim under the *droit de suite*, there are reciprocity provisions in such cases.[58] The right does not apply to all sales;

[56.] This section relies heavily on the LLM dissertation on this topic by Linda Scales, University College Dublin (1995).

[57.] In 1920 and 1921 respectively. On French inaction to reform the law - see (1993) 24 IIC 686.

[58.] These are probably invalid as a result of the *Phil Collins* litigation.

private dealers as distinct from public sales have until recently successfully resisted the expansion of the resale right into their sphere of business. In California the right, introduced in 1976 and later amended in 1982, provides that a 5% tariff of the consideration is to be payable to the artist or the artist's agent when a work of fine art has been sold. The sale may take place at auction by a dealer, broker, museum or gallery but does not apply to purely private transactions; there are a number of quite substantial exemptions such as first sale by the artist and where the resale results in a loss for the dealer. The right applies to sales that take place in California and can be claimed by US citizens or persons resident in California for a minimum of two years.

[19.26] While this short sketch should give some flavour of what the right consists of in two jurisdictions, there are a substantial number of particular issues that cause substantial differences as between *droit de suite* regimes. Some jurisdictions restrict the right to artists and blood dependants[59] while most other jurisdictions make the right freely transmissible under national inheritance legislation. The question of duration has also caused significant differences of approach. Because some countries regard the right as a matter of copyright, it enures for the duration of the artist's other economic rights, namely life and seventy years pma.[60] In California, the right lasts for the author's life and twenty years pma. Further points of departure involve the definition of original works for there is no agreed definition and where the work is not unique - an engraving, print or lithograph for example - the basis of protection is uncertain. Even unique items such as an author's original literary manuscript are normally excluded even though such items do enjoy a vibrant resale market. The economic implications of the right for fine arts businesses as well as national interests in supporting a vibrant national and international market for fine arts highlighted by an examination of the kinds of transaction that are either caught or exempted from the *droit de suite*. Should all public auction sales and dealer/broker sales be caught? A small number of countries even include private sales eg Brazil, although aspirational and unworkable provisions of this kind are thought to have contributed towards making the *droit de suite* completely ineffective in such jurisdictions. The picture is further complicated by exempting the first sale and certain fairly immediate resales by a dealer from the right (eg in California). International debate or the essential nature of the right is also inconclusive, for while most regard the right as an author's right it is often characterised by opponents as a tax, a perception that is often sharpened by the

---

59. France: see the *Utrilla* decision discussed in Pierredon Fawcett, *Droit de Suite* (Centre for Law and the Arts, Columbia University School of Law (1991)) discussed by Scales *op cit*.
60. The period provided in the Term Directive: see Ch 10.

State's intervention in some collection mechanisms and by the flat nature of the levy.

[19.27] However, the most trenchant criticisms of the *droit de suite* tend to concentrate on the unrealistic and inefficient nature of the right. While accepting that measures that sponsor and encourage a realistic return to the artist are of themselves 'a good thing', several critics have observed that the economic and cultural climate has moved on since the nineteenth century. As *Price* observed in 1968:[61]

> "The *droit de suite* springs from a nostalgic recollection of the late nineteenth century. It is a case, not unusual, of legislation passed or posed to correct a situation that no longer exists with the intensity that provoked reform.
>
> The *droit de suite* evolved from a particular conception of art, the artist and the way art is sold. At is core is a vision of the starving artist, with his genius unappreciated, using his last pennies to purchase canvas and pigments which he turns into a misunderstood masterpiece. The painting is sold for a pittance, probably to buy medicine for a tubercular wife. The purchaser is a canny investor who travels about artists' hovels trying to pick up bargains which he will later turn into large amounts of cash. Thirty years later the artist is still without funds and his children are in rags. Meanwhile his paintings, now the subject of a Museum of Modern Art retrospective and a Harry Abrams parlour-table book, fetch small fortunes at Park-Bernet and Christie's. The rhetoric of the *droit de suite* is built on this peculiar understanding of the artist and the art market. It is the product of a lovely wistfulness for the nineteenth century with the pure artist starving in his garret, unappreciated by a philistine audience and doomed to poverty because of the stupidity of the world at large. The *droite de suite* is *La Boheme* and *Lust for Life* reduced to statutory form. It is an expression of the belief that (1) the sale of the artist's work at anything like its 'true' value only comes late in his life or after his death; (2) the postponement in value is attributable to the lag in popular understanding and appreciation; (3) therefore the artist is subsidising the public's education with his poverty; (4) this is an unfair state of affairs; (5) the artist should profit when he is finally discovered by the new sophisticated market."

[19.28] It is sometimes pointed out that sponsorship of the artistic community by levying taxes on resale is inefficient because of the probability that many sales will be undetected, will take place in order to take advantage of exemptions and will fail to provide any income at all to the heirs of the artist because the dictates of fashion may simply make most artists unsaleable at certain stages, particularly when the market is subject to cyclical economic patterns. Far better to provide subsidies, bursaries and grants during the artist's creative life, so the

---

[61.] (1968) 77 Yale LJ 1333 at 1335: see generally Ulmer (1975) 6 IIC 12; for California see Neumann (1992) 23 IIC 45: Kretsinger [1993] Hastings Comm & Ent LJ 967.

argument runs. However, the debate on the *droit de suite* in Europe has taken on a different aspect in recent years because the European Commission has investigated this topic with a view to considering whether the presence of a *droit de suite* in some Member States[62] constitutes a distortion of competition insofar as the art market in non *droit de suite* jurisdictions operates at a competitive advantage due to the absence of the *droit de suite* 'levy' on sales in those countries. While the Commission has not been specific in its assertion that economic data exists to verify this position, the Commission probably has in mind the analogous situation of differential VAT or sale tax rates and how such imbalance can lead to market displacement.[63] In the *Joseph Beuys* case[64] decided in Germany in 1992, a decision to sell paintings by that artist in London rather than Germany was made by a collector on the basis of absence of *droit de suite* in the UK. The heirs of Joseph Beuys unsuccessfully claimed on the *droit de suite* because the sale was held to have been in London and thus the right could not be asserted in such circumstances. This displacement argument has been highlighted by the *Phil Collins* case which allows EU nationals to claim *droit de suite* in *droit de suite* states but does not allow *droit de suite* nationals to claim in respect of sales taking place in non *droit de suite* Member States. As the debate currently stands within the European Union, the United Kingdom is hostile to the introduction of a *droit de suite* harmonisation measure, the Dutch seem to be sceptical about such measures while the position of the Irish Government officials appears to be ambivalent about this question. United Kingdom opposition to legislation is in part due to the hostility of the Whitford Committee[65] to the introduction of a *droit de suite*, a feeling that measures of this kind may actually harm the position of young, unknown artists, but most important of all, a fear that the fine arts market may be displaced to Switzerland and the main US centres where *droit de suite* does not exist. While art displacement measures such as lower tariffs for highly priced works is seen as a possible riposte to these UK objections, it is clear that UK opposition is ferocious and sincerely felt.

[19.29] In Australia, the issue of introduction of a *droit de suite* was considered in 1989 by the Australian Copyright Council.[66] This empirical study of art resale in Australia reached the conclusion that creative endeavour would be

---

62. France, Belgium, Italy, Germany, Portugal, Luxembourg, Spain, Denmark, Finland, Sweden and Greece. However, the law has not been implemented in Italy and Luxembourg.
63. In Ireland, for example, differential VAT rates on bloodstock sales as between the UK and Ireland have led to reports about higher sales volumes in Ireland because VAT in 1994 and 1995 was much lower on such sales.
64. (1993) 24 IIC 139.
65. Cmnd 6732 Ch 17.
66. 'Droit de Suite: the Art Resale Royalty and its Implications for Australia' (1989).

encouraged via a mechanism of this kind which would give visual artists a share in the accumulating value of their original creative work. However, the practical constraints behind this right were not ignored by the Copyright Council and the royalty rate was to be set at a level which did not discourage sales of fine art or encourage avoidance via placing these sales on overseas markets. However, there are no real signs of legislative action in Australia at the present time, but the cautionary note set in the 1989 Report finds a significant echo in the work of the European Commission in its 13 March 1996 document on the Resale Right.[67]

The Proposed Directive

[19.30] The Commission justify the need for a harmonisation measure on the basis of internal market considerations and a perceived shifting of sales of works of art to what the proposal describes as "low tax countries where the artist's resale right is not applied". However, apart from the *Joseph Beuys* case there is no compelling proof of this phenomena in the proposal. The only really compelling reason for harmonisation set out in the proposal is essentially one of community cohesion and solidarity, for the net effect of the *Phil Collins* decision is that the reciprocity rule inherent in the *droit de suite* rule found in Berne cannot operate within the context of infra-community trade. Therefore, nationals of countries without a *droit de suite* could claim a resale right in those eight countries of the Community that operate a system of resale right, while the same claim could not be made in the seven other Member States where the resale right does not operate. The European Commission, at a public hearing held on 24 February 1995 decided that a harmonisation measure was required for a majority of States favoured such a solution in preference to outright repeal of *droit de suite* national legislation.

[19.31] Article 1 of the Proposed Directive requires Member States to provide, for the benefit of the author of an original work of art, a resale right, which is to be an inalienable right to receive a percentage of the sale price obtained from an resale of the work. The first sale by the author is not included within the concept of resale, nor are sales made by individuals acting in their private capacity. The 'original work' is defined in Article 2 as:

> "manuscripts and works of plastic art such as pictures, collages, paintings, drawings, engravings, prints, lithographs, sculptures, tapestries, ceramics and photographs, provided they are made by the artist himself or are copies considered to be original works of art according to professional usage in the Community."

[67.] *Proposal for a European Parliament and Council Directive on the Resale Right for the Benefit of the Author of an Original Work of Art* (Com) 96 97 Final.

The royalty threshold[68] is triggered at 1,000 Ecu, although Member States could lower this figure if so desired - the current German figure is set at 100 marks for example, which is around 1/18 of the 1,000 Ecu limit. The royalty rate is set on a sliding scale by Article 4 of the Proposed Directive in a deliberate attempt to win acceptance for the Proposal. Between a sale price of 1,000 Ecu and 50,000 Ecu 4% of the sale price will be gleaned. At a price between 50,000 Ecu and 250,000 Ecu it drops to 3% of the sale price, and for sales above 250,000 Ecu the resale right percentage drops to 2%. These relatively modest percentages are fixed so as to make the likelihood of art sales displacements less likely for the cost of freight and insurance, it is hoped, may persuade the seller that there would be nothing to be gained in selling the work in, say, New York, as distinct from London or Paris. Collective management of the input is possible but the right is to be administered in favour of the artist or, following the artist's death, those entitled under the artist. The rights last for the life of the artist and seventy years pma.[69] The Directive does not, therefore, embrace a distribution of income to the artistic community generally. Furthermore, attempts by some interests to introduce the concept of public ownership of a work (*domaine public payant*) have been rejected.[70] Nevertheless, this modest proposal has been subject to devastating criticism on the basis that the European Commission simply fails to understand the market and ignores the importance and role of collectors and museums as legitimate elements in the fine arts community.[71]

---

68. Article 3.
69. Article 6.
70. See Recital 16.
71. Merryman [1997] IPQ 16.

Chapter 20

Copyright - Irish Legislative Developments in the Twentieth Century

IRISH LAW - PAST AND PRESENT

[20.01] With the establishment of Saorstát Éireann as a result of the Treaty of 6 December 1921, and the resulting legislation,[1] the issue of the status of the Copyright Act 1911 arose for debate in Saorstát Éireann. Legislation to consolidate and amend existing legislation in the intellectual property field was initiated in the form of an Industrial and Commercial Property (Protection) Bill, which was introduced in 1925, but this legislation was withdrawn and re-introduced the following year by another omnibus measure which became the Industrial and Commercial Property (Protection) Act 1927. The provisions of Part VI on copyright broadly reflected the provisions set out in the 1911 legislation. Thus, copyright in published works were given, if the work was first published in the State, and in the case of an unpublished work, copyright subsisted if at the time of making the work the author was a citizen of, or resident in the State.[2] Save in cases where International Conventions provided to the contrary, a power was given to extend copyright to foreign citizens through the Governor General by order made on the advice of the Executive Council.[3] Through this mechanism, copyright protection for works published other than within the British Dominions[4] or in the Berne Union would be given as long as there was reciprocity of treatment. At this time the USA was regarded as the most significant jurisdiction outside either the British Copyright Union or the Berne Convention. The provisions in the 1927 Act on the nature of copyright, the kinds of infringement and duration of copyright, including the compulsory licensing exceptions[5] were also based on the 1911 Act. Issues that had to be dealt with even included the granting of a State Copyright[6] and the lodging of new books with certain copyright libraries within the State and in Britain.[7] Apart

---

[1.] Eg, Irish Free State (Agreement) Act 1922.
[2.] Industrial and Commercial Property (Protection) Act 1927, s 154.
[3.] This procedure was amended by the Industrial and Commercial Property (Protection) Act 1929.
[4.] On which, see s 175.
[5.] Sections 156 and 157.
[6.] Section 168.
[7.] Section 178.

from attempts by some well meaning parliamentarians who sought to introduce a manufacturing clause in relation to the printing of books, debates on the 1927 legislation were relatively unexceptional and it was certainly the view that this Act repealed and replaced the 1911 Act within the State. However, in a remarkable piece of litigation, the status of the 1911 Act was called into question by the Supreme Court although this decision was in turn overruled by the Judicial Committee of the Privy Council in *Performing Rights Society v Bray UDC*.[8] In that case, the defendant permitted a band to perform two musical works in the course of a number of summer concerts in 1926. Despite assurances to the contrary given to the defendant by the band, the band did not have a performing rights licence from the plaintiff. The works had been written before 6 December 1921 but assignments took place after that date in favour of PRS. The issue before the Irish courts was whether the 1911 Act was in force after the foundation of the State, for it was not, no infringement could have taken place in the summer of 1926. The Supreme Court[9] held that the Irish Free State, as a self governing dominion, had not declared the 1911 Act to be in force[10] and thus the 1911 Act was not carried over into Irish law. The Judicial Committee of the Privy Council held that the phrase, 'self governing dominion', within the 1911 Act, had a specific meaning and that the Irish Free State could not come within it. Their Lordships also noted that a Schedule to the 1927 Act certainly repealed the 1911 Act, an unnecessary measure if the Supreme Court's reasoning was correct. No remedy other than costs was available to the PRS however, because in the period between the 1927 Act and the Supreme Court's decision[11] the Oireachtas had passed amending legislation which had revested copyright as from 5 December 1921, but that legislation had also declared that no remedies were to be available prior to implementation of this amending Statute.[12]

[20.02] The 1927 Act continued to be the primary copyright law until replaced by the 1963 Act. After the *Bray UDC* litigation, pressure for amending legislation seems to have been virtually non-existent. The Industrial and Commercial Property (Protection) (Amendment) Act 1929 made significant amendments to the foreign national procedure and introduced licensing provisions in respect of translations of works into Irish in an attempt to stimulate interest in the Irish language, and those provisions were also the primary copyright matters contained in the Industrial and Commercial Property (Protection) (Amendment) Acts of 1957 and 1958.

---

8.   [1930] IR 509.
9.   [1928] IR 506.
10. Copyright Act 1911, s 25(1).
11. Handed down on 7 July 1928.
12. Copyright (Preservation) Act 1929 (24 July 1929).

[20.03] The Copyright Bill 1962 was introduced into Dáil Éireann on 28 November 1962 for a number of reasons. First, the 1927 legislation, itself based on the 1911 Act, clearly had outlived its usefulness and the Minister for Industry and Commerce, Mr Jack Lynch, indicated that the UK Act of 1956 took account of modern developments whereby ideas can be conveyed by radio, television films and recordings as well as the print media; this 1956 legislation had proved a model for other countries and "it is the basis upon which much of the present Bill has been prepared". The second factor mentioned by Mr Lynch was the influence of International Conventions and International Agreements. While Ireland was party to both the Berne Convention and the Geneva Convention,[13] legislation to give greater protection to broadcasts was of particular importance in such a context. The Minister also indicated that the October 1961 Rome Convention on *International Protection of Performers, Producers of Phonograms and Broadcast Organisations* required legislative changes to be made. Part III of the Act gave films and recordings specific copyrights, *qua* films and recordings and not entitlement as a kind of dramatic or musical work. The Minister noted that such a move was not only internationally mandated but a matter of good sense because "there is frequently no personal author in the sense in which the word is used in relation to dramatic or musical works".[14] Although the 1963 Act, by recognising broadcast copyright made a significant advance, the 1963 Act defined broadcast organisations so as to include the national broadcasting agency, Radio Éireann (RTE) and in fact it was only in 1991 that independent broadcasting services established under the Radio and Television Act 1988 were given a copyright in respect of broadcasts.[15]

[20.04] Even though the 1927 Act had been used to extend protection to foreign nationals, eg, the Copyright (Foreign Countries) Order 1959,[16] the technological and economic importance of copyright was pointed to by the Supreme Court in *PRS v Marlin Communal Aerials Ltd*.[17] In that case, PRS claimed infringement of copyright by a licensed wireless retransmission company who in diffusing the boosted signal of UK television companies was causing the PRS repertoire to be heard contrary to s 8(6)(e) of the 1963 Act. However, the authors of these works, not being qualified persons, had to rely on international rights available under the Berne Convention but no

---

[13.] Ie, the Universal Copyright Convention (Paris, 1974). The earlier 1955 Act is binding on Ireland.

[14.] 198 Dáil Debates Col 242.

[15.] SI 101/1991 as from 23 April 1991.

[16.] SI 50/1959.

[17.] [1977] FSR 51.

order had been made under s 43 of the 1963 Act at this time. The relevant order[18] under the 1927 Act did not make cable diffusion of works a restricted act. The Supreme Court declined to interpret the transitional provisions in the 1963 Act as having the effect of supplanting a s 43 order. The legally correct, but embarrassing situation for the Irish State was ultimately resolved by a number of statutory orders made one year later.[19] A number of separate orders have been made which deal with copyright for countries not covered by the Berne Convention or International Organisations within s 44 of the 1963 Act.[20] However, the Copyright (Foreign Countries) Order 1996[21] provides copyright protection in respect of the authors of literary, dramatic, musical or artistic works and the makers of films as long as the author or maker, as the case may be, are citizens of countries of the Berne Union, UCC States, or members of the World Trade Organisation on or after 30 January 1996.

SUBSTANTIVE LAW REFORM AND UK INFLUENCES

[20.05] Since the 1927 legislation was passed, the main features of Irish copyright law, in terms of substantive law, have remained largely unaltered. Even the introduction of the Part III copyrights in 1963 did not mark any significant departure from the primary features of the UK 1911 Act, and the history of legislative debate on both the 1927 Act and the 1963 Act point to the fact that the principles which shaped Irish law were largely externally determined. Efforts to introduce manufacturing clauses into what became the 1927 Act were resisted because of the Berne Convention and some very sensible efforts to abridge the duration of copyright itself similarly foundered during those debates.[22] Since the 1963 Act was passed, the only primary legislation on copyright to go through the Oireachtas[23] is the Copyright (Amendment) Act 1987, a short two section Act that improved powers of search and seizure of counterfeit goods and amended the law on artistic copyright to take functional designs out of copyright. It is universally agreed that the law is in serious need of complete revision as a result of technological and market developments, EU obligations and treaty changes. The Department of Enterprise and Employment, through its Intellectual Property Unit, is actively involved in drafting a new Bill but this will not appear until 1998 at the earliest. It is however possible to

---

[18.] SI 50/1959 as amended by paragraph 35 of the First Schedule to the 1963 Act.

[19.] SI 1321978; SI 133/1978 and SI 134/1978, effective as from 9 May 1978.

[20.] Eg, Copyright (Republic of Indonesia) Order 1988 (SI 155/1988).

[21.] SI 36/1996.

[22.] 17 Dáil Debates Cols 544 and 591.

[23.] A Copyright (Amendment) Bill 1984 was introduced by the Government but this modest Bill, to enhance s 27 infringement penalties, grew to become the 1987 Amendment Act.

anticipate some of the features of the new Bill and it is to the shape of things to come that we now turn.

[20.06] The changes recently made to the UK copyright law may be expected to have some impact upon the forthcoming legislation, for a number of reasons. The 1988 legislation was the result of prolonged process of review and debate in the UK, most significantly through the Whitford Report,[24] the Green Paper,[25] and the White Paper *Intellectual Property and Innovation*[26] of 1986. The Copyright, Designs and Patents Act 1988 therefore can be said to represent a relatively up-to-date benchmark by which to measure the task ahead, and its merits, in terms of substantive law reform, are many. For example, the expansion of literary copyright to cover speech,[27] the expansion of rights to cover issuing copies of works to the public[28] as distinct from publication *simpliciter*, the clarification of primary and secondary infringement concepts and the strengthening of civil and criminal laws aimed at counteracting piracy, such as providing protection against unauthorised broadcast reception[29] are only a few of the measures that would be useful to adapt to Irish conditions. However, the 1988 Act has many critics because of the length and complexity of the Act and the drafting style adopted. *Laddie, Prescott and Vittoria*[30] observe that while the 1988 Act does not confine itself simply to copyright matters

> "diversity of subject matter does not account for all of its greatly increased length. Consider, for example, Chapter III of Part I of the 1988 Act. Here one may find no less than 49 sections setting forth in (too great) detail what are the exceptions to copyright protection. Some of these regulations will soon be out of date, and an embarrassment. Others can only have been invented by persons who did not think out properly what they were supposed to be achieving. How much better the Americans do it with their simple, flexible 'fair use' exception! (A concept which originated on these shores by the way)."[31]

It is to be hoped that this kind of comment is taken to heart by those involved in drafting the Irish Act. The UK legislation is far too cumbersome - is it really necessary to have 16 sections[32] on moral rights, particularly when they

---

24. Copyright - Copyright and Design Law (Cmnd 6732) (1977).
25. Reform of the Law Relating to Copyright, Designs and Performers Protection (Cmnd 8302) (1981).
26. Cmnd 9712.
27. Section 3(1).
28. Section 16.
29. Sections 297-299: contrast *News Datacom v Lyons* [1994] 1 ILRM 545.
30. *The Modern Law of Copyright and Designs* 2nd ed (Butterworths, 1995).
31. Preface, p v.
32. Sections 77-89, 94-95, 103.

are so modest in nature? The Act is also out of date in the sense that EU Directives have supplanted many of the elements that inspired the 1988 Act (eg, computer programs) and the process of implementing EU Directives has not been a happy one.[33]

EUROPEAN UNION LEGISLATION

[20.07] In a legal context, the impact of European Union Law in the field of intellectual property law tends to focus upon the importance of competition rules and related concepts such as exhaustion of rights.[34] The general principles of EU law and how they affect intellectual property rights (which, in this field are largely national in operation) are not allowed to hamper Community trade, wherever possible. However, given the fact that, despite the Berne and Rome Conventions, Member States do operate under quite diverse laws of copyright, it is inevitable that the ECJ should take the view that national restrictions on free movement of goods, and perhaps, services, are permitted in certain instances. In such a context, the focus, in recent years, has switched dramatically to the possibility of approximation, and even harmonisation, of national laws on copyright and neighbouring rights. In terms of legislative competence, the engine behind these initiatives must be the need to complete the internal market and in the area of intellectual property legislation generally, Directorate General III (DG III), later re-organised and merged with DG XV, took on the task of producing draft legislation in accordance with a set of priorities identified in 1988 by the Commission in the document *Green Paper on Copyright and the Challenge of Technology - Copyright Issues Requiring Immediate Action.*[35] While the Green Paper rightly disclaimed any pretensions toward comprehensiveness in relation to copyright issues requiring immediate attention, it has, despite protestations to the contrary, proved to be a blueprint for Community action between 1988 and 1992. The issues identified and addressed in the 1988 Green Paper were seen as priorities for immediate action although several of the problem areas such as legislation to improve anti-piracy laws within Member States were outside the legislative competence of the European Community.

[20.08] The Commission published a follow-up to the Green Paper in January 1991[36] and in this document the Commission set out a number of proposed

---

[33.] The UK Government, like the Irish Government, tends to implement Directives by Statutory Instrument which is both inelegant and confusing for users and substantively dangerous. Incorrect transposition of the Computer Program Directive is being alleged by the European Commission against the UK in Article 169 proceedings.

[34.] See Tritton, *Intellectual Property in Europe* (Sweet & Maxwell, 1995).

[35.] Com (88) 172 Final.

[36.] Com (90) 584 Final.

actions. In terms of specific legislation, legislation harmonising copyright in such areas as software protection, database protection, duration of copyright, the harmonisation of neighbouring rights, legislation on commercial rental of works, and legislation on the co-ordination of copyright and neighbouring rights applicable to satellite and cable broadcasting. The follow-up document also recommended that the Council should make a decision requiring all Member States to accede to the 1971 Paris Act of the Berne Convention and the 1961 Rome Convention by the end of 1992.

[20.09] Although the legislative timetable in the follow-up document suggested that such legislative action would be taken before 31 December 1991, this timetable proved to be somewhat over-ambitious[37] in terms of the substantive topics to be covered and the time needed to process draft legislation through the Co-Operation Procedure.[38] Nevertheless, the success rate achieved by the Commission looks extremely impressive and Community legislation in certain key areas of harmonisation of copyright have proved extremely influential; the proposed WIPO Database Treaty, for example, is modelled on the 1996 Database Directive.

[20.10] For the sake of completeness, the measures adapted in the form of Directives are as follows.

The Software Directive

[20.11] This Directive, agreed on 15 May 1991[39] gave protection to computer programs as literary works in whatever form the program existed. Thus, object code became protected as a literary work. This Directive has been transposed into Irish law[40] and is discussed elsewhere in this book. However, there are issues that the Directive does not address, as recent Irish case-law demonstrates.[41]

The Directive on Rental, Lending and Neighbouring Rights

[20.12] The Directive[42] agreed on 19 November 1992, gives the authors of works exclusive rights to authorise rental and lending of those works, as defined in the Directive. Rental is defined as "making available for use, for a limited period of time and for direct and indirect economic or commercial advantage" but it is not intended that this covers the distribution of films for

---

[37.] Action on home copying of works, for example, never got off the ground.

[38.] See Article 100A of the Treaty.

[39.] 91/250/EEC. OJ 1991 L 122/42.

[40.] SI 26/1993.

[41.] *New Datacom v Lyons* [1994] 1 ILRM 545.

[42.] 92/100/EEC. OJ L 346/61. See, generally, Reinbothe & Von Lewinski, *The EC Directive on Rental and Lending Rights and Piracy* (Sweet & Maxwell, 1993).

public performance or broadcasting.[43] The distribution of physical copies is involved here and it is not intended to cover the distribution of on-line information or other forms of electronic rental such as video-on-demand services. Lending of works is also covered and this is defined as making available for use, for a limited period of time and not for direct or indirect economic advantage, when it is made through establishments which are accessible to the public, but this does not cover inter-establishment lending (eg, strict inter-library loans).[44]

[20.13] The public lending provisions were included to ensure that commercial rental was not endangered by unfair competition from publicly funded institutions. Existing Irish law does not currently make lending or rental of any kind a restricted act and attempts to regulate rental of works, for example, is currently achieved through contract or marketing practices such as making copies of films available for rental only and charging rental outlets accordingly. The Directive does not apply to the rental or lending of buildings and works of applied art, that is, industrial designs. Works protected in a Member State on 1 July 1994 qualify for these rental and lending rights[45] but no implementing legislation has been passed in Ireland, so although the works in respect of which these rights are to attach are protected under existing Irish copyright law, non-implementation of these rights for authors by the due date for implementation (not later than 1 July 1994) is regarded by the Irish government, apparently, as not being likely to involve State liability to rightholders under the *Francovich*[46] principle.

[20.14] Another new area that the Directive addresses is the probable introduction of a public lending right. Irish law does not give the authors of books, (much less all literary works, musical works, dramatic works, artistic works, sound recordings or films) any remuneration from the lending to the public of these works. Article 5 of the Directive opens the door to this possibility for it provides that States may derogate from the lending right - that is, not implement this right as exclusively an author's right - but the State must give remuneration to the authors of works made available via lending. One of the most controversial aspects of the Directive is the broad definition of author - it includes film directors *vis-à-vis* cinematographic films. Performers also acquire

---

43. Article 1.2 and Recital 13.
44. Article 1.3.
45. Article 44.
46. *Francovich v Italy* [1991] ECR 5359. However, non-implementation by Ireland and four other States (Luxembourg, Portugal, Netherlands and the UK have resulted in non-implementation proceedings being commenced: See OJ L 303/34, *Thirteenth Annual Report on Monitoring the Application of Community Law 1995*.

rights but the Directive contain presumptions and methods whereby these rights will, or may, under national legislation, be assigned to film producers, publishers, record companies and the like. It is likely that the Irish law, when it appears, will reflect the economic weakness of most performers and authors, for example, and statutory transfers of the rights will be made. However, the assignment or transfer cannot displace the author's right to equitable remuneration[47] and it is likely that such rights will ultimately be administered for performers and authors by collecting societies. This right, however, does not have to be introduced until 1 July 1997. Authors who have concluded contracts to exploit their works after the date of adoption of the Directive but before the implementation deadline (ie between 19 November 1992 and before 1 July 1994) must have asserted their rental right before 1 January 1997 or the right cannot be available.[48]

[20.15] Chapter II of the Directive, which is a harmonisation measure that aims to create equivalent rights in respect of performers, sound recordings, films and broadcasts, has less of an impact on Irish law because the 1963 Act broadly implemented the provisions of the 1961 Rome Convention. However, the granting of neighbouring rights to performers is extremely significant.[49]

The Directive on Satellite Broadcasting and Cable Retransmission

[20.16] This Directive[50] agreed on 27 September 1993, addresses several of the copyright issues that the earlier Television without Frontiers Directive[51] failed to resolve. Although a primary objective of that Directive was the distribution and promotion of European television programmes, the Directive did not address differences in national copyright laws, nor did it address the question of which law or laws governed issues of copyright clearance. The 1993 Satellite and Cable Directive regulates the communication to the public by satellite of broadcasts and it makes it clear that the broadcasting right conferred under Directive 92/100/EEC, considered above, is to be within the concept of a broadcast, whether the satellite broadcast is a DBS or point-to-point satellite communication.[52] The Directive provides a choice of origin rule whereby the law of the country where the broadcaster introduces the programme carrying signals intended

---

47. Article 4.
48. Article 13.
49. See Ch 12 *ante*.
50. 93/83/ECC; OJ L 248/15.
51. 89/552/EEC.
52. See *Dietz* (1989) 20 IIC 135; *Kern* [1993] EIPR 276.

for reception by the public in an uninterrupted chain is to apply *vis-à-vis* the clearance of authors' rights that are exploited in the broadcast.

[20.17] Chapter II of the Directive gives the author the exclusive right to authorise communication to the public by satellite of copyright works and because Article 2 requires all Member States to give authors such a broadcasting right, if the act of communication occurs in a Member State, copyrights and copyright clearances will be uniform.[53] However, if the act of communication to the public takes place in a third country that does not give these Chapter II rights, evasion is avoided by rules which direct that either the Community State where the up-link station is located or, failing that, the Member State where the broadcasting organisation has its principal establishment, should be deemed the place where communication to the public occurs. Article 4 of the Directive gives the right of communication to the public by satellite to performers, phonogram producers and broadcast organisations.

[20.18] The Directive has not yet been transposed into Irish law[54] and the definition of broadcast in the 1963 Act[55] does not appear to cover satellite broadcasts of any kind.

[20.19] The other major area of concern relates to cable retransmission by cable operators of television and radio broadcasts originally from another Member State. In cases of simultaneous retransmission of that signal, the Directive applies but if there is any retransmission delay, or the cable operator produces independently a cable service of programmes, the Directive does not apply. The Directive requires that authors, performers, phonogram producers and film producers should have their copyrights respected but these rights are to be exercised through collecting societies who may act even on behalf of rightholders who refuse to transfer such rights to a collecting society.[56] Broadcast organisations, however, are free to refuse to allow their broadcast signal to be retransmitted.[57]

[20.20] This area of cable retransmission (or causing the transmission of a work to subscribers of a diffusion service)[58] is a controversial one in Ireland and it is clear that non-implementation of the Directive has serious economic

---

[53.] Compulsory licensing is not possible and Article 3 envisages collective licensing of rights under contract.

[54.] It should have been implemented before 1 January 1995. Article 169 letters have been sent to defaulting States - see OJ L 303/34.

[55.] Section 2(2).

[56.] Article 9.

[57.] Article 10.

[58.] Section 2(5).

consequences for rightholders for many cable operators in the South and South West do not comply with licensing schemes currently operated in Ireland.[59]

The Directive on Copyright Duration

[20.21] This Directive,[60] agreed on 27 October 1993, broadly extends the duration of copyright for Part II works to 70 years pma and confirms the duration of Part III works to 50 years while it changes certain of the 'triggering' conditions. It has been transposed into Irish law by SI 158/1995.[61]

The Database Directive

[20.22] This Directive[62] eventually agreed on 11 March 1996, provides significant additional protection for compilations of works through copyright and a separate right to prevent extraction and/or re-utilisation of the contents of a database.[63]

Other Matters

[20.23] The above list of directives represents a considerable measure of success, but other proposals or initiatives flagged in the January 1991 follow-up document[64] did not proceed into legislative form, whether draft or otherwise. Studies that were to prepare the ground for an evaluation of the need for further reforms addressed the areas of moral rights, reprography[65] the resale right (or *droit de suite*) and collective management of rights. In relation to those studies, the Commission held a number of follow-up public hearings, the most important of which, on moral rights, concluded that there was no consensus in Europe for further action. The resale right debate has also raged across the Community with the UK and Ireland being resistant to the introduction of such a right but a proposed Directive emerged in 1996.[66] No specific initiatives have emerged in relation to collective management of copyrights although, as we shall see, the Commission continues to monitor the position. On the vexed topic of home copying of works, particularly film and sound recordings, the Green Paper and follow-up documents promised

---

[59.] See the discussion in the *IMRO/Cable Broadcast* Decision No 384 by the Competition Authority.

[60.] 93/98/EEC. OJ L 290/9.

[61.] See Ch 10 *ante*.

[62.] 96 9 EC. OJ L 77/20.

[63.] See Ch 14 *ante*.

[64.] Com (90) 584 Final.

[65.] Ie, photocopying.

[66.] Com (96) Final.

much but the efforts of the Commission to address the private copying of works, principally by technical methods of prevention and the introduction of a blank tape levy have not been able to muster sufficient support to allow a proposal for legislation to emerge despite an extensive consultation process.[67]

New Developments

[20.24] In July 1995 the Commission issued a new Green Paper *Copyright and Related Rights in the Information Society*.[68] The rationale for this initiative can be simply put: the digitisation of existing and future works, and their distribution in the form of bitstreams rather than in tangible form via the Information Superhighway, whether on-line or by satellite, or in tangible form such as CD or CD-i, makes immediate Europe-wide legislative action an imperative. This is an imperative, not simply because the economic climate for investment in such products would suffer due to legal uncertainty in Europe, but because major non-European competitors in the form of Japan and the USA are extremely active in creating or adapting their own legal climates to satisfy market and technological conditions and needs. The Green Paper identified a number of issues that require attention. Two general questions that appeared to the Commission to be of concern were, first, whether the law governing a particular act of exploitation should continue to be that of the place of exploitation[69] (ie, where the film is shown or the broadcast takes place). The Commission noted that the Cable and Satellite Directive opted for another rule (ie country of origin) and that contractual practice may seek to avoid certain rules, thus resulting in turn in mandatory rule that cannot be displaced (eg, the back-up copy rule in the Software Directive). The Commission's apparent preference for developing a Community rule on applicable law, based on place of origin (thereby meaning that a rightholder could select a location that gives an extensive bundle of rights and utilise those rights in countries where the work or service has been provided, even if less extensive rights are not available there) has not subsequently been endorsed and most commentators have indicated a preference for retaining existing contractual practices and private international law rules while at the same time clarifying issues such as liability for Internet type services.[70]

[20.25] The second general question raised in the 1995 Green Paper, the issue of exhaustion of rights, has also proved controversial. Existing Community rules provide that a rightholder who has consented to the sale of copies of that work anywhere in the Community cannot object to parallel importation of such

---

[67.] See DGXV, *Consultation Paper on Private Copying* (1993).

[68.] Com (95) 382 Final.

[69.] Known as the country where protection is sought under national treatment rules in International Treaties, such as Berne.

[70.] Follow-up to the Green Paper Com (96) 568 Final p 22-24.

copies, but the right to control reproduction of copies, or distribution in the form of services such as rental, lending or broadcasting, is not caught by the exhaustion principle. In the absence of any international rules on exhaustion, the Commission asked, should the Community legislate a general rule against a principle of international exhaustion of rights and should the Community affirm that the exhaustion principle does not apply to services? Comments made in the follow-up to the Green Paper by most Member States favour a Community exhaustion rule only and the Commission have opted for legislation which will direct that any first sale in the Community will exhaust the distribution right. Some countries, such as Germany, which apply an international exhaustion rule, will therefore have to amend their national law. This will be important for it will maintain the existing position adopted via case-law which allows the partition of copyrights where goods are first marketed in non-EU States, such as the USA. National laws blocking parallel imports as acts of secondary infringement will remain in force.[71] The Commission also intends to declare the exhaustion rule does not apply to services such as on-line provision of works.[72]

[20.26] The Green Paper set out a number of issues that require specific attention. Some of these are familiar to those who have followed the development of Community interest in copyright matters. The scope of the reproduction right was identified as being of central importance in the new digital environment. The Green Paper noted that some Member States have already acted to consider specific issues such as photocopying and other methods of copying works that produce identical quality copying and it was suggested that these issues need to be addressed, particularly in the context of identifying the range and kind of exceptions to the reproduction right, for law and practice on fair dealing exceptions varies dramatically across Europe. The Follow-up document has indicated that, building on Article 9.2. of the Berne Convention, a Community initiative will make it clear that digitisation of works and practices such as optical scanning, uploading and downloading of works, are covered by the reproduction right. Thus, the document indicates that private copying initiatives mentioned above will be revived, along with specific reference being made to an unspecified range of fair use exceptions and other limitations that are intended to balance the interests of users or the public at large.[73] Although the initiative has to some extent been overtaken by attempts at a redefinition of reproduction in the 1996 Protocol to Berne,[74] the Commission's attempts to set out detailed

---

[71.] See CA 1963, s 11.

[72.] Follow-up to the Green Paper, p 17-19.

[73.] Com (96) 568 Final, pp 9-12.

[74.] While final agreement was not reached in Geneva in December 1996 the conference declared that existing reproduction rights under Berne covered digital reproduction: see *Conference Resolution on the Reproduction Right.*

exceptions will trigger a lobbying process unlike any other.[75] However, the Commission intends to go further and provide an additional right to allow works to be communicated to the public,[76] the view being asserted in the Green Paper[77] that reproduction would not necessarily occur if information services are available to the public via interactive or on-line systems: video-on-demand for instance need not involve an act of reproduction, nor an act of broadcast for such communications may occur *via* a telecommunications network.[78] Again, this proposal has been overtaken by events in Geneva in 1996 but the Commission intends to set out exceptions to this right, something that was not attempted in the Berne Protocol.

[20.27] The other significant Community initiative flagged by the Follow-up document relates to technical methods of identifying works (so called digital tattooing) and technical methods of preventing or limiting the number of copies that may be made of a work. While the Berne Treaties have addressed this point for the first time in an international treaty context[79] the Community initiative will take the form of measures to encourage standardisation of these technical devices and methods, bearing in mind the principle of proportionality. Hints at making penalties for infraction and defences somewhat standardised are also made.[80]

[20.28] While the Follow-up document does not promise[81] that all those measures will result in specific legislation in the form of Directives on each particular topic, it is clear that those matters form the European Commission's agenda for future copyright harmonisation. Even though most of these measures address points that Irish law is currently silent on, it is clear that even the forthcoming Copyright Bill would appear to be something of an interim measure on certain technological issues, even if the drafting of that Bill should take account of the Geneva 1996 Treaties.

[75.] The lobbying over the Software Directive 91/250/EEC is legendary but pales into insignificance over this proposal.

[76.] Follow-up, pp 12-14.

[77.] Com (95) 382 Final p 53.

[78.] The Follow-up document indicates that this right will be closely modelled on existing rights in relation to the communication of works to the public, but states that no satisfactory definition exists! Note that no legislative work is currently proposed in relation to the digital dissemination or transmission right or the digital broadcasting right: Green Paper, ss V and VI.

[79.] See Articles 11 and 12 of the Protocol, Articles 18 and 19 of the New Instrument (Treaty 1 and Treaty 2 respectively), see Vinje [1996] EIPR 431.

[80.] Follow-up, pp 15-17.

[81.] Other topics that the Commission intend to keep a weather eye open for are, the broadcasting right, applicable law (discussed above), management of rights and moral rights.

INTERNATIONAL STIMULI FOR CHANGES IN IRISH LAW

[20.29] Apart from European Union initiatives towards harmonisation of copyright there are a number of International Treaties that provide the Irish legislature with additional reasons for making significant changes in copyright law. While Ireland is a member of the Berne Union, Irish law does not currently give effect to the most recent version of the Berne Convention, that is, the Paris Act 1971, and in certain respects, particularly in the area of moral rights, legislation is needed, for EEA Treaty obligations required the ratification of the Paris Act before 1 January 1994. The entire climate for International Treaty revisions and developments has been transformed by the adherence of the United States, China and many of the former Eastern Block States to the Berne Union - the USA joined in 1989 - and the successful conclusion of the GATT/TRIPS Agreement[82] has added a further element of broad agreement on the shape of copyright within the International Community of States. While the copyright provisions of the GATT/TRIPS Agreement do not require any legislative changes for Ireland[83] (the obligation to ratify the Paris Act[84] excludes the moral rights provisions in Article 6 *bis* of Berne) the expansion of neighbouring rights for broadcasting organisations, performers and phonogram producers hold out the prospect for greater concerted action against copyright pirates. The GATT/TRIPS Agreement is being used by the USA, along with threats of ending most favoured treatment, against States which are perceived to condone wholesale piracy, the most visible instances being the dispute between the USA and China in relation to pirated software and sound recordings. The EU has also used the threat of trade sanctions to force Thailand to address what the EU see as Thai indifference to wholesale piracy of sound recordings and proceedings before the World Trade Organisation under Part V of TRIPS has been commenced by the EU in relation to Japanese reluctance to meet obligations in relation to sound recordings for EU citizens.[85] However, the most significant international events took place at a diplomatic conference in Geneva in December 1996.

[82.] Agreement of Trade Related Aspects of Intellectual Property Rights Including Trade in Counterfeit Goods (15 December 1993).

[83.] Ireland ratified the WTO Agreement, including TRIPS on 15 November 1994; *Allen & Hanburys Ltd v Controller* [1997] 1 ILRM 416.

[84.] Articles 1-21 and the Appendix - see Article 9 of the GATT/TRIPS Agreement. On the TRIPs generally, see *Worthy* [1994] EIPR 195.

[85.] See 'EC wants Japan to pay for Old Hits', *Times* 24 February 1996.

The Berne Convention and the 1996 Geneva Treaties

[20.30] Work commenced in 1989 on preparing a Protocol to the Berne Convention in order to clarify existing international copyright norms, as found in the Paris Act 1971, and also to consider whether new international norms were needed. WIPO had then proposed establishing a Committee of Experts to examine the issue of revision but by 1992 it had been resolved[86] to establish two such Committees, one being charged[87] with examining the possible Protocol to the Berne Convention (hereafter 'the Protocol') and the second Committee addressing[88] the provisions of a possible New Instrument, or separate treaty (hereafter 'the New Instrument') on the protection of the rights of performers and the producers of phonograms. The work of these Committees was based upon preparatory documents provided by the International Bureau of WIPO. Acting upon a recommendation made to the Committees of Experts, a diplomatic conference was convened, in Geneva, between 2 December 1996 and 20 December 1996. Work on the texts of the Conference was entrusted to the chairman of the Committee of Experts and those texts were circulated to the States involved in the proposed conference by the WIPO International Bureau who then in turn produced the draft final clauses of the treaty or treaties. In fact, three treaties were before the December 1996 Conference: the two documents mentioned above, ie, the Protocol[89] and the New Instrument[90] were joined by a draft treaty on databases.[91] When the Conference closed and the smoke cleared, two treaties had been agreed in the form of the Protocol and the New Instrument. However, agreement could not be reached on the third treaty nor on the central issue posed in the New Instrument, namely, whether the performers' rights provisions should extend beyond performances in relation to sound recordings and embrace audio-visual performances also. A further conference was convened for 20 and 21 March 1997 in the hope that agreement could be reached or these matters.

[20.31] The first Treaty or Protocol to the Berne Convention[92] is a special agreement within Article 20 of Berne Convention and it is to have no connection with any Convention[93] other than the Berne Convention, and is not to derogate from any of the provisions of Berne itself.[94]

---

86. By the Assembly and the Conference of Representatives of the Berne Union.
87. Seven sessions were held between 1991 and May 1996.
88. Six sessions were held between 1993 and May 1996.
89. WIPO document CRNR/DC/4 (30 August 1996).
90. WIPO document CRNR/DC/5 (30 August 1996).
91. WIPO document CRNR/DC/6 (30 August 1996).
92. WIPO document CRNR/DC/89 (20 December 1996).
93. Article 1(1).
94. Article 1(2), ie, the Paris Act - Article 1(3). See, however Article 10.

[20.32] Some of the provisions of the Treaty repeat provisions found in the TRIPS agreement,[95] for example, the provisions declaring that copyright protection extends to expressions and not ideas, procedures, methods of operation or mathematical concepts as such.[96] Article 4 makes provision for the protection of computer programs as literary works, as defined in Article 2 of the Berne Convention "whatever may be the mode or form of expression" and Article 5 provides protection to compilations of data or other material in any form if their selection and form constitutes intellectual creations. This software and database protection mirrors Article 10 of TRIPS but the Protocol provisions are wider in certain respects.[97]

[20.33] Article 6(1) of the Treaty provides that authors shall enjoy an exclusive right of authorising the making available of the original and copies of their works through sale or other transfer of ownership. This provision thus adds a distribution right to authors, the international treaties previously not recognising this right. The controversial issue of exhaustion of rights is addressed in Article 6(2) which retains the existing position whereby this is a matter of national competence. The proposed options in the preliminary draft treaty, in Article 8 of the draft have been dropped, as has the reference to an importation right in one of the proposed drafts.

[20.34] Article 7 addresses the question of rental rights and this issue, while often regarded as an aspect of distribution rights in some countries, is dealt with along the lines set out in Article 11 of TRIPS; the Berne Convention does not address the issue at all. The authors of computer programs, cinematographic works and works embodied in phonograms are to enjoy an exclusive right of authorising commercial rental to the public of the originals or copies of their works.[98] Efforts to broaden the rental right to cover all works (with some opt out provisions) foundered due to strong resistance from the USA and some other States. The inclusion of phonograms is however a positive move but national competence is reserved for determining what works are to come within this category. The exclusive right is not to apply where the computer program is not the essential object of the rental (eg, hardware is rented also) and the right in relation to films is limited by the so-called impairment test found in the TRIPS agreement.[99]

[95.] Eg, Article 10 on limitations and exceptions mirrors Article 13 of TRIPS.

[96.] Article 2.

[97.] TRIPS only mentions programs in source or object code only: see however the Draft Agreed Statement Convening Treaty No 1.

[98.] The Rental and Lending Directive 92/100/EEC goes much further of course.

[99.] The right only applies if "such commercial rental had led to widespread copying of such works materially impairing the exclusive rights of reproduction".

Opt-out provisions[100] for countries that had and continue to have equitable remuneration for authors of phonograms that have been rented out may continue to operate under this system.[101]

[20.35] Article 8 is an important provision for authors insofar as the authors of works may find that works may be communicated to the public by wire or wireless means. The distribution of works in electronic form such as the digital diffusion of a work - digital distribution of musical works by cable or to a personal computer via telecommunications link or by satellite, on-line distribution of literary works, video on demand, to name just three examples - do not, arguably, come within existing reproduction or broadcasting rights. Article 8, therefore, in giving the author an exclusive right of this kind gives to authors protection against many kinds of commercial exploitation of a work, particularly on-demand distribution systems in which a tangible copy of the work is not transferred. This right does not prejudice provisions in the Berne Convention that also deal with "communication to the public".[102] However, failure to agree at the Conference on a definition of the reproduction right so as to cover digital works is regrettable; although the Conference apparently had no difficulty with regarding a digital representation of a work as being a reproduction, agreement could not be reached on temporary or ephemeral reproductions and exceptions to the reproduction right, so the article[103] was not carried over into the Treaty, but Article 10 of the Treaty allows Member States to address issues of this kind, consistent with the Berne Convention itself.[104]

[20.36] Articles 11 and 12 of the Treaty address two important matters, namely, the issues of technological methods of exercising the author's exclusive right and technological methods of rights management. States are obliged to provide adequate and effective legal remedies against persons who attempt to render such initiatives ineffective or less effective (eg, remove electronic 'tags' from a work).

[20.37] The Second Treaty[105] provides the International Community with an opportunity to expand the rights of performers and record companies in accordance with both the Rome Convention[106] and GATT/TRIPS. The Second

---

100. Article 7(3).
101. Crucial date is 15 April 1994, the date the GATT/TRIPS Agreement came into force.
102. Articles 11(1)(ii); 11 *bis* 1(i) and (ii); 11 *ter* 1(ii); 14(1)(ii) and 14 *bis* (1).
103. Article 7 of the draft in document CRNR/DC/4.
104. See the Draft Agreed Statements Conveying Treaty No 1 on Article 10 and the Resolution on the Reproduction Right.
105. WIPO Document CRNR/DC/90 (20 December 1996).
106. International Convention for the Protection of Performers, Producers of Phonograms and Broadcasting Organisation (Rome 26 October 1961).

Treaty is not to allow contracting parties to the Rome Convention to derogate from any of the obligations set out in that Convention.[107] The definitions found in Article 2 are extremely significant. The definition of a performer goes further than that found in the Rome Convention by including performers of expressions of folklore and the definition of phonogram makes it clear that digital representations of a work are to be included in the term phonogram: doubts had been expressed about whether traditional definitions of a 'record' were broad enough to deal with digital technology.[108] The definition of 'fixation' also covers digital representations of sound and the definition of broadcasting similarly is recast to cover the broadcasting of digital works. Satellite transmissions are also included in the definition of broadcast, as are encrypted signals where the public have been given the means of decrypting the signal by the broadcasting organisation, or with its consent.[109] The definition of 'communication to the public' is also of crucial importance for it makes it clear that cable transmissions which are outside the notion of a broadcast (eg, works made available via the Internet) are also to be regulated under this Treaty. In relation to the beneficiaries of the Treaty, the Rome Convention is used whereby coverage to nationals of other contracting parties is to be available to performers and phonogram producers on the basis of a national treatment rule,[110] although reservations are possible in relation to the Article 15 right to equitable remuneration for use made in connection with broadcasts or communication to the public.

[20.38] Article 5 makes provision for moral rights in relation to performers in respect of live aural performances, by which is meant performers who speak or sing a work or expression of folklore. Audio-visual performers are not covered by this provision, which is modelled on Berne Convention, Article 6 *bis*. Therefore, performers are to enjoy rights of paternity and integrity in accordance with the legislation of the contracting party where the protection is claimed.[111]

[20.39] Articles 6, 7 and 8 give performers exclusive economic rights in relation to authorising the broadcasting communication to the public and fixation of their unfixed performances,[112] the authorisation of reproductions

---

107. Article 1(1) of the Second Treaty.
108. See our outdated definition in CA 1963, s 2(1) for an example.
109. Article 2 of the Second Treaty.
110. Articles 3 and 4.
111. Article 5. Article 22(2) permits States to limit the moral rights provision to performers which occurred after entry into force of the Treaty.
112. Article 6.

of performances fixed in phonograms[113] and authorisations of distributions of an original or copies of fixed performances on phonogram through sale to the public or other transfer of ownership.[114] These performer's exclusive rights go much further than either the Rome Convention or the TRIPS provision which only gave performers "the possibility of preventing" such acts when they were undertaken without the authorisation of the performer. Article 9 also gives performers an exclusive right to authorise commercial rental to the public of performances fixed in phonograms, subject to national law of contracting parties and the possibility of displacement by prior[115] national regimes giving equitable remuneration.

[20.40] Article 10 addresses the issue of distribution of fixed performances by way of satellite or digital diffusion to members of the public who may access these performances from a time or place individually chosen by them. Digital diffusion services of this kind are now subject to the performers exclusive right to authorise the making available of such works, and the right thus given by Article 10 of this Treaty mirrors Article 8 of the Protocol which was given to the authors of works made available by way of 'on demand' services of this kind.

[20.41] These provisions on performers' rights are far reaching but it is significant that the definition of performer and phonogram were drawn up so as to exclude performances by way of audio-visual fixations, largely because of opposition by the Film Industry based in certain countries. Phonogram producers on the other hand found that exclusive rights to authorise reproduction of a recording "in any manner or form",[116] rights of authorisation of sales of the original or copies of a recording,[117] commercial rental[118] and authorising wire or wireless accessing by the public of recordings, including on demand services[119] were obtained during the conference with only a few amendments being made to these provisions, which are much more extensive than either the Rome or TRIPS provisions in relation to sound recording rights. Article 15 of the Treaty in essence repeats[120] the performers and phonogram producers right to single equitable remuneration if a phonogram which has been

---

[113.] Article 7. The right covers direct or indirect reproduction, thus covering reproduction by a person who uses a telecommunications network. However, the article does not address the question of temporary or ephemeral reproduction eg, loading or recording onto a hard disk for a short period of time.

[114.] Article 8.

[115.] Prior to 15 April 1994 - see Article 9(2).

[116.] Article 11.

[117.] Article 12.

[118.] Article 13.

[119.] Article 14.

[120.] See Article 12 of the Rome Convention.

published commercially is broadcast or communicated to the public. This is payable by the person who makes direct or indirect use of the phonogram. Whether this provision will be incorporated into Irish law is uncertain because the provision in both the Rome Convention and the Treaty[121] can be limited or not adopted at all, and Irish law does not currently set out such a right. Performer's protection is to run for 50 years following the end of the year in which the performance was fixed in the phonogram[122] while the phonogram producer's right runs for 50 years following on the year of publication, absent which, 50 years from the end of the year in which fixation was made.[123] Articles 18 and 19 set out the same technological protection of rights measures and rights management information provisions as are found in the First Treaty *vis-à-vis* author's rights.

[20.42] Both Treaties require an Assembly to be created. States are to appoint one delegate each and the Assembly is to deal with matters concerning the maintenance and development of the Treaties. Each Treaty is open for signature by any WIPO Member State and the EU until 31 December 1997 and will enter into force three months after 30 instruments of ratification or accession have been deposited with the Director General of WIPO.

SUMMARY

[20.43] Ireland is about to make significant changes to its legislative basis for identifying and maintaining copyright law. Recent international developments, in Europe and in the leading international forum of WIPO provide the raw material for Irish legislators to address the challenge of the digital era and it is to be hoped that the forthcoming Bill manages to integrate traditional concepts with the new economic and technological challenges presented to the draftsman addressed in recent EU Directives and in the new treaties.

[121.] This is the only permissible reservation: see Article 21.
[122.] Article 17(1).
[123.] Article 17(2).

Chapter 21

Semiconductor Chip Protection

INTRODUCTION

[21.01] Semiconductor chips are products which perform electronic or related functions. Semiconductors are elements or compounds that in part allow (or prevent) electricity being conducted and they stand between conductors (eg, metals) and insulators (eg, rubber). Semiconductors that are used include silicon and gallium arsenide. Those products are made *via* a photographic process which build a pattern of circuits upon layers or wafers of semiconducting material and *via* this process allow the design or mask work - normally a glass disc with the circuit pattern engaged upon it - to be produced as a composite product. More recent technology dispenses with the use of physical masks and relies upon an etching process whereby light or laser technology can etch a mask onto each layer of the chip. It is the physical mask and the information that goes into creating the circuit *via* digital plots, light emission technology, that represent the intellectual property that is the subject matter of protection.[1] The technology allows the development of integrated circuits which can perform a number of logical or analogue functions which increase the processing power of computers, reduce production costs and save both space and energy. Apart from obvious applications in the computer games industry, many semiconductors are now embedded into a number of consumer goods, from fuel efficiency elements in motor vehicles to microwave ovens and personal computers. Chips are valuable in themselves - witness the growth of computer chip thefts from offices and other commercial premises - and worthy of protection from industrial piracy. The investment needed to produce semiconductor products is substantial, but reverse engineering techniques allow a pirate to replicate a legitimate product at a fraction of the cost of developing that product.

[21.02] In describing the problems of providing protection, *Hart* drew a parallel between this technology and the earlier problem of protecting the layout of a printed circuit board.[2] Design protection *via* the law of copyright could be available under artistic copyright but *Hart* drew attention[3] to the danger that a

---

[1.] Hart [1985] EIPR 258; Hart (1986) 2 YLCT 93; Laddie, Prescott & Vittoria, *The Modern Law of Copyright and Designs* (Butterworths, 1995) Ch 45.

[2.] [1985] EIPR 258, at 260.

[3.] This was prescient: see the reasoning of the majority of the High Court of Australia in *Computer Edge Pty v Apple Computer* (1986) 60 ALJR 313.

three dimensional replication of the two dimensional design may fail to pass the non-expert test[4] whereby such a non-expert would be able to see a link between works - the masks or digital plots - and the infringing chip. So, even if artistic copyright could be available under Berne Convention principles,[5] there were problems of proof that were not to be easily overcome. In any event, this theoretical problem, for no Irish cases arose on the point, disappeared altogether when s 2 of the Copyright (Amendment) Act 1987 removed artistic copyright from purely functional designs that had been used to manufacture more than 50 copies of the product.[6] Given that the protection available for registered design protection under the 1927 Act requires the design to satisfy an eye appeal test, purely functional, or hidden design features of the kind that the semiconductor mask work epitomises, are not likely to be protected at all under Irish law. So, whatever areas are explored, protection for the semiconductor designs or works under domestic Irish intellectual property law were fraught with difficulties.

INTERNATIONAL DEVELOPMENTS

[21.03] In the international arena WIPO produced a Treaty on Integrated Circuits and Layout Designs[7] in 1989 but no EU States have to date signed this Treaty and the two major semiconductor producing States outside the EU actually opposed the adoption of the Washington Treaty, so the prospects of this Treaty obtaining international acceptance are slender indeed.[8] The reasons for this can be gleaned by considering the fact that some national legislations, and the EU Directive of 1985, had already produced *sui generis* measures of protection that differed quite radically from the Washington Treaty. The Washington Treaty departed significantly from pre-existing national legislation in relation to definitions of protected works, the period of protection, the nature of the infringing acts and the possibility, or not, of compulsory, non-exclusive licenses.

The US Semiconductor Chip Protection Act 1984

[21.04] Rather than wait for developments at the level of international treaty law, in the form of a WIPO Treaty or *via* the Berne Convention, the USA created an entirely new international context by passing legislation which protected 'mask works' that is, "images ... having or representing the pre-

---

4. In Ireland, see CA 1963, s 14(7).
5. Article 2(1) - "illustrations, maps, plans, sketches and three dimensional works relative to geography, topography, architecture or science".
6. To reverse *Allibert SA v O'Connor* [1982] FSR 317.
7. Washington, 26 May 1989 (The IPIC Treaty).
8. Note that many of these Treaty provisions, not least the provisions in Articles 2-7 (excluding Article 6(3), the compulsory licensing provision) are acceptable, for Articles 35-38 of GATT/ TRIPs obliges WTO states to implement some of the IPIC Treaty provisions.

determined three-dimensional pattern of metallic, insulating or semi-conductor material ... of a semiconductor chip product." If the work is original, first exploited in the US, or elsewhere by a US national or domiciled person, that person acquires an exclusive right to reproduce, import or distribute the mask work, or products containing the work. The right lasts for ten years from the registration of the work or its first commercial exploitation, whichever is the earlier. In the light of US anti-trust and fair use laws, the 1984 Act has generous reverse engineering provisions which all competitors may use to produce compatible (and thus competing) products or improved products. Substantial investment and originality must be shown if the competitor is to justify the use of the pre-existing mask work design, for independent creation not mere plagiarism, lies behind the legitimisation of reverse engineering in this context.

[21.05] The real significance of the US legislation, however, is found in the area of geographical scope. Because semiconductor products were not within the Berne system, and because international industrial design law was (and is) still in its infancy, no problem of national treatment for non-US citizens or non-US domiciliaries arose. Thus, foreign (eg, EU) rightholders could not come within US protection rules, in this most vital of markets, unless their countries had entered into Treaty agreements with the US Administration and those countries granted US citizens with equivalent protection in national law on the basis of reciprocity. By setting this agenda, the US hoped to be able quickly to force the pace in creating a new world regime on a bilateral treaty basis.[9] This objective has, broadly, been realised as the result of the reluctance of the European Community[10] to allow a trade war, or protectionism, to disfigure international trade in computer chip and chip enhanced products.

THE 1986 DIRECTIVE

[21.06] Council Directive of 16 December 1986 on the Legal Protection of Topographies of Semiconductor Products[11] was processed very quickly by Community institutions as a matter of urgency.[12] This Directive required all Member States to adopt legislative provisions conferring exclusive rights in respect of semiconductor product topographies. Ireland adopted legislation in the form of the European Communities (Protection of Topographies of Semiconductor Products) Regulations 1988,[13] Regulations which come into

---

[9.] Stern (1986) 17 IIC 486; Dreier (1988) 19 IIC 427.

[10.] Cohen Jehoram [1987] EIPR 35.

[11.] 87/154/EEC; OJ L 24/26.

[12.] The proposal was published in December 1985: OJ 1985 C360/14.

[13.] SI 101/1988.

effect on 13 May 1988[14] in Ireland. These Regulations[15] provide an exclusive right - called a topography right - in favour of the creator of a topography of a semiconductor product.[16] The Regulations do not define a semiconductor product but Article 1 of the Directive defines a semiconductor product thus:

(a) a 'semiconductor product' shall means the final or an intermediate form of any product:

    (i) consisting of a body of material which includes a layer of semiconducting material; and

    (ii) having one or more other layers composed of conducting, insulating or semiconducting material, the layers being arranged in accordance with a predetermined three-dimensional pattern; and

    (iii) intended to perform, exclusively or together with other functions, an electronic function.

The same Article goes on to define a topography as:

a series of related images, however fixed or encoded;

    (i) representing the three-dimensional pattern of the layers of which a semiconductor product is composed; and

    (ii) in which series, each image has the pattern or part of the pattern of a surface of the semiconductor product at any stage of its manufacture.

[21.07] Article 3 of the 1988 Regulations define the conditions of entitlement as depending upon the typography being able to satisfy an originality test that has since become part of the *'acquis communitaire'* - the topography must be "the result of the creator's own intellectual effort".[17] The Regulations also in that Article reinforce this by requiring that the topography not be "commonplace within the industry" but goes on to provide that where the topography consists of elements that are so commonplace, protection under the Regulation exists "only to extent that the combination of such elements, taken as a whole, fulfills" the non-commonplace standard. The requirement that the topography must be viewed as a whole is important, for many topographies will consist of standard cell or pre-existing configurations, and by analogy with compilations of pre-existing works in areas like compilations and computer programs produced from

---

14. The deadline set for implementation under the Directive was 7 November 1987. Only France, Germany and the Netherlands met the deadline.
15. SI 101/1988.
16. Articles 2(1) and 3(1).
17. This originality standard re-surfaced later in both the Computer Program and the Database Directives.

standard code, it is the totality of the work that may produce protection.[18] Whether computer generated works may satisfy the originality standard is open to debate, and the answer may turn on the distinction between computer aided and computer generated works, which are matters of fact.[19]

[21.08] For the creator[20] of the topography who overcomes such problems, protection under the Regulations will turn on whether a nationality test set by the Regulations can be satisfied. The individual creators must be, according to Article 3(3) of the Regulations:

(a) natural persons who are nationals of a Member State or who habitually reside on the territory of a Member State, or

(b) persons having a real and effective industrial or commercial establishment on the territory of a Member State.

[21.09] Regulation 3(3)(b) is obviously intended to confer rights on a human person or corporate body that takes the exclusive right by virtue of an assignment, *via* an employee or through commissioning that topography, and the actual human person or persons creating the topography are not EU nationals or habitually resident in the EU. Further, even if these tests of nationality or residence are not satisfied, Article 3(5) of the Regulations provides protection if the rightholder markets the topography *via* an EC national or person resident in the EU and the topography is first exploited commercially[21] in a Member State and that agent is exclusively authorised to exploit the topography throughout the EU. However, the Directive itself makes it clear that protection is available to the persons who are within Regulation 3(3) of the 1988 Regulations, as distinct from the EU rightholder who has authorised the Community national who is exclusively authorised to commercially exploit the work within the Community.[22] As soon as the topography is a protected work within these provisions, the protection is available to any successor in title, regardless of nationality or habitual residence.[23]

[21.10] The exclusive rights given by the Regulations are reproduction and commercial exploitation in Ireland, or importation for the purpose of commercial exploitation.[24] The same Article sets out an exception to the

---

[18.] Eg *A-One Accessory Imports Pty v Off-Road Imports Pty* (1996) 34 IPR 306; *Ibcos Computers v Barclays Mercantile Highland* [1994] FSR 275.

[19.] Eg, see the South African case of *Payen Components South Africa Ltd v Bovic Gaskets* (1995) IPR 407.

[20.] The right is, of course, assignable eg to a company, and where the creator is an employee, or it has been commissioned, the employer or commissioner prevails.

[21.] See the Directive, Article 1(c).

[22.] Directive, Article 3(4).

[23.] Directive, Article 3(5); 1988 Regulations, Article 3(6).

[24.] 1988 Regulations, Article 4.

reproduction right in respect of non-commercial reproductions and reproduction for analysis or evaluation or teaching purposes, and a further exception is given in relation to reproduction which results in the evaluation of another topography which in turn is the intellectual creation of the person who is responsible for that resulting topography.

[21.11] The commencement and duration of these rights are also fixed by the Regulations. Article 5 provides:

> (1) A right to protection in a topography shall commence:
>
>> (a) when the topography is first fixed or encoded, provided, however, these Regulations shall not apply to any topography created before the coming into operation of these Regulations, or
>>
>> (b) in a case falling within Regulation 3(5) of these Regulations, from the date of first commercial exploitation anywhere in the world.
>
> (2) The rights subsisting in a topography by virtue of these Regulations shall come to an end 10 years from the end of the calendar year in which the topography is first commercially exploited anywhere in the world, or, where it has not been commercially exploited anywhere in the world, within a period of 15 years from its first fixation or encoding.

[21.12] Infringement of rights are actionable at the suit of the owner of the topography right but there is an innocent infringer defence[25] which limits the innocent infringer to being liable in damages only: further, damages are to be measured by reference to a licensing measure - a reasonable royalty payment.[26]

[21.13] While the Directive provided that Member States could impose a registration of rights and deposit of materials procedures as a precondition to protection,[27] the Irish Regulations do not make provision for this, apart from a marking of a topography option in Article 7 of the Regulations. The topography right does not exist in relation to topographies created prior to 13 May 1988, but topographies created after that date acquire protection under the Regulation from the time of fixation or encoding, or in the case of topographies that acquire protection under Article 3(5), from the date of first commercial exploitation. Protection lasts for 15 years from the date of fixation or encoding if there is no subsequent commercial exploitation of the topography anywhere in the world,

---

[25.] See CA 1963, s 24(3).
[26.] Article 6 of the Regulations: *Stovin-Bradford v Volpoint* [1971] 3 All ER 570.
[27.] Directive, Article 4(1).

but if the work is so commercially exploited, protection ends ten years after first commercial exploitation.[28] Of course, the limited originality test in the Regulations make any enhanced product likely to attract new and distinct rights in any event as these expiry rules seem quite adequate for exploitative purposes.

Reciprocity and International Requisition of Rights

[21.14] The US position under the 1984 Act, mentioned above, permitted protection to non-US nationals or domiciliaries if *via* Presidential proclamation, the President of the US is satisfied that the foreign State in question affords protection to US owners of mask works. This reciprocity requirement is moderated by provisions which give the US Secretary of Commerce the power to issue interim orders giving protection to countries that are, *inter alia*, making progress toward enacting legislation that would trigger the issuing of a Presidential proclamation. The EC Member States and others, have benefited from this Interim Order Procedure while the USA has also been the subject of a number of interim measures in the form of Council Decisions.[29] The President with effect from 1 July 1995, issued the necessary proclamation[30] of protection to Members of the European Community, and that proclamation extended protection to all World Trade Organisation Members with effect from 1 January 1996. A Council Decision of 22 December 1994 extends topography protection in European Community Member States to all members of the World Trade Organisation with effect from 1 January 1996,[31] so the Irish Permanent And Temporary Protection Orders[32] have effectively been superceded by Community legislation.

[28.] 1988 Regulations, Article 5(2). The Regulations put the expiry events around the other way, as does the Directive.

[29.] 87/532/EEC; 90/511/EEC; 93/16/EEC; 94/4/EEC; 94/373/EEC; 95/237/EEC.

[30.] *Proclamation 6780 to Implement Certain Provisions of Trade Agreements Resulting from the Uruguay Round of Multilateral Trade Negotiations.*

[31.] 94/824/EC; OJ L 349.

[32.] SI 208/1988; SI 318/1991; SI 310/1993.

Chapter 22

Industrial Designs

INTRODUCTION

[22.01] Most countries have a system of registration whereby it is possible to protect a new design applied to a product but the dilemma is how to pitch such protection between that afforded by a patent and copyright in an artistic work. With the increasing liberalisation of trade mark laws, it is also now possible to register certain shapes of goods or their packaging which before would have been the sole prerogative of design law. It is possibly due to the overlap with other forms of intellectual property and uncertainty as to the boundaries of design law which has led to the low profile and under-utilisation of the system of design registration.[1] Design law is a recognition that, similar to the position with inventions, there are many instances where much time, energy and effort is injected into the design of a product, which once disclosed, can be copied at minimal cost. A design right protects the appearance of a specific article to which the design has been applied and in respect of which it has been registered.

[22.02] The principal legislation dealing with registered industrial designs is found in Part IV of the Industrial and Commercial Property (Protection) Act 1927.[2] The 1927 Act dealt with patents, copyright, trade marks and designs but now only remains in force in so far as it relates to designs and a provision dealing with the overlap with copyright law.[3] It is this overlap in s 172 which is fundamental in the consideration of industrial design law. The author of an artistic work may, at first glance, feel that he can in all instances, rely on copyright law and a system of automatic protection for an original work without the necessity of the expense of registration. Section 9 of the Copyright Act 1963 provides for protection in respect of artistic works and this includes protection against reproduction by turning a two dimensional work into a three dimensional form and *vice versa*, subject to the lay recognition test. This lay recognition test is contained in s 14(7) of the Copyright Act 1963 and states that the making of any object of any description which is in three dimensional form, shall not be taken to constitute an infringement of the copyright in an artistic

---

[1] 461 applications were filed in 1995.
[2] No 16/1927; Industrial and Commercial Property (Protection) Act 1927 (Commencement) Order (SI 60/1927).
[3] Section 172.

work in two dimensions if the object would not appear to persons who are not experts in relation to objects of that description to be a reproduction of the artistic work. In practice, it is difficult for a defendant to raise this defence.[4] In *King Features Syndicate Inc v OM Kleeman*[5], the House of Lords in dealing with corresponding provisions of the UK law, held that the production of 'Popeye The Sailor Man' dolls amounted to copyright infringement because without consent, there had been reproduction of the drawings in a material form albeit in a different dimension. The making of an article depicted in a drawing infringed the copyright under the concept of what has become known as indirect copying.

[22.03] What an author/artist has to consider very closely is whether or not their artistic work is capable of being registered as a design because there cannot be duality of protection. Under s 172 of the 1927 Act, copyright protection is denied in respect of designs which are capable of being registered under the 1927 Act and are used or intended to be used as models or patterns to be multiplied by an industrial process. An illustration of how this works in practice can be seen in the case of *Pytram Ltd v Models (Leicester) Ltd*[6] which considered the design of a wolf cub's head used on totem poles. Under the then equivalent provisions of UK law, Clawson J held that there was neither copyright nor design protection. Copyright did subsist but protection was denied because the work was capable of being registered as a design. A design only returns to the category of works protected by copyright if it is one which is not used or intended to be used as a model or pattern to be multiplied by any industrial process. This was not the case in respect of the newly designed totem poles and since design registration had not been sought, the plaintiff was stripped of all forms of protection.

[22.04] It is the artist's intention when the original drawings are created which determines whether or not it was the intention that such be used as a model or pattern to be applied by an industrial process. If a work enjoys copyright protection under the 1963 Act, it does not then lose such protection simply because it is subsequently used as a model for mass production.[7]

WHAT IS REGISTERABLE AS A DESIGN?

[22.05] A design is defined in s 3 of the 1927 Act as:

---

4. *Dorling v Honnor* [1964] RPC 160; *Allibert SA v O'Connor* [1981] FSR 613.
5. [1941] AC 417.
6. [1930] 1 Ch 639.
7. *King Features Syndicate Inc v O&M Kleeman* [1941] AC 417.

... only the features of shape, configuration, pattern, or ornament applied to any article by any industrial process or means, whether manual, mechanical, or chemical, separate or combined, which in the finished article appeal to and are judged solely by the eye, but does not include any mode or principle of construction, or anything which is in substance a mere mechanical device.

The word 'article' is also defined in s 3 as "any article of manufacture and any substance, artificial or natural or partly artificial and partly natural". This is very broad and can be applied to a wide range of articles such as, for example, containers, furniture, lamp shades, vehicles, chocolates and cutlery. A design registration is not restricted to three dimensional articles and can, for example, be surface decoration applied to clothing or wall paper. The definition of a design was considered by Costello J in *Allibert SA v O'Connor*.[8] Costello J broke down the definition into two parts, the first providing that a 'design' means, *inter alia*, those features of the shape and configuration of the finished article which appeal to and are judged solely by the eye. The second part excludes from the definition anything which is in substance a mere mechanical device. At issue in the *Allibert* case was the plaintiff's claim to ownership of copyright in drawings relating to fish boxes. The plaintiff also owned registered designs in relation to such but introduced evidence to show *inter alia* that the novelty in the shape of the boxes was dictated by its function of improved nesting and stacking. Costello J applied the statement of Luxmore J in *Kestos Limited v Kempat Limited*[9] that a mere mechanical device is a shape in which all the features are dictated solely by the function or functions which the article has to perform. If the shape does not possess some features beyond those necessary to enable the article to fulfil the particular purpose, then the drawing cannot be regarded as a design within s 3 of the 1927 Act.[10] Costello J went on to hold that the designs of the plastic fish boxes should not have been registered under the 1927 because all of the features were dictated by their function. As a consequence, copyright subsisted under s 9 of the Copyright Act 1963.

[22.06] The definition of a design was amended in England by s 1(3) of the Registered Designs Act 1949 and in *AMP Inc v Uitilux Proprietary Ltd*,[11] the House of Lords considered the definition which included reference to visual appeal. It was held that an electric terminal for a washing machine was not registerable. The terminal was located inside the machine and was not visible except to someone servicing the machine. Lord Porter stated:

[8.] [1981] FSR 613.

[9.] (1936) 53 RPC 139, at 151.

[10.] *Stenor Limited v Whitesides (Clitheroe) Limited* (1948) 64 RPC 1.

[11.] [1971] RPC 103, at 114.

"no doubt another shape of fuse and another type of machine could be invented to perform the same task. However, that may be, the only object of using the registered shape now under discussion is to perform the functional purpose of making the machine work".

The Copyright (Amendment) Act 1987[12]

[22.07] The effect of the judicial interpretation of the statutory provision[13] which denied registered design protection to functional designs meant that the owners of such could rely on copyright in the original drawings and enjoy protection under the Copyright Act 1963. Therefore, functional designs enjoyed protection for the life of the author plus 50 years, far exceeding that of either registered designs or patents. This created a number of problems, particularly for manufacturers of spare parts and components. Also, because copyright under the 1963 Act is an unregistered right, it is often very difficult to determine ownership. The UK courts had to grapple with the difficult problem of spare parts in the case of *British Leyland Motor Corp v Armstrong Patents Co*[14] on the issue of copyright protection in original drawings of vehicle exhaust pipes. The Court of first instance and the Court of Appeal adopted the traditional copyright line that by copying a British Leyland exhaust pipe in order to supply the market with competing spares, the defendant infringed copyright in the original drawings. The House of Lords, by a majority, accepted that copyright did exist in original drawings of functional designs such as a car exhaust pipe but nevertheless felt that this was so anti-competitive that copyright could not be allowed to interfere with the rights of car owners to repair their vehicles. Lord Templeman likened allowing motor manufacturers to monopolise the spare parts market to the consequence that car owners then "sell their souls to the company store" because a manufacturer could charge what it wished and the car owner would have no alternative but to buy from this source.

[22.08] The Irish courts were not called upon to address this problem and will not have to do so by virtue of s 1 of the Copyright (Amendment) Act 1987. Under the 1987 Act, protection is denied under the Copyright Act 1963 to artistic works reproduced in three dimensions where the shape, configuration and pattern that appear in the work and are applied to the object, are wholly or substantially functional. A second requirement is that the object must be one of a number, in excess of fifty, of identical objects which have been manufactured and made commercially available by the owner of the copyright or by a person authorised by him in that behalf. This effectively means that mass produced functional designs are no longer protected under copyright law. They also

---

12. No 24/1987.
13. Definition of design: Industrial and Commercial Property (Protection) Act 1927, s 3.
14. [1986] FSR 221; [1986] 2 WLR 400.

cannot be protected by way of a registered design or under trade mark law.[15] In some instances, patent protection can be sought and it is conceivable that a case of passing off might be made in an exceptional set of circumstances. Apart from this, functional designs are now a neglected species under Irish intellectual property law. There are no equivalent provisions to those contained in the UK Design Copyright Act 1968 or the UK Copyright, Designs and Patents Act 1988 and therefore there is currently quite a divergence from UK design law and, for example, no unregistered design right exists under Irish law.

Novelty Requirement

[22.09] Section 64(1) of the 1927 Act states the requirement that the design must be new or original. Unlike patent law, there is no requirement of universal novelty but only that it has not been published or used in the State prior to the application for registration. Similar to the position under patent law, there is a provision allowing for prior disclosure at a certified industrial or international exhibition. The exhibitor is required to give notice of their intention to exhibit and the application must be filed within six months of the opening of the exhibition.[16] Another exception to prior publication destroying novelty lies in s 72 and deals with disclosure in confidence. The disclosure must be in such circumstances as would make it contrary to good faith for that other person to use or publish the design.

[22.10] In the UK case of *Aspro-Nicholas Ltd's Design Application*,[17] the 'or' in 'new or original' was held not to be used in a disjunctive sense and that accordingly to qualify for registration, a design had to be both new *and* original, which meant that something more than bare originality was required. If this reasoning is followed by the Irish courts, then the tests applied in patent cases, (except that lack of novelty or originality is not a ground for cancellation of a registered design), would equally apply in relation to designs.[18] Publication in the State prior to the filing of an Irish design application is also possible if the applicant has filed, claiming priority from a foreign application prior to the Irish disclosure. Similar to the position under patent law,[19] under the Paris Convention for Industrial Property 1883, a person who has applied for registration of a design in a convention country may file a corresponding application in another convention country within six months of the first application, and be entitled in the second country to the priority right afforded by the first application. This also means, for example, that an Irish applicant can

---

15. TMA 1996, s 8(2)(b).
16. Section 76.
17. [1974] RPC 645.
18. See *Rosedale Associated Manufacturers Ltd v Airfix Products Ltd* [1957] RPC 239.
19. Except that the period is six months for designs and twelve months for patents.

file an Irish design application and then disclose internationally in the knowledge that provided he files in other jurisdictions within six months of the Irish date and claims priority, the disclosure will not invalidate any foreign design registration.

[22.11] In *Costelloe v Johnston*,[20] Blayney J had to consider a claim of infringement in respect of the registered design of a door. At the trial, the novelty was stated as residing in two segments below four panels which formed a semi-circle at the top of the door. However, the design registration was in respect of the entire door and it was the shape and configuration of such in which the novelty was claimed. Blayney J evaluated the difference between the prior art and the registered design by the test of impression which was created by the eye. He found as a matter of fact that the defendant had imported a very similar door prior to the filing of a design application and held that the resemblance between this door and the plaintiff's registered design was such that the former constituted a prior publication of the design.

Duration of a registered design

[22.12] A design when registered is registered as of the date of application for registration.[21] Where convention priority is claimed the design is registered as of the date claimed. The initial duration is for a five year term but is renewable for a further two periods of five years up to a maximum of 15 years from the date of registration.[22]

Infringement

[22.13] The rights granted by a registered design are stated in s 78 of the 1927 Act and are the exclusive rights as follows:

(a) for the purposes of sale to apply or cause to be applied to any article in any class of goods in which the design is registered the design or any fraudulent or obvious imitation thereof, except with the licence or written consent of the registered proprietor, or to do anything with a view to enable the design to be so applied; or

(b) while knowing that the design or any fraudulent or obvious imitation of the design has been applied to any article without the consent of the registered proprietor, to publish the article or expose it or cause it to be published or exposed for sale.

---

20. [1991] 1 IR 305.
21. Section 64(6).
22. Section 70.

The crux of any design infringement claim is the issue of substantiality. However, unlike copyright, it is not a question of the extent to which there has been copying but a comparison of differences between the respective design with designs which form the prior art. It is not a comparison of the articles in their entirety but only those aspects embraced by the design registration. Consequently, in some instances, it is advisable to register a number of designs to include the overall shape and configuration of an entire article such as, for example, a car and then separate designs for individual novel features of the car such as wing mirrors, bumpers, etc. provided there are non-functional aspects of the design for such. An example of the consequences of failing to do so can be seen in *Best Products Ltd v FW Woolworth & Co Ltd*.[23] In that case, the plaintiff's design was in respect of the entirety of a whistling kettle comprising three features, the shape of the body, handle and spout. The alleged infringement resembled the design in all, save the spout which was remarkably different. There was held to be no infringement because the respective spouts were held to be substantially different. The spout was an important and prominent feature of the design as a whole.

[22.14] Whether or not copying has taken place is in fact irrelevant to infringement of a registered design because a court is concerned with the extent of similarity and not the derivation of the design.[24] The test is a comparison of those features that appeal to and are judged by the eye. The relevant eye being that of a customer likely to be interested in the design of the articles in question. In *Gaskell & Chambers Ltd v Measure Master Ltd*,[25] Aldous J concluded that the Court must assume that the interested customer compared the registered design and the alleged infringement side by side and then went away and came back later to the alleged infringement. In this way, the Court could conclude which features of the design would strike the eye and be remembered, and then decide whether the designs were or were not substantially different. If only small differences separate the registered design from what has gone before, then equally small differences between the alleged infringement and the registered design will be held to be sufficient to avoid infringement.[26] On the other hand, the greater the advance over the prior art in the registered design, then in general, the greater will be the scope of the protection afforded by the registered design.

[23.] [1964] RPC 226.

[24.] *Gaskell & Chambers Ltd v Measure Master Ltd* [1993] RPC 76; see also Viscount Maugham in *King Features Syndicated Inc v O & M Kleeman Ltd* [1941] AC 417.

[25.] [1993] RPC 76.

[26.] *Kevi A/S v Suspa-Verein UK Ltd* [1982] RPC 173, at 179.

[22.15] In *Three Stripe International Ltd v Charles O'Neill & Company Limited*,[27] Costello J considered infringement of a registered design in respect of a football jersey. The plaintiff was the exclusive supplier of certain sportswear to the Football Association of Ireland (FAI). When the Irish team qualified for the European finals in 1988, the plaintiff designed a jersey to be worn by the team and which had a special collar. The design of this jersey was registered. The defendant produced two types of supporter's jerseys, one had a v-neck which it was accepted did not infringe the design, but the plaintiff claimed the second collared version infringed the registered design. At the hearing for an interlocutory injunction, Costello J held that there was a serious question of infringement. The onus was on the plaintiff to show that the defendant applied to their jersey a design which was a fraudulent or 'obvious imitation' of the registered design under s 78 of the 1927 Act. By way of summation of s 78 and the effect of such on the issue being tried, Costello J stated:

> "the plaintiff does not have to establish deliberate copying and will succeed in its claim if on a comparison of the rival jerseys, the defendant's appears to be an 'obvious imitation' of the plaintiff's, even if it was produced solely as a result of its knowledge of the trade and intelligent guesswork about trends in sportswear fashions. On the issue of 'obvious imitation', I cannot hold that the plaintiff's claim is a frivolous one and I think it has raised a serious question to be tried. The features of novelty claimed in its registration are the features of pattern or ornament and the pattern created by the tonal contrast applied to the article as shown in the representation. I do not consider that the Court will hold that this registration gives any right to an exclusive use of a green-coloured jersey (it is the pattern created by the contrasting colour that is protected; see: Morris and Quest: *Design: The Modern Law and Practice* (1987)) but applying long established principles (namely, that the test is to the eye alone, that small differences in detail will not necessarily prevent the occurrence of an infringement and that if under normal conditions of user, the eye would not confuse the two designs, then the claim will fail), the plaintiff has shown that it has raised a serious question as to whether its copyright has been infringed".

[22.16] Damages and injunctive relief are available to the proprietor of a registered design[28] but there is no statutory provision for an account of profits, delivery up or destruction of infringing articles.

Cancellation

[22.17] There are only two grounds for seeking cancellation of a registered design and these are stated in s 75 of the 1927 Act, namely:

[27.] [1988] IR 144.
[28.] Section 78(2).

(a) prior publication in the State or in the United Kingdom prior to the establishment of the State; or

(b) non-manufacture in the State to an extent as is reasonable.

Lack of novelty or originality which is a requirement for registration is not a ground of cancellation.[29]

[22.18] In relation to prior publication, undoubtedly the Irish courts will draw on the extensive case law in the field of patents but the difference in the field of designs is that it is only prior publication in the State which is taken into account. Section 72 of the 1927 Act allows for prior disclosure in such circumstances as would make it contrary to good faith for that other person to use or publish the design and also the acceptance of a first and confidential order for goods bearing a new or original textile design intended for registration. Costello J in *Three Stripe International Ltd v Charles O'Neill & Co Ltd*[30] expressed the view that the words 'textile design' meant a design for a textile and not to a design which is applied to textile material. Also, while disclosure of a design for the purpose of securing an order is *prima facie* evidence of its disclosure,[31] circumstances may be such that disclosure by a buyer would amount to a breach of good faith.

[22.19] Section 76 of the 1927 Act which allows for prior publication at an industrial or international exhibition certified by the Minister, requires notice to be given to the Controller and that the application for registration of the design be filed within six months from the date of the opening of the exhibition.

[22.20] The grounds for cancellation on the grounds of non-working[32] must now be read in the context of the EU law which does not allow (as contrary to Articles 30 and 36 of the Treaty of Rome) laws which discriminate between manufacturers in different EU Member States. The TRIPS Agreement[33] does address the area of industrial designs[34] but unlike patents, does not have any special prohibition on discrimination based on whether a product is imported or locally produced.[35] The proviso to s 75(1)(b) has been repealed by s 6 of the Industrial and Commercial Property (Protection) (Amendment) Act 1957[36] and now provides that if the Controller is satisfied that the time which has elapsed

---

[29.] *Radnall's Registered Design* (1934) 51 RPC 164.

[30.] [1988] IR 144.

[31.] *Gunston v Winox Ltd* [1921] 1 Ch 664.

[32.] Section 75(1)(b).

[33.] Agreement on Trade Related Aspects of Intellectual Property Rights. See para **[2.80]**.

[34.] Articles 25 and 26.

[35.] Article 27(1) - see *Allen and Hanburys Limited and Glaxo Group Ltd v Controller and Clonmel Healthcare Limited* [1997] FSR 1.

[36.] No 13/1957.

from registration has been insufficient for manufacture in the State, then the Controller may adjourn the application for a period deemed sufficient to allow for manufacture. Alternatively, instead of cancellation, the Controller may order the grant of a compulsory licence.

REGISTRATION PROCEDURE

[22.21] The information and documentation required in support of an application for registration are stated in the Industrial Property Rules 1927.[37] Rules 83-85 require the following:

(a) The surname, Christian names, nationality, trading style (if any) and full address of the applicant.

(b) A declaration that the applicant claims to be the proprietor of the design. This can simply be a statement made by the applicant's representative in the form of application.

(c) A brief description of the design and a statement of the feature or features of novelty claimed for the design. The statement can be very brief and for example can read "the novelty claimed is in the shape and configuration as applied to the article". What is important is that where appropriate it should be specific to the part of an article in which novelty is claimed. Otherwise, it will be the entire article against which a comparison with the prior art will be made.[38] Unlike a patent specification, the novelty claim does not have to be elaborate on any detail and is just an identification of whether it is the shape, configuration, pattern or ornament or any combination of these features for which novelty is claimed. If, for example, the design was in respect of a chocolate, the novelty might reside in a novel shape or pattern applied to the chocolate or indeed to both.

(d) It is necessary to state the class in which registration is desired. The importance of such lies in the fact that infringement only arises in respect of the class of goods for which the design is registered.[39] The classification system adopted is known as the Locarno Classification. The Locarno Union is a union of countries concerning the international classification of industrial designs and was founded by an agreement signed on 8 October 1968 and which took effect on 27 April 1971 which is also the date when Ireland became a member.

---

37. SI 78/1927.
38. *Costelloe v Johnston* [1991] 1 IR 305. *Best Products Ltd v FW Woolworth & Co Ltd* [1964] RPC 226.
39. Section 75(1)(a).

There are 32 different classes of goods (1 to 31 and an additional miscellaneous Class 99). Most classes have a sub-class which the Controller also requires to be identified in the application. Most classes are quite broad and, for example, a design registration in respect of a pattern applied to a necktie would also afford protection in respect of a wide range of items of clothing including handkerchiefs but would not, for example, extend to wallets which fall into a different class. Rule 80 of the 1927 Rules provides for a single registration embracing a set of articles. 'Set' is defined to mean a number of articles of the same general character ordinarily on sale together, or intended to be used together, all being of the same design with or without modifications not sufficient to alter the character or not substantially affecting the identity thereof. An example of a set of articles would be items of cutlery. There is no restriction on the number of classes in which a design may be registered.[40]

(e) A statement of the article or articles to which the design is to be applied.

(f) If the design has been already registered for other goods, the registration number and the class or classes in which previously registered. The fact of the existence of a design registration in other classes cannot lead to refusal of a design application on the grounds of either lack of novelty or originality or prior publication. However, a new registration cannot extend longer than the design arising from the earlier registration.[41]

(g) Details of any priority claimed under the Paris Convention and specifically the date of the earlier application for registration. Under s 152 of the 1927 Act as amended by s 7(3) of the Industrial and Commercial Property (Protection) (Amendment) Act 1957.[42] If priority is claimed, then the Irish application must be filed within six months from the foreign application from which priority is claimed. It is also necessary either at the time of application or within three months to file a certified copy of the foreign application. The certification must be from the national authority (usually the Patents Office) of the foreign country from which priority is claimed.

(h) If an agent is appointed, then the full name and address of the agent must be provided and who must be resident or have a place of business in the State.

[40.] Section 64(3).
[41.] Section 67.
[42.] No 13/1957.

(i) The application must be signed by the applicant or by an authorised agent on behalf of the applicant. In the latter case, the agent must furnish at the time of application or subsequently, a form of authorisation in their favour, signed on behalf of the applicant.

(j) The requisite official fee.

(k) A drawing or tracing in ink, photograph or other representation of a permanent character showing the design as applied. In the case of a shape, this involves depicting the article from various views showing all of the important features. Four sets of representations must be furnished. In the case of a set, the representation must show all the several arrangements in which it is proposed to apply the design to the articles included in the set. It is possible initially to file a rough sketch of the design provided it is sufficiently definitive to identify the design. Thereafter, formal representations must be filed within three months.

[22.22] If there are any words, letters or numerals forming part of the design, then these must be disclaimed.[43] If the design includes the name or representation of a person living or deceased within fifty years, the Controller may, before allowing registration, require the consent of the person or their legal representative.[44]

[22.23] If through default of an applicant, an application is not completed within twelve months, the Controller must give notice of non-completion. The applicant then has fourteen days to complete or apply for an extension of time which cannot exceed three months.[45]

[22.24] If the design application is approved by the Controller, a certificate of registration issues.[46] There is no opposition procedure to a design application. The fact of registration is advertised in the Official Journal and the design is entered on the Register. The details in the Journal are minimal and simply provide a registration number, date and description of the article(s) against which a design has been registered. Full details of the design including the representations are not open to public inspection for a period of two years from the date of registration.[47] An exception is made in the case of a refusal of a design on the grounds of identity with an existing registration. In such a situation, the applicant of the design being refused registration may inspect the

---

[43.] Rule 81.

[44.] Rule 82.

[45.] Rule 88.

[46.] Section 68(1); Rule 131.

[47.] Section 73; Rule 94.

prior design registration. Where an application for a design has been abandoned or refused, the application and any drawings, photographs, tracings, representations or specimens left in connection with the application, are not at any time open to public inspection or published by the Controller.[48]

[22.25] It is not possible for the public to directly carry out searches to establish the existence or otherwise of a registered design. This search must be carried out by the Controller upon application, paying the requisite official fee and identifying the design against which a search is required.[49]

EUROPEAN UNION DEVELOPMENTS

Introduction

[22.26] In June 1991, the EU Commission published a Green Paper on the Legal Protection of Industrial Designs[50] and subsequently in December 1993, published a draft Harmonisation Directive on the Legal Protection of Designs[51] and a proposed Regulation on the Community Design.[52] The Economic and Social Committee adopted a first opinion on 6 July 1994[53] and an additional opinion on 22 February 1995.[54] The European Parliament adopted its opinion on the Directive during its plenary session of 9-13 October 1995 and an amended proposal was sent to Council on 21 February 1996.[55]

[22.27] Similar to the position with the Trade Mark Harmonisation Directive, the purpose of the draft Design Harmonisation Directive is to approximate the substantive issues of design law throughout the European Union. These issues have been identified as the definition of a design, requirements for obtaining protection, scope and term of protection, grounds for refusal or invalidity, definition of rights conferred, including their limitation and, exhaustion of rights. There is currently a great disparity in design law throughout the EU. Greece has no specific design protection law. Design law in Germany and France protects against copying only, which contrasts with the position under Irish law where independent conception is no defence to infringement. The duration period varies considerably from 50 years in France, 25 years in the United Kingdom, 20 years in Germany and only 10 years in Spain. The draft Directive provides for cumulative protection between a registered design and

---

48. Section 79.
49. Section 74.
50. 111/F/5131/91-EN.
51. OJ No C345, 23 December 1993, Com (93) 344.
52. OJ No C29, 31 January 1994, Com (93) 342.
53. OJ No C388, 31 December 1994.
54. OJ No C110, 2 May 1995.
55. Com (96) 66.

copyright law[56] and consequently, the prohibition on such in s 172 of the 1927 Act will have to be removed. The extent and conditions under which copyright protection is conferred, including the degree of originality, is still a matter to be determined under national law. The Directive follows the main provisions of the Regulation on the basis that the content of national design protection law should as far as possible be the same as the content of the Regulation on a Community design.

[22.28] The objective of the Regulation is to create a system for obtaining a Community design to which uniform protection is given with uniform effect throughout the EU. The Regulation does not replace the national registration systems but it is envisaged that the attractiveness of a system which allows for community wide protection through one application made to one office with a single procedure, will greatly diminish the number of national registrations. The Office for Harmonisation in the Internal Market (OHIM) based in Alicante, Spain and which deals with applications under the Trade Mark Regulation will also do likewise in respect of designs. The right granted will be called a Registered Community Design conferring an exclusive right to use a design for a maximum term of 25 years. There will also be what is termed an Unregistered Community Design being a more limited right protected without any formalities and lasting three years from the date on which the design was first made available to the public.

Definitions of 'design' and 'product'

[22.29] There are definitions of both 'design' and 'product' in the Regulation. A design is defined in the Regulation to mean:

> the appearance of the whole or a part of a product resulting from the specific features of the lines, contours, colours, shape and/or materials of the product itself and/or its ornamentation.

The official commentary on the Regulation states that this definition is meant to indicate that any feature of appearance which can be perceived by the human senses as regards sight and tactility, are features of design. The commentary goes on to state that it is only some specific elements of which a design may consist which have been enumerated and the enumeration is not meant to be exhaustive. Weight and flexibility have been cited as examples of what may in some cases be design features. The definition requires no evaluation on whether a design feature is aesthetic or functional in nature and this distinction in Irish law will have to be removed. The definition in the Directive refers to the "outwardly visible appearance". Therefore, under the Directive, a design which

---

[56.] Article 18.

is protectable is one which gives an added value to the product so as to influence the choice of the consumer.

[22.30] A 'product' is defined in the Regulation to mean:

> any industrial or handicraft item, including parts intended to be assembled into a complex item, sets or compositions of items, packaging, get-ups, graphic symbols and typographic typefaces, but excluding a computer program or a semi-conductor product.

The exclusion of semi-conductor products does not exist in the Directive and therefore in keeping with the Directive on the Legal Protection Of Semi Conductor Products,[57] allows national design legislation to be the mode of implementation of its provisions. This is an option not taken up by the Irish legislature. The definition of product clarifies that a design may encompass both industrial and craft-made products. Unlike the Copyright (Amendment) Act 1987, the number of products manufactured will have no bearing on the protection available.

Exclusions from protection

[22.31] Certain designs will be excluded from protection. These are identified in Article 9 of the Regulation and Article 7 of the Directive. The first of these is a design "to the extent that the realisation of a technical function leaves no freedom as regards arbitrary features of appearance". While there is no distinction in the Regulation between aesthetic and functional designs, the rationale behind this particular provision is that in extremely rare cases, the form follows the function without any possibility of variation. In such cases, the designer cannot claim that the result is due to personal creativity and consequently, the design is viewed as having no individual character. It is envisaged that it would only be in exceptional cases that the whole design would be unprotectable and the exclusion relates only to that part of the design which lacks freedom as regards arbitrary elements of design. The draft Directive currently uses the words "features of appearance of a product which are solely dictated by its technical function" which is a concept that we are already used to under Irish law.[58] The Copyright (Amendment) Act 1987 goes further and excludes from protection both wholly and substantially, functional features of design.

[22.32] A second exclusion is:

> a design to the extent that it must necessarily be reproduced in its exact form and dimensions in order to permit the product in which the design is

---

57. 87/54/EEC - 16 December 1986.
58. *Allibert SA v O'Connor* [1981] FSR 613.

incorporated or to which it is applied to be mechanically assembled or connected with another product.[59]

This has been termed as the 'must fit' clause and an example which has been given is the dimensions of the fittings of an exhaust pipe which are dictated by the necessity of fitting the exhaust pipe to a specific car model and cannot constitute a protectable design element since the dimensions are dictated by those of the underside of the car. Despite this exclusion, a design right is still available for interconnections of modular products, possibly the most obvious example of which would be LEGO bricks but the Irish High Court also considered an example of such with the stackable and plastic fish boxes in the case of *Allibert SA v O'Connor.*[60]

[22.33] A third exclusion of a design right is a design, the exploitation or publication of which is contrary to public policy or to accepted principles of morality.[61]

Requirements for protection

[22.34] A design is protectable under both the draft Directive and Regulation 'to the extent that it is new and has an individual character'.[62] A design is considered as new if no identical design has been made available to the public prior to the date of application or priority claimed. Designs are deemed to be identical if their features differ only in immaterial details. Novelty is determined by reference to the position world-wide and accordingly a change in Irish law will be required. A design is deemed to have been available to the public if it has been published following registration or otherwise exhibited, used in trade or otherwise disclosed with an exception for disclosure to a third party under explicit or implicit conditions of confidentiality.

[22.35] A design is considered to have an individual character if the overall impression it produces on the informed user differs significantly from the overall impression produced on such user by a previously existing design. Under the draft Regulation, this existing design must be a design which has been commercialised in the market place or published following registration as a Community or national design of a Member State and in relation to which protection has not expired. The 'informed user' is not to be considered as an expert. It will usually be the end consumer but in some cases, the end consumer will be totally unaware of the appearance of the product, for example, if it is an internal part of a machine or a mechanical device replaced in the course of a

---

59. Directive Artilce 7; Regulation Article 9.
60. [1981] FSR 613.
61. *Masterman's Design* [1991] RPC 89.
62. Directive, Article 3 ; Regulation, Article 4.

repair. In such cases, the 'informed user' is the person replacing the part. In order to assess individual character, the draft Directive states that the degree of freedom of the designer in developing the design, shall be taken into consideration.

[22.36] Both the draft Regulation and Directive provide for what is termed a 'non-prejudicial disclosure'. This is a twelve month period prior to the date of filing of an application and during which a design can, for example, be tested in the market without breaching the novelty and individual character requirements. The disclosure must take place by the designer or their successor in title or where the disclosure is the result of an abuse in relation to the designer or their successor in title. The latter does not apply if the breach of confidence has led to a registration of a Community design or by a design right under the laws of a Member State by a person not entitled to seek such registration. In such circumstances the true owner of the design may seek a transfer of the registered right.

Ownership

[22.37] The ownership of a Community Design vests in the designer or his successor in title.[63] Where a design is developed by an employee in the execution of his duties or following instructions given by an employer, the Community Design right vests in the employer unless otherwise provided by contract.[64] A Community Design is assignable and can be held jointly. Commissioned designs are not addressed in the draft Regulation or Directive.

Rights conferred and term of protection

[22.38] When considering the rights conferred, it is necessary to differentiate between a registered design and an unregistered design.

[22.39] Infringement of an unregistered Community Design which is a creature of the Regulation, requires unauthorised copying of the design or use of a design resulting from such copying.[65] Consequently, there is no right of action against innocent infringers. This can be contrasted with a Registered Design Right which has an absolute monopoly[66] and does not require proof of copying against an infringer. It confers an exclusive right to use the design and includes protection against making, offering, putting on the market or use of a product in which the design is incorporated or to which it is applied, or from importing, exporting or stocking such a product for those purposes.

[63.] Article 14(1), Regulation.
[64.] Article 14(2).
[65.] Article 20, Regulation
[66.] Article 21, Regulation; Article 12, Directive.

[22.40] A design which has been protected as an unregistered Community design can be still protected as a registered Community design provided that an application for registration is made within one year from the date that the design was first made available to the public. The duration of an Unregistered Community Design is three years from first marketing of the design.[67] A Registered Design both Community and national, has a maximum term of twenty five years with renewal every five years.[68]

[22.41] Design rights do not extend to preclude:[69]

(a) acts done privately and for non-commercial purposes;

(b) acts done for experimental purposes;

(c) acts of reproduction for the purposes of making citations or of teaching, provided that such acts are compatible with fair trade practice and do not unduly prejudice the normal exploitation of the design, and that mention is made of the source; and

(d) equipment on ships and aircraft registered elsewhere and temporarily entering a Member State, and the importation of spare parts and accessories to repair such craft or the execution of repairs on such craft.

Repairs

[22.42] This is the most controversial aspect of the draft Regulation and Directive. There is a recognition that if a part is external and meant to be seen, then ideally an end consumer would wish the part to match the overall appearance of the complex product. Public policy will not allow a consumer who has bought a long lasting and perhaps expensive product such as, for example, a car, to be tied indefinitely to the manufacturer of the complex product when seeking external parts. Therefore, what is termed the 'must match' exemption arises.[70] This exemption provides that a registered design right cannot be exercised against third parties, who, after three years from the first marketing of a product incorporating the design or to which the design has been applied, use the design in compliance with three conditions, namely:

(a) the product incorporating the design or to which the design is applied, is a part of a complex product upon whose appearance the protected design is dependant;

[67.] Article 12, Regulation.
[68.] Articles 13 and 53, Regulation; Article, 10 Directive.
[69.] Article 22, Regulation; Article 13, Directive.
[70.] Article 23, Regulation; Article 14, Directive.

(b) the purpose of such a use is to permit the repair of the complex product so as to restore its original appearance; and

(c) the public is not misled as to the origin of the product used for repair.

[22.43] If competitors were only allowed to enter the market after the expiry of the design right, it is unlikely that they would wish to do so because it would no longer be commercially viable. Thus the legislation seeks to strike a balance between allowing a designer a reasonable opportunity to recoup research and development costs and at the same time, allowing the competition access to the market at a time when the investment in product can realistically be considered by the competition. The 'must match' exemption was devised specifically with the car industry in mind.

HAGUE AGREEMENT

[22.44] There is considerable support for a Regulation which allows for a single Registered Community Design which can be acheived through one application resulting in a single registration embracing all 15 countries of the EU. Similar to the position under the Community Trade Mark Regulation, an action brought before a Community Design Court which is a national Court or Tribunal designated by a Member State, may be enforceable throughout the EU. The only current streamlined system for the registration of designs is the Hague Agreement Concerning the International Deposit of Industrial Designs, 1925 which has 25 members. These do not include Ireland or the United Kingdom. States who are signatories include France, Germany, Spain, Italy and the Benelux countries. The Hague Agreement, which is quite similar in its procedure to the Madrid Agreement on Trade Marks, is a unified system for registering designs by deposit. Application is made centrally before the World Intellectual Property Organisation in Geneva and Member States have a set period of time within which to refuse registration otherwise registration is presumed. The Agreement works well in practice in Member States which operate a deposit system with no examination as to novelty. Attempts are being made to attract new members by concluding a revised Agreement, in particular to secure membership from the remaining EU Member States, the US and Japan. When the Community design protection system by way of the Regulation enters into force, it may become necessary to provide for a link between the Community design and the revised Hague Agreement similar to the Protocol relating to the Madrid Agreement concerning the International Registration of Marks establishing a link between the Community Trade Mark and the Madrid Agreement. The spare parts controversy, in particular, is making progress towards a Design Harmonisation Directive and Regulation, a slow and tortuous task and concern still remains over the novelty and individual character requirements which are higher than those currently in place in many EU countries.

Chapter 23

The Duty of Confidence

INTRODUCTION

[23.01] The duty to observe a confidence is an important element in the overall legal structure which recognises and protects intellectual property rights. Where such a duty exists it can overlap with certain copyright, patent and contractual remedies available to a rightholder, but in certain circumstances the law relating to confidence can take on a life of its own. For example, duties to observe express or implied terms in a contract or licence cannot bind third parties who are strangers to the contract unless some agency, fiduciary or trust relationship can be located. Further, because the law of copyright protects against unauthorised dealings in works which exist in a certain form, copyright cannot protect against the unauthorised use of information or an idea that exists in an unprotectable format (ie it has not been written down or drawn).[1] In these and other situations, the courts have developed the notion that a duty of confidence may exist, although as we shall see, this area of judge-made law is not without its uncertainties and contradictions, so much so that the English Law Commission, for example, have called for legislation to put the duty of confidence onto a statutory footing.[2] Academic commentators have also argued that some legislative measures would be useful in clarifying this somewhat arcane but policy-fraught area of intellectual property law.

[23.02] The modern law of confidence has evolved from a number of different sources, although it is generally recognised that the basic rationale behind both the cause of action and the available remedies are equitable in nature.

[23.03] It is the decision of the Lord Chancellor Lord Cottenham in *Prince Albert v Strange*[3] that represents the clearest early case in which the duty is recognised. Prince Albert and Queen Victoria arranged to have certain etched plates that they had created sent to Brown, a printer in Windsor so as to allow

---

[1.] *Fraser v Thames Television* [1983] 2 All ER 101. Note however that the inherent vagueness of the underlying idea may be held fatal to a confidence action: *De Maudsley v Palumbo* [1996] FSR 447; Phillips [1997] IPQ 135. Note the Irish courts refusal to rule that a patent application may waive a copyright claim: *House of Spring Gardens v Point Blank Ltd* [1984] IR 611.

[2.] Law Com No 110 *Breach of Confidence* (1981). See generally, Gurry, *Breach of Confidence* (1984) (OUP); Lavery, *Commercial Secrets* (Round Hall Sweet & Maxwell, 1996).

[3.] (1849) 1 Mac & G 25.

etchings to be made therefrom, the etchings to be kept for their own private amusement. Middleton, an employee of Brown, wrongfully kept copies for his own purposes and these copies came into the possession of Strange who arranged a catalogue intending to exhibit these works to allow the public "admire ... the eminent artistic talent of both" - a likely story! While these facts would clearly be seen today as involving a primary infringement of copyright in an unpublished work by Middleton, and an act of secondary infringement by Strange insofar as the unauthorised impressions made by Middleton, and the catalogue describing them, would be reproductions in a material form or adaptations of the plaintiff's works, Lord Cottenham granted injunctions restraining the circulation of the catalogues and the holding of the exhibition, because the defendants had dealt in the works in "breach of trust, confidence or contract". It is the notion that equitable remedies can be used to enjoin a threatened breach of contract, that marks this decision as an important one, although the fact that the Lord Chancellor identified the basis of the duty as resting upon a property right in the etching plates can be seen as a limiting circumstance. In the Irish case of *Turner v Robinson*[4] the defendant paid sixpence in order to view the painting, "the Death of Chatterton" by Wallis, exhibited by the plaintiff in order to raise demand for copies in the form of engravings. The defendant thereafter arranged a group of persons so as to reproduce the scene in the picture in order to photograph it, thereby undercutting any market for the engraving. An action to restrain the defendant from selling photographs or slides was taken in the Irish Courts of Chancery. The plaintiff's claim, resting upon the common law because statute at that time did not protect paintings, was described by Brady LC as resting upon the author's rights of ownership in personal property and he described the decision in *Prince Albert v Strange* as proceeding upon the principle that there is:

> "this peculiar property in such works of art as drawing and etchings remained in the authors, so long as they kept them for their own private use, or allowed them to be copied under any restrictions".[5]

[23.04] In fact the plaintiff had warned that attempts at reproduction by others would be met by legal proceedings, thus making it clear that the owner's right of property would be insisted upon. The Court of Appeal in Chancery thus affirmed the decision of the Master of the Rolls to grant an injunction restraining further publication.

[23.05] While the actual decision in *Turner v Robinson* is narrower in scope than *Prince Albert v Strange* insofar as principles of common law, copyright and

---

4. (1860) 10 Ir Ch R 121, 510.
5. *Ibid* at 514.

even implied contract are discernible, these two decisions demonstrate great judicial willingness to fill in gaps when other statutory reliefs are of perhaps doubtful utility.

[23.06] Some of the earlier cases that had been relied upon in *Prince Albert v Strange*, however, do not seem to rest on either implied contract or property rights, perhaps the most graphic being Lord Eldon's *dicta* that if one of George III's physicians had kept a diary of what he heard and saw, the Courts of Chancery would not have permitted publication during the King's lifetime.[6] Such conduct would clearly be professionally unethical, possibly even if publication took place after the Monarch's death, but this example serves to point up the privacy or confidentiality based aspects of the jurisdiction, based on notions of duty or trust. In *Morison v Moat*[7] the plaintiff's partner communicated verbally the details of a secret recipe for an unpatented medicine to the defendant in breach of a contractual duty of confidentiality. It was observed that the communication here took place in breach of faith and could thus be the subject of an injunction restraining use of this secret recipe. It is clear, however, that the property theory and the implied contract theory cannot adequately explain the diverse range of circumstances in which the equitable jurisdiction operates, and it is accepted that it is the judgment that the defendant stood in a confidential relationship with the plaintiffs, or one of them, that is the basis of the equitable duty of confidence.[8] As we shall see, the modern cases throw up a diverse range of relationships and circumstances within which the equitable duty will arise.

CONTEMPORARY JUDICIAL VIEWS ON THE DUTY OF CONFIDENCE

[23.07] In *Attorney General v Guardian Newspapers Ltd and Others (No 2)*[9] Lord Griffiths had this to say about the law of confidence:

> "It is judge-made law and reflects the willingness of the judges to give a remedy to protect people from being taken advantage of by those they have trusted with confidential information."[10]

[23.08] Lord Goff of Chieveley, without purporting to provide an exhaustive study of the subject, stated the following broad principle:

> "a duty of confidence arises when confidential information comes to the knowledge of a person (the confidant) in circumstances where he has notice, or

---

6. In *Wyatt v Wilson* (1820) cited in *Prince Albert v Strange* (1849) 1 Mac & G 25, 46.
7. (1851) 9 Hare 241.
8. See *EI du Pont de Nemours Powder Co v Masland* 244 US 100, 102 (1917) *per* Holmes J.
9. [1988] 3 All ER 545.
10. *Ibid* at p 648.

is held to have agreed, that the information is confidential, with the effect that it would be just in all the circumstances that he should be precluded from disclosing the information to others. I have used the word 'notice' advisedly, in order to avoid the (here unnecessary) question of the extent to which actual knowledge is necessary, though I of course understand knowledge to include circumstances where the confidant has deliberately closed his eyes to the obvious. The existence of this broad general principle reflects the fact that there is such a public interest in the maintenance of confidences, that the law will provide remedies for their protection.

I realise that, in the vast majority of cases, in particular those concerned with trade secrets, the duty of confidence will arise from a transaction or relationship between the parties, often a contract, in which event the duty may arise by reason of either an express or an implied term of that contract. It is in such cases as these that the expressions 'confider' and 'confidant' are perhaps most aptly employed. But it is well-settled that a duty of confidence may arise in equity independently of such cases; and I have expressed the circumstances in which the duty arises in broad terms, not merely to embrace those cases where a third party receives information from a person who is under a duty of confidence in respect of it, knowing that it has been disclosed by that person to him in breach of his duty of confidence, but also to include certain situations, beloved of law teachers, where an obviously confidential document is wafted by an electric fan out of a window into a crowded street, or when an obviously confidential document, such as a private diary, is dropped in a public place, and is then picked up by a passer-by. I also have in mind the situations where secrets of importance to national security come into the possession of members of the public, a point to which I shall refer in a moment."[11]

[23.09] To be sure, this decision of the House of Lords raised specific problems on the scope of the law of confidence that involve significant issues of constitutional law and public policy that have not yet been broadly addressed in Ireland. The basis of the duty of confidence has, however, been considered by the High Court and the Supreme Court in *House of Spring Gardens Ltd v Point Blank Ltd*.[12] In that case the plaintiffs sought damages for breach of contract, infringement of copyright and breach of confidence by the defendants who had variously used confidential information acquired during the process of developing a bullet-proof vest as part of a venture involving the plaintiffs, who held various rights, including copyrights in drawings as artistic works, in the products in question. In his examination of the claim relating to the misuse of confidential information Costello J in the High Court examined the leading English cases and summarised the law as resting upon a moral obligation.[13]

[11.] *Ibid* at p 658-9.
[12.] [1984] IR 611.
[13.] *Ibid* at 663-664.

While the Supreme Court endorsed Costello J's assessment of the law relating to misuse of confidential information, McCarthy J, in his judgment observed, somewhat elliptically, that "the obligation of secrecy, whilst enforced by equitable principles, depends more upon commercial necessity than moral duty".

[23.10] The significance of this observation will become evident when we come to consider the 'springboard' doctrine below.

THE LAW OF CONFIDENCE AND BROAD DUTIES OF SECRECY

[23.11] While the duty of confidence was a stable and recognised equitable principle by the end of the last century,[14] most explanations for the concept at this time adopt an implied contract theory even though other judges present breach of trust, or breach of the general duty as either an alternative or the true judicial basis[15] for relief in equity. Once we disentangle contract, copyright and other related phrases such as non-derogation of grant[16] from the range of possible explanations for judicial activism we can see that the moral, commercial, and public and private interest considerations that shape this cause of action are indeed complex.

[23.12] In *Attorney General v Guardian Newspapers Ltd and Others (No 2)*[17] the House of Lords indicated that while in most instances the plaintiff obtains relief because breach of the duty will result in financial detriment to the confider, there are instances where the duty will arise in cases where the right to personal privacy will be of legitimate concern for the courts, indeed Lord Keith indicated that "the right to personal privacy is clearly one which the law should in this field seek to protect."[18] Indeed, the signs are that this area of equitable duty is being used in the English courts, and to a lesser extent in Ireland, to make up for the absence of overt constitutional or statutory provisions governing the privacy of individuals. In these instances the individual can invoke equitable relief not because the statement or information is untrue and harmful (as in defamation) but because the information is probably true and harmful and is to be disclosed against the wishes of the person who confided it to others.

---

14. *Tipping v Clark* (1843) 2 Hare 383; *Merryweather v Moore* [1892] 2 Ch 518; *Robb v Green* [1895] 2 QB 315.
15. Eg *Tuck & Sons v Priester* (1887) 19 QBD 629; *Pollard v Photographic Co* (1880) 40 Ch D 345; *Exchange Telegraph Co v Gregory* [1896] 1 QB 147; *Exchange Telegraph Co v Central News Ltd* [1897] 2 Ch 48.
16. *Trego v Hunt* [1896] AC 7; *Gargan v Ruttle* [1931] IR 152.
17. [1988] 3 All ER 545.
18. *Ibid*, at 639.

[23.13] In the context of communications between a husband and wife it has been held that the law of confidence may prevent one of the partners from disclosing these communications as part of the relationship of trust that exists as between them, even if the proposed disclosure is to take place within the context of an acrimonious divorce case.[19] This principle was reshaped and extended further in *Stevens v Avery*[20] where Browne-Wilkinson VC refused to strike out an action in which the plaintiff invoked the law of confidence against a close friend who had passed on to a Sunday tabloid newspaper confidential information concerning the plaintiff's lesbian relationship with the victim of an unlawful killing which resulted in a much publicised trial in which the victim's husband was convicted of manslaughter. Browne-Wilkinson VC rejected a submission that the law of confidence would not protect information about sexual proclivities, save where married partners are involved and the learned judge observed that information about a person's sex life is "high on their list of those matters which they regard as confidential".[21] However, the absence of any general right of privacy in English law has led some courts to deny a plaintiff any remedy on the ground that a duty of confidence cannot arise as between a person seeking to make a private communication, on the one hand, and the communications organisation or individuals generally, on the other hand.[22]

[23.14] In *Kaye v Robertson*[23] the Court of Appeal was also unable to provide a remedy against intrusive press coverage of the celebrity plaintiff's struggle for life following a horrific road accident, even though all members of the Court of Appeal noted the need for parliamentary legislation to address this shortcoming in English law.

[23.15] In *Kaye v Robertson* the defendant and the plaintiff had no prior contractual or other link that could raise the prospect of some kind of implied duty or contract. If, however, there is some duty or obligation imposed upon an individual to provide information to some other person or agency, recent English cases signal the possibility of broader duty of confidence which is rooted in the privacy interests of the confider. This has been acknowledged in

---

19. *Duchess of Argyll v Duke of Argyll* [1967] Ch 302.
20. [1988] 2 All ER 477.
21. *Ibid*, at 481. Note also the possibility of persons who have been involved in criminal behaviour which gives a prospect of anonymity when such persons are released - so called Mary Bell Orders - by preventing press coverage of that person's life and whereabouts and the criterion in the case of Flora Keays: *The Observer* 18 January 1996.
22. *Malone v Commissioner of Police for the Metropolis* [1979] 2 All ER 620. In *Malone v UK* (1984) 7 EHRR 14, the European Court of Human Rights found the United Kingdom to be in breach of Article 8 of the European Convention on Human Rights. This led to the Interception of Communications Act 1985. In Ireland, see the Interception of Postal Packets and Telecommunications Messages (Regulation) Act 1993.
23. [1991] FSR 62; see also *Mrs R v Independent Television* [1994] 3 WLR 20.

relation to documents disclosed under some court order or discovery procedure.[24] In *Hellewell v Chief Constable of Derbyshire*[25] the duty of confidence was held to apply to the police who fingerprinted and photographed the plaintiff in connection with theft offences for which he was later convicted. The police later released the photographs to traders who were concerned to identify persons who may have been involved in a spate of shoplifting and harassment of shopkeepers in the Nottingham area. Laws J held that a duty of confidence could exist, after the *Spycatcher* litigation, simply out of a relationship between the parties without a need for express notice. The police were thus under a duty, which in this instance required them to make reasonable use of such information as they possessed. Laws J concluded, however, that there were sufficient surrounding circumstances to justify the limited disclosure that had taken place.

[23.16] The most highly publicised recent advance in relation to the duty of confidence has occurred in England and in other common law jurisdictions, including Ireland, when the State, in the form of State Security Agencies, has tried to restrain former operatives from profiting from memoirs which may compromise the interests of national security. In *Attorney General v Guardian Newspapers Ltd and Others (No 2)*[26] the House of Lords indicated that a member of MI5, Peter Wright, owed a life-long, world-wide duty of confidence to the Crown which he had breached by publishing his book '*Spycatcher*' initially in the United States of America, an act which Lord Jauncey described as one that 'reeked of turpitude'. Their Lordships had to consider the extent to which newspapers that had either reported or reviewed the book or overseas proceedings intended to restrain overseas publication, or serialise the work, could be restrained by injunction in the English courts. In affirming the decision of the Court of Appeal, their Lordships endorsed a number of earlier cases in which civil servants[27] and cabinet Ministers[28] who sought to put confidential information into the public domain by publication with a third party were caught by the equitable duty but that publication could be permitted unless the State can show that publication would be harmful to the public interest. It may be that a privacy interest and another legitimate interest, such as the desire to ensure the efficient and dignified administration of justice, may combine to counterbalance the broader public interest in freedom of the press.[29]

[24.] *Marcel v Commissioner of Police of the Metropolis* [1992] 1 All ER 72.

[25.] [1995] 4 All ER 473. See Fenwick and Phillipson (1996) CLJ 447; Wee Loon [1996] EIPR 307.

[26.] [1988] 3 All ER 545.

[27.] *Commonwealth of Australia v John Fairfax & Sons Ltd* (1980) 32 ALR 485.

[28.] *Attorney General v Jonathan Cape Ltd* [1975] 3 All ER 484.

[29.] *Wiggington v Brisbane TV Ltd* (1992) 25 IPR 58.

[23.17] One of the significant features of the *Spycatcher* litigation concerned the extent to which one State would uphold a duty of confidence owed not to its own State but to those of a friendly democratic State.[30] In Australia, the High Court held that an Australian court should decline to accept jurisdiction to enforce a duty of confidence owed to a foreign government. The New Zealand decision in *AG v Wellington Newspapers Ltd*[31] suggested that jurisdiction would be taken but no real public interest to justify the award of an injunction was evident. In Ireland the approach taken by Carroll J in *AG for England and Wales v Brandon Books*[32] is broadly in sympathy with the view that Irish constitutional requirements outweigh the secrecy interests of foreign powers for here the High Court refused to grant an injunction to restrain the defendant from publishing *One Woman's War*, the memoirs of a British security operative during the Second World War. Carroll J observed of the duty of secrecy visited on Crown employees in the context of Irish law:

> "The publication which is sought to be prevented here is not a private confidence or trade information but information shared between a government and a private individual. It seems to me that a distinction can and should be drawn between a government and a private person. This was considered in the Australian case *Commonwealth of Australia v John Fairfax & Sons Ltd*[33] Mason J says as follows:
>
>> 'The equitable principle has been fashioned to protect the personal, private and proprietary rights of the citizen, not to protect the very different interests of the executive government. It acts, or is supposed to act, not according to standards of private interest, but in the public interest. This is not to say that equity will not protect information in the hands of the government, but it is to say that when equity protects government information it will look at the matter through different spectacles.
>>
>> It may be a sufficient detriment to the citizen that disclosure of information relating to his affairs will expose his actions to public discussion and criticism. But it can scarcely be a relevant detriment to the government that publication of material concerning its actions will merely expose it to public discussion and criticism. It is unacceptable in our democratic society that there should be a restraint on the publication of information relating to government when the only vice of that information is that it enables the public to discuss, review and criticise government action.

---

30. *AG (UK) v Heinemann Publishers Australia Property* (1988) 78 ALR 449.
31. High Court, unrep, 28 April 1988.
32. [1987] ILRM 135.
33. (1980) 147 CLR 39.

Accordingly, the Court will determine the government's claim to confidentiality by reference to the public interest. Unless disclosure is likely to injure the public interest, it will not be protected.'(at p 51)

I consider that correctly states the law. Mason J was talking there in the context of the Government of Australia asking the courts of Australia to restrain publication where the question of public interest did arise and which would arise here if the Government of Ireland were the plaintiff. But here the plaintiff is the representative of a foreign government. There is no question of the public interest of this State being affected. The considerations which would move the courts in the United Kingdom in this matter are different to the considerations here."[34]

[23.18] Whether Irish law will develop along the same lines as the more recent English decisions *vis-à-vis* the privacy interest is perhaps in doubt because Irish constitutional law recognises a number of personal rights such as the right of a citizen to a good name[35] and the right to a livelihood[36] as well as the right to protect property.[37] These rights must be balanced and are not such as to require the State to provide absolute guarantees to citizens, so many of the factors that are relevant in a confidence action are broadly relevant to judicial activism under these constitutional parameters. While caselaw on Articles 40.3.2° and 43 are somewhat inconclusive on many points of detail concerning these express constitutional rights, the courts have identified an unenumerated personal right to privacy in Article 40.3. While the decisions on this initially addressed privacy within the context of marital and sexual privacy,[38] the decision in *Kennedy and Arnold v Ireland*[39] involved a case where Ministerial authorisation of wiretapping which failed to meet a number of internal administrative guidelines was conceded to be unlawful by the State. However, Hamilton P went further in finding the State had infringed the citizens' right to privacy and damages were awarded to the plaintiffs. Hamilton P indicated that the right is not absolute and is subject to the requirements of public order and morality. On the facts of this case there was no real attempt to argue that the State security interest would take priority over the citizens' privacy right. *Kennedy and Arnold* however highlights a different solution to the privacy plea so unsuccessful in the High Court decision in England in *Malone v Commissioner of Police for the Metropolis*,[40] at least on the issue of the possibility of a plea of invasion of privacy as a specific

---

34. [1987] ILRM 135, at 136-137
35. Article 40.3.2° eg *In Re Haughey* [1972] IR 217.
36. Article 40.3.2° eg *Lovett Transport v Gogan* [1995] 2 ILRM 12.
37. Article 40.3.2° and Article 43.
38. *McGee v Attorney General* [1974] IR 284; *Norris v Attorney General* [1984] IR 36.
39. [1987] IR 587.
40. [1979] 2 All ER 620.

cause of action.[41] In *X v Drury*[42] interlocutory injunctions were sought by a young woman who had been the complainant in a sexual abuse case. She had given interviews to members of the press, including the defendant and sought to prevent publication on the grounds, *inter alia*, that the journalists had not respected her constitutional right to privacy. Costello J expressly distinguished English case-law on privacy, pointing out that constitutionally protected rights to privacy were at issue in the instant proceedings. While referring to the contrasting interests of freedom of the press and the right of journalists to communicate and carry out their professional duties, the balance of convenience lay in protecting the privacy rights of the plaintiff *vis-à-vis* her family life. It should be noted that this case goes further than *Stevens v Avery*[43] insofar as the decision of Browne-Wilkinson VC was simply that the confider's action to protect her confidence was not to be struck out. In *X v Drury* the court was more pro-active in granting a broad measure of interlocutory relief. However *X v Drury* is not the last word on this point for in *MM v Drury*[44] O'Hanlon J limited the concept of marital privacy by holding that such rights could not prevent an estranged husband from giving to the press details about his wife's sexual affair with a Roman Catholic priest: here the balancing process was held to favour the freedom of the press and the approach of O'Hanlon J in *MM v Drury* appears to be in sharp contrast to the English decision of *Duchess of Argyll v Duke of Argyll*.[45] This balancing exercise is also evident in *Oblique Financial Services v The Promise Production Co*[46] when the publishers and editor of *The Phoenix* magazine were the subject of interlocutory proceedings brought to prevent the firm publishing confidential information which was the subject of an express contractual provision between the plaintiffs and the defendant's sources. Keane J held that the constitutional rights of citizens to convey information arose under Article 40.3.1° and that this right could be subject to other rights and duties, particularly the right to confidentiality. The injunction was granted. This balancing exercise will not always come out in favour of a confidentiality clause being upheld because countervailing constitutional principles, to say nothing of the restraint of trade doctrine, may be invoked to tilt the balance the other way.

[41.] The decision in *Malone v UK* (1984) 7 EHRR 14 however made it necessary for Irish administrative practices on telephone tapping to be put on a statutory footing through the interception.

[42.] High Court, unrep, 19 May 1994.

[43.] [1988] 2 All ER 477.

[44.] [1994] 2 IR 8.

[45.] [1967] Ch 302.

[46.] [1994] ILRM 74.

THE DUTY OF CONFIDENCE IN A COMMERCIAL CONTEXT

[23.19] While the discussion in the preceding paragraphs suggest an enhanced role for the law of confidence, it should be noted that most of the modern cases have addressed the duty within the context of commercially valuable information, a context which does not readily raise privacy or other human rights issues. The decision of the Court of Appeal in *Saltman Engineering Ltd v Campbell Engineering Co Ltd*,[47] decided in 1948, represents the most significant reformation of the equitable duty for later cases, particularly in the extremely active period between 1963 and 1969, defer to this case as the most influential summary of the law in such a context. The plaintiffs provided the defendants with access to design drawings needed by the defendants in furtherance of a contract whereby the defendants would manufacture machine tools on behalf of the plaintiffs. The defendants used the drawings for their own purposes and were the subject of proceedings for breach of contract and breach of confidence. Lord Greene MR characterised the rights of action as existing without the necessity of there being a contractual relationship and he approved, as the basic principle, that where:

> "a defendant is proved to have used confidential information, directly or indirectly obtained from a plaintiff, without the consent, express or implied, of the plaintiff, he will be guilty of an infringement of the plaintiff's rights."[48]

[23.20] Lord Denning MR in *Seager v Copydex Ltd*[49] followed the judgment of Lord Greene MR in *Saltman Engineering* and observed that:

> "The law on this subject does not depend on any implied contract. It depends on the broad principle of equity that he who has received information in confidence shall not take unfair advantage of it. He must not make use of it to the prejudice of him who gave it without obtaining his consent."[50]

[23.21] However, in an Irish context, the decision of Megarry J in *Coco v AN Clark (Engineers) Ltd*[51] and the decision of the same judge in *Thomas Marshall (Exports) Ltd v Guinle*[52] provide the basis for formulating the leading judicial statement on what must be provided to sustain a breach of confidence action.

[23.22] In *House of Spring Gardens v Point Blank Ltd*[53] Costello J said:

[47.] 65 RPC 203. The case was decided in 1948 but more widely reported at [1963] 3 All ER 413.

[48.] 65 RPC 203, at 211, cited with approval by O'Higgins CJ in *House of Spring Gardens v Point Blank Ltd*.

[49.] [1967] 1 WLR 923.

[50.] *Ibid* at p 931, cited with approval by Griffin J in *House of Spring Gardens v Point Blank Ltd*.

[51.] [1968] FSR 415.

[52.] [1978] 3 All ER 193.

[53.] [1984] IR 611.

"The court, it should be borne in mind, is being asked to enforce what is essentially a moral obligation. It must firstly decide whether there exists from the relationship between the parties an obligation of confidence regarding the information which has been imparted and it must then decide whether the information which was communicated can properly be regarded as confidential information. In considering both (i) the relationship and (ii) the nature of the information, it is relevant to take into account the degree of skill, time and labour involved in compiling the information. As to (i), if the informant himself has expended skill, time and labour on compiling the information, then he can reasonably regard it as of value and he can reasonably consider that he is conferring on its recipient a benefit. If this benefit is conferred for a specific purpose then an obligation may be imposed to use it for that purpose and for no other purpose. As to (ii), if the information has been compiled by the expenditure of skill, time and labour by the informant then, although he has obtained it from sources which are public, (in the sense that any member of the public with the same skills could obtain it had he acted like the compiler of the information) the information may still, because of its value, be regarded as 'confidential' information and subject to an obligation of confidence. Furthermore, the court will readily decide that the informant correctly regarded the information he was imparting as confidential information if, although based on material which is accessible to the public, it is of a unique nature which has resulted from the skill and labour of the informant. Once it is established that an obligation in confidence exists and that the information is confidential, then the person to whom it is given has a duty to act in good faith, and this means that he must use the information for the purpose for which it has been imparted, and he cannot use it to the detriment of the informant."[54]

[23.23] This approach must be regarded as the definitive Irish statement on the general judicial approach to breach of confidence actions for in the Supreme Court O'Higgins CJ specifically endorsed this part of Costello J's judgment while Griffin J concurred with the Chief Justice on the basic approach to be adopted, confining himself to issues of assessment and quantum. It is to the specific issues that Costello J's judgment addresses that we must now turn.

(1) The relationship between the parties - does it create an obligation of confidence *vis-à-vis* the information imparted?

The contract

[23.24] The most obvious relationship in which the duty may arise is a contractual relationship. Clearly if the parties have a contractual relationship which raises a number of positive obligations, breach of those obligations, express or implied, will be actionable contractually and under the duty of

---

[54.] *Ibid* at 663.

confidence. Thus, giving design drawings,[55] preparatory material like moulds[56] or plates[57] for the use of others imports express/implied duties of confidence. Specific contractual relationships, however, create a range of circumstances in which there may or may not be commensurate duties of confidence. In the arena of employment contracts, for example, an employee owes a duty of fidelity to the employer and while the major features of this duty depend upon the existence of the contractual relationship, there are certain duties that survive the termination of the employment relationship and it is also possible of course, for the scope of these duties to be broadened, both in scope and duration, by express agreement. Thus, the employee, during the currency of the contract, is not to use his master's own time and facilities to further his own interests by making use of information[58] soliciting customers of the master[59] even if the employee intends to do business with those persons after the termination of the contract. Nor is the employee to compete with the master during the currency of the employment contract or aid a competitor by 'moonlighting' outside of contracted hours.[60] The duty is based upon the relationship of trust and confidence that is a consequence of the contract. However, the ability of the employer to rely upon this implied duty to protect information from post-termination use by an employee is now circumscribed by the decision of the Court of Appeal in *Faccenda Chicken Ltd v Fowler*,[61] a case which tilts the balance in favour of allowing information, which is not seen as a trade secret but rather part of the general mode of doing business, to be used by competitors when an employment contract is at an end.

[23.25] The Court of Appeal limited the scope of the implied contractual term against disclosure of commercially valuable information to two instances:

> "[i] While the employee remains in the employment of the employer the obligations are included in the implied term which imposes a duty of good faith or fidelity on the employee. For the purpose of the present appeal it is not necessary to consider the precise limits of this implied term, but it may be noted: (a) that the extent of the duty of good faith will vary according to the nature of the contract (see *Vokes Ltd v Heather*); (b) that the duty of good faith will be broken if an employee makes or copies a list of the customers of the

---

55. Eg *Tuck & Sons v Priester* (1887) 19 QBD 629.
56. *Ackroyds (London) Ltd v Islington Plastics Ltd* [1962] RPC 97.
57. *Prince Albert v Strange* (1849) 1 Mac & G 25; *Bancode Portoga v Waterlow* (1933) 47 TLR 214.
58. *Robb v Green* [1895] 2 QB 1; *AF Associates v Ralston* [1973] NI 229; *Universal Thermosensors Ltd v Hibben* [1992] FSR 361.
59. *Robb v Green* [1895] 2 QB 1; *Wessex Dairies v Smith* [1935] 2 KB 80.
60. *Hivac Ltd v Park Royal Scientific Instruments* [1946] Ch 169.
61. [1986] 1 All ER 617. Purvis and Turner [1988] EIPR 3; Hull [1989] EIPR 319; Stewart [1989] EIPR 88 cites *Faccenda* and its use in other jurisdictions.

employer for use after his employment ends or deliberately memorises such a list, even though, except in special circumstances, there is no general restriction on an ex-employee canvassing or doing business with customers of his former employer (see *Robb v Green* [1895] 2 QB 31; [1895-9] All ER Rep 1053 and *Wessex Diaries Ltd v Smith* [1935] All ER Rep 75).

[ii] The implied term which imposes an obligation on the employee as to his conduct after the determination of employment is more restricted in its scope than that which imposes a general duty of good faith. It is clear that the obligation not to use or disclose information may cover secret processes of manufacture such as chemical formulae (see *Amber Size and Chemical Co Ltd v Menzel* [1913] 2 Ch 239), or designs or special methods of construction (see *Reid Sigrist Ltd v Moss Mechanism Ltd* (1932) 49 RPC 461), and other information which is of a sufficiently high degree of confidentiality as to amount to a trade secret. The obligation does not extend, however, to cover all information which is given to or acquired by the employee while in his employment, and in particular may not cover information which is only 'confidential' in the sense that an unauthorised disclosure of such information to a third party which the employment subsisted would be a clear breach of the duty of good faith".[62]

[23.26] This decision is a controversial one, and it has not been followed by later judges in all respects.[63] However, the implied term, as a judicially constructed device, does possess the merits of flexibility and responsiveness. The nature of the term, the duration of the term, and the boundary between compliance and breach, can be set on a case by case basis.[64] The most important instances of unauthorised appropriation of information in the context of breaches of implied terms have involved the unauthorised dissemination of information by subscribers to an information service. Third party disclosure which prejudiced the interests of the service provider was held to constitute a flagrant breach of an implied contract. These decisions,[65] while nearly a century old, will prove very pertinent in the age of electronic database subscription services.

[23.27] Whether the scope of the duty will be universal in the sense that all employees will be caught by it to the same degree is unlikely. Clearly an employee who comes into contact with trade secrets, confidential information and the like will be caught by the duty, but where the employee is menial[66] as distinct from being a director or managing director[67] there may be no obvious

---

62. *Per* O'Neill LJ at p 625.
63. *Systems Reliability Holdings plc v Smith* [1990] IRLR 377.
64. *Liverpool City Council v Irwin* [1977] AC 239.
65. Eg *Exchange Telegraph v Gregory* [1896] 1 QB 147; *Exchange Telegraph v Central News* [1897] 2 Ch 48.
66. *Nova Plastics v Froggatt* [1982] IRLR 146.
67. *Roger Bullivant Ltd v Ellis* [1987] FSR 172. *Balston Ltd v Headline Filters Ltd* [1990] FSR 385; *Marshall v Industrial Systems and Control Ltd* [1992] IRLR 294.

commercial interest worthy of protection. Certain employees are not to be the subject of intimidatory injunctive proceedings where they simply propose to compete, even if some preparatory acts take place during the currency of the employment contract.[68] Although some cases seem to be unduly favourable to employers, insofar as injunctions have been awarded when little or no legitimate interest was disclosed in the proceedings,[69] the courts are generally vigilant to permit former employees to compete whenever possible *pace Faccenda Chicken*, even if the employee has expressly agreed not to compete after leaving employment. The general view is that the employer may, by express contract, obtain additional protection from misuse of information by a former employee and attention has been drawn to the fact that *Faccenda Chicken* was based upon the implied duty of confidentiality only. Express restraints which specifically seek to either prevent former employees from using both trade secrets and know-how, or which attempt to prevent former employees from using that information or skill by way of blanket non-competition clauses are subject to the restraint of trade doctrine but they remain valid[70] and indeed are encouraged by the judges because clauses of this kind are subject to the reasonableness tests within the restraint of trade doctrine.[71] However, the success of such clauses requires precise and very skilful drafting if they are to either broaden the implied duty or survive the restraint of trade clause. In both *Ixora Trading Inc v Jones*[72] and *Triangle Corp v Carnsew*[73] the express clauses forbidding disclosure were held not to add to the *Faccenda* duty. *Ixora* goes further by showing that, save in trade secrets or soliciting cases or cases where the non-competition clause can be justified in context, express clauses are not likely to be very effective,[74] thus making the implied duty of great importance.[75]

[23.28] Other contractual relationships that have produced duties of confidence involve agents and subcontractors,[76] and banker-customer.[77] The law relating to fiduciaries is also invoked although the recent expansion of confidence makes this less necessary.[78]

---

[68]. *Ixora Trading Inc v Jones* [1990] FSR 251.
[69]. Compare *Hivac Ltd v Park Royal Scientific Instruments Ltd* [1946] Ch 169 with *Laughton v Bapp Industrial Supplies Ltd* [1986] ICR 634.
[70]. See *Printers and Finishers Ltd v Holloway* [1964] 3 All ER 731, at 736.
[71]. *Balston Ltd v Headline Filters Ltd* [1987] FSR 330, at 351-2.
[72]. [1990] FSR 251.
[73]. (1994) 29 IPR 69.
[74]. Eg *John Orr Ltd and Vescom BV v John Orr* [1987] ILRM 702.
[75]. See Stewart [1989] EIPR 88.
[76]. Eg *Fortuity Property Ltd v Barcza* (1995) 32 IPR 517.
[77]. *Tournier v National Provincial and Union Bank of England* [1924] 1 KB 461.
[78]. For a recent case involving sales agents and the interaction of these various heads of action, see *Ecrosteel Pty Ltd v Perfor Printing Pty* (1996) 37 IPR 22.

Proposed Joint Ventures

[23.29] The fact that information has been disclosed as part of a negotiating process that does not result in the formation of a contract between the parties is not an impediment to the application of the duty of confidentiality.[79] In *Coco v AN Clark*[80] the plaintiff designed a moped engine, disclosing details of its operation to the defendants, including a prototype of the engine. No agreement was reached about development of the engine and the defendants proposed to make their own moped engine to a different design. The plaintiff complained that the defendant was using confidential information for the defendant's own purpose without the consent of the plaintiff. Megarry J imported the duty of confidence as an equitable obligation because in his view the "circumstances of the disclosure in this case seem to me to be redolent of trust and confidence".[81] The strength of the duty here is that the confider is able to utilise the duty even if the information disclosed does not exist in some other protectable form. In *Fraser v Thames Television Ltd*[82] the plaintiffs provided a script writer and television company with the idea for a television comedy drama series upon condition that the plaintiffs had the right to appear in and contribute music towards the programme. The defendants ultimately used the ideas to create a successful television series but did not use the plaintiffs, arguing that the mere idea was not copyrightable and could not be the subject of a duty of confidence because of its tentative character. The defendants were nevertheless held liable for the idea was sufficiently developed and original even though it was not copyright protected.

Involuntary Relationships

[23.30] Where the relationship exists by force of circumstance, as in cases where information is obtained on the foot of a court order, eg discovery,[83] or under the exercise of police search powers[84] or powers of arrest and inquiry.[85] In *Hellewell*[86] Laws J observed that the police, when photographing suspects during investigations into criminality, were not free to do whatever they thought proper with that photograph:

[79.] *Saltman Engineering Ltd v Campbell Engineering Co Ltd* (1948) 65 RPC 203.

[80.] [1968] FSR 415.

[81.] *Ibid* at 424.

[82.] [1983] 2 All ER 101.

[83.] *Distillers Co (Biochemicals) Ltd v Times Newspapers Ltd* [1975] Q 613; *Riddick v Thames Board Mills Ltd* [1977] QB 881.

[84.] *Marcel v Commissioner for Police for the Metropolis* [1992] 1 All ER 72.

[85.] *Wiggington v Brisbane TV Ltd* (1992) 25 IPR 58; *Hellewell v Chief Constable of Derbyshire* [1995] 4 All ER 473.

[86.] *Ibid.*

"The circumstances in which the photograph is taken when the suspect has no choice save to insist that physical force be not used upon him, impose obligations on the police, breach of which may sound in an action at private law ... they [the police] may make reasonable use of it for the purpose of the prevention and detection of crime, the investigation of alleged offences and the apprehension of suspects or persons unlawfully at large ... they must have these and only these purposes in mind and must, as I have said, make no more than reasonable use of the picture in seeking to accomplish them."[87]

Bona Fide Third Party Defendants

[23.31] Can a defendant avoid the application of the duty of confidence on the ground that the defendant unwittingly came into possession of confidential material, having paid full value for this information? In *Stevenson Jordan & Harrison Ltd v MacDonald and Evans*,[88] the trial judge declined to accept the validity of such a plea. It is arguable that where a defendant does not actually know of the breach of confidence by another, or is in breach of duty negligently, without owing a contractual duty to the confider, there are few grounds upon which to visit a duty of conscience upon that defendant.[89] Lord Denning MR in *Fraser v Evans*[90] indicated that the duty can attach to the innocent recipient of information once that person gets to know that the information was originally given in confidence. We will return to the issue of the 'innocent infringement' in the next chapter.

(2) The requirement that the information must be secret - not in the public domain

[23.32] In *Attorney General v Guardian Newspapers and Others (No 2)*[91] Lord Goff observed:

"once information has entered what is usually called the public domain (which means no more than that the information in question is so generally accessible that, in all the circumstances, it cannot be regarded as confidential) then, as a general rule, the principle of confidentiality can have no application to it."[92]

Lord Goff considered this to be a limiting principle or a defence, but it is perhaps more proper to regard this as a necessary proof for the successful maintenance of a breach of confidence action.[93] Where the plaintiff is seeking to restrain a defendant from breaching the duty of disclosure, the action of the

---

[87.] *Ibid* at p 478-9.
[88.] (1951) 68 RPC 190. This defence was not at issue; *Stevens v Avery* [1988] 2 All ER 477.
[89.] *Weld-Blundell v Stephens* [1920] AC 956; See Law Commission No 110, paras 3.8 and 4.14.
[90.] [1969] 1 QB 349, at 361.
[91.] [1988] 3 All ER 545.
[92.] [1988] 3 All ER 545, at 659. *Attorney General v Blake* [1996] 3 All ER 903.
[93.] See Law Commission Report No 110 at para 4.15.

plaintiff may prejudice any such claim. The leading case is *O Mustad & Son v Dosen*.[94] In that case the plaintiff sought to prevent a manufacturing process from being disclosed by a former employee. However, the plaintiff had successfully filed a patent in relation to this process and was thus held not to be entitled to an injunction, for once the secret has been confided by the confider to the world "the secret, as a secret, has ceased to exist".[95] However, Lord Buckmaster indicated that if the plaintiff can show that the disclosee had obtained knowledge of ancillary secrets not disclosed in the patent invention but which would be of service in exploiting the information publicly available, then the duty of confidence will remain in place.

[23.33] In *House of Spring Gardens Ltd v Point Blank Ltd*,[96] Costello J applied the *dicta* by holding that despite the fact that two patents had been applied for in which much of the confidential information held by the disclosees was thus in the public domain, other valuable secrets not included in the patent specifications remained in the possession of the defendants who had misused it. The natural reluctance of the courts to allow one person to trade on the back of another explains the somewhat limited view of 'the public domain' in this particular context. Even if the information is a trade secret that could not be patentable because it would be obvious, once disclosed, this fact is no bar to the continued application of the duty.[97] Nor does the fact that information is a known element in the state of the art, for an expert, prevent that information from being caught by the duty *vis-à-vis* a lay or non-specialist confidant.[98] The courts may hold that even though information could be compiled from other sources or created by using research skills and data analysis, will not prevent the duty from being applicable once it appears that the confidant eschewed the opportunity to obtain or create the information in this way. In *Under-Water Welders & Repairers Ltd v Street*[99] a simple cleaning technique for cleaning ships could be protected even though others had the means and opportunity to use their brains so as to produce the same result through honest endeavour. The basic issue is whether the secret is known to the trade or particular to the confider.[100]

[23.34] Perhaps the most controversial element in the law of confidence centres around the problem of unauthorised disclosure of confidential information by

---

[94.] Decided in 1928 but reported in 1963; see [1963] 3 All ER 416.

[95.] [1963] 3 All ER 416 at 418 *per* Lord Buckmaster; *Franchi v Franchi* [1967] RPC 149.

[96.] [1984] IR 611.

[97.] *House of Spring Gardens Ltd v Point Blank Ltd* [1984] IR 611, at 664.

[98.] *Ibid.*

[99.] [1968] RPC 498.

[100.] *Triplex Safety Glass Co v Scorah* (1938) 55 RPC 21.

someone other than the confider. If information is put into the public domain by the confidant, or a third party, can the duty survive? The narrow approach to this issue depends upon judicial willingness to characterise the defendant as someone who is likely to unscrupulously profit from the privileged position they were previously in, rather than being a mere member of the public who is free to compete with others. The moral nature of the law of confidence is highlighted by several judicial statements which deny to the confidant the right to use 'public domain' information to steal a march on competitors, a view often described as the 'springboard' doctrine.

[23.35] In *Terrapin Ltd v Builders Supply Co (Hayes) Ltd*[101] the plaintiff designed portable buildings which were obviously open to use and inspection by others. The defendant manufactured these buildings on the plaintiff's behalf but then began to manufacture similar and competing products. Roxburgh J held for the plaintiff:

> "a person who has obtained information in confidence is not allowed to use it as a springboard for activities detrimental to the person who made the confidential communication, and springboard it remains even when all the features have been published or can be ascertained by actual inspection by any member of the public ... the possessor of the confidential information still has a long start over any member of the public."[102]

[23.36] It should be noted that in this case there had not been a complete and full disclosure to the public, for the central plank in the defence was that the disclosure of brochures describing the buildings by the plaintiff was tantamount to publication of plans, specifications and other know-how. Roxburgh J rejected this noting also that, while a skilled carpenter could dismantle these buildings and thus see how they were built, this possibility was not a publication which would discharge the confidential obligation. The defendant's 'head start' thus justified the 'special disability' they were under as against a trade competitor who could possibly imitate the plaintiff's product.[103] In later cases the *Terrapin* decision was expressly followed on this notion of a limited concept of public domain information. In *Cranleigh Precision Engineering Ltd v Bryant*[104] the defendant acquired information about a Swiss patent application during his employment with the plaintiff company, suppressed this information from the plaintiffs, intending to use confidential information and the patent information

---

[101] [1960] RPC 128, at 130.

[102] [1967] RPC 375.

[103] Of course artistic copyright may counteract even this possibility. For a recent decision which pushes out the boundaries on both fronts, see *Creation Records Ltd v NewsGroup Newpapers, Times*, 29 April 1997.

[104] [1964] 3 All ER 289.

for his own purposes. In awarding relief to the plaintiffs, Roskill J characterised the release of information as being a third party release which was not caught by the decision in *O Mustad & Son v Dosen*[105] even though it was of course open to him to argue that it was the advantage gleaned from his position of trust and confidence that allowed Bryant to profit from information about the Swiss patent he would otherwise not have come across. While *Cranleigh* has been criticised because of Roskill J's willingness to take an easy, but intellectually unsatisfying way out through distinguishing the *Mustad* decision, the *Cranleigh* decision is supportable if only because the evidence revealed a breach of trust and confidence in using secret and commercially useful information which this defendant, firstly, could not show had been acquired legitimately and, secondly, the breach of trust clearly gave a commercial advantage over others. On this basis Lord Goff of Chieveley in the *Spycatcher* case approved of Roskill J's judgment as representing nothing more than an extension of the springboard doctrine.

[23.37] The balance between preventing the free use of publicly available information and unfair use of information is at times a delicate one. In *Seager v Copydex Ltd*[106] Denning MR, who gave the leading judgment for the Court of Appeal, considered the scope of these principles where the information is mixed in the sense that some is publicly available (ie patented) while the remainder was disclosed confidentially (ie for purposes of joint development negotiations), Denning MR said:

> "when the information is mixed, being partly public and partly private, then the recipient must take special care to use only the material in the public domain. He should go to the public source and get it or, at any rate, not be in a better position than if he had gone to the public source. He should not get a start over others by using the information which he received in confidence. At any rate, he should not get a start without paying for it."[107]

[23.38] At this juncture the approach of the courts comes closer to the approach to an infringement of copyright claim as distinct from one of patent infringement and proof of misuse is unlikely to be excused by a claim that the material was publicly available. In *Roger Bullivant Ltd v Ellis*[108] the defendant took a card index containing his employer's customers' names and addresses intending to use them for his own purposes. The Court of Appeal held that even accepting that some of these names and addresses could have been recalled or found in other public sources, the 'ready and finite'[109] list of potential customers

---

105. [1963] 3 All ER 416.
106. [1967] 1 WLR 923.
107. *Ibid* at p 933.
108. [1987] FSR 172.
109. *Ibid* p 181 following *Robb v Green* [1895] 2 QB 315.

was still a valuable short-cut for the defendants in their canvassing activities; Nourse LJ made short shrift of the public domain defence:

"having made deliberate and unlawful use of the plaintiff's property he cannot complain if he finds that the eye of the law is unable to distinguish between those whom he could, had he chose, have contacted lawfully and those whom he could not."[110]

[23.39] The springboard doctrine, properly understood, turns upon a finding that the defendant has not used the publicly available source and this fact, combined with the use of information collected from another confidential source, makes it improper to allow the defendant to steal a march on others. It is a limited qualification of the *Mustad* decision but after the *Spycatcher* litigation in which the House of Lords accepted both *Mustad* and *post Terrapin* developments, there can be no real doubt about the usefulness of 'springboard' as being an essentially moral imperative, as well as a notion that ensures economic probity in terms of countering unfair competition while avoiding any taint of punishing a defendant. The primary relief of an injunction is to last only for so long as the advantage may reasonably be expected to continue - to cancel the headstart the defendant would otherwise get. This is a matter of fact tested by reference to any express terms, implied terms and the like in each individual case.[111] However, the approach of Lord Goff of Chieveley in the *Spycatcher* case tends to eliminate from the springboard doctrine two somewhat irrational features of it. Lord Goff doubted[112] whether the obligation of confidence could survive if a third party put the confidential information, *in toto*, into the public domain. In so doing, Lord Goff was clearly not able to support the decision in *Cranleigh Precision Engineering*, insofar as it rests upon the distinguishing of the *Mustad* case. Lord Goff also indicated that the duty of confidence will not survive an act of publication by the confidant (ie Peter Wright and his publishers in overseas locations), the learned judge indicating that *Speed Seal Products Ltd v Paddington*[113] could not be supported. Lord Goff was the only member of the House of Lords in *Spycatcher* to address these features of the 'springboard' doctrine and he was prepared to canvass the possibility that while the information so disclosed may lose its confidential nature, some kind of 'springboard' doctrine could be used to prevent the confidant from benefiting from his own iniquity. The problem for the United Kingdom Government in this case was the unsatisfactory nature of the pecuniary and other remedies because

---

[110.] *Ibid.*

[111.] *Potters Ballotini Ltd v Weston-Baker* [1977] RPC 202; *Harrison v Project & Design Co (Redcar) Ltd* [1978] FSR 81; *Fisher-Karpark Industries Ltd v Nichols* [1982] FSR 351.

[112.] [1988] 3 All ER 545 at 661-2.

[113.] [1986] 1 All ER 91.

Wright and his overseas publishers were outside the jurisdiction of the 'English courts'.[114]

The Public Interest

[23.40] The equitable principle operates because of the circumstances in which information was provided by the confider and not because the information was 'owned' by the confider; ownership in information is not possible under the Larceny Act 1916, although some limited movement in this direction is in evidence in the Oireachtas[115] and in the recent deliberations of the Law Reform Commission.[116] However, in this area of judge-made law the courts have traditionally balanced the interests of persons from being taken advantage of by those to whom they have entrusted confidential information with the broader public interest in counteracting serious misconduct and maintaining the integrity of the State. In *Spycatcher* Lord Goff of Chieveley compared existing English law or freedom of expression and the duty of confidence (as contrasting English law principles), with Article 10 of the European Convention on Human Rights, remarking that in the jurisprudence of the European Court of Human Rights the right to freedom of expression is qualified by restrictions based on pressing social need and noting also that the English courts qualify the duty of confidence by reference to similar considerations. However, recent case-law indicates that different approaches are to operate depending on whether the information is concerned with private law secrets and government secrets; in the first case the onus will lie in favour of upholding confidence while in the other case, the case for secrecy will have to be made out.

[23.41] The basis of the public interest exception is normally attributed to the words of Wood VC in *Gartside v Outram*:[117]

> "there is no confidence as to the disclosures of iniquity. You cannot make me the confidant of a crime or a fraud and be entitled to close up my lips upon any secret which you have the audacity to disclose to me relating to any fraudulent intention on your part; such a confidence cannot exist."[118]

[23.42] While cases in the early parts of this century have doubted the existence, not to say the scope, of such a principle[119] when the confidant sought to invoke it to excuse the publication of libellous material or information that would disclose the basis of some other kind of private civil cause of action, there is no doubt

---

[114.] See Lord Goff at [1988] 3 All ER 664.
[115.] Criminal Damage Act 1991.
[116.] Report on Dishonesty LRC 43-1992.
[117.] (1856) 26 LJ Ch 113.
[118.] *Ibid* at 114.
[119.] Eg Warrington LJ in *Weld-Blundell v Stephens* [1919] 1 KB 520, at 535.

that a wider duty owed to the State or to other citizens could, in a proper case, outweigh the contractual or equitable basis of the duty of confidence. The trick has always been where to draw the line in this area, as well as in analogous fields such as denying a plaintiff a successful cause of action for breach of contract because of some common law defence such as illegality or restraint of trade. In *Initial Services Ltd v Putterill*[120] the plaintiffs sought to strike out a defence to their action for breach of contract, brought against a former employee who had taken away with him, when he left employment, documents which tended to show involvement in a price fixing cartel which was a restrictive practice. The defendant passed these documents on to the second defendant, a national newspaper. Counsel for the plaintiffs relied heavily on *Weld Blundell v Stephens* arguing that even if proved their conduct was neither a crime nor a fraud. Lord Denning MR's view, although he may have misunderstood[121] the plaintiffs' argument, was:

> "The exception should extend to crimes, frauds and misdeeds, both those actually committed as well as to those in contemplation, provided always, and this is essential, that the disclosure is justified in the public interest."[122]

[23.43] Counsel's reliance on earlier cases was also directed at the identity of the person who is informed, in breach of confidence; was a national newspaper a proper person to be informed of the 'iniquity'? While the Court of Appeal accepted this proposition they were ultimately unprepared to strike out the defence for neither facet of it were such as to be unarguable. Later cases indicate that this public interest exception does not extend towards revelations that a particularly obnoxious military government elsewhere in Europe has engaged a firm of public relations consultants to improve its public image in other parts of Europe, even if the regime itself has a poor human rights record.[123] On the other hand, the disclosure of details about courses devised by the head of a religious organisation who was prepared to countenance powerful coercive methods to maintain the integrity of the church was certainly a powerful enough interest to deny interlocutory relief to the head of that church in confidence/copyright proceedings.[124]

[23.44] The case that establishes the public interest defence in English law, with greater clarity and precision than any other case is *Lion Laboratories Ltd v*

[120.] [1968] 1 QB 396.
[121.] See [1968] 1 QB 396, at 400D and Salmon LJ at 409A; Contrast Denning MR at 405E.
[122.] *Ibid* p 405.
[123.] *Fraser v Evans* [1969] 1 All ER 8.
[124.] *Hubbard v Vosper* [1972] 1 All ER 1023.

Evans,[125] a decision of the Court of Appeal which fully examined both the nature of the iniquity and the factors relevant to the balancing process.

[23.45] The Home Office had approved an intoximeter produced by Lion Laboratories for use by the police in detecting drunk drivers. The defendants who were technicians employed by Lion Laboratories leaked information which revealed that these devices were not completely reliable and this information appeared in the national press. Leonard J gave an interlocutory injunction restraining disclosure or use of confidential information but, following use of this information by the press, an application to have the injunction discharged was sought in the Court of Appeal. In the light of the much fuller argument in the Court of Appeal, that Court stated that the relevant principles necessitated the discharge of the injunction. While the Court of Appeal agreed with Leonard J that there were two primary interests to be balanced, namely, the protection of confidential documents and the freedom of the press to investigate matters of public concern, there were other relevant factors to be brought into play. First, the Court of Appeal pointed out that there is a wide difference between what is interesting to the public and what is in the public interest *vis-à-vis* open disclosure of facts; private matters may interest the public but be matters of no real public concern. Secondly, newspapers have a separate interest - boosting readership and circulation - which is not to be used to confuse the public interest issue. Thirdly, the public interest may often best be served by discretion in the sense that details should be given to the police or other bodies charged with investigative powers. Fourthly, the basic rule against a confidence being maintained in an iniquity was of importance. Using these supplementary rules, the Court of Appeal held that the balancing exercise should work in favour of disclosure. While the plaintiff company was not itself the author of an iniquity, it merely manufactured the device and unlike the Home Office did not specifically control its use, the failure to meet a manufacturing standard would raise the possibility of wrongful convictions and loss of liberty for citizens. On the issue of the appropriateness of resorting to the media, the Court of Appeal allowed a degree of latitude. Stephenson LJ went so far as to say that in a case of this kind the media may be under a duty to publish, even if information has been obtained in flagrant breach of confidence and even if some other motive (such as vengeance) could be shown to exist on the part of the informer. However, press freedom cannot be pushed too far; a countervailing interest that is similarly powerful is the public interest in facilitating the proper administration of justice through a leakproof system of discovery, for example.[126] The removal of the duty of confidence from a defendant using the iniquity exception will only be

---

[125.] [1984] 3 WLR 539.
[126.] *Distillers Co v Times Newspapers Ltd* [1975] QB 613.

tolerated if the removal of the duty presents the only realistic way in which "the press" can put this information, on a matter of public interest, before the public.[127] While an exegesis of the law relating to press freedom would be out of place at this juncture it should be recalled that third party disclosees who happen to be journalists cannot invoke any special privilege against disclosure of sources.[128]

[23.46] The most recent example of the iniquity defence being invoked in the English courts involved litigation over the pre-publication release of the Thatcher Memoirs by the *Daily Mirror* newspaper prior to the Conservative Party Conference in 1993. Forbes J ruled that the *Sunday Times* and Harper Collins, who owned the serialisation and publication rights respectively could not obtain an injunction against Mirror Newspapers because it was in the public interest that the public be aware of tensions within the Government party at a time when that party was attempting a show of unity which the memoirs tended to give the lie to. Forbes J followed *Lion Laboratories*. While the Master of the Rolls dismissed this appeal on different grounds, the decision was a cause of great surprise to many, especially the *Sunday Times*.[129] The fact that the confidant himself intends to make the information known at some time in the near future may undermine the confider's efforts to obtain an injunction, for as part of the balancing process a public interest argument may thus outweigh what is in essence an effort to protect the commercial value of the information rather than its secrecy.[130] The balance will go the other way if a legitimate privacy interest is at stake[131] although in some cases publication will be allowed if the confider cannot show that the confidant was really the recipient of 'exclusive' information and the information related to a person in the public eye who has acted improperly in a public place.[132] If there is any real risk of the public being physically harmed as a result of upholding the confidence then a public interest defence may prevail for it will be evident in some cases that the real interests of the public and the parties to the information may coincide.[133]

[23.47] Where the information in question is held by the Government, as distinct from being 'private' information, a rather different emphasis has been placed on

---

[127.] See in particular Templeman LJ in *Schering Chemicals Ltd v Falkman Ltd* [1981] 3 All ER 321, at 347 where he noted both the financial motive of the journalist and the 'public domain' nature of much of the information.

[128.] McGonigle, *Media Law* (Gill & Macmillan, 1996).

[129.] See 'For Authors Back to the Law of the Jungle' *Sunday Times*, 10 October 1993.

[130.] This was the basis of Bingham MR's decision in the Thatcher Memoirs appeal: *Ibid.*

[131.] *Francome v Mirror Group Newspapers Ltd* [1984] 2 All ER 408.

[132.] Contrast *Woodward v Hutchins* [1977] 2 All ER 751 with *Stevens v Avery* [1988] 2 All ER 477; *X v Y* [1988] 2 All ER 648.

[133.] *W v Edgell* [1989] 1 All ER 1089.

the availability of relief via the law of confidence. In *Attorney General v Jonathan Cape Ltd*[134] the Attorney General sought an injunction to restrain the publication of the Crossman Diaries on the ground that certain Cabinet discussions were relayed therein, in breach of confidence. However, it was for the Attorney General to show not only that publication would breach confidence but also that the public interest required that publication be restrained and that other facets of the public interest were not present which contradicted or were more compelling than the public interest requiring secrecy. This approach has been endorsed both in the High Court of Australia[135] and by various members of the House of Lords in *Spycatcher*.[136] In *Spycatcher*, however, the public interest in maintaining the integrity of the secret service was held clearly to outweigh any countervailing public interest in investigating wrongdoing (although it should be recalled that neither Wright nor his publishers were before the English courts to argue this point). Had the issue been whether an injunction should be given to restrain first publication in Britain there is no doubt that the Attorney General would have prevailed but in *Spycatcher* the issue was whether publication should be restrained when the work was widely available due to overseas publication and widespread importation into Britain. In the view of the House of Lords, broad injunctive relief would not be appropriate, for no confidence remained due to Wright's breach of duty and its world-wide dissemination. If, however, there is no allegation that the information provided to the Crown servant was secret or confidential, the recent decision of Scott VC in *Attorney General v Blake*[137] indicates that the Crown interest in maintaining an air of secrecy around the security services will not be sufficient to warrant an injunction: the countervailing public interest in freedom of speech and a person's right to earn a living will be predominant.

[23.48] This issue has arisen in recent times as a result of publication of the memoirs of former SAS members, the most important instance being Chris Ryan's *The One that Got Away*, televised in February 1996 and based on Chris McNab's *Bravo Two Zero*. The lack of activity in the form of attempts to injunct publication presumably indicates that this kind of publication is thought by the Attorney General to fall on the other side of the *Spycatcher* line, even though some danger to serving members is apprehended in certain circles.[138] Despite the

---

134. [1976] QB 752.
135. [1996] 3 All ER 903. See in particular Mason J in *Commonwealth of Australia v John Fairfax and Sons Ltd* (1980) 32 ALR 485, at 492-493.
136. See Lord Keith at [1988] 3 All ER 642; Lord Griffiths at 650-651, Lord Goff at 660.
137. [1996] 3 All ER 903.
138. See 'He who dares faces a law suit' *Observer* 25 February 1996. The article indicates that confidentiality agreements with members is being actively considered to provide a firmer legal basis for enforcing confidentiality. See 'Latest SAS TV drama fuels calls for secrecy' *The Times* 2 March 1996.

force of the earlier cases in which the onus was placed on the State, recent Australian case law, however,[139] has tended to emphasise that even if a public interest defence in exposing criminality is invoked against an agency of the Federal Government, the defendant will have to go some way towards substantiating this claim if he is to be relieved of the duty to keep confidence as a government employee.

Skill, Time and Labour in compiling the Information

[23.49] In *House of Spring Gardens Ltd v Point Blank Ltd*,[140] Costello J indicated that in determining the nature of the relationship and the information, the expenditure of skill, time and labour in compiling the information is relevant in determining whether the duty of confidence arises. Costello J was, of course, considering these factors in the context of industrial trade secrets, some of which were already in the public domain and these remarks are therefore to be seen in context. In general terms, however, if the information is seen as being management data rather than a trade secret the action will fail.[141] If the information is seen as being an essential part of the personal skill and know-how of the confidant[142] the duty will not arise thus making express clauses against competition necessary.[143] Although the memory test is not a part of English law[144] evidence that a confidant has taken or copied documents will tend towards a conclusion that the confidant knew that it had been given within a relationship of confidence and that the information was subject to a duty to use it only for certain purposes or not at all,[145] unless that information is characterised as little more than gossip or tittle-tattle.[146] If the information is vaguely expressed or little more than an idea this may point away from there being anything confidential at all, as in the case of an idea for a nightclub theme.[147]

REMEDIES IN RELATION TO BREACH OF CONFIDENCE

[23.50] As a broadly equitable doctrine, the remedies available in relation to a threatened or actual breach of confidence are closely linked to the traditional range of equitable remedies such as declaratory orders, injunctions and account of profits. While the basic principles that operate in relation to these remedies *vis-à-vis* other intellectual property rights are generally applicable, there are

---

[139.] *DCT v Rettke* (1995) 31 IPR 457.
[140.] [1984] IR 611.
[141.] *Herbert Morris Ltd v Saxelby* [1916] 1 AC 668; *Ixora Trading Corp v Jones* [1990] 1 FSR 251.
[142.] *Printers and Finishers Ltd v Holloway* [1965] 1 WLR 1.
[143.] Eg *Triangle Corp v Carnsew* (1994) 29 IPR 69.
[144.] See Heydon, *The Restraint of Trade Doctrine* (1971) pp 91-92.
[145.] *AF Associates v Ralston* [1973] NI 229; *Roger Bullivant Ltd v Ellis* [1987] FSR 172.
[146.] *Beloff v Pressdram Ltd* [1973] 1 All ER 241.
[147.] *De Maudsley v Palumbo* [1996] FSR 447.

specific problems in key areas which make it desirable for the law to be put on a statutory footing, particularly in relation to the remedy of damages.

Injunctions

[23.51] The principles expounded in *American Cyanamid Co v Ethicon Ltd*[148] have been accepted as governing this area of law although certain of the leading cases pre-date the decision of the House of Lords on this point.[149] It is by no means clear whether a defendant who is intent on pleading that disclosure was made in the public interest can be the subject of an interlocutory injunction. In *Hubbard v Vosper*[150] the Master of the Rolls, Lord Denning, said:

> "We never restrain a defendant in a libel action who says he is going to justify. So, in a copyright action, we ought not to restrain a defendant who has a reasonable defence of fair dealing. Nor in an action for breach of confidence if, the defendant has a reasonable defence of public interest. The reason is because the defendant, if he is right, is entitled to publish it; and the law will not intervene to suppress freedom of speech except where it is abused."[151]

[23.52] It has to be said that Lord Denning was the most enthusiastic exponent of this view and other judges have tended to decide not to award injunctions on the balance of convenience issue[152] rather than by reference to this rule, and there must be significant doubt about the existence of any such rule in the light of subsequent decisions in which interlocutory relief was given.[153] Factors that affect the balance of convenience in favour of upholding the confidence via an interlocutory injunction include whether publication would result in a breach of the criminal law[154] and whether damages would not be an adequate remedy for the plaintiff.[155] Injunctions are less likely where the defendant is innocent and has changed his position irrevocably[156] but *bona fide* purchasers are not immune from injunctions: *Stevenson, Jordan and Harrison Ltd v MacDonald and Evans*.[157] As long as the *American Cyanamid* test is applied, the fact that the defendant is likely to be driven out of business as a result of upholding the confidence via an interlocutory injunction is not a barrier to the relief.[158] Nor is

---

[148.] [1975] AC 396.

[149.] Eg *Amber Size and Chemical Co v Menzel* [1913] 2 Ch 239; *Coco v AN Clark Ltd* [1968] FSR 415.

[150.] [1972] 2 QB 84.

[151.] *Ibid* at 96-7.

[152.] *Woodward v Hutchins* [1977] 1 WLR 760.

[153.] *Schering Chemicals Ltd v Falkman Ltd* [1981] 2 WLR 848.

[154.] *Francome v Mirror Group Newspapers* [1984] 2 All ER 408.

[155.] *ECI European Chemical Industries Ltd v Bell* [1981] ILRM 345.

[156.] *Seager v Copydex Ltd* [1967] 2 All ER 415.

[157.] (1952) 69 RPC 10.

[158.] *Roger Bullivant Ltd v Ellis* [1987] FSR 172.

an injunction to be denied simply because the loss to the defendant is hard or impossible to quantify for, as Keane J said in *Oblique Financial Services Ltd v The Promise Production Co*:[159]

> "If that proposition were correct, then it would follow that in cases where breach of confidentiality arises it would, in effect, be impossible for the courts to grant interlocutory relief, however unjust the consequences, if the respondents were, as in the present case, publishers in magazines or periodicals of a large volume of information and comment other than the impugned material."[160]

Other equitable relief may be sought in the form of an order, given by the Court within the context of equitable principles, whereby the name of the person responsible for breaching the confidence may be disclosed to the applicant by the third party defendant. Again, knowledge, actual or constructive of the breach of confidence appears to be a precondition to relief.[161]

Damages

[23.53] While damages are awarded in cases of breach of confidence, the position of a plaintiff who has no contractual link with the defendant is somewhat perilous as the authorities now stand. The issue of the measure of damages is somewhat more satisfactorily settled.

Quantum of Damages

[23.54] The case that is most frequently cited on the issue of quantum is the Court of Appeal's decision in *Seager v Copydex (No 2)*.[162] In this case the defendants were approached by an inventor who wanted the defendants to licence others to use a carpet grip that he had devised; the defendants used information thus received to make their own product which competed with a carpet grip that the plaintiff himself sold, although the two products were different in design. The plaintiff sought compensation for the loss to his business that he suffered as a result of giving the defendants information which they had exploited, albeit innocently, to the detriment of the plaintiff's business. Denning MR said that the approach to be taken was to be based on the analogy provided by damages for conversion or trover. Once damages are paid, the property becomes that of the defendant, a satisfied judgment having the effect of transferring property to the defendant, the problem was one of valuing the 'property':

[159.] [1994] ILRM 74.
[160.] *Ibid* at 80.
[161.] *NEAP Pty v Ashton* (1995) 33 IPR 281.
[162.] [1969] 2 All ER 718.

"If there was nothing very special about it, that is, if it involved no particular inventive step but was the sort of information which could be obtained by employing any competent consultant, then the value of it was the fee which a consultant would charge for it; because in that case the defendant company, by taking the information, would only have saved themselves the time and trouble of employing a consultant. But, on the other hand, if the information was something special, as for instance if it involved an inventive step or something so unusual that it could not be obtained by just going to a consultant, then the value of it is much higher."[163]

[23.55] In this judgment Lord Denning MR considered that the approach to take is to look to an appropriate figure; thus on the lower end of the scale, ie where the information is 'not special' the consultant fee basis would be the quantum, while at the other end of the scale Lord Denning MR had in mind the possibility of looking to the royalty that confidential information could have attracted and then capitalising the value of that royalty, presumably over the commercial life of that information, that is, the lead-in time before competitors could enter the market and use this information for themselves.

[23.56] However, Lord Denning MR's speech in *Copydex (No 2)* has not fared well and it has been held in subsequent cases[164] not to lay down any rule which qualifies the broad compensatory principle by which damages are calculated. In *Dowson and Mason Ltd v Potter*[165] the Court of Appeal considered *Copydex (No 2)* in the context of an action where the first defendant gave to his new employer, the second defendant, information concerning technical equipment which he acquired while in the plaintiff's employment. In finding a breach of confidence the defendants were ordered to compensate the plaintiffs for their loss of profits resulting from the wrongful disclosure. The defendants appealed, characterising the information disclosed as being within the first category stated by Lord Denning MR, ie information available elsewhere, as distinct from information within the exclusive control of the plaintiff. In such a case, the defendants argued, the damages should be the value of the article (the information) as between a willing buyer and a willing seller. The Court of Appeal, relying upon the decision of the House of Lords in *General Tire and Rubber Co v Firestone Tyre and Rubber Co*[166] restated the basic principle that in economic torts the purpose of an award of damages would be to put the plaintiff in the position he would have been in if the plaintiff had not sustained the wrong. The Court of Appeal added to the *Copydex (No 2)* test a requirement to

---

[163.] *Ibid* at 719-20.
[164.] Eg *General Television v Talbot* [1981] RPC 1.
[165.] [1986] 2 All ER 418.
[166.] [1975] 2 All ER 173, especially Lord Wilberforce at 177.

look to the particular position of the plaintiff. If, as in *Copydex (No 2)*, the plaintiff is prepared to allow others to use information for a fee, on a non-exclusive basis, then that fee should be the quantum. If, however, the information is not to be licensed, even if others could ultimately discover and use the information from other sources, the non-exclusive nature of that information, or relatively prosaic nature of the information, is not to deprive the plaintiff of the profit he would have obtained as a result of being ahead of the competition via the exclusivity of the information, judged at the time of the wrong done to him. Slade LJ, in particular, drew a contrast between the relevant quantum where the plaintiff did not intend to manufacture the finished products; the relevant measure here should be a licensing measure. In contrast, where the plaintiff did manufacture that item, the licensing measure would be inappropriate, for it is manufacturing profits that the plaintiff has lost. A similar attempt to restrict damages in *House of Spring Gardens Ltd v Point Blank Ltd*[167] was unsuccessful, for the plaintiffs, in opting for an account of profits, which were multi-million pound figures, were able to side-step the defendants' assertion that as between a willing seller and buyer the information would be worth around £630,000 under a royalty agreement.

[23.57] The nature of the information, however, may be important in the final analysis of just how much of the defendant's business can be attributed to the nature of the defendant's misuse of information. Certainly, where the information consists of customer names and addresses, the plaintiff is often given the benefit of the doubt, but if in the assessment of damages it is found that the defendant used little or no confidential information and that the defendant's success is down to other factors then nominal damages and a successful counterclaim may result.[168]

[23.58] Where the plaintiff's claim is based on a contractual relationship with the defendant, the award of damages may be possible because of that contractual link. However, where the plaintiff is bringing an action against someone with whom there is no such link (eg a third party disclosee) then the issue arises whether damages are possible. Certainly in cases of a threatened breach of confidence, where the plaintiff seeks interlocutory relief, the court has a discretion to award damages "in lieu of or in addition to an injunction" under the Chancery Amendment Act 1858 (Lord Cairn's Act), a reforming piece of legislation intended to rationalise litigation by allowing a common law remedy to be available in a court of equity in circumstances where an injunction would be within the jurisdiction of the court but an inappropriate or inadequate relief in

---

[167.] [1984] IR 611, especially the judgment of Griffin J on this point.
[168.] *Universal Thermosensors Ltd v Hibben* [1992] FSR 360.

the case at bar. Several of the leading cases are to be regarded as cases where the court awarded damages in lieu of an injunction,[169] the damage being awarded to cover loss occasioned by previous and possible future breaches of confidence. It is, however, necessary for the non-contractual claimant to seek to prove that the claimant had some claim to an injunction for if there is no real prospect of an injunction being awarded, as where the breach of duty has already occurred and an injunction is not necessary to deter future breaches of duty, then, in the absence of some other cause of action for damages there seems no prospect of Lord Cairns' Act being applicable.[170] This issue was considered extensively in the Northern Ireland case of *O'Neill v DHSS*.[171] In that case the plaintiff made an application to her local DHSS office for maternity benefit. She was unmarried at the time and apart from the father of the child and her doctor, no other person was aware of the pregnancy. Shortly after this application was made, the plaintiff miscarried. A neighbour later indicated that he knew that she was pregnant indicating that the source of this information was his sister who had dealt with the plaintiff's initial maternity benefit claim. This caused the plaintiff to be upset and she told the salient facts to her mother as a result of this distress, although she initially wanted to withhold her condition from her mother. While the DHSS accepted that information of this kind was given in confidence and while Carswell J held that the facts came within the *Coco v AN Clark*[172] threefold test, Carswell J indicated that there is no common law tort of breach of confidence and because there was no prospect of the plaintiff getting an injunction in the case before him, damages in lieu of an injunction were not possible. Carswell J also observed that if the disclosure made by the DHSS clerk was made negligently then there may have been a further obstacle to awarding damages for in his view any such tort should be limited to deliberate disclosures. Carswell J also took the view that while the DHSS clerk may well have been within a *Hedley Byrne* special relationship, or also in the position of a fiduciary, liability under such headings for true statements would cause difficulties for the plaintiff. Carswell J also opined that mere nervous shock, aside from some other sustainable claim to protect other interests, is not recoverable *per se*. The plaintiff was also not able to fix the State with liability since the wrong done was outside the concept of vicarious liability and protected by Crown immunity.

---

[169] See Slade J's view of *Seager v Copydex* in *English v Dedham Vale Properties Ltd* [1978] 1 WLR 93, at 111.

[170] *Proctor v Bayley* (1889) 42 Ch D 390; *Malone v Metropolitan Police Commissioner* [1979] 2 All ER 620; contrast Harman J in *Nichrotherm Electrical Co v Percy* [1957] RPC 207.

[171] [1986] 5 NI 290.

[172] [1968] FSR 415, at 420-1.

[23.59] While *Capper*[173] has made valiant efforts to suggest that a more pro-plaintiff spin can be put on both the facts and the law, *O'Neill v DHSS* represents an almost unimpeachable argument for statutory modification of the remedial aspects of the equitable duty of confidence.

[23.60] The decision in the *O'Neill* case also raises the issue of non-pecuniary loss. Had the plaintiff made out a cause of action, could there be an award of damages for distress, vexation, injured feelings and annoyance caused by the breach of duty? In cases where the information is commercial in nature, transferred within a context of this kind, general principles may dictate that financial distress rather than injury to feelings is the foreseeable kind of loss, and the Irish courts on both sides of the border have taken the view that injury to feelings and mental stress is not generally recoverable.[174] If, however, the nature of the confidence is such that no pecuniary or financial interest can be shown to have been prejudiced, then damages, if available at all, should be assessed so as to compensate the plaintiff for injury to reputation, anxiety, loss of self esteem and general distress caused by the breach of duty, certainly in cases of deliberate disclosure even if the facts disclosed are true. The appropriate analogy here is with holiday cases[175] and the many decisions involving "the wedding reception from hell".[176] Similar uncertainties surround the availability of punitive damages (save in cases of State misuse of confidential information) or damages intended to prevent unjust enrichment of a plaintiff under the *Hickey v Roches Stores* *dictum*[177] that damages for breach of contract or some other wrong can be assessed to deprive a '*mala fide*' defendant of the fruits of his wrongdoing.

[23.61] There are of course several cases in which the plaintiff is able to make out a number of different causes of action, breach of confidence being only one of them. It is clear that the plaintiff cannot obtain damages under each cause of action for damages are cumulative. The plaintiff has some opportunity to nominate both the cause of action and the relevant measure, but the courts may determine that the appropriate measure of damages in breach of confidence is the actual value of the information rather than profits earned by the defendant. In *Interfirm Comparison v Law Society of NSW*[178] the plaintiff was able to support actions for breach of confidence and infringement of copyright. The plaintiff

---

[173.] (1986) 37 NILQ 273; (1994) 14 Legal Studies 313.

[174.] *Kelly v Crowley* High Court, unrep 5 March 1985; However, Keane J in the later case of *Lennon v Talbot Ireland* High Court, unrep 20 December 1985 awarded modest damages for "general anxiety and inconvenience" caused by premature termination of a motor dealership. In Northern Ireland see *Smith v Huey* [1993] 8 NIJB 49.

[175.] *Jarvis v Swans Tours* [1973] 2 QB 233.

[176.] Eg *Hotson v Payn* [1988] CLY 409.

[177.] High Court, unrep 14 July 1976; (1978) 26 NILQ 128.

[178.] (1975) 6 ALR 445.

was held entitled to one lot of damages to cover two breaches of obligation, and that the normal copyright measure, that is, the depreciation caused by the infringement to the chose in action - the copyright work - is not a universal measure. In that case the court compared the work, as an unpublished work, to an unauthorised disclosure in breach of confidence, and said that the relevant measure is the value of the information disclosed in breach of duty. In *Fortuity Property Ltd v Barcza*[179] this approach was taken even further for here the Court held that either measure was impossible to calculate so a reasonable sum by way of damages was ordered as compensation for the defendants' breaches of duty.

An Account of Profits

[23.62] This is an equitable remedy that the plaintiff may elect to chose, in contrast with the remedy of damages. The election is to take place at a time prior to the conclusion of the litigation although recent case-law has indicated that the plaintiff is entitled to make an informed choice which will necessitate the defendant providing details of accounts prior to the election.[180] Most judicial opinion is of the view that an account of profits is a messy and unsatisfactory business.[181] In two recent cases however, the English and the Irish courts have extolled the virtue of an account of profits in cases where the courts have already obtained access to the accounts of the defendant and the ordering of an account will have the additional advantage of deterring wrongdoers who are thus denied any incentive to breach the confidence and hope that damages will not disgorge from the defendant all his ill-gotten gains.[182] Furthermore, because the plaintiff need only elect after adequate information has been provided by the infringer, new lines of authority suggest the courts may order a form of discovery, or require affidavits from responsible persons which will serve to inform the plaintiff of the likely outcome of the account.[183] However, practical difficulties may arise in sorting out the profits made legitimately from those made as a result of the breach of confidence and in such cases the court's discretion may led to the award of damages.[184]

[179.] (1995) 32 IPR 517.

[180.] *Island Records Ltd v Tring International plc* [1995] 3 All ER 444; *Tang Man Sit (decd) v Capacious Investments Ltd* [1996] 1 All ER 193.

[181.] Eg *Siddell v Vickers* (1892) 9 RPC 152; *Wedderburn v Wedderburn* (1848) 4 My & Cr 41.

[182.] *Peter Pan Manufacturing Corp v Corsets Silhouette Ltd* [1964] 1 WLR 108; *House of Spring Gardens Ltd v Point Blank Ltd* [1984] IR 611.

[183.] *Island Records v Tring* [1995] 3 All ER 444; *LED Builders Pty v Eagles Homes Pty (No 2)* (1996) 36 IPR 293.

[184.] *Fortuity Property Ltd v Barcza* (1995) 32 IPR 517.

Miscellaneous

[23.63] Within the law of confidence some discussion has taken place about the number of possible reliefs, apart from the obvious dichotomy between injunctive relief and damages. In cases where confidential information has been used to create a business or trading activity, it has been suggested that the profits and indeed the business should be capable of being transferred or held in constructive trust for the plaintiff.[185] In the *Spycatcher* litigation several members of the House of Lords indicated that ownership in the book may well rest in the Crown although these observations were made *obiter. Spycatcher*[186] of course also opens up the possibility that certain injunctive reliefs may be available in order to discourage or prevent unjust enrichment if the person in breach of duty brings himself within the jurisdiction of the court. Indeed, in recent litigation involving a former domestic servant of the Prince and Princess of Wales, who has published a book, in breach of confidence, disclosing details of the ill-fated marriage of the couple, the Prince was held entitled to recover all profits made by the defendant even though she is living in Canada and will only be exposed to the jurisdiction if she and the profits come back into the jurisdiction of the British courts. There is some suggestion that quantum meruit claims may be maintained in this context[187] and destruction and delivery up of items that are the result of the breach of duty may be ordered but this is an exceptional remedy.[188]

[185.] Eg *LAC Minerals Ltd v International Corona Resources Ltd* (1989) 6 DLR (4th) 14; *Fortuity Property Co v Barcza* (1995) 32 IPR 517.

[186.] [1988] 3 All ER 545.

[187.] *Fractionated Care Technology Ltd v Joseph Ruiz Avila* (1987) 8 IPR 502, being available to both parties presumably.

[188.] *Industrial Furnaces Ltd v Reaves* [1970] RPC 605; *Franklin v Giddins* [1978] Qd 72.

Chapter 24

Remedies in Tort

PASSING OFF

Historical Origins[1]

[24.01] While the basic features of the cause of action for passing off have been clearly identified in modern jurisprudence as resting upon the law relating to misrepresentation, this rationalisation has not always been agreed upon. In historical terms, the approach of equity and the common law courts did not coalesce until the end of the nineteenth century, and the early cases demonstrate a variety of possible motives for judicial intervention when goods or services were offered or supplied by a defendant in controversial circumstances.

[24.02] In two early seventeenth century cases[2] Dodderidge J gave as an early instance of the vitality of the common law in this field, an earlier Tudor case in which a Gloucester clothier's mark of reputation was fixed upon cloth inferior to that of the Gloucester clothier by the defendant. Dodderidge J observed that an action could lie upon the wrong of the defendant although it is by no means clear that the action was available to the user of the mark or a purchaser of the inferior cloth who relied upon the mark.[3] However, the nineteenth century cases that followed made it clear that the action at law was available to the trader whose mark had been used by the defendant and that the basis of the right to common law damages[4] is deceit on the part of the defendant. In equity, however, the availability of injunctive relief proceeded on somewhat different grounds. Early cases like *Blanchard v Hill*[5] indicated that one trader could not injunct another trader from using the plaintiff's mark, although Lord Hardwicke LC observed *obiter*, that while use of the mark *per se* could not ground relief, doing so with fraudulent intent to either sell bad goods or draw away customers from the plaintiff could merit relief. By the beginning of the nineteenth century, however, equity had awarded injunctive relief to protect authors from having inferior works sold under the author's name[6] and to prevent traders from occupying

---

1. See Wadlow, *Passing Off* (2nd Ed) (Sweet & Maxwell, 1994) Ch 1.
2. *Southern v How* (1618) Cro Jac 468; *Dean v Steel* (1626) Latch 188 reported in law french.
3. See Wadlow *supra*.
4. *Sykes v Sykes* (1824) 3 B & C 541; *Crowshay v Thompson* (1842) 4 Man & G 427.
5. (1742) 2 Atk 484.
6. *Byron v Johnson* (1816) 2 Mer 29.

premises previously used by the plaintiff and imitating their nature and mode of business.[7] The decision in *Millington v Fox*,[8] however, suggested that equity was not simply following the law in regarding intention to deceive as an essential proof, for in this case an injunction was given to restrain the defendant from using the plaintiff's mark even though the original use was innocent, insofar as the defendant did not know it was the plaintiff's mark but rather, was a technical or descriptive mark. So, while innocent original use was not a defence in equity, the approach at common law was fully considered in *Perry v Truefitt*.[9]

[24.03] In *Perry v Truefitt*, the plaintiff successfully manufactured and sold a hair product under the name 'Perry's Medicated Mexican Balm' for several years. The defendant produced a rival product which he described as 'Medicated Mexican Balm'. The plaintiff complained that in the mind of the public the phrase 'Medicated Mexican Balm' was connected with Perry. Lord Langdale declined to give an injunction saying however:

> "A man is not to sell his own goods under the pretence that they are the goods of another man; he cannot be permitted to practice a deception, nor to use the means which contribute to that end. He cannot, therefore, be allowed to use names, marks, letters or other indicia, by which he may induce purchasers to believe that the goods which he is selling are the manufacture of another person".[10]

[24.04] The observation of Lord Langdale MR about the basis of the action being a desire to counteract deception is heightened by his doubts about the possibility of there being any property right in a name or a mark, and his lordship also observed that the principle is the basis of both common law and equitable reliefs. In Ireland, *Perry v Truefitt* was followed in *Foot v Lea*[11] some eight years later. The well known Dublin firm of Lundy Foot & Co[12] sought an injunction to prevent a former employee from selling 'A Lea Dublin Snuff', the defendant advertising the fact that he was a former employee of the plaintiffs who manufactured 'Lundy Foot & Co Irish Snuff'. The labels used by the defendant were said by the court to have been made so as to intentionally mislead the public, but on these facts an injunction would not be issued. The jurisdiction at law and in equity were said to be one and the same, *pace Perry v Truefitt*, and the liability of the defendant was left to be tested in a trial of the action. Shortly after *Foot v Lea* an Irish court held that an agreement to allow

---

7. *Crutwell v Lye* (1810) 17 Ves Jn 335.
8. (1838) 3 Myl & Cr 338.
9. (1842) 6 Beav 66, 418.
10. (1842) 6 Beav 66 at 73.
11. (1850) 13 IR Eq R 484.
12. Mentioned by James Joyce in *Ulysses*.

persons to trade in products that deceive the public would be unenforceable as a fraud on the public.[13]

[24.05] The emphasis on misrepresentation or deception was not the only rationalisation however. In a number of cases, Lord Westbury gave the view that the basis of the plaintiff's cause of action in relation to trade marks was a right of property[14] and this view was espoused by an Irish judge in *Wheeler v Johnson*.[15] In that case the plaintiffs had bottled water using an ancient well in Belfast under the name Cromac Springs, a geographical appellation. The defendants began to sell water using the name Cromac Springs pointing to the number of wells and springs in that area. Chatterton VC had no doubt that a geographical name of this kind could become a trade mark, observing that rights to marks acquired by usage and reputation are in the nature of property rights and he granted an injunction restraining the defendants from using the phrase Cromac Springs in such a way as to indicate a connection with the plaintiff's business.

[24.06] However, the property right rationalisation did not take root and after *Singer Manufacturing Co v Loog*[16] little is heard of the Westbury view. By the end of the nineteenth century the Irish courts had given a considered view of the basis of the cause of action in two cases. In *Bodega Company v Owens*,[17] Chatterton VC adopted the view of James LJ in *Levy v Walker*[18] that a man:

> "has a right to say, you must not use a name, whether fictitious or real, you must not use a description, whether true or not, which is intended to represent, or calculated to represent to the world that your business is my business, and so, by a fraudulent misstatement deprive me of the profits of the business that would otherwise come to me. That is the principle and the sole principle on which this court interferes."

[24.07] Chatterton VC extended this *dictum* by allowing the plaintiff to succeed even without any proof of fraud, holding that both the fact of registration and the undoubted reputation of the plaintiffs gave them rights to their trade name independent of any statute. The Vice Chancellor held that:

> "On the evidence now before me, to the use of the word [Bodega] as a trade name in connection with his trade and business: this, however, does not give him an exclusive right to it, but only the right to restrain any other person from

---

[13.] *Oldham v James* (1863) 14 IR Ch R 81.

[14.] Eg *Hall v Barrows* (1863) 4 De GJ & S 150; *Leather Cloth Co v American Leather Cloth Co* (1865) 11 HLC 523.

[15.] (1879) 3 LR (Ir) 284.

[16.] (1882) 8 App Cas 15.

[17.] (1888) 23 LR (Ir) 371.

[18.] (1879) 10 Ch D 436, at 448.

using it in such a way as to represent that the business carried on by that person is his business."[19]

The Modern Basis for Passing Off

[24.08] In *Jameson v Dublin Distillers Co*[20] the plaintiff carried on the business of whiskey distilling under the name of John Jameson & Son Limited. There was another distillery which distilled and sold whiskey under the name of William Jameson and Company. Both companies had been founded in the eighteenth century. However, after the defendant company acquired William Jameson and Company they began to trade under the style of Jameson's Whiskey, dropping the prefix of William from the product label. The plaintiffs asserted that the William Jameson product was inferior and cheaper in price and that 'Jameson's Whiskey' in the public mind was associated with them. Chatterton VC gave an injunction to prevent the defendant trading in their product without prefacing the phrase 'Jameson's Whiskey' with the name of William. In treating this case as turning solely on the misuse of a name, Chatterton VC indicated that a court of equity would protect a person whose name has been used in trade or manufacture from use by others if such use leads others to think that the trade of the person using the name is that of the plaintiff and that for such relief to be obtained it is enough to show that the conduct complained of will tend to mislead ordinary persons. While Chatterton VC throughout this judgment refers to fraud, parallel developments in England suggest that some English judges were also persuaded that deceit remained at the heart of a passing off action.[21] However, in *AG Spalding v AW Gamage Ltd*[22] the true basis of a passing off action was enunciated by Lord Parker. In that case the learned Lord of Appeal observed that the basis of the relief is a false representation by the defendant and he reformulated the basis of the cause of action thus:

> "A cannot, without infringing the rights of B, represent goods which are not B's goods or B's goods of a particular class or quality to be B's goods or B's goods of that particular class or quality."

[24.09] While rejecting the notion of deceit and noting that reliefs could be obtained even against innocent defendants, Lord Parker observed that the right that the plaintiff may invoke is a right of property. The right is not a right of property in the name, mark or other *indicia* but, rather, a right of property in the business or goodwill that the plaintiff has created.[23] Lord Parker thus provided

---

[19.] (1888) 23 LR (Ir) 371, at 389-90.

[20.] [1900] 1 IR 43, 73, 466.

[21.] Eg Lord Davey in *Edge & Sons v Gallon & Son* (1900) 17 RPC 557, at 566.

[22.] (1915) 32 RPC 273.

[23.] Following on this point Lord Herschell in *Reddaway v Banham* [1896] AC 199, at 209.

not only a more satisfying rationale for passing off as a strict liability economic tort, he also provided a more flexible basis for relief when the misrepresentation is not linked to names, marks, etc, but to non-trade mark material such as a shape[24] or an advertising campaign.[25] The *Spalding* decision is seen as the basis of the most influential of all recent appellate utterances on liability for passing off for the formula devised by Lord Parker in *Spalding* came into its own in a series of cases in which marks *per se* were not used by the defendants but the defendants were seen to be appropriating the reputation and integrity of the plaintiff's goods by misdescribing their own products. The first case in this sequence, *Bollinger v Costa Brava Wine Co*[26] involved an action brought by producers of champagne from the Champagne district of France, who produced this wine from particular grapes by a particular method of production, who sought to prevent the defendants from using the phrase 'Spanish Champagne' to describe their own beverage. In that case Danckwerts J held that the misdescription would enable each and every shipper of sparkling wine from the Champagne region, whose wines met the requirements of the appellation, to protect the goodwill built up in England from damage caused by the defendants' misrepresentation to, and deception of, the public. This approach was extended in later cases to the producers of sherry from Jerez[27] and Scotch whisky.[28] The leading case which upholds the integrity of these decisions which afford to the producers of collective and individual rights to protect the integrity of a descriptive term that is used to market goods so as to exploit the public's esteem for those goods is the *Advocaat* case.[29] In that case, the manufacturers of an egg and gin drink, made to Dutch governmental standards, sought to prevent the defendants from marketing a cheaper product made up from a mixture of eggs and wine, from selling this as 'Old English Advocaat'. The plaintiffs, who were the market leader for the Dutch Advocaat were able to show that the name Advocaat had a significance and a reputation in England and that the defendant's product, being wine based rather than spirit based, did not meet consumer expectations and that, accordingly, the public would be deceived, to the detriment of the plaintiffs.

[24.10] In his speech, Lord Diplock, with whom the other law lords concurred[30] identified five elements in the tort of passing off:

---

24. *Reckitt & Colman Products v Borden* [1990] 1 All ER 873.
25. *Cadbury Schweppes v Pub Squash* [1981] 1 All ER 213.
26. [1960] Ch 262.
27. *Vine Products Ltd v MacKenzie* [1968] FSR 625.
28. *Walker (John) and Sons v Henry Ost & Co* [1970] 2 All ER 106.
29. *Warnink v Townsend & Sons (Hull)* [1979] AC 731.
30. Lords Dilhorne, Salmon and Scarman concurred with both Lord Diplock and Lord Fraser's speeches but Lord Fraser's speech is more narrowly focused and has not proved influential.

(1) a misrepresentation,

(2) made by a trader in the course of trade,

(3) to prospective customers of his or ultimate customers or ultimate consumers of goods or services supplied by him,

(4) which is calculated to injure the business or goodwill of another trader (in the sense that this is a reasonably foreseeable consequence) and

(5) which causes actual damage to a business or goodwill of the trader by whom the action is brought or (in a *quia timet* action) will probably do so.[31]

[24.11] In *Reckitt & Colman Products Ltd v Borden*,[32] Lord Oliver addressed the issue of the essential elements in passing off:

"[The plaintiff] must establish a goodwill or reputation attached to the goods or services which he supplies in the mind of the purchasing public by association with the identifying get-up (whether that consists simply of a brand name or trade description or the individual features of labelling or packaging) under which his particular goods or services are offered to the public, such that the get-up is recognised by the public as distinctive, specifically as the plaintiff's goods or services. Second, he must demonstrate a misrepresentation by the defendant to the public (whether or not intentional) leading or likely to lead the public to believe the goods or services offered by him are the goods or services of the plaintiff ... Third, he must demonstrate that he suffers or in a *quia timet* action that he is likely to suffer damage by reason of the erroneous belief engendered by the defendant's misrepresentation that the sources of the defendant's goods or services is the same as the sources of those offered by the plaintiff."[33]

[24.12] Lord Jauncey, in a concurring judgment gave his view of the proofs needed to succeed in the tort of passing off:

"In a case such as the present, where what is in issue is whether the goods of A are likely to be passed off as those of B, a plaintiff, to succeed, must establish

(1) that his goods have acquired a particular reputation among the public,

(2) that persons wishing to buy his goods are likely to be misled into buying the goods of the defendant and

(3) that he is likely to suffer damage thereby."[34]

[31.] [1979] AC 731 at 742.

[32.] [1990] 1 All ER 873; *Neutrogen Corp v Golden Ltd* (1995) 34 IPR 406.

[33.] [1990] 1 All ER 873, at 880.

[34.] *Ibid* at p 880.

[24.13] Lord Oliver's formulation has the merit of being more elaborately structured and it has been endorsed in recent English litigation as a valuable restatement of the Diplock approach. In *Consorzio del Prosciutto di Parma v Marks & Spencer plc*[35] Nourse LJ regarded the approach of both Lord Oliver and Lord Jauncey in *Reckitt v Coleman* as signalling a welcome return to the classical approach to the elements of a passing off action, an observation endorsed by Harman J in the *Fortnum and Mason* case[36] when he observed that the judgments of Lords Oliver and Jauncey are to the same effect "save that the Scotsman compresses it more than the Englishman".

[24.14] Modern Irish pronouncements on passing off have tended to follow the classical English approaches in cases such as *Reddaway v Banham*, *Spalding* and the *Advocaat* case.[37] The most expansive statement on passing off in recent times is the judgment of Budd J in *Polycell Products Ltd v O'Carroll*.[38]

> "To establish merchandise in such a manner as to mislead the public into believing that it is the merchandise or product of another is actionable. It injures the complaining party's right of property in his business and injures the goodwill in his business. A person who passes off the goods of another acquires, to some extent, the benefit of the business reputation of the rival trader and gets the advantage of his advertising."[39]

As we shall see this observation must be noted in its context of being a case involving get-up rather than use of names or marks.

GOODWILL

[24.15] In the *Polycell* case, Budd J emphasised that the vital interest that is being protected is a property right in the business or trade carried on by the plaintiff. It must therefore be established by the plaintiff that goodwill exists, defined in the leading English tax case of *Inland Revenue Commissioners v Muller & Co's Margarine Ltd*[40] as:

> "the benefit and advantage of the good name, reputation, and connection of a business. It is the attractive force which brings in custom. It is the one thing which distinguishes an old established business from a new business at its first start."[41]

---

35. [1991] RPC 351.
36. *Fortnum & Mason plc v Fortnums Ltd* [1994] FSR 438.
37. Eg Murphy J in *Falcon Travel Ltd v Owners Abroad Group plc* [1991] 1 IR 175; Kinlen J in *An Post v Irish Permanent* [1995] 1 ILRM 336.
38. [1959] Ir Jur Rep 34.
39. *Ibid* at 36.
40. [1901] AC 217, followed in *Independent Newspapers Ltd v Irish Press Ltd* [1932] IR 615.
41. *Ibid* at 213.

It must also be established that the plaintiff is responsible for developing nay reputation and goodwill, and passing off will fail if it is shown that the words that provoke the litigation are slang or colloquial terms, in common usage, that the plaintiff could not have contributed towards the language, as in 'the box' to describe television-related products and services: *Box Television Ltd v Box Magazines Ltd.*[42]

[24.16] While goodwill and a business activity are generally present when the plaintiff is successful, there are instances where goodwill can subsist even if the plaintiff does not have a business, eg trading has recently ceased. In order to establish the element of goodwill, the plaintiff must demonstrate a trading presence within a locality or public. In *Stannard v Reay*[43] the plaintiff traded as a mobile fish and chip shop in holiday resorts on the Isle of Wight for several weeks before the defendant started his own enterprise using the same business name. Even though the business itself was peripatetic and the composition of the customer body, many of them being holidaymakers or trippers, hardly constant, an interlocutory injunction was given because trade in this seasonal kind of business had built up very quickly. Goodwill will be easier to establish, even if trading has not been carried out for a long period of time, if the business is distinctive in terms of its trading sphere or business image.[44] There are cases where a defendant has sought to avoid liability by arguing that the plaintiff, as a professional person[45] or non-profit making entity has no goodwill because customers rely on that person's professional and personal skills rather than any trading reputation. In the case of charities, churches, clubs and associations[46] and the like, the absence of any direct market or business motivation has been invoked by defendants. In both instances these defences have been ineffective for the professional person, no more than the charity, church or club may find his reputation and professional standing tarnished if others may appropriate his name. The possibility that members of an association or the association itself may be subject to some later legal liability has also been used to justify the grant of interlocutory relief in *BMA v Marsh*.[47]

[42.] *Times* 1 March 1997.

[43.] [1967] RPC 589. It may be that neither party can establish goodwill; *Nationwide Building Society v Nationwide Estate Agents* (1987) 8 IPR 609; a trade promotion board does not trade; *An Bord Tráchtála v Waterford Foods* [1994] FSR 316.

[44.] *Compatibility Research Ltd v Computer Psyche Co* [1967] RPC 201; contrast *BBC v Talbot Motor Co* [1981] FSR 228.

[45.] *Burchell v Wilde* [1900] 1 Ch 551.

[46.] *British Diabetic Association v Diabetic Society Ltd* [1995] 4 All ER 812; *AG (Elisha) v Holy Apostolic and Catholic Church of the East (Assyrian)* NSW (1989) 16 IPR 619; *British Legion v British Legion Club (Street) Ltd* (1931) 48 RPC 555; *BMA v Marsh* (1931) 48 RPC 565.

[47.] *Ibid*; Inglis & Stevens [1996] EIPR 166.

[24.17] However, it has been held that political parties are not engaged in commercial activities[48] and in *Independent Newspaper Ltd v Irish Press Ltd* in 1932, Meredith J observed "Mr Yeats could not transfer the goodwill of his business as a poet".

[24.18] Where the plaintiff has ceased to trade or has perhaps abandoned[49] the use of some trading *indicia*, then the plaintiff may find it difficult to establish any goodwill or reputation sufficient to sustain a passing off action. In *Independent Newspapers Ltd v Irish Press Ltd*[50] the plaintiffs had acquired the title in the Evening Telegraph newspaper in 1925 but until the date of the application for a *quia timet* injunction, the plaintiffs had not since 1925 published a newspaper under that name; they, however, reserved the right to use the title at some time in the future. The defendants announced their intention to re-title their evening newspaper, the *Evening Press*, as the *Evening Telegraph*. Meredith J declined to grant the injunction sought, pointing out that particularly in *quia timet* cases the onus of showing an appropriation of goodwill and damage to be a heavy one for a plaintiff. Meredith J saw a distinction between a trader using premises vacated by a plaintiff for similar trading purposes and using an abandoned business name; in the latter case a business name has a peculiar function - to designate and identify. While there could not be a proprietary right in a name *simpliciter*, the seven year interval in trading and the remote possibility that purchasers who had recently returned to Ireland, following a long absence abroad, might be misled into thinking the new evening paper was the plaintiff's product made the injunction inappropriate given the improbability of damage.[51] While some vague intention to continue or return to trade is not sufficient, evidence that the plaintiff is active in trying to return to a trading situation will be influential,[52] but at issue is whether the business actually has any goodwill left. A temporary interruption in trading while relocating to other premises[53] or due to planning or other difficulties will not eliminate goodwill. So, in *Ad-Lib Club v Granville*[54] an injunction was issued to restrain the defendant from opening a club under the name Ad-Lib Club, even though the plaintiff had spent five years unsuccessfully trying to find premises in which he could resume to trade as a place of entertainment under the same name. The selection of the name by the defendant was held to indicate that some reputation must have survived the (temporary) closure of the plaintiff's club and

---

[48.] *Kean v McGiven* [1983] FSR 119.
[49.] *Elders IXL Ltd v Australian Estates Pty* (1987) 10 IPR 575.
[50.] [1932] IR 615.
[51.] Leave to re-enter the application if proof of damages could be shown was reserved.
[52.] *Star Industrial v Yap* [1976] FSR 256.
[53.] *Berkeley Hotel v Berkeley International* [1971] FSR 300.
[54.] [1971] 2 All ER 300.

because the name had no geographical or activity, based point of reference, the plaintiff was entitled to exploit this residual goodwill.[55] At some stage, however, goodwill will cease because the business will cease to be distinctive.[56]

Goodwill and Reputation Contrasted

[24.19] A number of leading English and Australian cases draw a distinction between goodwill and reputation. Where the plaintiff is able to establish that his product has a reputation or cache in the minds of the public, then the orthodox view is that this alone will not justify intervention by the courts, for a reputation may exist in isolation from any business activity, but goodwill, the appropriate basis for protection, can only arise and subsist through trading activities.[57] It must be doubted whether this distinction is a hard and fast one, for many judges use the word reputation to describe the plaintiff's obligation to show distinctiveness as well as the likelihood that the public are likely to be misled. Indeed in *Muckross Park Hotel Ltd v Randles and Others*[58] Barron J observed that:

> "'Goodwill' is a term used in some of the reported cases. However, it seems to me that 'reputation' is a more correct word in the context of passing off. 'Goodwill' is essentially a balance sheet term. It is an intangible asset. It is in my view, *inter alia,* the additional sum which would be paid for premises to carry on a particular business there which has either now or in the past been carried on and which will accordingly have a fund of customers already in existence. The value in the name is in the same position. Its importance lies in the number of people who know it and what it stands for."[59]

[24.20] Barron J, in preferring 'reputation' is not alone for even in *Jif Lemon*, Lords Jauncey and Oliver talked about 'reputation' and 'goodwill and reputation' respectively but the law lords were probably using the word 'reputation' in the context of distinctiveness. It is, however, likely that Barron J's preference will attract judicial support in Ireland and elsewhere because the courts in most common law jurisdictions are increasingly prepared to protect traders and corporations with international or regional trading reputations from parasitic or imitative trading, even though the plaintiff may only be able to demonstrate a reputation within that jurisdiction. A typical case is point is the decision of the Federal Court of Australia in *Al Hyat Publishing Co v Sotarno*[60]

[55.] See also *Elders IXL Ltd v Australian Estates Pty* (1987) 10 IPR 575.

[56.] *Kark v Odhams* [1962] RPC 163. On the converse issue of whether liability can be avoided if the defendant pleads no intention to trade, see the discussion by Karet [1996] EIPR 47 and cases cited therein.

[57.] *Anheuser-Busch Inc v Budejovicky Budvar NP* [1984] FSR 413 (the *Budweiser* case); *Athlete's Foot Marketing Associates Inc v Cobra Sports Ltd* [1980] RPC 343.

[58.] High Court, unrep, 10 November 1992.

[59.] *Ibid* p 12 of transcript.

[60.] (1996) 34 IPR 214; *Congra Inc v McCain Foods (Aust) Pty* (1992) 23 IPR 193.

where efforts to launch a newspaper with the *Al Hyat* title in Australia was the subject of successful interlocutory relief proceedings by the UK parent company that published this title internationally, even though the plaintiffs could only show reputation, and not the fact of trading, in Australia. In the context of global markets, international advertising and brand and consumer awareness, the English view, as espoused in *Budweiser*, looks increasingly archaic. This will be considered below.

[24.21] The basic principle upon which the courts operate is that the plaintiff must establish goodwill within the jurisdiction in which relief is sought. A person cannot complain about customers being deceived if he has no customers[61] who do business with the plaintiff. Whether goodwill exists on the part of the manufacturer, importer, distributor, retailer or some other person responsible for putting the goods or services before the public, is a question of fact. Some of the early cases indicate that the plaintiff should have some kind of trading presence within the jurisdiction but this is not the current state of the law. In *Grant v Levitt*[62] the defendant proposed to trade in Dublin under the style of Globe Furnishing Company. The plaintiffs traded in Liverpool under that name, a significant element in their business being mail order customers in Ireland who were targeted through advertising in Ireland. To similar effect is *C & A Modes Ltd v C & A (Waterford) Ltd*[63] when the plaintiff company, who traded in Northern Ireland, but had no retail business within the Republic, obtained an injunction to force the defendants to discontinue trading under the 'C & A' style of the plaintiffs. The plaintiff's advertising within the United Kingdom reached into the homes of residents of the Irish Republic and shopping expeditions to the plaintiff's Belfast store were extremely popular until 1969 and although business had declined from the Republic, the Supreme Court accepted that the plaintiffs enjoyed a significant goodwill in their C & A symbol in the Irish Republic. In England, the question of whether the plaintiff will succeed, if he does not have any customers within that jurisdiction, is somewhat uncertain. One early case, *Alain Bernadin et CIE v Pavilion Properties Ltd*[64] decided that the plaintiffs, proprietors of the famous Crazy Horse Saloon in Paris, could not obtain an injunction to prevent the defendant from using that name in England. The distribution of promotional literature in England to create or enhance a reputation in the hope that English visitors to Paris would patronise the plaintiff's establishment was insufficient to establish a customer base in England. However, this decision was not followed in *Maxim's v Dye*[65] where Graham J permitted the proprietors of Maxim's in Paris to prevent the defendant

---

[61.] See Oliver LJ in the *Budweiser* case [1984] FSR 413.
[62.] (1901) 18 RPC 361.
[63.] [1976] IR 198.
[64.] [1967] RPC 581; *Taco Bell Pty Ltd v Taco Co of Australia* (1982) 42 ALR 177.
[65.] [1978] 2 All ER 55.

from trading in Norwich under that name. The judge was unable to distinguish the *Crazy Horse* case but nevertheless took the view that on the facts a sufficient reputation and goodwill could be established in England by the plaintiff. Further, a decision denying relief simply because the plaintiff did not trade in England would be contrary to Article 59 of the Treaty of Rome by inhibiting the plaintiff from setting up any future business in England. In the *C & A* case the Supreme Court disapproved of the distinction between trading within a State and advertising within a State and declined to follow the reasoning in the *Crazy Horse* case. The *Crazy Horse* case, however, has not been disapproved in England, at least within the context of cases without a European Community context. In *Athlete's Foot Marketing Associates v Cobra Sports Ltd*,[66] Walton J declined to give an injunction to an American company who found that the name for their chain of sports footwear shops was being used by the defendant for a shop in London. While Walton J disapproved of the Irish Supreme Court's rejection of the *Crazy Horse Saloon* distinction, the actual decision in *Athlete's Foot* is supportable. While some English customers may have patronised the plaintiff's stores in the USA, there was no evidence of any efforts to advertise or franchise the plaintiff's name in England, much less create a reputation or goodwill in relation to their retailing activities. Some preliminary advertising, expenditure or preparatory work which indicates the possibility of goodwill being created via consumer expectations may, however, be enough to persuade a court that there is a serious issue to be tried.[67]

[24.22] Attention should be drawn to the fact that the debate on whether customers within one country can be identified is a somewhat sterile approach. In essence, we should be considering the likelihood that customers who know of the plaintiff are going to be deceived by a defendant when the customer seeks out the kind of product that the plaintiff offers because the customer believes, wrongly, that it is the plaintiff who is offering that product. For high value, branded products where quality is important, the *Crazy Horse* decision seems inappropriate[68] because it damages the marketability of the plaintiff's name in potential future markets. While recent cases indicate that even a few customers in another jurisdiction may suffice[69] when the plaintiff enjoys a substantial reputation, the trade-in-this-country view survives in England.[70] A Hong Kong court in *Ten Ichi Co v Jancar Ltd*[71] has gone even further in preventing a Hong

---

66. [1980] RPC 343.
67. *My Kinda Bones Ltd v Dr. Pepper's Store Co* [1981] FSR 228.
68. See *Apple Computer Inc v Apple Leasing Industries Ltd* (1991) 22 IPR 257; *Calvin Klein Inc v International Appard Syndicate* [1995] FSR 515.
69. *Orkin Exterminating Co v Pestco* (1985) 19 DLR (4th) 90.
70. *Tie Rack plc v Tie Rack Stores Pty Ltd* [1989] 4 SA 427; *Fortnum & Mason plc v Fortnams Ltd* [1994] FSR 438.
71. [1990] FSR 151.

Kong restaurant from using the name and trading style of an up-market chain of Japanese Tempura restaurants on the ground that a considerable volume of Japanese tourists may easily visit Hong Kong and that such persons may believe they were trading with the plaintiff. Here the case goes much further than the *C & A* case because there was no evidence that the plaintiff company advertised or sought to cultivate any market for its services in Hong Kong nor was there any evidence of an intention to trade in Hong Kong in the immediate future, much less expenditure to create goodwill in this regard. If the plaintiff trades within a number of cities or a region within a particular jurisdiction, the defendant will be unlikely to persuade a court not to grant relief because the defendant intends only to trade in another city or region where the plaintiff is not active for markets and customers are flexible and modern advertising and communications make the likelihood of reputations spreading beyond a trading sphere to be somewhat inevitable[72] unless the business only has a localised appeal[73] or lacks distinctiveness.

[24.23] The Trade Marks Act 1996 alters this position significantly in order to protect well-known marks[74] which are the property, not simply of EU nationals (the *Maxim* case) but persons who are nationals of Paris Convention States when those marks are well-known. Section 2 of the GATT/TRIPS agreement is also relevant here.

Who owns the Goodwill?

[24.24] It may also be of the utmost importance to establish who enjoys the goodwill in question. Where goods are manufactured to the order of a seller, the goodwill vests in the seller rather than the manufacturer, unless the manufacturer alone is held out as the sole trader involved or the defendant falsely asserts authorised distributor status.[75] Where a foreign manufacturer appoints a local distributor then the foreign manufacturer, if identified, will generally possess goodwill[76] unless the local distributor or representative is identified as the source of the goods, the foreign manufacturer being undisclosed to purchasers.[77] Where a licensee obtains rights of manufacture under a licensing agreement then the licensor obtains goodwill *vis-à-vis* third parties.[78] The recent

---

[72.] *Chelsea Man Menswear Ltd v Chelsea Girl Ltd* [1987] RPC 189; *The Last Aussie Fish Caf Pty Ltd v Almove Pty Ltd* (1989) 16 IPR 376.

[73.] *Clock Ltd v Clock House Hotel Ltd* (1936) 53 RPC 269; *A Levey v Henderson-Kenton (Holdings) Ltd* [1974] RPC 617.

[74.] So called Marque Notoire - TMA 1996, s 59.

[75.] *Hirsch v Jones* (1876) 3 Ch 584; *Nishika Corp v Goodchild* [1990] FSR 371.

[76.] *Manus (A/B) v R J Fulwood & Bland Ltd* (1949) 66 RPC 71.

[77.] *Sturtevant Engineering Ltd v Sturtevant Mill Co* [1936] 3 All ER 137; *Grange Marketing Ltd v M & Q Plastic Products Ltd* High Court, unrep, 17 June 1976, distinguishing *Dental Manufacturing Co v de Trey & Co* [1912] 3 KB 76.

case of *Colgate Palmolive Ltd v Markwell Finance Ltd*[79] points out the importance of joining all parties as co-plaintiff since the late joinder of a parent company had a deleterious effect on the award of costs to the successful plaintiff in the action.

MISREPRESENTATION

[24.25] The basis of passing off is a false representation by the defendant that goods or services offered by him are the goods of another person. It is generally true to say that express misrepresentations are not the most frequent instances of passing off, but examples exist where the defendant supplies customers with the goods of a third party when the customer requested the plaintiff's goods by name and has not consented to third party goods as a substitution.[80] In most cases, however, the misrepresentation takes place because marks, names, get-up or the image or marketing techniques used by the defendant are likely to cause confusion in the mind of customers about the source of the product, or, in the case of merchandise licensing, about whether the plaintiff has licensed or authorised the defendant to produce the goods in question. The misrepresentation must take place in a context whereby the statements are calculated, ie likely to deceive. The plaintiff cannot assert an infringement by passing off simply because the defendant uses a mark, name or other indicia which is identified as the 'property' of the plaintiff if no misrepresentation takes place.[81] It may be that the defendant is doing nothing more than using, trading or advertising materials that are common or universal within a trade or profession as in the case of *Hennessy & Co v Keating*[82] where the use by the defendant of brandy labels, which featured a grape and leaf motif but did not incorporate any of the Hennessy marks, was held not to constitute a passing off. The defendant, for example, is entitled to truthfully describe his present or former link with the plaintiff company[83] but to describe the defendant company incorrectly as agent of or the successor to the plaintiff company when there is no link and the plaintiff company is still in existence, is a passing off.[84] It is also a misrepresentation to represent goods that have been withdrawn from sale by the manufacturer as substandard, as being the latest version of that product.[85] Filling

---

[78.] *Alfred Dunhill Ltd v Sunoptic* [1979] FSR 337.

[79.] [1990] RPC 197.

[80.] *British Leather Cloth Manufacturing v Dickens & Cooper Ltd* (1914) 31 RPC 337; *Procea Products Ltd v Evans & Sons* (1951) 68 RPC 210.

[81.] *Singer Manufacturing Co v Loog* (1882) 8 App Cas 15.

[82.] [1908] 1 IR 43, at 73 affirmed by the House of Lords at 466.

[83.] *Pompadour Laboratories v Frazer* [1966] RPC 7.

[84.] *Kent Adhesive Products Co v Ryan* High Court, unrep, 5 November 1993.

[85.] *Spalding v Gamage* (1915) 32 RPC 117; contrast *Revlon Inc v Cripps & Lee* [1980] FSR 85.

branded product containers with inferior versions of that product is also clearly a misrepresentation.[86] The range of, and possibilities for, misrepresentation cannot be catalogued; suffice it to say that if the statement is false and likely to deceive the public and damage the plaintiff, then it is in all probability actionable.

[24.26] While it is not necessary to show an intention to defraud in order to establish passing off because there is no mental element involved in the cause of action, the plaintiff may find it useful to establish dishonest intent by a defendant, for the courts will readily infer that the defendant has achieved his objective of deceiving members of the public by way of the misrepresentation.[87] If the defendant is an innocent infringer, this may operate so as to lead the court not to infer the likelihood of deception or damage[88] and an innocent infringer will be inhibited from trading by way of an injunction, but there may be some effect on the right to damages or an account of profits. The innocent infringer, once put on notice, will be liable to compensate the plaintiff for post notice damages but older cases indicate that because fraud was a proof in common law passing off cases, only nominal damages are available against the innocent infringer.[89] The basic standard by which the misrepresentation is to be tested is whether the misrepresentation is likely, on an objective basis, to deceive a 'careless and casual person'.[90] The defendant may seek to justify his conduct by stressing that the public, as an educated body of persons, would inspect and compare the goods and not be deceived, but the courts will, however, consider whether a substantial body of persons would nevertheless be likely to be deceived. In *Taittinger v Allbev Ltd*[91] the effect of this test was graphically illustrated. The defendant manufactured a non-alcoholic drink called Elderflower Champagne which he sold at £2.45 per bottle. The drink was sold in the thick heavy bottles associated with champagne and foil caps and mushroom shaped corks were also incorporated. The plaintiff, a Champagne House, brought a representative action alleging, *inter alia*, a passing off. At first instance, Mervyn Davies J found a misrepresentation but held that there was no likelihood of damage. Before the Court of Appeal, the defendants cross-appealed that the judge had been incorrect in holding a material misrepresentation, arguing that members of the public, seeing a bottle of this

---

[86.] *Jameson (John) & Sons Ltd v Clarke* (1902) 19 RPC 255.

[87.] *Parker-Knoll Ltd v Knoll International* [1962] RPC 265; *Telmac Teleproducts Aust Pty Ltd v Coles Myer Ltd* (1989) 12 IPR 297; *Congra v McCain Foods* (1992) 23 IPR 193.

[88.] *Grange Marketing Ltd v M & Q Plastic Products Ltd* High Court, unrep, 17 June 1976; *Petersville Sleigh Ltd v Sugarman* (1987) 10 IPR 501.

[89.] *Crawshay v Thompson* (1842) 4 Man & G 357; *Draper v Trist* [1939] 3 All ER 513.

[90.] *Per* Holmes LJ in *Hennessy v Keating* [1908] 1 IR 43, at 101; applying *Singer Manufacturing Co v Loog* (1882) 8 App Cas 15 at 18 *per* Lord Selborne ("ignorant and unwary").

[91.] [1994] 4 All ER 75.

kind at £2.45 would inspect the product and conclude that it was not champagne or linked with champagne. Peter Gibson LJ agreed with Mervyn Davies J who had observed that a simply unworldly man may know nothing of Elderflower Champagne as an old cottage drink and may know nothing of champagne prices. Such persons are not a majority of the public or even a substantial sector of the public, but there must be many persons who would think that Elderflower is Champagne. The other members of the Court of Appeal indicated that the real danger is that persons could believe this beverage was in some way associated with French champagne and thus 'dilute' the goodwill in Champagne.[92]

[24.27] The need for the defendant to make a representation to customers or potential customers of the plaintiff has been a significant factor in limiting the scope of a successful passing off action. In the absence of any registered trade mark or copyright or design right protection, the courts permit imitative or even derivative trading if the plaintiff's own badges of trade are not distinctive, are generic, or attributable to a fashion that the plaintiff cannot identify as being of his making. In *Adidas Sports Schuhfabriken Adi Dassler KA v Charles O'Neill & Co*[93] O'Higgins CJ said of the plaintiff's right to prevent the defendant from using a three stripe design on their own sportswear when that design was, on the evidence, not associated in the public mind with Adidas products and no other trader:

> "In this case, if the complaint had been that the name 'Adidas' or a name similar thereto or an imitation thereof had been used in association with O'Neill's goods, although no Adidas products were on sale in this country, I have no doubt that a goodwill and a potential in relation to customers would have been established and protection given. We are dealing, however, not with a well known name but with a particular design and its exclusive association with the goods of Adidas in Ireland must be established if the claim made is to succeed. One other matter should be mentioned. The fact is that Adidas have, over the years, projected their products with the three-stripe design in every advertising medium available. This fact, however, does not give title to Adidas to complain if a trader, attracted by the design or susceptible to the fashion which its prominence creates, decides to copy or imitate. The mere copying of a design or the anticipation of a fashion or the taking advantage of a market or demand created by another's advertising is not of itself sufficient to support an action for passing off if the trader against whom the complaint is made has sufficiently distinguished his goods so that confusion is not created."[94]

[24.28] In contrasting the use of a name as distinct from a design, O'Higgins CJ is emphasising that certain badges of trade are more effective than others in

---

92. Carty (1996) 112 LQR 632.
93. [1983] ILRM 112.
94. [1983] ILRM 112 at 116-7.

allowing the plaintiff to establish that his products and services are distinctive of the plaintiff's trade. The use of the plaintiff's trade marks or logo (or deceptively similar marks) names, descriptive terms or geographical statements of origin are the most frequent sources of the misrepresentation but impersonation of goods by adopting the style or get-up of the plaintiff's goods without using the plaintiff's marks or in conjunction with distinguishing terms or names identifiable with the defendant, may suffice to ground liability as in *Gabicci plc v Dunnes Stores*[95] where sweaters produced by the defendants were made up in the same factory as the plaintiff's branded goods, sold at half the price under the defendant's St. Bernard label. Carroll J held an injunction should be granted for at point of sale the public could not distinguish these garments, thinking that the defendants must have got the plaintiff's goods under an arrangement at a special price. Similarly in *R Griggs Group and Others v Dunnes Stores*[96] the actual get up of a Doc Martens Shoe was replicated by the defendant's product, but for the sake of injunction proceedings, the misrepresentation relied upon was a verbal description given by the defendant's employees of the disputed product being 'Docs'.

Names

[24.29] While the plaintiff cannot assert a proprietary right in his personal name he is entitled to trade in his own name even if the use of that name is likely to result in some confusion.[97] This right is limited to cases where the person uses his name as a style of trading and it is a very limited concession for it is generally agreed that the defence is available to natural persons who do nothing further which could cause confusion and who act honestly.[98] This requirement of acting honestly and *bona fide* is an important one and there are several Irish cases in which the defendant has been prevented from trading in his own name because of the context within which the name has been used.

[95.] High Court, unrep, 31 July 1991.

[96.] High Court, unrep, 4 October 1996.

[97.] Older cases assert this right but more modern decision suggest otherwise. *Taylor Bros Ltd v Taylors Group Ltd* (1990) 14 IPR 353; *Guccio Gucci SPA v Paolo Gucci* [1991] FSR 89; for older cases that suggest the right subsists see in particular, *Rodgers v Rodgers* (1924) 41 RPC 277; *Marengo v Daily Sketch* (1948) 65 RPC 242.

[98.] *Parker-Knoll Ltd v Parker Knoll International Ltd* [1962] RPC 265; *Boswell-Wilkie Circus Pty v Brian Boswell Circus Property Ltd* [1985] FSR 434, affirmed at [1986] FSR 479; *Noel Leeming Television Ltd v Noel's Appliance Centre Ltd* (1985) 5 IPR 249. This issue has resurfaced in England when the Forte hotel and restaurant chain discontinued proceedings against a Winchester tea-room proprietor who traded in his own name of 'The Forte Tea-rooms' *Times* 8 August 1996. *Wadlow* doubts the existence of any such exception to this confusion principle.

[24.30] In *Valentine v Valentine*[99] the plaintiffs had previously traded as Valentine & Co, tea merchants at 23 Corn Market, Belfast. When their lease expired the defendants obtained a lease of those premises and traded as J Valentine & Co, also as tea merchants. It was held that such conduct was calculated to deceive the public. In *Glenny v Smith*[100] the defendant used his own name to describe his business but added that he was 'From T & G' his former employer. The use of the former employer was held to have been misleading and upon proof of persons being misled, the use of the phrase was restrained by injunction and the view that persons should not describe goods sold by way of a surname that may mislead has been endorsed in Irish case law[101] although, even if the defendant is held to be liable for passing off, injunctive relief will be limited to discontinuing the misleading usage: the defendant may still be able to use his own name[102] but the adoption of a surname that has no link with any of the defendants will be regarded as an attempt to appropriate the name of a reputable trader[103] unless businesses are dissimilar and the company name is explained away.[104]

[24.31] Even if the trader uses his own name in a *bona fide* manner, and there are few cases which actually establish this as a positive finding of fact, the plaintiff can still succeed if the defendant has marked or marketed goods or services by reference to a mark that is distinctive of the plaintiff's goods or services. In *Baume & Co v Moore (AH) Ltd*[105] the marketing of watches which were factually correctly identified by a mark that was similar to the plaintiff's mark was the subject of an injunction even though the defendant was held to have acted honestly. His failure to attempt to distinguish, or disclaim, his goods from those of the plaintiff was a significant element here. Initials may also be distinctive and protected via injunction[106] when these have become distinctive.

Descriptive Words

[24.32] Where the defendant has used a word or phrase to describe or identify his goods or services, the plaintiff may complain that the use of that descriptive

---

99. (1892) 31 LR Ir 488. Contrast *Burgess v Burgess* (1853) 3 Deg M & G 896 and *Turton v Turton* (1889) 42 Ch 128.
100. (1862) 2 Dr & Sm 476.
101. *Jameson v Dublin Distillers Co* [1900] 1 IR 43.
102. *Dickson v Dickson* [1909] 1 IR 204.
103. *Lloyds & Dawson Bros v Lloyds, Southampton Ltd* (1912) 29 RPC 433; *Dockrell v Dockrell* (1941) 75 ILTR 226.
104. *Fortnum & Mason plc v Fortnam Ltd* [1994] FSR 439.
105. [1958] Ch 907. See 'Restraining Orders Put on Firm Marketing Footwear Dryer', *Irish Times* 1 May 1997.
106. *Kinahan v Botton* (1863) 15 IR Ch R 75; *C & A Modes Ltd v C & A (Waterford) Ltd* [1976] IR 198.

phrase may confuse customers into believing that the goods or services are connected with the plaintiff's business. The plaintiff is required to establish that the phrase has acquired a secondary meaning. The leading case is *Reddaway v Banham*.[107] Here, the plaintiff manufactured a product called 'camel hair belting' and was in fact the market leader. A former employee set up his own business manufacturing camel hair belting made up from camel hair. The House of Lords held that it had been established that in the minds of purchasers this product was identified as the product of Reddaway for here the phrase went beyond being merely descriptive insofar as it was connected with the business of the plaintiff. Some phrases, however, will be so common that they will not be capable of producing a secondary meaning. In *Office Cleaning Services Ltd v Westminster Office Cleaning Association*[108] the House of Lords held that the only possible mark was the activity of cleaning offices, that as a mark this was a non-starter because it was simply a description of what each party did. The plaintiff should be able to point to a name which identifies what the goods or services provided actually are and at the same time point to a descriptive phrase or brand that is distinctive of the plaintiff's trading activities. In the absence of such proofs the plaintiff may find that the defendant can use descriptive phrases such as 'oven chips'[109] 'vacuum cleaner',[110] 'linoleum',[111] for here the phrase will be held to be descriptive or generic in nature and thus not distinctive. A striking example of a successful argument for a secondary meaning can be found in *Kettle Chip Company Pty Ltd v Apand Pty Ltd*[112] The plaintiffs in 1989 manufactured potato chips by reference to a particular method of cooking by hand in batch cookers and sold those chips under the name of Kettle Chips. The defendants later made chips of a similar texture using different methods of cooking but described the product as Kettle style chips. Holding that the word 'Kettle' does not naturally describe a potato chip the court held that the word had acquired the status of a brand. Even if the word was descriptive, insofar as it referred to the method of cooking, it had also acquired a secondary meaning with the Australian public insofar as it was linked to the plaintiff's potato chip products.

[107.] [1896] AC 199. See 'Golden Pages gets injunction against publisher' *Irish Times* 11 July 1996 when injunctions against the use of the words 'Golden' and 'Yellow' pages were given against an Internet-based advertiser.

[108.] [1946] 1 All ER 320; *County Sound v Ocean Sound* [1991] FSR 367.

[109.] *McCain International v Country Fair Foods Ltd* [1981] RPC 69.

[110.] *British Vacuum Cleaner Co v New Vacuum Cleaner Co* [1907] 2 CH 312.

[111.] *Linoleum Manufacturing Co v Nairn* (1878) 7 Ch 834.

[112.] (1993) 27 IPR 321.

[24.33] Descriptive words such as 'Solartint' for sunglasses[113] are inherently descriptive. Some descriptive words have been categorised as being distinctive rather than descriptive, such as Fantasyland for an amusement park.[114] Foreign words may be held to be descriptive as in the case of 'Chi Yip' which means 'acquire property', thus a descriptive phrase in the area of real estate companies in Hong Kong.[115]

Geographical Names

[24.34] Place names, whether local, national or international are clearly capable of distinguishing or identifying the plaintiff's goods or services. In *Montgomery v Thompson*[116] the town of Stone was the place of the plaintiff's brewery and his beers were sold as Stone Ales. The defendant was prevented from building his own brewery and selling his ales under the name of Stone Ales. In the recent case of *Muckross Park Hotel Ltd v Randles*[117] the plaintiffs were able to show that the reputation of their long established hotel in Muckross, Co. Kerry was such that 'the Muckross' was known nationally and internationally as connoting the Muckross Park, so that when the defendant changed the name of their hotel from the Dromhall Hotel, following refurbishment and an extension of the premises, to the 'Muckross Court Hotel' the geographical fact that their premises were in the district of Muckross and situated on the Muckross Road could not provide a justification for this user for a secondary meaning had been established. It will not, however, always be possible to establish a secondary meaning for products as in *My Kinda Town v Soll*[118] where the phrase 'Chicago Pizza' was held not to be such as to conjure up a secondary meaning.

Get-Up

[24.35] The whole visible external appearance of the goods, as they are presented to the public prior to purchase, is capable of being misrepresented. Where the external appearance of the goods is in essence due to the shape, colour, size and composition of the container the recent *Jif Lemon* case[119] illustrates that once a distinctive reputation is established as a mater of fact, then the defendant may be prohibited from trading in goods that are packaged in an imitative way, even if the defendant does not use the plaintiff's trade mark and

---

[113.] *Dodds Family Investments v Lane Industries* (1993) 26 IPR 261.

[114.] *Walt Disney Productions v Fantasyland Hotel Inc* (1994) 31 IPR 233.

[115.] *Land Power International Holdings Ltd v Inter-Land Properties Ltd* (1995) 31 IPR 163; See also *Bodega Company v Owens* (1888) 23 LR (Ir) 371.

[116.] [1891] AC 217.

[117.] High Court, unrep, 10 November 1992.

[118.] [1983] RPC 407.

[119.] *Reckitt and Coleman Products v Borden Inc* [1990] 1 All ER 865; *Dalgety Spillers Foods Ltd v Food Brokers Ltd* [1994] FSR 505; Mills [1994] EIPR 307.

some efforts have been made to distinguish the defendant's goods by way of his own mark or distinctive labelling. The external appearance of goods and the similarity between them does not, in itself, provide the plaintiff with an open and shut case of passing off, for the courts tend towards the view that buyers are likely to purchase by reference to brands and brand names rather than a possibly generic appearance. In Ireland, the cases involving misdescription by way of packaging have tended to go in favour of the plaintiff. In *Grange Marketing Ltd v M & Q Plastic Products Ltd*[120] the products in question were exercise machines which were being sold by the defendants in boxes that were the same size and shape as that of the plaintiffs, with point of sale material copied from the plaintiffs' own material and using the plaintiffs' box design and advertising slogan. In *Polycell Products Ltd v O'Carroll and Others*[121] the defendants sold wallpaper paste in packages similar to those used by the plaintiff and while the brand names were quite dissimilar, the danger of confusion was such as to merit interlocutory relief. Injunctions have also been obtained to prevent the sale of non-dairy spreads from being sold in containers under a get-up that closely resembles another product already in the market but in these cases the defendant's brand name itself has tended to be very close to the plaintiff's name.[122] In some cases the court is able to find parasitic copying of the packaging and get-up as a deliberate act by the defendant and where this occurs relief can be expected.[123] Where, however, the shape or style of the goods themselves is at issue, there are few cases in which the plaintiff has succeeded when the extent of the copying relates to functional items as distinct from decoration.[124] Even where decoration is involved, the decision in the *Adidas* case[125] suggest that distinctiveness may not be easy to establish. In the case of pharmaceutical products the size, shape and colour of the product itself is the only real method of distinguishing, for the medicines themselves may be much the same as between brands.[126] Generally, mixtures of colours will be held to be much more distinctive than single colours unless the colour of the item or get-up has significance for the customer (eg the market is an illiterate one that buys in ignorance of brands or in reliance on colour or get-up alone).

---

[120] High Court, unrep, 17 June 1976.

[121] [1959] IR Jur Rep 38.

[122] *Mitchelstown Co-Operative Agricultural Society Ltd v Goldenvale* High Court, unrep, 12 December 1985; *R & C Products v Sterling Winthrop* (1993) 27 IPR 223.

[123] *Cantrell & Cochrane Ltd v Savage Smith & Co* High Court, unrep, 16 October 1975.

[124] *Edge (William) & Sons Ltd v William Niccolls & Sons* [1911] AC 693; *Tot Toys v Mitchell* (1992) 25 IPR 337.

[125] [1983] ILRM 113; See Phillips (1983) 5 DULJ (ns) 105.

[126] *Hoffman La Roche v DDSA Pharmaceuticals* [1972] RPC 1; *Beecham Group v Eiraj Pharmaceuticals Ltd* High Court, unrep, 27 March 1985; *Irish Times*, 28 March 1985; *Ciba-Geigy Canada Ltd v Apotex Inc* (1992) 24 IPR 652.

Inverse Passing off

[24.36] If the misrepresentation made by the defendant is to the effect that the goods or services the defendant is providing are the defendants when in fact they are those of another, recent case-law indicates that such cases of 'inverse passing off' may be relieved against, as where the defendants advertising material claimed that ornamental conservatories produced by the plaintiffs were in fact produced by the defendant: *Bristol Conservatories v Conservatories Custom Built Ltd.*[127]

The Likelihood of Deception and Damage

[24.37] The plaintiff will have to prove, in a number of different ways, that his reputation is such that the defendant's trading activity is likely to cause the public to believe that the defendant is providing goods or services that are linked with those provided by the plaintiff, thus causing substantial damage to the plaintiff's property in the goodwill of his business. In *Stringfellow v McCain Foods*[128] the plaintiff was the proprietor of a night club in London which was at that time successful and popular with the affluent and glamorous sector of London society. The defendant used the name Stringfellow to launch an oven chip product that was long and thin in shape. The advertising campaign for the product involved scenes from a discotheque and in the view of the Court of Appeal involved an element of misrepresentation. However, there was no proof of damage; the word Stringfellow could have a reference to the 'stringy' nature of the chip. In *Newsweek Inc v BBC*[129] the title 'Newsweek' was adopted by the BBC for their current affairs programme. The proprietors of Newsweek Magazine sought to prevent this usage claiming it would deceive the public into thinking that the publication was in some way involved. However, it was held that the BBC would distinguish the broadcast by way of distinctive titles, credits and BBC logos, thus avoiding any deception. If the defendant seeks to trade in competition with a brand leader by putting onto the market goods that are produced in a similar get-up, the likelihood of confusion may, in most cases, be avoided by emphasising different brand names[130] or by selling the goods in a different markets.[131] Where evidence of this kind is before the Court passing off will not be established for it is likely that 'only a moron in a hurry' would be deceived; *Morning Star Co-operative Society Ltd v Express Newspapers.*[132]

[127.] [1989] RPC 455; Carty [1993] EIPR 370. See also *John Robert Powers Scholl Inc v Tessensohn* [1995] FSR 947 (a Singapore case).

[128.] [1984] RPC 501.

[129.] [1979] RPC 441.

[130.] *Rizla Ltd v Bryant & May Ltd* [1986] RPC 389.

[131.] *Financial Times v Evening Standard* [1991] FSR 8; *Borthwick v Evening Post* (1888) 37 Ch 449.

[132.] (1978) 1A IPR 661.

[24.38] The courts will tend to infer damage in cases where fraudulent trading is established or where the plaintiff can show a falling volume of sales. Damage is normally made up from a reduction in the volume of sales,[133] injurious association with the defendant because the defendant's goods are inferior, or because the plaintiff may become embroiled in disputes with others or suffer loss of goodwill. A recent illustration of this occurred in *Associated Newspapers plc v Insert Media Ltd*.[134] The proprietors of two national newspapers objected to the practice of inserting advertising leaflets into their daily newspapers. After finding that there was an element of misrepresentation - that the leaflets formed a part of the newspaper - Browne-Wilkinson VC went on to consider whether there was any evidence of substantial damage[135] occurring if this practice were permitted:

> "The evidence disclosed that, on occasion, readers who had responded to advertisements in the plaintiff's newspapers and had been less than satisfied with the results had complained to the publishers, who had taken steps, usually effectively, to right wrongs which the readers suffered. It is true that such letters of complaint cannot be tied in with any one reader ceasing to take the plaintiff's newspapers though, as the judge held, that is not decisive. If the third defendant can procure newsagents to make inserts without the knowledge and approval of the plaintiffs, there must be a real risk that the Daily Mail will be thought by the readers to be responsible for the accuracy and honesty of those advertisements. The publishers will have no control over the nature of the advertisements, or their honesty or their quantity. There is therefore an obvious, appreciable, risk of loss of goodwill and reputation by the publishers."[136]

Despite *Taittinger v Albev*, a majority of the Court of Appeal has reiterated the view that if the public are not likely to be confused by the use of a name, but such sue has the danger of harming the plaintiffs reputation but not the plaintiff's goodwill, this is not sufficient to sustain a passing off action: *Harrods v Harrodian School*.[137]

[24.39] The requirement that there be substantial damage may help to explain the recent Irish case of *B & S v Irish Auto Trader*.[138] There the plaintiffs sought an injunction to prevent the defendants from launching an Irish edition of their magazine 'Auto Trader'. The plaintiffs had produced a magazine which had used the word Autotrader as a heading for their used car section. An injunction

---

[133.] *Singer v Loog* (1888) 8 App Cas 15.

[134.] [1991] 3 All ER 535.

[135.] See Peter Gibson LJ in *Taittinger v Allbev* [1994] 4 All ER 75, at 83.

[136.] [1991] 3 All ER at 542.

[137.] (1996) 35 IPR 355.

[138.] [1995] 2 ILRM 252; See also *Private Research Ltd v Brosnan* [1995] 1 IR 534.

was refused because McCracken J held that it was unlikely that car dealers would be deceived but that if members of the public bought the defendant's magazine thinking it was the plaintiffs, they would quickly realise that this was not the case.

[24.40] The most interesting recent decision on damage is the decision of Murphy J in *Falcon Travel Ltd v Owners Abroad Group*.[139] The plaintiffs, a small retail travel agency had traded under the name Falcon Travel since 1970. In 1988 the defendants started to sell package holidays, as tour operators, on the Irish market using the name Falcon. This caused market confusion insofar as the plaintiff complained that "I am afraid that everybody thinks I am the defendants". Was confusion enough or did the plaintiff have to show a real tangible risk of damage resulting from the confusion? While damage is normally an essential proof,[140] Murphy J held that in cases where the plaintiff can show that the defendant has appropriated the plaintiff's reputation, submerging that reputation into that of the defendant, the tort is completed, whether or not any other damage has been shown to follow from "that invasion of the right of property". This decision must be regarded as incorrect, for damage to goodwill is the basis of liability rather than appropriation of any supposed property right. Rather than awarding nominal damages, Murphy J awarded damages as a rough estimate of loss intended to allow the plaintiffs to advertise and re-establish their identity with the public and the trade.

Proof of Damage

[24.41] If damage is not inferred, and two Irish cases indicate that this may well occur when improper use is proved,[141] the plaintiff will have to establish the likelihood of deception and damage.[142] If the action is *quia timet* then proof may be impossible to obtain. While some cases involved the testimony of traders, wholesalers and the like, this evidence may not always be admissible, for the basic issue will be whether, at the point of sale, a customer is likely to be deceived and the judges have tended to say that they are a more suitable point of reference for this test than someone actively involved in business, and although actual evidence of deception is helpful, the independent judgment of the court should always be exercised.[143] Trade evidence of customer behaviour is

---

[139.] [1991] 1 IR 175. Carty [1996] EIPR 487.

[140.] Citing *Unitex Ltd v Union Texturing Co* [1973] RPC 119.

[141.] *C & A Modes v C & A (Waterford) Ltd* [1976] IR 198 and *Falcon Travel Ltd v Owners Abroad Group (Supra)*.

[142.] See in particular *Harrods v Harrodian School* (1996) 35 IPR 355, at 369-370 *per* Millet LJ; Lai (1996) 146 NLJ 874.

[143.] *Payton & Co v Snelling Lampard & Co* [1901] AC 308; *Symonds Cider & English Wine Co v Schwepps (Ireland)* High Court, unrep, 10 January 1997.

increasingly being admitted[144] in areas where specialist knowledge is needed and the area is one where the court is ignorant of the specific market in question. Many courts have traditionally been hostile to market survey or opinion survey evidence, fearing that the survey itself may be flawed because of the way in which it has been conducted.[145] Whiteford J in *Imperial Group Ltd v Philip Morris Ltd*[146] set out a number of guidelines by which the veracity of the survey evidence can be trusted. In the *Jif Lemon* case survey evidence was gathered by surveying customers in shops and supermarkets about their perceptions of the rival products and the House of Lords endorsed the trial judge's view that this evidence was admissible. Survey evidence played a significant role in the hearing in *An Post v Irish Permanent plc*[147] where two surveys were admitted to show that advertisements for savings certificates were associated in the minds of 81% of the public, who were aware of this product, with An Post's Saving Certificate and that of those persons aware of the Irish Permanent product, a significant number of such persons (3 out of 10) were confused between that product and the An Post product. This survey evidence was subjected to considerable criticism by the defendant and it seems that for this reason Kinlen J put the survey evidence to one side and determined the issue of confusion without relying upon either survey.

Character Merchandising

[24.42] One important area of commercial activity relates to the practice of character merchandising and the possibility that the defendant may appropriate the person or image of a real or invented character for his own ends. In this context, the act of appropriation, with consent, does not lead the courts to impute damage to the plaintiff's goodwill. The plaintiff will generally have to prove that members of the public would believe the plaintiff had licensed the use of the image or character in circumstances where damage to the goodwill in the business would be prejudiced. The licensing of an image or an invented character is as much a commercial enterprise as the actual sale of goods or services. At first, English courts struggled with recognition of this problem. Radio personalities and actors who found that either their name had been appropriated to promote a product with which they had no conceivable point of contact could not point to any cause of action because their goodwill was based upon their 'business' as entertainers - there was no common field of activity in relation to the plaintiff's professional persona and the defendant's marketing of

---

144. *Guccio Gucci SPA v Paolo Gucci* [1991] FSR 89.
145. *United Biscuits (UK) Ltd v Burtons Biscuits* [1992] FSR 14.
146. [1984] RPC 293; *The European Ltd v Economist Newspapers* [1996] FSR 431.
147. [1995] 1 ILRM 336.

a breakfast cereal.[148] Similarly, the impersonation of a distinguished actor's voice in order to promote products by way of radio advertisements was held not to be actionable despite evidence that listeners thought that the voice was that of the plaintiff.[149] English courts adhered to this approach in cases involving the pop group ABBA,[150] the fictional detective Kojak[151] and the Wombles.[152] These cases suggested that the creators of an image or a character could not control unauthorised use of that image unless some artistic copyright design right or trademark had been used in replicating the character and that mere use of a name could not be actionable without more. In the *ABBA* case, the group had begun to fix the group's name and image to a limited range of products but unfortunately for them they diversified into clothing, T Shirts or bedlinen and thus could not show any likelihood of confusion. In the case of the *Kojakpop* lollipop, the defendant was in fact claiming to be an authorised licensee of the rightholder in the Kojak character but this did not prevent Walton J from granting an injunction in favour of the plaintiff who had no such authority and happened to be the first to exploit the Kojak name. Walton J was clearly sceptical of both the scope and public benefit of the practice of character licensing, observing that the man in the street would not conclude from the mere use of an invented character's name that the defendant had been given a licence to use that name and that the use of the name carried a guarantee of quality in the product.[153]

[24.43] However, a line of Australian cases has in effect subverted the English approach. The first in this sequence, *Henderson v Radio Corporation*[154] involved an application for injunction restraining the defendant from releasing an album of dance music under a cover which reproduced a photograph of the plaintiffs, professional ballroom dancers. No copyright infringement in the photograph occurred but the defendants, in using the photograph, were held to indicate 'sponsorship'[155] of the defendant's products. More significantly, while there was a common field of activity as between the parties, insofar as the album would be used in dance and dance tuition, activities which both parties had a commercial interest in, the court distanced itself from both the common field of

---

148. *McCulloch v May* [1947] 2 All ER 845. Recently doubted in *Harrods Ltd v Harrodian School* (1996) 35 IPR 355.
149. *Sim v H J Heinz* [1959] 1 All ER 547.
150. *Lyngstad & Others v Anabas Products Ltd* [1977] FSR 62.
151. *Tavener Rutledge v Trexaplam* [1977] RPC 275.
152. *Wombles Ltd v Wombles Skips Ltd* [1975] FSR 488.
153. The Judge Dredd case is an honourable exception to the English line of authority; see *IPC Magazines v Black & White Music Corp* [1983] FSR 348.
154. [1969] RPC 218.
155. *Per* Manning J.

activity test and the result in *McCulloch v May*, and the Supreme Court of New South Wales argued for a return to basic principle, namely:

> "once it is proved that A is falsely representing his goods as the goods of B or his business to be the same as or connected with the business of B, the wrong of passing off has been established and B is entitled to relief."[156]

[24.44] The crucial factor here is whether there is some commercial connection between the plaintiff and the defendant by way of the use by the defendant of the image or indicia. In *Hogan v Pacific Dunlop*[157] the defendants sold leather shoes by utilising the knife scene in the film *Crocodile Dundee* although the actor playing the role of Mick Dundee in the advertisement could not be confused with the plaintiff, Paul Hogan. The Federal Court of Australia found a misrepresentation, for the public would be deceived into thinking that the shoes had some authorised link with Crocodile Dundee, perceived to be a persona of the plaintiff by the Australian public, in Burchett J's view. The Australian courts have also granted injunctions to restrain the unauthorised marking of T shirts with the 7 Up Fido-Dido character, a decision that is important because it was followed by Browne-Wilkinson VC in *Mirage Studios v Counter-Feat Clothing Co*.[158] In that case, the plaintiffs obtained an injunction to prevent the defendant from trading in sportswear that depicted humanoid turtles engaged in sporting rather than martial arts activities, but the evidence indicated a similarity with the plaintiff's Ninja Turtles characters and the fact that the defendant's artwork was derived from that of the plaintiffs via a re-design exercise. While the actual decision is a somewhat narrow one, insofar as the plaintiffs could point to artistic copyright infringement, the Vice Chancellor indicated that the evidence was that the public were now much more sophisticated in relation to character merchandising than previously:[159]

> "The critical evidence in this case is that a substantial number of the buying public now expect and know that where a famous cartoon or television character is reproduced on goods, that reproduction is the result of a licence granted by the owner of the copyright or owner of other rights in that character. Mr Smith, the defendant, accepted that evidence subject to this; he said that was only true where the reproduced matter was an exact reproduction of the character in the cartoon or television show, whereas in his case the defendants' turtles were different. I cannot accept that. If, as the evidence here shows, the public mistake the defendants' turtles for those which might be called genuine plaintiffs' Turtles, once they have made that mistake they will assume that the

---

[156.] *Per* Evatt CJ and Myers J.

[157.] (1989) 12 IPR 225, 14 IPR 398; *Hogan v Koala Dundee Pty Ltd* (1988) 12 IPR 508.

[158.] [1991] FSR 145.

[159.] Or possibly that Walton J in the *Kojak* case took an unrealistic view of the character merchandising phenomenon, even in 1977.

product in question has been licensed to use the Turtles on it. That is to say, they will connect what they mistakenly think to be the plaintiffs' Turtles with the plaintiffs. To put on the market goods which the public mistake for the genuine article necessarily involves a misrepresentation to the public that they are genuine. On the evidence in this case, the belief that the goods are genuine involves a further misrepresentation, namely that they are licensed."[160]

[24.45] On the other important point of proof of damage, Browne-Wilkinson VC said that where the plaintiff can show that a part of his business profile involves the licensing of others to use the character, then the plaintiff will establish depreciation in the value of the image and thus damage to the licensing right. In following the trend set out in Australian case law,[161] the Vice Chancellor indicated that while both the *ABBA* case and the *Wombles* case were probably still good law insofar as there was no use made of copyright material, the decision in *Kojak*, based on the evidence of consumer awareness before the Vice Chancellor, was simply not reliable and could only be defended on the ground that there could be no copyright in a name. However, the *Ninja Turtles* case does not suggest that the proprietor of rights in a character or image will always succeed in a passing off action when the defendant has used that character to produce a rival, for the requirement of misrepresentation may operate as an obstacle. In *Tot Toys Ltd v Mitchell*[162] the plaintiffs were the proprietors of a 'Buzzy Bee' toy which the defendant used to produce a rival product which he marketed as 'Kiwi Bee'. Significantly, design right protection for the 'Buzzy Bee' had expired and no copyright protection could be claimed. The plaintiff was thus forced to argue that there was a deception which injured, *inter alia*, the plaintiff's character merchandising rights. Fisher J, however, refused to follow the Australian decisions for two reasons: firstly, it could not be shown in all character merchandising cases that a deception had been practised and, secondly, the argument that the defendant is damaging the plaintiff's merchandising rights assumes that a right always exists - a circular argument. Fisher J observed that the Australian courts were guilty of turning passing off into a cause of action based more on a property right than deception, and he approved of certain academic comments which described the Australian cases as being based in unfair competition or appropriation of personality rather than misrepresentation.[163] One recent English commentator also sees the Australian cases as jettisoning goodwill and protecting the plaintiff because of loss of

---

[160.] [1991] FSR 145 at 155.

[161.] *Children's Television Workshop Inc v Woolworths (NSW) Ltd* [1981] RPC 187 and *Fido-Dido Inc v Venture Stores Retailers* (1988) 16 IPR 365.

[162.] (1992) 25 IPR 337.

[163.] *Terry* (1991) 65 ALJ 587; *Howell* (1991) 6 IPJ 197.

future merchandising opportunities.[164] In any event, Fisher J held that the plaintiff's claim did not succeed because the defendant had taken adequate steps to distinguish their product from the 'Buzzy Bee'. Notwithstanding this cautionary New Zealand decision, English courts are making significant strides in favour of broad brand or name protection since the repudiation of the common field of activity element in the tort.[165] The character merchandising protection available in respect of imaginary persons may also extend to character goods, ie, goods that are not traded in but which are associated with a character. In *Twentieth Century Fox v South Australian Brewing*[166] Homer Simpson's favourite tipple, Duff Beer, was poached by the defendants without the consent of 'The Simpsons' rightholder. Applying *Pacific Dunlop*, the Federal Court of Australia found both a misrepresentation in the form of conjuring an association between the product and the plaintiffs and damage in the form of lost licensing opportunities.

[24.46] Where the defendant has appropriated the image of real personalities for product endorsement the plaintiff has generally been unsuccessful,[167] save in the *Crocodile Dundee* case where the Hogan/Dundee persona have tended to be regarded as the same. In one recent case, the artist Michael Jackson sought to prevent the unauthorised release of recordings on the ground that this would infringe Jackson's right to publicity, but the application failed because Australian law does not recognise any such right.[168] Lockhart J in the Federal Court of Appeal resisted the temptation to enquire into whether cases such as *Henderson v Radio Corporation* could be the basis of such a right in Australian law.

[24.47] In Ireland, the constitutional protections in relation to property and a good name would arguably assist any Irish litigant whose name has been used prejudicially from obtaining vindication in the courts, but there is no judicial recognition of any tortious right to personality in Irish case-law.

Application of Personality

[24.48] In some jurisdictions the appropriation of aspects of a human personality, whether it be image, voice name or other *indicia* of identity, may be

---

[164.] *Carty* (1993) 13 LS 289. Note, however, that in the *Ninja Turtles* case, Browne-Wilkinson VC seems to have regarded market entry as a *sine qua non*.

[165.] Eg *Lego System v Lego M Lemilstritch Ltd* [1983] FSR 155.

[166.] (1996) 34 IPR 225.

[167.] *10th Cantanac Pty v Shoshana Pty* (1987) 10 IPR 289; *Wickham v Associated Pool Builders Property* (1986) 7 IPR 392; *Honey v Australian Airlines* (1990) 18 IPR 185.

[168.] *Sony Music Australia Ltd & Michael Jackson v Tansing* (1993) 27 IPR 649. See also *Gould Estate v Stoddart Publishing* (1996) 30 OR (3d) 520.

actionable under the tort of appropriation of personality.[169] In the United States this tort is known as the right to publicity.[170] The *Ninja Turtles* decision indicated a willingness to subsume this tort under passing off, but at the time of writing the issue of whether such a tort exists in England has been litigated unsuccessfully on behalf of the estate of Elvis Presley but only on the narrow issue of trade mark registration.[171]

INJURIOUS OR MALICIOUS FALSEHOOD

[24.49] Some practices in trade that harm the plaintiff may not be protected *via* passing off and in the absence of broader laws on unfair competition the plaintiff may have to resort to one of the lesser torts to vindicate his business reputation. Trade libels, whereby the defendant deliberately disparaged the goods or business of the plaintiff, were possible[172] but the decision of the House of Lords in *White v Mellin*[173] indicated that statements which simply praise the defendant's goods as superior to the plaintiff's brand are not actionable as an injurious falsehood and the general elements of the tort are narrow in order to minimise the scope of liability in the cut and thrust of business practices. The classic statement on liability is that the plaintiff must prove:

(1) that the statements complained of were untrue;

(2) that they were made maliciously - ie without just cause or excuse;

(3) that the plaintiffs have suffered special damage thereby.[174]

[24.50] If the statement is false it matters not that the plaintiff is not likely to suffer any loss of reputation or public esteem as long as his business contacts or customer base is likely to be dissuaded from contracting with him, eg by falsely asserting that the plaintiff intends to cease trading either generally or specifically.[175] However *Allason v Campbell*[176] held that special damage need not be specifically pleaded under the Defamation Act 1961 s 20(1). There is some recent support for the view that where the defendant intends to plead justification then an injunction will not issue[177] although injunctive relief is

---

[169.] In Canada see *Athens v Canadian Adventure Camps* (1973) 40 DLR (3d) 15. The Australian judges regard the problem as amenable to passing off rules (see the above fn 168) but a separate tort seems inevitable. In Jamaica see the *Robert Marley Foundation v Dino Michelle Ltd* High Court, unrep, 12 May 1994, discussed by St Michael Hytton and Goldson (1996) 55 CLJ 56.

[170.] See Fraser (1983) 99 LQR 281.

[171.] *The Times* 3 and 4 March 1997; judgment of Laddie J reported in the *Times*, 25 March 1997.

[172.] Eg *Herman Loog v Bean* (1884) 26 Ch 306.

[173.] [1895] AC 154. See *Cooke v McGuigan* (1926) 61 ILTR 45.

[174.] Lord Davey in *Royal Baking Powder Co v Wright, Crossley & Co* (1901) 18 RPC 95 at 99.

[175.] *Radcliffe v Evans* [1892] 2 QB 524.

[176.] *Times* 8 May 1996.

[177.] *Alan H Reid Engineering v Ramset Fasteners* (1990) 20 IPR 15.

relatively easy to obtain if the defendant acts outrageously to damage the reputation of the plaintiff.[178]

UNLAWFUL INTERFERENCE WITH ECONOMIC RELATIONS

[24.51] It is beyond the scope of this book[179] to explore the history of this particular tort although the Irish courts have had occasion to consider whether it exists at all from a somewhat early date. In the case of *Higgins v O'Donnell*[180] it was held that the obstruction of the plaintiff's customers by the defendant to the prejudice of the plaintiff's business was not actionable because no interference with a proprietary right or contract could be pointed to. Later Irish courts have tended to the view that this tort certainly exists within the sphere of employment contracts[181] and despite some judicial ambivalence on this point[182] the Supreme Court has recently affirmed that this tort is part of Irish law. In *Charles O'Neill & Co v Adidas Sports Schuhfabriken and Others*[183] the plaintiffs complained that the defendants had provided sports shirts for a charity event, but finding that none of theirs were suitable they used shirts manufactured by the plaintiffs and put Adidas symbols on the shirts in two places. Blayney J dismissed the plaintiff's application for injunctive relief and damages for the tort of unlawful interference in the plaintiff's business interest on the basis that there was no evidence that the plaintiff intended to harm the business of the plaintiff. In the Supreme Court, Finlay CJ endorsed the analysis of the tort set out in *Clerk and Lindsell on Torts*[184] where three ingredients of the tort are set out, namely:

(1) interference by unlawful means with a man's trade or activities of an economic or commercial nature;

(2) with the intent to damage the plaintiff;

(3) and which causes such damage.

In the view of the Supreme Court, the plaintiff had failed to make out either of factors (2) or (3) to the satisfaction of Blayney J at first instance and the trial judge was therefore entitled to dismiss the action.

[178.] *Kaye v Robertson* [1991] FSR 62.

[179.] See *Carty* (1988) 104 LQR 250.

[180.] (1869) Ir R 4 Cl 91.

[181.] *Cooper v Millea* [1938] IR 749.

[182.] *Bula Ltd v Tara Mines (No 2)* [1987] IR 95; *Pine Valley Developments Ltd v Minister for the Environment* [1987] ILRM 747.

[183.] Supreme Court, unrep, 25 March 1992 *ex tempore, Irish Times Law Report* 17 August 1992.

[184.] (15th Edition) p 747.

Chapter 25

Introduction to Trade Mark Law

[25.01] Under Irish law, rights to a trade mark are governed by the provisions of the Trade Marks Act 1996,[1] the Community Trade Mark Regulation[2] or by use of a mark leading to goodwill sufficient to sustain an action for passing off. The statutory protection does not affect the laws of passing off[3] and indeed, until the 1996 Act, passing off was the only legal remedy available to the owners of marks used in respect of services. Registration under the 1996 Act and earlier trade mark legislation enables a trade mark proprietor to produce a certificate of registration showing that they are the *prima facie* owner of the mark and subject to certain limitations, can claim exclusivity to that mark and sue for any infringement. The existence of a trade mark register also assists parties in determining what rights, if any, exist in a particular mark and the scope of protection.

COMPANY NAMES AND BUSINESS NAMES

[25.02] Rights to a trade mark exist neither by virtue of the incorporation of a company under a particular name under the Companies Acts 1963-1990 nor the existence of a business name registration under the Registration of Business Names Act 1963. Under s 21 of the Companies Act 1963, there is a provision whereby the Minister may, within six months after incorporation, compel a company to change its corporate name if the name is too similar to that of a company which has already been incorporated. The Registrar of Companies adopts a liberal attitude towards the approval of company names and will more or less approve any name unless it is identical, or extremely close, to that of a company name already on the Register.Unfortunately, there is no cross searching between the Company Names Register and the Register of Trade Marks. The Registrar of Companies will approve a company name even though a third party already holds a trade mark registration for such. The effect of this is that even though a party may incorporate a company under a particular name, use of that name could constitute trade mark infringement and/or passing off. Indeed, the Irish courts have gone even further and have held that the mere

---

[1.] Which implements the Trade Mark Harmonisation Directive 89/104/EEC.
[2.] Regulation 40/94.
[3.] Section 7(2).

incorporation of a company under a name can also amount to passing off. In the Supreme Court in *C & A Modes v C & A (Waterford) Limited*,[4] Kenny J stated:

> "the legal wrong known as passing off includes the incorporation in the Republic of Ireland of a company with a name likely to give the impression to the public that it is a subsidiary or branch of or is associated or connected with another company which has an established goodwill, whether the latter company is incorporated in the Republic or outside it. The incorporation with the name selected may have been with the intention of creating that impression, *Lloyds and Dawson Bros v Lloyds (Southampton) Ltd* [1939] 3 All ER 513; (1912) 29 RPC 433; *Harrods Ltd v R Harrod Ltd* (1924) 41 RPC 74 or innocently without knowing the existence of the well known company, *Ewing v Buttercup Margarine Co. Ltd* [1917] 2 Ch 1. In either event, the wrong of passing off may be restrained by the company with the established goodwill".

[25.03] This *obiter dictum* was more recently approved as "a sound statement of the law" by Carroll J in the unreported case of *Rittal Werk Rudolph Loh GmbH v Rittal (Ireland) Limited*.[5] In that case the defendant was ordered to change its corporate name even though it was not trading and had undertaken not to trade in the plaintiff's field of activity.

[25.04] Under the Registration of Business Names Act 1963, the registration of a business name is a legal requirement imposed upon a person who uses a name which is different from his own individual, corporate or firm name. The purpose of such a registration is that the public can carry out a search in the Register of Business Names and ascertain who is behind a particular trading name at a particular address. The registration of a business name does not confer any proprietary rights in the name. Section 14(3) specifically states that the registration shall not be construed as authorising the use of that name if apart from such registration, the use thereof could be prohibited. The Registrar of Business Names has no power to refuse a registration based on what is already on the Business Names Register and a multiplicity of different and unconnected persons can, and often do, hold identical or confusingly similar business name registrations.

THE FUNCTION OF A TRADE MARK

[25.05] The reason why persons seek to protect their trade mark(s) must be considered in the context of the functions which a trade mark performs. Perhaps the most immediate function that springs to mind is that the trade mark is an indication as to the origin of the goods or services and thus, for example, in the Trade Marks Act 1963, the statutory definition of a trade mark was:

---

4. [1976] IR 198.
5. High Court, unrep, 11 July 1991.

a mark used or proposed to be used in relation to goods for the purpose of indicating, or so as to indicate, a connection in the course of trade between the goods and some person having the right either as proprietor or as registered user to use the mark, whether with or without any indication of the identity of that person.

[25.06] As a consequence of this definition, in many instances, the courts felt compelled to adopt a narrow interpretation of a trade mark and issues such as whether "an inference of identity of origin would be drawn"[6] were raised in determining issues of similarity between marks. Also, the UK courts refused registration of a cartoon character "Holly Hobbie"[7] by an applicant because the owner intended to grant licences in such a way that the mark was being dealt with primarily as a commodity in its own right and so there would be no real trade connection between the owner of the mark and the goods to which the mark was to be applied. Both the UK Trades Mark Act 1938 and the Irish Trade Marks Act 1963 included a provision against facilitating trafficking in a trade mark.[8]

[25.07] In a group of cases involving parallel imports of re-packaged pharmaceuticals, the ECJ reaffirmed that the essential function of a trade mark is to guarantee to the consumer or end-user the identity of the trade marked product's origin by enabling him to distinguish it without any risk of confusion from products of different origin. That guarantee of origin means that the consumer or end user can be certain that a trade marked product offered to him has not been subject at a previous stage of marketing to interference by a third person, without the authorisation of the trade mark owner, in such a way as to affect the original condition of the product.[9]

[25.08] The ECJ has drawn attention to a further function of a trade mark which is to guarantee certain attributes of goods and/or services and thus ensure customer satisfaction. Recognition of this guarantee function can be seen in the case of *SA CNL-Sucal NV v Hag AG*:[10]

> "trade marks reward the manufacturer who consistently produces high quality goods and they thus stimulate economic progress. Without trade mark protection, there would be little incentive for manufacturers to develop new products or to maintain the quality of existing ones. trade marks are able to achieve that effect because they act as a guarantee, to the consumer, that all

---

6. *McDowell's Application* (1926) 43 RPC 313.
7. *American Greetings Corporation's Application* [1984] RPC 329.
8. Section 36(6).
9. *Bristol-Myers Squibb v Paranova; Eurim-Pharm v Beiersdorf; MPA Pharma v Rhone-Poulenc* [1997] FSR 102.
10. [1990] 3 CMLR 571.

goods bearing a particular mark have been produced by, or under the control of, the same manufacturer and are therefore likely to be of a similar quality."

[25.09] The recognition of the function of a trade mark as a commodity in its own right can now be seen in the Trade Marks Act 1996 which grants rights to prevent dilution by use of a third party even in respect of goods and/or services which are dissimilar to that in which the trade mark owner trades. However, this is only likely to arise in a limited number of instances and it is the product/ service differentiation function of a trade mark which is now prevalent under the 1996 Act, ie a trade mark should distinguish the goods or services of one undertaking from that of other undertakings.[11]

[25.10] Given these important functions of a trade mark and increased consumer awareness due to extensive advertising, there has been an increased awareness in the importance of trade marks which has resulted in efforts at brand valuation. In 1991, Rank Hovis McDougall plc. calculated that its brand names were worth £583.5 million and valuations of $39.5 billion and $33.4 billion have been suggested for MARLBORO and COCA-COLA respectively.

REGISTRATION

[25.11] Most countries, including Ireland, have taken steps to protect trade marks through a system of registration rather than rely solely on common law rights which may exist and which have limitations such as the need to show damage or a likelihood of damage. The evolution of trade mark statute law up to 1927 was summarised by Johnston J in *Fry-Cadbury (Ireland) Limited v Synott*.[12] The Industrial and Commercial Property (Protection) Act 1927 dealt with intellectual property matters generally and Part IV of the Act dealt with trade marks. The first trade mark to be advertised in Irish Official Journal was DÉANTA IN ÉIRINN and logo held by the Industrial Development Association. As far as trade marks were concerned, the 1927 Act was repealed by the Trade Marks Act 1963 which had a two part Register, Part A and Part B, depending on whether or not a trade mark was adapted to distinguish or capable of distinguishing.

[25.12] One of the principal failures of the 1963 Act was to provide for the registration of marks in respect of services. Although this has been dealt with under the 1996 Act, Ireland was in fact the last EU country to provide for such and the commencement date of the 1996 Act, 1 July 1996, was long after the implementation date set down by the Trade Mark Harmonisation Directive,[13] ie

---

[11.] Section 6(1).

[12.] [1935] IR 700.

[13.] 89/104/EEC.

31 December 1992. The question arises as to whether or not there is direct effect of provisions allowing for the registration of marks in respect of service marks.[14] On any reading of the Harmonisation Directive, it appears to be clear that the Directive applies to marks in respect of both goods and services.

[25.13] In 1993, the Irish Patents Office started to accept receipt of service mark applications and indeed, prior to the 1996 Act, it is estimated that approximately 7,000 such applications had been filed. These applications were all simply held in abeyance and although given a number, were not given an official filing date. The transitional provisions of the 1996 Act[15] provided that all of these applications were to be given the same date, 1 July 1996, the commencement date of the 1996 Act and will be examined under the 1996 Act. This means that for many service mark applications, there was a loss of rights from the filing date, which in some cases could, of course, be important. The situation was further worsened by the State's failure to implement the 1996 Act prior to 1 April 1996, which was the effective date of the Community Trade Mark Regulation. This means that in many cases, owners of CTMs have service mark registrations which were effective in Ireland before it was possible to secure such nationally. Also, if a CTM is abandoned, it can be converted into a national application in Ireland and retain the CTM date of application. This means that the Irish Patents Office may have to deal with national service mark applications bearing a date earlier than provision for such in the 1996 Act. It is regrettable that the State's failure to introduce the new trade mark law prior to the Directive's implementation date and worse still, the effective date of the CTM has left in its wake, a legal quagmire. In fact, Michael McDowell, TD introduced a Private Member's Trade Marks Bill 1993[16] which did implement the provisions of the Directive and introduce service marks. Although this was gratefully received, the Government decided to pursue its own legislation.

[14.] See *Service Mark Registrations in Ireland* [1994] 4 EIPR 167.
[15.] Third Schedule - para 15.
[16.] No 12 of 1993.

Chapter 26

Irish Trade Mark Law and International Conventions

THE PARIS CONVENTION

[26.01] Under the Paris Convention,[1] "trade marks, service marks, trade names, indications of source or appellations of origin, and the repression of unfair competition" are all specifically stated as being industrial property rights and the objective in relation to which is to provide protection. Similar to the position in relation to other forms of industrial property, nationals of all Member States should enjoy the same rights as those which prevail in a particular State. No requirement as to domicile or establishment may be imposed.[2] Article 2 of the GATT Agreement on Trade-related Aspects of Intellectual Property Rights (TRIPS) requires Member States to comply with Articles 1-12 and 19 of the Paris Convention.

[26.02] There are several references to the Paris Convention in the 1996 Act and such is specifically defined in s 60(1)(a). Reference is also made to a Convention country which simply means a State (other than Ireland) which is party to the Convention.

[26.03] The Paris Convention provides for 'priority' and this is set out in s 40(1). This means that where any person who has filed a trade mark application in a Convention country, if they or their successor in title subsequently file in Ireland within six months of the first application, then they can claim rights from the date of the first application. The Irish trade mark application must correspond to the first application in that the trade marks must be the same and the goods or services must fall within the specification of the first application. The Irish application is not dependant on the outcome of the application from which priority is claimed.[3] The purpose of the priority provision is to enable trade mark owners to file just one trade mark application and preserve their position for at least six months knowing that they can, during this time, market products and services under a trade mark, carry out market research and undertake searches, etc. and yet avoid being pre-empted by filing

---

[1.] See Ch 2.
[2.] Article 2(2)
[3.] Article 4(3); s 40(3)

in other States within the six month period. Priority in relation to trade marks is not as important as in relation to patents because pre-application trade mark use does not invalidate any subsequent registration. Less than twenty per cent of trade mark applications before the Irish Patents Office claim priority.

[26.04] Under the 1963 Act,[4] the effect of claiming priority was that the date of registration was the same date as the date of the application from which priority was claimed.

[26.05] However, under s 40(2) of the 1996 Act, the date of registration will be the date of the actual Irish application but "the relevant date for the purposes of establishing which rights take precedence, shall be the date of filing of the first Convention application". This means that when carrying out trade mark searches and subsequently filing an application for a period of six months, one cannot provide any certainty that a third party right may take precedence even with a subsequent Irish filing date. Strictly speaking, the Irish Patents Office, when examining an application, should refrain from carrying out searches against earlier rights for a period of six months from the date of filing, in order to be sure that all prior conflicting applications/registrations are on record, but in practice this does not occur.

[26.06] In certain circumstances, a subsequent Convention application will be treated as the first Convention application where the previous application has been withdrawn, abandoned or refused without having been laid open to public inspection and without leaving any rights outstanding.[5] It must also not yet have served as a basis for claiming a right to priority.[6] The applicant for the Irish application does not have to be the same as that for the Convention application, since under s 40(6) provision is made for an assignment or transmission of the application from which priority is claimed. It is also provided that the provision relating to priority could extend to non-Convention countries in certain instances and would also extend to a CTM application.[7]

[26.07] The transitional provisions of the 1996 Act raise some interesting issues by virtue of their failure to address the position *vis-à-vis* a claim to priority of a trade mark which is dated prior to 1 July 1996, being the commencement date of the 1996 Act. A person who was fortunate enough to file a Convention application post 1 January 1996 and claim priority will find that they have rights prior to the commencement date which did not exist under the old law and which could pre-empt applications which bear the commencement date of the

---

4. Section 70.
5. Section 40(4)(a).
6. Section 40(4)(b).
7. Section 41.

1996 Act. If we take, for example, an application in respect of a trade mark for the shape of goods or their packaging which was unregisterable under the 1963 Act. An application for such not claiming priority and filed prior to 1 July 1996 would be refused registration and the only possibility would have been to convert the application so that it would have been examined under the new law. The effect of conversion was that the applicants lost the filing date which was replaced by 1 July 1996, which is subsequent to the rights which are afforded to an applicant of a priority based application fortunate enough to have a priority date within six months prior to 1 July 1996. The inequity of such is even stronger in relation to service marks where the Controller has accepted applications since 1993 but under s 15 of the Third Schedule, these have all been given the date of 1 July 1996. However, it is possible to claim rights in a service mark filed prior to this date again by virtue of a priority based claim which is dated after 1 January 1996.

[26.08] The position *vis-à-vis* the right of an applicant to claim priority from an Irish service mark filed prior to 1 July 1996 is far from certain. Although the Controller allotted an application number, no date of application was afforded to such and paragraph 15, the transitional provisions, states that the date of filing is to be the commencement date, ie 1 July 1996. However, it could, of course, be argued that under the Paris Convention, a national filing simply means "any filing that is adequate to establish the date upon which the application was filed in the country concerned, whatever may be the subsequent date of the application". In other words, it is the *filing* date that is important, not the *application* date afforded by a national Patents Office.

[26.09] There is no requirement for a home application or registration in order to prosecute and register a mark in other Convention countries.[8]

Well Known Trade Marks

[26.10] The term "well known trade marks" appears in Article 6 *bis* of the Paris Convention and s 61 of the 1996 Act gives statutory effect to this provision which allows the owner of a well known trade mark, whether or not they carry on business or have any goodwill in the State, to obtain injunctive relief against the use of an identical or similar mark in relation to identical or similar goods or services where the use is likely to cause confusion. The trade mark must be well known in the State. Section 11(1)(c) also includes such as an earlier mark which forms the basis for opposing or seeking rectification of a conflicting mark. It could be argued that the rights granted to a well known trade mark under statute do in fact simply reflect the position at common law and as illustrated in the

---

8. Article 6(2).

Supreme Court decision in the case of *C & A Modes v C & A (Waterford) Ltd.*[9] In that case the Supreme Court criticised the UK authorities and held that the plaintiff possessed a protectable reputation in the State even though it did not trade in the State. The law of passing off is not dependant on use within the State and if we equate reputation with a mark being well known as appears to have been done in the *C & A case*, then a legal remedy was available prior to the 1996 Act. In the *C & A case*, Finlay J actually used the words "well known" when referring to the reputation through advertising circulating in the State and this was repeated by Kenny J in the Supreme Court. The decision would also suggest that the level of recognition required of a trade mark to make it well known should not be equated with too high a level of notoriety. As stated by Henchy J:

> "if there are in this State sufficient customers of a plaintiff's business to justify his claim to have a vested right to restrain and expand that custom, then there is ample authority in principle and in the decided cases for the conclusion that, no matter where the plaintiff's business is based, he is entitled to be protected against it being taken away or dissipated by someone whose deceptive conduct is calculated to create a confusion of identify in the minds of existing or potential customers."

An obvious way of trying to show how well a mark is known is by way of survey evidence[10] but apart from being expensive, its conclusions, given the number of variables, are not the result of exact science. For example, who is to be surveyed? Presumably, although not stated, the term "well known" is to be directed towards likely consumers and not necessarily to the population generally.

[26.11] The rights granted to a well known trade mark under s 61 are limited to an injunction and, for example, does not include damages although such can be included as part of a claim in respect of passing off. Section 61(3) differs from paragraph 3(2) of the transitional provisions and there appears to be an inconsistency. Under the transitional provisions, it is not an infringement under the 1996 Act to continue to do an act which was not an infringement under the 1963 Act. However, in relation to well known trade marks, the pre-1996 Act use must also be *bona fide*.

[26.12] Although a well known trade mark under the Paris Convention is deemed to be an "earlier trade mark" for opposition or rectification purposes, a different phrase "earlier right" is used in s 15 to determine if there exists a defence to infringement proceedings. What is strange is that if a well known trade mark is to be embraced within the phrase "earlier right" which one would

---

9. [1978] FSR 126.
10. See paras **[31.31]-[31-35]** *post*.

expect, then the whole of the State must be viewed as a "locality" under s 15(3) and which would appear to be a strange interpretation of this word.

National and State Emblems

[26.13] Article 6 *ter* of the Paris Convention deals with national and international organisation emblems including flags and is dealt with in ss 62 to 64 of the 1996 Act, complying with Article 3(1)(h) and 3(2)(c) of the Harmonisation Directive.[11]

[26.14] Essentially, flags, armorial bearings or State emblems, official signs or hallmarks of Convention countries cannot be registered without authorisation from the appropriate authority. In relation to flags, the Controller can dispense with such authorisation "if it appears to the Controller that use of the flag in the manner proposed is permitted without such authorisation".[12] No such exception exists in relation to armorial bearings or State emblems which must be notified in accordance with Article 6 *ter*.[13] The protection afforded to official signs or hallmarks adopted by a Convention country which indicate control and warranty, must be protected under the Paris Convention and the restriction on registration applies only in relation to goods or services of the same or a similar kind.

[26.15] The restrictions do not apply to applications made by a national of a country who is authorised to make use of a State emblem or official sign or hallmark of that country, notwithstanding that it is similar to that of another country.[14] Injunctive relief is available to restrain use of a mark which could not be registered without authority.[15] In relation to national flags, State emblems, official signs or hallmarks, the protection also extends to imitations from an "heraldic point of view".[16]

[26.16] The position *vis-à-vis* armorial bearings, flags or other emblems and abbreviations or names of international intergovernmental organisations and any imitations of an emblem from a heraldic point of view is that a Member State is not compelled to prevent registration or use where such "is probably not of such a nature as to mislead the public as to the existence of a connection between the user and the organisation".[17] Again, these emblems must be protected under the Paris Convention, a pre-requisite of which is notification in accordance with

---

[11.] 89/104/EEC.
[12.] Section 62(1); see para **[31.59]** *post* re unauthorised use of State emblems.
[13.] Section 62(2).
[14.] Section 61(5).
[15.] Section 61(6).
[16.] Section 61(4).
[17.] Article 6 *ter* (1)(c); s 63.

Article 6 *ter*.[18] The Irish Government has lodged both the shamrock and harp devices as protected State emblems under Article 6 *ter*.

Unauthorised applications

[26.17] Article 6 *septies* of the Paris Convention is implemented by s 65 of the 1996 Act and deals with a situation where, without permission, a trade mark application is made by a person who is an agent or representative of the owner of the trade mark in another Convention country. In such a situation, the State is obliged to refuse registration upon opposition or the proprietor can demand cancellation. Irish law also allows for a declaration of invalidity against such a registration[19] or for the proprietor to be substituted as the registered proprietor.[20]

[26.18] There is a defence by which the agent or representative can justify their action. Article 6 *septies* provides that "domestic legislation may provide an equitable time limit within which the proprietor of a mark must exercise the rights provided". In this regard, Irish law provides for a three year time limit which runs from knowledge of the registration.[21] The proprietor can also obtain an injunction to restrain use by the agent or representative.[22] It is, of course, also likely that in a case of this type, there would also be a claim for breach of a contractual relationship between the parties.

Unfair Competition

[26.19] Article 10 *bis*, is a provision which must be complied with under the TRIPS Agreement, requires the State to provide effective protection against unfair competition which is stated to be "any act of competition contrary to honest practices in industrial or commercial matters" and Article 10 *bis* goes on to give the following examples, namely:

(1) all acts of such a nature as to create confusion by any means whatever with the establishment, the goods, or the industrial or commercial activities, of a competitor;

(2) false allegations in the course of trade of such a nature as to discredit the establishment, the goods, or the industrial or commercial activities, of a competitor;

(3) indications or allegations the use of which in the course of trade is liable to mislead the public as to the nature, the manufacturing

---

18. Section 64.
19. Section 65(3)(a)
20. Section 65(3)(b); see also *ZOPPAS Trade Mark* [1965] RPC 381.
21. Section 65(6).
22. Section 65(4).

process, the characteristics, the suitability for their purpose, or the quantity, of the goods.

[26.20] It could be argued that the State has not fulfilled its obligation under TRIPS by failing to include provisions in the 1996 Act corresponding to Article 10 *bis*. However, the Irish courts have shown a willingness to expand the traditional horizons of the law of passing off. In *C & A Modes*,[23] Henchy J stated "it is to prevent unfair competition of that kind that the action for passing off lies". Essentially, in so far as the concept of unfair competition exists under Irish law it does so in the form of passing off, defamation and injurious falsehood.

TRIPS AGREEMENT

[26.21] Trips is the Agreement on Trade Related Aspects of Intellectual Property, including trade in counterfeit goods. TRIPS was opened for signature on 15 April 1994 and is the intellectual property portion of the Uruguay round of the World Trade Organisations agreements which amended GATT. TRIPS resulted from the desire stated in the preamble:

> ... to reduce distortions and impediments to international trade, and taking into account the need to promote effective and adequate protection of intellectual property rights, and to ensure that measures and procedures to enforce intellectual property rights do not themselves become barriers to legitimate trade.

TRIPS sets forth minimum international standards in the provision of principles concerning the availability, scope and use of trade related intellectual property rights including trade marks and geographical indications. Members must treat nationals of all member nations, including their own, equally with regard to intellectual property rights and must comply with Articles 1-12 and 19 of the Paris Convention.

[26.22] Trade marks are dealt with in Part II, s 2 of the TRIPS Agreement (Articles 15-21). Article 15 is headed 'Protectable Subject Matter' and defines what may constitute a trade mark in terms which are already reflected in the 1996 Act, namely signs capable of distinguishing the goods or services of one undertaking from those of other undertakings. Section 6(1) of the Trade Mark Act 1996 which also requires that a sign be capable of being represented graphically, is an option allowed Member States who may require that signs be visually perceptible. Where signs are not inherently capable of distinguishing the relevant goods or services, Member States may make registerability dependant on distinctiveness acquired through use. Actual use cannot be a condition for filing a trade mark application but (as is currently the position

---

[23.] [1978] FSR at 139.

under US law), it can be a prerequisite to registration. However, an intent to use application must not be refused solely on the grounds that the intended use has not taken place before the expiry of a period of three years from the date of the application. Given Article 6 *quinquies* of the Paris Convention, it is permissible to deny registration of marks which designate the kind, quality, intended purpose, value or place of origin of the goods or which are considered contrary to morality or public order. However, the nature of the goods or service to which trade mark is to be applied, cannot be a bar to registration. Trade marks must be published and a reasonable opportunity afforded to third parties to seek cancellation. As under Irish law, members can also provide for opposition but pre-registration opposition proceedings are not mandatory.

[26.23] Article 16 deals with the rights conferred by a trade mark registration and these are already reflected under Irish law. The owner has the exclusive right to prevent third parties from using identical or similar signs for goods or services which are identical or similar to those for which the trade mark is registered where such use would result in a likelihood of confusion. If signs are identical, the likelihood of confusion is assumed.

[26.24] TRIPS applied Article 6 *bis* of the Paris Convention dealing with well known trade marks and extends such to service marks. In addition, if a mark is well known and its use by a third party indicates a connection with the trade mark owner, and the interests of the trade mark owner are likely to be damaged, then its use may be prohibited even if it is being used for dissimilar goods or services. Section 14(3) of the 1996 Act which also provides for infringement in respect of dissimilar goods, appears to be stricter in requiring proof that the use is detrimental to the distinctive character or the reputation of the trade mark. There is no definition of 'well known' in the Paris Convention or the 1996 Act but there is a statement in Article 16(2) of TRIPS that in determining whether a trade mark is well known, account shall be taken of the knowledge of the trade mark in the relevant sector of the public, including knowledge obtained as a result of the promotion of the trade mark.

[26.25] TRIPS allows Member States to make registered trade marks subject to any existing prior rights and this is the position under s 15 of the 1996 Act. Rights may also exist on the basis of use, such as passing off under Irish law.

[26.26] Article 17 allows limited exceptions to the rights conferred by a trade mark such as fair use of descriptive terms, provided that such exceptions take account of the legitimate interests of the owner of the trade mark and of third parties. This can be seen in s 15(2) of the 1996 Act which provides for certain exceptions to infringement provided that the "use is in accordance with honest practices in industrial and commercial matters".

[26.27] The minimum term of protection is dealt with in Article 18 which allows for renewal indefinitely. Initial registration and each renewal must be for not less than seven years.

[26.28] In Article 19, use may be required to maintain a registration and registrations may be cancelled for non-use but only after a minimum of three years unless valid reasons based on the existence of obstacles to such use are shown by the trade mark owner. Circumstances arising independently of the will of the owner such as government restrictions or other requirements, are recognised as valid reasons for non-use. Such is the position under s 51(1)(b) of the 1996 Act as governmental restrictions would be considered proper reasons for non-use. The non-use period under Irish law is five years. When subject to the control of its owner, use of a trade mark by another person shall be recognised as use of the trade mark for the purpose of maintaining the registration.

[26.29] Article 20 provides that members cannot unjustifiably encumber the manner in which a trade mark is used. Examples given of such are requirements to use a trade mark in conjunction with another trade mark or in a special form. It is, however, possible to impose a requirement prescribing the use of the trade mark identifying the undertaking producing the goods or services along with, but without linking it to, the trade mark distinguishing the specific goods or services in question of that undertaking.

[26.30] Provisions dealing with the licensing and assignments of trade marks are contained in Article 21. The owner of a registered trade mark has a right to assign the trade mark with or without the transfer of the business to which the trade mark belongs. This differs from the Paris Convention which required the transfer of the business or goodwill.

[26.31] TRIPS explicitly prohibits compulsory licensing of trade marks. Article 6 states that outside the scope of the TRIPS Agreement are any provisions dealing with the issue of the exhaustion of intellectual property rights.

[26.32] Part III of TRIPS contains enforcement provisions. Enforcement procedures must be fair and equitable and must not be unnecessarily complicated, costly or entail unreasonable time limits or unwarranted delays. The remedies must include injunctive relief and damages. In the case of wilful trade mark counterfeiting, criminal penalties must be provided for, including monetary fines and/or imprisonment as well as seizure, forfeiture and destruction of infringing goods.

THE TRADEMARK LAW TREATY

[26.33] The Trademark Law Treaty[24] (TLT) came into effect on 1 August 1996. Although it started out with more ambitious aims, it is essentially an international treaty harmonising procedural aspects of the filing of trade mark applications and their maintenance. It is directed principally at countries where there are cumbersome and expensive procedural requirements. Thirty six countries, not including Ireland, signed the draft treaty on 27 October 1994. By 27 October 1995, more than fifty countries had signed the Treaty including the Member States of the European Union. The TLT became effective on 1 August 1996 being three months after deposit by seven States.[25]

[26.34] The TLT applies to marks which are described as visual marks and also to three dimensional marks where a Contracting State allows for registration of such. The TLT does not apply to holograms, sound, or to collective or certification marks.

[26.35] Article 3 of the TLT provides for certain maximum requirements in the filing of a trade mark application. In certain countries, it is necessary to furnish a certificate or an extract from a local Chamber of Commerce and in other countries, evidence of a corresponding registration in other jurisdictions. These requirements are not permitted under the TLT.

[26.36] A Contracting State must allow for the filing of a multi-class application covering both goods and/or services resulting in a single registration. Irish law already provides for such under the 1996 Act but for example, in the European Union, Spain and Portugal do not. The CTM Regulation also allows for multi-class applications and registrations. Under Article 7, trade mark owners can divide applications in those cases where, for example, certain classes encounter opposition. The divided application maintains the filing date of the initial application and the benefit of priority, if any. The 1996 Act already allows for such division.[26]

[26.37] Article 9 of the TLT outlaws the practice in some countries[27] of allowing registration in respect of a specification reading "all goods/services in class ...". It is necessary to identify the specific goods and/or services by name. The practice of the Controller under the 1963 Act had been to allow a registration covering all goods in a given class but only in exceptional circumstances where an applicant was able to show trading or an intent to trade in an extremely broad range of goods in that class. As is already the position under Irish law, goods/

---

24. Concluded in Geneva on 27 October 1994.
25. Moldova, Ukraine, Sri Lanka, Czech Republic, United Kingdom, Monaco & Guinea.
26. Trade Mark Rules 1996, Rule 28 (SI 199/1996).
27. Particularly Scandinavian countries such as Denmark, Finland, Norway and Sweden.

services will not be considered similar just because they have the same class number and also goods/services will not be considered dissimilar just because they have different class numbers.

[26.38] Article 13 of the TLT deals with duration and renewal. The duration of the initial period of the registration and the duration of each renewal period must be ten years. Trade Mark Offices cannot require proof of use at renewal or a re-examination of the mark as to its validity. Proof of use can, however, be required at times other than renewal and this is the position under current US law.

[26.39] The TLT regulations establish standard forms for applications, renewals, change of address, change of name or ownership and powers of attorney. These must be accepted by the national Trade Mark Offices when presented in the manner prescribed by the TLT.

[26.40] The only substantive features of the TLT are that all contracting parties must comply with the provisions of the Paris Convention concerning marks and allow for the registration of marks in respect of services.

THE MADRID AGREEMENT

[26.41] The Madrid Agreement Concerning the International Registration of Marks of 14 April 1891 entered into force on 13 July 1892 and a number of revisions have been made subsequently.[28] It would be fair to say that the title to the Agreement is somewhat a misnomer. First, the Agreement does not register marks and secondly, it is not truly international and apart from Ireland, notable absentees include the USA, UK, Japan, Australia, South Africa, New Zealand and the Scandinavian countries. Both the Agreement and Protocol are closed systems which means that the users of the systems must be citizens or legal entities from a Member State which includes a company regardless of its place of incorporation having a real and effective industrial and/or commercial establishment in a Member State.

[26.42] The purpose of the Agreement is to enable the owner of a national registration to obtain protection in other Member States by way of a single application.

Procedure

[26.43] The first requirement is the holding of a home national registration. Once this is acquired, then an application for an international registration can be filed with the National Registry of the country of the applicant. The application

---

28. Brussels, 14 December 1900; Washington, 2 June 1911; The Hague, 6 November 1925; London, 2 June 1934; Nice, 15 June 1957; Stockholm, 14 July 1967.

must be made in French and is directed to the World Intellectual Property Organisation (WIPO) based in Geneva. The application seeks extension of the home registration to Member States which the applicant designates. Once the National Registry has examined the application as to formalities, it is then forwarded to WIPO. The goods and/or services must correspond with or be more limited than the home registration. WIPO will only make a formal examination which is mainly restricted to checking on the specification of goods/services and classification. WIPO will allocate a number and publish the registration in the journal: *Les Marques Internationales*. WIPO also notifies the National Registries of all countries designated by an applicant.

[26.44] Each National Registry will then treat the national registration as if it was filed as a national application. This means, for example, that the German part of the international registration can be refused by the German Patent Office or can be opposed by the owners of earlier conflicting marks on the National German Register. However, each National Registry has only a period of twelve months within which to refuse registration. Such refusal can be provisional or final. In the absence of a notification of refusal within the twelve months, registration is deemed to have been accepted by that country.

[26.45] Although what results is a bundle of national registrations, renewals, changes of name and assignments are all dealt with centrally through WIPO. A licence cannot be recorded centrally and must be done before the National Registries which allow for such. An accepted international registration enjoys exactly the same protection as a national registration and the major advantage of the Madrid Agreement is a considerable cost saving from the alternative of filing individual national applications. This cost saving includes the possibility of filing multi-class applications which is not possible when filing nationally in some Member States, eg Spain and Portugal. It is also possible to extend protection to other countries at any time by way of a simple formality. The Agreement has proved a great success and is heavily utilised particularly in Germany, Benelux, France, Italy, Spain and Portugal.

Dependency on National Registration

[26.46] The international registration remains dependant on the basic home national registration for the first five years of its existence. If, during that five year period, the national mark ceases to enjoy protection whether by voluntary withdrawal, non-renewal, cancellation or rectification, the international registration is no longer valid in those countries for which the mark has been accepted. After the five year period has expired, the international registration becomes independent from the basic national registration. This provision is often referred to as the dependency clause or the central attack system.

PROTOCOL TO THE MADRID AGREEMENT[29]

[26.47] For many years, WIPO tried to attract a wider membership of the Madrid Agreement, especially important industrial countries who remained outside despite the advantages offered by the Agreement. The principal reasons for non-membership could not be addressed by amendment to the Agreement because such amendments would have suppressed some of the main advantages of the Madrid Agreement itself. Therefore, a separate Agreement was concluded and is termed the Protocol. Where possible, the Protocol followed the terms of the Madrid Agreement itself but the following are the main differences.

(a) Home application is sufficient instead of a home registration

[26.48] This was perceived to be necessary because in countries where there was a more substantive examination, nationals would be disadvantaged by the consequential delays in obtaining the basis upon which to found a Madrid Agreement Registration.

The innovation of the Protocol is that while a home registration is still accepted as a basis for an International Protocol application, it is not a requirement. A home application is sufficient although such must mature to registration at the latest five years after the application for the international mark.

(b) Extended time limit for refusing registration

[26.49] Under the Protocol, notification of refusal of protection by the National Registry where protection is sought can be extended to eighteen months and even later in the event of opposition. The UK has exercised this option and it is expected that Ireland will do likewise upon membership. Again, like the Madrid Agreement, if there is no notification of refusal during the time period allowed, then registration is deemed automatic.

(c) Fees for extending protection to a given country can be equal to the national filing fees instead of a flat fee per country

[26.50] National Registries were concerned about a considerable loss of income by joining the Madrid Agreement because the fees charged for a designation via Madrid were often much lower than the official fees charged for national applications. Indeed, this is one of the main advantages of the Madrid Agreement. Unfortunately, such an advantage had to be sacrificed so that National Registries could maintain at their option, the same charges irrespective of whether an application is under the Protocol or a national application. The UK, Sweden, Norway, Finland and Denmark have all struck designation fees which are very close to the national filing fees.

[29.] 28 June 1989.

(d) Conversion following central attack

[26.51] The Protocol retains the principle of central attack but in certain circumstances, a Protocol trade mark can be transformed into a national trade mark application and still retain the date of filing of the Protocol mark.[30] In this way, cancellation of a home national registration may not necessarily lead to a loss of rights in countries, although it will be necessary to file a second time under each national system.

(e) Duration

[26.52] The duration of a Protocol mark is every ten years as opposed to a twenty year renewal under the Madrid Agreement.

(f) Languages

[26.53] Under the Protocol, applications can be filed in either French or English and publications will occur in both languages. Under the Madrid Agreement, it is only French.

LINK BETWEEN MADRID AGREEMENT AND PROTOCOL

[26.54] There is no relationship between countries who are only members of the Madrid Agreement and countries who are only members of the Protocol because although having many common elements, they are to be viewed as separate and succinct Conventions. However, in a situation where a country is a member of both conventions, it is the Madrid Agreement which prevails[31] and therefore by way of example, the country where protection is sought must send its refusal notification within twelve months of the date of the international mark as provided in the Madrid Agreement as opposed to eighteen months under the Protocol.

LINK WITH CTM

[26.55] The Protocol provides for a link with the CTM system on the basis that the EU is an intergovernmental organisation that can become a member. This means that if ratified by the EU, an applicant with an existing registration or application in a Protocol country may file a single application at WIPO in Geneva and designate the CTM system.

[30.] Article 9 *quinquies*.
[31.] Article 9 *sexies*.

INFRINGEMENT

[26.56] As an international or Protocol mark is essentially a bundle of national rights, enforcement of a right is dependant on the national laws of the country concerned in the same way as infringement of a national registration. Invalidity proceedings are dealt with in the same way but details of any invalidity, cancellation, etc. are recorded on the National Register. Use in each designed State is required to maintain validity.

[26.57] The Protocol came into force on 1 April 1996 and as of that date, the Member States were Spain, UK, Denmark, Sweden, Finland, Norway, China, Cuba and Germany. Ireland has not yet ratified but is expected to do so in 1998. Section 59 of the 1996 Act enables the Minister to give effect to the provisions of the Madrid Protocol.

Chapter 27

The Community Trade Mark

INTRODUCTION AND BRIEF HISTORY

[27.01] The objective of the Community Trade Mark ("CTM") is to fulfil the recognised need for an arrangement for trade marks whereby undertakings can, by means of one procedural system, obtain a single registration to which uniform protection is given, and which has effect throughout the entire area of the European Union. It does not replace the national trade mark laws of the various EU countries but is a complimentary system for undertakings who require a more cost effective and streamlined system for protecting trade marks in a number of EU countries. Prior to the CTM, an Irish company wishing to register its trade mark throughout the EU had to file, prosecute and register through the national trade marks office of each country. The only exception being a single Benelux registration covering the Netherlands, Belgium and Luxembourg.

[27.02] The Regulation governing the CTM has been long in the offing. The major obstacles to adoption were political, namely the location of the Community Office and the selection of the official languages. On 29 October 1993, the EU Council of Ministers decided that the Community Trade Marks Office, or to give it its correct but cumbersome name, The Office for Harmonisation in the Internal Market ("OHIM") would be located in Spain and later the Spanish authorities decided on establishment in the city of Alicante in South East Spain. The language problems were resolved on 7 December 1993.

[27.03] On 20 December 1993, the Council of the EU issued Regulation No 40/94. The Regulation was published in the Official Journal on 14 January 1994 and came into force on 15 March 1994. Although OHIM has accepted applications since January 1996, the effective date was 1 April 1996.[1] However, similar to the transitional provisions in the Irish Trade Marks Act 1996, it was still possible to claim Paris Convention priority of an earlier filed application and thus effectively secure a right earlier than 1 April 1996.

[1.] The number of applications filed before OHIM during 1996 exceeded most expectations and was in excess of 40,000.

PRINCIPAL FEATURES OF THE CTM

Unitary character

[27.04] Article 1(2) provides:

> A Community Trade Mark shall have a unitary character. It shall have equal effect throughout the Community; it shall not be registered, transferred or surrendered or be the subject of a decision revoking the rights of the proprietor or declaring it invalid, nor shall its use be prohibited, save in respect of the whole community.

It is thus not possible to hold a CTM registration excluding one or more EU countries. It is all or nothing. A single prior conflicting earlier trade mark, for example, on the national register in just one EU country can form the basis for opposition against the entire CTM application. If an opposition is successful, an applicant must abandon the application or alternatively may convert into a series of national applications and enjoy the same date of filing and priority or seniority of the CTM application.

Who may apply

[27.05] Under Article 5, both natural and legal persons may apply for and hence own a CTM registration. Legal persons are covered by a broad definition. Companies or firms and other legal entities shall be regarded as such if, under the terms of the law governing them, they have the capacity in their own name to have rights and obligations of all kinds, to make contracts or accomplish other legal acts and to sue and be sued. Apart from nationals of EU Member States, the CTM system may also be availed of by non-EU nationals provided that they are nationals of countries which are party to the Paris Convention or to the World Trade Organisation Agreement.[2] The CTM is also available to nationals domiciled in, or which have their seat in or which have a real and effective industrial or commercial establishment within either the EU or a State which is a party to the Paris Convention. It is also provided that trade mark owners not falling into these categories may still secure a CTM if their own country accords reciprocal protection to all EU nationals.

Definition of a Community Trade Mark

[27.06] Article 4 provides as follows:

> A Community Trade Mark may consist of any signs capable of being represented graphically, particularly words, including personal names, designs, letters, numerals, the shape of goods or of their packaging, provided that such

---

[2.] Article 5(1)(b) as amended by Article 1(1) Regulation 3288/94.

signs are capable of distinguishing the goods or services of one undertaking from those of other undertakings.[3]

This broad definition corresponds to Article 2 of the Harmonisation Directive and s 6 of the Trade Marks Act 1996. The explanatory memorandum to the Regulation states that "no type of sign is automatically excluded from registration" and would therefore include colours, sounds, smells, phrases, slogans, gestures, surnames, get-up and trade dress. For registration purposes all signs must be capable of distinguishing. The explanatory memorandum to the Regulation states that the purpose of these words is to focus attention on the question whether:

> ... the relevant sign is capable of performing the basic function of a trade mark. That function in economic and legal terms, is to indicate the origin of goods or services and to distinguish them from those of other undertakings.

Languages

[27.07] The provision *vis-à-vis* languages was a compromise position and is therefore quite intricate. Under Article 115, the OHIM official languages are English, French, German, Spanish and Italian.

However, an application for a CTM may be filed in any one of the eleven official EU languages[4] but an applicant must always select a second language which must be one of the five OHIM languages.

If the applicant is the sole party to any proceedings, then the language of these proceedings is the language used for filing. If, however, the language used for filing is not one of the five official OHIM languages, then the OHIM may choose the second language as the language for communication.

[27.08] All notices of oppositions and all applications for revocation or invalidity must be in one of the official OHIM languages, a translation period of one month being provided.[5]

All information published under the Regulation including all entries in the register will be in all of the eleven EU official languages.

ABSOLUTE GROUNDS FOR REFUSAL

[27.09] Because a trade mark registration grants exclusivity of use, there is an examination as to whether or not the trade mark fulfils the requisite requirement of being distinctive and thus capable of distinguishing the goods or services of one undertaking from those of other undertakings and that there is therefore no

---

[3.] Directive 89/100/EEC.
[4.] Danish, Dutch, English, Finnish, French, German, Greek, Italian, Portuguese, Spanish and Swedish.
[5.] Article 115(5).

inconsistency with the rights being conferred. There is an exhaustive list of the absolute grounds for refusal[6] and these are as follows:

(A) Marks falling outside the definition of a sign in Article 4.[7]

(B) Trade marks which are devoid of any distinctive character.

(C) Trade marks which consist exclusively of signs or indications:

- which may serve in trade, to designate the kind, quality, quantity, intended purpose, value, geographical origin or the time of production of the goods or of rendering of the services or other characteristics of the goods or services; and/or

- have become customary in the current language or in the bona fide and established practices of the trade. Thus, generic Marks are excluded.

(D) Signs being exclusively shapes either resulting from the nature of the goods, necessary to obtain a technical result or give a substantial value to the goods.

(E) Trade marks contrary to public policy or morality.

(F) Deceptive trade marks.

(G) Trade marks pursuant to Article 6 *ter* of the Paris Convention.

(H) Public interest badges, emblems or escutcheons.

(I) Trade marks for wines or spirits which contain or consist of a geographical indication and where the wine or spirit does not have this origin.[8]

These absolute grounds apply notwithstanding that the basis for non-registerability pertains only in part of the EU.[9] This could arise, for example because of the meaning of the word in just one language. In relation to (B) and (C) above, use can be taken into account and if the trade mark can be shown to be distinctive through use, then registration will be allowed.

[27.10] It is not possible to file an opposition to a CTM application on any of the grounds in Article 7. However, it is possible to file observations following publication.

---

6. Article 7.
7. *Supra.*
8. Article 7(1) as amended by Article 1(3) - Regulation 3288/94.
9. Article 7(2).

SEARCHES[10]

[27.11] The OHIM do not cite prior conflicting marks on the CTM or any national register as a basis for refusing registration and hence differs from the examination before certain national trade mark offices, including examination under the Irish Trade Marks Act 1996. The OHIM will conduct a search of prior CTM Marks. National registries may search their own registers for conflicting marks but are not obliged to do so.[11] However, if a national registry does conduct a search, then it is obliged to send the results of the search to the OHIM. The results of all of these searches are sent to the applicant who must then decide whether or not to proceed with their application. This procedure is modelled on Benelux law and the OHIM will not raise objections based on the search report. Given that there are no citations, it does mean that there are likely to be a large number of oppositions and that owners of marks will have to be vigilant and monitor applications which have been approved and published for opposition purposes.

OPPOSITIONS AND RELATIVE GROUNDS FOR REFUSAL

[27.12] Not more than three months following publication, a proprietor of, or his authorised licensee under an earlier trade mark and other specified persons with interests in marks can lodge an opposition[12] to the CTM application. An opposition may be brought on the basis of any or all of the relative grounds for refusal[13] in Article 8. An "earlier trade mark" is defined as:

- a CTM;
- national trade mark in an EU country or the Benelux; and
- an International (Madrid Arrangement or Madrid Protocol) trade mark effective in an EU country.

Article 8.2(c) also provides for opposition based on a trade mark which is well known in an EU country under Article 6 *bis* of the Paris Convention. Under Article 8.4, opposition is also possible by the proprietor of an unregistered trade mark used in the course of trade and of more than mere local significance. The unregistered trade mark must have been acquired before the CTM application or its priority date. The law in a particular EU country must be such as to confer a right on the proprietor to prohibit the use of a subsequent trade mark.

[10.] Article 39.

[11.] Only Germany, France and Italy have indicated that they will not carry out national searches.

[12.] Article 42.

[13.] Article 8.

[27.13] Normally, opposition is based on a trade mark which is identical or similar for identical or similar goods/services to that of the opposed trade mark. However, Article 8.5 does provide for opposition by the proprietor or licensee of an earlier trade mark which is registered for goods/services not similar to those for which the CTM is to be registered where, in the case of an earlier CTM, the mark has a reputation in the EU and, in the case of an earlier national trade mark, the mark has a reputation in the State concerned. It is also necessary for the opponent to show that the use without due cause of the trade mark applied for, would take unfair advantage of, or be detrimental to, the distinctive character or the repute of the earlier trade mark.

DURATION AND RENEWAL[14]

[27.14] A CTM registration has a registration period of ten years from the date of filing of the application and may be renewed for further ten year periods. No evidence of use is required for renewal.

EXTENT OF PROTECTION CONFERRED BY CTM

[27.15] A CTM registration confers an exclusive right to prevent others from using in the course of trade, an identical or confusingly similar sign on identical or similar goods/services anywhere in the EU.[15] Rights can also extend to prevent use in respect of dissimilar goods/services where the CTM has a reputation in the EU and where the unauthorised use without due cause, takes unfair advantage of, or is detrimental to, the distinctive character or repute of the CTM. The rights conferred by a CTM prevail against third parties from the date of publication of registration of the CTM. However, damages can be claimed from the date of publication of the application.

[27.16] In relation to an infringement claim in respect of a non-identical trade mark and/or goods/services, it is necessary to prove "there exists a likelihood of confusion on the part of the public". It is further stated that "the likelihood of confusion includes the likelihood of association between the sign and the trade mark". This corresponds to the provision in s 14(2) of the Trade Marks Act 1996. Likelihood of association is a concept which in particular, has been developed by Benelux case law. The Benelux law recognises that the function of a trade mark is not just as an indication of origin but also as a carrier or reputation and goodwill. The public may be in a position to distinguish the respective marks but may nevertheless associate the trade marks and attribute the goodwill to one and the same source and presumes an economic or

---

14. Article 46 and 47.
15. Article 9.

contractual link between the owners of the respective Marks. A question which arises is whether likelihood of confusion is a separate criterion to be satisfied, or whether likelihood of association is sufficient. In the preamble to the Regulation, the following statement appears:

> Whereas an interpretation should be given of the concept of similarity in relation to the likelihood of confusion; whereas the likelihood of confusion, the appreciation of which depends on numerous elements and, in particular, on the recognition of the trade mark on the market, the association which can be made with the used or registered sign, the degree of similarity between the trade mark and the sign and between the goods or services identified, constitutes the specific condition for such protection.

[27.17] This, in very tortuous language, appears to indicate that the likelihood of confusion forms the basis for protection and likelihood of association is one of the determining factors. If the goodwill function of a trade mark is to be recognised, then likelihood of confusion should be interpreted in such a way that this likelihood will already exist if the phonetical, visual or conceptual similarity between the trade mark and the sign is such that somebody confronted therewith, will associate one with the other. However, in the UK case of *Wagamama Ltd v City Centre Restaurants plc*,[16] Laddie J concluded that "confusion" is meant to be confusion as to the source or origin of the goods. He did not accept a concept of likelihood of association which would mean that it will be trade mark infringement if, on seeing the alleged infringing sign, the registered trade mark would be called to mind even if there is no risk of confusion as to the origin of the goods.

[27.18] Article 9(2) contains a non-exhaustive list of acts which can be considered to be use of a trade mark in the course of trade. The following may constitute infringement:

- affixing a sign to the goods or to the packaging thereof;
- offering the goods, putting them on the market or stocking them for these purposes under that sign, or offering or supplying services thereunder;
- importing or exporting the goods under that sign; or
- using the sign on business papers and in advertising.

[27.19] The registration of a CTM does not entitle the proprietor to prohibit the use of that trade mark in relation to goods which have been put on the market in the EU under that trade mark by the proprietor or with his consent.[17] Parallel

---

16. [1995] FSR 713.
17. Article 13.

imports of products covered by the CTM registration from countries which are not members of the EU are not subject to this rule and to this limitation, with the exception of those countries party to the agreement on the European Economic Area. This exhaustion principle does not apply where there exists legitimate reasons for the proprietor to oppose further commercialisation of the goods, especially where the condition of the goods is changed or impaired after they have been put on the market.

JURISDICTION

[27.20] Jurisdiction for proceedings relating to infringement and the validity of a CTM is governed by the Regulation[18] and also the Brussels Convention on Jurisdiction and the Enforcement of Judgments in Civil and Commercial Matters. Jurisdiction for proceedings other than infringement and validity is governed solely by the Brussels Convention on the basis that the CTM is treated as if it were a national trade mark registration.[19]

[27.21] The Regulation did not set up a special court to deal with CTM matters but rather each Member State was obliged to nominate a limited number of courts and tribunals in their own jurisdiction entitled to handle CTM cases.[20] These are referred to as "Community Trade Mark Courts" and the court so nominated by the Irish Government was the High Court. These courts have exclusive jurisdiction for proceedings relating to CTM infringement and validity actions, declarations of non-infringement (if allowed under national law) and counterclaims for revocation or for a declaration of invalidity. Also claims for reasonable compensation for use of a CTM between the date of publication of the application and the date of grant.

[27.22] Essentially, the jurisdiction of a Community Trade Mark court is governed either by domicile or where the act of infringement is taking place. Firstly, in relation to jurisdiction based on domicile, the following rules apply:

(a) the proceedings must be brought in the CTM court of the Member State in which the defendant is domiciled or if it is not domiciled in any Member State, in which it has an establishment which means a real and effective industrial or commercial establishment;

(b) if the defendant is not domiciled and does not have an establishment in any Member State, the proceedings must be brought in the CTM court of the Member State in which the plaintiff is domiciled or if it is

---

[18.] Articles 91 to 94.

[19.] Article 102.1.

[20.] Article 91(1).

not domiciled in any Member State in which it has an establishment; and

(c) if the plaintiff is similarly neither domiciled nor has an establishment in any Member State, the proceedings shall be brought in the Spanish CTM courts since OHIM has its seat in Alicante, Spain.

[27.23] The parties can agree that a different CTM court has jurisdiction and then Article 17 of the Brussels Convention clicks into place, it being provided:

If the parties, one or more of whom is domiciled in a contracting State, have agreed that a court or courts of a contracting State are to have jurisdiction to settle any dispute which have arisen ... that court or those courts shall have exclusive jurisdiction. Such an agreement conferring jurisdiction shall be either in writing or evidenced in writing or in international trade and commerce in a form which accords with practices in that trade and commerce of which the parties are or ought to have been aware. Where such an agreement is concluded by parties, none of whom is domiciled in a contracting State, the courts of other contracting States shall have no jurisdiction over their disputes unless the court or courts chosen, have declined jurisdiction ... if an agreement conferring jurisdiction was concluded for the benefit of only one of the parties, that party shall retain the right to bring proceedings in any other court which has jurisdiction by virtue of this Convention.

[27.24] In addition, if a defendant enters an appearance before a CTM court which would not otherwise have jurisdiction, then Article 18 of the Brussels Convention applies. This means that this CTM court has jurisdiction provided that the defendant has not entered an appearance solely to contest jurisdiction. In all of these cases, the CTM court decision has extra-territorial effect. The decision in a particular Member State CTM court has effect throughout the EU.

[27.25] An infringement claim can always be brought in a CTM court in the EU country in which infringement is occurring or threatened. In such a case, the decision of the CTM court does not have extra territorial effect. The remedies will only extend to acts in that EU State.

[27.26] Article 99 of the Regulation provides for "provisional relief". An interim or interlocutory injunction may be sought in a CTM court or a national court in the same way as would be available if that was in respect of a national trade mark. If such an action is based on the rules of domicile, then extra-territorial provisional relief can be granted.

[27.27] Validity may only be put in issue in proceedings before a CTM court by way of a counterclaim or by way of defence. If a person wishes to challenge the validity of a CTM other than in infringement proceedings, then the action must be before the OHIM for revocation or a declaration of invalidity.

[27.28] Article 96.7 provides that a CTM court hearing a counterclaim for revocation or declaration of invalidity may on application, stay proceedings and require the defendant to submit the matter to the OHIM for their decision on revocation or a declaration of invalidity. The CTM court may also make an order for provisional relief pending the outcome of the application to the OHIM. Article 95 provides that in the case of a defence, a defendant may put validity in issue only to the extent that the plea relates to non-use of the CTM in issue or an earlier right of the defendant, otherwise the CTM court must treat the CTM as being valid. The validity of a CTM may not be put in issue in an action for a declaration of non-infringement.

[27.29] All of the above leads to one of the major advantages for the owner of a CTM, namely that in many cases, they may have a choice of forum within which to take infringement proceedings.

ASSIGNMENT

[27.30] A CTM may be assigned in respect of some or all of the goods/services but only for the whole of the EU. A CTM cannot be assigned for individual Member States.[21] The assignment must be in writing and executed by both parties. Until recordal is entered on the register, rights cannot be invoked and third parties without knowledge of the transfer will not be affected. Assignments need not include the goodwill but must not mislead the public.

LICENSING

[27.31] A CTM may be licensed for some or all the goods/services and for the whole or part of the EU.[22] A licence may be exclusive or non-exclusive. The holder of an exclusive licence may bring infringement proceedings if the proprietor, after formal notice, does not himself bring the proceedings.

REVOCATION AND INVALIDITY

[27.32] Both an application for revocation and for a declaration of invalidity can be made to the OHIM or by way of a counterclaim in infringement proceedings.[23] The grounds of revocation are as follows:

(1) A CTM registration will be revoked if there is non-use during a five year period.[24] The trade mark must have been put to genuine use in the EU in connection with the goods or services for which it is

---

21. Article 17.
22. Article 22.
23. Articles 50, 51, and 52.
24. Article 15.

registered and provided there are not proper reasons for non-use. The five year period runs from the date of registration. A resumption of use can cure previous non-use but a three month period before revocation or a counter claim is discounted. The genuine use must be in the EU and thus use in only a single EU country will suffice. This is a significant advantage of the CTM system over both the national trade mark and Madrid systems.

(2) That as a consequence of the inactivity of the proprietor, the trade mark has become the common name in the trade for a product or service for which it is registered, ie the mark has become generic.

(3) As a consequence of the use by the proprietor, or with his consent, the mark is liable to mislead the public.

(4) The proprietor is not within the category of persons entitled to hold a CTM registration.[25] This is also one of the grounds for invalidity.

The absolute grounds for refusal[26] are a basis for invalidity but usage after registration is to be taken into account in determining whether the trade mark has acquired a distinctive character. A CTM may be declared invalid where the applicant was acting in bad faith when he filed the application.

[27.33] The registration of a CTM may also be declared invalid because the mark conflicts with earlier rights of third parties. Article 52(2) sets out a non-exhaustive list of some earlier rights to include right to a name, a right of personal portrayal, a copyright and an industrial property right.

ACQUIESCENCE

[27.34] If the proprietor of a CTM or national registration has acquiesced for five years to the use of a later CTM, the owner of that earlier CTM or national mark is barred from applying for a declaration that the later CTM is invalid and from opposing the use of the later CTM in respect of goods or services for which it is being used, unless the registration of the later CTM was applied for in bad faith.[27]

CONVERSION INTO NATIONAL APPLICATION

[27.35] A CTM application or registration may be converted into separate national applications and retain the CTM filing date, priority or seniority as is

---

25. Article 5.
26. Article 7.
27. Article 53.

appropriate.[28] Conversion cannot take place if there has been revocation on the grounds of non-use.

SENIORITY

[27.36] The owner of a CTM may claim the seniority of one or more national registrations in those EU countries where the trade mark is registered nationally.[29] The proprietor of the national registration from which seniority is claimed must be the same person as the owner of the CTM. The trade marks should also correspond and the goods/services of the national registration should be identical with or contained within the specification of the CTM. The claim to seniority may be made either at the time of the CTM application or within two months of the filing date or after registration. If seniority is claimed and the proprietor surrenders his national registration or allows it to lapse, he will continue to have the same rights as he would have had if his earlier national registration had been retained.

OVERVIEW

[27.37] A CTM registration arises through a single application and examination. Only one renewal is required and recordal of assignments, change of name, licences, etc. can all be done centrally before the OHIM. It is also particularly advantageous to trade mark owners who are only using a mark in some but not all EU countries. Genuine use in one EU country constitutes use throughout the EU. Unlike the Madrid systems, there is no requirement for a national registration or application. Opposition proceedings are through one forum, ie the OHIM and there are no citations. Also included in the cost of application are search reports of prior CTMs and national registrations with the exception of France, Germany and Italy. The decision of a single CTM court can have effect throughout the EU. Seniority will, in some cases, allow a trade mark owner to tidy up their portfolio and maintain just a single registration without loss of rights. With a CTM, a single certificate can be used for filing with customs authorities in order to activate customs' monitoring.[30]

[27.38] Because a single national conflicting prior right can form the basis of successful opposition, it is likely that registration will be difficult to achieve and that oppositions are likely to be numerous. There is a two month cooling-off period following Notice of Opposition and within which an applicant can withdraw or convert to national applications without incurring any liability for Opponent's costs but to a large extent, the success of the CTM will be dependant

[28.] Article 108.
[29.] Article 34.
[30.] Regulation No 40/94 of 20 December 1994.

on the extent to which there are oppositions and how these are resolved by the OHIM. The number of CTM applications filed in the first year exceeded almost all expectations and was in excess of 50,000. This has had the effect of delaying the examination of applications and the first CTM applications were not advertised for opposition purposes until March 1997. For the initial three or four years of the CTM Regulation it is expected that there will be long delays in the registration procedure.

Chapter 28

Trade Marks Act 1996 - Registrability

INTRODUCTION

[28.01] The Trade Marks Act 1996 has a commencement date of 1 July 1996[1] and apart from generally modernising the statutory law *vis-à-vis* trade marks, it enabled the State to fulfil its obligations under EU law. The substantive provisions regarding the types of marks registrable, grounds upon which to oppose and seek rectification, scope of protection, user requirements and the new concept of acquiescence, are all requirements under the First Council Directive of 21 December 1988 to approximate the laws of the Member States relating to trade marks.[2] The 1996 Act introduces registration in respect of marks used for services[3] and for collective marks. New to Irish law is the concept that the scope of protection granted by a registration extends beyond the exact goods/services and in some cases, to dissimilar goods/services. Rights to a trade mark through registration effective in the State can now be secured under the Community Trade Mark Regulation[4] and provision is made for the recognition of such and also the Madrid Protocol[5] when ratified by the State. Procedurally, it is now possible to file multi-class applications, renewals are every ten years and procedures relating to licensing and assignments are simplified. For trade mark applications after 1 July 1996, the distinction between Parts A and B of the Register no longer exists. Although the 1963 Act is repealed, the transitional provisions provide that it still applies to the validity of existing registrations and therefore the distinction between an old Part A and Part B registration may still be important. This is an example of a difference between the Irish Act and its UK counterpart.[6] Another example is the retention of compulsory disclaimers in the 1996 Act. The rigid registered user requirements are gone and any use with the consent of the proprietor will defeat revocation on the ground of non-use. Associations are no longer imposed and when agreed between parties, the Controller has no discretion to refuse to allow to co-exist on the Register identical or confusingly similar marks held by

---

[1.] SI 199/1996.
[2.] 89/104/EEC.
[3.] See para **[25.12]** and **[25.13]** *supra*.
[4.] Council Regulation (EC) 40/94 of 20 December 1993 on the Community Trade Mark.
[5.] Sections 58 & 59.
[6.] The Trade Marks Act 1994 which came into effect on 31 October 1994.

different proprietors. The 1996 Act also gives effect to certain provisions of the Paris Convention.[7]

DEFINITION OF A TRADE MARK

[28.02] Section 6(1) of the 1996 Act defines a trade mark as:

> Any sign capable of being represented graphically which is capable of distinguishing goods or services of one undertaking from those of other undertakings.

A non-exhaustive list of examples are given such as "words (including personal names), designs, letters, numerals or the shape of goods or their packaging". This definition and the non-exhaustive list of examples are taken from Article 2 of the Trade Mark Harmonisation Directive. The definition imposes three requirements for a trade mark:

(a) it must be a sign;

(b) it must be capable of being represented graphically; and

(c) it must be capable of distinguishing goods or services of one undertaking from those of other undertakings.

The word 'sign' is to be interpreted broadly. The UK White Paper[8] includes a quote from an explanatory memorandum issued by the Commission in relation to the corresponding provision of the CTM Regulation (which was then in draft form) as follows:

> "No type of sign is automatically excluded from registration as a Community Trade Mark. Article 3 lists the types of signs used most frequently by undertakings to identify their goods or services, but is not an exhaustive list. It is designed to simplify the adoption of administrative practices and court judgments to business requirements and to encourage undertakings to apply for Community Trade Marks.
>
> Depending on the circumstances, therefore, the Trade Marks Office, the National Courts, or in the last resort, the Court of Justice, will be responsible for determining whether, for example, solid colours or shades of colours, and signs denoting sound, smell or taste, may constitute Community Trade Marks".[9]

[28.03] The requirement that the sign must be capable of being represented graphically is logical in order that parties are aware of the scope of protection and, for example, can, by carrying out searches, ascertain rights which exist under trade marks either pending or on the Register. Also, trade marks are

---

[7.] Sections 60-65.

[8.] *Reform of Trade Marks Law*, September 1990.

[9.] *Bulletin of the European Communities*, Supplement 5/80.

advertised for opposition purposes and the Journal must be able to represent exactly what the trade mark is. It is a procedural requirement of registration alone and this is confirmed by s 2(2) which states that:

> ... references in this Act to use (or any particular description of use) of a trade mark, or of a sign identical with, similar to, or likely to be mistaken for a trade mark, include use (or that description of use) otherwise than by means of a graphic representation

Examples of trade marks which are prima facie registrable but which may be difficult to represent graphically, are sound marks, smells and tastes.

Sounds

[28.04] In relation to sounds, the US practice has been to simply describe such as, for example, "for the mark consisting of the sound of a creaking door" or "the mark consists of the sound of clop, clop, clop, moo". In some instances, the mark can be described by reference to the name of a well known song or musical work such as, for example, Bach's *Air On A G-String*, immediately recognisable from advertising campaigns for Hamlet cigars. The perceived problem with simply using musical notation is that part of the distinctiveness may lie in the emphasis given to a particular instrument and whether or not it is accompanied by vocals. In some cases, it will be necessary to accompany musical notation with a written description.

Smells

[28.05] During the passage of the UK Bill, there was much discussion over whether or not a smell can be represented graphically in such a way that the scope of protection can be determined. There are various classification systems for odorants such as chromatography and methods of chemical analysis which can be detailed. However, to a searcher, such an analysis is unlikely to assist in determining the nature of the smell without performing the chemical analysis itself. Therefore, it may well be decided that the graphic representation in itself does not adequately portray the sign. Smells can, of course, be graphically represented by a description such as in the US case of a registration in respect of embroidery yarn for "a high-impact, fresh floral fragrance reminiscent of plumeria blossoms". In the UK, applications have been filed in respect of the smell of stale beer for darts and the smell of roses for vehicle tyres.

Colours

[28.06] Even under the 1963 Act, colour has been held to be a trade mark. In *Parke Davis and Company's Application*,[10] Kenny J allowed registration in Part

---

[10.] [1976] FSR 195; see also *Smith Kline & French Laboratories Ltd v Sterling-Winthrop Group Ltd* [1976] RPC 511.

A of the Register of a coloured band around a capsule containing a pharmaceutical preparation. In almost all cases where colour is sought to be registered as a trade mark, it will be necessary to show capacity to distinguish through use which would include showing that there is no compelling need to use a particular colour and that the colour serves no utilitarian or functional purpose.

Slogans

[28.07] Although slogans have never been considered by the Irish courts, there are two UK decisions which show how such have been considered. In the decision, *I CAN'T BELIEVE IT'S YOGHURT Trade Mark*[11] emphasis was placed on the fact that the slogan was used on its own without any other trade mark and "as seen on a pot of yoghurt, the public will take the phrase to be a brand name". In the second decision, *HAVE A BREAK Trade Mark*,[12] the slogan was viewed as no more than an exhortation to buy, ie a phrase used purely in an advertising sense and not therefore in a trade mark sense at all. There is a recognition that some slogans serve both functions but as stated in the *I CAN'T BELIEVE IT'S YOGHURT* decision, "it may be necessary to show by evidence that there is a branding function in addition to there being an advertising slogan". The distinction drawn by the UK courts appears to be artificial given that a trade mark need not actually be applied to goods and that advertising is clearly trade mark use.

The shape of goods or their packaging

[28.08] Given the specific inclusion of the shape of goods or their packaging in s 6(2) of the 1996 Act, it is readily apparent that the House of Lords decision in *Coca-Cola*,[13] where the bottle shape was refused registration, would now be decided differently. There is no longer a requirement that a "sign" must consist of something which is different from the goods themselves and which had been the practice of the Irish Patents Office. For example, the *Coca-Cola* bottle shape is in fact also used graphically on labelling and this would already have been registrable even under the 1963 Act. There is an obvious overlap between the provision which allows for registration in respect of the shape of goods and registered design law which also allows for such under the Industrial and Commercial Property (Protection) Act 1927.[14] The additional requirement of capacity to distinguish may mean that at least in the initial years of a new shape, it may be necessary to rely on the protection afforded to a registered design.

[11.] [1992] RPC 533.
[12.] [1993] RPC 217.
[13.] [1986] RPC 421.
[14.] No 16 of 1927.

[28.09] A question which will arise is in relation to get-up or trade dress which is not packaging. Examples would be the decor of a restaurant or a petrol station forecourt. Again, provided the criterion as to capability of distinguishing is satisfied, there is no reason why such should not be registrable simply because it comprises a number of signs. It has certainly been the practice in the US to allow such registrations.

Capable of distinguishing

[28.10] Graphical representation is only one requirement and it is still necessary to show a capability of distinguishing goods or services of one undertaking from those of other undertakings. The expression "capable of distinguishing" is not new and under the 1963 Act, the Register was divided into two parts. Part A of the Register was for marks which were considered to be "adapted to distinguish" whereas Part B was for marks which were "capable of distinguishing".[15] It could therefore be argued that the test under the 1996 Act should correspond to the criteria for Part B registration under the 1963 Act, including the important factor that where a mark is shown to be distinctive in fact, it will be registrable. This was a concept with which the English courts struggled but in the Irish Supreme Court decision in *WATERFORD Trade Mark*,[16] the English authorities were rejected and despite its geographical signification, registration of WATERFORD was allowed in respect of cut crystal glassware. It was accepted that the mark had been used continuously since 1952 and that when used in relation to cut crystal glassware, had in fact achieved 100% factual distinctiveness. O'Higgins CJ in reviewing the English authorities stated:

> "Eighteen years later, however, in *Liverpool Electric Cable Co's Application* [1929] 46 RPC 99, the same Court, having accepted that factual distinctiveness had been established in relation to the words LIVERPOOL CABLES, held that the word being geographical in part, lacked capacity to be distinguished in law ... I feel that in relation to the Part B application the Court at the time had turned against geographical words and faced with the fact that no discretion to refuse was possible under the section once the factual distinctiveness was established, introduced a requirement of "capacity in law" which was not within the words used in the section ... The Liverpool case and similar cases were followed in subsequent decisions and the line of authority which these represent, no doubt led to the recent House of Lords decision in *York TM*.[17] It involves interpreting section 10(2)(b) of the United Kingdom Trade Marks Act, 1938 (which is identical in terms with section 18(2)(b) of the Trade Marks Act, 1963) as if it only applied to words which could be regarded as "capable in

---

15. TMA 1963, ss 17 & 18.
16. [1984] FSR 390.
17. [1982] FSR 111.

law" of distinguishing. It seems to me, as I have already indicated, that this is to ignore the plain words which are used or to seek to alter the meaning. I cannot accept such a view as being correct so far as this jurisprudence is concerned".

[28.11] How the criteria in the 1996 Act differ from the 1963 Act is that there is no longer a requirement of a connection in the course of trade between the goods and a person entitled to use the mark, ie use as a means of denoting the source or origin of the goods[18] so that consumers recognise the goods bearing the mark as emanating from the same source.[19] The new criteria move from treating a trade mark as an indicator of origin to a means of distinguishing, which somewhat ironically was the test used in the past when assessing whether or not a trade mark was adapted to distinguish and so worthy of Part A registration under the 1963 Act. As stated by Kenny J in *Mothercare Ltd's Application*:[20]

> "I think that this must mean that there is some feature of the word which makes it suitable to distinguish the goods of one trader from another."

[28.12] The new regime faced by the Courts raises consideration of factors similar to the old Part B criterion but with a change in emphasis as to the function of a trade mark which makes the criteria harder to follow. The tendency may be to maintain the view of a trade mark as an indicator of origin/source and simply consider the function of distinguishing as a means of achieving this objective. The Trade Mark Harmonisation Directive does, after all, in its preamble, describe the function of a trade mark as being in particular, an indication of origin.

[28.13] Prior to the 1996 Act and principally because of the absence of service mark registration, many trade mark owners sought to maintain a footing on the Register by registering what was essentially a service mark but in respect of goods. Thus, banks, insurance and car hire companies used to register their trade marks in respect of printed publications (Class 16). The validity of a number of these registrations must be questionable given that such still remains to be determined under the 1963 Act[21] and hence the need for a trade mark proprietor to show a connection in the course of trade with the goods of registration. It is true that the Supreme Court in *ITT World Directories Inc v Controller*[22] did retreat from Kenny J's statement that "the goods which are to bear the trade mark must be sold in the course of trade"[23] and did not require an actual sale but if, for example, the use on printed publications is simply a means of advertising

---

[18.] *Bismag v Amblins (Chemists) Ltd* (1940) 57 RPC 209.
[19.] *McDowell's Application* (1926) 43 RPC 313.
[20.] [1968] IR 359.
[21.] TMA 1996, s 13; Third Schedule.
[22.] [1985] ILRM 30 (GOLDEN PAGES Trade Mark).
[23.] *Bank of America National Trust & Savings Association's Trade Mark* [1977] FSR 7.

services on different goods, then the requisite connection in the course of trade does not exist.[24] This is also the position likely to be adopted under the 1996 Act and to quote from the UK White Paper:

> "The goods 'of' an undertaking can in this context only sensibly mean the goods which the undertaking makes or sells - in short, goods which it deals with in the course of trade - and not for example goods which it merely repairs or delivers. Likewise, the services 'of' an undertaking mean those services (banking, repairing, cleaning, etc.) which the undertaking is in the business of providing."

RETAIL SERVICES

[28.14] During the passage of the UK Trade Marks Bill, attempts were made to include a specific provision allowing for the registration of marks in respect of retail services. Under the UK 1938 Act, which corresponded to the Irish 1963 Act, registration in respect of retail services was refused but the decision was primarily based on the wording of the 1938 Act, as amended by the UK Trade Marks (Amendment) Act 1984, which required that the provision of a service had to be for money or moneys' worth, which is no longer a requirement under the new 1994 UK Act or the Irish 1996 Act. This was not the only reason for refusal, the Court of Appeal in *DEE Corporation plc & Others' Application*[25] also expressed the view that the specification "retail services" was too indefinite and that the activities were merely ancillary to the business of trading in goods in the stores. The UK Trade Marks Office has decided to refuse applications in respect of retail services, which is in keeping with the statements for entry in the Minutes of the Council Meeting at which the CTM Regulation was adopted and which states with regard to Article 1(1):

> The Council and the Commission consider that the activity of retail trading in goods is not as such a service for which a Community Trade Mark may be registered under this Regulation.

[28.15] Retail services is also not a specific entry in the Nice Classification of goods or services. In other common law countries such as USA, Australia, Hong Kong and South Africa, registration in respect of retail services is permissible and it is hoped that the Irish courts will adopt a more liberal approach and will also allow for such. In the *Golden Pages*[26] decision, the Supreme Court has already determined registrability, not on the basis of what is actually sold but on the substance of the product provided to customers. There appears to be no

---

[24.] See *KODAK Trade Mark* [1990] FSR 49.

[25.] [1990] RPC 159.

[26.] [1985] FSR 27.

logical distinction between other services such as restaurants and photocopying where charges are made in respect of goods supplied.

USE OR INTENTION TO USE

[28.16] There is no requirement of actual usage to secure registration under Irish law. The 1963 Act stated that the mark had to be "used or proposed to be used in relation to the goods".[27] Section 37(2) of the 1996 Act provides that an applicant must state that the trade mark is being used or that the applicant has a bona fide intention that it should be so used. This provision appears to have no teeth because it is not specifically identified as one of the absolute grounds for refusing registration. However, it must follow that an application to register without a *bona fide* intention to use is likely to be considered as an application made in bad faith.[28] The registration of a "ghost mark" is not *bona fide* as evidenced in the case of *Imperial Group Ltd v Philip Morris & Co Ltd*.[29] In that case, the plaintiff wished to use the word MERIT in respect of cigarettes but understandably considered the word to be unregisterable as being laudatory. In order to gain a footing on the Register, they registered the word NERIT and also made token use with the objective that the registration would not be liable to cancellation on the ground of non-use. This failed and it was held that there was no bona fide use, the Court of Appeal equating the words *"bona fide"* with the need for use to be genuine use, ie use in the context of a course of trading embarked upon as an end in itself and not as embracing an activity which, although in the nature of trading, is in reality subordinate to a wholly independent objective.

[28.17] One major advantage of the 1996 Act for trade mark owners is that the applicant for registration no longer has to be the actual or intended user of the mark or to file a simultaneous registered user application. An applicant and subsequent registered proprietor can be a holding company. However, since invalidity of registrations dated prior to 1 July 1996 are determined under the 1963 Act, this is still an important issue for Part B registrations of less than seven years standing.[30] An application invalidly filed under the 1963 Act by failure to include the user by way of a simultaneously filed registered user application, cannot be subsequently remedied by filing a registered user application since the requirement under s 37(1)(b) was for the registered user application to accompany the trade mark application itself.[31]

---

[27] TMA 1963, s 1.

[28] TMA 1996, s 8(4)(b).

[29] [1982] FSR 72.

[30] TMA 1963, s 21.

[31] See *Gillette Co's Application* (1972) Supp OJ No. 1160 p 9. This decision was affirmed on appeal by the High Court.

Chapter 29

Trade Marks Act 1996: Absolute Grounds for Refusal of Registration

[29.01] Because a trade mark registration grants the proprietor exclusivity, it is not unnatural that there are limitations on what is registerable. Grounds for refusal can be divided into *absolute* grounds and *relative* grounds. Absolute grounds for refusal means that they are not dependant on earlier rights. Relative grounds are also a basis for refusal but because of earlier rights and not because of something inherently wrong with the applied for trade mark itself.

[29.02] The absolute grounds for refusal are stated in s 8 of the Trade Marks Act 1996 and these, together with ss 62 and 63 which deal with flags and emblems under Article 6 *ter* of the Paris Convention, implement the compulsory grounds for refusal under Article 3 of the Trade Mark Harmonisation Directive and also most of the optional grounds. Not included is Article 3(2)(b) of the Directive allowing refusal of a trade mark which "covers a sign of high symbolic value, in particular, a religious symbol" and only to a limited extent, Article 3(2)(c) which allows for refusal in respect of badges, emblems and escutcheons of public interest but outside Article 6 *ter* of the Paris Convention.[1]

[29.03] The absolute grounds are mandatory but in contrast to the 1963 Act state the specific grounds for refusal rather than laying down positive requirements necessary for registration. This would suggest that there is a presumption of registerability. The absolute grounds are as follows.

SIGNS WHICH ARE NOT TRADE MARKS

[29.04] Under s 8(1)(a), it is necessary that a sign fall within the definition of a trade mark contained in s 6(1)[2] and must therefore be capable of being represented graphically and capable of distinguishing the goods or services of one undertaking from those of other undertakings. An aspect of this ground of refusal is that evidence of use even showing factual distinctiveness is not sufficient to overcome this particular objection. A broader view of what is capable of distinguishing must be taken than that which existed under the Trade Marks Act 1963. Geographical place names must generally be viewed as

---

[1.] See TMA 1996, s 9(2).
[2.] See para **[28.02]**.

capable of distinguishing because such can acquire a distinctive character through usage as recognised in the proviso to s 8(1).[3] The Irish Supreme Court in the WATERFORD trade mark decision had already allowed for the registration of well known place names upon evidence of factual distinctiveness through usage but the English courts proceeded differently.[4]

TRADE MARKS DEVOID OF DISTINCTIVE CHARACTER

[29.05] Under this ground for refusal contained in s 8(1)(b), unless the words "capable of distinguishing" are interpreted broadly, it is at a first glance hard to see how a trade mark can pass the test of being capable of distinguishing and still be devoid of distinctive character. The key to the interpretation must surely lie in the word 'capable'. The definition of a trade mark does not require actual distinctiveness but only a capability of distinguishing. Therefore, a trade mark can be devoid of distinctive character at a particular moment in time but may earn distinctiveness through usage. Examples of such would be one and two letter or numeral marks. It will be a matter of interpretation as to whether or not a common surname is likely to be considered devoid of distinctive character.

[29.06] Under the 1963 Act, the Controller determined whether or not the ordinary signification of a word was that of a surname by consideration of the number of times the word appeared in both the Irish and a number of foreign telephone directories, a practice which the Irish courts considered could not be applied too rigidly.[5] This practice may still be followed by the Controller but is even less likely to be an important consideration by the courts since the prohibition does not result from the fact of being a surname but from such being devoid of distinctive character. The Community Trade Marks Office have stated that they will not raise objection to surnames unless such has a further meaning which takes it into the realm of lacking distinctiveness, eg 'farmer' in respect of agricultural products.

[29.07] Personal names are specifically stated in s 6(2) as being an example of a trade mark and under German law, the registration of even well known surnames is allowed, one of the arguments being that the very purpose of a surname is as a means of distinguishing between persons. It is, of course, true that surnames do have a capacity to distinguish, eg FORD, COLEMANS, MURPHYS, and it remains to be seen whether or not this is sufficient in its own right or will at least common surnames require use in order to illustrate that they are not devoid of distinctive character. It should be borne in mind that the

---

3. See also *WATERFORD Trade Mark* [1984] ILRM 565.
4. *YORK Trade Mark* [1982] FSR 111.
5. *Kreuzer* [1978] FSR 239.

registration of a surname cannot be asserted to stop a third party from using their own name provided such use is honest.[6]

[29.08] The word 'devoid' might suggest that if the trade mark has a number of elements, then the existence of a single distinctive element in the composition should make the overall trade mark registerable. However, such is not necessarily always the position. If, for example, one takes the word 'super' which may have a very distinctive stylisation of the letter 'S' and which might accordingly be registerable in its own right. The inclusion of such stylisation in the word 'super' is likely to be viewed as insignificant to the overall mark and therefore the total mark remains devoid of distinctive character.

DESCRIPTIVE TRADE MARKS

[29.09] In s 8(1)(c), these are defined as:

> Trade marks which consist exclusively of signs or indications which may serve, in trade, to designate the kind, quality, quantity, intended purpose, value, geographical origin, the time of production of goods or of rendering of services, or other characteristics of goods or services.

The rationale behind this provision is essentially that marks which should legitimately be open to use by traders in general cannot be registered. The use of the word 'exclusively' would indicate that use of a descriptive word in conjunction with other elements means that the overall mark would fall outside this prohibition. This appears to be the position but the mark can still fall foul of s 8(1)(b) as being devoid of any distinctive character.[7] What is different from s 8(1)(b) is that a trade mark could be viewed as distinctive by consumers but may nevertheless be trade terminology and accordingly refused. Even operating under the former law, the trade mark *SUPERWOUND*[8] was refused registration in respect of guitar strings. The evidence showed that the word 'wound' was used by the trade and was therefore descriptive. In *Fry-Cadbury (Ireland) Limited v Synott*[9], an application was brought seeking rectification of the Register by cancellation of the trade mark 'CRUNCH' in respect of confectionery. Both the High and Supreme Courts agreed that the trade mark was essentially descriptive. Many of the Controller's decisions[10] on trade marks having a direct reference to the character or quality of the goods under the 1963 Act would still apply. There is also no reason to believe that phonetic equivalents to descriptive words will not be caught under this provision.[11] The

---

6. TMA 1996, s 15(2)(a).
7. See paras **[29.05]** to **[29.08]** *supra*.
8. [1988] RPC 272.
9. [1936] IR 700.
10. See Tierney, *Irish Trade Marks Law and Practice* (Gill & Macmillan, 1987).

proviso to s 8(1) applies to subsection (c) and therefore use showing a distinctive character will be sufficient to overcome an objection, eg BUDGET for care hire. It is only pre-application use which can be taken into account in determining the question of distinctiveness under the proviso. In the absence of sufficient use, well known geographical locations are still likely to be refused registration. However, because the test is based on the legitimacy of the likely wish by traders to use the trade mark, then where there is no plausible connection between the goods and the geographical location, registration should be allowed. Thus DETROIT for motor vehicles would be refused but ICELAND for coconuts would not. A trade mark application for a protected designation of origin or geographical indication should also be refused registration under s 8(1)(c) at least in so far as the application relates to the agricultural product or foodstuff covered by Regulation No 2081/92.[12] Article 14 of the Regulation specifically provides for refusal in relation to "the same type of product" if the trade mark application is dated subsequent to the publication of approval of the protected designation or geographical indication.

CUSTOMARY LANGUAGE IN A TRADE

[29.10] Under s 8(1)(d), an absolute ground for refusal arises in respect of:

> Trade marks which consist exclusively of signs or indications which have become customary in the current language or in the bona fide and established practices of the trade.

Some commentators have equated this provision with a trade mark being generic but unlike the revocation provision in s 51(1)(c), the words 'common name' are not used and which are also the words used in Regulation No 2081/92 dealing with geographical indications or designations of origin and whether such should be considered as generic. The word 'customary' suggests a somewhat lower standard than 'common' and certainly a lower standard than 'well known' which were the words used in the 1963 Act.[13] However, what is similar to the 1963 Act is that the test is trade use and it is not use by the general public which decides this issue[14]. Unlike s 8(1)(c), it is what traders are actually doing as opposed to what they may be likely to wish to do at a future date. It is not just words that might fall foul of this provision. In the *Cimetidine* trade mark[15] case, Smith Kline & French Laboratories Ltd sought to register the

---

[11.] *Electrix Ltd's Application* [1959] RPC 283.

[12.] 14 July 1992 - On the protection of geographical indications and designations of origin for agricultural products and foodstuffs.

[13.] TMA 1963, s 23.

[14.] *Daiquiri Rum* [1969] RPC 600; *Gramaphone Co's Application* [1910] 2 Ch 423.

[15.] [1991] RPC 17.

colour pale green as a trade mark for pharmaceutical preparations on varying shapes of tablets. Registration was denied, it being found to be common practice for pharmaceutical tablets to be supplied in a visible single colour although not pale green. If this case had been decided under the 1996 Act, it is unlikely that it would be held to fall foul of s 8(1)(d) given that it was not customary in the trade to use pale green. The fact that the trade mark owner himself has misused the trade mark by using it in a descriptive sense[16] may make it devoid of distinctive character but it is not customary trade usage and although it may lead to such at a future date, this is not a basis for refusal under s 8(1)(d). It is, however, a factor that is likely to be taken into account in determining whether or not an applicant can avail of the proviso to s 8(1) allowing use to show that a trade mark has in fact acquired a distinctive character.[17] If an applicant is using a word as a name of an article and not as a trade mark, then distinctiveness cannot be proved. The danger by failing to take a passing off action is that when applying to register any use by the third party, may well be a factor in determining whether or not use is customary in the trade. Dependant on the type of industry, use by a small number of traders may be sufficient to uphold this ground of refusal.

SHAPES

[29.11] Although the definition of a trade mark in s 6 includes the "shape of goods or of their packaging", there are certain shapes which will be excluded from registration and these are set out in s 8(2) which states:

> A sign shall not be registered if it consists exclusively of:
>
> (a) the shape which results from the nature of the goods themselves;
>
> (b) the shape of goods which is necessary to obtain a technical result; or
>
> (c) the shape which gives substantial value to the goods.

[29.12] The rationale behind these provisions is a compromise. Firstly, the view that to allow the registration of the shape of goods or containers would lead to an unacceptable restriction on the choice of shapes available to traders, ie an attempt to expand the boundaries of intellectual property and to convert a protective law into a source of monopoly.[18] The law provides for a monopoly right for a shape by way of a Registered Design under the Industrial and Commercial Property (Protection) Act 1927. However, the shape must be new and upon expiry of the maximum fifteen year duration, enters the public domain. The concept of registered trade mark protection for a shape, contrasts

16. *Shredded Wheat Co Ltd v Kelloggs* [1940] 57 RPC 137.
17. *Portogram Radio Electrical Co's Application* (1952) 69 RPC 241.
18. *Coca-Cola* [1986] RPC 421.

strongly and therefore sits uncomfortably with registered design law, by not requiring any novelty and being indefinite in duration. A second and contrasting view is reflected in paragraph 2.18 of the UK White Paper.[19]

> "It is a fact of the market place, however, that some shapes are recognised by consumers as distinctive of the products of a particular trader. Allowing the registration of such shapes would therefore not be conferring a monopoly - it would merely recognise that a *de facto* monopoly already exists."

[29.13] In the *Jif Lemon* case[20], the House of Lords held that the Jif lemon shape was protected under the law of passing off since all the ingredients to sustain such an action were present including get-up by way of the shape which was associated in the minds of substantial numbers of the purchasing public specifically and exclusively with the Jif lemon juice. The reluctance with which the House of Lords reached their decision can be seen in the following statement of Lord Bridge of Harwich:

> "The result seems to be to give the respondents a *de facto* monopoly of the container as such which is just as effective as *de jure* monopoly. A trader selling plastic lemon juice would never be permitted to register a lemon as his trade mark, but the plaintiffs have achieved the result indirectly that a container designed to look like a real lemon is to be treated, *per se*, as distinctive of their goods. If I could find a way of avoiding this result, I would. But difficulty is that the trial judge's finding of fact, however surprising they may seem, are not open to challenge".

Section 8(2) is taken from Article 3(1)(e) of the Trade Mark Harmonisation Directive which has its roots in the corresponding provisions of the Benelux Trade Marks Act.[21] The Benelux Court of Justice in the case involving Burberry's tartan patterns[22] held that shapes only cover three dimensional and not two dimensional designs. In the Minutes to the Community Trade Mark Regulation, it is also stated "the Council and the Commission consider that where goods are packaged, the expression 'shape of the goods' includes the shape of the packaging".

[29.14] When looking at the exceptions, it should be noted that these only arise if the trade mark consists exclusively of the shape. It is, of course, possible that the inclusion of further matter to the mark may still not be sufficient to avoid refusal under s 8(1)(b), ie devoid of distinctive character.

[19.] *Reform of Trade Marks Law*, September 1990.
[20.] *Reckitt & Colman Products Ltd v Borden Inc* [1990] RPC 341.
[21.] Article 1(2) of Benelux Trade Mark Law, 1971.
[22.] *Burberrys v Bossi* [1992] NJ 596.

(a) 'The shape which results from the nature of the goods themselves'

[29.15] This involves consideration of both the shape and the goods and would cover, for example, the shape of a pineapple in respect of pineapples. Not precluded would be the shape of a pineapple for ice buckets. Because of the words "which results from the nature of", it is broader than a mere representation of the product itself and may, for example, cover a caricature of a pineapple, again in respect of pineapples. A bottle shape would not generally come under this provision because its contents, being the goods, are not reflected in the shape itself. This is not always the case and one could, for example, have orange juice in a bottle resembling an orange. Some guidance on this whole issue can be taken from US law.[23] The rationale behind this exception is that one cannot impose on the industry or the trade restrictions on the use of a shape which is indispensable to the manufacture or the distribution of the product.

(b) 'The shape of goods which is necessary to obtain a technical result'

[29.16] An example of how this is likely to be applied can be seen in the Irish design case of *Allibert SA v O'Connor*[24] where Costello J considered the shape of a fish box and whether or not a valid registered design existed in such. The criteria used by Costello J was whether all the features were dictated by the function to be performed which in this case, was ease of stacking. The provision is directed at functional shapes such as in the US case of *Shenango Chemicals Inc.*[25] and the shape of rim on the underside of china to protect against breakage. In most cases it is unlikely that the whole shape will be unprotectable. The provision provides for unprotectability only to the extent that there is no freedom as regard arbitrary elements of design since almost all three dimensional items will fulfill a certain technical function.

(c) 'The shape which gives substantial value to the goods'

[29.17] This provision is likely to be extremely difficult to interpret and certainly would seem to cover a large number of products which are often bought for their aesthetic qualities such as jewellery, ornaments, china, bags and fashion items. If a person's reason for purchasing a product is its aesthetic qualities, then it appears to be caught by this provision. It is these very aesthetic qualities which make it more likely to be a suitable candidate for a Registered Design. Although there is no prohibition on a shape being protected by both a Registered Design and a trade mark registration, it will perhaps be this duality

---

[23] *North American Philips Corp.* (1983) 217 USPQ 926 relating to the face plate of a three headed electric razor.
[24] [1981] FSR 613.
[25] [1962] 362 F 2d 287.

that will influence a Court in adopting a position that it is the aesthetic quality in the shape that gives substantial value to the goods. But, of course, a shape can serve as a trade mark and also be aesthetic. Then the question which might appropriately be asked is which factor influenced the purchase? The answer may be, of course, a combination of factors. In the Dutch Supreme Court case of *Wokkels*,[26] it was held that the shape of a particular cracker did increase market share but the intrinsic value was in the actual taste which was accordingly the determining factor. It would be strange if a manufacturer of a product with expensive packaging was to be penalised by being refused registration in respect of an attribute to the product which assists in its promotion but which in most cases, must be secondary to the product itself. In a case involving the BURBERRY check in the Benelux it was held that if the effect on the market value has its origin in the attractive power connected with the shape's reputation as a distinctive sign and not in the aesthetic attractiveness of the shape, the exception should not apply. Certainly in the US, the aesthetic function is no longer viewed as the correct criteria for registerability of product shapes.[27]

[29.18] Section 8(2) does not have a proviso similar to s 8(1) and consequently an applicant cannot avoid refusal in respect of a shape by showing that through use, the shape has in fact acquired a distinctive character.

TRADE MARKS CONTRARY TO PUBLIC POLICY OR TO ACCEPTED PRINCIPLES OF MORALITY

[29.19] This provision in s 8(3)(a) is unlikely to be interpreted very differently than that part of s 19 of the 1963 Act which provided for mandatory refusal of marks "contrary to law or morality or any scandalous design". Although public policy is specifically included, it was also the rationale behind the provision in the 1963 Act which existed not merely for the benefit of traders but for the benefit of the public at large.[28] The section would also presumably prevent registration in respect of marks which would cause offence to a section of the public on matters such as race, sex, religious belief and even general matters of taste and decency. It is also likely to cover Article 3(2)(b) of the Trade Mark Harmonisation Directive which was an optional provision relating to refusal on the grounds that "the trade mark covers a high symbolic value, in particular, a religious symbol" but given that this is an additional ground, it must, at least have been perceived that not all trade marks of 'high symbolic value' were also necessarily contrary to public policy. The HALLELUJAH trade mark[29] was

---

26. [1985] BIE 23.
27. *DC Comics Inc* (1982) 689 F2d 1042.
28. *Livron* (1937) 54 RPC 161.
29. [1976] RPC 605.

Department of
Agriculture, Fisheries & Food

library *and* information service

23 June 2009

You are responsible for books on loan to you. If they are not returned you or your section will be **required to replace them.**

Sending reminders is very time consuming. Please cooperate by returning books on time.

31637 **Contract law.** (+ accompanying CD-ROM if applicable)

Date due: **14/7/2009**

Do not mark books by underlining or highlighting or any other means

Books must be returned
BY HAND OR REGISTERED POST
(If returned by van please ensure it is signed for in the Library)
Do NOT return in a circulation envelope

BR: **Conor O'Mahony**

If an extension is required please contact **Caroline Edney**
PLEASE RETAIN THIS SECTION

Library and Information Service, Department of Agriculture, Fisheriesand Food, Agriculture House, Kildare Street, Dublin 2, Ireland.
Tel: 6072803   Fax: 6072079   Email: Caroline.Edney@agriculture.gov.ie

refused registration in respect of women's clothing and the following observation was made by the UK Registrar:

> "to be contrary to morality the use of a mark would, I think, have to offend the generally accepted mores of the time, while the adverse use of the Registrar's discretion would be warranted if registration would be reasonably likely to offend persons who might be in a minority in the Community, yet be substantial in number".

[29.20] In the design case of *Masterman's Design*,[30] a design for a kilted doll with mimic male genitalia was allowed, it being considered that simply because a section of the public would find it distasteful, was not a valid reason for refusal. Public safety is, of course, a matter of public policy and therefore the question arises as to whether or not it is a ground for refusal to register where the trade mark is identical or confusingly similar to an existing trade mark where co-existence may be of concern to public safety. An example of such is in the case of trade marks for pharmaceutical purposes but it could also arise in respect of dissimilar goods and where the Controller's searching would not raise the earlier mark as a citation. In the case of the JARDEX trade mark,[31] application for JARDEX in respect of disinfectants was refused upon opposition by the owners of the trade mark JARDOX in respect of extract of meat despite the possibility of a serious accident being remote and probably could not occur without negligence on the part of one or more persons. The UK Assistant-Comptroller stating:

> "I do think that I can take cognisance of the fact that negligence is a human failing from which few, if any, of us are entirely free, and the consequence of a mistake such as that just referred to, might be so disastrous, that it is obviously necessary for me to consider carefully whether, as a public official exercising a discretionary power, I ought to take any step that would encourage the placing upon the market of a food and a poisonous disinfectant sold under almost identical marks, knowing that the two articles may ultimately come to be used in proximity with each other."[32]

[29.21] The difference between the Trade Marks Act 1996 and the 1963 Act is that in the 1963 Act, there was a definite dual obligation on the Controller, not just to protect the owners of earlier marks, but to avoid confusion amongst the public. This was evidenced by s 31 of the 1963 Act and the association requirement whereby owners of identical or similar marks could only assign associated marks together, preventing them from being held by different owners. In the 1996 Act, there is no association requirement and indeed, the

---

30. [1991] RPC 89.
31. (1946) 63 RPC 19 - See also *UNIVER Trade Mark* [1993] RPC 239.
32. See also *Motorine* (1907) 24 RPC 585.

transitional provisions remove such for existing registrations.[33] More salient is s 10(6) whereby a consent by the owner of an earlier trade mark is sufficient to overcome any objection by the Controller on the relative grounds of refusal based on an earlier conflicting right. However, s 10(6) is limited to objection under s 10 itself and therefore appears to be overridden by public policy including public safety objectives. Article 4(5) of the Trade Mark Harmonisation Directive does allow for consent as an optional provision but only in 'appropriate circumstances' and public policy is a mandatory provision under Article 3(1)(F).

DECEPTIVE TRADE MARKS

[29.22] Section 8(3)(b) provides for refusal if a trade mark "is of such a nature as to deceive the public, for instance, as to the nature, quality or geographical origin of the goods or service". Section 19 of the 1963 Act also provided for refusal in respect of trade marks "likely to deceive or cause confusion". It was common practice for the Controller to raise objection on this basis and applicants were often faced with the dilemma of a trade mark which was either descriptive of the goods or alternatively, was deceptive in that it described an attribute of a product which did not exist. The often quoted UK ORLWOOLA trade mark[34] is a good illustration of this point, Fletcher Moulton LJ, finding that the trade mark ORLWOOLA for textile goods was utterly unfit for use as a trade mark being directly descriptive for goods that were all wool and deceptive of goods that were not. The 1996 Act puts applicants in the same position by virtue of a possible descriptiveness objection[35] and/or a deceptiveness objection.[36] However, no amount of use can overcome a deceptiveness objection under s 8(3)(b). The device of a crocodile was held by the High Court and affirmed by the Supreme Court as being deceptive of clothing and footwear not made from genuine crocodile skin.[37] In the Irish case of American Cyanamid's application to register STRESSTABS,[38] it was held that such was likely to deceive or cause confusion if the mark were used on goods which were not in the form of tablets for the relief of physical stress. Examples of decisions relating to deceptiveness as to the nature of the goods are CHINA-TERM[39] for insulated cups and tumblers made of plastic, such mis-describing the character of the goods since people were likely to believe the goods were made of china. CONSARC[40] in

---

[33.] Third Schedule s 2(3).
[34.] (1909) 26 RPC 683.
[35.] TMA 1996, s 8(1)(c).
[36.] TMA 1996, s 8(3)(b).
[37.] *La Chemise Lacoste* - unrep 1974 No. 38 Sp.
[38.] 1980 Supp OJ No 1367 p 11, decision aff'd on appeal to the High Court (unrep).
[39.] [1980] FSR 21.
[40.] [1969] RPC 179.

respect of electrical welding apparatus and electric furnaces on the grounds that the mark suggested arc welding apparatus; SOFLENS[41] for contact lenses held to be deceptive if used for hard contact lenses. An example as to deceptiveness of quality can be seen in the case of SAFEMIX[42] in respect of thermostatically controlled valves for mixing hot and cold water. It was held that the use of the word 'SAFE' as part of the mark was deceptive and such could be regarded as inducing purchasers to believe that goods bearing the mark were safe to use since the goods were of a kind which could be possibly dangerous to a user.[43] The issue of deception is directed to 'the public' but it is likely that this will be interpreted as deceptive to the public who are likely to purchase the goods or avail of the services in question. Trade marks in respect of goods in a specialised market directed to persons engaged in a particular trade and not goods sold to the general public for consumption and domestic use should be considered accordingly.[44] However, the fact that the goods are not bought without due enquiry is not of itself sufficient to avoid an argument of deceptiveness. In the BLACK MAGIC[45] trade mark, Morton J stated "the mark must be held to offend if it is likely to cause confusion or deception in the minds of persons to whom the mark is addressed, even if actual purchasers will not ultimately be deceived".

[29.23] In relation to marks falsely suggesting a particular geographical origin, it is not the use of the place name itself which is objectionable. Whether the use of a place name is in fact deceptive will in part depend on the nature of the product and the likelihood of its being thought of as coming from the place suggested. The trade mark ROMAN HOLIDAY[46] was allowed registration in respect of perfumes, it being held that the fact that to some persons the mark will indicate a connection with the modern City of Rome, did not mean that such persons will believe that the connection has anything to do with the origin of the goods. In the Australian case of *Re Bali Brassiere Co Inc's Application*,[47] it was commented by Windeyer J as follows:

> "There is no evidence that any one has thought that BALI BRAS are made in Bali. It seems to me most unlikely that members of the public who buy brassieres in Australia, would think so. Bali is not famed or known as a country where such goods are made. Balinese women are not notable for wearing brassieres."

[41.] [1976] RPC 694.
[42.] [1978] RPC 397.
[43.] See also VITASAFE [1963] RPC 256.
[44.] *GE Trade Mark* [1973] RPC 297.
[45.] (1941) 58 RPC 91.
[46.] [1964] RPC 129.
[47.] (1968) 118 CLR 128.

[29.24] The ADVOKAAT trade mark[48] was refused registration in respect of an alcoholic beverage from Belgium because Advokaat of Dutch origin enjoyed such a reputation and a substantial number of the purchasing public associated that alcoholic drink with Dutch origin. It was common practice under the 1963 Act to overcome a deceptiveness objection due to geographical origin by agreeing to a condition of registration which would read:

"It is a condition of registration that the mark shall be used only in relation to goods manufactured in ...".

[29.25] Indeed, this was a condition imposed upon registration of the WATERFORD trade mark.[49] Under the transitional provision of the 1996 Act,[50] these conditions ceased to have effect. Another way of overcoming a deceptiveness objection but which will presumably stay under the 1996 Act is to simply add a statement in the specification itself, ie "... all being goods of ... origin" or "... all being goods emanating from ...". An application should be refused registration in respect of a protected designation of origin or geographical indication under Regulation No 2081/92 governing agricultural products and foodstuffs.

[29.26] The list of possible deceptive characteristics contained in s 8(3)(b) is not exhaustive. It would presumably cover references in a trade mark to protection by way of other forms of intellectual property and which cannot be justified such as 'patent', 'copyright', 'design', etc. This was specifically provided for in Rule 12 of the 1963 Trade Mark Rules.[51] Rule 15 of the Trade Mark Rules 1996 grants the Controller a discretion to refuse to accept any application in which the word 'patent', 'patented', 'registered', 'copyright' or any other word or any symbol with a like signification appears. Also disallowed may be marks which falsely suggest affiliation or sponsorship. An example of such can be seen in the Australian case of *Radio Corp Pty Ltd v Disney*.[52] In this case, the name 'MICKEY MOUSE' was denied registration in respect of radio transceiving sets as it suggested in some way, an association with Walt Disney. There is an overlap with the provisions for refusal on absolute grounds in s 10 because a mark conflicting with an earlier right can, of course, deceive as to origin. Hence, s 19 of the 1963 Act was often pleaded in opposition proceedings and there is no reason to suspect that such will not also be the position under s 8(3)(b). If it can be shown that the result of the user of the mark will be that a number of persons

---

[48.] [1978] RPC 252.
[49.] See all *TONINO* [1973] RPC 568.
[50.] Third Schedule - Section 2(4)
[51.] SI 268/1963.
[52.] (1937) 57 CLR 448.

will be caused to wonder whether it might not be the case that the two products come from the same source is an example of deception.[53]

[29.27] The absence of the word 'likely' in s 8(3)(b) and which appeared in s 19 of the 1963 Act might suggest that actual deception must be shown. This is unlikely to be interpreted in this way because a trade mark application can, of course, be based on an intent to use and it is only when actual use commences, will actual instances of deception become apparent. Also, in many instances, an Examiner will not have any knowledge of whether or not there is actual usage.

[29.28] The Consumer Information Act 1978 makes it an offence to make a false trade description. There are a wide range of statements which fall within the definition of a trade description including statements as to place or country in which goods are manufactured, mode of manufacture and material of which any goods are composed. It is also an offence to publish any advertisement misleading the public and thereby causing loss, damage or injury. The fact that a trade description is a trade mark or part of a trade mark does not prevent it from being a false trade description.

TRADE MARKS, THE USE OF WHICH ARE PROHIBITED BY LAW

[29.29] Section 8(4)(a) provides that a trade mark shall not be registered if or to the extent that the use is prohibited in the State by any enactment or rule of law or by any provision of community law. This is an optional provision contained in Article 3(2)(a) of the Trade Mark Harmonisation Directive. Examples of Irish legislation which prohibit use of certain trade marks are The Red Cross Act 1938 as amended by The Red Cross Act 1954 which disallows use of the heraldic emblem of the Red Cross on a white background formed by reversing the federal colours of Switzerland or the words 'Cross Dearg', 'Cross Na Geineibhe', 'Red Cross' or 'Geneva Cross'. In the National Lottery Act 1986 there is a prohibition on use in relation to a lottery game other than the National Lottery of the names 'Irish National Lottery' or 'National Lottery' or of their equivalents in the Irish language or names so closely resembling "as to be reasonably capable of leading to the belief that either of those names or either of those equivalents is being referred to".

[29.30] Under Community law, there are already a number of regulations governing what are considered to be protected names. The Community Trade Mark Regulation itself has already been amended by Article 1(3) of Regulation No 3288/94 and whereby an absolute ground for refusal is:

[53.] *JELLINEK'S Application* (1946) 63 RPC 59 - See also *SMITH HAYDEN* (1946) 63 RPC 97.

Trade marks for wines which contain or consist of a geographical indication identifying wines or for spirits which contain or consist of a geographical indication identifying spirits with respect to such wines or spirits not having that origin.

[29.31] Both 'champagne'[54] and 'cognac' are protected names. The Commission are also considering a large number of trade marks for which protection has been sought in respect of geographical indications and designations of origin for agricultural products and foodstuffs.[55]

TRADE MARKS APPLIED FOR IN BAD FAITH

[29.32] Section 8(4)(b) contains a prohibition in respect of trade mark applications to the extent that such was applied for in bad faith. The words 'to the extent' suggest that the bad faith may only relate to a part of the application such as, for example, a specification which includes goods/services for which there is no bona fide intention to use the mark in accordance with s 37(2). So called 'ghost' marks[56] registered simply to block a competitor or to secure a footing on the Register to protect an unregisterable mark would be examples of trade marks applied for in bad faith.

[29.33] It is bad faith for an application to be made by an agent or representative of a trade mark proprietor. This is also a basis for opposition under s 65 of the 1996 Act but attractively for a proprietor is the fact that bad faith is an absolute ground to be taken into account by the Controller on examination. The question is, of course, how will the Controller be aware of any such agent/representative relationship without opposition. This can be done by way of observations to the Controller. A dilemma for the Controller is an obligation to refuse an application if he suspects such has been made in bad faith but at the same time, allow an applicant to present their own evidence in this regard. It is therefore unlikely that this particular aspect of bad faith will be raised at examination stage but will be left to opposition proceedings except if the trade mark is also well known under s 61.

[29.34] The 1963 Act did require an applicant to make a claim as to proprietorship of the trade mark. In *Al Bassam Trade Mark*,[57] the Court of Appeal considered that all that was required at the time of application was that the claim was *bona fide*, ie an honest belief that it had a good claim to be registered. Whether or not there is a *bona fide* application is a question of whether or not the applicant was aware of proprietary rights of a third party.

---

54. *Taittinger SA v Allbev Ltd* [1993] FSR 641.
55. Regulation No 2081/92.
56. *Imperial Group Ltd v Philip Morris & Co Ltd* [1982] FSR 72.
57. [1995] RPC 511.

These rights could be other intellectual property rights such as copyright[58] or registered designs, employer rights against an application by an employee.[59]

[29.35] The mere fact that another party has a trade mark registration or has used their trade mark in other countries does not mean an application has been made in bad faith. The proprietary right, if it exists from outside the State, then it must be as a consequence of a reputation which nevertheless exists within the State.[60] However, an earlier proprietary right through use is a separate ground of opposition. In *Gaines Animal Foods' Application*,[61] the use was not deemed to be sufficient to establish a reputation but nevertheless, the conduct of the applicant in attempting to register a number of different marks used in the US, illustrated bad faith. A further illustration is the RAWHIDE trade mark[62] where again, reputation for the goods was not proven but bad faith arose because the applicant chose the trade mark because in the hope of gaining some benefit from the publicity through television broadcasts of the opponent's film. Cross J drew the following distinction:

> "It is one thing to say that a man who is using or proposes here and now to use a mark on his goods is entitled to be registered notwithstanding that his reason for choosing that mark is the hope of getting the benefit of publicity for which he has not paid, but it is quite another thing to say that a man can put himself in the position of reaping the advantage of any publicity which may subsequently attach to the name though he has no intention of making any substantial use of the mark unless and until it is clear that publicity will attach to it."

Bad faith relates to the motive of the applicant and knowledge of the trade mark is simply an aspect for consideration in determining the motive. However, generally trade marks are registered on a territorial basis and that is why an exception which does exist is limited to well known trade marks under Article 6 *bis* of the Paris Convention.[63]

INVALIDITY AND OPPOSITION ACTIONS ON ABSOLUTE GROUNDS

[29.36] Unlike the position under Article 42 of the Community Trade Mark Regulation, opposition to an Irish trade mark application is possible based on the absolute grounds of refusal in s 8. Also when registered, an invalidity action is possible on the absolute grounds.[64] There is a recognition that a trade mark which might have been invalid at the time of application, may have acquired

---

58. *Karo Step* [1977] RPC 255.
59. *Casson's Trade Mark* (1910) 27 RPC 65.
60. *C & A Modes* [1976] IR 198.
61. [1958] RPC 312.
62. [1962] RPC 133.
63. TMA 1996, s 61.
64. TMA 1996, s 52(1).

distinctiveness post registration. This implemented the optional provision in Article 3(3) of the Harmonisation Directive and allows post registration use to be taken into account in relation to an invalidity action which claims lack of distinctiveness,[65] descriptiveness[66] or customary language in a trade mark.[67]

REGISTRATIONS PRIOR TO 1996 ACT (TRANSITIONAL PROVISIONS)

[29.37] Section 13 of the transitional provisions in the Third Schedule to the 1996 Act, exercised the option available to States under Article 3(4) of the Trade Mark Harmonisation Directive and provides:

> "The old law shall continue to apply as regards the validity of the registration of an existing registered mark; and no objection to the validity of such a registration may be taken on the grounds of failure to satisfy the requirements of this Act".

The reasoning for such which differs from the position taken in the UK, was stated by the Minister in the Dáil Debates as simply being due to advice given by the Attorney General concerning a possible constitutional challenge that the basis upon which personal property right was being held was to be varied. This view was not shared by Deputy Michael McDowell who pointed out that "there is no constitutional law which states, when one has acquired a property right under the Trade Marks Act, that the right cannot be qualified, varied, reduced, affected or prejudiced if the State considers it has a good reason to do so. There is every good reason to introduce a single law of invalidity in respect of existing and future marks. They should all be decided by the same canons of validity.[68]

[29.38] The effect of the transitional provision is that the grounds for invalidity under the 1963 Act remain for trade marks registered under the 1963 Act. This means that for pre-1996 Act registrations, the distinction between Part A and Part B of the Register is still important. Under s 21 of the 1963 Act, registration of a trade mark in Part A of the Register is conclusive as to validity after the expiration of seven years from the date of registration unless the registration was obtained by fraud or offended against s 19 of the 1963 Act. On the other hand, the validity of a Part B registration could always be declared invalid irrespective of the time it had been on the Register. Section 19 of the 1963 Act concerns marks which are likely to deceive or cause confusion and such a mark, even on Part A of the Register, can be removed from the Register although it has been on

---

[65.] TMA 1996, s 8(1)(b).
[66.] TMA 1996, s 8(1)(c).
[67.] TMA 1996, s 8(1)(d).
[68.] 462 Dáil 683.

it for over 7 years. This arises even if the trade mark was validly registered but has subsequently become likely to deceive or cause confusion.[69]

[29.39] However, the further grounds of invalidity under the 1963 Act will for pre-1996 Act registrations, remain indefinitely in the case of Part B registrations. This includes trade marks which although invalidly registered at the time of application, have become distinctive through usage. This contracts with the saving proviso in s 52(1) of the 1996 Act. Ironically, it was noticeable that in anticipation of the 1996 Act, the Irish Patents Office had already relaxed examination and many trade marks were approved in Part B of the Register even though on a strict interpretation of the 1963 Act, registration should have been refused. It was this very liberalisation of the registerability requirements under the 1996 Act which prompted the Irish Patents Office into a more pro-registration position but as a consequence, the validity of a number of marks under the 1963 criteria would be questionable. This would include well known surnames or geographical[70] place names allowed upon evidence of minimal use and also three letter trade marks not forming a pronounceable word[71] and again, without sufficient evidence of distinctiveness through usage at the date of application. Three letter trade marks forming a pronounceable word were allowed under the 1963 Act.[72]

[29.40] A number of trade marks which would be invalid under the 1963 requirements are those which did not comply with the definition of a trade mark in s 2 of the 1963 Act, namely:

> "A mark used or proposed to be used in relation to goods for the purpose of indicating, or so as to indicate, a connection in the course of trade between the goods and some person having the right either as proprietor or as Registered User to use the mark, whether with or without any indication of the identity of that person ...".

This definition, in conjunction with s 25 of the 1963 Act, meant that the applicant for registration must be the actual or intended user of the mark or at the time of application, there must have been in place a registered user identifying an actual or intended user. Without such a registered user, an application, for example, by a holding company would be invalid and could not be saved later by a subsequent user entry. Such a registration in Part B under the 1963 Act will continue to remain invalid. Even if there was a registered user entry, it does not necessarily save the position if the Irish Courts follow the

---

[69] *Sterling Winthrop Group Ltd v Farbenfabriken Bayer AG* [1976] RPC 469.
[70] *DENT Trade Mark* [1979] FSR 205.
[71] *SFD Trade Mark* [1975] RPC 607.
[72] *SAF Trade Mark* [1982] ILRM 207; see also *ACEC Trade Mark* [1964] IR 20.

reasoning of the House of Lords in *Holly Hobbie*[73] and refuse registration on the grounds of trafficking in the trade mark.[74] This was a case of character merchandising where the owner intended to grant Licences in such a way that the mark was being dealt with primarily as a commodity in its own right and no real trade connection between the owner of the mark and the goods to which the mark was to be applied.

SPECIALLY PROTECTED EMBLEMS

[29.41] In s 9, there is a prohibition on registration of a trade mark consisting of or containing any state emblem without consent from the Minister. The prohibition also extends to marks that are so nearly resembling, that they may be mistaken to be such an emblem. Various state emblems of Ireland have been notified under Article 6 *ter* of the Paris Convention, namely arms of Ireland, harp and shamrock symbols and escutcheons in various forms as used by the State.

[29.42] Article 7 of the Irish Constitution defines the Irish flag as the tricolour of green, white and orange. There is no general prohibition as to registration of trade marks consisting of or containing the Irish flag except to the extent that such is misleading or grossly offensive. To this extent, the protection afforded to the Irish flag is less than that given to the flags of other Paris Convention countries where registration is to be refused without authorisation from the Authorities in that country "unless it appears to the Controller that use of the flag in the manner proposed is permitted without such authorisation".[75]

[29.43] The Controller also has a discretionary power to refuse to register a trade mark which consists of or contains any badge, device or emblem of a public authority unless there is consent to such.[76] What is strange with s 9 is that it sits in isolation and unlike the corresponding provision in the UK Act, it is not listed as one of the absolute grounds of refusal and is not therefore a ground of invalidity under s 52.

---

73. [1984] FSR 199.
74. TMA 1963, s 36(6).
75. TMA 1996, s 62(1).
76. TMA 1996, s 9(3).

Chapter 30

Trade Marks Act 1996: Relative Grounds for Refusal of Registration

INTRODUCTION

[30.01] The relative grounds for refusal of registration of a trade mark are based on prior conflicting rights owned by proprietors of earlier trade marks or other earlier rights. The sections in the 1996 Act dealing with relative grounds for refusal are as follows:

> Section 10 - Statement of the basic prohibition.
>
> Section 11 - Definition of what is meant by an earlier trade mark.
>
> Section 12 - Exception to the prohibition based on honest concurrent use.
>
> Section 52(2) - Earlier trade mark or earlier right as a basis of invalidity of a registration.

Sections 10, 11 and 52(2) are based on Article 4 of the Trade Mark Harmonisation Directive.[1] Section 12 dealing with honest concurrent use is modelled on the corresponding provision in the Trade Marks Act 1963.[2] The relative grounds should be read in conjunction with s 61 which provides for prior rights based on trade marks which are well known[3] and s 65 where there is an agent/representative relationship with the trade mark proprietor.[4]

[30.02] The sources available to assist in the interpretation of the statutory provisions are quite numerous. In many cases, it is possible to look at decisions decided under the 1963 Act and UK 1938 counterpart because prior trade marks which formed a basis for opposition and invalidity under the 1963 Act included not just identical marks for identical goods but also identical or similar marks for similar goods. In addition, the 1996 Act includes prior rights which can be raised even where there is dissimilarity of goods/services. In due course, decisions of the Community Trade Mark Office and ultimately the ECJ on the interpretation of the corresponding provision in Article 8 of the CTM

---

[1] 89/104/EEC.
[2] Section 20(2).
[3] Article 6 *bis* - Paris Convention.
[4] Article 6 *septies* - Paris Convention.

Regulation will be important. Since the main thrust of the relative grounds are based on mandatory provisions in the Trade Mark Harmonisation Directive, decisions by courts in other EU countries are likely to be drawn upon, particularly in the Benelux upon whose law prior to the Directive, certain of these provisions have been based. There will also need to be cross-referencing to decisions based on the infringement provisions in s 14 of the Trade Marks Act 1996 because the scope of protection afforded by a registration corresponds to the relative grounds of refusal. This differs from the 1963 Act where the scope of protection afforded to a registration was limited to the exact goods of registration but refusal extended to a question of similarity of goods.

[30.03] Conflicts with earlier trade marks or rights can arise at three different stages in the life of a trade mark. Firstly, the Controller carries out a search upon examination of a trade mark application and can raise a conflicting mark as a basis for refusing registration. This *ex officio* search and citation procedure is not a mandatory requirement under Community law and many EU countries including Germany, France, Benelux and Italy do not carry out such official action. Also, the Community Trade Marks Office, under the Community Regulation, does not cite prior conflicting marks on either the CTM or national registers and leaves it to the owner of a prior trade mark or antecedent right to institute opposition proceedings.

[30.04] Secondly, an application for registration can be opposed on relative grounds following advertisement in the Patents Office Journal.[5] This opposition must be filed within three months of advertisement with no extension of time permissible.[6]

[30.05] Thirdly, even when registered, the relative grounds are a basis for securing cancellation or part cancellation of a registration due to invalidity.[7] The prior trade marks or rights which can form the basis for a refusal of an application or invalidity of a registration on relative grounds are as follows.

EARLIER TRADE MARK

[30.06] An earlier trade mark can be a trade mark registered or pending[8] on either the Irish Register, the CTM Register or the International Register. The latter by virtue of s 58, means a trade mark which has been registered with the International Bureau of WIPO under the Madrid Protocol and protection for which has been extended to the State. This will not arise until the State ratifies

---

5. Section 43.
6. Trade Mark Rules 1996, r 18(1).
7. Section 52(2).
8. Section 11(2).

the Madrid Protocol.[9] Whether a trade mark is to be deemed earlier, is determined by the filing date or any priority date if claimed under the Paris Convention.[10]

[30.07] Also included in the list of earlier trade marks is a later filed CTM but with a valid seniority claim bearing an earlier date. Under Articles 34 and 35 of the CTM Regulation, the proprietor of an Irish registered trade mark who applies for and secures registration for an identical trade mark under the CTM Regulation may surrender or allow the Irish registration to lapse but retain seniority for such. This means that the trade mark proprietor is deemed to continue to have the same right as if the earlier Irish registration had been maintained.[11]

[30.08] Under s 11(1)(c) of the 1996 Act, reference to an earlier mark also includes a mark which is not registered but which at the priority date of the mark in question, was entitled to protection under the Paris Convention as a well known trade mark.[12] A question which may arise is whether or not the Irish owner of an unregistered mark can rely on this provision because s 61 refers to the mark of a national of a 'Convention application' which in s 60, excludes the State itself. Ironically, this means that an Irish trade mark may have to rely on s 10(4)(a) with the possible heavier evidential burden of having to show rights equivalent to sustain an action for passing-off.

[30.09] It is still necessary to take into account earlier trade marks on the pertinent Register which may have lapsed. This is because of s 11(3) and includes as an earlier trade mark, a registration which has expired within the previous year unless the Controller is satisfied that there was no *bona fide* use of the trade mark during the two years immediately preceding the expiry. This provision does not wholly reflect the optional provision in Article 4(4)(f) of the Trade Mark Harmonisation Directive which limits this inclusion as an earlier trade mark to a situation where the expiry was only because of non-renewal and can be avoided if "the proprietor of the earlier trade mark gave his agreement for the registration of the later mark or did not use his trade mark".

[30.10] If there is an earlier trade mark as defined, then the issue is one of comparison with the conflicting mark.

---

9. See para **[26.47]**.
10. Section 40.
11. Section 11(1)(b).
12. Section 61.

IDENTICAL MARKS FOR IDENTICAL GOODS OR SERVICES

[30.11] This is the most straightforward situation and does not require any proof of a likelihood of confusion. It is presumed that although the respective trade marks must be identical, it is only necessary that some of the goods/services must correspond directly to that of the earlier trade mark. It is the advantage of not having to show a likelihood of confusion which is attractive to the owner of an earlier trade mark availing of this section. At a first glance, it would appear that the owner of an earlier registration would have to show identicality of goods/services to that of the registration. However, the words used in the section refer to an identicality with the earlier mark as protected, as opposed to as registered. Thus, it could be argued that since protection extends to similar goods/services to those embraced by the actual registration, that identicality is only necessary with such similar goods/services.

SIMILAR OR IDENTICAL TRADE MARKS FOR SIMILAR OR IDENTICAL GOODS/SERVICES

[30.12] Section 10(2) of the 1996 Act covers the following:

-   where the respective marks are identical and the goods or services are similar;
-   where the respective marks are similar and the goods or services are identical;
-   where the respective marks are similar and the goods or services are similar.

In all cases, there is a requirement that there exists a likelihood of confusion which includes the likelihood of association.

[30.13] It is the concept of similarity which is the key factor and in the 1996 Act, as under the 1963 Act, there is no legislative statement as to what is meant by this term. The wording is taken from Article 4(2) of the Harmonisation Directive and some guidance can be drawn from a recital in the Directive which states that the likelihood of confusion depends on a number of elements and in particular:

-   the recognition of the trade mark on the market;
-   the association which can be made with the used or registered sign; and
-   the degree of similarity between the respective marks and the goods/ services.

[30.14] The tendency will be to look at decisions of the Irish and UK courts in determining the issue under s 20 of the 1963 Act and its UK equivalent.[13]

---

13. UK Trade Marks Act 1938, s 12(1).

Section 20 prohibited registration of an identical trade mark or a mark so nearly resembling an existing trade mark as to be likely to deceive or cause confusion for the same goods or goods of the same description.[14]

SIMILARITY OF THE RESPECTIVE MARKS

[30.15] It is unlikely that the words 'nearly resembles' in the 1963 Act and 'similar' in the 1996 Act will be interpreted any differently and the word 'similar' is probably incapable of definition. The Irish Supreme Court in *Coca-Cola v F Cade & Sons Ltd*[15] applied the tests expounded by Parker J in *PIANOTIST*[16] and stated:

> "You must take the two words. You must judge of them, both by their look and by their sound. You must consider the goods to which they are to be applied. You must consider the nature and kind of customer who would be likely to buy the goods. In fact, you must consider all the surrounding circumstances; and you must further consider what is likely to happen if each of those trade marks is used in a normal way as a trade mark for the goods of the respective owners of the marks. If, considering all those circumstances, you come to the conclusion that there will be a confusion - that is to say, not necessarily that one man will be injured and the other will gain illicit benefit, but there will be a confusion in the minds of the public which will lead to confusion in the goods - then you may refuse the registration, or rather you must refuse the registration in that case".

IDEAS CONVEYED BY A TRADE MARK

[30.16] It has been long established that the idea or image conveyed by the respective marks is a primary consideration. As stated in *Kerly's Law of Trade Marks*,[17] "two marks, when placed side by side, may exhibit many and various differences, yet the main idea left on the mind by both may be the same". In *Broadhead's Application*,[18] the trade mark ALKA-VESCENT was refused in the face of the trade mark ALKA-SELTZER given that the suffix VESCENT suggested effervescence and so conveyed the same underlying idea as the ALKA-SELTZER fizzy alkaline tablet. In *Harry Reynolds v Laffeaty's LD*,[19] the suffix MATIC was common but similarity was found to exist between the trade mark AQUAMATIC and WATERMATIC in respect of water pistols as both brought the same idea to mind. Trade marks can, however, be viewed as similar

---

[14.] *Seixo v Provezende* (1865) LR 1 Ch 192.
[15.] [1957] IR 196.
[16.] (1906) 23 RPC 774.
[17.] Twelfth Edition, p 439.
[18.] (1950) 67 RPC 209.
[19.] [1958] RPC 387.

even if they convey two different meanings. In *Beecham Group Ltd v Goodalls of Ireland*,[20] Kenny J held that TANG was likely to deceive or cause confusion with the trade mark TANGO, both being used in respect of non-alcoholic beverages.

IMPROPER RECOLLECTION

[30.17] In *Sandow Ltd's Application*,[21] Sarjant J cautioned against over-reliance on a detailed examination of the respective trade marks side by side as follows:

> "The question is not whether if a person is looking at two trade marks side by side there would be a possibility of confusion; the question is whether the person who sees the proposed trade mark in the absence of the other trade mark, and in view only of his general recollection of what the nature of the other trade mark was, would be liable to be deceived and to think that the trade mark before him is the same as the other, of which he has a general recollection."

[30.18] It is the first impression which is the important factor. The customers whose imperfect recollection is to be considered are persons of ordinary intelligence and memory who are not to be credited with any high perception or habitual caution but on the other hand, stupidity or exceptional carelessness may be disregarded.[22]

TRADE MARKS AS A WHOLE/COMMON ELEMENTS

[30.19] Regard should be had to the trade mark as a whole and not by dividing the trade mark into segments. In *Bailey's Application*,[23] Farwell J refused registration of ERECTIKO in the face of a prior mark ERECTOR, both for toys, and stated:

> "I do not think it is right to take a part of the word and compare it with a part of the other word; one word must be considered as a whole and compared with the other word as a whole ... I think it is a dangerous method to adopt to divide the word up and seek to distinguish a portion of it from a portion of the other word".

[30.20] However, where an element which is common to marks under comparison is descriptive or in common use generally or in the trade, its presence must, to some extent, be discounted in deciding on confusing similarity. It is common practice to carry out a trade investigation and a search

---

[20.] High Court, unrep, 1977 (No 4662).
[21.] (1914) 31 RPC 196.
[22.] *Australian Wooden Mills v FS Walton* (1937) 58 CLR 641.
[23.] (1935) 52 RPC 136.

of other marks on the Register to determine the existing state of the Register concerning marks with the same common element. The Supreme Court found that the trade mark PHILCO[24] was not likely to deceive or cause confusion because of prior trade marks for the same description of goods consisting of the same prefix PHIL and Kennedy CJ cautioned against the extent to which a registration of a mark with a common element can be used to prevent others from adopting marks also including such a common element. Similarly, the Supreme Court found that the trade mark CADA COLA was not confusingly similar with COCA COLA, the common feature being the descriptive word COLA.[25]

Importance of first syllable

[30.21] In *London Lubricants*,[26] Sarjant LJ observed on the tendency of persons using the English language to slur the termination of words and which had the effect necessarily that the beginning of words is accentuated in comparison. Consequently, the first syllable of a word is, as a general rule, the most important for the purpose of assessing similarity. However, if the latter part of a word is more unusual and distinctive, then emphasis is likely to be placed on such.[27] The visual consideration of a monosyllabic trade mark may require that greater significance be attached to the first letter of the mark.[28]

Visual and aural comparison necessary

[30.22] The respective trade marks must be judged by both their look and sound. Trade marks can be similar phonetically although visually very different. This is a recognition that in many cases, products are bought over the telephone.[29] There is an argument that with modern shopping where goods are for the most part picked up in circumstances where the marks will be clearly visible, the question of sound is perhaps becoming of diminishing importance.[30] There are also circumstances where despite phonetic similarity, the trade marks will not be confused because of the nature of the goods. In *Lancer*,[31] it was held that there was no risk of confusion between LANCER and LANCIA for cars since a car is

---

[24.] *Philadelphia Storage Battery Co v Philips* [1935] IR 575; see also *Mediline AG's App* [1970] IR 169.

[25.] *Coca-Cola v F Cade & Sons Ltd* [1957] IR 196; see also *Coca-Cola Co (Canada) Ltd v Pepsi-Cola* (1942) 59 RPC 127.

[26.] (1925) 42 RPC 264.

[27.] *Parker-Knoll Ltd. v Knoll International* [1962] RPC 265.

[28.] *FIF Trade Mark* [1979] RPC 355.

[29.] *Morcream Products Ltd v Heatherfresh (Foods) Ltd* [1972] RPC 799.

[30.] *Mars GB Ltd v Cadbury Ltd* [1987] RPC 387, at 395.

[31.] [1987] RPC 303.

unlikely to be purchased over the telephone and the matter will usually be considered with some care, assisted by an abundance of literature.

[30.23] Another factor to be considered is a comparison of the respective marks as they would be seen in actual usage when fairly and honestly used.[32] It is also possible for a word mark to be viewed as similar to a device mark. In *Dewhurst's Application*,[33] the words THE GOLDEN FAN BRAND were refused registration in the face of a prior mark of a fan which was coloured gold in usage.

[30.24] It is reasonably common for traders to adopt and register a series of trade marks with a common element such as, for example, the same prefix but a suffix which denotes a particular product in the range of products for which the prefix is the source indicator. In *SEMIGRES Trade Mark*,[34] the opponent had a number of SEM prefixed marks and it was accepted that evidence showed that SEM used as a prefix in relation to flooring tiles, indicated their products. In *FRIGIKING*,[35] Whitford J commented on the decision in *Ravenhead Brick v Ruabon Brick & Terra Cotta*:[36]

> "It can, I think, be said upon the basis of the judgment in the *Ravenhead Brick* case that it is not necessary to success in an objection of this character that the objector should be able to establish the use of a series of marks if he has in fact used some mark which is highly distinctive or some mark which has some highly distinctive part, but only used one such mark, for, if somebody comes along and takes that highly distinctive mark and adds something to it or takes a highly distinctive mark or part of the mark and makes an addition or a substitution, then it may still be possible that people will be confused and will think that the new mark indicates the same source of origin - the same sort of connection - as the old mark indicated. This sort of approach does necessarily involve some enquiry as to the inherent distinctiveness of the part which is common to both marks under consideration".

The emphasis in these instances is the distinctiveness of the common element in its own right. In *FRIGIKING*, the earlier mark was THERMO-KING, the complained of common element being KING which was held to be highly distinctive and hence to succeed, the opponent would have had to show a reputation in a series of KING suffixed marks. However, in SEMIGRES, it was considered that the common element SEM was capable of standing on its own as a trade mark. In *TURBOGAZ*,[37] an application to register the mark in respect of

---

[32.] *Lyle & Kinahan's Application* (1907) 24 RPC 37 & 249.
[33.] [1896] 2 Ch 137; see also *Baldwin & Walker v Prescott* [1941] Supp OJ No 384, p 76.
[34.] [1979] RPC 330.
[35.] [1973] RPC 739.
[36.] (1937) 54 RPC 341.
[37.] [1978] RPC 206.

blow torches was opposed by the proprietor of an earlier TURBOTORCH registration. It was claimed that since the applicant had a series of GAZ suffixed trade marks, it indicated the source of origin and was simply one more of a series of marks. It was held that since GAZ was the French for the word gas, it was not highly distinctive and did not sufficiently detract from the prefix TURBO so as to make the whole mark distinguishable from TURBOTORCH.

[30.25] There have been a number of cases in Australia where the courts have allowed an opponent to call on a combination of elements of different marks which they held. Opposition was upheld against FIBROBESTOS on the basis of trade marks FIBROLITE and DURBABESTOS.[38] In a similar manner, CAT-TRAX was refused on the basis of the opponent's use of CAT and TRAXCAVATOR.[39] The basis of these decisions is that a compound of earlier marks could 'bridge over' the distinction between the earlier marks themselves and create confusion. Stretching the principle even further is the UK case of *Taylor Drug Co Ltd's App*[40] where an application to register the word GERMOCEA was refused on the grounds of the existence of two registered marks GERMOLINE and HOMOCEA, held by different proprietors on the grounds that the new word bridged over the distinction between the two registered marks and might create confusion between the goods offered for sale under each of the marks.

SIMILARITY OF GOODS OR SERVICES

[30.26] The word 'similar' used in the context of goods or services is something which the Irish courts and Patents Office have already become attuned by virtue of s 20(1) of the 1963 Act and the determination whether or not respective goods were 'of the same description'. The test followed by the Irish courts has been that propounded in *Jellinek's Application*,[41] namely a comparison of:

(a) the nature and composition of the goods;

(b) the respective uses of the articles; and

(c) the trade channels through which the commodities are bought and sold respectively.

The question is one of fact in each case and it is not necessary for all three elements to be satisfied.

[38.] *James Hardie & Co Ltd v Asbestos Products Ltd* (1937) 7 AOJP 767.
[39.] *Freestone v Caterpillar Tractor* (1985) AIPC 90-237.
[40.] (1923) 40 RPC 193.
[41.] (1946) 63 RPC 59.

[30.27] The UK *Jellinek* decision was reached long before the introduction of service mark registration in the UK but the UK Trade Marks Registry adopted the principles in respect of a comparison of services as follows:

(a) the nature of the services;

(b) the purpose of the services;

(c) the users of the services; and

(d) whether the two services could be provided in the course of normal business relations.

If any two or more of these were the same, then this was regarded as an indication that the services were of the same description.

[30.28] The above were only guidelines and there is no single conclusive test for deciding whether or not goods are of the same description. Ultimately, the matter is one of judgment and degree.[42] This was the view expressed by Jacob J in allowing registration for different fungicides, one for the pharmaceutical trade and the other for agricultural purposes. The nature of the goods were the same but the uses and trade channels were different. It is an open question whether or not this decision would be the same under the new UK 1994 Act corresponding to the Irish 1996 Act. It could be argued that similarity should be a lesser test than a determination whether or not goods are of the same description. Two products could be similar but the same description would not be applied to them. The counter argument is that it would be unreasonable to look at similarity in isolation. For example, certain instances of similarity such as colour, size, weight, etc. might all exist but are not determining factors and in many cases, can be disregarded. It is similarity in the context of what is likely to cause confusion that gives rise to the importance of questions concerning trade channels and actual usage. In *SEAHORSE Trade Mark*,[43] an application for the trade mark in respect of inboard marine engines exceeding 5,000 bhp was allowed despite the existence of an identical mark for outboard motors. The similarity that both goods powered vessels was outweighed by the sizes and prices of engines and the different vessels to which they would be applied so that there was no real and tangible risk of confusion.

[30.29] The question of similarity of goods must be answered irrespective of the mark in issue and any reputation that might exist. In other words, the decision should be determined without reference to the marks in question. It is also sufficient if any of the goods covered by the application are similar to any of the goods covered by the earlier mark. It does not matter if most of the goods

---

42. *INVICTA* [1992] RPC 541.
43. [1980] FSR 250.

covered by the application or the prior mark are not similar if there is a small residue which is.[44]

LIKELIHOOD OF CONFUSION

[30.30] In addition to the requisite similarity between the respective trade marks and the goods or services, it is also a requirement under s 10(2) that:

> there exists a likelihood of confusion on the part of the public, which includes the likelihood of association of the later mark with the earlier trade mark.

This provision is derived from Article 4(1)(b) of the Harmonisation Directive[45] and modelled on Article 13A of the uniform Benelux Trade Mark Law of 1971. The test adopted by the Benelux Supreme Court in interpreting their law does not focus on the question of confusion but whether the public are likely to draw an association between the respective marks. ANTI-MONOPOLY was held likely to be associated with the trade mark MONOPOLY on board games. Even though there was no confusion as to the origin of the products, there was a calling to mind of the earlier case of *MONOPOLY Trade Mark*.[46] The decisive factor was not the use of the trade mark as an indicator of origin, but instead its function as a means of encapsulating goodwill. If these tests are followed, what will occur is an application of certain principles which have developed from the law of passing-off. In particular, the Irish Supreme Court has already viewed likelihood of association as a grounds for maintaining an action for passing-off. In the *C & A Modes*[47] case, Kenny J stated:

> "the legal wrong known as passing-off includes the incorporation in the Republic of Ireland of a company with a name likely to give the impression to the public that it is a subsidiary or branch of or is associated or connected with another company which has a substantial goodwill."

[30.31] What is at issue is whether or not what is meant by association is the extent to which the public call to mind the earlier trade mark. In *HP Bulmer Ltd v J Bollinger SA*,[48] the UK Court of Appeal cautioned that not every type of connection will amount to passing-off and quoted with approval Harman J in the *Treasure Cot*[49] case that what was required was a connection in the mind of the public that the goods were "something for which the plaintiffs were responsible". However, the Irish Court approved Kenny J's statement in the *C &*

---

44. *Bensyl* [1992] RPC 529.
45. 89/100/EEC.
46. *MONOPOLY Trade Mark*, Dutch Supreme Court [1978] BIE 39; see also *Union v Union Soleure* [1984] BIE 137 and *Always v Regina* [1993] IER 22.
47. [1976] IR 198.
48. [1978] RPC 79.
49. (1950) 67 RPC 89 - See also *LEGO* [1983] FSR 155 and *GLENLIVET* [1993] RPC 461.

A case and compelled a company to change its corporate name even though it was not trading.[50] The use of the term 'mere incorporation' by Kenny J would suggest that to succeed in a passing-off action, it is sufficient that an association can be drawn by the public even if that association does not result in an actual belief that an offending product originated from the same source as the owner of the reputation. As stated by Carroll J in the *RITTAL* case approving of the statement made by Kenny J:[51]

> "It is urged on behalf of the defendants that this should not be adopted as the law because it is obiter dictum. However, it seems to me whether it is obiter or not it is a sound statement of the law. The company was incorporated with the purpose of gaining an advantage from the use of the word RITTAL. It had to be in the context that it would give the impression that it was a subsidiary or branch or was associated or had a connection with the plaintiffs. The defendants have therefore committed the tort of passing off. While the plaintiffs have a proved reputation for excellence in a particular field both in this country and internationally in my opinion the company is not limited to trading only in that field. If it expands its business it is entitled to use its market name and the defendants are not entitled to appropriate the name for any purpose."

[30.32] The wording in s 10(2) is ambiguous because it is not clear whether the likelihood of association is an additional requirement to a likelihood of confusion or is the likelihood of association simply an example of an instance of the likelihood of confusion. The problem with the first interpretation is that it is hard to envisage a situation where there is a likelihood of confusion but not necessarily association. Nevertheless, this was the preferred interpretation by Laddie J in the case of *Wagamama Ltd v City Centre Restaurants plc*[52] who stated "it is unconventional use of language to provide that the smaller (ie likelihood of confusion) includes the larger (ie likelihood of association)". Significantly, Laddie J rejected any obligation to draw any inference from interpretation by the Benelux Courts and stated:

> "... if the broader scope (ie likelihood of confusion) were to be adopted, the Directive and our Act would be creating a new type of monopoly not related to the proprietor's trade but in the trade mark itself. Such a monopoly would be likened to a quasi-copyright in the mark. However, unlike copyright, there would be no fixed duration for the right and it would be a true monopoly effective against copyist and non-copyist alike."

Laddie J went on further to state:

[50.] *Rittal Werk Rudolf LOH GmbH & Co KG v Rittal (Ireland) Ltd*, High Court, unrep, 11 July 1991 (376P/1989), Carroll J.

[51.] *Supra.*

[52.] [1995] FSR 713.

"... if it had been the intention to make the Directive identical with Benelux law on this important issue, it could have said so. Indeed, in view of the fact that to have done so would have been significantly to expand trade mark rights and thereby significantly restrict the freedom of traders to compete. I would have expected any such expansion to have been stated in clear and unambiguous words so that traders throughout the European Union would be able to appreciate that their legislators had created a new broad monopoly ... It follows that this Court cannot follow the route adopted by the Benelux on this issue ... Nevertheless, the natural inclination to come to a conclusion which would further harmony on this issue is not so strong that I am prepared to agree that a new millstone round the neck of traders has been created when that is not my view."

[30.33] It remains to be seen if the Irish courts will follow the views expressed by Laddie J but it is considered unlikely. The broad interpretation already given to the law of passing off indicates that likelihood of association without an instance of a likelihood of confusion is not as radical as might immediately be perceived. The concept of likelihood of association is necessarily wider than the concept of confusion and is dependant to a large extent on the recognition of the earlier trade mark. The German Federal Supreme Court has recently stated a case to the ECJ on the question of the extent to which the term "confusion" in the directive also includes "likelihood of association". A decision in the case of *Puma v Sabel* is expected in early 1998, The Advocate General's decision having been delivered on 29 April 1997.

SIMILAR OR IDENTICAL TRADE MARKS FOR DISSIMILAR GOODS/ SERVICES

[30.34] Section 10(3) incorporates both a mandatory provision in Article 4(3) and an optional provision in Article 4(4)(a) of the Harmonisation Directive.[53] The mandatory provision required Member States to recognise that in some instances, an earlier Community mark can be a basis for opposition or seeking invalidity even if the identical or similar complained of mark is in respect of dissimilar goods or services. The optional provision allowed Member States to extend this principle to an earlier national trade mark registration. The requirement in each case in s 10(3) is that if the earlier mark is a CTM, then there must be a reputation in the EU. If it is a national registration, there must be a reputation in the State. The use of the later mark must also be without due cause and take unfair advantage of or be detrimental to, the distinctive character or the repute of the earlier trade mark.

[53.] 89/104/EEC.

[30.35] There is certainly scope for argument that s 10(3) does not correctly implement the Directive. Section 10(3)(b) requires a comparison of the goods or services of the later mark with those for which the earlier trade mark is 'protected' as opposed to the Directive's statement that the comparison is with the goods or services of the earlier mark as 'registered'. Protection extends beyond the exact goods or services of a registration where there exists a likelihood of confusion.[54] It could be argued that since 'protection' extends to similar goods or services, the comparison to establish if there is dissimilarity is to be made between the exact or similar goods or services of an earlier trade mark and the goods or services of the complained of mark. This would mean that fewer cases might arise under s 10(3) than might have been expected because there would be fewer instances of dissimilarity between the respective goods or services. A further divergence from the Directive is that s 10(3)(a) comes into play in respect of an 'earlier trade mark' which as defined in s 11 includes well known trade marks under the Paris Convention. The Directive does not provide for such and therefore, the proprietor claiming an earlier trade mark by virtue of a well known mark and who seeks to rely on s 10(3) may find a challenge that the statutory provision is in breach of Community law.

[30.36] The requirement to show a reputation under the earlier trade mark will undoubtedly draw upon principles established under the law of passing-off in determining whether or not there is the requisite reputation. In broad terms as expressed by O'Higgins CJ in the Supreme Court decision in the case of *Adidas v Charles O'Neill & Co Ltd*,[55] it arises where the trade mark "is clearly associated in the public mind with its products, and with those of no other trader" and the degree to which the same or a similar mark has been used by third parties is important. At a practical level, the question of reputation is a matter of fact which takes into account the duration, extent and geographical area in which the trade mark is used together with the amount spent on advertising and channels of trade.

[30.37] Very similar evidential requirements were imposed under the Trade Marks Rules 1963[56] in order to show distinctiveness through usage and it is this possible dilution to the distinctive character or reputation of the earlier mark which is the rationale behind this provision. In *Taittinger SA v Allbev Ltd*,[57] the plaintiffs were champagne producers who succeeded in preventing the use of the trade mark 'Elderflower Champagne' on a non-alcoholic soft drink. Bingham LJ in the Court of Appeal stated:

---

54. Section 10(2).
55. [1983] FSR 76, at 84.
56. SI 268/1963, r 20(2).
57. [1993] FSR 641.

"a reference to champagne imports nuances of quality and celebration, a sense of something privileged and special. But this is the reputation which the champagne houses have built up over the years, and in which they have a property right. It is not in my view unfair to deny the defendants an opportunity to exploit, share or (in the vernacular), cash in on that reputation, which they have done nothing to establish. It would be very unfair to allow them to do so if the consequence was, as I am satisfied, it would be, to debase and cheapen that very reputation".

[30.38] The concept equates with that of dilution under US law and from which guidance can be sought. Anti-dilution laws in the US are designed to prevent the gradual whittling away or the dispersion of the identity and hold upon the public mind. If we take the case of champagne, its use upon non-alcoholic beverages, then confectionery items and then restaurants, etc. would gradually erode and make the trade mark commonplace thus losing its identity. Another form of dilution is possible damage to the positive attributes which may be enjoyed under a reputation. This is recognised under Benelux law and in the case of *Claeryn v Klarein*,[58] the owner of CLAERYN Dutch gin was able to prevent the use of KLAREIN in respect of a household cleaning product.[59] The words 'without due cause' in s 10(3) would suggest that there are some instances where it is possible to take unfair advantage of an earlier mark. This is hard to imagine except where there has been consent from the owner of the earlier mark or there has been honest concurrent use under s 12. Production diversification into dissimilar goods is an increasing phenomenon and, for example, the WATERFORD trade mark is now being used on linen products and could conceivably be used on other luxury goods items such as leather bags. Taking 'unfair advantage' may include an act which is likely to prevent such a product diversification. In *Lego System v Lego M Lemelstrich Ltd*,[60] it was put by Falconer J as follows:

"because of the reputation of LEGO (meaning the plaintiffs' toy construction products), there would be an opportunity for licensing or franchising the mark LEGO in other fields, that, because of the nature of the LEGO products, primarily plastic bricks, the plastic area would be a likely one to exploit and that garden implements would be an ideal market for franchising LEGO ... Obviously, the possibility of licensing or franchising another trader to use LEGO in the gardening equipment area would be lost if the defendants are allowed to continue using LEGO in this country in relation to their products. The effect, therefore, of the defendants continuing to use LEGO in this country in relation to their products would be to destroy that part of the plaintiff's

---

58. (1976) 7 11C 420.
59. See also *Parfums Givenchy v Designer Alternative Labels* [1994] RPC 243.
60. [1983] FSR 155.

reputation in their mark LEGO and goodwill attached to it which extends to such goods".

The courts will have to determine in many cases whether or not loss of exclusivity to the proprietor of an earlier mark is the taking of an unfair advantage.

EARLIER RIGHTS

Unregistered trade marks

[30.39] The right to oppose a trade mark application based on an unregistered mark existed under s 19 of the Trade Marks Act 1963 which provided that:

> it shall not be lawful to register as a trade mark or part of a trade mark any matter the use of which would, by reason of its being likely to deceive or cause confusion or otherwise, be disentitled to protection in a Court of Law or would be contrary to law or morality, or any scandalous design.

Unlike s 10(4)(a), no reference to passing-off was made. Indeed, under s 19 of the 1963 Act, the evidential burden for an opponent to a trade mark registration was not as heavy to sustain as an action for passing-off. The Irish courts have applied the statement of Evershed J in *Smith Hayden & Co Ltd's Application*:[61]

> "having regard to the reputation acquired by the [earlier mark], is the Court satisfied that the mark applied for, if used in a normal and fair manner in connection with any goods covered by the registration proposed, will it not be reasonably likely to cause deception and confusion amongst a substantial number of persons".

Unlike passing-off, it was not necessary to prove a likelihood of damage caused by the deception. Indeed, in *BALI Trade Mark*,[62] Lord Upjohn went further and stated "I think the learned Judge was wrong to use the words 'reputation acquired by', it should have been 'the user of'". Lord Upjohn went on to say:

> "... it is not necessary ... to prove that there is an actual probability of deception leading to a passing off ... It is sufficient if the result of the registration of the mark will be that a number of persons will be caused to wonder whether it might not be the case that the two products came from the same source. It is enough if the ordinary person entertains a reasonable doubt, but the Court has to be satisfied not merely that there is a possibility of confusion; it must be satisfied that there is a real tangible danger of confusion if the mark which it is sought to register is put on the Register."[63]

---

61. [1946] 63 RPC 97, at 101.
62. [1969] RPC 472.
63. See also *Pioneer Hi-Bred Corn Company v Hi-Line Chicks Pty Ltd* [1979] RPC 410.

[30.40] The difference between s 10(4)(a) and s 19 of the 1963 Act, although both allow opposition based on unregistered rights, is nevertheless quite significant. The requirement under s 10(4)(a) is that the owner of the claimed earlier right must be able to show that he would have a legal basis for prohibiting use of the subsequent mark. The legal basis is described as "by virtue of any rule of law (in particular, the law of passing-off)". Section 10(4)(a) will require the owner of the claimed earlier right to submit proofs in the same way as would be required to prove passing-off, putting the subsequent mark into the notional position as if it were being used. This is meant to reflect the optional provision in Article 4(4)(b) of the Harmonisation Directive but does not do so entirely. The Directive makes it clear that the basis of the claim to a non-registered trade mark must have been acquired prior to the date of application or priority date of the subsequent mark. The Directive refers to "rights to a non-registered trade mark" which "confers on its proprietor the right to prohibit the use of a subsequent trade mark". This would include certain statutes which prevent certain names from being used such as, for example, under the Industrial Research and Standards Act 1961 and the National Lottery Act 1986.

Other intellectual property rights

[30.41] Section 10(4)(b) implements the optional provision in Article 4(4)(c) of the Harmonisation Directive and prohibits registration if use could be prevented by virtue of an earlier right "in particular, by virtue of the law of copyright, registered designs or any other law relating to a right to a name, a right of personal portrayal or an industrial property right". Essentially, the owner of an earlier right would have to show that he would have a legal basis for prohibiting use. In the case of copyright, this would entail showing that he is a qualified person and the owner of an original work and that the subsequent mark amounts to a reproduction of a substantial part of the work. Under provisions corresponding to s 19 of the 1963 Act, the UK courts have allowed copyright in an artistic work as a basis for revocation of a registration of a device mark which was deemed 'contrary to law'.[64] A registered design arises by virtue of the Industrial and Commercial Property (Protection) Act 1927[65] and provides for protection by way of registration in respect of novel shapes, configurations, patterns or ornaments as applied to an article. The shape of goods or their packaging may be registrable[66] subject to certain limitations.[67] Even though a certain shape may not itself be registrable as a trade mark, for example, being 'a shape which gives substantial value to the goods'[68], it may nevertheless be a

---

[64.] *KARO STEP* [1977] RPC 255; see also *OSCAR* [1979] RPC 173.
[65.] See Ch 22 *ante*.
[66.] Section 6(2).
[67.] Section 8.

Registered Design and form the basis for opposition or revocation. Once the Registered Design right expires, so will the basis for opposition or revocation. The right to a name or the right of personal portrayal are matters which would generally fall under the law of passing off and so fall outside s 10(4)(b) and into s 10(4)(a), the effect of which is the same. Unauthorised character merchandising using a name can amount to passing-off.[69] In *Hogan v Koala Dundee*[70] and *Hogan v Pacific Dunlop*,[71] the actor Paul Hogan obtained injunctions against a retail shop displaying pictures of a koala bear with a bush hat and a crocodile tooth necklace and a television advertisement for shoes which parodied a scene from the *Crocodile Dundee* film. Rights to a name which would fall outside the field of passing-off would be rights of privacy and against defamation.

[30.42] Section 10(6) provides that a consent from the proprietor of an earlier mark shall dispense with the prohibition based on any of the relative grounds for refusal. In practice, this will mean that there are likely to be a large amount of requests to owners of earlier trade marks which may have been cited by the Controller. This is a practice which is common in Scandinavian countries and has also operated in the United Kingdom since 1994. If the cited mark is vulnerable to cancellation on the grounds of non-use, then a consent is likely to be forthcoming. In many cases, a consent is furnished in return for undertakings which may, for example, restrict the form of the trade mark to be used and the goods or services of use and registration. There is also no legal prohibition on the owner of an earlier trade mark from seeking a consideration in return for furnishing a consent and refusing to provide such if it is not forthcoming. The UK Registry have indicated that they will not take into account the question of whether or not the proprietor of an earlier mark requires payment for a consent. Apart from the danger of a likelihood of confusion, before giving a consent, the proprietor of an earlier trade mark should bear in mind that under s 51(1)(d), it is possible for revocation to be upheld on the grounds that the consent has resulted in use which is liable to mislead the public. A licence confers no proprietary rights on a licensee[72] and therefore, no opposition or revocation action is possible by a licensee on the relative grounds if the registered proprietor has given consent to such trade mark application/registration.

---

68. Section 8(2)(c).
69. *Muppets-Childrens' Television Workshop v Woolworths* [1981] RPC 187.
70. (1988) 12 IPR 508.
71. (1989) 14 IPR 398.
72. *Northern & Shell Plc v Conde Nast & National Magazine Distributors Ltd* [1995] RPC 117.

HONEST CONCURRENT USE

[30.43] The provisions dealing with honest concurrent use are contained in s 12 of the 1996 Act and were introduced during the passage of the Bill where it was argued at committee stage for provisions corresponding to that previously contained in s 20(2) of the 1963 Act. Essentially, honest concurrent use allows for an otherwise conflicting mark to be registered and is designed to reflect on the Register the reality of the market place and in a situation, where the proprietor of an earlier mark is not prepared to furnish a consent. Section 12(3) expressly states that the criteria as to what constitutes honest concurrent use, are to be determined in accordance with s 20(2) of the 1963 Act and therefore, it is clear that authority can be taken from appropriate case law under s 20(2) of the 1963 Act and the equivalent UK provision.[73] The leading authority is the House of Lord's decision in *Alexander Pirie & Sons Ltd*[74] where Lord Tomlin identified the factors which may be taken into consideration. These are:

(a) the extent of use of the mark for which registration is sought. Extent would include duration of use, quantity and geographical spread within the State;

(b) the degree of confusion likely to arise;

(c) the honesty of the concurrent use;

(d) whether any instances of confusion have been proven; and

(e) the relative inconvenience if the mark was allowed registration.

[30.44] These are only guidelines and every case is decided on its own merits. As a rough rule of thumb, the Irish Patents Office sought evidence of about seven years' pre-application use on a reasonably sizeable basis. In *PEDDIES App*,[75] two and a quarter years was sufficient and in *GRANADA Trade Mark*,[76] two years and ten months was held to be a comparatively short period for the exercise of such a discretion but was nevertheless allowed. Because it is a discretionary provision, there is considerable reluctance to allow a trade mark under this honest concurrent use provision in a situation of what is termed, triple identity, ie if the respective marks, goods/services and geographical areas of trade are all identical. In the case of triple identity, confusion is deemed to be inevitable.[77] However, even in cases of triple identity, the discretion can still be exercised.[78] Honest concurrent use recognises and takes into account the fact

---

[73.] UK Trade Marks Act 1938, s 12(2).
[74.] (1933) 50 RPC 147.
[75.] (1944) 61 RPC 31.
[76.] (1979) RPC 303.
[77.] *LION Brand* [1940] 57 RPC 248.
[78.] *BUD* [1988] RPC 535.

that the relevant public can, by familiarity brought about by concurrent use, learn that two similar marks are in use.[79] In *BULER*,[80] the goods were in each case watches but the respective customers were different because of the considerable price divergence and so the risk of confusion was slight. In that case, the applicant's trade was in fact larger than the opponent's but this is not a requirement.[81]

[30.45] There are some factors which differentiate s 12 from s 20(2) of the 1963 Act. First, it is restricted to honest concurrent use alone and does not provide for 'other special circumstances' to be taken into account. Secondly, it may be more difficult to distinguish marks because unlike the 1963 Act no limitations or conditions can be imposed, except a limitation by consent under s 17 of the 1996 Act. In *Bass Ratcliffe & Gretton Ltd v Nicholson & Son Ltd*[82] the fact that there was a limitation in the form of different containers differentiated the goods and was a determining factor but this may no longer afford the degree of comfort that a court might require before exercising its discretion in favour of an honest concurrent user. Thirdly, it was not clear under the 1963 Act whether or not an honest concurrent user could apply where the earlier trade mark had been used but not registered. Section 12 makes it clear that both registered trade marks and unregistered earlier rights can be overcome by an honest concurrent user.

[30.46] To establish how the honest concurrent user provision will apply in practice, it is important to look at s 12(2) which indicates that if the Controller establishes honest concurrent use, he will allow the application to proceed to advertisement but an opponent with an earlier trade mark or right may still succeed in opposition proceedings despite the existence of honest concurrent use. The effect of honest concurrent use in opposition proceedings will be to show that under s 10(2), there is no likelihood of confusion given that there has already been use without confusion.

[30.47] Indeed, one of the honest concurrent user tests is whether any instances of confusion have been proved and if such is not the case, then it serves towards showing an unlikelihood of future confusion. If an opposition is based on s 10(1), then it seems that honest concurrent use will not be sufficient to defeat such because it is not necessary for an opponent to show a likelihood of confusion. In this instance, at least two elements of the triple identity, ie identical trade mark and goods/services are present so that honest concurrent use would have been hard to demostrate even under the 1963 Act. If opposition is

---

[79.] *L'AMY* [1983] RPC 137.
[80.] [1975] RPC 275.
[81.] *BAINBRIDGE* (1940) 57 RPC 248.
[82.] (1932) 49 RPC 88.

under s 10(3), honest concurrent use may go to show that there will be no unfair advantage taken of the earlier trade mark.

[30.48] The EU Trade Mark Harmonisation Directive[83] does not provide for honest concurrent use and there is an argument that the inclusion of such is a breach of the State's obligations under Community law. Article 4 expressly states that a trade mark shall not be registered when it conflicts with an earlier trade mark or right as defined. The provision of a consent is an option and exception provided in Article 4(5) of the Directive but the addition of a further exception by way of honest concurrent use is not provided for. The owner of an earlier trade mark or right could challenge a decision to allow a registration based on honest concurrent user or seek invalidity of any such registration as being in breach of the Directive. The other side of the argument is that honest concurrent user is simply being used as a criterion in determining the question of a likelihood of confusion under Article 4(1)(b) or whether the later mark takes unfair advantage or is detrimental to the earlier mark under Article 4(3).

[30.49] The Directive in fact uses the words "a trade mark shall not be registered or if registered, shall be liable to be declared invalid" on the basis of an earlier conflicting trade mark or right. In a number of EU countries, the National Trade Marks Offices do not cite earlier trade marks as a basis for refusal and it is up to the owners of an earlier trade mark to oppose or seek invalidity. Indeed, in the Benelux, there is not even an opposition procedure. The State can therefore argue that its decision not to cite an earlier trade mark because of honest concurrent use but allow such proceed to advertisement is not, itself in breach of the Directive. There is in fact no statutory obligation on the Controller to carry out searches of prior trade marks either on the Irish or Community Registers but such is provided for in the Rules[84] and policy in this regard may, of course, vary.

[30.50] The honest concurrent user provisions do not have a bearing on the absolute grounds of refusal or on invalidity proceedings. This means that subject to any acquiescence under s 53, the owner of an earlier trade mark or right may, where honest concurrent use has been pleaded, be better served by refraining from opposition and seeking invalidity once registration has taken place. The downside of such a course of action is that under s 15(1), no infringement occurs while the trade mark remains on the Register.

[83.] 89/04/EEC.
[84.] Trade Marks Rules 1996, r 16 (SI 199/1996).

Chapter 31

Trade Marks Act 1996: Infringement and Remedies

INTRODUCTION

[31.01] A trade mark registration confers on the proprietor exclusivity of rights therein[1] and there is no requirement to prove a reputation or to show actual or likely damage, which are constraints under the law of passing off. It could be argued that the wording in s 13(1) of the 1996 Act does not correctly transpose Article 5(1) of the Trade Mark Harmonisation Directive[2] because Article 5(1) appears to be broader in that the right to prevent unauthorised use is only part of the overall entitlement granted by virtue of a registration. Section 13(1) links the exclusive right as being limited to prevention of unauthorised use of the trade mark. It is customary to focus on the exclusivity of use but a trade mark is a proprietary right and as such, rights extend beyond mere usage and to, for example, other dealings such as assignment or as a security interest. In addition, the protection afforded under s 14 includes infringing acts which do not amount to trade mark usage.

[31.02] It is not possible to bring infringement proceedings prior to the date of publication of registration[3] but the effective date of registration is the application date[4] and therefore damages for infringement can be claimed from this date.

[31.03] The proprietor of an Irish trade mark registration can only sue on foot of infringement within the State.[5] However, s 14(4)(c) contains a prohibition against infringing use by way of export under the offending trade mark. In *George Ballantine & Son Ltd v Ballantyne Stewart & Co Ltd*,[6] it was held that the likelihood of deception is to be considered as against the public in the country where the article is to be sold. Section 61 deals specifically with the rights of the proprietor of a well known trade mark and which arises irrespective of registration.[7] Similarly, s 65 grants the proprietor a right of action against unauthorised acts of an agent or representative.[8]

---

1. Section 13(1).
2. 89/104/EEC.
3. Section 13(4)(a).
4. Sections 13(3) & 45(3).
5. Section 13(1); s 101.
6. [1959] RPC 273.
7. Article 6 *bis* - Paris Convention.
8. Article 6 *septies* - Paris Convention.

INFRINGEMENT

[31.04] The Trade Marks Act 1963 limited the scope of protection by way of an infringement action to the goods embraced by the registration. Section 14 of the 1996 Act, in implementing Article 5 of the Trade Mark Harmonisation Directive, increases the scope of such protection to unauthorised use of an identical or similar sign on goods or services similar to that of the registration and in some instances, to even dissimilar goods or services.[9] To this extent, the grounds of infringement correspond to those for determining whether or not an earlier trade mark right exists under s 10. However, the infringement provisions in s 14 also require not just a comparison of the respective marks and the goods/services but also an examination of the nature of the complained of act and despite the constraints of the 1963 Act, the Irish courts were already moving in this direction. In *Gallaher (Dublin) Ltd v The Health Education Bureau*,[10] Costello J found infringement by use on printed matter by virtue of a registration in respect of tobacco products. The defendant used the identical trade mark on an imitation cigarette packet containing printed matter used as an aid to stop smoking. This was held to be use in relation to cigarettes and thus an infringement.

[31.05] Under s 14, an infringing act requires use of a sign in the course of trade. One of the first issues which will have to be determined by the Irish courts is whether or not s 14 embraces non-trade mark usage. Many cases under the 1963 Act and the corresponding provision in the UK 1938 Act were decided on this issue. In *Mars (GB) Ltd v Cadbury Ltd*,[11] the registered trade mark TREETS in respect of confectionery was deemed not to be infringed by the use of the words 'treat size' as such was not used as a trade mark. In *Mothercare (UK) Ltd v Penguin Books Ltd*,[12] it was stated by Dillon LJ as follows:

> "Indeed it stands to reason that a Trade Marks Act would only be concerned to restrict the use of a mark as a trade mark or in a trade mark sense, and should be construed accordingly. If descriptive words are legitimately registered in Part A of the Register, there is still no reason why other people should not be free to use the words in a descriptive sense, and not in only a trade mark sense".

[31.06] In *Unidoor Ltd v Marks & Spencer plc*,[13] the plaintiff held a Part B registration for COAST TO COAST in respect of articles of clothing. The defendants used COAST TO COAST as a slogan on their own T-shirts and it was held that this was not in a manner which constituted trade mark usage.

---

9. Section 14(3); *BASF plc v CEP (UK) plc* [1996] ETMR 51.
10. [1982] ILRM 240.
11. [1987] RPC 387.
12. [1988] RPC 113, at 118-119.
13. [1988] RPC 275.

[31.07] In *Trebor Bassett Limited v The Football Association*[14] the plaintiff manufactured candy sticks the packaging of which included collectable insert cards. Some of these cards depicted soccer internationals in English team jerseys on which the Football Association logo appeared. The plaintiff was granted a declaration of non-infringement and Rattee J found that the logo was not being used a 'sign' in respect of its cards.

[31.08] There are certainly arguments as to why these cases might still apply under the new law. The preamble to the Harmonisation Directive states "whereas the protection afforded by the registered trade mark, the function of which is in particular to guarantee the trade mark as an indication of origin". The definition of a trade mark in s 6(1) reinforces this statement and s 13 states infringement as being in relation to use of that trade mark. In contrast, the definition of 'use' in s 2(2) distinguishes between a trade mark and a sign and envisages both by using the word 'or'. In the first decision in the UK courts which addresses this issue, Jacob J in *British Sugar plc v James Robertson & Sons Ltd*[15] held that the section covers non-trade mark use and considered the important matter to be the language of the Directive which has not been exactly transposed into either UK or Irish law. Jacob J did not view the language corresponding to s 13 as of assistance in interpreting s 14 being "really no more than a chatty introduction to the details set out in s 14, itself adding no more than that the acts concerned must be done without consent".

[31.09] Section 14(4) includes a non-exhaustive list of examples of what constitutes use of a sign, namely:

(a) affixing it to goods or the packaging thereof;

(b) offering or exposing goods for sale, putting them on the market or stocking them for those purposes under the sign, or offering or supplying services under the sign;

(c) importing or exporting goods under the sign; or

(d) using the sign on business papers or in advertising.

Even under the 1963 Act, the trade mark did not have to appear at the point of sale.[16] In *CHEETAH Trade Mark*,[17] it was held that use of a registered trade mark on invoices and delivery notes was just as much an infringement as stamping the mark on a container for the goods. Also, the use of a registered

---

[14]. [1997] FSR 211.
[15]. [1996] RPC 281.
[16]. *Esquire Electronics Ltd v Roopanand Bros* [1991] RPC 425.
[17]. [1993] FSR 263.

trade mark on an invoice, even if rendered long after sale and delivery, was still use in the course of trade.

[31.10] The infringement provisions require use in the course of trade. 'Trade' is defined in s 2 to include any business or profession and use includes otherwise than by means of a graphic representation.[18] Thus, oral use can amount to an infringement which was not possible under the 1963 Act which required "use of a printed or other visual representation of the mark". However, use in the course of trade was a requirement under the 1963 Act and therefore recourse can be made to decisions under the 1963 Act. The High Court adopted a broad interpretation in *Gallaher (Dublin) Ltd v Health Education Bureau*[19] and conferred protection against any use which damaged the trade mark. This can be contrasted with the UK decision in *M Ravok (Weatherwear) Ltd v National Trade Press Ltd*[20] in which the defendant incorrectly attributed ownership of a trade mark in a directory. It was held that there was no infringement since the defendant had not used the mark in the course of trade in the goods for which it was registered.

[31.11] Section 14(5) provides for contributory infringement in circumstances where a person applies a registered trade mark to certain materials where that person knew or had reason to believe that such was unauthorised. The words 'had reason to believe' were considered in the case of *LA Gear Inc v Hi-Tech Sports Plc*[21] and held to involve the concept of knowledge of facts from which a reasonable man would arrive at the relevant belief and that facts from which a reasonable man might suspect the relevant conclusion was not enough. It was stated by Morritt J that "the phrase does connote the allowance of a period of time to enable the reasonable man to evaluate those facts so as to convert the facts into a reasonable belief".

Comparative Advertising

[31.12] There are different forms of comparative advertising and such is defined in the amended proposal for an EU Directive on comparative advertising[22] as: "any advertising which explicitly or by implication identifies a competitor or goods or services of the same kind offered by a competitor". In some instances, comparative advertising does not refer to a specific competitor and, for example, a slogan which states a courier service to be faster than the rest or a supermarket to be better value is a form of comparative advertising. There are differing views

---

[18.] Section 2(2).
[19.] [1982] ILRM 240.
[20.] (1955) 72 RPC 110.
[21.] [1992] FSR 121.
[22.] OJ 1991 C180/14.

as to whether or not comparative advertising should be allowed and for example, German laws are very restrictive in this regard. The matter was never tested in the Irish courts under the 1963 Act but there is no reason to believe that the principles adopted by the UK courts would not be equally applicable in this jurisdiction. It is clear that comparative advertising is not just a question of trade mark law and in cases of false or misleading statements, involves the issues of trade libel or injurious falsehood. In *Kaye v Robertson*,[23] Glidewell LJ stated the essential requirements in the tort of injurious or malicious falsehood, namely:

> "that the defendant has published about the plaintiff words which are false, that they were published maliciously, and that special damage has followed as the direct and natural result of their publication ... Malice will be inferred if it be proved that the words were calculated to produce damage and that the defendant knew when he published the words that they were false or was reckless as to whether they were false or not."

[31.13] The EU Directive concerning misleading advertising[24] has been implemented by way of the European Communities (Misleading Advertising) Regulations 1988.[25] However, advertising standards are in the main ensured by means of self regulation, the principal body being the Advertising Standards Authority for Ireland which administers the Code of Advertising Standards for Ireland and the Code of Sales Promotion Practice. Tobacco advertising is regulated directly by specific legislation, principally, the Tobacco Products (Control of Advertising, Sponsorship and Sales Promotion) Act 1978 and the Tobacco Products, (Control of Advertising, Sponsorship and Sales Promotion) Regulations 1991, both under the responsibility of the Department of Health.

[31.14] Under the European Communities (Misleading Advertising) Regulations 1988[26] an individual can apply to the High Court to restrain a misleading advertisement if it can be shown that such misleading advertisements will cause harm or damage to the competitor. The High Court may require the advertiser to furnish evidence as to the accuracy of any factual claims made in any advertisement. In determining whether advertising is misleading, account is taken of all its features including the characteristics of the goods, their nature, composition and method of manufacture.

[31.15] Comparative advertising can result in an action for passing off in circumstances where there is a misrepresentation whereby customers are deceived into believing that the defendant's product is that of the plaintiff. In

---

[23.] [1991] FSR 62; see also *Compaq Computer Corp v Dell Computer Corp* [1992] FSR 93.

[24.] 84/450/EEC.

[25.] SI 134/1988.

[26.] *Ibid*.

McDonald's Hamburgers Ltd v BurgerKing (UK) Ltd,[27] the defendant advertised by way of a card with the words 'It's not just Big, Mac' beside a reference to their own hamburger called the 'WHOPPER'. Whitford J held that there was passing off, the words conveying the impression that the burger being advertised was an improved version of the BIG MAC or drew an association between the BIG MAC and the defendant. Whitford J came to the conclusion that a significant number of people reading the advertisement would find in it a misrepresentation as to the possible source or origin from which the BIG MAC could be obtained and stated "advertisements are not to be read as if they were some testamentary provision in a will or a clause or in some agreement with every word being carefully considered and the words as a whole being compared."

[31.16] In *Ciba-Geigy plc v Parke Davis & Co Ltd*,[28] the defendant only referred to the plaintiff's trade mark in an indirect manner while emphasising the equivalent quality but cheaper price for its own product. It was held that there was no actual misrepresentation because the advertisement made it clear that the product came from the defendant. Although the defendant used the device of an apple which was associated with the plaintiff, the advertisement did not result in confusion as to the source of the defendant's product. Aldous J quoted from the House of Lords decision in *Erven Warnick BV v J Townend & Sons (Hull) Ltd*[29] and the statement by Lord Diplock that:

> "exaggerated claims by a trader about the quality of his wares that they are better than those of his rivals, even though he knows this to be untrue, have been permitted by the common law as venial 'puffing' which give no cause of action to a competitor even though he can show that he has suffered actual damage to his business as a result."

The difficulty of showing passing off in the case of comparative advertising is that in many cases, there is no question of customer confusion as to the origin of the product. This is particularly so in cases where the advertisement refers indirectly to the attributes of a rival product. Examples given by Aldous J in the *Ciba Geigy* case were "A's flour is as good as B's" or "A's flour can be substituted in all recipes for B's flour". The position under the law of passing off was mirrored for registered trade marks prior to the 1963 Act.[30] However, s 12(1)(b) of the 1963 Act extended protection to prevent use in advertising issued to the public in the course of trade. This was considered by the Court of Appeal under the corresponding provision in the UK Trade Marks Act 1938 in

---

[27] [1986] FSR 45.
[28] [1994] FSR 8.
[29] [1979] AC 731.
[30] See *Irving's Yeastvite Ltd v Horsenail* (1934) 51 RPC 110.

the case of *Bismag Ltd v Amblins (Chemists) Ltd.*[31] It was held that although the section was obscure, it essentially prevented traders from using registered trade marks of others as a springboard to the promotion of their own products even in cases where there was no confusion as to origin.[32] The only way around the provision for a person wishing to engage in comparative advertising was to avoid using a registered trade mark. In *Duracell International Ltd v Ever Ready Ltd,*[33] the defendant used the corporate name of its competitor and a black and white picture of a battery similar to the get-up of the plaintiff's goods, but in neither case infringed a registered trade mark. A possible defence under the 1963 Act available to a defendant engaged in comparative advertising was s 13(2) of the 1963 Act and in circumstances where the trade mark was registered in Part B of the Register. This was a statutory defence to infringement proceedings where the defendant can show that despite the use being made, it is not likely to deceive or cause confusion or indicate a connection in the course of trade with the proprietor.[34]

[31.17] The position now under s 14(6) of the 1996 Act is that it is permissible to engage in comparative advertising by use of another person's registered trade mark for the purpose of identifying the goods or services of the proprietor of the registered trade mark or their licensee. However, such use must be in accordance with honest practices in industrial or commercial matters and should not without due cause take unfair advantage of, or be detrimental to, the distinctive character or reputation of the trade mark. Section 14(6), although mimicking the provisions in s 10(6) of the UK Trade Marks Act 1994, is not taken directly from any particular single provision of the Harmonisation Directive[35] but draws from both Articles 5(5) and 6(1) of the Directive, the words "*bona fide* and established practices of the trade" also being used in the Paris Convention.

[31.18] Attempting to strike a balance between allowing comparative advertising in the interest of consumers but at the same time limiting the extent to which the products of a competitor, through its trade mark can be denigrated, means that the courts will have a very difficult task in interpreting s 14(6). The use of the expression 'honest practices' does not help because it could be argued that such practices did not exist to a large extent by virtue of the restrictive provisions in the 1963 Act. The courts may, of course, look at practices in accordance with standards operated in different industries and where, for

---

[31.] (1940) RPC 209.

[32.] *Chanel Ltd v Triton Packaging Ltd* (1993) RPC 32.

[33.] [1989] FSR 71.

[34.] *Montana Wines Ltd v Villa Maria Wines Ltd* [1985] FSR 400; see also *Pompadour Laboratories v Frazer* [1966] RPC 7.

[35.] 89/104/EEC.

example, in the car industry, it is more common to engage in comparative advertising than in, for example, the food industry.

[31.19] However, again it would be difficult for the courts to adopt varying standards dependant on the product/service line. Such an approach would certainly make it very difficult for guidelines to be interpreted from judicial pronouncements. Indeed, it is just as likely that the courts will turn to guidelines established by regulatory bodies such as the Advertising Standards Authority to establish what is likely to be viewed as an honest practice. The likely criteria to be taken into account by the courts are the following standards of comparative advertising, namely:

(a) the advertisement should be fair and not misleading;

(b) it should be clear as to what is being compared, and on what basis;

(c) it should compare like with like;

(d) it should not confer an artificial advantage;

(e) the points of comparison must be capable of substantiation and not unfairly selected; and

(f) it should not include generalised superiority claims based on selective comparisons or claims that a competitive product is generally unsatisfactory based on the highlighting of selected advantages only of the advertised product.

[31.20] The word 'honest' would lean towards a subjective test but the courts in the UK have already been faced with the difficulty of such a test in interpreting the words '*bona fide*'. In *Provident Financial plc v Halifax Building Society*,[36] it was observed by Aldous J that:

> "the test of *bona fide* use as enunciated by the Court of Appeal is subjective, namely whether the defendant honestly thought that no confusion would arise and had no intention of wrongfully diverting business to himself. I have always found it difficult to believe that this was the correct test, because the test tends to the result that the uninformed fool could have a defence ... whereas the properly informed reasonable man would not."

When the word 'honest' is read in conjunction with 'practices' as appearing in s 14(6), the courts are likely to adopt an objective as opposed to a subjective test and by reference to the trade. In *Barclays Bank plc v RBS Advanta*,[37] Laddie J held that it was indeed an objective test and depended on whether the use would be considered honest by members of a reasonable audience.

[36.] [1994] FSR 81.

[37.] [1996] RPC 307.

[31.21] It could be argued that comparative advertising is in fact covered by s 14(4)(d) but the Minutes of the Council Meeting at which the European Trade Mark Regulation was adopted specifically stated that the corresponding Article 9(2)(d) "does not cover the use of a Community trade mark in comparative advertising". Section 14(6) in extracting the wording from Article 5(5) of the Harmonisation Directive and requiring without due cause an unfair advantage or an act detrimental to the distinctive character or reputation of the registered trade marks means that reference can be had to the interpretation under s 14(3) and 10(3). The use of these words is strong in this context because it appears to suggest that it is only proprietors of well established trade marks by virtue of a reputation, who can prevent comparative advertising. A more logical explanation is that the legislative provision is designed to protect disparaging or negative advertising which is likely to have a detrimental effect and which by its very nature, detracts from the registered trade mark. It was stated by Laddie J in *Barclays Bank plc v RBS Advanta*,[38] that the proviso that:

> "if the use without due cause takes unfair advantage of, or is detrimental to, the distinctive character or repute of the trade mark in most cases adds nothing of significance to the first part of the proviso. An advertisement which makes use of a registered mark in a way which is not honest will almost always take unfair advantage of it and vice versa. At the most these final words emphasise that the use of the mark must take advantage of it or be detrimental to it. In other words the use must either give some advantage to the defendant or inflict some harm on the character or repute of the registered mark which is above the level of *de minimis*."

In *Vodafone Group plc v Orange Personal Communications Services Ltd*[39] Jacob J applied the test in *Barclays Bank plc v RBS Advanta* and affirmed that the primary objective of s 14(6) is to facilitate comparative advertising, provided it is honest. In the *Vodafone case*, the advertisement complained of, which was directed to mobile phone users, stated "On average, Orange users save £20 a month compared to Vodafone and Cellnet equivalent tariffs." Vodafone sued both for malicious falsehood and infringement and failed on both counts. In relation to the claim as to malicious falsehood it was held that as a notional jury, the judge had to decide upon a single natural and ordinary meaning of the words taking into account the fact that the public expect a certain amount of hyperbole in advertising. However, the more precise and specific the claim, the more likely it was that the public would take it seriously. Jacob J accepted that the most likely meaning was that asserted by Orange, ie Orange users would save £20 a month compared to what they would be paying if they

---

38. [1996] RPC 307.
39. [1997] FSR 34.

made the same use of their telephones but using the Vodafone network to make calls. That meaning was not false. If the slogan had been misleading then infringement would have been upheld.

[31.22] A draft proposal for a Council Directive concerning comparative advertising and which also amends the misleading advertising Directive,[40] was published in June 1991[41] and a second draft published in April 1994.[42] The objectives are stated in the preamble with a recognition that under certain conditions, comparative advertising can stimulate competition between suppliers of goods and services to the consumer's advantage. To achieve this objective, it is stated that:

> "whereas such use of another's trade mark or trade name does not breach this exclusive right in cases where it complies with the conditions laid down by the Directive and does not capitalise on the reputation of another trade mark, but is intended solely to distinguish between them and thus objectively highlight differences."

[31.23] Under the proposed Directive, comparative advertising will be permitted provided that it objectively compares the material, relevant, always verifiable, fairly chosen and representative features of the competing goods and services and that it:

(a) does not mislead;

(b) does not create the risk of confusion in the market place between the advertiser and a competitor or between the advertiser's trade marks, trade names, other distinguishing marks, goods or services and those of a competitor;

(c) does not discredit, denigrate or bring contempt on the trade marks, trade names, goods, services or activities of a competitor and does not principally capitalise on the reputation of a trade mark or trade name of a competitor; and

(d) does not refer to the personality or personal situation of a competitor.

It will also be necessary for comparative advertising to indicate the length of time during which the characteristics of the goods or services compared shall be maintained where these are the subject of a special or limited duration offer.

[40.] 84/450 EEC.
[41.] 91/C 180/15.
[42.] 94/C 136/04.

Infringement Proceedings pursuant to s 14(1)

[31.24] Infringement under s 14(1) arises in circumstances where the respective marks are identical and the goods or services under the offending mark fall within the scope of the registered trade mark. In such a case, there is no requirement to show any likelihood of confusion. There is, for example, no defence available corresponding to that which existed for Part B registration under the 1963 Act where a defendant could show their use is not likely to deceive or cause confusion or to be taken as indicating a connection in the course of trade. On the question of identicality of goods/services, reference should be made to corresponding provisions in s 10(1).[43] In *British Sugar plc v James Robertson & Sons Ltd*,[44] Jacob J held that a spread was not a desert sauce or a syrup and stated "when it comes to construing a word used in a trade mark specification, one is concerned with how the product is, as a practical matter, regarded for the purposes of trade. After all a trade mark specification is concerned with use in trade". Jacob J went on to confirm the test in *Origins Natural Resources Inc v Origin Clothing Ltd*,[45] that a comparison of a mark with the sign being used by the defendant:

> "requires the Court to assume the mark of the plaintiff is used in a normal and fair manner in relation to the goods for which it is registered and then to assess the likelihood of confusion in relation to the way the defendant uses its mark, discounting added matter or circumstances."

Infringement Proceedings pursuant to s 14(2)

[31.25] Section 14(2) is divided into two parts, ie an identical sign or similar goods or services in s 14(2)(a) and a similar sign for identical or similar goods or services in s 14(2)(b). Both are treated equally and in each case, there must exist a likelihood of confusion on the part of the public because of the identicality or similarity. The provision in s 14(2) introduces a major change from the 1963 Act and for the first time, extends infringement to goods or services not covered by the Registration. The wording is taken from Article 5(1)(b) of the Harmonisation Directive and some guidance can be sought from the preamble which states that the likelihood of confusion "depends on numerous elements, and in particular, on the recognition of the trade mark on the market, of the association which can be made with the used or registered sign, of the degree of similarity between the trade mark and the sign and between the goods or services identified". The issue of recognition and association suggest that certain proofs used in passing off actions may be imposed on a trade mark proprietor.

---

43. See Ch 30.
44. [1996] RPC 281.
45. [1995] FSR 280.

This is strange in itself because a registered trade mark may not even have been used at the time of an infringement action and thus possesses no recognition on the market. It is illogical to suggest that such a mark cannot avail of s 14(2) and the comparison should still remain between the defendant's sign as used and the plaintiff's registered trade mark.[46] Recognition becomes a factor presumably if an argument is being made that there is an association. The concept of 'likelihood of association' was developed by Benelux case law, a point made in the Council Minutes at which the EU Trade Mark Regulation was adopted. In the Benelux case of *Union v Union Soleure*,[47] it was stated that:

> "there is similarity between a trade mark and a sign when, taking into account the particular circumstances of the case, such as the distinctive power of the trade mark, the trade mark and the sign, each looked at as a whole and in relation to one another, demonstrate such auditive, visual or conceptual resemblance, that associations between sign and trade mark are evoked merely on the basis of this resemblance."

Thus, calling to mind an association is not to be equated with confusion as to origin and is well illustrated with the case of *Monopoly v Anti-Monopoly*[48] where the Benelux Court held that ANTI-MONOPOLY, when used on a game, infringed the MONOPOLY trade mark even though given the very different nature of the ANTI MONOPOLY game, it was highly unlikely that the public would be confused into believing that the games come from the same source. The infringement lay in the association and not public confusion. However, already the UK courts have shown their reluctance to follow this broad interpretation as "creating a new type of monopoly not related to the proprietor's trade but in the trade mark itself.[49]

[31.26] On the question of similarity of goods/services, the courts have already had much experience through their interpretation of s 20 of the 1963 Act where the courts had to determine what is meant by goods of the same description. The UK courts have already drawn on the older cases and in *British Sugar plc v James Robertson & Sons Ltd*,[50] Jacob J used the following criteria:

    (a) the respective uses of the respective goods or services;

    (b) the respective users of the respective goods or services;

    (c) the physical nature of the goods or acts of service;

[46.] *Portakabin Ltd v Powerblast Ltd* [1990] RPC 471. See also *Origins Natural Resources Inc v Origin Clothing Ltd* [1995] FSR 280.

[47.] [1984] BIE 137.

[48.] [1978] BIE 39.

[49.] *Wagamama Ltd v City Centre Restaurants Plc* [1995] FSR 713.

[50.] [1996] RPC 281.

(d) the respective trade channels through which the goods or services reach the market;

(e) in the case of self-serve consumer items, where in practice they are respectively found or likely to be found in supermarkets and in particular whether they are, or are likely to be, found on the same or different shelves; and

(f) the extent to which the respective goods or services are competitive. This enquiry may take into account how those in trade classify the goods, eg, whether market research companies, who of course act for industry, put the goods or services in the same or a different sector.

These tests are very much a modern version of the old *JELLINEK*[51] criteria namely the nature of the goods, their uses and the trade channels.

Infringement Proceedings pursuant to s 14(3)

[31.27] Section 14(3) implements the optional provision in Article 5(2) of the Harmonisation Directive[52] and extends infringement to use of an identical or similar sign on dissimilar goods in circumstances where the registered trade mark has a reputation in the State and the use of the sign is without due cause and takes unfair advantage of, or is detrimental to, the distinctive character or the reputation of the registered trade mark. Essentially, the provision is a recognition of possible dilution which is a concept long recognised by the Benelux courts and certain US State laws and arises in instances of damage despite the absence of any confusion. There are a number of aspects pertaining to the concept of dilution and this includes a blurring of the distinctiveness of a mark towards non-distinctiveness. The Benelux courts have found such, for example, in relation to DUNHILL for glasses and MARLBORO for cosmetics. In *HP Bulmer Ltd v J Bollinger SA*,[53] Buckley LJ moved towards recognising dilution when he stated:

> "the exclusivity of the association of the name, mark or get-up with A's business might, perhaps, be shown to be itself a valuable asset as a powerful means of bringing A's goods to the notice of the public, thus maintaining and promoting A's competitive position on the market."

[31.28] The more recognisable instances of dilution are cases where there is damage to the positive attributes which the mark conveys to the public. In the Benelux, the proprietor of a Dutch gin under the trade mark *CLAERYN* prevented the use of KLAREIN in respect of a liquid cleanser.[54] In the British

---

[51.] (1946) 63 RPC 59. See also *DAIQUIRI RUM* [1969] RPC 600.

[52.] 89/104/EEC.

[53.] [1978] RPC 79, at 94.

[54.] (1976) 7 11C 420.

case of *Taittinger SA v Allbev Ltd*,[55] the defendant sold as 'Elderflower Champagne', a non-alcoholic fruit drink in a bottle of a same shape, size and colour as champagne, with labels and wired corks similar to those used for champagne. The Court of Appeal upheld an injunction in favour of the champagne producers and the Master of The Rolls, Sir Thomas Bingham stated:

> "The first plaintiffs' reputation and goodwill in the description Champagne derive not only from the quality of their wine and its glamorous associations, but also from the very singularity and exclusiveness of the description, the absence of qualifying epithets and imitative descriptions. Any product which is not Champagne but is allowed to describe itself as such must inevitably, in my view, erode the singularity and exclusiveness of the description Champagne and so cause the first plaintiffs' damage of an insidious but serious kind."

[31.29] What is strange is that the protection afforded under s 14(3) by use on dissimilar goods could be argued to be stronger than that under s 14(2) because there is no requirement to show any likelihood of confusion. This argument was rejected in the case of *Baywatch Production Co Inc v The Home Video Channel*.[56] Mr M Crystal QC sitting as a deputy judge of the Chancery Division held that it would be illogical for the UK equivalent to s 14(3) to give a greater protection in relation to non-similar goods or services by dispensing with the ingredient of a likelihood of confusion than the protection afforded to similar goods under s 14(2). It was considered that the requirements under s 14(3) are:

(1) A sign which is similar to the trade mark, so that there is a likelihood of confusion on the part of the public, is used in relation to goods and services which are not similar to the mark;

(2) The mark has a reputation in the State;

(3) The use of the sign, being without due cause, takes advantage of, or is detrimental to the distinctive character or the repute of the trade mark.

[31.30] In the case of *BASF plc v CEP (UK) plc*[57] Knox J also held that confusion is an essential ingredient for infringement to occur under s 14(3).[58] In relation to the requirement to show a reputation, the Supreme Court has already held in *C & A Modes v C & A (Waterford) Ltd*,[59] that this can arise even though there is no actual use in the State. The factors taken into account by the courts in determining reputation, will be similar to those in a passing off action and would include:

[55.] [1993] FSR 641.
[56.] [1997] FSR 22.
[57.] [1996] ETMR 51.
[58.] For a contrasting ciew see Tony Martino, *Trade Mark Dilution* (Claredon Press, 1996).
[59.] [1978] FSR 126.

- The degree of inherent or acquired distinctiveness of the mark.

- The duration and extent of use of the mark in connection with the goods or services.

- The duration and extent of advertising and publicity of the mark.

- The geographical extent of the trading area in which the mark is used.

- The channels of trade for the goods or services with which the proprietor's mark is used.

- The degree of recognition of the proprietor's mark in its and the defendant's trading areas and channels of trade.

- The nature and extent of use of the same or any similar sign by third parties.

What is meant by use 'without due cause' will have to be determined by the courts but will presumably embrace claims such as prior rights, authorisation by the trade mark proprietor, necessity due to legal requirements or the trade mark proprietor's abuse of a dominant position.

Survey Evidence

[31.31] Apart from the reliability of survey evidence, a question arises as to whether such is *prima facie* hearsay. A person answering a questionnaire is not on oath and unless called cannot be cross examined. An unsworn questionnaire is not itself admissible as illustrated in the case of *LANCER Trade Mark*[60] following the practice established in the *Glastonbury* case[61] where Lord Russell of Killowen stated:

> "The applicants circularised ninety-one members of the public asking them to answer the following question: 'if you were offered in the ordinary way of trade slippers described as 'Glastonbury Slippers' what would the word 'Glastonbury' mean to you? They received eighty three replies. To save expense they only filed affidavits by eleven of those who had replied; but in order to prove that the eleven were a proper and fair sample of the bulk, the remaining seventy-two replies were exhibited to an affidavit. This procedure was the subject of severe comment in the Court of Appeal. No doubt it was technically wrong; but the appellants not unnaturally shrank from the great expense of filing some seventy affidavits. It will be wiser perhaps in a similar case in the future to file an affidavit merely stating the number of the other answers which have been received, and that they are open to inspection by the other side's advisers. The Court will then be protected from the embarrassment of being in possession of documents which are in no sense evidence of the facts stated therein."

[60.] [1987] RPC 303, 319.
[61.] *Bailey & Co Ltd v Clark, Sun & Morland* (1938) 55 RPC 253.

At face value there appears to be no better way of illustrating to a court the reputation enjoyed by a trade mark or the likelihood of confusion between respective marks than by producing survey evidence. However, the weight and reliance placed by the courts on such which is usually undertaken at great expense, is generally so minimalistic as to raise the question whether it is in fact a futile exercise. In *Imperial Group plc v Philip Morris Ltd*[62] Whitford J observed as follows:

> "However satisfactory market research surveys may be in assisting commercial organisations as to how they can best conduct their business, they are by and large, as experience in other cases has indicated, an unsatisfactory way of trying to establish questions of fact which are likely to be matters of dispute."

The dilemma for litigants is that despite statements such as those by Whitford J the courts often find such surveys helpful and of evidential value. In the case of *Unilever plc's Trade Mark*[63] Falconer J criticised the absence of such evidence.

[31.32] In the New Zealand case of *Custom Glass Boats Ltd v Salthouse Bros Ltd*[64] Mahon J concluded that survey evidence was admissible as being an exception to the strict hearsay rule and "as proving an external fact, namely, that a designated opinion is held by the public or a class of public, which is not a matter of hearsay at all."

[31.33] What is readily apparent is that it is the methodology behind any survey which is closely scrutinised and which is the usual crux as to the acceptability of survey evidence. In *Imperial Group plc v Philip Morris Ltd*[65] Whitford J set out the following criteria for surveys:

1. The interviewees must be selected to represent a relevant cross-section of the public;

2. The size of the sample must be statistically significant;

3. The survey must be conducted fairly;

4. All the surveys carried out must be disclosed, including the number carried out, how they were conducted, and the totality of persons involved;

5. The totality of the answers given (and the requisite details) must be made available to the opposite party before trial;

6. The questions must not be leading nor should they lead the person answering into a field of speculation he would never have embarked

---

[62.] [1984] RPC 293, at 302.
[63.] [1984] RPC 155, at 181
[64.] [1976] RPC 589.
[65.] [1984] RPC 293.

upon had the question not been put. In *Scott Ltd v Nice-Pak Products Ltd*[66] the interviewees were shown the defendant's product and asked questions about it. However, the product in question was not available in the UK. It was held that the entire premise upon which the questions were put was false.

7. The exact answers and not some abbreviated form must be recorded;

8. The instructions to the interviewers as to how to carry out the survey must be disclosed;

9. Where the answers are coded for computer input, the coding instructions must be disclosed.

[31.34] It is important that the survey is not made under conditions remote from the conditions in which people are going to look at marks when they are in a shop, thus in the *Laura Ashley* case[67] Whitford J rejected evidence by way of the results of readings from a tachistoscope which is an instrument used in perception studies. A tachistoscope comprises a viewing chamber and an eyepiece. Material is exposed on an illuminated screen by an operator. Over a period of time the image gradually becomes clearer and records are kept of the time period taken for recognition of the trade mark Whitford J held that 'trademarks had to be considered in a business context and in the context of laboratory experiments" and such was rejected as being a "perfectly useless exercise".[68] A typical way of conducting a survey in a real context is to approach purchasers having made a purchase or potential purchasers picking up and examining a product.[69] It is also important that a subject is given ample time to consider their response.[70]

[31.35] The importance of survey evidence really resides in marginal cases and is reflected by the statement of Jacob J in *Neutrogena Corporation v Golden United*:[71]

"Ultimately the question is one for the court, not for the witnesses. It follows that if the judge's own opinion is that the case is marginal, one where he cannot be sure whether there is a likelihood of sufficient deception, the case will fail in the absence of enough evidence of the likelihood of deception. But if that opinion of the judge is supplemented by such evidence then it will succeed. And even if one's own opinion is that deception is unlikely though possible, convincing evidence of deception will carry the day."[72]

---

[66] (1989) FSR 100.

[67] *Laura Ashley Ltd v Coloroll Ltd* [1987] RPC 1.

[68] See also *Saville Perfumery Ltd v June Perfect Ltd* (1941) 58 RPC 147.

[69] *Reckitt & Colman v Borden* (1987) FSR 505.

[70] *Unilever plc v Johnson Wax Ltd* (1989) FSR 145.

[71] [1996] RPC 473, at 482.

[72] Cited with approval in *Neutrogena Corporation v Golden United* [1996] RPC 473, at 492.

Jacob J also stated the preference for evidence in chief by direct oral examination[73] and indeed the costs of survey evidence often make the oral evidence of a small number of witnesses a more attractive proposition for many litigants.

Transitional Provisions (Third Schedule)

[31.36] The transitional provisions are contained in the Third Schedule to the 1996 Act. In relation to the rights conferred by a registration, as and from the date of commencement of the 1996 Act, ie 1 July 1996, the distinction between Part A and B of the register is removed and consequently, the Part B defence under the 1963 Act no longer applies, ie it is not a defence for the defendant to show no likelihood of deception or confusion.[74] However, for use occurring prior to 1 July 1996, then it is the 1963 Act which applies in determining whether or not there is infringement.[75] It remains questionable if a Part B defence is available in such an instant because the use was still deemed an infringement and the Part B defence only provided for denial of injunctive or other relief and accordingly was not a defence to the infringement itself. For acts of infringement after 1 July 1996, it is necessary to determine if the plaintiff's mark is an 'existing registered mark' within Schedule 3, paragraph 1(1). This is defined as "a trade mark or certification trade mark, within the meaning of the Act of 1963, registered under that Act, immediately before commencement". Consequently, in most cases, it will be clear if the plaintiff's mark is an existing registered mark. The difficulty lies in cases where a trade mark application has been filed under the 1963 Act but which had not proceeded to registration by 1 July 1996. Such a mark does not appear to be caught by the definition of an existing registered mark because it was not registered "immediately before commencement". Under Schedule 3, paragraph 1(2), it would be treated as pending by virtue of not having been finally determined. It is unfortunate that 'finally determined' is not defined, but presumably, it would at least mean the expiry of the opposition period following advertisement and no opposition having been encountered.

[31.37] As and from 1 July 1996, the rights conferred on an existing registration are those under the 1996 Act.[76] However, it is not an infringement of an existing registered mark to continue after 1 July 1996 any use which did not amount to an infringement under the 1963 Act.[77] This provision also extends to a registered trade mark of which the distinctive elements are the same or substantially the

---

[73.] See also *Wagamama Ltd v City Centre Restaurants plc* [1995] FSR 713.
[74.] Trade Marks Act 1963, s 13(2).
[75.] Schedule 3, para 3(2).
[76.] Schedule 3, para 3(1).
[77.] Schedule 3, para 3(3).

same as those of an existing registered mark and which is registered for the same goods or services.[78] This is designed to protect a defendant against a plaintiff who applies to register the same mark and who in the absence of this provision, could allege infringement of the second registration. The reference to 'services' is erroneous because it is not possible to have an existing registered mark in respect of services since such were not provided for under the 1963 Act.

[31.38] A defendant claiming use prior to 1 July 1996 and thus a defence to infringement under the 1996 Act, must show a use which has 'continued'. The words 'continuously used' appeared in s 15 of the 1963 Act and reference to court decisions interpreting such will, no doubt, be made. Although there must be more than occasional use of the mark, it can still be somewhat intermittent.[79]

REMEDIES FOR INFRINGEMENT

[31.39] The 1996 Act provides for both civil and criminal remedies for infringement of a trade mark.

CIVIL REMEDIES

[31.40] An infringement is actionable by the trade mark proprietor.[80] It is also possible for an exclusive licensee to take an infringement action in specified circumstances.[81] Although rights extend from the date of filing, no infringement is possible until the trade mark is registered.[82] Section 18(2) of the 1996 Act, provides that damages, injunctions, accounts and other reliefs are available as in the case of infringement of any other intellectual property right.

Damages

[31.41] An award of damages is essentially an attempt to put the proprietor into the same position as if the infringement had not occurred. The methodology used to calculate damages in other areas of intellectual property is often by reference to the notional reasonable licence. In other words, if the infringer was a licensee under an arms length agreement, what royalty would have been expected? This is generally less suitable in cases of trade mark infringement where damages are more likely to be calculated based on lost sales to the proprietor but it is unlikely that every infringing sale will be viewed as a loss to

---

[78.] Schedule 3, para 3(3)(b).
[79.] *Smith Bartlett & Co Ltd v British Pure Oil, Crease & Carbide Co Ltd* (1934) 51 RPC 157.
[80.] Section 18(1).
[81.] Section 34.
[82.] Sections 13(3) and 13(4).

the plaintiff.[83] Innocence on the part of an infringer is no defence to a claim to damages.[84]

Account of Profits

[31.42] This is an alternative remedy to damages and being an equitable remedy it is discretionary. It is essentially an accountancy exercise and deprives the defendant of profits made as a result of the infringing activity. When a plaintiff elects in favour of an account of profits, he will in the normal case, get an account of what the defendant expended upon manufacturing the goods, the price received for their sale and obtain an order for the difference.[85]

Injunctions

[31.43] The normal criteria governing injunctive relief applies in relation to trade mark infringement. The Irish courts apply the decision of the Supreme Court in *Campus Oil Limited v Minister for Energy*[86] in determining whether or not to grant an interlocutory injunction. The test applied is whether a *bona fide* question has been raised by the person seeking relief. Secondly, the court considers the balance of convenience, and finally what irreparable damage would follow from any denial of the interlocutory injunction to the plaintiff. A decision on trade mark infringement and/or passing off at interlocutory stage, although designed to preserve the *status quo* pending a full hearing, tends to finally determine the issue particularly for a defendant against whom an injunction has been granted. The reality of the market is that a defendant will have relaunched a product under a different trade mark and is unlikely to pursue an action in respect of a trade mark which has now been superseded. The balance of convenience will usually favour the plaintiff unless there has been undue delay and it is impossible to calculate damages to the reputation of a plaintiff's trade mark by the existence of the defendant's product on the market since issues such as product quality come into focus as well as the obvious diminution of market share which may not be recoverable. The plaintiff who obtains an interlocutory injunction has to give a cross-undertaking as to damages to compensate the defendant for any damage caused by the injunction if it is lifted at a full hearing.

Other injunctive reliefs available are:

---

83. *Dormeuil Freres SA v Feraglow Ltd* [1990] RPC 449.
84. *Gillette UK Ltd v Edenwest Ltd* [1994] RPC 279.
85. *House of Spring Gardens Limited v Point Blank Ltd* [1983] FSR 489.
86. [1983] IR 88.

(a) Anton Piller Order

[31.44] An Anton Piller order arises where there is a serious risk that a defendant will destroy documents or evidence upon notice of the proceedings. It is consequently held ex parte and the jurisdiction of the court to make such an order is found under s 28 of the Judicature (Ireland) Act 1877. The order authorises entry and inspection and directs the defendant to give permission for such.

(b) Mareva injunction

[31.45] A *Mareva* injunction is a court order freezing the defendant's assets to ensure that they are not dissipated up to a certain value pending the trial of the action. Again, the basis for this injunction is to be found in s 28 of the Judicature (Ireland) Act 1877. It must be just and convenient which means that the balance of convenience lies with the plaintiff.[87] The presence of money or assets within the State, does not automatically confer a jurisdiction on the court to grant a *Mareva* injunction.[88]

(c) Quia Timet injunction

[31.46] This is an order preventing a defendant from carrying out a threatened act in violation of a plaintiff's right, even though such an act has not yet taken place. The proof required is "a well founded apprehension of injury - proof of actual and real danger - a strong probability almost amounting to a moral certainty".[89]

Erasure of Offending Sign

[31.47] This remedy is to be found in s 19 of the 1996 Act and only arises in cases where infringement has been found. As an alternative to delivery up, the High Court may instead order the offending sign to be removed from the infringing goods. If this is not reasonably practicable, then the High Court may order destruction. In the event of non-compliance or if the Court believes non-compliance is likely, an order may direct delivery to an authorised person for compliance.

Order for Delivery up of Infringing Goods, Material or Articles

[31.48] Sections 20, 22 and 23 of the 1996 Act, should be read together. Section 20 enables the trade mark proprietor to obtain a court order[90] for delivery up of any infringing goods, materials or articles. Subject to certain exceptions

---

87. *Harry Fleming & Ors v Ranks (Ireland) Ltd* (1983) ILRM 541.
88. *Serge Caudron & Ors v Air Zaire & Ors* [1986] ILRM 10.
89. *AG v Rathmines & Pembroke Joint Hospital Board* (1940) IR.
90. Includes Circuit Court - s 96.

concerning the disability of the trade mark proprietor or fraud or concealment on the part of the infringer, an order cannot be made after the end of a period of six years from the date on which the trade mark was applied to the goods, their packaging or the material or in the case of articles, the date on which they were made.[91] In interpreting similar delivery up provisions in the UK Copyright, Designs & Patents Act 1988, it was held in *Lagenes Limited v It's At (UK) Ltd*,[92] that an order may be made against a person who has an infringing copy in his possession in the course of business regardless of the existence of any knowledge on the part of that person that the copy is an infringing copy. All that is required is that 'a person' has possession, custody or control in the course of business and that person may not be the actual infringer. Thus, delivery orders could be made against persons engaged in storage or transportation. Section 20 does not limit the granting of an order to a situation in which infringement has been found to have occurred, unlike the position under s 19 dealing with erasure. No order will be made unless the court also makes or it appears to the court that there are grounds for making an order for destruction or forfeiture under s 23. If there has been an order for delivery up and no order for destruction or forfeiture, then the infringing goods, material or articles are retained by the person to whom there has been delivery up until a determination by the court.[93]

Order for Disposal of Infringing Goods, Materials or Articles

[31.49] Where an order for delivery up has been made under s 20, the High Court or the Circuit Court[94] may also order destruction or forfeiture.[95] In determining whether to grant such an order, the Court will have regard to whether other remedies are available which would be adequate to compensate and to protect the interests of the proprietor and any licensee[96] and, for example, a court may determine that damages are sufficient and order return of the goods, material or articles.[97] Section 23 sets out procedures whereby any person with an interest in the goods, materials or articles must be notified and their entitlement to appear in both proceedings for an order or an appeal against such an order.

'Infringing Goods, Material or Articles'

[31.50] The provisions dealing with the various remedies refer to infringing goods, material or articles. These are defined individually in s 21 of the 1996 Act.

[91.] Section 22.
[92.] [1991] FSR 492.
[93.] Section 20(3).
[94.] Section 96.
[95.] Section 23(1).
[96.] Section 23(2).
[97.] Section 23(5).

(a) Infringing goods

[31.51] This includes goods themselves or their packaging and which must bear a sign identical or similar to a registered trade mark. The application of the sign to the goods or their packaging must amount to an infringement. It is also provided that infringing goods include goods or their packaging which have been or are proposed to be imported into the State in circumstances where application of the mark in the State would constitute infringement. This is subject to the doctrine of exhaustion under EU law.[98] In consideration of a similar provision under UK copyright law, it was held that the relevant person to be considered is the person making the goods abroad and notionally this was taken to have been done in the UK to determine if there is infringement.[99] Infringing goods also include a situation where a sign has otherwise been used in relation to the goods in such a way as to infringe the trade mark registration.

(b) Infringing material

[31.52] This covers use on packaging, labelling, business paper and advertising material. Again, the material should bear a sign identical or similar to the registered trade mark in such a way as to infringe or it must be intended to be so used and such use would infringe.

(c) Infringing articles

[31.53] This covers articles specifically designed or adapted for making copies of an identical or similar sign and would, for example, include printing plates, moulds, photographic negatives, etc. These must be in the possession, custody or control of a person who knows or has reason to believe that they have been or are to be used to produce infringing goods or material. Once such a person is put on notice, then they have the requisite knowledge. In a scenario where a person who has control of the articles has the requisite knowledge but the person in possession does not, the articles are still deemed to be infringing articles.

Power of Seizure and Search

[31.54] Section 25 of the 1996 Act was introduced during the passage of the Bill through the Dáil and allows the District Court by way of an order to authorise a member of the Garda Síochána to seize infringing goods, material or articles without a warrant and by way of a warrant to enter premises. The goods, material or articles must then be brought before the Court which can order delivery up, destruction or forfeiture or that the goods are to be dealt with in any other way the court thinks fit.

---

98. See paras **[32.14]**-**[32.24]**.
99. *CBS United Kingdom v Charmdale Record Distributors* [1981] Ch 91.

Seizure by Customs Authorities

[31.55] Council Regulation (EC) No 3295/94[100] and Commission Regulation (EC) No 1367/95[101] have been implemented by the European Communities (Counterfeit and Pirated Goods) Regulations 1996.[102] These Regulations enable the proprietor or an authorised user of a registered trade mark or design or a copyright owner to apply to the Revenue Commissioners seeking the interception and detention of counterfeit and pirated goods. It is necessary to submit evidence of ownership of the requisite intellectual property and pay a £400 fee. The notification must be renewed and an additional fee paid every three months. The application can also be made by a representative of the right holder or authorised user. The normal procedure is for the Revenue Commissioners to supply a sample of goods taken from a consignment so that it can be confirmed that such is indeed a counterfeit or a pirated copy. It is necessary for an applicant to indemnify the Revenue Commissioners by way of security against all actions, proceedings, claims or demands consequent upon detention of the goods. Criminal sanctions are imposed against any person who makes a declaration for the release for free circulation, for export or for re-export in respect of goods found to be counterfeit or pirated.

CRIMINAL REMEDIES

[31.56] Criminal remedies exist in respect of certain acts identified in ss 92 to 94 and s 97 of the 1996 Act.

(a) Fraudulent Use of a Trade Mark

[31.57] Under s 92, it is an offence to carry out specified acts when there is no entitlement to use the mark in relation to the goods in question or there is no authorisation by a person who is so entitled. The specified acts are the application, selling, hiring, offering, exposing for sale or hire or the distribution of goods bearing a registered trade mark or to materials used or intended to be used for labelling, packaging or advertising goods. A slight variant of the registered trade mark will not be a defence because the provision also includes a mark so nearly resembling a registered trade mark. Also covered within the specified acts stated to constitute an offence, is the use of material bearing the mark in the course of a business for labelling, packaging or advertising the goods. It is also an offence to possess in the course of a business, goods or materials with a view to carrying out any of the offences or in order to assist a third party, knowing or having reason to believe that the third party has no

---

[100.] 22 December 1994; OJ L 341, 30.12.94, p 8.

[101.] 16 June 1995; OJ L133, 17.6.95, p 2.

[102.] SI 48/1996.

entitlement. There is no requirement that the goods upon which the offending mark is being used, actually fall within the specification of a registered trade mark. However, it is a defence to show a belief on reasonable grounds that there was an entitlement to use the mark on the goods in question. Counterfeiters would be unlikely to be in a position to avail of this defence but if there was legal uncertainty on issues such as whether or not the complained of mark was similar to the registered trade mark or the goods being identical or similar, then there is considerable scope for the defence to operate. An offence only arises if a person acts within a view to gain for himself or another, or with intent to cause a loss to another. Both inevitably arise in the case of counterfeit products. There is no provision for criminal liability in respect of unauthorised use of a mark in relation to services. Under s 13(4)(b), no offence arises in respect of acts carried out prior to publication of registration of the mark. On summary conviction, the liability is to a term of imprisonment not exceeding six months or a fine not exceeding £1,000 or both. On conviction on indictment, a term of imprisonment not exceeding five years or a fine not exceeding £100,000 or both, arises.

(b) Falsification of the Register

[31.58] Under s 93, it is an offence to make a false entry on the register knowing or having reason to believe such to be false. It is also an offence to produce a document which falsely purports to be an entry in the register.

(c) Falsely representing a Trade Mark as being registered

[31.59] Under s 94 of the 1996 Act, it is an offence to falsely represent a trade mark as being registered, knowing or having reason to believe that the representation is false. This includes use of the word 'registered' or any other word or device importing a reference to registration, express or implied. This would include an abbreviated term of the word registered such as 'regd' and also presumably the symbol ® which is a recognised abbreviation for registered. The initials TM simply stand for trade mark. They do not imply registration and consequently, no offence arises where TM is used in conjunction with an unregistered trade mark. There is no offence if it can be shown that the reference is in fact to registration outside the State for the goods or services upon which the trade mark is being used.[103] This results from the decision in *Pall v Dahlhausen*[104] where it was held that a provision in German unfair competition law which prohibited the circulation of goods with the R symbol where the mark was not registered, contravened Article 30 of the Treaty of Rome. However, this defence in s 94(2) is not limited to instances where the trade mark is only registered in another EU country. In the UK case of *Johnson v Puffer*,[105] an

---

[103.] Section 94(2).
[104.] [1990] ECR 4827.
[105.] (1930) 47 RPC 95.

interlocutory injunction was denied in a passing off action where the plaintiff falsely indicated its trade mark as being registered, but questions have been asked whether this is still good law and whether such is likely to be followed at any full hearing of an action.[106] A person guilty of an offence under this section is liable on summary conviction to a fine not exceeding £1,000 and in the case of a continuing offence, to a further fine not exceeding £100 for every day on which the offence continues.[107]

Unauthorised Use of State Emblems of Ireland

[31.60] Under Article 6 *ter* of the Paris Convention, the Irish government have registered both the harp and shamrock devices as being State emblems. These emblems or any future emblems which may be registered by the State, cannot be used in connection with any business without the authority of the Minister.[108] The prohibition also extends to emblems so closely resembling the State emblems as to be calculated to deceive or to lead to the belief that there is authorisation. The Minister can injunct such use.[109] A defence to the prohibition arises if the user is the owner of a registered mark containing the emblem.[110] Indeed, there are a large number of trade mark registrations on the Irish Register containing the shamrock device. Under the Trade Mark Rules 1963,[111] the Controller had a discretion to refuse a mark in which the device of a shamrock or where the word SHAMROCK appeared in relation to goods other than goods expressly of Irish origin.[112] This meant that if the trade mark proprietor amended the specification to indicate Irish origin or made it a condition of registration that the goods were of Irish origin, the Controller allowed the application. Under the 1996 Act, it remains to be seen if the Minister will give a consent to an application containing a state emblem because without such, a trade mark application must be refused.[113] At least in relation to the device of a shamrock, this is really more an indication of Irish origin and provided an applicant undertakes to use the trade mark on goods or services of Irish origin, there is no reason for the Minister to refuse to consent to registration and/or use of what is already a heavily utilised trade mark by many Irish entities.

[31.61] The Minister also has power to issue proceedings abroad against the use or registration of trade marks which are deceptive if not used in relation to Irish

---

[106.] Kerly's *Law of Trade Marks* (12th ed) p 478; *Jamieson v Jamieson* (1898) 15 RPC 169, at 191.

[107.] Section 94(3).

[108.] Section 97(1).

[109.] Section 97(3).

[110.] Section 97(4).

[111.] SI 268/1963.

[112.] Rule 12(1)(b).

[113.] Section 9.

goods or services.[114] This is not limited to emblems registered under Article 6 *ter* of the Paris Convention. It would, for example include the words 'Ireland' or 'Irish'.

Offences committed by Partnerships and Bodies Corporate

[31.62] Proceedings in respect of any offence committed by a partnership under the 1996 Act, must be brought against the partnership in the name of the firm and not in that of the partners.[115] Every partner is also subject to proceedings and punished if there has been an offence by the partnership unless they can prove that they were ignorant of the commission of the offence or attempted to prevent it.[116] In relation to a company, if the offence was committed with the consent, connivance of or attributable to any neglect by a director, manager, secretary or similar officer, then such a person is subject to the same set of proceedings and fines as against the company.[117]

GROUNDLESS THREATS OF INFRINGEMENT PROCEEDINGS

[31.63] Section 24 of the 1996 Act makes provision for certain forms of relief in the event of groundless threats of infringement. Similar provisions exist under the Patents Act 1992 and formerly under the Patents Act 1964. Prior to the 1996 Act, relief had to be sought through the laws of trade libel and it was necessaryto show not just that the threat was calculated to injure the plaintiff's trade or to diminish the value of his goods but also that the party had acted in bad faith.[118] In *Bestobell Paints Ltd v Bigg*,[119] Oliver J stated that:

> "no interlocutory injunction will be granted in defamation proceedings, where the defendant announces his intention of justifying, to restrain him from publishing the alleged defamatory statement until its truth or untruth has been determined at the trial, except in cases where the statement is obviously untruthful and libellous"

and extended this principle to trade libel. An interlocutory injunction was granted to restrain threats of passing off in *Essex Electric (Pte) Ltd v IPC Computers (UK) Ltd*,[120] it being held that there is jurisdiction in a court to restrain, either completely or partially, the commencement of proceedings which the court would regard as an abuse of its process and as a corollary, there must likewise be jurisdiction to restrain in some instances, the making of threats to

---

[114] Section 98.
[115] Section 95(1).
[116] Section 95(3).
[117] Section 95(4).
[118] *Colley v Hart* (1890) 7 RPC 101. *Speed Seal v Paddington* [1986] 1 All ER 91.
[119] [1975] FSR 421, at 430.
[120] [1991] FSR 690.

commence proceedings.[121] Also, the normal rules granting an interlocutory injunction may apply if the plaintiff's case is based on a defendant's unlawful interference with the plaintiff's contractual relations with third parties.[122] The statutory provision appears to be primarily designed to protect against threats made to parties other than an alleged primary infringer. A typical example would be a manufacturer's customer who may be more inclined to switch suppliers rather than risk an infringement suit with the resultant loss of business. No right of action for groundless threats exists where the alleged infringement is said to arise out of:

(a) the application of the mark to goods;

(b) the importation of goods to which the mark has been applied; or

(c) the supply of services under this mark.

What remains are a number of instances where a trade mark owner or their legal representative must be extremely cautious in the issuance of a cease and desist letter threatening proceedings for trade mark infringement. This includes instances where the alleged infringer is affixing the mark to packaging, offering as opposed to supplying services and using the mark in advertising and would cover wholesalers, retailers and distributors.

[31.64] The reliefs available to the aggrieved party are an injunction to stop the threats from continuing, a declaration that the threats are unjustified and damages sustained as a result of the threats. A defendant will usually plead justification and counterclaim for infringement. The injunctive relief is important because at an interlocutory stage, the balance of convenience would usually favour a plaintiff seeking a cessation of the threats prior to a full hearing of the action. In almost all cases, it will be readily apparent as to whether or not a person is an aggrieved party. It would obviously include the persons against whom the threat is made and manufacturers, suppliers or distributors of the pertinent goods. The relief is equally available to the owner of a CTM and an international mark entitled to protection in the State.[123] The onus is on a defendant to show that the threats were justified and that the complained of acts do constitute an infringement.[124] If the plaintiff can prove invalidity or revoke the registration in any relevant respect, then there is an entitlement to the relief.[125]

[121.] See also *Landi Den Hartog BV v Sea Bird (Clean Air Fuel Systems) Ltd* [1976] FSR 489.
[122.] *Microdata Information Services Ltd v Rivendale Ltd* [1991] FSR 681.
[123.] Section 57(4). Section 59(3).
[124.] Section 24(3).
[125.] Section 24(4).

[31.65] A mere notification that a trade mark is registered or that an application for registration has been made, does not constitute a threat. Since the threat must be made against another, a general threat placed in an advertisement and not directed to a particular person is not actionable. A court will decide on what constitutes a threat through the eyes of a reasonable and normal recipient. Verbal statements can amount to threats.[126] The fact that it is not explicit that infringement proceedings will be taken is not conclusive because a threat can be veiled or implied just as much as it can be explicit. Also, a communication may constitute a threat against a person other than the recipient.[127] What is quite bizarre is that apart from the law of trade libel, there is no prohibition on threats to take an action for passing off or criminal proceedings for counterfeiting. However, if a party threatens passing off and in the same communication notifies the recipient of the existence of trade mark registrations, this is likely to be viewed as an implied threat of infringement and thus actionable.

[31.66] In *Symonds Cider & English Wine Co Ltd v Showerings (Ireland) Ltd*[128] Laffoy J had cause to consider s 24 which was raised by way of a counterclaim in defence of proceedings seeking an interlocutory injunction and commented:

> "At the time the defendant initiated its application under s 24 the jurisdiction conferred by s 24 was spent. The jurisdiction conferred by s 24 relates to threats of proceedings. When as happened here, a threat of proceedings burgeons into an action in this court against the party threatened, in my view, it is not open to the party against whom the action has been taken to retaliate by invoking s 24. It is true that on this construction of s 24 a party threatening proceedings may pre-empt an application under s 24 by issuing a plenary summons. However, I believe this is what the legislature intended in enacting s 24. Once a plenary summons is issued, the matter is within the seisin of this court and, if necessary, the party who was threatened can invoke the rules of procedure of this court to ensure that the issue between him and the party who issued the threat is dealt with."

[31.67] In *Trebor Bassett Ltd v The Football Association*[129] the plaintiff successfully brought an action for groundless threats and obtained a declaration of non-infringement. The defendant's cross action for infringement was held to be an abuse of the process of the court and was struck out.

---

126. *Lunar Advertising Co Ltd v Burnham & Co* (1928) 45 RPC 258.
127. *Bowden Controls Ltd v Acco Cable Controls Ltd* [1990] RPC 427.
128. High Court, unrep, 10 January 1997 (6155P/1996).
129. [1997] FSR 211.

Chapter 32

Trade Marks Act 1996: Limitations On Rights Conferred

USE OF A REGISTERED TRADE MARK

[32.01] The provisions of s 15(1) of the Trade Marks Act 1996 are similar to those of s 12(4) of the Trade Marks Act 1963 and provides a defence to an infringement action in circumstances where there is concurrent registration by the defendant and use of the mark on goods or services embraced by the defendant's registration. This provision is subject to s 52(6) and where the defendant's mark is subsequently declared invalid then to the extent of the invalidity the registration is deemed never to have been made. The section will undoubtedly be narrowly interpreted and will require use by the defendant in the exact form in which its trade mark is registered. There is no equivalent to s 51(2) which allows for use in a form differing in elements which do not alter the distinctive character of the mark. For this reason, it is particularly important to register a mark in the exact form in which it is used. It will also be necessary for the defendant to use its registered trade mark in respect of the exact goods and/ or services embraced by the registration. Use outside the goods of registration will mean this defence is not available in respect of those particular goods and/ or services. It should be noted that this particular defence is not provided for under the Trade Mark Harmonisation Directive[1] and consequently, it could be argued that this is in breach of Community law. Indeed, it does not fit easily into the system under the CTM Regulation[2] whereby there is no citation of a prior registered mark and it is left to the proprietor of an earlier registration to formally oppose following advertisement. This requires proprietors of registered marks to be vigilant, not just in the market place, but by closely observing the Irish, CTM and international registers otherwise they may find that at least interlocutory relief will be denied and no remedy will be available until the conclusion of an invalidity action. This statutory defence does not affect the position at common law and consequently a possible action for passing off.

[1.] 89/104/EEC.
[2.] 40/94.

DESCRIPTIVE USES

Use of one's own name and address

[32.02] Section 15(2)(a) provides that the use by a person of his own name or address shall not amount to an infringement of a registered trade mark. A similar provision existed under s 16 of the 1963 Act which required that such use be *bona fide*. A proviso to s 15(2) requires that the use be in accordance with honest practices in industrial and commercial matters which is the wording used in Article 6(1)(a) of the Trade Mark Harmonisation Directive[3] except that the word "or" is used as opposed to "and". However, this is unlikely to have any significance in practice. What will have to be determined by the courts is whether or not use by a company of its incorporated name amounts to a defence. It would still have to fulfil the criteria of being an honest practice and this would exclude parties who had knowledge of the plaintiff's rights. In *Parker-Knoll Ltd v Knoll International Ltd*,[4] the defence was held to extend to the *bona fide* use by a company of its incorporated name with or without use of its corporate status, eg 'Ltd'. However, whether or not this will remain the position is doubtful given the minutes of the Council Meeting at which the CTM Regulation was adopted and which stated that the Council and the Commission consider that the words "his own name" apply only in respect of natural persons. This is consistent with the law of passing off and whereby *bona fide* use of one's own name is not a defence if the name was used on goods.[5]

Description of the Goods or Services

[32.03] Section 15(2)(b) provides as follows:

(2) A registered trade mark shall not be infringed by ...

(b) the use of indications concerning the kind, quality, quantity, intended purpose, value, geographical origin, the time or production of goods or of rendering of the service or other characteristics of goods or services; ...

Again, this is subject to the proviso that such use is in accordance with honest practices in industrial and commercial matters. The wording is taken from Article 6(1)(b) of the Harmonisation Directive.[6] The difference between this provision and that in s 16(b) of the 1963 Act is that to avail of the defence under the 1963 Act, it was necessary to show that the *bona fide* description was not likely to impart a reference as having the right to use the mark by virtue of being the registered proprietor or registered user. The type of question which will arise

---

3. 89/104/EEC.
4. [1962] RPC 265.
5. *Rodgers v Rodgers* (1924) 41 RPC 277.
6. 89/104/EEC.

to be determined under s 15(2)(b) is the question of using a third party's trade mark to describe, for example, an ingredient in a product or that it is compatible with a particular product. Thus, it becomes necessary to read s 15(2)(b) in conjunction with s 14(6) which generally allows use of a third party's trade mark for the purpose of identifying goods or services of the registered proprietor. Taking the example of identification of an ingredient in a finished product by reference to a registered trade mark, this would come under s 14(6). As for the finished product itself, the use is not use as a trade mark in relation to the finished product but it is attributing a certain characteristic to the finished product and would consequently be a defence under s 15(2)(b). It will be necessary that no undue prominence is given to the registered trade mark, otherwise it is arguable whether or not the use is honest. The courts will have to proceed with caution and it will be noted that unlike s 15(2)(c), there is no statement in s 15(2)(b) that there can be use of a trade mark, but what is being allowed is use of an *indication*. The difference in wording between the two provisions in (b) and (c) suggests that (b) must be more limited on its scope of application. There will be instances in which what might normally have been considered an indication has, through usage, acquired a distinctiveness and become registerable as a trade mark. The courts may consider such as no longer an indication when used on products not genuinely having a characteristic due to the trade mark owners' own product/service even if it is, for example, a quality or quantity descriptor or describes the geographical origin of the goods/services. In *British Sugar plc v James Robertson & Sons Ltd*,[7] Jacob J considered the corresponding section under the UK Trade Marks Act 1994[8] and held that if a word was being used as a trade mark for the defendant's goods, then it would not be covered by the defence, even if outside the context of such use it was descriptive.

Use of a Trade Mark to Indicate Intended Purpose: Accessories and Spare Parts

[32.04] Section 15(2)(c) provides:

(2) A registered trade mark shall not be infringed by ...

(c) the use of the trade mark where it is necessary to indicate the intended purpose of a product or service, in particular, as accessories or spart parts;

Provided that such use is in accordance with honest practices in industrial and commercial matters.

[7.] [1996] RPC 281.
[8.] Section 11(2).

This provision corresponds to Article 6(1)(c) of the Harmonisation Directive.[9] A problem for a defendant in seeking to rely on this provision is the requirement that such use must be "necessary". The provision in s 12(3)(b) of the 1963 Act used the words "reasonably necessary" and a court will have to determine if an absolute necessity is required under s 15(2)(c). Even if this restrictive interpretation were adopted by the courts, it may not have too profound an impact because in most instances, a defendant will be entitled to avail of the defence in s 15(2)(b) as an indication of the intended purpose.

Honest Practices in Industrial and Commercial Matters

[32.05] All of the defences in s 15(2) require that the defendant's use be in accordance with honest practices in industrial and commercial matters. These words are totally new to Irish trade mark law and there are no definitions given as an aid to interpretation. In due course, the courts will have to address this question not jut under s 15(2) but also under s 14(6) which also uses the words "honest practices". In *Barclays Bank plc v RBS Advanta*,[10] Laddie J held that this test is objective and is determined by reference to members of a reasonable audience and disagreed that the court should look to statutory or industry agreed codes of conduct to determine whether the advertisement is honest. Laddie J went on to hold that "honesty has to be gauged against what is reasonably to be expected by the relevant public". This interpretation seems to ignore the reference to industrial and commercial matters which requires the courts to apply a subjective test by reference to trade practices. The reluctance to apply a subjective test does, of course, lead to anomalies which were expressed by Aldous J in *Provident Financial plc v Halifax Building Society*,[11] namely it results in an uninformed fool having a defence whereas a properly informed reasonable man would not. However, the difference between the 1996 Act and the provision in s 16 of the 1963 Act is that the actions of the defendant must be compared against what would be considered honest practice in a particular trade. In most cases, what is dishonest applies right across industry generally and decisions under the 1963 Act where there is *male fides* or dishonesty would still be upheld under s 15.[12] However, instances will arise where trade practices are such that the conduct of a defendant will not be viewed as dishonest and, for example, in the computer industry, it is the norm to prominently refer to another company's trade mark in the context of compatibility.

---

9. 89/104/EEC.
10. [1996] RPC 307.
11. [1994] FSR 81, at 93.
12. *Teofani Co Ltd v Teofani* (1913) 30 RPC 446; *IZAL Trade Mark* (1935) 52 RPC 399.

Use of an Earlier Right

[32.06] Section 15 of the 1963 Act provided a defence to infringement in the case of continuous use by the defendant from a date prior to registration or use by the registered proprietor. A somewhat similar, but more limited, provision exists under s 15(3) of the 1996 Act which provides:

> (3) A registered trade mark shall not be infringed by the use in the course of trade in a particular locality of an earlier right which applies only in that locality.

It is still a requirement that use by the defendant be continuously made but it is limited to a particular locality and does necessitate the defendant showing an earlier right by way of any rule of law and in particular, the law of passing off which would protect use in that particular locality.

[32.07] Section 15(3) implements Article 6(2) of the Harmonisation Directive[13] but in doing so, does not follow the exact wording. The Directive indicates that the earlier right is a defence to an infringement claim whereas s 15(3) states that use of the earlier mark does not actually amount to an infringement and thus no cause of action arises in the first place. Section 15(4) is stated as defining what is meant by an earlier right for the purposes of s 15(3). This definition differs from that of an earlier right in s 11 and s 15(4) would probably overrule the definition in s 2 which states that an earlier right should be defined by reference to s 11. An earlier right in s 15(3) means an unregistered trade mark or other sign which has been continuously used in relation to goods and services from a date prior to the use of the registered trade mark or its registration, whichever is the earlier.

[32.08] Article 6(2) of the Harmonisation Directive states:

> The trade mark shall not entitle the proprietor to prohibit a third party from using, in the course of trade, an earlier right which only applies in a particular locality if that right is recognised by the laws of the Member State in question and within the limits of the territory in which it is recognised.

There is no definition in either the Directive or the 1996 Act as to what is meant by a locality and it remains to be decided if in fact it can embrace a whole country and it is notable that no similar provision exists under the CTM Regulation.[14] The concept of the CTM is alien to that of local trade marks and treats the whole of the European Union as one territory. If a national registration were treated on the same footing, then the whole of Ireland would not be viewed as a locality. The rationale of the provision is to cater for the position where there are localised earlier rights and to this limited extent, co-existence is

---

13. 89/104/EEC.
14. 90/94.

tolerated. If the earlier rights extend to the whole State, then an action for invalidity is appropriate under s 52(2) or alternatively, there may be a defence that a likelihood of confusion does not exist.

[32.09] What is meant by continuous use in the context of s 15(4) in determining whether or not an earlier rights exists, will have to be decided in conjunction with the requirement that the use is such that it would sustain an action for passing off. This would mean that use can be somewhat interrupted. There are many instances in which plaintiffs have succeeded in passing off actions where their businesses have been shut down for some time.[15] The courts are likely to look at any circumstances surrounding the interrupted use and whether such has affected the goodwill rather than simply taking a liberal meaning of the word continuous. Even the words "continuously used" in s 15 did not carry this literal interpretation.[16] It is somewhat an anomaly that the continuous use must be in relation to the goods or services of the registration and does not extend to similar goods or services which are now protected by way of registration under s 14(2). This is unlikely to have been the intention of the legislature because clearly, if there is an earlier right which meets the other criteria in s 15(4), then there is an even stronger case that it should lie as a defence against an action for infringement based on similar goods.

[32.10] Although s 15(3) requires continuous use prior to use or registration by the proprietor, it does not state that the goodwill must exist at that time. A scenario could exist whereby there was a small amount of continuous use prior to registration or use by the proprietor but the defendant's goodwill accrued through subsequent usage. Again, it is doubtful that this was the intention of the legislature but it arises from a failure to properly define an earlier right as necessitating the requisite goodwill prior to the registrant's own rights and which appears to be the position under Article 6(2) of the Harmonisation Directive.

Use in order to identify proprietor's own goods or services

[32.11] Section 14(6) provides for a defence to infringement in circumstances where there is:

- use for the purposes of identifying the goods or services of the trade mark owner or licensee; and

---

[15.] *Ad-Lib Club Ltd v Granville* [1972] RPC 673; *A Levey v Henderson-Kenton (Holdings) Ltd* [1974] RPC 617.

[16.] *Smith, Bartlett & Co v British Pure Oil Grease and Carbide Co* (1934) 51 RPC 157, at 163.

-   where such use without due cause, does not take unfair advantage of or is detrimental to, the distinctive character or reputation of the trade mark.

It is quite legitimate to use another person's trade mark to describe the compatibility or suitability of a particular product being, for example, a spare part or accessory. In the computer industry, it is common to identify software or hardware compatibility by reference to another company's trade mark. A regular instance of use of another's mark is in comparative advertising.[17] This defence was successfully raised in the case of *Barclays Bank plc v RBS Advanta*[18] where in considering the corresponding section in the UK Trade Marks Act 1994, the High Court held that the primary objective was to allow for comparative advertising. So long as the use of the competitor's mark is honest, then there is nothing wrong with informing the public of the relative merits of competing goods or services and using registered trade marks to identify them. What was honest was held to be an objective test by reference to members of a reasonable audience. It was stated by Laddie J:

> "The fact that the advertising pokes fun at the proprietor's goods or services and emphasises the benefits of the defendant's is a normal incidence of comparative advertising. Its aim will be to divert customers from the proprietor. No reasonable observer would expect one trader to point to all the advantages of its competitor's business and failure to do so does not *per se* take the advertising outside what reasonable people would regard as 'honest'. Thus mere trade puffery, even if uncomfortable to the registered proprietor, does not bring the advertising within the scope of trade mark infringement. Much advertising is recognised by the public as hyperbole. The Act does not impose on the courts an obligation to try to enforce, through the back door of trade mark legislation, a more puritanical standard. If, on the other hand, a reasonable reader is likely to say, on being given the full facts, that the advertisement is no honest, for example, because it is significantly misleading, then the protection from trade mark infringement is removed."

The nature of the goods or services may affect the reasonable perception of what advertising is honest. There is no requirement to identify the owner or licensee of the trade mark or that it is in fact a trade mark by, for example, use of the initials TM.

ACQUIESCENCE

[32.12] This is a totally new concept to Irish trade mark law and its introduction in s 53 of the 1996 Act is by way of implementation of Article 9 of the Trade

---

[17.] See Ch 31.
[18.] [1966] RPC 307.

Mark Harmonisation Directive.[19] Acquiescence arises where the proprietor of an earlier trade mark or right has acquiesced for a continuous period of five years in the use of a later registered trade mark in the State. It is required that the proprietor of the earlier trade mark or right was aware of such usage. The effect of acquiescence is that it is no longer possible to seek invalidity of the later registration or to oppose continued use for those goods or services in relation to which there has been acquiescence. It would not prevent an action against use on similar goods/services to that for which the acquiescence took place. Essentially, what takes place if s 53 is invoked is an enforced co-existence of trade marks, since even in the case of acquiescence, the proprietor of the later mark cannot invoke its mark against use of the earlier mark or exploitation of the earlier right. Each party must tolerate each other's usage. A claim of acquiescence will not be upheld if it can be shown that the registration of the later trade mark was applied for in bad faith.

[32.13] Acquiescence is stated to deny the proprietor of the earlier trade mark or right the ability "to oppose the use of the later trade mark". This strange wording leaves open an argument that all that is denied is injunctive relief, and that damages or other remedies may still be available, which is a bizarre scenario with which the courts are unlikely to find favour. The acquiescence must be to the use of a registered mark. However, the knowledge required is in relation to *use* as opposed to *registration*. Thus, a situation could possibly exist where the owner of the earlier trade mark may know of the existence of a registration for over five years but will not have acquiesced where their knowledge of use of the later registered mark is less than five years. Although the courts are likely to adopt constructive notice as a criteria, it is reasonably common for many marks to be registered for some time before being used. Therefore, the mere fact of registration should not constitute constructive notice that the mark is in actual use. There is no provision for acquiescence where the later trade mark is unregistered. Section 53 is limited to acquiescence in the use of the mark which is on the register.

EXHAUSTION OF RIGHTS/PARALLEL IMPORTS

[32.14] This limitation on the right to enforce a trade mark is common to intellectual property law in general. The doctrine is specifically stated in s 16 of the 1996 Act and Article 7 of the Trade Mark Harmonisation Directive. A registered proprietor cannot pursue an infringement action if the goods are the proprietor's own goods which have been put onto the market in the European economic area either by the proprietor or with its consent, for example, by a subsidiary or licensee. The doctrine is a reconciliation between the right to

---

[19.] 89/104/EEC.

enforce an intellectual property right weighed against the objective of allowing the free movement of goods throughout the European Union. Article 30 of the Treaty of Rome provides that: "Quantitative restrictions on imports and all measures having equivalent effect shall be prohibited between Member States".

[32.15] Normally this means that goods lawfully put on sale in one EU country must be acceptable throughout the EU and national laws cannot prohibit free movement. Article 36 provides for a derogation on several grounds which include the protection of industrial and commercial property, ie intellectual property, where such does not constitute a means of arbitrary discrimination or a disguised restriction on trade between Member States. Thus, Article 36 recognises that the owner of a national trade mark registration can rely on the protection afforded by such to prevent the importation of goods under a trade mark which infringes that national registration even though the trade mark is legitimately used in other countries of the EU. However, if the goods are those of the proprietor or a licensee, then any attempt to prevent importation by the proprietor is in effect, a disguised restriction on trade. What is permitted is control by the proprietor of the first marketing in the European Economic Area.

[32.16] Initially, cases were decided under the anti-competition laws of the Treaty of Rome and in particular, Article 85. In *Grundig & Consten v Commission*,[20] an agreement was held by the ECJ to be a deliberate attempt to use trade marks to prevent price competition by way of parallel imports. The agreement was between the German manufacturer Grundig and its sole distributor in France, Consten. Under the agreement, the distributor was allowed to register in its own name, the trade mark GINT. Grundig not only applied its own GRUNDIG trade mark to products but also the trade mark GINT and thus the distributor claimed infringement when a parallel import occurred. The ECJ considered that the aim of the agreement was to isolate the French market for Grundig products and distort competition. The Court went on to draw a distinction between recognition of the existence or ownership of intellectual property rights as stated under Article 222 of the Rome Treaty and the exercise of such rights which can be curtailed in certain circumstances such as anti-competitive agreements under Article 85(1). The early cases saw a general hostility to trade marks as exclusive rights limited by national registrations and in *Sirena Srl v Eda Srl*,[21] the ECJ stated:

> "The exercise of a trade mark right is particularly apt to lead to a partitioning of markets, and thus to impair the free movement of goods between states which is essential to the common market. Moreover, a trade mark right is

---

20. [1996] ECR 299.
21. [1971] ECR 69.

distinguishable in this context from other rights of industrial and commercial property in as much as the interests protected by the latter are usually more important, and merit a higher degree of protection, than the interests protected by an ordinary trade mark".

[32.17] Continuing with the principle of distinguishing between the existence and exercise of an intellectual property right, the ECJ considered subsequent cases under Articles 30 to 36 of the Treaty of Rome and developed the doctrine of exhaustion. In *Deutsche Grammophon v Metro SB*[22] which was a copyright case, the ECJ held that a German record company could not rely on copyright to stop a supermarket from selling sound recordings bought from the record company's French distributor. The application of the doctrine of exhaustion to trade marks was illustrated in *Centrafarm BV v Winthrop BV*[23] and where the ECJ gave a definition as what the court viewed as the specific subject matter of a trade mark:

> "In relation to trade marks, the specific subject matter of the industrial property is the guarantee that the owner of the trade mark has the exclusive right to use that trade mark, for the purpose of putting products protected by the trade mark into circulation for the first time, and is therefore intended to protect him against competitors wishing to take advantage of the status and reputation of the trade mark by selling products illegally bearing that trade mark".

This narrow interpretation of the function of a trade mark led to a rigorous application of the doctrine of exhaustion in *Van Zuylen Freres v Hag Ag (Hag I)*[24] which is a heavily criticised decision of the ECJ and their attempt to deal with what is termed trade marks of common origin. Prior to the Second World War, a German company owned the HAG trade mark in Germany and a subsidiary of the German company held the registration in Belgium. After the Second World Ward, the rights in Belgium were sequestrated and assigned to Van Zuylen. The German company commenced selling goods under the trade mark in Belgium and it was claimed that this amounted to infringement. The ECJ held that because the registrations had a common origin, the German product was to be considered as a parallel import and did not constitute infringement. The Court viewed the basic function of a trade mark as being to guarantee to consumers that the product has the same origin. In *Terrapin v Terranova*,[25] the ECJ emphasised that national trade mark rights held by different undertakings could prevent importation, provided that there were no agreements restricting competition and no legal or economic ties between the

---

22. [1971] ECR 487.
23. [1974] ECR 1183.
24. [1974] ECR 731.
25. [1976] ECR 1039.

undertakings and their respective rights had arisen independently of one another. A national registration can even be used to stop importation under a non-distinctive trade mark as illustrated in *Deutsche Renault AG v Audi AG*[26] where the word QUATTRO meaning the number four in Italian was registered in Germany on evidence being provided of distinctiveness through usage.

[32.18] The ECJ has more recently recognised the importance of trade marks not just to owners but to consumers and have relaxed the boundaries of the doctrine of exhaustion by emphasising the need for full consent by the trade mark proprietor or its licensee to the first marketing. This was already recognised under patent law where a compulsory licence was not viewed as a consent.[27] The ECJ was prepared to disapprove of their decision in *Hag I* and in *CNL-Sucal NV v HAG AG (Hag II)*,[28] reached a different decision to *Hag I* although factually the cases could not be distinguished. In *Hag II*, there was a reverse set of facts whereby the Belgium company sought to sell into the German market. The ECJ stated:

> "Trade mark rights are, it should be noted, an essential element in the system of undistorted competition which the Treaty seeks to establish and maintain. Under such a system, an undertaking must be in a position to keep its customers by virtue of the quality of its products and services, something which is possible only if there are distinctive marks which enable customers to identify those products and services. For the trade mark to be able to fulfil this role, it must offer a guarantee that all goods bearing it have been produced under the control of a single undertaking which is accountable for their quality".

The ECJ emphasised the determining factor to be the absence of any consent on the part of the proprietor of the trade mark protected by national legislation in a situation where the first marketing is by an undertaking which is economically and legally independent. The ECJ also pointed out that the essential function of the trade mark would be jeopardised because of possible confusion by the public. In *IHT Internazionale Heiztechnick GmbH v Ideal Standard GmbH*,[29] the ECJ had to consider the situation of trade marks of common origin and a voluntary assignment to an unconnected assignee. It was held that the consent implicit in any assignment is not the consent required for application of the doctrine of exhaustion of rights. For that, the owner of the right in the importing State must, directly or indirectly, be able to determine the products to which the trade mark may be affixed in the exporting State and to control their quality.

---

[26] [1993] 1 CMLR 421.
[27] *Pharmon BV v Hoechst AG* [1985] ECR 2281.
[28] [1990] ECR 1-3711.
[29] [1994] ECR 1-2789.

That power was held to be lost if, by assignment, control over the trade mark is surrendered to a third party having no economic link with the assignor.

[32.19] It is no defence to a claim of exhaustion to show that first marketing was in a Member State where there was in fact no protection[30] or that there is a divergence between the laws of the EU Member States concerned.[31]

[32.20] It is doubtful whether the Irish courts will allow international exhaustion. The wording in s 16(1) does specify that the trade mark proprietor should put the product on sale in the European economic area. In *EMI Records Ltd v CBS*,[32] the ECJ held that Article 30 did not apply to goods coming from outside the EU. The trade mark owner could rely on a national registration to prevent importation from the USA. It is left to each Member State to determine whether or not to adopt the minimum EEA exhaustion or international exhaustion. In the UK under their Trade Marks Act 1938, corresponding to the Irish 1963 Act, the Court of Appeal did not support international exhaustion in the case of *Revlon Inc v Cripps & Lee Ltd*[33] but this was distinguished in *Colgate-Palmolive v Markwell Finance Ltd*[34] where the quality of the product first sold in Brazil did not correspond to that on sale under the trade mark in the UK.[35]

[32.21] Exhaustion of rights does not take effect where the goods have been changed or impaired after they have been put onto the market and consequently under s 16(2) there exists legitimate reasons for the proprietor of the trade mark to oppose further dealings in the goods.[36] The question of repackaging and re-labelling of trade marked goods has already been considered by the ECJ in a number of cases. In *Hoffmann La Roche & Co v Centrafarm*,[37] the importer purchased valium in the UK, repacking it in different quantities for the German market, adding the trade mark with its own name and address. The ECJ held that it was permissible to oppose the importation and sale. The essential function of a trade mark was to guarantee to consumers the original identity of the trade marked product. This requires that the goods have not been tampered with. The ECJ set out guidelines under which an importer could avoid infringement. Thus, in *Pfizer Inc v Eurim-Pharm GmbH*,[38] repackaging took place but the packaging

---

30. *Merck & Co v Stephar BV* [1981] ECR 2063.
31. *Keurkoop BV v Nancy Kean Gifts BV* [1982] ECR 2853.
32. [1976] ECR 811.
33. [1980] FSR 85.
34. [1989] RPC 497.
35. See also *Castrol Ltd v Automotive Oil Supplies Ltd* [1983] RPC 315.
36. Section 16(2).
37. [1978] ECR 1139.
38. [1981] ECR 2913.

clearly indicated that the goods were repackaged and imported and consumers were not misled as to origin, hence there was no infringement.

[32.22] In *Bristol-Myers Squibb v Paranova*[39] the ECJ emphasised that the parallel importer should engage in the least amount of tampering with the original packaging necessary to market in the Member State of importation and stated:

> "The owner may oppose the repackaging of the product in the new external packaging where the importer is able to achieve packaging which may be marketed in the Member State of importation by, for example, affixing to the original external or inner packaging new labels in the language of the Member State of importation, or by adding new user instructions or information in the language of the Member State of importation, or by replacing an additional article not capable of gaining approval in the Member State of importation with a similar article that has obtained such approval."

In a series of cases[40] the ECJ listed stringent requirements with which a parallel importer must comply when repackaging goods, particularly pharmaceutical products, namely:

(a) he must indicate on the external packaging who repackaged the product and who manufactured the product, printed in such a way as to be understood by a person with normal eyesight exercising a normal degree of attentiveness;

(b) if the parallel importer has added an extra article to the package, he must ensure that its origin is indicated in such a way as to dispel any impression that the trade mark owner is responsible for it;

(c) he must give the trade mark owner advance notice of the product being put on sale. The trade mark owner may also require the parallel importer to supply him with a specimen of the repackaged product before it goes on sale.

It is not necessary for the parallel importer to state that the repackaging was carried out without the authorisation of the trade mark owner.

[32.23] In *Centrafarm v American Home Products*,[41] the ECJ considered the question of re-affixing a trade mark. American Home Products sold tranquillisers under the trade marks SERENID in the UK and SERESTA in the Netherlands which were considered to be identical products. The parallel importer imported SERENID into the Netherlands and applied the trade mark

---

[39.] [1997] FSR 102.

[40.] *Bristol-Myers Squibb v Paranova; Eurim-Pharm v Beiersdorf; MPA Pharma v Rhone-Poulenc* [1997] FSR 102.

[41.] [1978] ECR 1823.

SERESTA. It was held that there was infringement but the ECJ cautioned that if a trade mark proprietor had deliberately pursued a policy of using different trade marks in EU countries in order to partition the market, then the exercise of the right may constitute a disguised restriction on trade within the meaning of Article 36.

[32.24] In *CHEETAH Trade Mark*,[42] the defendant purchased a herbicide in Belgium and sold it in the UK without altering the packaging. However, the defendant did use the plaintiff's different UK trade mark on delivery notes and invoices. Infringement was upheld. The use of different marks in different countries, in the absence of other evidence, was held not to be a disguised restriction on trade.

DISCLAIMERS OR LIMITATIONS

[32.25] Section 17 of the 1996 Act provides for both voluntary and mandatory disclaimers, the latter being introduced during the passage of the Trade Marks Bill during the Dáil and Irish law differs from UK law in this regard. The purpose of a disclaimer was well stated in the Trade Mark Rules 1963 as being "in order that the public generally may understand what the applicant's rights, if his mark is registered, will be".

[32.26] The imposition of a disclaimer requirement on an applicant under s 22 of the 1963 Act was a common occurrence and this is likely to continue under the 1996 Act. A disclaimer statement would read "registration of this trade mark shall give no right to the exclusive use of ...". Thus, on examination, it might be considered that the overall trade mark was sufficiently distinctive but contained certain elements which in isolation, might be considered non-distinctive. By use of a disclaimer condition, the Controller is able to grant exclusivity in the overall mark but at the same time, ensure to the public that the scope of such exclusivity does not extend to prevent third party use in respect of a particular part of the trade mark. In the case of *VIRGINIA SLIMS Trade Mark*,[43] Costello J considered the circumstances under which the Controller could exercise his discretion to impose a disclaimer condition under s 22 of the 1963 Act and accepted that just because a feature of a mark is of a non-distinctive character, it does not follow that a disclaimer should be entered as a matter of course. The court should bear in mind the disadvantages which the applicant will suffer if the disclaimer is required and weigh them against the public's interest in having the applicant's rights clarified by means of a disclaimer. The danger of the absence of a disclaimer is, of course, unjustifiable claims to a monopoly right. Even though a

---

[42.] [1993] FSR 263.
[43.] High Court, unrep, 7 October 1980.

disclaimer entry does not exist, it does not mean that rights extend to such element. It depends amongst other things on the nature of the element and the prominence of such in the overall mark. There are many instances in which it would be self apparent that despite the absence of a disclaimer, no exclusivity could extend to a particular element. Although there is no provision providing for disclaimers under the Trade Mark Harmonisation Directive, it is to be noted that provision for such exists under the CTM Regulation and s 17(2) is clearly modelled on Article 38(2) of the CTM Regulation.

[32.27] A registration with a disclaimer does not affect the proprietor's rights under the law of passing off and it is, of course, true that a disclaimer entry is in effect, a snap shot at the date of registration or that the disclaimed element may now have become distinctive through usage. It is always possible for a trade mark proprietor to re-apply for registration and argue against a disclaimer condition subsequently and once the trade mark has been used for a number of years. Although a disclaimer means that infringement proceedings will be precluded, there are advantages of owning a registration even with such a disclaimed element. When carrying out examination, the Controller can still cite under s 10, an earlier trade mark where the similarity resides in the disclaimed element. In *GRANADA Trade Mark*,[44] it was held that in opposition proceedings, regard was to be had to a disclaimed element since a disclaimer does not affect the significance which a mark conveys to others.[45] A disclaimer element is entered on the register and should be picked up by third party searching and may thus serve as a deterrent by giving notice as to possible common law rights and citation and/or opposition to an application even though usage will not amount to infringement.

[32.28] A limitation may be entered on a voluntary basis and s 17(1)(b) specifically states such to be, for example, a territorial limitation and whereby it would be agreed only to use the mark in a particular part of the State or for export use. A limitation as to a particular colour or colours may be self-imposed by an applicant in an attempt to show distinctiveness as, for example, in colour schemes for tablet capsules.[46]

[32.29] Under the transitional provisions of the 1996 Act, a disclaimer or limitation entered previously on the register, was transferred to the new register under the 1996 Act[47] but conditions ceased to have any effect.

[44.] [1979] RPC 303.
[45.] See also *L'AMY Trade Mark* [1983] RPC 137.
[46.] *Parke Davis App* [1976] FSR 195.
[47.] Third Schedule - s 2(5).

TRANSITIONAL PROVISIONS

[32.30] In respect of acts committed prior to 1 July 1996[48] which is the commencement date of the 1996 Act, it is the 1963 Act which determines whether or not there is infringement.[49] This means that the scope of protection is limited to unauthorised third party use in the course of trade in relation to the goods embraced by the registration. If the registration is in Part B of the Register, then for acts committed prior to 1 July 1996, the defence under s 13(2) of the 1963 Act is available to a defendant who can show that the use of which the plaintiff complains is not likely to deceive or cause confusion or indicate a connection in the course of trade with the trade mark proprietor.

[32.31] It is also not an infringement to continue to use a mark after 1 July 1996 which did not amount to an infringement under the 1963 Act.[50]

[32.32] As and from 1 July 1996 and for acts committed after that date, the distinction between Parts A and B of the Register, as far as the scope of protection is concerned, is removed.

---

48. Third Schedule - s 2(4).
49. Third Schedule - s 3(2).
50. Third Schedule - s 3(3).

Chapter 33

Trade Marks Act 1996: Registration Procedure and Ownership

REGISTRATION PROCEDURE

Searches

[33.01] Prior to making an application to register a trade mark before the Patents Office, it is normal to carry out a search to establish what registrations/ applications of a conflicting nature already exist. The search must embrace not only trade marks on the Irish register but also the CTM register. When Ireland ratifies the Madrid Protocol,[1] it will also be necessary to search against international trade marks registered under the Madrid Agreement extending to Ireland. The searches in the various trade mark registers should be in the international class covering the goods/services for which the mark is to be used and cross-referencing to further classes covering similar goods/services. Despite these searches, it should be borne in mind that in some cases, a trade mark application can be refused even in the case of dissimilar goods/services under s 10(3). This arises where use of the mark would take unfair advantage of, or be detrimental to, the distinctive character or reputation of the earlier mark on the register. This requirement is such that the earlier mark would have such a reputation that it would almost certainly be known to an applicant, but as a precautionary measure, it is normal for a search to identify at least an identical mark in all classes. More difficult to identify are common law rights which are unregistered and well known marks under s 61 of the 1996 Act and which can also be unregistered. Searches can be made in trade and telephone directories, company and business name registers, etc. However, this will not necessarily disclose the prior mark because there is no requirement for there to be trading under the prior mark in the State. However, generally if a mark meets the statutory requirement of being well known[2] or an unregistered trade mark sufficient to sustain an action for passing off,[3] then an applicant would know of the existence of this prior mark. In relation to shape trade marks, a search of the

---

1. See para [26.47].
2. Section 61.
3. Section 10(4)(a).

design register is also advisable because an industrial design can also be a basis for refusal of such an application.[4]

Application

[33.02] When filing an Irish trade mark application, there are certain minimum formalities required in order to secure a filing date and unless subsequently lost, this will be the eventual date of registration for all purposes under the 1996 Act.[5] Once registration takes place, an infringement action can claim damages from the filling date since the rights have effect from that date.[6] In order to secure this date documents must be filed:

(a) indicating that registration of a trade mark is sought and containing the name and address of the person requesting registration;

(b) containing a representation of the mark for which registration is sought; and

(c) in which the goods or services are stated.[7]

If not filed at the date of application, then subsequently an applicant must lodge the prescribed Form 1 which is scheduled to the Trade Mark Rules 1996.[8] This form includes the statement in s 37(2) that the trade mark is being used by the applicant or with their consent or that the applicant has a *bona fide* intention that it should be so used. What is strange is that the Form No 1 actually separates the statements so that an applicant has to identify whether use has actually commenced and which is not a requirement under the Act. It is also not clear whether use or intention to use relates to the position in the State. Although there are no specific statements as to the consequences of making a false statement, it would probably be considered to be an application made in bad faith.[9] The statement also pertains to the entire goods and/or services so the practice of including specifications which are actually broader than the intended use, may also constitute an application made in bad faith. Such bad faith is a grounds for refusal and invalidity. In relation to invalidity, under s 52(5), the trade mark should only be declared invalid in so far as it relates to those goods or services for which no intention to use existed.

[33.03] Under the 1996 Act, there is no longer a requirement that the applicant be the actual or intended user or that such user be identified by way of a simultaneously filed registered user application.

---

4. Section 10(4)(b).
5. Section 45(3).
6. Section 13(3).
7. Trade Marks Rules 1996, SI 199/1996, r 12.
8. SI 199/1996 - Schedule Two.
9. Section 8(4)(b).

[33.04] When filing, it is necessary to identify the goods and/or services in the application. There is an International Classification of Goods/Services[10] and goods and services should be classified accordingly. Under the 1963 Act, a separate application was required in each class. Under the Trade Mark Rules 1996,[11] a multi-class application is possible with an additional official fee required for each class. Ultimately, the Controller is the final arbiter as to the appropriate class and a decision of the Controller in this regard is final.[12] Classification is not usually a problem given that most goods/services are indexed in the Nice Classification. If in doubt, a procedure exists whereby WIPO can be asked to adjudicate on a matter of classification. Classification is a significant aid to searching.

[33.05] If official application fees are not paid at the date of application, then they must be paid within one month of the filing date otherwise the application will be deemed abandoned.[13]

[33.06] It is possible to file under one application what is called a series of trade marks. This is defined in s 46(2) to mean a number of trade marks which resemble each other as to their material particulars and differ only in respect of matter of a non-distinctive character which does not substantially affect the identity of the trade mark. The most common examples would be trade marks in upper/lower case lettering or trade marks in black and white or colour. There is no restriction on the number of marks which may appear in a series.

Priority

[33.07] If priority is to be claimed under the Paris Convention,[14] then such an application must be filed within six months from the date of filing of the first Convention application.[15] The application can cover some or all of the goods/ services of the application from which priority is claimed. What is not clear from the Rules is whether or not a claim to priority can be made subsequent to the filing date but still within the six month period allowed under the Paris Convention. Rule 12(2)(b) simply states that where a right to priority is claimed, the information required by Form No 1 concerning claims to priority shall be furnished in the form. Since Form No 1 does not have to be filed in order to secure a filing date, it would seem that a claim to priority can be delayed until

---

[10.] Arrangement of Nice Classification for dividing goods into 34 Classes (1-34) and services into a further 8 Classes (35-42).
[11.] Rule 14.
[12.] Section 39(2).
[13.] Rule 12(5).
[14.] See para **[26.03]**.
[15.] Section 40(1).

the filing of the form and provided this is still within the six month period. There is a three month period from the filing date within which to file the priority document by way of evidence of the first Convention application from the competent authority[16] which is usually the Patents Office in that country.

[33.08] It is a requirement that the first application be what is termed a regular national filing which means that it must be possible to determine the date of filing. It is not necessary that such an application itself proceeds to registration.[17] The application from which priority is claimed must be the first one in any Convention country for that trade mark. Section 40(4) does contain a limited exception where at the time of the subsequent application from which priority is being claimed:

(a) the previous application has been withdrawn, abandoned or refused, without having been laid open to public inspection and without leaving any rights outstanding; and

(b) it has not yet served as a basis for claiming a right of priority.

It is not understood how this provision can ever have application because a trade mark is open to public inspection within a very short space of time after filing.

[33.09] A merging of applications is possible[18] but only under very limited circumstances which are prescribed in the Trade Mark Rules 1996.[19] The merger must take place before a notice of acceptance has issued in relation to any of the applications. This could arise when the first official action issues from the Patents Office or when advertisement takes place in the Official Journal. All the applications must bear the same date and be in respect of the same trade mark. This means that there will be very few instances of merger except in the early days of the 1996 Act. Prior to 1 July 1996, over 7,000 service mark applications had been filed and a system which required separate applications in each class. An applicant who had a number of simultaneously filed applications for the same mark in different service classes has advantage in merger because of reduced registration fees and future renewal fees.

[33.10] It is also possible to merge registrations. Again, the registrations must be for the same mark and have the same date. Any registrable transaction must be recorded against all of the marks being merged and each mark must have the same disclaimer or limitation, if any. It is not possible to merge collective or certification mark registrations.

---

16. Rule 13.
17. Section 40(3).
18. Section 46(1)(b).
19. SI 199/1996 - Rule 29.

[33.11] It is also possible to divide an application into several applications, each of which will have the same filing date as the original application.[20] Division is limited under the Trade Mark Rules to applications in relation to which a notice of acceptance has not yet issued[21] or which has been opposed. In practice, it is the latter which will cover almost every situation in which an applicant is likely to wish to divide an application. In particular, a multi-class application which has been opposed and where the opposition relates to only certain but not all of the classes, an applicant is able to divide the application and allow the remaining classes to proceed. If the opposition is defeated, then merger can take place subsequently. What is unfortunate is that if an application is advertised and threatened with opposition, it is not possible to divide until the actual notice of opposition has been lodged.

Formalities

[33.12] Once a trade mark application is filed, a receipt issues from the Patents Office. This receipt allocates a number to the application and acknowledges the date upon which the application was received. The numbering system is simply the last two digits of the year followed by a number which is the next number in respect of applications filed that year eg 97/2090 would be the two thousand and ninetieth application filed in 1997. The details of the application by way of the trade mark, number, date and applicant's name together with classes and goods/services are entered onto a database for searching purposes.

[33.13] There is no statutory time period within which the trade mark application must be examined by the Patents Office. Examination takes place to establish whether or not the requirements of the 1996 Act and Rules have been met.[22] This means that there is examination both as to formalities and to substantive matters. It is extremely important for an applicant to fulfil the minimum requirements to establish a filing date[23] because although formality irregularities in this regard may be remedied, the filing date will be the date when all such formalities are complete. Similarly, it is also important to pay all class fees within one month of the filing date. The Controller, on examination of formalities, will identify the absence of correct fees but such examination may well take place more than one month after filing. If an application fee is not submitted within the prescribed one month period, the application is deemed abandoned. It is uncertain as to what will happen in the case of a wrong calculation in the official fee payable for example, on a multi-class application.

[20.] Section 46(1)(a).
[21.] Rule 28.
[22.] Section 42(1).
[23.] Section 38; Rule 12(1).

Presumably at a minimum, the entire application will not be deemed abandoned and the Controller will allow the filing date in so far as it relates to the number of classes in respect of which the official application fee has been paid. The remaining formal requirement over which there is a statutory time limit, is the filing of the priority document where priority is claimed.[24] Failure to file this document within the prescribed three month period means that an applicant must relinquish the claim to priority. However, this particular time period is extendible, provided such extension request is made before the expiry of the normal period.[25]

[33.14] The most common formality requirements raised by a Controller relate to the specification of goods/services. Although it is possible to file in respect of a specification which reads "all goods in class ...", this is not normally allowed. An applicant will be asked to specify the exact goods/services in the particular class. An exception arises if an applicant can illustrate that they trade across a very broad range of goods/services in a particular class, it is possible to use the class heading, with the exception of class 42 which is the miscellaneous service class. If the Controller is unsure whether the goods/services fall into the class indicated by an applicant, then clarification will be sought and if necessary, amendment made to the specification. The Controller who ultimately decides on all matters of classification, may insist on deletion of certain goods/services or on additional class fees being paid.[26]

[33.15] If colour is claimed as part of a trade mark, it is necessary to furnish coloured representations. An application in respect of a three dimensional mark requires representations by way of a photographic reproduction or a graphic representation showing different perspectives not exceeding six in total.[27]

Substantive Requirements

[33.16] The Controller also carries out a substantive examination of the application which will relate to the following:

(a) whether the mark is a trade mark within the definition in s 6(1) which requires the mark to be capable of being represented graphically and of distinguishing the applicant's goods/services from those of other undertakings;

[24.] Rule 13.
[25.] Rule 63.
[26.] Rule 14(3).
[27.] Rule 12(3)(c).

(b) the absolute grounds of refusal in s 8 and which includes an examination as to distinctiveness and whether or not the mark is deceptive or contrary to law or public policy;

(c) whether under s 9, the mark includes a specially protected emblem of the State or the national flag;

(d) whether under ss 62 or 63, the mark includes national flags or State or other emblems which have been notified under Article 6 *ter* of the Paris Convention;[28] and

(e) the relative grounds of refusal under s 10 in so far as they relate to earlier trade marks. This necessitates the Controller carrying out searches of the Irish, CTM and international registers but the Rules simply state the scope and methodology of such a search shall be as determined by the Controller.[29] In practice, the search is not limited to identical conflicting earlier trade marks and there is also cross searching to related classes in order to assess the position *vis-à-vis* similarity of goods/services.

[33.17] If the examination of either the formalities or the substantive requirements results in the Controller taking the view that the requirements have not been met, then an official action issues to the applicant or their authorised agent, providing an opportunity to make representations or to amend the application. There is no specific statutory time period within which to respond to an official action and the time period allowed is stated by the Controller[30] in the official communication and is extendible.[31] In practice, there are often a number of exchanges of communication between an applicant or their agent and the Controller dealing with the official action. If the applicant fails to respond or satisfy the Controller that the requirements for registration have been met, or to amend the application to the Controller's satisfaction, then the application is refused.[32] This is subject to the right to request a hearing before the Controller[33] and which requires payment of an official fee.[34]

[33.18] If the requirements of registration are met, then the application is accepted[35] and allowed to proceed to publication (advertisement). This should be contrasted with the position under the 1963 Act where it was possible for the

---

[28] See para **[31.59]**.

[29] Rule 16.

[30] Section 42(2).

[31] Rule 63.

[32] Section 42(3).

[33] Section 71.

[34] Rule 61.

[35] Section 42(4).

Controller to advertise a trade mark prior to acceptance and then if necessary, to re-advertise. This does not appear to be an option open to the Controller under the 1996 Act.

Publication/Advertisement

[33.19] Advertisement takes place in the Patents Office Journal which is published fortnightly. The purpose of advertisement is to give third parties an opportunity to oppose an application before it is allowed to proceed to registration. Under the 1963 Act, the opposition period was one month from the date of advertisement but this period was extendible upon request for extension being received within the one month period. The 1996 Act introduces a new regime of a three month opposition period which is not extendible.[36] This is likely to substantially increase the number of oppositions as parties will wish to preserve their position pending attempts to settle the matter between the parties.

[33.20] There is no specific listing of the grounds of opposition and therefore, the grounds which exist must be the same as those which form the basis for a trade mark application to be refused generally. There is no restriction on who can lodge an opposition but such must be by way of a written statement of the grounds of opposition accompanied by an official fee.[37] In practice, the opposition including the statement of grounds is in broad terms simply identifying the sections under the Act upon which the opposition is to be based. It is sent in duplicate to the Controller who sends a copy to the applicant or their agent.[38] Within three months, the applicant must file with the Controller in duplicate, a counter-statement[39] with the prescribed official fee. The counter-statement is a denial or admittance of any of the grounds of opposition. This period of three months is also non-extendible.[40] If the counter-statement is not filed, the application is deemed to have been withdrawn.[41] The Controller sends a copy of the counter-statement to the opponent. There subsequently follows a three month time period which is extendible and within which the opponent, and subsequently the applicant, must file with the Controller their evidence by way of statutory declaration[42] and furnish the other side with a copy.

[33.21] When the applicant furnishes their evidence, a further two month extendible period is given to the opponent to file further statutory declarations if

---

[36.] Rule 18(1).
[37.] Section 43(2); Rule 18(2).
[38.] Rule 18(3).
[39.] Rule 19(1).
[40.] Rule 63(2).
[41.] Rule 19(2).
[42.] Rules 20 & 21.

desired, but which must be confined to matters strictly in reply.[43] The Controller has a discretion to accept further evidence.[44] When the evidence is complete, the Controller invites the parties to attend at a hearing and to pay the requisite official fee within seven days of the notice. It is normal practice for parties to attend such a hearing at which they are usually represented by their trade mark agent or counsel. Following a hearing, the Controller notifies the decision to the parties who have a one month extendible period within which to request the written grounds of the decision.[45] This decision can be appealed to the High Court.[46] Section 79 states that unless provided otherwise by the rules of the Court, the appeal must be lodged within three months from the date of the Controller's decision. This means that it may be necessary to lodge an appeal before actually being in receipt of the written grounds.

[33.22] Once advertised, it is also possible for any person to make written observations to the Controller as to why they consider that an application should be refused.[47] The applicant is notified of such observations and although not stated, presumably the identity of the party making the observations. A person who simply makes observations does not become a party to proceedings.[48]

[33.23] The purpose of making observations is to try and persuade the Controller to withdraw acceptance and without the need to engage in the expense of opposition. Section 45 does allow for an acceptance to be withdrawn on the grounds that such acceptance was erroneous having regard to matters subsequently coming to the attention of the Controller. The observations do not have to be made within the three month opposition period but is advisable to do so if seeking withdrawal of acceptance as an alternative to opposition. However in reality, a potential opponent is always obliged to lodge an opposition to preserve their opposition since a decision from the Controller may not issue within the three months or may be again reversed in favour of an applicant following further submissions. It is arguable whether under such circumstances, the Controller is obliged to re-advertise the mark.

[33.24] It is possible to withdraw or amend a trade mark application. A common amendment is to restrict the specification of goods/services. It is not possible to broaden a specification. If the application has already been advertised, any withdrawal or restriction is also subsequently advertised in the Patents Office Journal. If the restriction occurs subsequent to any opposition, then an opponent

---

43. Rule 22.
44. Rule 23.
45. Rule 27.
46. Section 79.
47. Section 43(3).
48. Section 43(4).

is given an opportunity to withdraw the opposition or to amend such if desired.[49] Any withdrawal of the application is irrevocable after the expiry of three months from the date of notice of the withdrawal.[50]

[33.25] Unlike the position under the CTM Regulation and the corresponding UK provision, it is also possible to make any other amendment which does not substantially affect the identity of the trade mark.[51] This includes, but is not limited to, correction of the name or address of the applicant, errors of wording or of copying, or obvious mistakes. If the application has not yet been advertised, it is only the amended mark which is published in the Patents Office Journal.[52]

TRANSITIONAL PROVISIONS

[33.26] All applications filed prior to 1 July 1996 are examined and oppositions determined under the criteria of the 1963 Act.[53] Although it is stated that Rules may allow for procedures to follow that of the 1996 Act, no such Rules were prescribed. This means that for applications filed prior to 1 July 1996, there is only a one month opposition period which is extendible but for applications filed as and from July 1 1996, a three month non-extendible opposition period applies. The procedure for applications filed prior to 1 July 1996 will be determined by the Trade Mark Rules 1963.[54]

[33.27] In relation to any application filed prior to 1 July 1996 which has not yet been advertised, it was possible to convert such an application so that it is examined and opposition determined under the criteria of the 1996 Act.[55] This conversion is irrevocable and request for such must have been made prior to 1 January 1997. Any such conversion means that the application loses its filing date and instead receives the commencement date for the 1996 Act, ie 1 July 1996. Thus, prior to any conversion, it was advisable to carry out searches to establish the position *vis-à-vis* conflicting marks between the filing date and 1 July 1996. If there were any conflicting marks, then conversion was a last resort.

[33.28] All applications for service marks filed prior to 1 July 1996 do not require any conversion and are automatically given a filing date of 1 July 1996

---

49. Rule 26.
50. Section 44(2).
51. Section 44(3).
52. Rule 26(3).
53. Third Schedule - para 8(2).
54. SI 268/1963.
55. Third Schedule - para 9.

and dealt with under the 1996 Act.[56] Over 7,000 service mark applications had been filed prior to 1 July 1996.

REGISTRATION

[33.29] If there is no opposition or if such has been withdrawn or decided in favour of the applicant, then upon payment of the final registration fee, a certificate of registration issues. An exception arises where, having regard to matters coming to the Controller's notice since acceptance, it is believed that the acceptance was made in error.[57] This would normally arise following a written observation[58] by a third party.

[33.30] The registration fee must be paid within two months of the request for such by the Controller[59] and the fact of registration is published in the Patents Office Journal.[60] This date of publication is important because it determines the date of completion of the registration procedure[61] which is the date from which the five year period runs for revocation on the grounds of non-use[62] and from which infringement proceedings can commence.[63] However, the date of *registration* is the date of filing of the application[64] and this is the effective date from which rights accrue to a trade mark proprietor.[65]

Duration and Renewal

[33.31] Under s 47, the duration of a trade mark registration is ten years from the date of registration (filing date) and is renewable for successive ten year periods. Unlike other forms of intellectual property, a trade mark registration can remain in force indefinitely upon payment of the requisite renewal fees. The 1963 Act provided for an initial registration period of seven years and then renewal periods every fourteen years. To determine the renewal date of a registration, it is necessary to establish the registration date. If such date is 1 July 1996 or after that date, then the renewal date is due on each ten year anniversary date. If the registration date is prior to 1 July 1996, then the next renewal date is determined under the 1963 Act, ie seven or fourteen years but subsequently every ten years.[66] A term of renewal takes effect from the expiry date of the registration

---

56. Third Schedule - para 15.
57. Section 45(1).
58. Section 43(2).
59. Rule 73.
60. Section 45(4).
61. Section 45(5).
62. Section 51(1).
63. Section 13(4).
64. Section 45(3).
65. Section 13(3).
66. Third Schedule - para 10.

and not from the date of payment of a renewal fee.[67] It is not possible to pay a renewal fee more than six months before the anniversary date[68] and the Controller is obliged to send a renewal notice at least one month before the anniversary date.[69] It is possible to make late payment of a renewal fee provided such is within six months of the anniversary date and the requisite fees including a late renewal fee are paid.[70]

[33.32] Even where a trade mark is removed from the register for non-payment of a renewal fee, it is still taken into account in determining the registrability of a later mark for a period of one year from the anniversary date. A removed trade mark can remain as a citation and thus a basis for refusal of an application during this period unless the Controller is satisfied that there was no *bona fide* use of the mark in the two years immediately preceding expiry.[71]

[33.33] Restoration is provided for in Rule 40[72] of the Trade Mark Rules 1996 but is limited to six months from the date of publication of removal of the mark in the Patents Office Journal. This time period is non-extendible.[73] It is also necessary to show to the satisfaction of the Controller that having regard to all the circumstances, it is just to restore the registration. This obviously requires an explanation to the Controller as to the reason for failure to renew and which, for example, could include the failure of the Patents Office to send out the renewal reminder.[74] Unlike the position under the Patents Act 1992, there is no provision dealing with the effect of late renewal or restoration on third parties. In relation to the six month grace period for late renewal, the trade mark must still be considered as a registered trade mark.[75]

[33.34] It is possible for the proprietor of a registered trade mark to add to or alter the registration in any manner not substantially affecting the identity of the registered mark.[76] This provision corresponds to that under s 43 of the 1963 Act but differs from the position under both the CTM Regulation and the UK Act where alteration is limited to the name or address of a proprietor which may appear in the mark.

[67.] Section 48(5).
[68.] Rule 38.
[69.] Rule 37.
[70.] Rule 39(1).
[71.] Section 11(3).
[72.] SI 199/1996.
[73.] Rule 63(2).
[74.] *Ling's Patent* [1981] RPC 85.
[75.] Section 48(4).
[76.] Section 49.

[33.35] The practice under the 1963 Act and the former UK Trade Marks Act 1938, was to view a change as being substantial even though it affected only one letter in the mark, if either the pronunciation or the appearance of the mark altered. Hence, the change from OTRIVIN[77] to OTRIVINE was not allowed. However, in the case of a non-invented word, there was a tendency to be more liberal and the change from PELICAN[78] to PELIKAN was allowed. An important factor taken into account was the effect of the alteration on the position of other parties as to possible infringement. This is the reason why the altered mark is advertised and open to opposition.[79]

[33.36] Under s 50 of the 1996 Act, it is also possible for a trade mark proprietor to surrender a Registration in respect of some or all of the goods or services for which it is registered. There are also provisions in Rule 36 for protecting the interests of other persons having a right in the registered trade mark. The Controller is obliged not to act upon a notice of surrender unless the proprietor certifies that they are not precluded by contract or other agreement from surrendering the mark. In addition, the proprietor must specify the name and address of each person entered in the Register as having an interest. Each of these persons must have been given three months notice and not objected to the surrender. Notice of the surrender or partial surrender is published in the Patents Office Journal and is effective from this date. However, no action for infringement lies in respect of any act carried out before that date.

PROPERTY RIGHTS IN TRADE MARKS

[33.37] Both a registered trade mark and a trade mark application are personal property rights.[80]

Jointly owned Marks

[33.38] Section 27 of the 1996 Act provides:

(1) Where the relations between two or more persons interested in a trade mark are such that no one of them is entitled, as between himself and the other or others, to use it except -

(a) on behalf of both or all of them, or

(b) in relation to an article with which both or all of them are connected in the course of trade,

those persons may be registered as joint proprietors of the trade mark.

[77.] *OTRIVIN Trade Mark* [1967] RPC 613.
[78.] *PELICAN Trade Mark* [1978] RPC 424.
[79.] Section 49; Rule 35.
[80.] Sections 26 & 31(1).

The same rights apply as if the trade mark had been vested in a single person.[81] Section 27(4) states that the rights of any person registered as a joint owner shall be deemed to be infringed by any of the other of the joint owners who uses the trade mark in physical or other relation to goods or services in respect of which the trade mark is registered but with which both or all of the joint owners are not and have not been connected in the course of trade.[82] If there are joint applicants, the Controller may call for confirmation either that none of the applicants will use the mark except on behalf of all or both of the joint applicants or alternatively, that the mark will be used in relation only to goods or services with which all joint applicants are connected in the course of trade. An example of such a connection would be where one joint owner is a manufacturer and the other is a distributor.[83] Section 27(2) precludes the registration of a mark to two or more persons who use or propose to use the mark independently of one another.

Assignments and Registrable Transactions

[33.39] Under s 28 of the 1996 Act, a registered trade mark or an application[84] can be assigned in the same way as other personal property either in connection with the goodwill of a business or independently. The 1963 Act, as interpreted by the Irish courts, had not allowed the assignment of a pending trade mark application.[85] The 1963 Act also contained restrictions on assignments, which were designed to protect the public from being misled. This included an association requirement whereby the Controller could compel the owner of an identical or similar mark when assigning the trade marks to do so *en bloc* so that confusingly similar marks would not be held separately. Associations have been dispensed with under the 1996 Act and even trade marks which were associated under the 1963 Act find that such associations no longer have any effect.[86] However, an assignment which renders the subsequent use of the trade mark likely to mislead the public, may lead to revocation of a registration under s 51(1)(d) of the 1996 Act.

[33.40] There was also a requirement under s 30(7) of the 1963 Act, that an assignment of a used trade mark other than in connection with the goodwill of the business in which it was being used, was required to be advertised. This is no longer a requirement under the 1996 Act. The statutory provision which allows

---

81. Section 27(3).
82. Section 27(4).
83. *Val Marks* (1923) 40 RPC 103; *Tarantella* (1910) 27 RPC 573 at 584.
84. Section 31(1).
85. *Western States Bank Card Association v The Controller* High Court, unrep, [1975] 126 Sp - 1 March 1978.
86. Third Schedule - para 2(3) - Transitional provision.

assignment separately from the goodwill of a business was required to abrogate the common law rule whereby a trade mark could not be assigned separately from its owner's business[87] because otherwise, a trade mark would become deceptive.[88] The common law principle still applies in relation to an unregistered mark which can only be assigned as part of the goodwill of a business.[89] The courts have shied away from giving any definition of what is meant by goodwill but such has been described as:

> "the benefit and advantage of the good name, reputation and connection of a business. It is the attractive force which brings in custom. It is the one thing which distinguishes an old established business from a new business at its start".[90]

[33.41] Section 28(2) of the 1996 Act allows for partial assignment in respect of some but not all of the goods[91] or services or relating to use of the trade mark in a particular manner or a particular locality. There is no discretion on behalf of the Controller to refuse to accept such an assignment and it is up to the trade mark proprietor to determine if they run the risk of revocation on the grounds that the trade mark is now deceptive.[92] Under Article 17(4) of the CTM Regulation, it is possible for the Community Trade Mark Office (OHIM) to refuse to record a transfer where such is likely to mislead the public as to the nature, quality or geographical origin of the goods or services. An assignment of a CTM must be for the whole of the Community.

[33.42] Where there is a licence under a registered trade mark which is subsequently assigned, then unless the licence states otherwise, it is binding on the successor in title.[93] Similar to the position under patent law, in order to be effective an assignment of a registered trade mark must be in writing.[94] A registered trade mark may be the subject of a charge in the same way as other personal property[95] and may be assigned by way of security.[96] The 1963 Act continues to apply in relation to assignments which took place prior to 1 July 1996.[97] Section 30 of the 1963 Act contained certain prohibitions on partial assignments likely to deceive or cause confusion.

---

[87] *Bowden Wire Co Ltd v Bowden Brake Co Ltd* (1914) 31 RPC 385.
[88] *Pinto v Badman* (1891) 8 RPC 181.
[89] Section 28(6).
[90] *Inland Revenue v Muller's & Co's Margarine Ltd* [1901] AC 217.
[91] *Sunbeam Motor Car Co* (1916) 33 RPC 389.
[92] Section 51(1)(d).
[93] Section 32(4).
[94] Section 28(3).
[95] Section 28(5).
[96] Section 28(4).
[97] Third Schedule - para 6(1).

[33.43] Provision is made in s 29 of the 1996 Act for recordal in the trade mark register of certain interests which are termed registrable transactions. These are assignments, licences, grants of security, assents and court orders or an order of any other competent authority transferring a registered trade mark or any right in or under it. Until an application has been made to record a registrable transaction, it is ineffective as against a person acquiring a competing interest in ignorance of the transaction. This would suggest that if an application has been made but not yet been entered on the register, a party is still nevertheless affixed with notice. Given that there may well be a lengthy period of time between application and recordal, this appears unreasonable if ignorance is taken to be actual rather than constructive notice. There is no requirement that a trade mark proprietor be actually entered on the register before taking an infringement action but a licensee in a position to take such an action must have at least applied to record such a licence on the register.[98]

[33.44] The penalties for not making application to record a registrable transaction do not arise unless six months have elapsed from the transaction date. Even then, the courts may excuse such upon being satisfied that it was not practical to make an application earlier and steps were taken as soon as practically possible.[99] The penalties are a denial of any entitlement to damages or an account of profits for infringement between the date of the transaction and the application for recordal.

[33.45] Section 99 of the Companies Acts 1963 as amended by s 122 of the Companies (Amendment) Act 1990 requires that a company register with the Registrar of Companies certain charges including a charge on goodwill or on a trade mark. On the requisite application being made, the Registrar enters the relevant particulars on the register including the date of creation of the charge, the amount secured, particulars of the property charged and particulars of the person entitled to the charge.

[33.46] The formalities for recordal of a registrable transaction are set out in Rule 45 of the Trade Mark Rules 1996[100] and require submission of a certified copy of the instrument or document upon which the claim is based. If the Instrument is chargeable with stamp duty, evidence that such has been paid is required. Although s 28(3) indicates that an assignment executed by the assignor alone is sufficient, Rule 45(1)(a) suggests that the assignment must be signed by or on behalf of both parties to the assignment before recordal can take place. The Rule in this regard is clearly *ultra vires* the Act. Even though a registrable

---

[98.] Section 29(3)(b).
[99.] Section 29(4)(a) and (b).
[100.] SI 199/1996.

transaction may be dated prior to 1 July 1996, provided application for recordal is subsequent to this date or still pending, the provisions and thus procedures under s 29 of the 1996 Act apply.[101]

[33.47] An equitable interest in a trade mark, such as an agreement to grant a licence, is enforceable but not recordable on the register.[102] The position *vis-à-vis* recordal of registrable transactions against a pending trade mark application is essentially the same as that of a registration.[103]

LICENSING OF TRADE MARKS

[33.48] Article 8 of the Trade Mark Harmonisation Directive states as follows:

1. A trade mark may be licensed for some or all of the goods or services for which it is registered and for the whole or part of the member state concerned. A licence may be exclusive or non-exclusive.

2. The proprietor of a trade mark may invoke the rights conferred by that trade mark against a licensee who contravenes any provision in his licensing contract with regard to its duration, the form covered by the Registration in which the trade mark may be used, the scope of the goods or services for which the licence is granted, the territory in which the trade mark may be affixed, or the quality of the goods manufactured or of the services provided by the licensee.

Under Article 10(3), use of a trade mark with consent is deemed to constitute use by the proprietor. These statements are not repeated in the 1996 Act and to some limited extent, can be extracted primarily from the licensing provisions in ss 32 and 33. However, there is no express provision corresponding to Article 8(2) and the normal remedy for a trade mark owner would be for breach of contract. Although licensing was also provided for under the 1963 Act, it necessitated recordal on the register by way of a registered user entry which required proof of a prescribed control relationship between the parties. Only use by a registered user could be attributed to the proprietor and, for example, a trade mark in use by a licensee was vulnerable to cancellation on the grounds of non-use if the licensee was not registered. The regime under the 1996 Act is to leave the contractual relationship between parties at their discretion in recognition of the fact that a trade mark proprietor will exercise due control over a licensee's use because it is in the proprietor's interest to maintain the integrity of the trade mark.

[101.] Third Schedule - paras 6(2) and 6(4).
[102.] Section 30.
[103.] Section 31(1).

[33.49] Section 32(2) gives examples of certain limited licences, namely a licence in respect of some but not all of the goods and services and for the use of a trade mark in a particular manner or a particular locality.

[33.50] A licence is not effective unless it is in writing signed by or on behalf of the grantor.[104] It is thus in the interest of both parties to conclude a written agreement, because in the absence of such a purported licensee is in fact an infringer. A licence is also a registrable transaction under s 29(2)(c) which means that non-recordal results in a number of disadvantages, in particular for a licensee. Firstly, the licence is ineffective as against a person acquiring a conflicting interest.[105] Secondly, a licensee will be unable to recover damages or an account of profits[106] and thirdly, a licensee will be unable to bring an infringement action in its own name.[107] A sub-licence is permissible but is a matter for the licence agreement itself.[108] Section 32(4) states that unless a licence provides otherwise, it is binding on a successor in title to the grantor's interest but s 29(3)(a) requires an application to record a licence on the register otherwise a 'transaction' is stated to be ineffective as against a person acquiring a conflicting interest in or under the registered trade mark in ignorance of such an interest. This would suggest that a distinction must be drawn between acquiring ownership by virtue of succession and an acquisition through purchase. In the case of inheritance subject to a specific provision to the contrary in the licence itself, the owner is bound by the licence. In the case of a purchase, the purchaser is not bound by the terms of the licence unless such has been recorded and the purchaser is on notice. It will therefore be common for a licensee to insist on recordal and for a vendor to warrant by way of disclosure, any licences which may exist under the trade mark.

[33.51] Article 10(3) of the Trade Mark Harmonisation Directive[109] states that use of the trade mark with the consent of the proprietor, shall be deemed to constitute use by the proprietor. The 1963 Act had a very similar provision[110] but quite ironically, there is no statement to this effect in the 1996 Act except in s 51(1)(a) dealing with revocation on the grounds of non-use. During the course of the debates on the UK Trade Marks Bill, it was stated that all use of the mark by the proprietor or with his consent is genuine use and that there was no need to spell such out. However, this is not so apparent and ss 51(1)(c) and (d) suggest

---

104. Section 32(3).
105. Section 29(3)(a).
106. Section 29(4) proviso.
107. Section 29(3)(b); s 34.
108. Section 32(5).
109. 89/104/EEC.
110. Section 36(2).

that use by a licensee may lead to the trade mark becoming a common name or misleading. Although this could also arise by virtue of the manner of use made by the proprietor, it could arise by virtue of the licensee generating their own goodwill under the mark. Therefore, in addition to quality control provisions, a trade mark owner would normally insist that a licensee indicate in their use that the trade mark is so used under the authority of the trade mark owner. A licence agreement also normally provides that the goodwill will belong to the trade mark owner and will be assigned upon request.

[33.52] Section 36(6) of the 1963 Act allowed the controller to refuse to register a user where it appeared that such would tend to facilitate trafficking in a trade mark. This provision was never interpreted by the Irish courts nor was it raised by the Controller in refusing applications under the 1963 Act. In the UK, the House of Lords in *American Greetings Corp's Application*[111] held that the HOLLY HOBBIE trade mark could not be registered because the owner intended to grant licences in such a way that the mark was being dealt with primarily as a commodity in its own right and that there would be no real trade connection between the owner of the mark and the goods to which the mark would be applied. Thus, trade mark owners engaged in character merchandising sometimes found it difficult to register their marks in the UK. Although neither the UK 1994 Act or the Irish 1996 Act contain this prohibition, it is still a matter which could arise in the Irish courts. This is because of the transitional provisions and whereby applications filed prior to 1 July 1996 and which have not been converted, will be determined under the 1963 Act.[112] In addition, the 1963 Act also applies in relation to licences granted prior to 1 July 1996.[113] The validity of existing registrations is also determined under the 1963 Act.[114]

Exclusive, Sole and Non-Exclusive Licences

[33.53] An exclusive licence is specifically defined in s 33 of the 1996 Act and is essentially a licence excluding all other parties including the licensor. In a sole licence, although there are no other licensees, the licensor is not precluded from exploiting the trade mark. In a non-exclusive licence, the licensor may grant further licences and also exploit the mark personally. An exclusive licence may be limited, for example, as to certain but not all of the goods or services covered by a registration or confined to a specific location.

---

[111] [1984] FSR 199.
[112] Third Schedule - paras 8, 7(3) and 7(4).
[113] Third Schedule - para 7(1).
[114] Third Schedule - para 13.

[33.54] The reason why an exclusive licence is specifically defined is that an exclusive licensee is granted certain rights and remedies under the 1996 Act which do not exist for a sole or non-exclusive licensee.

[33.55] Section 33(2) states that an exclusive licensee has the same rights against a successor in title who is bound by the licence as the exclusive licensee has against the person granting the licence. A successor in title will not be bound if the licence provides otherwise.[115]

Licensee's Right to take Infringement Proceedings

[33.56] Section 34 provides that a licensee can bring infringement proceedings in its own name but this particular provision does not apply to exclusive licensees who have a right to bring proceedings in their own name under s 35. Under s 34(2), if the terms of a licence do not provide otherwise, then a licensee is entitled to call on the proprietor of the registered trade mark to take infringement proceedings in respect of any matter which affects the licensee's interests. This would obviously include any infringement of the mark covered by the licence. If the goods of the infringer's use fall outside the scope of the licence agreement, there is still a strong argument that a licensee's interests might be affected, for example, because of inferior quality goods similar to that of the licence agreement.

[33.57] The licensee must call upon the trade mark proprietor to institute proceedings and the proprietor must refuse or fail to do so within two months of receiving the request.[116] Also, a licensee cannot avail of the provisions of either ss 34 or 35 until application has been made to record the licence on the register.[117]

[33.58] If the requirements are met, then the licensee may bring the proceedings in its own name as if it was the proprietor. Without leave of the Court, the proprietor must be joined as a party to the proceedings. An exception is made in the case of interlocutory relief where such may be sought by a licensee alone.[118] A proprietor who is added as a defendant shall not be liable to any costs unless they take part in the proceedings.[119] A court is directed to take into account any loss suffered or likely to be suffered by a licensee even where proceedings are brought in the name of the trade mark proprietor and may direct the extent to which the proceeds of any pecuniary remedy is held on behalf of a licensee.[120]

[115.] Section 32(4).
[116.] Section 34(3).
[117.] Section 29(3)(b).
[118.] Section 34(4).
[119.] Section 34(5).
[120.] Section 34(6).

[33.59] The position of an exclusive licensee is covered by s 35 except to the extent that a licence provides otherwise. A licence may give an exclusive licensee the same rights and remedies as if the licence had been an assignment.[121] An exclusive licensee, in such a position, may bring proceedings in its own name without, for example, putting the proprietor on notice and awaiting the two month period under s 34. Such an exclusive licensee may institute proceedings immediately and, for example, may avail of additional remedies such as delivery up.

[33.60] An exclusive licensee under s 35 is deemed to have rights and remedies concurrent with that of the trade mark proprietor.[122] This means that both the trade mark proprietor and exclusive licensee must, unless they have the leave of the Court to do otherwise, join the other party to the proceedings. An exception is made in the case of interlocutory relief. Where a proprietor or licensee is added to the proceedings as a defendant, then they will not be liable for costs unless they take part in the proceedings.[123] Because an exclusive licensee is essentially put in the same position as the trade mark proprietor, s 35(4) allows a defendant to avail of any defence that would have been available if the action had been brought by the trade mark proprietor. The position *vis-à-vis* damages and an account of profits is also dealt with in such a way as to ensure that an infringer is not held doubly liable and that there is apportionment between the concurrent rights.[124] The trade mark proprietor must notify an exclusive licensee with a concurrent right before applying for an order of delivery up[125] and a Court may, for example, upon application, order delivery up to the licensee as opposed to the trade mark proprietor. The whole of s 35 dealing with the concurrent rights of certain exclusive licensees, is subject to any contractual rights to the contrary[126] and also recordal of the licence agreement.[127]

COMPETITION LAW ASPECTS OF ASSIGNMENTS/LICENSING

[33.61] Any assignment or a licence agreement must be considered in the context of EU competition law and the domestic equivalent, namely the Competition Act 1991. Article 30 of the Treaty of Rome states that:

[121.] Section 35.
[122.] Section 35(3).
[123.] Section 36(2).
[124.] Sections 36(3) & 36(4).
[125.] Section 36(5).
[126.] Section 36(6).
[127.] Section 29(3)(b).

Quantitative restrictions on imports and all measures having equivalent effect shall, without prejudice to the following provisions, be prohibited between Member States.

National intellectual property rights fall within Article 30 but Article 36 recognises an exception such as intellectual property rights where such are necessary to achieve the reasonable purposes for which they were introduced.[128] Trade mark rights cannot serve as a means of arbitrary discrimination or as a disguised restriction on trade.

[33.62] In the case of a trade mark licence, the rule of exhaustion applies in relation to the licensee. Under Article 7 of the Trade Mark Harmonisation Directive,[129] it is provided that a trade mark shall not entitle the proprietor to prohibit its use in relation to goods which have been put on the market in the Community under that trade mark by the proprietor or with his consent. Consent being the key word in relation to a licensee and the ECJ has in this context, viewed all entities within a corporate group as operating under consent from the trade mark proprietor.[130]

[33.63] Assignments are viewed differently with regard to the operation of the principle of exhaustion of rights.[131] In *IHT Internazionale Heiztechnick GmbH v Ideal Standard GmbH*,[132] it was held that a national trade mark right which had been voluntarily assigned, could be used to prevent importation by a successor in title to the assignee. However, as stated by the ECJ, where undertakings independent of each other make trade mark assignments following a market sharing agreement, the prohibition against anti-competitive agreements under Article 85 applies. In determining whether a trade mark assignment can be treated as giving effect to an agreement prohibited under Article 85, it is necessary to analyse the context, the commitments underlying the assignment, the intention of the parties and the consideration for the assignment.

Block Exemptions

[33.64] Article 85 prohibits agreements between undertakings, decisions by associations of undertakings and concerted practices which may affect trade between Member States and which have as their objective or effect the prevention, restriction or distortion of competition within the common market. Agreements which infringe Article 85 are void. There is provision in Article 85(3) for the Commission to exempt certain agreements provided they satisfy

---

128. *Officier Van Justitie v De Peijper* [1976] ECR 613.
129. 89/104/EEC.
130. *Centrafarm BV v Winthrop BV* [1974] ECR 1183.
131. See para **[32.14]-[32.24]**.
132. [1994] ECR 2789.

the criteria set out in Article 85(3) whereby there are positive attributes of the agreement which outweigh the anti-competitive provisions. The agreement must contribute to the improvement of the production or distribution of goods, or promote technical or economic progress. Also, a fair share of the resultant benefit must be passed to consumers.

[33.65] To avail of such an exemption, the parties must notify the agreement to the Commission. It is also possible to obtain a negative clearance whereby the agreement is submitted to the Commission to establish if it is compatible with competition policy. Given the large number of notifications, the Commission has issued a number of block exemption regulations. The effect of these regulations is to indicate guidelines by way of clauses which are permitted (white clauses) and those which are prohibited (black clauses) in certain types of agreements. If the type of agreement falls within the Regulation and it includes permitted clauses and none of the prohibited clauses, then it may be exempted from Article 85 without notification. There is no block exemption regulation pertaining to trade mark licence agreements although ancillary trade mark provisions are considered in connection with other intellectual property rights. The relevant block exemptions are:

- Regulation (EEC) 1983/83 - Categories of Exclusive Distribution Agreements Block Exemption.[133]

- Regulation (EEC) 4087/88 - Franchise Agreements Block Exemption.[134]

- Regulation (EC) 240/96 - Technology Transfer Agreements Block Exemption.[135]

It is not permissible for parties to rely on these Regulations to claim exemption from what is essentially a trade mark licence agreement. In *Moosehead Breweries Ltd v Whitbread & Co's Agreement*,[136] it was held that the principal interest of the parties lay in the exploitation of the trade mark rather than the know-how, and in the circumstances the provision of the agreement relating to trade marks was not ancillary and therefore, Regulation 556/89 which was a know-how licence agreement block exemption did not apply. Exemption necessitated notification of the agreement to the Commission.

[33.66] In *Consten & Grundig*,[137] it was argued that the prohibition in Article 85(1) only applied to so-called *horizontal agreements*, namely agreements made

---

133. OJ 1983 L173/1.
134. OJL 359, 28 December 1988 p 46.
135. OJ L31/2, 1996.
136. [1994] 4 CMLR 391.
137. [1964] CMLR 489.

by undertakings that would otherwise compete with each other at the same level of trade or industry, eg between manufacturers or between retailers of competing products. This was not accepted by the ECJ who held that it applied equally to *vertical agreements*, namely between firms at different levels of trade or industry such as a supplier and customer or licensor and licensee. In this case, a distribution agreement infringed Article 85 on a number of fronts including a provision whereby the distributor was allowed to register the manufacturer's trade mark so as to keep out goods from other distributors in a crude attempt to avoid the principle of exhaustion of rights.

[33.67] In *Davide Campari-Milano SpA*,[138] it was held that an exclusive trade mark licence agreement automatically falls within Article 85(1) although it is sometimes acceptable for a limited degree of territorial exclusivity to be conferred on a trade mark licensee.

[33.68] In *Nungesser v Commission (Maize Seed Case)*,[139] the ECJ held that an open exclusive licence is not itself contrary to Article 85(1). An open exclusive licence is described by the ECJ as an agreement whereby the owner merely undertakes not to grant other licences in respect of the same territory and not to compete himself with the licensee in that territory. Such a licence allows parallel imports of the protected product into the designated territory.

[33.69] The ECJ has recognised in a number of cases that quality control provisions in a licence agreement may be necessary to protect the essential or specific subject matter of the trade mark. In *DDD Ltd & Delta Chemie's Agreement*,[140] strict requirements imposed by a licensor on the manner in which stain removers were to be manufactured and packaged, were considered not to fall within Article 85(1).

[33.70] The exclusive distribution block exemption includes in the white list of permissable clauses the obligation to resell the goods only under the trade mark. This only applies in cases of resale of products and therefore a licence of trade mark rights alone would not benefit from the block exemption. If exclusive trade mark licences fall within Article 85(1), it is necessary to make an individual notification and seek an exemption. There is a *de minimus* exemption[141] which states that agreements between undertakings with a combined annual turnover of less than ECU 300 million and a combined relevant market share of less than 5 per cent are generally presumed to be incapable of affecting market conditions

---

138. [1978] 2 CMLR 397.
139. [1982] ECR 2015.
140. [1989] 4 CMLR 535.
141. Commission Notice on Agreements of Minor Importance, OJ 1986 C231/2, 12 September 1986 as last amended by OJ 1994 C368, 23 December 1994.

and therefore such agreements do not need to be notified to the Commission. The relevant market is usually narrowly defined and as a consequence an exclusive trade mark licence agreement will rarely fall within the *de minimus* exemption. In *Hilti v The Commission*[142] the ECJ defined the relevant market as being nails designed for use in a specific nail gun. Products bearing a particular trade mark might be determined as constituting a separate market.

[33.71] Agreements which are reached in order to avoid confusion between marks are examined very closely even if the parties are unconnected. This is particularly so if parties are completely prevented from marketing their goods in the other's territory.[143] It is necessary to consider the validity of the trade mark forming the basis of the delimitation. An invalid registration means that there is a genuine conflict between the parties.[144] If there is a genuine conflict between unconnected companies, then the agreement may be ruled as falling outside Article 85.[145] The case of *PERSIL Trade Mark*[146] is an example of a trade mark dispute settled not by exclusion from certain markets but by means of colour and certain additions thereto whereby the trade marks could be identified and utilised concurrently throughout the European Union.

[33.72] In *Pronuptia*,[147] the ECJ considered what it termed "distribution franchising" whereby the franchisee operated as an independent business while at the same time, using the name and know-how of the franchisor. The ECJ favourably viewed such franchising as a means by which an undertaking can derive financial benefit from another's expertise and without investing its own capital. It was held that provisions strictly necessary in order to ensure that know-how and assistance provided by the franchisor did not benefit competitors did not constitute restrictions of competition for the purposes of Article 85(1). Examples of such were clauses prohibiting the franchisee, during the period of the validity of the contract and for a reasonable period after its expiry, from opening a shop of the same or a similar nature in an area whereby he may compete with a member of the franchise network. The same may be said of the franchisee's obligation not to transfer his shop to another party without the prior approval of the franchisor. The franchisor is also entitled to take measures necessary for maintaining the identity and reputation of the network bearing his business name or symbol. Examples are obligations to apply certain business methods, to sell goods only in premises at particular locations with certain

---

[142.] [1994] ECR 1667.
[143.] *Sirdar Ltd* [1975] 1 CMLR D93.
[144.] *Bat Cigaretten Fabriken* [1985] 2 CMLR 363.
[145.] *Penney's Trade-Mark* [1978] 2 CMLR 100.
[146.] [1978] 1 CMLR 395.
[147.] [1986] ECR 353.

layouts and for all advertising to be approved by the franchisor. In some cases, there is also no practical solution other than for a franchisor to insist that the franchisee sell only products which have been supplied by the franchisor or by suppliers selected by the franchisor. Such a provision may not have the effect of preventing the franchisee from obtaining those products from other franchisees.

[33.73] The Franchise Block Exemption No 4087/88[148] only applies to franchises for the distribution of goods or supply of services. It does not apply to industrial franchises where the franchisee provides goods, or to wholesale franchises. To fall within the Regulation an agreement must include obligations relating to:

- The use of a common name or shop sign and a uniform presentation of contract premises and/or means of transport;

- The communication by the franchisor to the franchisee of know-how;

- The continuing provision by the franchisor to the franchisee of commercial or technical assistance during the life of the agreement.

[33.74] By definition, the know-how has to be secret, substantial and identified. Therefore, in many cases, franchise agreements will not fall within the block exemption. Some of the permitted provisions (white clauses) under the block exemption are an obligation on a franchisor in a defined area of the European Union not to grant the right to exploit all or part of the franchise to third parties. A franchisee can be obliged to operate only from licensed premises and not to sell goods competing with that of the franchisor. Black listed is any ban on passive sales. Thus, a franchisee cannot be prevented from meeting unsolicited orders simply because of a customer's place of residence.

Abuse of a Dominant Position

[33.75] Article 86 states that any abuse by one or more undertaking(s) of a dominant position within the Common Market or in a substantial part of it, shall be prohibited as incompatible with the common market in so far as it may affect trade between Member States. In *United Brands*,[149] it was stated that:

"The dominant position referred to in this Article relates to a position of economic strength enjoyed by an undertaking which enables it to prevent effective competition being maintained on the relevant market by giving it the power to behave to an appreciable extent independently of its competitors, customers and ultimately of its consumers."

---

148. [1988] OJ L359.
149. [1978] 1 CMLR 429.

The existence of an intellectual property right, such as a trade mark, is not evidence in its own right that the owner has a dominant position.[150] However in combination with other factors, an abuse of a dominant position can occur. An example would be for an undertaking in a dominant position to register a mark knowing such to be in use by a competitor. An undertaking in a dominant position which cashes in on the reputation of a brand name known and valued by customers, cannot stop supplying a long standing customer who abides by regular commercial practice, if the orders placed by this customer are in no way out of the ordinary.[151] In a case involving the acquisition of the trade mark WILKINSON SWORD, the Commission held that the transfer and certain delimitation of trade mark rights infringed Article 86 and ordered a divestiture of the mark.[152]

THE REGISTER

[33.76] The Controller is obliged to maintain a register of trade marks.[153] This is now kept in computer form[154] and is open to public inspection.[155] Rule 43 of the Trade Mark Rules 1996[156] prescribes the information which must be available on the Register upon registration, namely:

(a) the name and address of the proprietor and the address for service. Every proprietor must have an address for service in the State;[157]

(b) the goods or services in respect of which the mark is registered and their class or classes;

(c) the date of filing, being the date of registration.[158] The importance of such lies in s 13(3) which provides the rights of the proprietor of a registered trade mark have effect from this date;

(d) details of any priority date claimed under s 40 or s 41 of the 1996 Act. This date is sometimes necessary to determine which rights take precedence;

(e) the date of publication of the registration[159] which is the date from which the five year non-use provision is calculated and consequently

---

[150.] *Deutsche Grammophon v Metro* [1971] ECR 487.
[151.] *Union Brands* [1978] ECR 207.
[152.] *Warner Lambert & Bic SA v Gillette & Eemland* [1993] 5 CMLR 559.
[153.] Section 66(1).
[154.] Rule 42.
[155.] Section 66(3)(a).
[156.] SI 199/1996.
[157.] Rule 10.
[158.] Section 45(3).
[159.] Section 45(5).

required for a determination whether a registration is subject to revocation on the grounds of non-use under s 51(1)(a) of the 1963 Act;

(f) if the mark is a collective or certification mark;

(g) any disclaimer or limitation subject to which the mark is registered. Such entries made under the 1963 Act are transferred to the Register and maintained by the Controller under the 1996 Act;[160] and

(h) details of any consent furnished by the proprietor of an earlier trade mark or right.[161]

[33.77] Information regarding registrations taken out prior to the 1996 Act are transferred to the Register and maintained under the 1996 Act.[162] This is important because the distinction between Part A and B registrations *vis-à-vis* invalidity has been maintained.[163] It is no longer necessary to maintain details of associations because these no longer have any effect.[164] Conditions entered on the former register are also not carried forward.[165]

[33.78] Also entered on the Register are details of assignments,[166] licences- including information on whether they are exclusive or non-exclusive and their duration,[167] security interests,[168] vesting assents by a personal representative[169] and any order, including a court order transferring any rights in or under the mark.[170]

[33.79] It is also possible to obtain limited details of pending applications which is imperative to enable proper searching of prior rights. The practice is for applications to be entered onto the database shortly after filing and thereafter, details of the trade mark applicant, date of application and goods/services together with their classes is made available. Rule 60(2) states the information made available on pending applications should in fact be that contained in the prescribed form of application (Form 1) and any certificate from the national authority in any country from which priority is claimed. Although the prescribed Form 1 is a requirement, such is not necessary in order to obtain a filing date but

---

160. Third Schedule - para 2(5).
161. Section 10(6).
162. Third Schedule - para 2(1).
163. Third Schedule - para 13.
164. Third Schedule - para 2(3).
165. Third Schedule - para 2(4).
166. Rule 44(a).
167. Rule 44(b).
168. Rule 44(c).
169. Rule 44(d).
170. Rule 44(e).

it is not the practice of the Controller to delay entry of the application onto the database until the prescribed form has been filed.

[33.80] Once a trade mark has been approved and advertised for opposition purposes, a number of documents on the file become open to public inspection,[171] namely:[172]

(a) the prescribed application Form 1 and priority certificate, if any. Form 1 requires an applicant to state at the time of application whether or not a trade mark is being used or alternatively whether there is a *bona fide* intention to use;

(b) written grounds of the Controller's decisions in any *inter partes* proceedings;

(c) notices of opposition to a trade mark application;

(d) an application to alter a registered trade mark, including the reasons and any evidence filed in support thereof;[173]

(e) notifications of surrender of a registered trade mark;[174]

(f) applications for revocation,[175] invalidity[176] or rectification of an error or omission in the register;[177]

(g) details of applications made to amend an application prior to advertisement and the Controller's decision;[178] and

(h) any instrument or document submitted as a registrable transaction and which has been retained by the Patents Office. Inspection of such is only possible with the consent of the party who submitted the instrument or document.

Prior to publication, the above information is not available without the consent of the applicant[179] unless the applicant has warned that upon registration, they will bring proceedings against that person in respect of acts done after publication of the application.[180] Regrettably, public access to files is in fact far more limited than that provided for under the corresponding UK provisions. It is possible for an applicant to file a statutory declaration as evidence of the extent

---

[171.] Section 70(1).
[172.] Rule 60(3).
[173.] Section 49(1); Rule 35(1).
[174.] Rule 36(1).
[175.] Section 51.
[176.] Section 52.
[177.] Section 67.
[178.] Section 44.
[179.] Section 70(3).
[180.] Section 70(4).

to which they have used a mark in the State in order to show distinctiveness. A copy of such evidence is not available to an opponent in opposition proceedings unless divulged during the course of such proceedings. It may therefore be difficult for a potential opponent to assess the likelihood of successful opposition or, for example, to determine whether or not a claim of honest concurrent use has been made.

[33.81] The proprietor of a registered trade mark can make application to record a change in their name or address.[181] It is also possible for the proprietor to amend a specification of goods, provided such is limiting and does not extend rights.[182] The failure to provide for amendment of a specification in respect of services appears to be an oversight. The proprietor may also enter a disclaimer or memorandum, provided such does not extend the rights granted by the registration.[183]

[33.82] Under s 67(1), any person having a sufficient interest may apply for the rectification of an error or omission in the Register. Rectification under s 67 does not relate to matters affecting the validity of a registration. The application can be made to the High Court or the to Controller except where proceedings concerning the trade mark are already in the High Court, then the application for rectification must be made to the High Court. Where the application is made by a person other than the proprietor, the Controller will send a copy of the application and the statement of grounds to the proprietor[184] who may within three months, oppose the application.[185] Unless otherwise directed, the effect of any rectification is that the error or omission in question is deemed never to have been made.[186]

[33.83] The Controller has the power to reclassify goods or services and to require a proprietor to amend a specification, failing which the Controller may cancel or refuse to renew the registration.[187]

---

181. Section 67(5)(a).
182. Section 67(5)(b).
183. Section 67(5)(c).
184. Rule 41(2).
185. Rule 41(3).
186. Section 67(3).
187. Section 68.

Chapter 34

Trade Marks Act 1996 - Revocation and Invalidity

REVOCATION OF REGISTRATION

[34.01] Because of the scope of protection granted by a registration and the more liberal regime under the 1996 Act as to what can be registered, there is likely to be an ever increasing number of registrations. Over time, a large percentage will be CTM registrations[1] and trade marks under the Madrid Protocol when ratified.[2] The clearance of a new mark will become increasingly problematic. Apart from earning revenue, one of the reasons behind the renewal fees charged by the State is to clear at least a certain amount of dead wood from the Register. Another way is to require that a trade mark be used. As stated in the preamble to the Trade Mark Harmonisation Directive:[3]

> Whereas in order to reduce the total number of trade marks registered and protected in the Community and, consequently, the number of conflicts which arise between them, it is essential to require that registered trade marks must actually be used or, if not used, be subject to revocation.

[34.02] In some countries such as the US, a proprietor must provide evidence of use at a specified stage during the lifetime of a registration in order to maintain the registration in force. Certain countries have elected for a system requiring evidence of use at the time of renewal. This is not a requirement under Irish law where non-use only leads to revocation where action is taken by a third party. Section 51(1) of the 1996 Act identifies the two instances where a registration can be revoked on the grounds of non-use as follows:

(1) if the mark has not been put to genuine use in the State in relation to the goods/services embraced by the registration within five years from when the trade mark was actually registered;[4] and

(2) where, after actual registration, genuine use in relation to the goods/ services is suspended for an uninterrupted period of five years.[5]

[1.] See Ch 27.
[2.] See para **[26.47]**.
[3.] 89/104/EEC.
[4.] Section 51(1)(a).
[5.] Section 51(1)(b).

In both instances, there is an exception where there are proper reasons for non-use.

[34.03] These non-use provisions implement Article 10(1) of the Harmonisation Directive and similar provisions also existed under the 1963 Act.[6] However, the 1963 Act did provide for revocation in the case of a registration less than five years old on the grounds that the applicant had no *bona fide* intention to use and there had in fact been no *bona fide* use. Under the 1996 Act, it will be necessary in such circumstances to rely on s 52(1) and claim invalidity on the grounds of bad faith because of a failure to comply with s 37(2) requiring a *bona fide* intention to use.

[34.04] Under the 1963 Act, the onus to show non-use lay on the party seeking revocation.[7] Section 99 of the 1996 Act now shifts the onus of proving use onto the trade mark proprietor. This is likely to lead to many speculative revocation actions because the expense of investigation into non-use can now be avoided. It will be necessary for the Courts to determine whether or not s 99 also requires a proprietor to prove a *bona fide* intent to use. It seems logical that this should be the position.

[34.05] The five year non-use period runs from completion of the registration procedure[8] which s 51(1) describes as the date of publication of the registration which should correspond to the time that the certificate of registration issues but may be earlier.[9]

[34.06] It is possible to commence or recommence use and thereby remedy a position whereby the registration was previously vulnerable to revocation on the grounds of non-use. However, use during the three month period immediately preceding the application for revocation is disregarded unless preparations for the commencement or resumption of use began before the proprietor became aware that the application for revocation might be made.[10] This means that it is possible to write to a trade mark proprietor seeking voluntary cancellation on the grounds of non-use. The proprietor may be prompted to commence use upon receiving such a communication but use for the first three months will be disregarded. It is therefore important for a third party not receiving a positive response within three months to preserve their position by filing an application for revocation. Under the 1963 Act, the use period disregarded was one month.

---

6. Section 34.
7. *Cheseborough Manufacturing Co's TM* 19 RPC 342; see *Anheuser-Busch Inc v Budweiser Budvar* High Court, unrep, 23 October 1996, Costello J.
8. Article 10(1) - EU Harmonisation Directive No 89/104/EEC.
9. Section 45(4). See Ch 33 *ante*.
10. Section 51(3).

[34.07] The onus is on the trade mark proprietor to show genuine use. Under the 1963 Act the use had to be *bona fide*. There is likely to be very little difference, if any, between the courts' interpretation of the word 'genuine' as opposed to the words '*bona fide*'. The Irish courts followed the Court of Appeal Decision in *Electrolux Ltd v Electrix Ltd*[11] in which *bona fide* use was held to mean substantial and genuine use of the mark judged by ordinary commercial standards. The words do not imply that there has to be a particular volume or duration of use. Provided the use was of a genuine commercial nature, the motive was irrelevant. In *Batchelors Limited v Goodalls of Ireland Limited*,[12] the plaintiff owned the trade mark TANGO and sued the defendant for the use of TANG in relation to a non-alcoholic beverage. The defendant counterclaimed for revocation and alleged that there had been non-use for a number of years and the mark had only been put to use for the express purpose of enabling the plaintiff to save the registration and sue for infringement. McWilliam J held that use effected for that purpose was nevertheless *bona fide* and stated:

> "the question of *bona fide* refers only to the use being genuinely for the purpose of marketing the owner's goods and has no reference to an opportune commencement of the use to the disadvantage of anybody else".

[34.08] The provision in s 51(3) which allows the proprietor to rely upon preparations to commence or resume use, although not in the 1963 Act, was a factor considered by the Controller in *Re Frisk*.[13] In that case, the only use of the trade mark had been in relation to a consignment of imported goods which had not cleared customs. It was held that this use was *bona fide* and the Controller refused to expunge the trade mark from the Register.

[34.09] In *CONCORD Trade Mark*,[14] the UK courts applied more stringent criteria and seemed to require that the use had to be for the purposes of establishing a goodwill in the mark so as to make trading under that mark profitable in itself.[15] In doing so, the emphasis was placed more on the requirement that the use be substantial than that it be genuine.

[34.10] In *Harold Radford & Austin Motor Company's Applications*,[16] it was held that advertisements for sale and orders resulting from such advertisements, did not constitute use of the trade mark. It was not, however, necessary that the goods exist concurrently with the advertisement. What was required was that the proprietor had at the time of advertisement, taken positive steps to trade in goods

---

[11.] (1954) 71 RPC 23.
[12.] High Court, unrep, (1977) No 4662P.
[13.] *Carnation Co v Ocean Harvest Ltd.* (1970) Supp OJ 111 p 17.
[14.] [1987] FSR 209 - See also *HERMES* [1982] RPC 425.
[15.] See also *Imperial Group Ltd v Philip Morris & Co Ltd* [1982] FSR 72.
[16.] (1951) 68 RPC 221; see also *REVUE Trade Mark* [1979] RPC 27.

marked with the trade mark. Advertising would usually be sufficient to at least fulfil the requirement that preparations for the commencement or resumption of the trade mark had begun.[17]

[34.11] Section 51(2) in implementing Article 10(2) of the Trade Mark Harmonisation Directive[18] allows the following to constitute use:

(a) use of the trade mark in a form differing in elements from the Registration but which does not alter the distinctive character of the mark in the form in which it was registered; and

(b) affixing of the trade mark to goods or to the packaging thereof in the State solely for export purposes.

[34.12] In relation to (a), a similar provision existed under s 38 of the 1963 Act. There has always been a tendency to register word trade marks in block capital letters on the basis that most stylisation or different casing of letters will be viewed as a difference from the registered mark which does not alter the distinctive character.[19] This provision is a recognition that over time, the format in which a trade mark is used may alter but the substantial identity remain intact. Where possible, a proprietor should register a series mark providing for different formats in the registration itself.[20] An example where the courts refused to accept use of a trade mark with just a one letter difference is *HUGGARS Trade Mark*[21] where use was made of HUGGERS. The Court was heavily influenced by the fact that although HUGGARS was meaningless, the word HUGGERS was descriptive in relation to the goods being clothing. Decisions made under s 49(1) in relation to permissible alterations to a trade mark registration are likely to be of considerable guidance. In *Seaforth Maritime Ltd's Application*,[22] an amendment was refused on the basis that the change in visual impression created by the alteration was substantial. It was held that what is important are "the features by which the mark will be recognised either by its meaning, phonetically or visually and which serve to distinguish the goods of the proprietor of the mark from the similar goods of other traders".[23] In *Spillers Ltd v Quaker Oats Ltd*,[24] it was held that use of a non-hyphenated word trade mark could be taken as equivalent for the use of the registered hyphenated version.

---

17. Section 51(3).
18. 89/104/EEC.
19. 1963 Act , s 38: 'Not substantially affecting its identity'.
20. Section 46(2). See para **[33.06]**.
21. [1979] FSR 310.
22. [1993] RPC 72.
23. See also *OTRIVIN Trade Mark* [1967] RPC 613 and *PELICAN Trade Mark* [1978] RPC 424.
24. (1969) FSR 510.

[34.13] The provision allowing for export use to be taken into account also existed under the 1963 Act. It is limited to the affixing of the trade mark to goods or their packaging and there is no inclusion of a service mark for export trade. No such use of a service mark will defeat an action for revocation.

[34.14] A revocation action can be defeated where it can be shown that there were proper reasons for non-use. There is no definition of what is meant by the words 'proper reasons'. Under the 1963 Act, a similar defence to revocation also arose if the registered proprietor could show that non-use was due to special circumstances in the trade and was not due to any intention not to use or to abandon the mark.[25] An example of proper reasons would be the need to secure regulatory approval before the launch of a pharmaceutical product. In *Manus AB v RJ Fulwood & Bland Ltd*,[26] a number of external restrictions on trade due to the Second World War were deemed sufficient reasons to justify non-use. An intention to use the mark as soon as the technical problems have been overcome has been held not to be sufficient reason for non-use.[27] It is possible that a similar decision would be reached under the 1996 Act and proper reasons are still likely to be external reasons common to the trade as a whole as opposed to business difficulties experienced by a particular trader. However in *Glen Catrine Bonded Warehouse Ltd's Application*[28] Tuck LJ considered that the word "proper" may be more liberally interpreted and a "Tribunal may, therefore perhaps be able to find that disruptive situations in which the registered proprietor's business alone is affected are, nonetheless proper" and that the word proper in the context of s 51 means "acceptable reasonable, justifiable in all the circumstances". It was also held that there is a statutory discretion in s 51 and that revocation is not automatic where there is non-use.

[34.15] A likely common occurrence is where there may be partial use, ie use on some but not all of goods/services covered by a registration. This is dealt with in s 51(5) which provides that "where grounds for revocation exist in respect of only some of the goods or services for which the trade mark is registered, revocation shall relate to those goods or services only". It is common practice to hold specifications for a broad range of goods/services and even in a few cases, for a specification reading 'all goods' in a particular class. In any application for revocation, it is important to identify the exact goods/services against which revocation is sought. Failure to do so may mean that a proprietor will simply furnish evidence of use in respect of certain goods/services and defeat the entire action since in the case of a wide specification, it is unlikely that the proprietor

---

[25] Section 34(3) - 1963 Act.
[26] (1949) 66 RPC 71.
[27] *Thermax* [1985] RPC 403.
[28] [1996] ETMR 56.

will be called upon to provide evidence of use in relation to the entire specification. The revocation action should properly define the scope of the relief sought, ie the extent to which revocation is sought. The 1963 Act contained a discretion to allow goods to remain in the specification despite non-use where there was use on goods of the same description in the specification and this discretion may also exist under the 1996 Act.[29]

[34.16] The definition of a trade mark in s 6(1) of the 1996 Act is also of critical importance in the context of revocation on the grounds of non-use because s 51(1) requires use as a trade mark. In *KODAK Trade Mark*,[30] revocation was sought against the KODAK registration in respect of clothing. Kodak Ltd did use their mark on T-shirts but it was held that this was not trade mark use and was simply advertising so as to encourage people to buy their photographic products. This decision was decided under the UK Trade Marks Act 1938, corresponding to the Irish 1963 Act. The definition of a trade mark under the 1963 Act was limited to the function of a trade mark as an indication of origin. Whether or not the KODIAK case will be followed under the 1996 Act depends on the extent to which the role of the trade mark is seen as a vehicle for advertising and promotion.

[34.17] Article 10(3) of the Harmonisation Directive[31] provides that use of the trade mark with the consent of the proprietor shall be deemed to constitute use by the proprietor. This consent is likely to be interpreted as meaning use by a party who is in the position of a licensee. A proprietor should ensure that there is proper control over a licensee. In *JOB Trade Mark*,[32] it was held that insufficient control of the licensee's activities was maintained and therefore use by the licensee could not be relied on. This decision was made under the UK Trade Marks Act 1938 but is still likely to be followed because uncontrolled licensing can be viewed as tantamount to an assignment of the trade mark. Uncontrolled use can also lead to a trade mark being considered misleading and subject to revocation under s 51(1)(d).

[34.18] It is not stated that the use must be by the registered proprietor and this would suggest that an assignee who has not recorded its ownership on the Register may nevertheless rely on its use.[33]

---

[29] *Glen Catrine Bonded Warehouse Ltd's Application* [1996] ETMR 56.
[30] [1990] FSR 49.
[31] 89/104/EEC.
[32] [1993] FSR 118.
[33] *TROOPER Trade Mark* [1994] RPC 26.

Generic use

[34.19] A further ground for revocation exists under s 51(1)(c) and arises where as a consequence of the acts or inactivity of the proprietor, the trade mark has become the common name in the trade for a product or service for which the trade mark is registered. It is important for a trade mark owner to ensure that it properly polices its trade mark so that it does not become generic or descriptive. It is the use being made by the trade as opposed to the public which is the determining factor and this is only natural, given that the public may refer to a product simply by way of its trade mark but such a trade mark still serves to distinguish the product from that of the competitor, eg WALKMAN denotes a Sony personal stereo system. Examples of trade marks which have become generic through trade use are ASPRIN and FORMICA.

[34.20] A similar provision did exist under s 23 of the 1963 Act but with one particularly important difference. The 1963 Act allowed for revocation in the case of generic use by the trade in relation to goods not covered by the registration, ie where the generic use is in respect of goods of the same description. This was somewhat ironic, given that the proprietor under the 1963 Act could not in fact take an infringement action against unauthorised use on goods not embraced by the registration and consequently may not have been in a position to prevent the generic use. In *Daiquiri Rum*,[34] the trade mark registered in respect of rum was removed from the Register on evidence of generic use by the trade in respect of a rum cocktail. This would not be the position under the 1996 Act given that the generic use must be in respect of a product or service embraced by the registration. Also, under the 1996 Act, the proprietor can also take an infringement action where goods or services are similar[35] and even in some cases dissimilar.[36]

[34.21] The trade mark must become the common name in the trade due to acts or inactivity of the proprietor. Such inactivity would typically be the failure to properly control use by a licensee or to continually allow the mark to be infringed. The acts by the proprietor would be to use the trade mark in a descriptive manner, for example, as a noun, verb or in plural form. Although there is no legal requirement to indicate a trade mark as being registered by use of the symbol ® or otherwise, apart from serving as a deterrent, it does help to indicate that the trade mark is not a product description but the subject of proprietary rights. Even if a trade mark is not registered, it is possible to use the initials TM.

---

34. [1969] RPC 600.
35. Section 14(2).
36. Section 14(3).

[34.22] A CTM grants broader protection under Article 10 of the CTM Regulation. If use of a CTM in a dictionary, encyclopaedia or similar reference work gives the impression that it constitutes the generic name of the goods or services for which the trade mark is registered, the publisher of the work shall, at the request of the proprietor of the CTM, ensure that the reproduction of the trade mark at the latest in the next edition of the publication, is accompanied by an indication that it is a registered trade mark.

Misleading use

[34.23] Under s 51(1)(d), revocation can arise due to use which is liable to mislead the public. Examples given as to the type of deception refer to the nature, quality or geographical origin of goods or services. This is not an exhaustive list and another example would be misleading use as to mode of manufacture. The position was similar under the 1963 Act but in *GE Trade Mark*,[37] the House of Lords ruled that if the likelihood of confusion did not exist at the time of registration but arose subsequently, then revocation was only possible due to some blameworthy act of the registered proprietor. While the 1996 Act requires that the misleading use must be as a consequence of use by or with the consent of the proprietor, there is no requirement of any culpability and could be inadvertent use.

[34.24] An example of misleading use would be to use a trade mark on a product of a particular origin and then without sufficient notice which would otherwise avoid public confusion, to subsequently use the trade mark on a product of a different origin.[38] It is important for a trade mark owner to exercise proper quality control provisions amongst its licensees. If the quality of a product varies between difference licensees selling under the same trade mark, there is certainly a strong argument that the public will be misled.

[34.25] Under the 1963 Act, it was possible for the Court or Controller to impose a condition on registration in an attempt to avoid any subsequent confusion. Thus, if the trade mark was a geographical location, a condition would typically read:

> "It is a condition of registration that the trade mark will only be used on goods manufactured in (that location)".[39]

If this condition was breached, then the registration was liable to cancellation. The imposition of such a condition is no longer possible under the 1996 Act and the transitional provisions[40] also caused existing conditions to cease to have

---

[37.] [1973] RPC 297.
[38.] See *Thorne & Sons Ltd v Pimms Ltd* (1909) 26 RPC 221.
[39.] See *WATERFORD Registration* No 110772.

effect. The onus has shifted from the Controller to protect against public confusion under the 1963 Act to the owner who may otherwise suffer the consequence of revocation under s 51(1)(d).

[34.26] Under Council Regulation No 2081/92, on the Protection of Geographical Indications and Designations of Origin for Agricultural Products and Foodstuffs, it is possible to register certain geographical and in some cases, even non-geographical names which identify origin.[41] Such a registration prevents unauthorised use in any way liable to mislead the public as to the true origin of the product. It is necessary for such a trade mark owner to use the trade mark in accordance with the product specification which must be furnished under Regulation No 2081/92, otherwise the product is likely to be viewed as misleading.

[34.27] Section 51(5) deals with the position vis-à-vis partial revocation where grounds for revocation exist in respect of only some of the goods or services for which the trade mark is registered, revocation relates to those goods or services only.

Application for revocation

[34.28] An application for revocation can be made by any person[42] and unlike the 1963 Act, does not require *locus standi* by way of a person aggrieved.[43] The most common instances are likely to be by way of a counterclaim in infringement proceedings in response to opposition proceedings or where the Controller has raised an earlier mark by way of a citation under the relative grounds for refusal. The applicant for revocation can elect to take the action before either the High Court or the Controller. It is expected that similar to the position in the 1963 Act, the vast majority of revocation actions will be taken before the Controller. If proceedings concerning the trade mark in question are pending in the High Court in, for example, an infringement suit, then the application for revocation must be made to the High Court.[44] If the application is made to the Controller, then he may at any stage refer the application to the High Court.[45]

[34.29] The procedure before the Controller is governed by Rule 41 of the Trade Marks Rules 1996. An application for revocation requires a statement of the grounds and when this is filed, a copy is sent by the Controller to the proprietor

---

[40.] Third Schedule, para 2(4).
[41.] See para **[36.12]**.
[42.] Section 51(4).
[43.] Sections 34 & 40 - 1963 Act.
[44.] Section 51(4)(a).
[45.] Section 51(4)(b).

of the registered mark. The proprietor has three months within which to lodge a counterstatement by way of defence. If the revocation action claims non-use under s 51(1)(a) or (b), then the proprietor must file evidence of the use upon which it is intended to rely. Failure to file such evidence means that the Controller has a discretion to dismiss the defence and grant the revocation. Subsequent procedures will be determined by the Controller but parties do have a right to be heard. In proceedings before the High Court, the Controller is entitled to appeal and be heard.[46] Unless otherwise directed by the High Court, the Controller may submit evidence by way of written statement.[47] An appeal from the Controller's decision lies to the High Court.[48] The Controller may award costs[49] and it is usual for such to follow the successful party. The awards made by the Controller under the 1963 Act tended to be nominal and did not compensate the successful party for the actual costs incurred.

Effective date of revocation

[34.30] The effective date of revocation is dealt with in s 51(6). Where the registration of a trade mark is revoked to any extent, the rights of the proprietor shall be deemed to have ceased to that extent as from:

    (a) the date of the application for revocation; or

    (b) if the Controller or the Court is satisfied that the grounds for revocation existed at an earlier date, that date.

If the revocation is by way of counterclaim in infringement proceedings, then it would be expected that an order be sought claiming that revocation should take effect from a date immediately prior to the alleged acts of infringement.

[34.31] Under the transitional provisions, applications for revocation on the grounds of non-use under sub-ss 51(1)(a) or (b) apply to all registrations including those registered under the 1963 Act.[50]

[34.32] It is unclear, however, whether the grounds under s 51(1)(c) or (d) apply to trade marks dated prior to 1 July 1996, ie the commencement date of the 1996 Act. The uncertainty arises because of the division in the 1996 Act between grounds for revocation (s 51) and grounds for invalidity (s 52).

[34.33] It is only the validity of existing registrations which the transitional provisions state will be determined under the 1963 Act. No objection to the validity of registrations under the 1963 Act may be taken on the grounds of

---

46. Section 78(1).
47. Section 78(2).
48. Section 79(1).
49. Section 72(1).
50. Third Schedule, para 11(2).

failure to satisfy the requirements of the 1996 Act.[51] The fact that the transitional provisions are silent on sub-ss 51(1)(c) and (d) might suggest that these grounds will be held not to be available against trade marks dated prior to 1 July 1996. However, Article 12 of the Trade Mark Harmonisation Directive does not allow States to derogate from the provisions in sub-ss 51(1)(c) and (d) in relation to existing registrations and therefore, it is likely that these grounds will also be held to exist against all registrations irrespective of their date. No application for revocation on grounds of non-use may be made in relation to a defensive trade mark until 1 July 2001, ie five years from the commencement date of the 1996 Act.[52]

INVALIDITY OF REGISTRATION

[34.34] The main grounds for challenging the validity of a trade mark registration are stated in s 52 of the 1996 Act which implements Articles 3 and 4 of the Harmonisation Directive[53] and provides that both the absolute and relative grounds for refusal also arise post-registration by way of an action for invalidity. Essentially, the action is available against trade marks which, although registered, should not have been. However, a situation may arise where a trade mark, although invalidly registered, has through use, acquired distinctiveness and can therefore remain on the register. This arises in the context of the absolute grounds in s 8. These grounds which form a basis on which the Controller can refuse an application and on which an application can be opposed following advertisement, are also grounds for invalidity. If, however, it is claimed that the trade mark is devoid of distinctive character,[54] purely descriptive[55] or is a trade use,[56] then the proprietor can rely on post-registration use to show that even if these grounds existed earlier, they no longer apply.[57]

[34.35] A common ground for seeking invalidity under the 1963 Act was a lack of a *bona fide* intention to use the trade mark on the goods of application. Under s 37(2) of the 1996 Act, it is also a requirement that there be use or at a minimum, a *bona fide* intention to use. Therefore, failure to comply with this requirement could also be considered a ground for invalidity by virtue of s 8(4)(b) as being an application made in bad faith. Post-registration use cannot subsequently remedy this position. The grounds for invalidity must exist at the time of registration and a trade mark cannot be declared invalid on the grounds

---

[51.] Third Schedule, para 13.
[52.] Third Schedule, para 11(3).
[53.] 89/100/EEC.
[54.] Section 8(1)(b).
[55.] Section 8(1)(c).
[56.] Section 8(1)(d).
[57.] Section 52(1).

that it has subsequently ceased to be distinctive. In such a case, it is necessary to consider whether the grounds for revocation under s 51(1)(c) or s 51(1)(d) are available.

[34.36] The transitional provisions contained in s 13 of the Third Schedule to the 1996 Act, state that the 1963 Act continues to apply as regards the validity of existing registrations, ie trade marks dated prior to 1 July 1996. This creates a number of problems. A trade mark registered under the 1963 Act may be declared invalid even though the grounds for invalidity do not exist under the 1996 Act. A proprietor cannot rely on post-registration use under the 1963 Act. It is necessary to consider both the grounds for invalidity under the 1963 Act and also whether or not the trade mark was registered under Part A or Part B of the Register. This is because under s 21 of the 1963 Act, a Part A registration after seven years is taken to be valid in all respects unless the registration was obtained fraudulently or was contrary to s 19 of the 1963 Act, ie trade marks likely to deceive or cause confusion or otherwise disentitled to protection in a court of law. In the case of a Part B registration or a Part A registration of less than seven years duration, then it is necessary to give consideration to invalidity on grounds including ss 2 and 25 of the 1963 Act and in particular, the definition of a trade mark. In the absence of service mark registration prior to the 1996 Act, trade mark owners sought to obtain a footing on the Register by registering in respect of certain goods although the trade mark owner's activities were purely in the services sector. For example, it was quite common for entities in the services industry to register marks in respect of printed publications (Class 16) and the validity of a number of these registrations is questionable. The Supreme Court in *ITT World Directories Inc v The Contoller*,[58] although accepting that it was not necessary to sell goods under the trade mark, still required a commercial activity under the mark. Such does not arise if use of a trade mark on the goods is simply as a means of advertising services.

[34.37] The relative grounds for refusal of an application in s 10 of the 1996 Act, form the basis for an action for invalidity under s 52(2) unless the proprietor of the earlier trade mark or earlier right has consented to the registration. It is not clear whether this ground is to be determined by reference to the position at the date of the application for invalidity or at the date of registration. The effect of a successful action which declares a registration invalid, is that the registration is deemed never to have existed.[59] This, and the fact that the grounds for refusal and invalidity are dealt with together in Article 4 of the Harmonisation Directive, suggest that the question should be determined by the position at the date of registration.

[58.] [1985] ILRM 30 (GOLDEN PAGES Trade Mark).
[59.] Section 52(6).

[34.38] Because of the transitional provisions which provide that the validity of registrations dated prior to 1 July 1996, must be determined under the 1963 Act, it is necessary to consider the grounds which exist under both the 1963 and 1996 Act.[60]

[34.39] If the trade mark being challenged is dated after 1 July 1996 and the earlier trade mark is an identical registration in respect of identical goods/ services, then no proofs by way of a likelihood of confusion are required. Under s 12(4)(b), no defence by way of honest concurrent use is available. If invalidity is sought against a registration dated prior to 1 July 1996, then it is necessary to establish if it is registered in Part A or B of the Register and the date of registration. If the registration is in Part A of the Register and more than seven years old, then the grounds for invalidity under s 20 of the 1963 Act are not available and it is necessary to rely on s 19 of the 1963 Act. Section 19 requires proof that the trade mark is likely to deceive or cause confusion because of the use of the earlier trade mark.

[34.40] In a case involving one of the following:

    (a) identical marks and similar goods or services;

    (b) similar marks and identical goods or services; and

    (c) similar marks and similar goods or services

then the 1996 Act requires a likelihood of confusion which includes the likelihood of association.[61] The position under the 1963 Act does not differ from that outlined above in relation to identical marks/goods and it is possible to raise a defence of honest concurrent use.

[34.41] The relative grounds which exist for dissimilar goods/services are new to Irish trade mark law and the 1963 Act did not include a provision corresponding to s 10(3) of the 1996 Act. Under the 1963 Act, it was necessary to rely on s 19. In *Gallaher (Dublin) Ltd v Health Education Bureau*,[62] Costello J stated:

> "It seems to me that if it can be shown that a person used another's trade mark in a way which means that the registered proprietor cannot use it again on the goods for which he obtained registration, then it is highly likely the use complained of must have been in relation to the goods in respect of which it was registered as otherwise, no damage would have been done to his mark. If there is a dispute as to whether or not the user of the mark complained of was 'in relation to' goods, the fact that the goodwill in the mark has been injured

---

[60.] Third Schedule, para 13.

[61.] See paras **[30.30]**-**[30.33]**.

[62.] [1982] ILRM 240.

does lend considerable support to a plaintiff's claim that there has been use of the mark in relation to the goods for which the mark was registered".

This is certainly supportive of the view that there are circumstances where a conflicting mark for dissimilar goods may be declared invalid because of possible damage to the proprietor's goodwill under an earlier trade mark.

[34.42] The grounds for invalidity based on unregistered trade mark rights under the 1996 Act are narrower than those which existed under the 1963 Act. Therefore, a trade mark registered under the 1996 Act is less susceptible to invalidity on this ground than trade marks registered under the 1963 Act. Section 52(2)(b) of the 1996 Act allows for invalidity on the basis of unregistered earlier rights identified in s 10(4)(a) & (b). This requires the proprietor of an earlier right to have enforceable intellectual property rights such as copyright, registered designs or grounds to sustain an action for passing off. On the other hand, the grounds for invalidity in s 19 of the 1963 Act, although requiring a need to show a likelihood of confusion or deception, did not require the same proofs as an action for passing off.[63] Section 19 was also interpreted to include grounds existing by virtue of unregistered rights in the form of other intellectual property rights such as copyright and registrations conflicting with such were viewed as 'contrary to law'.[64]

[34.43] The definition of 'earlier trade mark' in s 11(1) of the 1996 Act, includes well known trade marks under Article 6 *bis* of the Paris Convention. Therefore, such a trade mark, even though unregistered, may form a basis for seeking invalidity of a later trade mark.

Application for Invalidity

[34.44] Similar to the position vis-à-vis revocation, an application for invalidity under s 52 of the 1996 Act, can be made by any person and not necessarily by a person aggrieved, and can be made to the High Court or the Controller.
Section 52(4) allows the Controller to seek a declaration of invalidity in the case of bad faith in the registration of a trade mark.

[34.45] Where the grounds for invalidity exist in respect of only some of the goods or services for which the trade mark is registered, the trade mark is declared invalid as regards those goods or services only.[65] Where the registration of a trade mark is declared invalid to any extent, the registration shall, to that extent, be deemed never to have been made with the exception of transactions past and closed.[66]

[63.] *BALI* [1969] RPC 472.
[64.] *KARO STEP* [1977] RPC 255.
[65.] Section 52(5).

[34.46] A person may be estopped from taking invalidity proceedings. The effect of acquiescence is now statutorily stated in s 53 of the 1996 Act which implements the provisions in Article 9 of the Trade Mark Harmonisation Directive.[67]

[34.47] The legislation will have to be read alongside the equitable doctrine of estoppel, an example of which can be seen in *JOB Trade Mark*[68] where a licensee was estopped from taking an action for rectification. Section 53 requires acquiescence for a continuous period of five years in the use of a registered trade mark in the State and while being aware of such use. The effect of such acquiescence is to deny a right to seek a declaration of invalidity but in keeping with the Directive, there is no such exclusion in relation to revocation proceedings.

[34.48] Section 65(3) of the 1996 Act[69] which implements Article 6 *septies* of the Paris Convention allows the proprietor of a mark to apply for a declaration of invalidity against an unauthorised registration taken out by an agent or representative. In an Italian decision, *Hifonics Europe v Denico Srl*[70] it was held that Article 6 *septies* of the Paris Convention does not apply to mere distributors. Under s 25 of the 1963 Act, it is also possible to claim invalidity by virtue of the fact that such an agent or representative falsely claimed to be the trade mark proprietor or that under s 19 of the 1963 Act use would be likely to deceive or cause confusion.[71]

---

66. Section 52(6).
67. 89/104/EEC.
68. [1993] FSR 118.
69. See Article 6 *septies* of the Paris Convention.
70. Court of Milan, 9 February 1995.
71. *K Sabatier* [1993] RPC 97.

Chapter 35

Certification and Collective Marks

CERTIFICATION MARKS

[35.01] A certification mark is defined in s 55 of the Trade Marks Act 1996 to mean a mark indicating that the goods or services in connection with which it is used are certified by the proprietor of the mark in respect of origin, material, mode or manufacture of goods or performance of services, quality, accuracy or other characteristics. The provisions dealing with certification marks are contained in the Second Schedule to the 1996 Act. The Trade Marks Act 1963 also provided for certification marks but only in respect of goods.

[35.02] A certification mark acts as a warranty that goods or services have particular characteristics. The owner can be an individual, but is more normally a trade association or other organised body who, although not trading in the goods or services, can by way of registration protect against traders using the mark and thereby falsely claiming certain attributes. An example of a certification mark is STILTON which is owned by The Stilton Cheese Makers Association which denotes cheese originating from a particular region and with certain characteristics as to quality. It is quite common for a certification mark to be used alongside a trade mark. The former identifying the individual trader, while the certification mark is a statement that such a trader produces goods or provides services which have certain characteristics with which any other user of the certification mark also comply. An example would be a group of traders in a particular location grouping together with a shared interest by way of a certification mark thus ensuring that such can only be used on goods originating from such a location but at the same time, each individual member would promote their own particular product. While there would be competition between individual members, there would be a common objective to prevent use of any false geographical indicator.

[35.03] The characteristics of a certification mark demand that the proprietor cannot carry on a business involving the supply of goods or services of the kind certified.[1] It must be owned by a proprietor not engaged in trade in the goods or services in relation to which the mark is used.

[1.] Second Schedule - para 4.

[35.04] The definition of a trade mark in s 6(1) of the 1996 Act is equally applicable to a certification mark[2] except that the capacity to distinguish is between goods or services which are certified from those which are not certified. Under the 1963 Act, it was necessary for a certification mark to be adapted to distinguish and therefore fulfil the requirements for registration in Part A of the Register. This is no longer a requirement under the 1996 Act and, for example, in keeping with other marks, it will be possible to register as a certification mark the shape of goods or their packaging which are capable of distinguishing. It will also be necessary that the mark is capable of being represented graphically.

[35.05] Article 15(2) of the EU Trade Mark Harmonisation Directive allowed Member States the option of allowing registration of certification marks which consist of signs or indications that designate geographical origin. This option has been implemented in the 1996 Act[3] and therefore nullifies the position which would have otherwise applied under s 8(1)(c) of the 1996 Act. There is a proviso that the proprietor of such a certification mark cannot restrain use in accordance with honest practices and in particular, use by a person who is entitled to use a geographical name.

[35.06] A certification mark must be refused registration if it is liable to mislead the public as to the character or significance of the mark, in particular, if it is likely to be taken to be something other than a certification mark.[4] The Controller may require the mark to include an indication that it is a certification mark and an application can be amended in this regard if necessary.[5]

[35.07] It is necessary for the applicant for registration of a certification mark to file with the Controller regulations governing the use of the mark. These regulations must indicate[6] at a minimum:

- who is authorised to use the mark;

- the characteristics to be certified by the mark;

- how the certifying body is to test the characteristics and to supervise use;

- the fees (if any) to be paid in connection with the operation of the mark; and

- procedures for resolving disputes.

---

2. Second Schedule - para 2.
3. Second Schedule - para 3.
4. Second Schedule - para 5(1).
5. Second Schedule - para 5(2).
6. Second Schedule - para 6(2).

The Minister must approve the regulations and, in addition to the minimum requirements, it is also necessary that the regulations are not contrary to public policy or to accepted principles of morality.[7] Public policy would include an obligation to allow any party to use the mark who meet with the characteristics and comply with the regulations. It is also usual for there to be a right of appeal to an independent body in the event of refusal to permit use or if such permission is withdrawn. The regulations also usually provide for a register of users and for the issue of a certificate to an authorised user. The Minister must also be satisfied with the competence of the applicant to certify the goods or services. This does not mean the applicant is actually bound to inspect the goods.[8]

[35.08] The regulations do not have to be filed at the date of application but must be lodged within six months of the Controller's initial decision to allow an applicant to proceed.[9] The regulations are open to public inspection from the date of advertisement in the Official Journal[10] and may be amended with the consent of the Minister.[11]

[35.09] Once advertised in the Official Journal, the normal three month period for opposition and/or observations applies. A notice of opposition must be filed with the Minister and a copy sent to the Controller.[12] The grounds for opposition include that the regulations do not comply with the requirements for registration.

[35.10] A certification mark can not be effectively assigned or transmitted without the consent of the Minister.[13]

[35.11] Generally, the normal infringement provisions apply equally in respect of a certification mark. However, the proprietor of a certification mark designating geographical origin is not entitled to restrain use in accordance with honest practices in industrial or commercial matters.[14] Unless there is an agreement to the contrary, an authorised user can call on the proprietor to take infringement proceedings in respect of any matter which affects the authorised user's interests.[15] If the proprietor refuses, then after two months, the authorised user may bring proceedings in their own name.[16] Without leave of the High

---

7. Second Schedule - para 7(1)(a).
8. Second Schedule - para 7(1)(b); *UNIS & UNIS FRANCE TM* (1922) 39 RPC 346.
9. Rule 33(1) - Second Schedule - paras 7(2) and 7(3).
10. Rule 33(4)(a).
11. Second Schedule - para 11; Rule 34.
12. Rule 33(4)(c).
13. Second Schedule - para 12.
14. Second Schedule - para 3.
15. Second Schedule - para 13(2).
16. Second Schedule - para 13(3).

Court, the proprietor must be joined as a plaintiff or added as a defendant.[17] If added as a defendant, unless they take part in the proceedings, the proprietor is not liable for costs.[18] Where infringement proceedings are brought by the proprietor of a certification mark, the High Court must take into account any loss suffered or likely to be suffered by authorised users. The Court may further direct that any award be held on behalf of such user(s).[19]

[35.12] The normal grounds for revocation contained in s 51 of the 1996 Act equally apply in relation to certification marks. However, there are additional grounds as follows:

(a) the proprietor has begun to trade in the goods or services certified, thus not complying with Paragraph 4 of the Second Schedule;[20]

(b) the manner in which the trade mark has been used has made it misleading to the public as regards the character or significance of the mark, in particular, if it is likely to be taken to be something other than a certification mark;[21]

(c) the proprietor has failed to observe or secure observance of the regulations governing the use of the mark;[22]

(d) there has been an amendment to the regulations which no longer comply with the statutory prescribed contents or are contrary to public policy or accepted principles of morality;[23] and

(e) the proprietor is no longer competent to certify the goods or services for which the mark is registered.[24] This ground was the subject of revocation proceedings in *SEA ISLAND COTTON Certification Trade Mark*[25] where it was held that there was no obligation to carry out any examination or investigation but the proprietor must have the legal and practical ability to certify. One must take into account the constitution of the certifying body and whether in practice, it could and did carry out the duty of certification.

[35.13] Revocation on the grounds identified at (a), (b) and (e) must be made to the Minister. The grounds for invalidity in s 52 of the 1996 Act also apply to certification marks. Also included as grounds for invalidity are regulations

---

[17.] Second Schedule - para 13(4)(a).
[18.] Second Schedule - para 13(4)(b).
[19.] Second Schedule - para 13(6).
[20.] Second Schedule - para 14(1)(a).
[21.] Second Schedule - para 14(1)(b).
[22.] Second Schedule - para 14(1)(c).
[23.] Second Schedule - para 14(1)(d).
[24.] Second Schedule - para 14(1)(e).
[25.] [1989] RPC 87.

which are contrary to public policy, or to accepted principles of morality or which do not fulfil the requirements stated in para 7(1) (Second Schedule) as being a pre-requisite to Ministerial approval.[26] Invalidity can arise through use liable to mislead the public as to the character or signification of the mark. A certification mark may also be declared invalid if the proprietor commences business involving the supply of goods or services of the kind certified.

COLLECTIVE MARKS

[35.14] Collective marks which are provided for under the EU Trade Mark Harmonisation Directive were introduced to Irish law by the 1996 Act.[27] No provision for such existed under the 1963 Act or earlier legislation. A collective mark is defined in s 54 to mean:

> A mark distinguishing the goods or services of members of the association which is the proprietor of the mark from those of other undertakings.

[35.15] The 1996 Act contains no definition of what is meant by association. However, Article 64 of the Community Trade Mark Regulation refers to such as:

> Associations of manufacturers, producers, suppliers of services, or traders which, under the terms of the law governing them, have the capacity in their own name to have rights and obligations of all kinds, to make contracts or accomplish other legal acts and sue and be sued, as well as legal persons governed by public law.

The same provisions governing the registration of marks generally also apply in relation to collective marks but the capacity to distinguish is as between the goods or services of the members of the particular association which is the proprietor of the mark from those of other undertakings which are not members of the association.[28]

[35.16] A geographical name may be registered as a collective mark even if such serves in the trade to designate the geographical origin of the goods or services.[29] Such a registration does not entitle the proprietor to prevent use by a third party, provided that the use is in accordance with honest practices in industrial or commercial matters.[30]

[35.17] As well as the normal absolute grounds for refusal, a collective mark cannot be registered if the public is liable to be misled in relation to the character

---

26. Second Schedule - para 15.
27. Section 54 and First Schedule.
28. First Schedule - para 2.
29. First Schedule - para 3(1).
30. First Schedule - para 3(2).

or significance of the mark.[31] This includes a belief that the mark is other than a collective mark. The Controller can call upon an applicant to amend a mark to include an indication that it is a collective mark.[32]

[35.18] An applicant for registration of a collective mark must file regulations governing the use of the mark[33] within six months of the date of application.[34] The regulations are required at a minimum to address the following:[35]

(a) persons who are authorised to use the collective mark;

(b) conditions of membership of the association; and

(c) where they exist, the conditions of use of the collective mark, including any sanctions against misuse.

Unlike certification marks, approval of regulations governing collective marks rests with the Controller[36] who must also be satisfied that such regulations are not contrary to public policy or to accepted principles of morality.[37]

[35.19] If the Controller accepts the application, then it is advertised for opposition purposes in the Official Journal and the regulations are open to public inspection.[38] There is a three month period for opposition or the making of observations.[39] The regulations may be amended but if amended are not effective until filed with, and accepted by, the Controller.[40]

[35.20] Unless there is an agreement to the contrary, an authorised user can call on the proprietor to take infringement proceedings in respect of any matter which affects the authorised user's interests.[41] If after a period of two months the proprietor refuses or fails to take proceedings, the authorised user may bring the proceedings in their own name.[42] Without leave of the High Court, the proprietor must be either joined as a plaintiff or added as a defendant.[43] A proprietor added as a defendant is not liable for costs unless they take part in the proceedings.[44] This does not affect the ability of an authorised user to seek interlocutory relief in their own right.[45]

[31.] First Schedule - para 4(1).
[32.] First Schedule - para 4(2).
[33.] First Schedule - para 5(1).
[34.] Rule 31(1).
[35.] First Schedule - para 5(2).
[36.] First Schedule - para 6(1)(a).
[37.] First Schedule - para 6(1)(b).
[38.] First Schedule - paras 8(1) and 9.
[39.] Rule 31(3).
[40.] First Schedule - para 10.
[41.] First Schedule - para 11(2).
[42.] First Schedule - para 11(3).
[43.] First Schedule - para 11(4)(a).
[44.] First Schedule - para 11(4)(b).

Infringement Proceedings Taken by the Proprietor

[35.21] Any loss or potential loss suffered by authorised users will be taken into account by the High Court. The High Court may give directions regarding the extent to which the plaintiff shall hold the proceeds of any pecuniary remedy on behalf of such authorised users.[46]

[35.22] The normal grounds for revocation exist as set out in s 51 of the 1996 Act but additional grounds also apply in relation to collective marks, namely:

(a) the manner of use by the proprietor has made the mark misleading to the public as to its character or significance, in particular, if it is likely to be taken as something other than a collective mark;[47]

(b) the proprietor has failed to observe or to secure the observance of the regulations governing the use of the mark;[48] and

(c) the regulations have been amended and no longer comply with the statutory requirements[49] or are contrary to public policy or to accepted principles of morality.[50]

[35.23] The grounds for invalidity contained in s 52 of the 1996 Act apply to collective marks but further grounds arise where at the time of registration:

(a) the mark was liable to mislead the public as regards its character or significance, in particular, if it is likely to be taken to be something other than a collective mark;[51] or

(b) the regulations governing use fail to comply with the prescribed requirements or are contrary to public policy or accepted principles of morality.[52]

[35.24] The minutes of the Council meeting at which the CTM Regulation was adopted state that it is considered that a collective mark which is available for use only by a member of an association which owns the mark is liable to mislead if it gives the impression that it is available for use by anyone who is able to use certain objective standards.

[45.] First Schedule - para 11(5).
[46.] First Schedule - para 11(6).
[47.] First Schedule - para 12(a).
[48.] First Schedule - para 12(b).
[49.] First Schedule - para 5(2).
[50.] First Schedule - para 12(c).
[51.] First Schedule - paras 13 and 4(1).
[52.] First Schedule - paras 13 and 6(1).

Chapter 36

Geographical Indications and Appellations of Origin

INTRODUCTION

[36.01] A geographical indication can have many facets. As an indication of source, it can be perceived by the public as indicating the origin of particular goods or services. There are, however, generic geographical indications which are merely descriptors for goods or services such as, for example, BERMUDA for a certain type of shorts. An appellation of origin is, however, a geographical indication used to designate goods or services which originate from the region or place in question and whose qualities and characteristics are due exclusively or essentially to the geographical environment.[1] It is this type of geographical indication for which there are different avenues of protection designed to prevent misuse and hence public confusion.

[36.02] Council Regulation (EEC) 2081/92 on the protection of geographical indications and designations of origin for agricultural products and foodstuffs is only a more recent attempt at creating a protective right. There are already in existence four multilateral treaties, namely:

- The Madrid Agreement for the Repression of False or Deceptive Indications of Source of Goods, 1891;

- The Paris Convention for the Protection of Industrial Propert, 1893;

- The Lisbon Agreement for the Protection of Appellations of Origin and their International Registration 1958;

- The TRIPS Agreement.

as well as EU Wine Regulations and the Stresa Convention on the Use of Appellations of Origin and Designations of Cheeses 1951.[2]

[36.03] In addition to these, there are laws at national level in countries such as Ireland which address such issues as consumer protection guarding against false or misleading descriptions,[3] as well as general trade mark law including the

---

1. TRIPS, Article 22.
2. Ireland is not a member. Denmark, France, Italy and the Netherlands have ratified this Convention.
3. Consumer Information Act 1978.

registration of certification and collective marks and the law of passing off/ unfair competition.[4]

[36.04] French law provides that a geographical denomination which constitutes an appellation of origin or any other mention conjuring up this denomination, may not be used in connection either with a similar product or with another product or service, whenever this use is likely to divest or weaken the renown of the appellation of origin.[5]

[36.05] There are also a number of bilateral agreements between France/ Germany, France/Italy, Germany/Switzerland, Germany/Spain, France/Spain and France/Switzerland. The agreement between France and Spain[6] has already come under scrutiny by the ECJ in a decision on 10 November 1992.[7] The effect of the agreement was to prohibit Spanish undertakings from using protected Spanish designations in France if they were denied the right to use them by Spanish law, and to prohibit French undertakings from using protected French designations in Spain, if they were denied the right to use them by French law. This agreement provided that certain names including 'Turron De Alicante' and 'Turron De Jijona' were reserved exclusively on French territory to Spanish goods and products and could only be used on the conditions provided for by Spanish legislation. It was held that even if the denomination in question was accompanied by terms such as 'type', 'kind' or 'style', Articles 30 and 36 of the Treaty of Rome do not preclude the application of rules laid down by a bilateral convention between Member States on the protection of indications of provenance and appellations of origin, provided that the protected designations have not acquired, either at the time of the entry into force of the agreement or subsequently from that time, a generic connotation in the country of origin.

[36.06] There are a number of limitations with the various multilateral agreements. Ireland is not a member of the Madrid Agreement. This Agreement does not provide for the repression of false or deceptive indications used in translation or together with correct qualifying terms such as 'kind', 'type', etc. Also, it does not protect indications of source against transformation into a generic name except for regional appellations concerning the source of products of the vine. Sanctions provided under the Agreement are also very limited.

[36.07] Article 1(2) of the Paris Convention specifically contains a reference to 'indications of source' and 'appellations of origin' in the list of objects of industrial property. There is an obligation to protect 'indications of source'

---

4. *Supra* passing off, para **[24.34]**.
5. *Champagne Perfume by Yves Saint Laurent*, Court of Appeal of Paris, 15 December 1993.
6. 27 June 1973.
7. *Exportus SA v Lor SA* C-3/91.

contained in Article 10. Article 10(1) provides that the sanctions (Article 9) also apply to a 'false indication or source'. The effect is that no indication of source may be used that refers to a geographical area from which the products in question do not originate. Use includes indirect use such as in advertising.

[36.08] Article 10 *bis* provides protection against unfair competition which includes misleading indications, and countries are obliged to ensure effective protection against such. Article 10 *ter* requires appropriate legal remedies in favour of federations and associations representing producers or merchants. A problem which arises is that Article 10(1) does not protect against uses which, although not false, may still be misleading. An example of this arises in situations where the same geographical name may exist in different countries or indeed within a country itself.

[36.09] Only sixteen countries are party to the Lisbon Agreement, only three from within the EU: France, Italy and Portugal. The Agreement provides for the registration of appellations of origin. Unlike the Madrid Agreement, the use of corrective/qualifying terms are not allowed (Article 3) and it prevents a registered appellation of origin from becoming a general name in the country of origin (Article 6). The problem with the Lisbon Agreement is the very narrow definition of 'Appellation of Origin' (Article 2(a)). There is a requirement of prior recognition and protection under a specific official act in the country of origin. This is all very well in countries such as France where there is a strong legislative tradition for enacting laws protecting specifically identified appellations of origin but such is not the case in Ireland and the United Kingdom where protection arises under the common law by way of an action for passing off.

[36.10] Article 22(2) of TRIPS provides that States must allow for remedies to prevent the public being mislead as to the geographical origin of goods or use which constitutes unfair competition under Article 10 *bis* of the Paris Convention. The remedies include opposition to or invalidation of marks if use of the indication in the trade mark for such goods in that Member State is of such a nature as to mislead the public as to the true place of origin. This arises even if the indication is literally true as to the territory, region or locality in which the goods originate but nevertheless, falsely represents to the public that the goods originate in another territory.[8]

[36.11] Despite the varying forms of protection already in existence, DG VI, the part of the EU Commission which deals with agriculture, formed a view that there was a requirement for protective provisions for agricultural products or

---

8. TRIPS, Article 22(4).

foodstuffs given the growing demand for such with an identifiable geographical origin, hence Regulation No 2081/92 on the Protection of Geographical Indications and Designations of Origin for Agricultural Products and Foodstuffs.[9]

PGIs and PDOs

[36.12] Regulation No 2081/92 entered into force on 26 July 1993 and as the preamble states, a distinction is drawn between 'Protected Geographical Indications' (PGI) and 'Protected Designations of Origin' (PDO). These terms are defined in Article 2.2. A PDO is the name of a region or place (even exceptionally a country) describing an agricultural product or foodstuff originating there. The quality and other characteristics of the product must be "essentially or exclusively due to a particular geographical environment with its inherent natural and human factors, and the production, processing and preparation of which take place in the defined geographical area". The definition suggests that it is equivalent to the already known term 'Appellation of Origin' as defined in Article 2 of the Lisbon Agreement.

[36.13] The definition of a PGI begins in the same way but the differences are that:

(a) the product only needs to possess a specific quality, reputation or other characteristic attributable to the location. This contrasts with the essential or exclusive connection of the PDO; and

(b) it is the production *and/or* processing *and/or* preparation taking place at the location which is required for a PGI. The PDO requires production, processing and preparation.

A PDO applies to products which have characteristic qualities that are due to conditions existing in the geographical area, whereas, a PGI applies to any products originating in the geographical area to which the indication refers. In the wine industry, this would be termed as 'Indication De Provenance'. Thus, for example, 'French wine' is an Indication De Provenance indicating simply the source of the product, whereas, 'Champagne' and 'Burgundy' would be 'Appellations De Origin' because of their characteristics in addition to the fact that they are also French wines. In other words, all Appellations of Origin (PDO) are PGIs but not all PGIs are Appellations of Origin (PDO). It can also be noted that under Article 2.3, "certain traditional geographical or non-geographical names" can be considered a PDO provided that other conditions are fulfilled. Perhaps the best known example would be FETA cheese. FETA is not a geographical location but is the Greek word for a slice.

[9.] 14 July 1992.

[36.14] The Regulation provides in substance for Community protection of designations of origin and of geographical indications of agricultural products and foodstuffs. Specifically excluded are wine products and spirit drinks. Specifically included are beer, natural mineral waters and spring waters, beverages made from plant extracts, bread, pastry, cakes, confectionery and other baker's wares, natural gums and resins, hay and essential oils. Also covered are meat, fish and most dairy products. The protection is secured by way of a registration.

DISENTITLEMENT TO REGISTRATION

[36.15] Article 3.1 states that "names that have become generic may not be registered", ie if it has become the common name for such goods. This may be a difficult question to answer because account may be taken of the meaning of the name throughout the Community. It has also been stated in a Commission paper that "responsibility for proving that a name is generic, rests with the party who claims that it is such".

[36.16] Under Article 3.3, a non-exhaustive list of generic names was meant to be published in the EU Official Journal prior to entry into force of the Regulation. This did not happen but the Commission did adopt a proposal which included as generic names, BRIE, CAMEMBERT, CHEDDAR, EDAM, EMMENTALE and GOUDA.

[36.17] Furthermore, under Article 3.2, a name may not be registered where it conflicts with the name of a plant variety or an animal breed *and* as a result, is likely to mislead the public as to the true origin of the product. In Article 14.3, there is a provision which states that a designation of origin or geographical indication shall not be registered where, in the light of a trade mark's reputation and renown and the length of time it has been used, registration is liable to mislead the consumer as to the true identity of the product. However, this is not a ground for objecting to an application under Article 7.4.

REGISTRATION PROCEDURE

[36.18] There is a normal registration procedure (Articles 5, 6 and 7) and for a period of time, there existed a simplified or fast track procedure (Article 17). Both procedures require specifications to be presented. Article 4 lays down what the specifications are to include and it commences with the words "to be eligible to *use*" a PDO or PGI ... "the product or foodstuffs must comply with a specification". Presumably, however, the word 'use' is incorrect and this should be a reference to registration. The specification is more than simply the name of goods and includes evidence of the link between the product and the PDO or

PGI, a description of the method of obtaining the product and inspection structures even though such is within the ambit of each Member State.

[36.19] An application is made by a group (as defined) subject to amending Regulation No 2037/93 which states that an applicant can be a natural or legal person "where the person concerned is the only producer in the geographical area defined at the time the application is submitted". The application may be accepted only where:

(a) the said single person engaged in authentic and unvarying local methods; and

(b) the geographical area defined possesses characteristics which differ appreciably from those of neighbouring areas and/or the characteristics of the product are different.

[36.20] The application is sent to the Member State in which the geographical area is located. If Member States believe the 'application is justified', and satisfies the requirements of the Regulation, it is then sent to the Commission. Although not stated in the Regulation, if a Member State refuses to pass on the application, it should state the reasons and give the applicant an opportunity to appeal.

[36.21] There is a vague reference to the fact that if an application concerns a name also situate in another Member State, that other State should be consulted before any decision is taken. There is no reference to what is meant by 'consultation' or the effect of failure to do so.

[36.22] Upon receipt of an application, the Commission has six months in which to advise a Member State as to whether the specification requirements have been met. This follows a stated 'formal investigation'. The question which immediately arises is whether or not the Commission can refuse to allow the application to proceed to publication if it does not make such a decision within six months. The Commission is certainly of the view that the six months is only for examination as to formalities and is not a substantive examination. This is not readily apparent because under Article 6.2, it is upon such 'formal investigation' that the Commission reaches its conclusion as to whether the name qualifies for protection and can decide not to proceed with publication under Article 6.5. If the Commission concludes that the name qualities for protection, details are published in the EU Official Journal[10] and if there are no objections notified, registration is automatic.

---

10. See, by way of example, Regulation Nos 1107/96 and 1263/96 although these applications were under the simplified/fast track procedure (Article 17).

Procedure for Lodging Objections

[36.23] Objection must be taken within six months of publication and must be made by a Member State. A legitimately concerned objector must send a statement of objection to the authority in the Member State where they reside or are established. Under Article 7, the objection must state that the application is either:

(a) outside the definition of a PDO or PGI; or

(b) would jeopardise the existence of an entirely or partly identical name or trade mark or the existence of products which are legally on the market as of 24 July 1992;[11] or

(c) generic in nature.

If the objection is deemed admissible, then it is for Member States to reach agreement and failing which the Commission will determine the issue "having regard to traditional fair practice and of the actual likelihood of confusion".

Simplified or Fast Track Procedure

[36.24] The time period for availing of this procedure expired on 26 January 1994 and there were no Irish applications filed under such.

[36.25] In order to avail of this procedure it was required that the name must have been protected in the Member State in accordance with national law. This included a system of protection based on case law. The big advantage for applicants who availed of the fast track procedure was that there is no opposition procedure (Article 7).

Inspection Structures

[36.26] Under Article 10, each Member State is obliged to have in place 'inspection structures' to ensure that the requirements laid down in the specifications are met.[12] Ultimately, a registration can be cancelled if the product specification is not being met.[13]

PROTECTION AFFORDED TO REGISTERED MARKS

[36.27] These are stated in Article 13 and apart from preventing direct or indirect commercial usage of the name in respect of the products registered, extends to any practice liable to mislead the public as to the trade origin. It also extends to 'comparable' products if the use exploits the reputation of the

---

11. The date of publication of Regulation No 2081/92.
12. European Communities (Protection of Geographical Indications and Designations of Origin for Agricultural Products and Foodstuffs) Regulations 1995 (SI 148/1995).
13. Article 11.4.

protected name. The use of expressions such as 'style', 'type', 'method', 'as produced in', 'imitation', is no defence. Article 13.2 allows these terms to be used for up to five years if:

(a) the products have been marketed legally using such expressions for at least five years before 24 July 1992; and

(b) the labelling clearly indicates the true origin of the product.

This is, however, a matter for national law and the exception does not allow the marketing of products freely in the territory of a Member State where such expressions are prohibited.

CONFLICT WITH TRADE MARKS

[36.28] Practitioners will have to be aware of PDO and PGI registrations under the Regulation and to search against such in order to advise their clients fully. Under Article 14, an application to register a trade mark which would be considered as prohibited from use under Article 13, must be refused registration where it relates to 'the same type of product'. This provision applies to trade mark applications which have been filed after the advertisement/publication of the PDO or PGI application in the Official Journal and also in cases of prior trade mark applications which are still pending at the time of advertisement/ publication.

[36.29] Article 14 goes on to deal with trade marks 'registered in good faith' but before the date that the PDO or PGI application was lodged. In such a case, the trade mark use may continue unless:

(a) the trade mark consists exclusively of signs or indications which may serve, in trade, to designate the kind, quality, intended purpose, value, geographical origin, or the time of production of the goods or of rendering of the service, or other characteristics of the goods or service. This ground is by reference to Article 3(1)(c) of the Trade Mark Harmonisation Directive[14] but there is no provision to deal with Article 3(3) and whereby a trade mark can acquire a distinctive character through use and thus fall as an exception to Article 3(1)(c);

(b) the trade mark is of such a nature as to deceive the public, for instance as to the nature, quality or geographical origin of the goods or service;[15] and

(c) in consequence of the use made by the proprietor or with his consent in respect of the goods or services for which it is registered, it is liable

---

14. 89/104/EEC.

15. Article 3(1)(g) - Harmonisation Directive - No 89/104/EEC.

to mislead the public, particularly as to the nature, quality or geographical origin of those goods or services.[16]

[36.30] A number of issues are unresolved by the Regulation including the following:

1. Does the refusal of a trade mark application arise at a national level and if so, is there an obligation on Member States to hold a substantive examination against PDO or PGI Registrations. There is currently no such examination by the Irish Patents Office.

2. What is meant by the expression 'same type of product'? It is probable that this can be equated with 'similarity of the goods or services' which is the language used in the EU Trade Mark Harmonisation Directive.

3. What is the position *vis-à-vis* trade marks registered in good faith prior to advertisement/publication of the PDO or PGI? There is a vacuum in these circumstances.

4. National trade mark registrations or applications held by the holder of a PDO or PGI.

5. The reference is to use of the trade mark being allowed to continue. Does this mean that there must already have been use and can a registration be maintained?

USE OF REGULATION NO 2081/92

[36.31] As of September 1996, over 1,400 applications had been filed but none from an Irish applicant. A wide variety of products have been covered including cheese, fresh meats, meat based products, fruit and vegetables, oils and fats, mineral and spring waters, honey and confectionery products. Regulation Nos 1007/96, 1263/96 and 123/97 contain lists of applications which have been approved for registration under the fast track procedure in Article 17. There have also been applications approved following the normal opposition procedure.[17] Some of the more well known names on the list include WHITE AND BLUE STILTON CHEESE as PDOs; NEWCASTLE BROWN ALE as a PGI and FETA as a PDO. When it can be seen that also on the list of registrations are SCOTTISH BEEF and SCOTTISH LAMB as PGIs, it is surprising that steps have not been taken to register IRISH BEEF and IRISH LAMB or indeed, for example, WICKLOW LAMB given further precedents of registerability for SHETLAND LAMB and ORKNEY LAMB as PDOs.

---

16. Article 12(2)(b) - Harmonisation Directive - No 89/104/EEC.
17. Regulation No 2400/96.

REGULATION NO 2082/92 ON CERTIFICATES OF SPECIFIC CHARACTER FOR AGRICULTURAL PRODUCTS AND FOODS[18]

[36.32] Under this Regulation, producers can identify specific characteristics to which their agricultural product or foodstuff adheres and obtain a Community certificate of specific character. The specific character is defined to mean "the feature or set of features which distinguishes an agricultural product or foodstuffs clearly from other products or foodstuffs belonging to the same category". This does not include presentation but is not restricted to qualitative, quantitative composition or to a mode or production.

[36.33] Registration is not permitted if the specific character is due to the product's provenance or geographical origin or solely to application of a technological innovation. A product specification must be filed which includes as being part of the requirements of registration, a description of the method of production, including the nature and characteristics of the raw material and/or ingredients used and/or the method of preparation of the agricultural product or foodstuff referring to its specific character. Protection by way of registration, subject to certain limitations, affords protection in respect of the name enjoying the specific character. Registration also enables the producers to use a community symbol, details of which are set out in Regulation No 2515/94[19] and which symbol includes the words in English, 'TRADITIONAL SPECIALITY GUARANTEED'.

---

18. Council Regulation on the Protection of Geographical Indications and Designations of Origin for Agricultural Products and Foodstuffs, 14 July 1992; OJ L 208, 24.7.92, p 1.
19. 9 September 1994.

Chapter 37

Taxation and Intellectual Property Rights

STAMP DUTY[1]

[37.01] Intellectual property rights are a form of personal property which can be licensed or assigned. Section 79 of the Patents Act 1992 states that the rules of law applicable to the ownership and devolution of personal property shall apply in relation to patent applications and patents as they apply in relation to other choses in action. Similarly, s 47 of the Copyright Act 1963 also specifically identifies copyright transmissible by assignment as personal property and furthermore, no assignment (whether total or partial) can have effect unless it is in writing signed by or on behalf of the assignor. Section 26 of the Trade Marks Act 1996 states that a registered trade mark is personal property and goes on to provide in s 28 that a registered trade mark is transmissible by assignment either in connection with the goodwill of a business or independently. These provisions also apply in respect of a trade mark application.[2] An assignment is not effective unless it is in writing.[3] A design under the Industrial and Commercial Property (Protection) Act 1927 is also referred to as a property right. Section 17(1) of the Plant Varieties (Proprietary) Rights Act 1980 also provides for assignment of such as a property right. In relation to topography rights in semiconductor products, although not specifically identified as a property right, by implication, they must be treated as such, given the rights which are conferred by statute.[4] The only form of intellectual property which it has been held does not constitute property for the purpose of stamp duty is 'know how'[5] and which is a form of unregistered right under the common law.

[37.02] Since stamp duty arises primarily on instruments which convey or transfer property, it is readily apparent that intellectual property rights fall within the ambit of the stamp duty provisions of finance legislation. Given the huge values that can be attributed to certain intellectual property rights and a top rate of 6% (if the amount or value of the consideration exceeds a low threshold of IR£60,000), the stamp duty on a transfer can be immense. Also, the granting

---

[1.] On stamp duty generally, see Donegan & Friel, *Irish Stamp Duty Law* (Butterworths, 1995).
[2.] Trade Marks Act 1996, s 31.
[3.] Trade Marks Act, 1996, s 28(3).
[4.] SI 101/1988.
[5.] *Musker v English Electric Company Limited* (1964) 41 TC 566; *John & E Strange Ltd v Hessel* (1975) 5 TC 573.

of an exclusive and irrevocable licence may be considered as equivalent to a conveyance of property.[6]

[37.03] Assignments of intellectual property are stamped as being conveyances on sale of property.[7] One of the consequences of which is that the stamp duty chargeable is calculated on the basis of the consideration rather than the actual value of the property. However, if the conveyance is a voluntary conveyance, *inter vivos*, then under s 74 of the Finance Act 1909-10, stamp duty is payable on the market value of the property conveyed or transferred instead of the amount of the consideration. Therefore, in almost all cases of an assignment of intellectual property, either the consideration represents the true value, ie there has been valuable consideration or alternatively, a voluntary disposition, *inter vivos*, arises because the conveyance confers a substantial benefit on the person to whom the property is conveyed. In both scenarios, duty is calculated on the market value of the property. The value placed on the property is to be determined objectively.[8] Section 104 of the Finance Act 1991 also provides that where a conveyance on sale includes consideration which cannot be ascertained at the date of execution, then the conveyance on sale is chargeable to duty as if the market value of the property conveyed were substituted for such consideration.

[37.04] The stamp duty provisions in the Finance Act 1991[9] introduced a number of new features into stamp duty law for instruments executed on or after 1 November 1991. The Stamp Duty Act 1891 imposed no direct legal obligation to pay duty on chargeable instruments relying on the fact that an unstamped or insufficiently stamped instrument could not be used by way of evidence in civil proceedings. Under s 94 of the Finance Act 1991, the payment of stamp duty is mandatory once an instrument which is liable to duty is executed. In order to avoid penalties, payment must be made not later than 30 days after execution. For intellectual property practitioners, this provision is draconian because in a large number of cases, an assignment is executed abroad and simply includes an Irish right as only part of a portfolio of rights in a number of countries. An instrument of assignment may only enter the State for recordal before the Irish Patents Office many months after execution. Under s 97(5), transfers of property for less than full consideration must be brought specifically to the attention of the Revenue Commissioners and a statement of market value for the property rights must be furnished. There is, of course, an inherent difficulty in attributing a value to an intellectual property right but there is an obligation on a

---

6. *Smelting Company of Australia Limited v Commissioners of Inland Revenue* (1897) 1 QB 175.
7. Stamp Act 1891, ss 54 and 59.
8. *Lap Shun Textiles Industrial Co Ltd v Collector of Stamp Revenue* [1976] 1 All ER 833.
9. Sections 94-100 and s 130.

practitioner to notify the Revenue Commissioners when in doubt. It is also necessary for practitioners in the preparation of any instrument to set out all the facts and circumstances affecting liability to duty.

[37.05] For instruments executed since 8 February 1995, if there is a beneficial change in ownership of intellectual property between associated companies, then stamp duty is zero rated.[10] Essentially, the relief is available to transfers between bodies corporate which are sufficiently connected so as to effectively mean that there has been no real change in ownership. Thus, for example, a transfer between a company and its only shareholder, does not qualify for the relief.

[37.06] The corporate bodies must be connected so that at least 90 per cent of the issued share capital in one of the companies is held by the other company, or at least 90 per cent of the issued share capital in both bodies corporate must be held by another body corporate. The relief is not available where the consideration is provided either directly or indirectly by an outsider. If the companies cease to be associated within two years of the transaction, then the instrument becomes chargeable to the full rate of duty without any exemption and the liability to pay such duty rests both jointly with the assignor and assignee. The claim for relief must be accompanied by a statutory declaration and requires adjudication. The instrument itself must be stamped, denoting that it is not chargeable with any duty.

[37.07] Section 56(1) of the Stamp Act 1891 deals with the position where the consideration consists of periodical payments to be charged for a definite period not exceeding twenty years. In such a situation, the commencing payment and all periodic payments which will fall due are totalled and duty is payable on the total amount. If the periodic payments fall due over a definite period in excess of twenty years, or in perpetuity, or for an indefinite period not terminable with a life, then it is necessary to consider both s 56(2) of the Stamp Act 1891 and s 104 of the Finance Act 1991. Under s 56(2), duty is chargeable "on the total amount which will or may, according to the terms of sale, be payable during the period of twenty years next after the day of the date of the instrument". If, however, the consideration cannot be ascertained, then under s 104, the market value is substituted for the consideration. It is, of course, true that most agreements involving periodic payments are licence agreements which are usually revocable and do not constitute a conveyance on sale. Consequently they do not attract stamp duty unless executed under seal, attracting a fixed duty of IR£10. However, what may purport to be a licence agreement could be

---

10. Finance Act 1995, s 143.

considered in effect to be a conveyance. An example of such would be an exclusive non-revocable patent licence for the duration of the patent (20 years).

[37.08] It is possible to claim reduced rates of stamp duty if a certificate of value clause can be furnished. Such certificate reads as follows:

> The transaction hereby effected does not form part of a larger transaction or a series of transactions, in respect of which the amount or value, or the aggregate amount or value of the consideration exceeds IR£____.

If the figure of IR£5,000 can be inserted in the certificate, then stamp duty is exempt. Above IR£5,000 and up to and including IR£60,000, reduced rates apply.

[37.09] Practitioners are regularly asked whether or not the certificate relates to simply transactions involving Irish intellectual property rights and not the global assignment. It often arises that a certificate can be provided if it related to just Irish property but that the global transaction of which the Irish property is only a small part will take the figure over the threshold level. The Stamp Act 1891 contains no restriction as to the nature of the larger transaction or series of transactions and from this could be summarised the fact that the Irish property transfer is only one of a number of transactions taking place in a number of different countries, does not prevent it from being one of a series of transactions. It is certainly the custom of the Revenue Commissioners in determining the applicability of the certificate of value to aggregate the total considerations, whether they are payable in respect of Irish property or not. Accordingly, it appears that a certificate of value cannot be given if the overall global assignment exceeds the valuation required to be given in the certificate.

[37.10] Stamp duty is chargeable on an instrument executed in the State or which, wherever executed, refers to property situated or things done or to be done in the State. Thus, to avoid paying stamp duty on intellectual property situated outside the State, the instrument of transfer should be executed outside the State. For example, an Irish company acquiring a portfolio of intellectual property rights is well advised to execute two separate assignments, one for the Irish rights and a second for the foreign rights. The latter, if executed outside the State, is not chargeable to duty. If a single instrument of transfer contains a portfolio of rights, both Irish and foreign which is executed outside the State, then it is necessary to apportion a value to the Irish rights and pay stamp duty in respect of such. A potential problem which was identified in the Dáil debates on the Trade Marks Act 1996, was stamp duty payable on the transfer of a CTM or an international Madrid Protocol mark designating the State. This has now been resolved by virtue of s 118(2) of the Finance Act 1996 which provides that:

stamp duty shall not be chargeable on an instrument relating to a Community Trade Mark or an international trade mark, or an application for any such mark, by reason only of the fact that such a mark has a legal effect in the State.

This wording would nevertheless suggest that if the instrument transferring the Community or international mark was executed in the State, it is still chargeable because the duty in such a case is not by virtue of the existence of a property right effective in the State but the mere fact of execution in the State.

[37.11] An equally strong case can be made for exclusion of stamp duty in respect of the transfer of a European patent application which designates the State. Under s 120 of the Patents Act 1992, an application for a European patent designating the State is treated as having the same rights as a national patent application.

[37.12] A further reason for the need to pay stamp duty arises in respect of intellectual property rights resulting through a system of registration, ie patents, designs and trade marks. In each of these cases, any application to record the change in proprietorship on the respective Registers in the Irish Patents Office necessitates submission of the instrument or a certified copy showing that the stamp duty has been paid or that alternatively, there is a IR£5,000 certificate of value clause which exempts the instrument from stamp duty. The Irish Patents Office will not, however, question the adequacy or otherwise of the duty which has been paid. The onus in this regard rests with an assignee. Because copyright is both an unregisterable right and without territorial limitations, more difficult questions arise.

[37.13] If the copyright was created in Ireland, then on the face of it, the right has its *situs* in the State and an instrument of transfer wherever executed will attract duty. Article 9 of TRIPS requires compliance with Articles 1-21 and the Appendix of the Berne Copyright Convention (1971). Article 5(2) of the Berne Convention states that the rights granted shall be independent of the existence of protection in the country of origin. It is also quite legitimate to transfer copyright in so far as it arises in different jurisdictions and, for example, retain copyright just in Ireland while transferring rights to the rest of the world. Consequently, it can certainly be strongly argued that separate assignments, one for Ireland and a further assignment in respect of the independent right to copyright which exists abroad, will mean that stamp duty need only be paid in respect of the value of the copyright in this jurisdiction. In the UK courts, there is already judicial authority that copyright can have a *situs* other than in the country of origin of the copyright work.[11]

[11.] *Novello & Company Limited v Hinrichsen Edition Limited & Anor* [1951] 1 All ER 779.

[37.14] The recent British case of *Brown & Root McDermott Fabricators Ltd v Coflexip Stena Offshore Ltd*[12] addressed the issue of replacing an existing formal assignment with a new one which identifies the value of the patent rights being transferred and so that the appropriate stamp duty could then be paid. In this case, the original patentee contracted by way of a single agreement to transfer to the respondent a ship, a large number of other assets and a number of patents, some of which were UK patents. The total purchase price was US$31.5 million. The patent agent prepared a short form of assignment (A1) of the patents which was duly executed. Upon learning that the original contract to assign was not stamped, it became apparent that the short form assignment needed a valuation for stamping before recordal on the register could take place. A fresh assignment (A2) was then executed which contained a valuation. A2 was stamped and then used as a basis for recording the change in ownership on the UK Patent Register. It was argued that A2 was void because A1 complied with the Patents Act in all respects and it was consequently A1 which vested the change in ownership and the register should be rectified by the removal of any reference to A2. This would mean that the register would then still show the original patentee as the owner. The importance of this to the applicant was that when A1 was subsequently stamped and recorded on the register, it would be too late for the respondent to claim damages or an account of profits given the provisions of s 68 of the UK Patents Act 1977 (of which there is no corresponding provision in the Irish Patents Act 1992 but there is under s 29(4) of the Trade Marks Act 1996). Jacob J accepted the somewhat circular argument that given that under s 14(4) of the Stamp Act 1891 an unstamped instrument cannot be given in evidence or made available for any purposes whatsoever, the first assignment (A1) could not be used to invalidate the second assignment (A2). This had the effect that it could not then be established that A2 was void since this could only be proved by reference to A1. Thus, on the admissible evidence, A2 had been properly registered. In conclusion, Jacob J stated:

> "I reach my conclusion without intellectual satisfaction. But there is some rough justice. It was an attempt to comply with the Stamp Act, 1891 which caused the trouble and it is the Stamp Act, 1891 which saves the position."

[37.15] Section 29(4) of the Trade Marks Act 1996 provides that late application for recordal[13] of the change in ownership on the register means that damages or an account of profits will be denied, this means that practitioners must be cautious in their use of a short form assignment following a much longer agreement which is expressed to be an assignment.

---

12. [1996] STC 483.
13. More than 6 months from date of transaction.

[37.16] The complexity of stamp duty legislation in the context of intellectual property rights which are extremely hard to value and where assignments are often concluded on a global basis without reference to Irish taxation provisions, has resulted in extreme difficulties for practitioners in ensuring both their client's compliance and also their personal obligations under the Finance Act 1991. The Irish Association of Patent and Trade Mark Agents have, on a number of occasions, made submissions to the Department of Finance, in an effort to relax the stamp duty regime or preferably abolish such as it relates to intellectual property. So far, with the limited exception of s 118 of the Finance Act 1996 which exempts CTMs and international marks, the archaic and punitive stamp duty provisions still remain in place.[14]

PATENT ROYALTIES[15]

[37.17] Section 34 of the Finance Act 1973 introduced an exemption from tax for income arising from patents for inventions devised within the State. The rationale was to encourage research and development in Ireland and to stimulate invention. The exemption was only available to residents of the State, which is defined to mean any person who is resident in the State for the purposes of income tax and who is not resident elsewhere. A company is regarded as so resident if it is controlled and managed in the State. To avail of this exemption it is necessary to possess a 'qualifying patent' which is stated in s 34 to mean:

> A patent in relation to which the research, planning, processing, experimenting, testing, devising, designing, developing or similar activity leading to the invention which is the subject of the patent was carried out in the State.

[37.18] It is not necessary that all of these activities took place within the State and the Revenue Commissioners recognised that in some instances part of the research and development may prove necessary to be done outside the State. The income from a qualifying patent which is exempt from tax is any royalty or other sum paid in respect of the user of the invention to which the qualifying patent relates and includes any sum paid for the grant of a licence to exercise rights under such a patent. The Corporation Tax Act 1976 extended the relief in s 34 to cover Corporation Tax.

[37.19] Section 34 does not require the patent holder to be the actual person who carried out the requisite research and development or other activity leading to a qualifying patent. It is quite legitimate for an Irish resident to acquire a qualifying patent and then claim the relief on foot of such. In the initial year of

---

[14.] For an excellent summary of stamp duty on intellectual property rights in Ireland, see article by Francis Hackett, Commercial Law Practitioner, March 1995.
[15.] See Judge, *Irish Income Tax 1996-97* (Butterworths) pp 959-972.

the relief, concern was expressed at the length of time that it took to obtain an Irish patent and the possibility that the tax incentive would not be available at the beginning of a product's lifecycle when it was needed the most. Possibly in recognition of such, the Revenue Commissioners simply required the grant of a patent in any country to satisfy them that it was a *bona fide* invention. Hence the practice developed of securing patents in Belgium and South Africa where minimum formalities allowed for speed of grant of patents. The Revenue Commissioners agreed to give the exemption from income tax after the grant of such a patent. This was backdated to the date of filing of the complete specification.

[37.20] Up until the mid-1980s s 34 was little availed of but as other tax exemptions were closed off an increased awareness of the relief arose. The first inroad into the s 34 relief arose under s 28 of the Finance Act 1994. Under s 28 the definition of "income from a qualifying patent" was amended so that if the licensor and licensee are connected then the income must be paid in respect of manufacturing activities. Whether the parties are connected was determined by reference to s 33 of the Capital Gains Tax Act 1975 which has recently been replaced by a new definition in the Finance Act 1996. However, it was still possible for a person to receive income in excess of the benefit derived from the patented invention and still qualify for the exemption.

[37.21] Section 32(1) of the Finance Act 1996 now imposes the need for an arms length agreement between parties at least in relation to the income claimed for exemption. The following proviso has been inserted in the definition of 'income from a qualifying patent':

> Provided that where the royalty or other sum exceeds the royalty or other sum which would have been paid if the payer of the royalty or other sum and the beneficial recipient thereof were independent persons acting at arm's length, the excess shall not be income from a qualifying patent.

[37.22] The excess patent income (whether royalty or lump sum) is liable to income tax under Case IV of Schedule D, subject to the particular provisions of ss 288 and 291 of the Income Tax Act 1967. Section 32 applies to all royalties paid on or after 23 April 1996 and embraces licence agreements already in existence. No criteria is included as to what factors will be taken into account in determining whether the payments are consequent on an arms length agreement. However, this would involve consideration of the strength of the patent itself and typically also the cost of the research and development leading to the patent together with the terms of the licence on issues such as exclusivity and territoriality.

[37.23] Under s 170 of the Corporation Tax Act 1976 dividends and other distributions paid by a company from patent income qualifying for exemption under s 34 of the Finance Act 1973 are tax free in the hands of the shareholders. Also embraced is a situation where a company receives the distribution from another company. The recipient is deemed to have 'disregarded income'. The effect of this being that the distribution of the second company paid out of disregarded income is also exempt from tax. Section 19 of the Finance Act 1992 had already imposed restrictions on this relief by requiring in certain circumstances that the shares be held by a person directly involved in the research and development activity leading to the invention. A further restriction was introduced by s 34(2) of the Finance Act 1996 in situations where the royalty income is by virtue of an agreement with a connected person and where the patented invention is used for the purpose of a manufacturing activity. This is now referred to as 'specified income'.

[37.24] A distribution made out of 'specified income' not exceeding the amount of aggregate expenditure incurred on research and development by the company and its 75% associated companies in the accounting period and the two previous accounting periods is treated as a distribution made out of disregarded income, thus maintaining its exempt status.

[37.25] Any distribution out of 'specified income' can be exempt from tax if such is in respect of a qualifying patent in respect of an invention which:

(a) involved radical innovation, and

(b) was patented for *bona fide* commercial reasons and not primarily for the purpose of avoiding liability to taxation.

There is no definition of the words 'radical innovation'. It is no longer enough for there to be a patent in place and some inventions which fulfil the criteria of patentability in being new and involving an inventive step will not be a substantial enough advance to secure the tax exemption. The Minister for Finance, Ruiarí Quinn, made the following statement during the passage of the Bill through Committee Stage in the Dáil:

"The term 'radical innovation' means the creation of something which is fundamentally novel. The degree of novelty cannot be other than a subjective judgement. However, there is an OECD precedent for classifying innovations as 'completely new', 'modestly improved' and 'merely a differentiation of an existing product or process'. In viewing the foregoing categories in the context of 'radical innovation' something completely new would come within its scope but a mere differentiation would not. The modestly improved product which is not a mere differentiation is more likely to be considered radical innovation than a modestly improved process ... A body of precedents exists to which inspectors can refer and the interpretation of 'radical' or 'innovative' can be reasonably adduced. This matter will be clarified with the taxation administration committee and guidelines will be given to domestic tax practitioners."[16]

ARTISTS' EXEMPTION FROM INCOME TAX

[37.26] Under s 2 of the Finance Act 1969 the income from certain works are exempt from tax.[17] The individual claiming the relief must be solely resident in the State and the work must be determined by the Revenue Commissioners or generally recognised as having cultural or artistic merit. Section 2 provides that a work must be an original and creative work falling under one of the following categories:

  (a) a book or other writing;

  (b) a play;

  (c) a musical composition;

  (d) a painting or like picture;

  (e) a sculpture.

[37.27] Section 14 of the Finance Act 1994 provided for An Comhairle Ealaíon and the Minister for Arts, Culture and the Gaeltacht to draw up a set of guidelines as an aid to determination on whether or not works are original and creative and whether they have, or are generally recognised as having, cultural or artistic merit. Since enactment of the Finance Act 1994 the following guidelines have been issued.

Cultural or artistic merit

A work has cultural merit if its contemplation enhances the quality of individual or social life by virtue of that work's intellectual, spiritual or aesthetic form and content.

A work has artistic merit when its combined form and content enhances or intensify the aesthetic apprehension of those who experience or contemplate it.

Original and creative

For the purpose of a determination under s 2 of the Finance Act 1969, the term "original and creative" encompasses any unique work which is brought into existence for the first time as an independant entity by the exercise of its creator's imagination.

A non-fiction work in category (a), a book or other writing will be considered original and creative only if:

[16.] *Select Committee on Finance and General Affairs* 24 April 1996, Col 199.

[17.] See Judge, *Irish Income Tax 1996-97*, (Butterworths) pp 667-671.

(i)   it comes within one of the following categories:

-   The following categories of literature (and any combination thereof) coming fully within the terms of reference of the Arts Council encompassing the subjects of fiction writing, drama, music, film, dance, mime or visual arts, and related commentaries by *bona fide* artists:

    Arts criticism;

    Arts history;

    Arts subject works;

    Arts diaries;

    Autobiography;

    Belles-lettres essays

    Cultural dictionaries;

    Literary translation;

    Literary criticism;

    Literary history;

    Literary diaries.

-   The following category of works coming fully within the terms of reference of the Heritage Council including works which, in their entirety, comprise one or more of the these categories:

    archaeology;

    publications associated with items or areas of significant heritage value.

-   The following categories of works coming fully within the terms of reference of the National Archives Advisory Council:

    Publications which relate to archives which are more than 30 years old concerning Ireland, and are based largely on research from such archives.

-   Categories of works which in their entirety comprise one ore more of the categories cited in the above paragraphs.

(ii) the essence of the work is the presentation of the author's own ideas or insights in relation to the subject matter, and the ideas or insights are of such significance that the work would be regarded as a pioneering work casting new light on its subject matter or changing the generally accepted understanding of the subject matter.

Exclusions from the ambit of "original and creative"

The following types of work in the categories set out in s 2 of the 1969 Act will not be regarded as coming within the ambit of "original and creative":

(a) A book or other writing (exluding those at (i) and (ii) above).

A book or other writing published primarily for, or which is or will be used primarily by students pursueing a course of study or persons engaged in any trade, profession, vocation or branch of learning as an aid to professional or other practice in connection with the trade, profession, vocation or branch of learning.

An article or series of articles published in a newspaper, magazine, book or elsewhere - except a book consisting of a series of articles by the same author connected by a common theme and therefore capable of existing independently in its own right.

(b) A play.

Types or kinds of plays written for advertising purposes which do not exist independently in their own right by reason of quality or duration.

(c) A musical composition.

Types or kinds of musical compositions written for advertising purposes which do not exist independently in their own right by reason of quality or duration. Arrangements, adaptations and versions of musical compositions by a person other than a bona fide composer who is also actively engaged in musical composition.

(d) A painting or like picture

Types or kinds of photographs or drawings (other than a set or sets of photographs or drawings that are collectively created for an artistic purpose) which are mainly of record, or which serve a utilitarian function, or which would not exist independently in their own right by reason of quality or by reference to their potentiality for inclusion as part of an art exhibition.

(e) A sculpture

Types or kinds of objects which are primarily functional in nature, objects produced by processes other than by hand, objects produced by persons other than those actively engaged in as bona fide artists in the field of the visual arts.

[37.28] In the case of the *Revenue Commissioners v Colm O'Loinsigh*[18] the respondent was a school teacher who wrote a series of four books entitled *Pathways to History* which were intended primarily for the education of school children. Murphy J in the High Court upheld the decision of the Appeal Commissioner that the books were original and creative within s 2 of the Finance Act 1969.[19]

---

18. High Court, unrep, 21 December, Murphy J.
19. See also *Mara v Hummingbird Ltd* [1982] ILRM 421; *Healy v Breathnach (Inspector of Taxes)* [1986] IR 105.

APPENDIX I

AGREEMENT ON TRADE-RELATED ASPECTS OF INTELLECTUAL PROPERTY RIGHTS, INCLUDING TRADE IN COUNTERFEIT GOODS

TABLE OF CONTENTS

AGREEMENT ON TRADE-RELATED ASPECTS OF INTELLECTUAL PROPERTY RIGHTS, INCLUDING TRADE IN COUNTERFEIT GOODS

Members,

Desiring to reduce distortions and impediments to international trade, and taking into account the need to promote effective and adequate protection of intellectual property rights, and to ensure that measures and procedures to enforce intellectual property rights do not themselves become barriers to legitimate trade;

Recognising, to this end, the need for new rules and disciplines concerning:

(a) the applicability of the basic principles of the GATT 1994 and of relevant international intellectual property agreements or conventions;

(b) the provision of adequate standards and principles concerning the availability, scope and use of trade-related intellectual property rights;

(c) the provision of effective and appropriate means for the enforcement of trade-related intellectual property rights, taking into account differences in national legal systems;

(d) the provision of effective and expeditious procedures for the multilateral prevention and settlement of disputes between governments; and

(e) transitional arrangements aiming at the fullest participation in the results of the negotiations;

Recognising the need for a multilateral framework of principles, rules and disciplines dealing with international trade in counterfeit goods;

Recognising that intellectual property rights are private rights;

Recognising the underlying public policy objectives of national systems for the protection of intellectual property, including developmental and technological objectives;

Recognising also the special needs of the least developed country Members in respect of maximum flexibility in the domestic implementation of laws and regulations in order to enable them to create a sound and viable technological base;

Emphasising the importance of reducing tensions by reaching strengthened commitments to resolve disputes on trade-related intellectual property issues through multilateral procedures;

Desiring to establish a mutually supportive relationship between the MTO and the World Intellectual Property Organization (WIPO) as well as other relevant international organisations;

Hereby agree as follows:

PART I: GENERAL PROVISIONS AND BASIC PRINCIPLES

Article 1

Nature and Scope of Obligations

1. Members shall give effect to the provisions of this Agreement. Members may, but shall not be obliged to, implement in their domestic law more extensive protection

than is required by this Agreement, provided that such protection does not contravene the provisions of this Agreement.

Members shall be free to determine the appropriate method of implementing the provisions of this Agreement within their own legal system and practice.

2. For the purposes of this Agreement, the term 'intellectual property' refers to all categories of intellectual property that are the subject of Sections 1 to 7 of Part II.

3. Members shall accord the treatment provided for in this Agreement to the nationals of other Members.[1] In respect of the relevant intellectual property right, the nationals of other Members shall be understood as those natural or legal persons that would meet the criteria for eligibility for protection provided for in the Paris Convention (1967), the Berne Convention (1971), the Rome Convention and the Treaty on Intellectual Property in Respect of Integrated Circuits, were all Members of the MTO members of those conventions.[2] Any Member availing itself of the possibilities provided in paragraph 3 of Article 5 or paragraph 2 of Article 6 of the Rome Convention shall make a notification as foreseen in those provisions to the Council for Trade-Related Aspects of intellectual Property Rights.

Article 2

Intellectual Property Conventions

1. In respect of Parts II, III and IV of this Agreement, Members shall comply with Articles 1-12 and 19 of the Paris Convention (1967).

2. Nothing in Parts I to IV of this Agreement shall derogate from existing obligations that Members may have to each other under the Paris Convention, the Berne Convention, the Rome Convention and the Treaty on Intellectual Property in Respect of Integrated Circuits.

Article 3

National Treatment

1. Each Member shall accord to the nationals of other Members treatment no less favourable than that it accords to its own nationals with regard to the protection[3] of intellectual property subject to the exceptions already provided in, respectively, the

---

[1] When 'nationals' are referred to in this Agreement, they shall be deemed, in the case of a separate customs territory Member of the MTO to mean persons, natural or legal, who are domiciled or who have a real and effective industrial or commercial establishment in that customs territory.

[2] In this Agreement, "Paris Convention" refers to the Paris Convention for the Protection of Industrial Property; "Paris Convention (1967)' refers to the Stockholm Act of this Convention of 14 July 1967 'Berne Convention', refers to the Berne Convention for the Protection of Literary and Artistic Works; 'Berne Convention (1971)' refers to the Paris Act of this Convention of 24 July 1971. 'Rome Convention' refers to the International Convention for the Protection of Performers, Producers of Phonograms and Broadcasting Organisations, adopted at Rome on 26 October 1961. 'Treaty on Intellectual Property' in Respect of integrated Circuits' (IPIC Treaty) refers to the Treaty on Intellectual Property in Respect of Integrated Circuits adopted at Washington on 26 May 1989.

[3] For the purposes of Articles 3 and 4 of this Agreement, protection shall include matters affecting the availability, acquisition, scope, maintenance and enforcement of intellectual property rights as well as those matters affecting the use of intellectual property rights specifically addressed in this Agreement.

Paris Convention (1967), the Berne Convention (1971), the Rome Convention and the Treaty on Intellectual Property in Respect of Integrated Circuits. In respect of performers, producers of phonograms and broadcasting organizations, this obligation only applies in respect of the rights provided under this Agreement. Any Member availing itself of the possibilities provided in Article 6 of the Berne Convention and paragraph 1(b) of Article 16 of the Rome Convention shall make a notification as foreseen in those provisions to the Council for Trade-Related Aspects of Intellectual Property Rights.

2. Members may avail themselves of the exceptions permitted under paragraph 1 above in relation to judicial and administrative procedures, including the designation of an address for service or the appointment of an agent within the jurisdiction of a Member, only where such exceptions are necessary to secure compliance with laws and regulations which are not inconsistent with the provisions of this Agreement and where such practices are not applied in a manner which would constitute a discussed restriction on trade.

Article 4

Most-Favoured-Nation Treatment

With regard to the protection of intellectual property, any advantage, favour, privilege or immunity granted by a Member to the nationals of any other country shall be accorded immediately and unconditionally to the nationals of all other Members. Exempted from this obligation are any advantage, favour, privilege or immunity accorded by a Member:

(a) deriving from international agreements on judicial assistance and law enforcement of a general nature and not particularly confined to the protection of intellectual property;

(b) granted in accordance with the provisions of the Berne Convention (1971) or the Rome Convention authorizing that the treatment accorded be a function not of national treatment but of the treatment accorded in another country;

(c) in respect of the rights of performers, producers of phonograms and broadcasting organizations not provided under this Agreement;

(d) deriving from international agreements related to the protection of intellectual property which entered into force prior to the entry into force of the Agreement Establishing the MTO, provided that such agreements are notified to the Council for Trade-Related Aspects of Intellectual Property Rights and do not constitute an arbitrary or unjustifiable discrimination against nationals of other Members.

Article 5

Multilateral Agreements on Acquisition or Maintenance of Protection

The obligations under Articles 3 and 4 above do not apply to procedures provided in multilateral agreements concluded under the auspices of the World Intellectual Property Organization relating to the acquisition or maintenance of intellectual property rights.

Article 6

Exhaustion

For the purposes of dispute settlement under this Agreement, subject to the provisions of Articles 3 and 4 above nothing in this Agreement shall be used to address the issue of the exhaustion of intellectual property rights.

Article 7

Objectives

The protection and enforcement of intellectual property rights should contribute to the promotion of technological innovation and to the transfer and dissemination of technology, to the mutual advantage of producers and users of technological knowledge and in a manner conducive to social and economic welfare, and to a balance of rights and obligations.

Article 8

Principles

1. Members may, in formulating or amending their national laws and regulations, adopt measures necessary to protect public health and nutrition, and to promote the public interest in sectors of vital importance to their socio-economic and technological development, provided that such measures are consistent with the provisions of this Agreement.

2. Appropriate measures, provided that they are consistent with the provisions of this Agreement, may be needed to prevent the abuse of intellectual property rights by right holders or the resort to practices which unreasonably restrain trade or adversely affect the international transfer of technology.

PART II: STANDARDS CONCERNING THE AVAILABILITY, SCOPE AND USE OF INTELLECTUAL PROPERTY RIGHTS

SECTION 1: COPYRIGHT AND RELATED RIGHTS

Article 9

Relation to Berne Convention

1. Members shall comply with Articles 1-21 and the Appendix of the Berne Convention (1971). However, Members shall not have rights or obligations under this Agreement in respect of the rights conferred under Article 6 *bis* of that Convention or of the rights derived therefrom.

2. Copyright protection shall extend to expressions and not to ideas, procedures, methods of operation or mathematical concepts as such.

Article 10

Copyright Programmes and Compilations of Data

1. Computer programs, whether in source or object code, shall be protected as literary works under the Berne Convention (1971).

2. Compilations of data or other material, whether in machine readable or other form, which by reason of the selection or arrangement of their contents constitute

intellectual creations shall be protect as such. Such protection, which shall not extend to the data or material itself, shall be without prejudice to any copyright subsisting in the data or material itself.

Article 11

Rental Rights

In respect of at least computer programs and cinematographic works, a Member shall provide authors and their successors in title the right to authorize or to prohibit the commercial rental to the public of originals or copies of their copyright works. A Member shall be excepted from this obligation in respect of cinematographic works unless such rental has led to widespread copying of such works which is materially impairing the exclusive right of reproduction conferred in that Member on authors and their successors in title. In respect of computer programs, this obligation does not apply to rentals where the program itself is not the essential object of the rental.

Article 12

Term of Protection

Whenever the term of protection of a work, other than a photographic work or a work of applied art, is calculated on a basis other than the life of a natural person, such term shall be no less than fifty years from the end of the calendar year of authorized publication, or failing such authorised publication within fifty years from the making of the work, fifty years from the end of the calendar year of making.

Article 13

Limitations and Exceptions

Members shall confine limitations or exceptions to exclusive rights to certain special cases which do not conflict with a normal exploitation of the work and do not unreasonably prejudice the legitimate interests of the right holder.

Article 14

Protection of Performers, Producers of Phonograms (Sound Recordings) and Broadcasting Organisations

1. In respect of a fixation of their performance on a phonogram, performers shall have the possibility of preventing the following acts when undertaken without their authorisation: the fixation of their unfixed performance and the reproduction of such fixation. Performers shall also have the possibility of preventing the following acts when undertaken without their authorisation: the broadcasting by wireless means and the communication to the public of their live performance.

2. Producers of phonograms shall enjoy the right to authorize or prohibit the direct or indirect reproduction of their phonograms.

3. Broadcasting organizations shall have the right to prohibit the following acts when undertaken without their authorisation: the fixation, the reproduction of fixations, and the re-broadcasting by wireless means of broadcasts, as well as the communication to the public of television broadcasts of the same. Where Members do not grant such rights to broadcasting organizations, they shall provide owners of

copyright in the subject matter of broadcasts with the possibility of preventing the above acts, subject to the provisions of the Berne Convention (1971).

4. The provisions of Article 11 in respect of computer programs shall apply *mutatis mutandis* to producers of phonograms and any other right holders in phonograms as determined in domestic law. If, on the date of the Ministerial Meeting concluding the Uruguay Round of Multilateral Trade Negotiations, a Member has in force a system of equitable remuneration of right holders in respect of the rental of phonograms, it may maintain such system provided that the commercial rental of phonograms is not giving rise to the material impairment of the exclusive rights of reproduction of right holders.

5. The term of the protection available under this Agreement to performers and producers of phonograms shall last at least until the end of a period of fifty years computed from the end of the calendar year in which the fixation was made or the performance took place. The term of protection granted pursuant to paragraph 3 above shall last for at least twenty years from the end of the calendar year in which the broadcast took place.

6. Any Member may, in relation to the rights conferred under paragraphs 1-3 above, provide for conditions, limitations, exceptions and reservations to the extent permitted by the Rome Convention. However, the provisions of Article 18 of the Berne Convention (1971) shall also apply, *mutatis mutandis*, to the rights of performers and producers of phonograms in phonograms.

SECTION 2: TRADEMARKS

Article 15

Protectable Subject Matter

1. Any sign, or any combination of signs capable of distinguishing the goods or services of one undertaking from those of other undertakings, shall be capable of constituting a trademark. Such signs, in particular words including personal names, letters, numerals, figurative elements and combinations of colours as well as any combination of such signs, shall be eligible for registration as trademarks. Where signs are not inherently capable of distinguishing the relevant goods or services, Members may make registrability depend on distinctiveness acquired through use. Members may require, as a condition of registration, that signs be visually perceptible.

2. Paragraph 1 above shall not be understood to prevent a Member from denying registration of a trademark on other grounds, provided that they do not derogate from the provisions of the Paris Convention (1967).

3. Members may make registrability depend on use. However, actual use of a trademark shall not be a condition for filing an application for registration. An application shall not be refused solely on the ground that intended use has not taken place before the expiry of a period of three years from the date of application.

4. The nature of the goods or services to which a trademark is to be applied shall in no case form an obstacle to registration of the trademark.

5. Members shall publish each trademark either before it is registered or promptly after it is registered and shall afford a reasonable opportunity for petitions to cancel the registration. In addition, Members may afford an opportunity for the registration of a trademark to be opposed.

Article 16

Rights Conferred

1. The owner of a registered trademark shall have the exclusive right to prevent all third parties not having his consent from using in the course of trade identical or similar signs for goods or services which are identical or similar to those in respect of which the trademark is registered where such use would result in a likelihood of confusion, in case of the use of an identical sign for identical goods or services, a likelihood of confusion shall be presumed. The rights described above shall not prejudice any existing prior rights, nor shall they affect the possibility of Members making rights available on the basis of use.

2. Article 6 *bis* of the Paris Convention (1967) shall apply, *mutatis mutandis,* to services. In determining whether a trademark is well-known, account shall be taken of the knowledge of the trademark in the relevant sector of the public, including knowledge in that Member obtained as a result of the promotion of the trademark.

3. Article 6 *bis* of the Paris Convention (1967) shall apply, *mutatis mutandis,* to goods or services which are not similar to those in respect of which a trademark is registered, provided that use of that trademark in relation to those goods or services would indicate a connection between those goods or services and the owner of the registered trademark and provided that the interests of the owner of the registered trademark are likely to be damaged by such use.

Article 17

Exceptions

Members may provide limited exceptions to the rights conferred by a trademark, such as fair use of descriptive terms, provided that such exceptions take account of the legitimate interests of the owner of the trademark and of third parties.

Article 18

Term of Protection

Initial registration, and each renewal of registration, of a trademark shall be for a term of no less than seven years. The registration of a trademark shall be renewable indefinitely.

Article 19

Requirement of Use

1. If use is required to maintain a registration, the registration may be cancelled only after an uninterrupted period of at least three years of non-use, unless valid reasons based on the existence of obstacles to such use are shown by the trademark owner. Circumstances arising independently of the will of the owner of the trademark which constitute an obstacle to the use of the trademark, such as import restrictions on or other government requirements for goods or services protected by the trademark, shall be recognized as valid reasons for non-use.

2. When subject to the control of its owner, use of a trademark by another person shall be recognized as use of the trademark for the purpose of maintaining the registration.

Article 20

Other Requirements

The use of a trademark in the course of trade shall not be unjustifiably encumbered by special requirements, such as use with another trademark, use in a special form or use in a manner detrimental to its capability to distinguish the goods or services of one undertaking from those of other undertakings. This will not preclude a requirement prescribing the use of the trademark identifying the undertaking producing the goods or services along with, but without linking it to, the trademark distinguishing the specific goods or services in question of that undertaking.

Article 21

Licensing and Assignment

Members may determine conditions on the licensing and assignment of trademarks, it being understood that the compulsory licensing of trademarks shall not be permitted and that the owner of a registered trademark shall have the right to assign his trademark with or without the transfer of the business to which the trademark belongs.

SECTION 3: GEOGRAPHICAL INDICATIONS

Article 22

Protection of Geographical Indications

1. Geographical indications are, for the purposes of this Agreement, indications which identify a good as originating in the territory of a Member, or a region or locality in that territory, where a given quality, reputation or other characteristic of the good is essentially attributable to its geographical origin.

2. In respect of geographical indications, Members shall provide the legal means for interested parties to prevent:

    (a) the use of any means in the designation or presentation of a good that indicates or suggests that the good in question originates in a geographical area other than the true place of origin in a manner which misleads the public as to the geographical origin of the good.

    (b) any use which constitutes an act of unfair competition within the meaning of Article 10 *bis* of the Paris Convention (1967).

3. A Member shall, *ex officio* if its legislation so permits or at the request of an interested party, refuse or invalidate the registration of a trademark which contains or consists of a geographical indication with respect to goods not originating in the territory indicated, if use of the indication in the trademark for such goods in that Member is of such a nature as to mislead the public as to the true place of origin.

4. The provisions of the preceding paragraphs of this Article shall apply to a geographical indication which, although literally true as to the territory, region or

locality in which the goods originate, falsely represents to the public that the goods originate in another territory.

Article 23

Additional Protection for Geographical Indications for Wines and Spirits

1. Each Member shall provide the legal means for interested parties to prevent use of a geographical indication identifying wines for wines not originating in the place indicated by the geographical indication in question or identifying spirits for spirits not originating in the place indicated by the geographical indication in question, even where the true origin of the goods is indicated or the geographical indication is used in translation or accompanied by expressions such as "kind", "type", "style", "imitation" or the like.[4]

2. The registration of a trademark for wines which contains or consists of a geographical indication identifying wines or for spirits which contains or consists of a geographical indication identifying spirits shall be refused or invalidated, *ex officio* if domestic legislation so permits or at the request of an interested party, with respect to such wines or spirits not having this origin.

3. In the case of homonymous geographical indications for wines, protection shall be accorded to each indication, subject to the provisions of paragraph 4 of Article 22 above. Each Member shall determine the practical conditions under which the homonymous indications in question will be differentiated from each other, taking into account the need to ensure equitable treatment of the producers concerned and that consumers are not misled.

4. In order to facilitate the protection of geographical indications for wines, negotiations shall be undertaken in the Council for Trade-Related Aspects of Intellectual Property Rights concerning the establishment of a multilateral system of notification and registration of geographical indications for wines eligible for protection in those Members participating in the system.

Article 24

International Negotiations; Exceptions

1. Members agree to enter into negotiations aimed at increasing the protection of individual geographical indications under Article 23. The provisions of paragraphs 4-8 below shall not be used by a Member to refuse to conduct negotiations or to conclude bilateral or multilateral agreements. In the context of such negotiations, Members shall be willing to consider the continued applicability of these provisions to individual geographical indications whose use was the subject of such negotiations.

2. The Council for Trade-Related Aspects of Intellectual Property Rights shall keep under review the application of the provisions of this Section; the first such review shall take place within two years of the entry into force of the Agreement Establishing the MTO. Any matter affecting the compliance with the obligations

---

4. Notwithstanding the first sentence of Article 42, Members may, with respect to these obligations, instead provide for enforcement, by administrative action.

under these provisions may be drawn to the attention of the Council, which, at the request of a Member, shall consult with any Member or Members in respect of such matter in respect of which it has not been possible to find a satisfactory solution through bilateral or plurilateral consultations between the Members concerned. The Council shall take such action as may be agreed to facilitate the operation and further the objectives of this Section.

3. In implementing this Section, a Member shall not diminish the protection of geographical indications that existed in that Member immediately prior to the date of entry into force of the Agreement Establishing the MTO.

4. Nothing in this Section shall require a Member to prevent continued and similar use of a particular geographical indication of another Member identifying wines or spirits in connection with goods or services by any of its nationals or domiciliaries who have used that geographical indication in a continuous manner with regard to the same or related goods or services in the territory of that Member either (a) for at least ten years preceding the date of the Ministerial Meeting concluding the Uruguay Round of Multilateral Trade Negotiations or (b) in good faith preceding that date.

5. Where a trademark has been applied for or registered in good faith, or where rights to a trademark have been acquired through use in good faith either:

(a) before the date of application of these provisions in that Member as defined in Part VI below; or

(b) before the geographical indication is protected in its country of origin;

measures adopted to implement this Section shall not prejudice eligibility for or the validity of the registration of a trademark, or the right to use a trademark, on the basis that such a trademark is identical with, or similar to, a geographical indication.

6. Nothing in this Section shall require a Member to apply its provisions in respect of a geographical indication of any other Member with respect to goods or services for which the relevant indication is identical with the term customary in common language as the common name for such goods or services in the territory of that Member. Nothing in this Section shall require a Member to apply its provisions in respect of a geographical indication of any other Member with respect to products of the vine for which the relevant indication is identical with the customary name of a grape variety existing in the territory of that Member as of the date of entry into force of the Agreement Establishing the MTO.

7. A Member may provide that any request made under this Section in connection with the use or registration of a trademark must be presented within five years after the adverse use of the protected indication has become generally known in that Member or after the date of registration of the trademark in that Member provided that the trademark has been published by that date, if such date is earlier than the date on which the adverse use became generally known in that Member, provided that the geographical indication is not used or registered in bad faith.

8. The provisions of this Section shall in no way prejudice the right of any person to use in the course of trade, his name or the name of his predecessor in business except where such name is in such a manner as to mislead the public.

9. There shall be no obligation under this Agreement to protect geographical indications which are not or cease to be protected in their country of origin, or which have fallen into disuse in that country.

SECTION 4: INDUSTRIAL DESIGNS

Article 25

Requirements for Protection

1. Members shall provide for the protection of independently created industrial designs that are new or original. Members may provide that designs are not new or original if they do not significantly differ from known designs or combinations of known design features. Members may provide that such protection shall not extend to designs dictated essentially by technical or functional considerations.

2. Each Member shall ensure that requirements for securing protection for textile designs, in particular in regard to any cost, examination or publication, do not unreasonably impair the opportunity to seek and obtain such protection. Members shall be free to meet this obligation through industrial design law or through copyright law.

Article 26

Protection

1. The owner of a protected industrial design shall have the right to prevent third parties not having his consent from making, selling or importing articles bearing or embodying a design which is a copy or substantially a copy of the protected design, when such acts are undertaken for commercial purposes.

2. Members may provide limited exceptions to the protection of industrial designs, provided that such exceptions do not unreasonably conflict with the normal exploitation of protected industrial designs and do not unreasonably prejudice the legitimate interests of the owner of the protected design, taking account of the legitimate interests of third parties.

3. The duration of protection available shall amount to at least ten years.

SECTION 5: PATENTS

Article 27

Patentable Subject Matter

1. Subject to the provisions of paragraphs 2 and 3 below, patents shall be available for any inventions, whether products or processes, in all fields of technology, provided that they are new, involve an inventive step and are capable of industrial application.[5] Subject to paragraph 4 of Article 65, paragraph 8 of Article 70 and paragraph 3 of this Article, patents shall be available and patent rights enjoyable without discrimination as to the place of invention, the field of technology and whether products are imported or locally produced.

[5.] For the purposes of this Article, the terms 'inventive step' and 'capable of industrial application' may be deemed by a Member to be synonymous with the terms 'non-obvious' and 'useful' respectively.

2. Members may exclude from patentability inventions, the prevention within their territory of the commercial exploitation of which is necessary to protect *ordre public* or morality including to protect human, animal or plant life or health or to avoid serious prejudice to the environment provides that such exclusion is not made merely because the exploitation is prohibited by domestic law.

3. Members may also exclude from patentability:

    (a) diagnostic, therapeutic and surgical methods for the treatment of humans or animals;

    (b) plants and animals other than micro-organisms and essentially biological processes for the production of plants or animals other than non-biological and microbiological processes. However, Members shall provide for the protection of plant varieties either by patents or by an effective *sui generis* system or by any combination thereof. The provisions of this sub-paragraph shall be reviewed four years after the entry into force of the Agreement Establishing the MTO.

Article 28

Rights Conferred

1. A patent shall confer on its owner the following exclusive rights:

    (a) Where the subject matter of a patent is a product, to prevent third parties not having his consent from the acts of: making, using, offering for sale, selling, or importing[6] for these purposes that product;

    (b) where the subject matter of a patent is a process, to prevent third parties not having his consent from the act of using the process, and from the acts of: using, offering for sale, selling, or importing for these purposes at least the product obtained directly by that process.

2. Patent owners shall also have the right to assign, or transfer by succession, the patent and to conclude licensing contracts.

Article 29

Conditions on Patent Applicants

1. Members shall require that an applicant for a patent shall disclose the invention in a manner sufficiently clear and complete for the invention to be carried out by a person skilled in the art and may require the applicant to indicate the best mode for carrying out the invention known to the inventor at the filing date or, where priority, is claimed, at the priority date of the application.

2   Members may require an applicant for a patent to provide information concerning corresponding foreign applications and grants.

[6.] This right, like all other rights conferred under this Agreement in respect of the use, sale, importation or other distribution of goods, is subject to the provisions of Article 6 above.

Article 30

Exceptions to Rights Conferred

Members may provide limited exceptions to the exclusive rights conferred by a patent, provided that such exceptions do not unreasonably conflict with a normal exploitation of the patent and do not unreasonably prejudice the legitimate interests of the patent owner, taking account of the legitimate interests of third parties.

Article 31

Other Use Without Authorisation of the Right Holder

Where the law of a Member allows for other use[7] of the subject matter of a patent without the authorisation of the right holder, including use by the government or third parties authorized by the government, the following provisions shall be respected:

(a) authorisation of such use shall be considered on its individual merits;

(b) such use may only be permitted if, prior to such use, the proposed user has made efforts to obtain authorisation from the right holder on reasonable commercial terms and conditions and that such efforts have not been successful within a reasonable period of time. This requirement may be waived by a Member in the case of a national emergency or other circumstances of extreme urgency or in cases of public non-commercial use. In situations of national emergency or other circumstances of extreme urgency, the right holder shall, nevertheless, be notified as soon as reasonably practicable. In the ease of public non-commercial use, where the government or contractor, without making a patent search, knows or has demonstrable grounds to know that a valid patent is or will be used by or for the government, the right holder shall be informed promptly.

(c) the scope and duration of such use shall be limited to the purpose for which it was authorized, and in the case of semi-conductor technology shall only be for public non-commercial use or to remedy a practice determined after judicial or administrative process to be anti-competitive.

(d) such use shall be non-exclusive;

(e) such use shall be non-assignable, except with that part of the enterprise or goodwill which enjoys such use;

(f) any such use shall be authorized predominantly for the supply of the domestic market of the Member authorizing such use;

(g) authorisation for such use shall be liable, subject to adequate protection of the legitimate interests of the persons so authorized, to be terminated if and when the circumstances which led to it cease to exist and are unlikely to recur. The competent authority shall have the authority to review, upon motivated request the continued existence of these circumstances.

(h) the right holder shall be paid adequate remuneration in the circumstances of each case taking into account the economic value of the authorization:

[7.] 'Other use' refers to use other than that allowed under Article 30.

(i) the legal validity of any decision relating to the authorization of such use shall be subject to judicial review or other independent review by a distinct higher authority in that Member;

(j) any decision relating to the remuneration provided in respect of such use shall be subject to judicial review or other independent review by a distinct higher authority in that Member;

(k) Members are not obliged to apply the conditions set forth in sub-paragraphs (b) and (f) above where such use is permitted to remedy a practice determined after judicial or administrative process to be anti-competitive. The need to correct anti-competitive practices may be taken into account in determining the amount of remuneration in such cases. Competent authorities shall have the authority to refuse termination of authorization if and when the conditions which led to such authorization are likely to recur;

(l) where such use is authorized to permit the exploitation of a patent ("the second patent") which cannot be exploited without infringing another patent ("the first patent"), the following additional conditions shall apply:

　　(i) the invention claimed in the second patent shall involve an important technical advance of considerable economic significance in relation to the invention claimed in the first patent;

　　(ii) the owner of the first patent shall be entitled to a cross-licence on reasonable terms to use the invention claimed in the second patent; and

　　(iii) the use authorized in respect of the first patent shall be non-assignable except with the assignment of the second patent.

Article 32

Revocation/Forfeiture

An opportunity for judicial review of any decision to revoke or forfeit a patent shall be available.

Article 33

Term of Protection

The term of protection available shall not end before the expiration of a period of twenty years counted from the filing date.[8]

Article 34

Process Patents: Burden of Proof

1. For the purposes of civil proceedings in respect of the infringement of the rights of the owner referred to in paragraph 1(b) of Article 28 above, if the subject matter of a patent is a process for obtaining a product, the judicial authorities shall have the authority to order the defendant to prove that the process to obtain an identical product is different from the patented process. Therefore, Members shall provide, in

---

[8.] It is understood that those Members which do not have a system of original grant may provide that the term of protection shall be computed from the filing date in the system of original grant.

at least one of the following circumstances, that any identical product when produced without the consent of the patent owner shall, in the absence of proof to the contrary, be deemed to have been obtained by the patented process:

(a) if the product obtained by the patented process is new;

(b) if there is a substantial likelihood that the identical product was made by the process and the owner of the patent has been unable through reasonable efforts to determine the process actually used.

2. Any Member shall be free to provide that the burden of proof indicated in paragraph 1 shall be on the alleged infringer only if the condition referred to in sub-paragraph (a) is fulfilled or only if the condition referred to in sub-paragraph (b) is fulfilled.

3. In the adduction of proof to the contrary the legitimate interests of the defendant in protecting his manufacturing and business secrets shall be taken into account.

SECTION 6 - LAYOUT-DESIGNS (TOPOGRAPHIES) OF INTEGRATED CIRCUITS

Article 35

Relation to IPIC Treaty

Members agree to provide protection to the layout-designs (topographies) of integrated circuits (hereinafter referred to as "layout-designs") in accordance with Articles 2-7 (other than paragraph 3 of Article 6), Article 12 and paragraph 3 of Article 16 of the Treaty on Intellectual Property in Respect of Integrated Circuits and, in addition, to comply with the following provisions.

Article 36

Scope of the Protection

Subject to the provisions of paragraph 1 of Article 37 below, Members shall consider unlawful the following acts if performed without the authorization of the right holder:[9] importing, selling, or otherwise distributing for commercial purposes a protected layout-design, an integrated circuit in which protected layout-design is incorporated, or an article incorporating such an integrated circuit only insofar as it continues to contain an unlawfully reproduced layout-design.

Article 37

Acts not Requiring the Authorization of the Right Holder

1. Notwithstanding Article 36 above, no Member shall consider unlawful the performance of any of the acts referred to in that Article in respect of an integrated circuit incorporating an unlawfully reproduced layout-design or any article incorporating such an integrated circuit where the person performing or ordering such acts did not know and had no reasonable ground to know, when acquiring the integrated circuit or article incorporating such an integrated circuit that it incorporated an unlawfully reproduced layout-design. Members shall provide that, after the time that such person has received sufficient notice that the layout-design

---

[9.] The term "right holder" in the Section shall be understood as having the same meaning as the term "holder of the right" in the IPIC Treaty.

was unlawfully reproduced, he may perform any of the acts with respect to the stock on hand or ordered before such time, but shall be liable to pay to the right holder a sum equivalent to a reasonable royalty such as would be payable under a freely negotiated licence in respect of such a layout-design.

2. The conditions set out in sub-paragraphs (a)-(k) of Article 31 above shall apply *mutatis mutandis* in the event of any non-voluntary licensing of a layout-design or of its use by or for the government without the authorization of the right holder.

Article 38

Term of Protection

1. In Members requiring registration as a condition of protection, the term of protection of layout-designs shall not end before the expiration of a period of ten years counted from the date of filing an application for registration or from the first commercial exploitation wherever in the world it occurs.

2. In Members not requiring registration as a condition for protection, layout-designs shall be protected for a term of no less than ten years from the date of the first commercial exploitation wherever in the world it occurs.

3. Notwithstanding paragraphs 1 and 2 above, a Member may provide that protection shall lapse fifteen years after the creation of the layout-design.

SECTION 7:   PROTECTION OF UNDISCLOSED INFORMATION

Article 39

1. In the course of ensuring effective protection against unfair competition as provided in Article 10 *bis* of the Paris Convention (1967), Members shall protect undisclosed information in accordance with paragraph 2 below and data submitted to governments or governmental agencies in accordance with paragraph 3 below.

2. Natural and legal persons shall have the possibility of preventing information lawfully within their control from being disclosed to, acquired by, or used by others without their consent in a manner contrary to honest commercial practices[10] so long as such information:

    -   is secret in the sense that it is not, as a body or in the precise configuration and assembly of its components, generally known among or readily accessible to persons within the circles that normally deal with the kind of information in question;

    -   has commercial value because it is secret; and

    -   has been subject to reasonable steps under the circumstances, by the person lawfully in control of the information, to keep it secret.

3. Members, when requiring, as a condition of approving the marketing of pharmaceutical or of agricultural chemical products which utilise new chemical

---

[10] For the purpose of this provision, "a manner contrary to honest commercial practices", shall mean at least practices such as breach of contract, breach of confidence and inducement to breach, and includes the acquisition of undisclosed information by third parties who knew or were grossly negligent in failing to know that such practices were involved in the acquisition.

entities, the submission of undisclosed test or other data, the origination of which involves a considerable effort, shall protect such data against unfair commercial use. In addition, Members shall protect such data against disclosure, except where necessary to protect the public, or unless steps are taken to ensure that the data are protected against unfair commercial use.

SECTION 8:   CONTROL OF ANTI-COMPETITIVE PRACTICES IN
                 CONTRACTUAL LICENCES

Article 40

1. Members agree that some licensing practices or conditions pertaining to intellectual property rights which restrain competition may have adverse effects on trade and may impede the transfer and dissemination of technology.

2. Nothing in this Agreement shall prevent Members from specifying in their national legislation licensing practices or conditions that may in particular cases constitute an abuse of intellectual property rights having an adverse effect on competition in the relevant market. As provided above, a Member may adopt, consistently with the other provisions of this Agreement, appropriate measures to prevent or control such practices, which may include for example exclusive grantback conditions, conditions preventing challenges to validity and coercive package licensing, in the light of the relevant laws and regulations of that Member.

3. Each Member shall enter, upon request, into consultations with any other Member which has cause to believe that an intellectual property right owner that is a national or domiciliary of the Member to which the request for consultations has been addressed is undertaking practices in violation of the requesting Member's laws and regulations on the subject matter of this Section, and which wishes to secure compliance with such legislation, without prejudice to any action under the law and to the full freedom of an ultimate decision of either Member. The Member addressed shall accord full and sympathetic consideration to and shall-afford adequate opportunity for, consultations with the requesting Member, and shall co-operate through supply of publicly available non-confidential information of relevance to the matter in question and of other information available to the Member, subject to domestic law and to the conclusion of mutually satisfactory agreements concerning the safeguarding of its confidentiality by the requesting Member.

4. A Member whose nationals or domiciliaries are subject to proceedings in another Member concerning alleged violation of that other Member's laws and regulations on the subject matter of this section shall upon request, be granted an opportunity for consolations by the other Member under the same conditions as those foreseen in paragraph 3 above.

PART III: ENFORCEMENT OF INTELLECTUAL PROPERTY RIGHTS

SECTION 1: GENERAL OBLIGATIONS

Article 41

1. Members shall ensure that enforcement procedures as specified in this Part are available under their national laws so as to permit effective action against any act of infringement of intellectual property rights covered by this Agreement, including expeditious remedies to prevent infringements and remedies which constitute a deterrent to further infringements. These procedures shall be applied in such a manner as to avoid the creation of barriers to legitimate trade and to provide for safeguards against their abuse.

2. Procedures concerning the enforcement of intellectual property rights shall be fair and equitable. They shall not be unnecessarily complicated or costly, or entail unreasonable time-limits or unwarranted delays.

3. Decisions on the merits of a case shall preferably be in writing and reasoned. They shall be made available at least to the panics to the proceeding without undue delay. Decisions on the merits of a case shall be based only on evidence in respect of which parties were offered the opportunity to be heard.

4. Parties to a proceeding shall have an opportunity for review by a judicial authority of final administrative decisions and, subject to jurisdictional provisions in national laws concerning the importance of a case, of at least the legal aspects of initial judicial decisions on the merits of a case. However, there shall be no obligation to provide an opportunity for review of acquittals in criminal cases.

5. It is understood that this Part does not create any obligation to put in place a judicial system for the enforcement of intellectual property rights distinct from that for the enforcement of laws in general, nor does it affect the capacity of Members to enforce their laws in general. Nothing in this Part creates any obligation with respect to the distribution of resources as between enforcement of intellectual property rights and the enforcement of laws in general.

SECTION 2:   CIVIL AND ADMINISTRATIVE PROCEDURES AND REMEDIES

Article 42

Fair and Equitable Procedures

Members shall make available to right holders[11] civil judicial procedures concerning the enforcement of any intellectual property right covered by this Agreement. Defendants shall have the right to written notice which is timely and contains sufficient detail, including the basis of the claims. Parties shall be allowed to be represented by independent legal counsel and procedures shall not impose overly burdensome requirements concerning mandatory personal appearances. All parties to such procedures shall be duly entitled to substantiate their claims and to present all relevant

---

[11.] For the purpose of this Part, the term 'right holder' includes federations and associations having legal standing to assert such rights.

evidence. The procedure shall provide a means to identify and protect confidential information, unless this would be contrary to existing constitutional requirements.

Article 43

Evidence of Proof

1. The judicial authorities shall have the authority, where a party has presented reasonably available evidence sufficient to support its claims and has specified evidence relevant to substantiation of its claims which lies in the control of the opposing party, to order that this evidence be produced by the opposing party, subject in appropriate cases to conditions which ensure the protection of confidential information.

2. In cases in which a party to a proceeding voluntarily and without good reason refuses access to, or otherwise does not provide necessary information within a reasonable period, or significantly impedes a procedure relating to an enforcement action, a Member may accord judicial authorities the authority to make preliminary and final determinations, affirmative or negative, on the basis of the information presented to them, including the complaint or the allegation presented by the party adversely affected by the denial of access to information, subject to providing the parties an opportunity to be heard on the allegations or evidence.

Article 44

Injunctions

1. The judicial authorities shall have the authority to order a party to desist from an infringement, *inter alia* to prevent the entry into the channels of commerce in their jurisdiction of imported goods that involve the infringement of an intellectual property right, immediately after customs clearance of such goods. Members are not obliged to accord such authority in respect of protected subject matter acquired or ordered by a person prior to knowing or having reasonable grounds to know that dealing in such subject matter would entail the infringement of an intellectual property right.

2. Notwithstanding the other provisions of this Part and provided that the provisions of Part II specifically addressing use by governments, or by third parties authorized by a government, without the authorization of the right holder are complied with. Members may limit the remedies available against such use to payment of remuneration in accordance with sub-paragraph (h) of Article 31 above. In other cases, the remedies under this Part shall apply or, where these remedies are inconsistent with national law, declaratory judgments and adequate compensation shall be available.

Article 45

Damages

1. The judicial authorities shall have the authority to order the infringer to pay the right holder damages adequate to compensate for the injury the right holder has suffered because of an infringement of his intellectual property right by an infringer who knew or had reasonable grounds to know that he was engaged in infringing activity.

2. The judicial authorities shall also have the authority to order the infringer to pay the right holder expenses which may include appropriate attorney's fees. In appropriate cases, Members may authorize the judicial authorities to order recovery of profits and/or payment of pre-established damages even where the infringer did not know or had no reasonable grounds to know that he was engaged in infringing activity.

Article 46

Other Remedies

In order to create an effective deterrent to infringement, the judicial authorities shall have the authority to order that goods that they have found to be infringing be, without compensation of any sort, disposed of outside the channels of commerce in such a manner as to avoid any harm caused to the right holder, or, unless this would be contrary to existing constitutional requirements, destroyed. The judicial authorities shall also have the authority to order that materials and implements the predominant use of which has been in the creation of the infringing goods be, without compensation of any sort disposed of outside the channels of commerce in such a manner as to minimise the risks of further infringements. In considering such requests, the need for proportionality between the seriousness of the infringement and the remedies ordered as well as the interests of third parties shall be taken into account. In regard to counterfeit trademark goods, the simple removal of the trademark unlawfully affixed shall not be sufficient, other than in exceptional cases, to permit release of the goods into the channels of commerce.

Article 47

Right of Information

Members may provide that the judicial authorities shall have the authority, unless this would be out of proportion to the seriousness of the infringement, to order the infringer to inform the right holder of the identity of third persons involved in the production and distribution of the infringing goods or services and of their channels of distribution.

Article 48

Indemnification of the Defendant

1. The judicial authorities shall have the authority to order a party at whose request measures were taken and who has abused enforcement procedures to provide to a party wrongfully enjoined or restrained adequate compensation for the injury suffered because of such abuse. The judicial authorities shall also have the authority to order the applicant to pay the defendant expenses, which may include appropriate attorney's fees.

2. In respect of the administration of any law pertaining to the protection or enforcement of intellectual property rights. Members shall only exempt both public authorities and officials from liability to appropriate remedial measures where actions are taken or intended in good faith in the course of the administration of such laws.

Article 49

Administrative Procedures

To the extent that any civil remedy can be ordered as a result of administrative procedures on the merits of a case, such procedures shall conform to principles equivalent in substance to those set forth in this Section.

SECTION 3: PROVISIONAL MEASURES

Article 50

1. The judicial authorities shall have the authority to order prompt and effective provisional measures:

    (a) to prevent an infringement of any intellectual property right from occurring, and in particular to prevent the entry into the channels of commerce in their jurisdiction of goods including imported goods immediately after customs clearance;

    (b) to preserve relevant evidence in regard to the alleged infringement.

2. The judicial authorities shall have the authority to adopt provisional measures *inaudita altera parte* where appropriate, in particular where any delay is likely to cause irreparable harm to the right holder, or where there is a demonstrable risk of evidence being destroyed.

3. The judicial authorities shall have the authority, to require the applicant to provide any reasonably available evidence in order to satisfy themselves with a sufficient degree of certainty that the applicant is the right holder and that his right is being infringed or that such infringement is imminent, and to order the applicant to provide a security or equivalent assurance sufficient to protect the defendant and to prevent abuse.

4. Where provisional measures have been adopted *inaudita altera parte*, the parties affected shall be given notice, without delay after the execution of the measures at the latest. A review, including a right to be heard, shall take place upon request of the defendant with a view to deciding, within a reasonable period after the notification of the measures, whether these measures shall be modified, revoked or confirmed.

5. The applicant may be required to supply other information necessary for the identification of the goods concerned by the authority that will execute the provisional measures.

6. Without prejudice to paragraph 4 above, provisional measures taken on the basis of paragraphs 1 and 2 above shall, upon request by the defendant, be revoked or otherwise cease to have effect, if proceedings leading to a decision on the merits of the case are not initiated within a reasonable period, to be determined by the judicial authority ordering the measures where national law so permits or, in the absence of such a determination, not to exceed twenty working days or thirty-one calendar days, whichever is the longer.

7. Where the provisional measures are revoked or where they lapse due to any act or omission by the applicant, or where it is subsequently found that there has been no

infringement or threat of infringement of an intellectual property right, the judicial authorities shall have the authority to order the applicant, upon request of the defendant, to provide the defendant appropriate compensation for any injury caused by these measures.

8. To the extent that any provisional measure can be ordered as a result of administrative procedures, such procedures shall conform to principles equivalent in substance to those set forth in this Section.

SECTION 4: SPECIAL REQUIREMENTS RELATED TO BORDER MEASURES[12]

Article 51

Suspension of Release by Custom Authorities

Members shall, in conformity with the provisions set out below, adopt procedures[13] to enable a right holder, who has valid grounds for suspecting that the importation of counterfeit trademark or pirated copyright goods[14] may take place, to lodge an application in writing with competent authorities, administrative or judicial, for the suspension by the customs authorities of the release into free circulation of such goods. Members may enable such an application to be made in respect of goods which involve other infringements of intellectual property rights, provided that the requirements of this Section are met. Members may also provide for corresponding procedures concerning the suspension by the custom authorities of the release of infringing goods destined for exportation from their territories.

Article 52

Application

Any right holder initiating the procedures under Article 51 above shall be required to provide adequate evidence to satisfy the competent authorities that, under the laws of the country of importation, there is *prima facie* an infringement of his intellectual property right and to supply a sufficiently detailed description of the goods to make them readily recognisable by the customs authorities. The competent authorities shall inform the applicant within a reasonable period whether they have accepted the application and,

---

[12.] Where a Member has dismantled substantially all controls over movement of goods across its border with another Member with which it forms part of a customs union it shall not required to apply provisions of this Section at that border.

[13.] It is understood that there shall be no obligation to apply such procedures to imports of goods put on the market in another country by or with the consent of the right holder or to goods in transit.

[14.] For the purposes of this Agreement:

- counterfeit trademark goods shall mean any goods, including packaging, bearing without authorisation a trademark which is identical to the trademark validly registered in respect of such goods, or which cannot be distinguished in its essential aspects from such a trademark, and which thereby infringes the rights of the owner of the trademark in question under the law of the country of importation.

- Pirated copyright goods shall mean any goods which are copies made without the consent of the right holder or person duly authorized by him in the country of production and which are made directly or indirectly from an article where the making of that copy would have constituted an infringement of a copyright or a related right under the law of the country of importation.

where determined by the competent authorities, the period for which the customs authorities will take action.

Article 53

Security or Equivalent Assurance

1. The competent authorities shall have the authority to require an applicant to provide a security or equivalent assurance sufficient to protect the defendant and the competent authorities and to prevent abuse. Such security or equivalent assurance shall not unreasonably deter recourse to these procedures.

2. Where pursuant to an application under this Section the release of goods involving industrial designs, patents, layout-designs or undisclosed information into free circulation has been suspended by customs authorities on the basis of a decision other than by a judicial or other independent authority, and the period provided for in Article 55 has expired without the granting of provisional relief by the duly empowered authority, and provided that all other conditions for importation have been complied with, the owner, importer, or consignee of such goods shall be entitled to their release on the posting of a security in an amount sufficient to protect the right holder for any infringement. Payment of such security shall not prejudice any other remedy available to the right holder, it being understood that the security shall be released if the right holder fails to pursue his right of action within a reasonable period of time.

Article 54

Notice of Suspension

The importer and the applicant shall be promptly notified of the suspension of the release of goods according to Article 51 above.

Article 55

Duration of Suspension

If, within a period not exceeding ten working days after the applicant has been served notice of the suspension, the customs authorities have not been informed that proceedings leading to a decision on the merits of the case have been initiated by a party other than the defendant, or that the duly empowered authority has taken provisional measures prolonging the suspension of the release of the goods, the goods shall be released, provided that all other conditions for importation or exportation have been complied with, in appropriate cases, this time-limit may be extended by another ten working days. If proceedings leading to a decision on the merits of the case have been initiated, a review, including a right to be heard, shall take place upon request of the defendant with a view to deciding, within a reasonable period, whether these measures shall be modified, revoked or confirmed. Notwithstanding the above, where the suspension of the release of goods is carried out or continued in accordance with a provisional judicial measure, the provisions of Article 50, paragraph 6 above shall apply.

Article 56

Indemnification of the Importer and of the Owner of the Goods

Relevant authorities shall have the authority to order the applicant to pay the importer, the consignee and the owner of the goods appropriate compensation for any injury caused to them through the wrongful detention of goods or through the detention of goods released pursuant to Article 55 above.

Article 57

Right of Inspection and Information

Without prejudice to the protection of confidential information, Members shall provide the competent authorities the authority to give the right holder sufficient opportunity to have any product detained by the customs authorities inspected in order to substantiate his claims. The competent authorities shall also have authority to give the importer an equivalent opportunity to have any such product inspected. Where a positive determination has been made on the merits of a case, Members may provide the competent authorities the authority to inform the right holder of the names and addresses of the consignor, the importer and the consignee and of the quantity of the goods in question.

Article 58

Ex Officio Action

Where Members require competent authorities to act upon their own initiative and to suspend the release of goods in respect of which they have acquired *prima facie* evidence that an intellectual property right is being infringed:

(a) the competent authorities may at any time seek from the right holder any information that may assist them to exercise these powers.

(b) the importer and the right holder shall be promptly notified of the suspension. Where the importer has lodged an appeal against the suspension with the competent authorities the suspension shall be subject to the conditions, *mutatis mutandis,* set out at Article 55 above.

(c) Members shall only exempt both public authorities and officials from liability to appropriate remedial measures where actions are taken or intended in good faith.

Article 59

Remedies

Without prejudice to other rights of action open to the right holder and subject to the right of the defendant to seek review by a judicial authority, competent authorities shall have the authority to order the destruction or disposal of infringing goods in accordance with the principles set out in Article 46 above. In regard to counterfeit trademark goods, the authorities shall not allow the re-exportation of the infringing goods in an unaltered state or subject them to a different customs procedure, other than in exceptional circumstances.

Article 60

De Minimis Imports

Members may exclude from the application of the above provisions small quantities of goods of a non-commercial nature contained in travellers' personal luggage or sent in small consignments.

SECTION 5: CRIMINAL PROCEDURES

Article 61

Members shall provide for criminal procedures and penalties to be applied at least, in cases of wilful trademark counterfeiting or copyright piracy on a commercial scale. Remedies available shall include imprisonment and/or monetary fines sufficient to provide a deterrent, consistently with the level of penalties applied for crimes of a corresponding gravity. In appropriate cases, remedies available shall also include the seizure, forfeiture and destruction of the infringing goods and of any materials and implements the predominant use of which has been in the commission of the offence. Members may provide for criminal procedures and penalties to be applied in other cases of infringement of intellectual property right, in particular where they are committed wilfully and on a commercial, scale.

PART IV: ACQUISITION AND MAINTENANCE OF INTELLECTUAL
                       PROPERTY RIGHTS AND RELATED INTER-PARTES
                       PROCEDURES

Article 62

1. Members may require, as a condition of the acquisition or maintenance of the intellectual property rights provided for under Sections 2-6 of Part II of this Agreement, compliance with reasonable procedures and formalities. Such procedures and formalities shall be consistent with the provisions of this Agreement.

2. Where the acquisition of an intellectual property right is subject to the right being granted or registered, Members shall ensure that the procedures for grant or registration, subject to compliance with the substantive conditions for acquisition of the right, permit the granting or registration of the right within a reasonable period of time so as to avoid unwarranted curtailment of the period of protection.

3. Article 4 of the Paris Convention (1967) shall apply *mutatis mutandis* to service marks.

4. Procedures concerning the acquisition or maintenance of intellectual property rights and, where the national law provides for such procedures, administrative revocation and *inter partes* procedures such as opposition, revocation and cancellation, shall be governed by the general principles set out in paragraphs 2 and 3 of Article 41.

5. Final administrative decisions in any or the procedures referred to under paragraph 4 above shall be subject to review by a judicial or quasi-judicial authority. However, there shall be no obligation to provide an opportunity for such review of decisions in cases of unsuccessful opposition or administrative revocation, provided that the grounds for such procedures can be the subject of invalidation procedures.

PART V: DISPUTE PREVENTION AND SETTLEMENT

Article 63

Transparency

1. Laws and regulations, and final judicial decisions and administrative rulings of general application, made effective by any Member pertaining to the subject matter of this Agreement (the availability, scope, acquisition, enforcement and prevention of the abuse of intellectual property rights) shall be published or where such publication is not practicable made publicly available, in a national language, in such a manner as to enable governments and right holders to become acquainted with them. Agreements concerning the subject matter of this Agreement which are in force between the government or a governmental agency of any Member and the government or a governmental agency of any other Member shall also be published.

2. Members shall notify the laws and regulations referred to in paragraph 1 above to the Council for Trade-Related Aspects of Intellectual Property Rights in order to assist that Council in its review of the operation of this Agreement. The Council shall attempt to minimise the burden on Members in carrying out this obligation and may decide to waive the obligation to notify such laws and regulations directly to the Council if consultations with the World Intellectual Property Organization on the establishment of a common register containing these laws and regulations are successful. The Council shall also consider in this connection any action required regarding notifications pursuant to the obligations under this Agreement stemming from the provisions of Article 6 *ter* of the Paris Convention (1967).

3. Each Member shall be prepared to supply, in response to a written request from another Member, information of the sort referred to ill paragraph 1 above. A Member, having reason to believe that a specific judicial decision or administrative ruling or bilateral agreement in the area of intellectual property rights affects its rights under this Agreement, may also request in writing to be given access to or be informed in sufficient detail of such specific judicial decisions or administrative rulings or bilateral agreements.

4. Nothing in paragraphs 1 to 3 above shall require Members to disclose confidential information which would impede law enforcement or otherwise be contrary to the public interest or would prejudice the legitimate commercial interests of particular enterprises, public or private.

Article 64

Dispute Settlement

1. The provisions of Articles XXII and XXIII of the General Agreement on Tariffs and Trade 1994 as elaborated and applied by the Understanding on Rules and Procedures Governing the Settlement of Disputes shall apply to consultations and the settlement of disputes under this Agreement except as otherwise specifically provided herein.

2. Sub-paragraphs XXIII: 1(b) and XXIII: l(c) of the General Agreement on Tariffs and Trade 1994 shall not apply to the settlement of disputes under this Agreement

for a period of five years from the entry into force of the Agreement establishing the Multilateral Trade Organisation.

3. During the time period referred to in paragraph 2, the TRIPS Council shall examine the scope and modalities for Article XXIII: l(b) and Article XXIII: 1(c)-type complaints made pursuant to this Agreement, and submit its recommendations to the Ministerial Conference for approval. Any decision of the Ministerial Conference to approve such recommendations or to extend the period in paragraph 2 shall be made by consensus, and approved recommendations shall he effective for all Members without further formal acceptance process.

PART VI: TRANSITIONAL ARRANGEMENTS

Article 65

Transitional Arrangements

1. Subject to the provisions of paragraphs 2, 3 and 4 below, no Member shall be obliged to apply the provisions of this Agreement before the expiry of a general period of one year following the date of entry into force of the Agreement Establishing the MTO.

2. Any developing country Member is entitled to delay for a further period of four years the date of application, as defined in paragraph 1 above, of the provisions of this Agreement other than Articles 3, 4 and 5 of Part I.

3. Any other Member which is in the process of transformation from a centrally-planned into a market, free-enterprise economy and which is undertaking structural reform of its intellectual property system and facing special problems in the preparation and implementation of intellectual property laws may also benefit from a period of delay as foreseen in paragraph 2 above.

4. To the extent that a developing country Member is obliged by this Agreement to extend product patent protection to areas of technology not so protectable in its territory on the general date of application of this Agreement for that Member, as defined in paragraph 2 above, it may delay the application of the provisions on product patents of Section 5 of Part II of this Agreement to such areas of technology for an additional period of five years.

5   Any Member availing itself of a transitional period under paragraphs 1, 2, 3 or 4 above shall ensure that any changes in its domestic laws, regulations and practice made during that period do not result in a lesser decree of consistency with the provisions of this Agreement.

Article 66

Least-Developed Country Members

1. In view of their special needs and requirements, their economic, financial and administrative constraints, and their need for flexibility to create a viable technological base, least-developed country, Members shall not be required to apply the provisions of this Agreement, other than Articles 3, 4 and 5, for a period of 10 years from the date of application as defined under paragraph 1 of Article 65 above.

The Council shall, upon duly motivated request by a least-developed country-Member, accord extensions of this period.

2. Developed country Members shall provide incentives to enterprises and institutions in their territories for the purpose of promoting and encouraging technology transfer to least-developed country Members in order to enable them to create a sound and viable technological base.

Article 67

Technical Co-operation

In order to facilitate the implementation of this Agreement, developed country Members shall provide, on request and on mutually agreed terms and conditions, technical and financial co-operation in favour of developing and at least developed country Members. Such co-operation shall include assistance in the preparation cf domestic legislation or on the domestic and enforcement of intellectual property rights as well as on the prevention of their abuse, and shall include support regarding the establishment or reinforcement of domestic affairs and agencies relevant to these matters, including the training of personnel.

PART VII: INSTITUTIONAL ARRANGEMENTS; FINAL PROVISIONS

Article 68

Council for Trade-Related Aspects of Intellectual Property Rights

The Council for Trade-Related Aspects of Intellectual Property Rights shall monitor the operation of this Agreement and, in particular, Members' compliance with their obligations hereunder, and shall afford Members the opportunity of consulting on matters relating to the trade-related aspects of intellectual property rights. It shall carry out such other responsibilities as assistance to it by the Members, and it shall, in particular, provide any assistance requested by them in the context of dispute settlement procedure, in carrying out its functions, the Council may consult with and seek information from any source it deems appropriate. In consultation with the World Intellectual Property Organization, the Council shall seek to establish, within one year of its first meeting, appropriate arrangements for co-operation with bodies of that Organization.

Article 69

International Co-Operation

Members agree to co-operate with each other with a view to eliminating international trade in goods infringing intellectual property rights. For this purpose, they shall establish and notify contact points in their national administrations and be ready to exchange information on trade in infringing goods. They shall, in particular, promote the exchange of information and co-operation between customs authorities with regard to trade in counterfeit trademark goods and pirated copyright goods.

Article 70

Protection of Existing Subject Matter

1. This Agreement does not give rise to obligations in respect of acts which occurred before the date of application of the Agreement for the Member in question.

2. Except as otherwise provided for in this Agreement, this Agreement gives rise to obligations in respect of all subject matter existing at the date of application of this Agreement for the Member in question, and which is protected in that Member on the said date, or which meets or comes subsequently to meet the criteria for protection under the terms of this Agreement. In respect of this paragraph and paragraphs 3 and 4 below, copyright obligations with respect to existing works shall be solely determined under Article 18 of the Bern Convention (1971), and obligations with respect to the rights of producers of phonograms and performers in existing phonograms shall be determined solely under Article 18 of the Berne Convention (1971) as made applicable under paragraph 6 of Article 14 of this Agreement.

3. There shall be no obligation to restore protection to subject matter which on the date of application of this Agreement for the Member in question has fallen into the public domain.

4   In respect of any acts in respect of specific objects embodying protected subject matter, which become infringing under the terms of legislation in conformity with this Agreement and which were commenced, or in respect of which a significant investment was made before the date of acceptance of the Agreement Establishing the MTO by that Member, any Member may provide for a limitation of the remedies available to the right holder as to the continued performance of such acts after the date of application of the Agreement for that Member. In such cases the Member shall, however, at least provide for the payment of equitable remuneration.

5. A Member is not obliged to apply the provisions of Article 11 and of paragraph 4 of Article 214 with respect to originals or copies purchased prior to the date of application of this Agreement for that Member.

6. Members shall not be required to apply Article 31, or the requirement in paragraph 1 of Article 27 that patent rights shall be enjoyable without discrimination as to the field of technology, to use without the authorization of the right holder where authorization for such use was granted by the government before the date this Agreement became known.

7. In the case of intellectual property rights for which protection is conditional upon registration, applications for protection which are pending on the date of application of this Agreement for the Member in question shall be permitted to be amended to claim any enhanced protection provided under the provisions of this Agreement. Such amendments shall not include new matter.

8. Where a Member does not make available as of the date of entry into force of the Agreement Establishing the MTO patent protection for pharmaceutical and agricultural chemical products commensurate with its obligations under Article 27, that Member shall:

    (i)   notwithstanding the provisions of Part VI above, provide as from the date of entry into force of the Agreement Establishing the MTO a means by which applications for patents for such inventions can be filed;

    (ii) apply to these applications, as of the date of application of this Agreement, the criteria for patentability as laid down in this Agreement as if those criteria were being applied on the date of filing in that Member or, where priority is available and claimed, the priority date of the application;

(iii) provide patent protection in accordance with this Agreement as from the grant of the patent and for the remainder of the patent term, counted from the filing date in accordance with Article 33 of this Agreement, for those of these applications that meet the criteria for protection referred to in sub-paragraph (ii) above.

9. Where a product is the subject of a patent application in a Member in accordance with paragraph 8(i) above, exclusive marketing rights shall be granted, notwithstanding the provisions of Part VI above, for a period of five years after obtaining market approval in that Member or until a product patent is granted or rejected in that Member, whichever period is shorter, provided that, subsequent to the entry into force of the Agreement Establishing the MTO, a patent application has been filed and a patent granted for that product in another Member and marketing approval obtained in such other Member.

Article 71

Review and Amendment

1. The Council for Trade- Related Aspects of Intellectual Property Rights shall review the implementation of this Agreement after the expiration of the transitional period referred to in paragraph 2 of Article 65 above. The Council shall, having regard to the experience gained in its implementation, review it two years after that date, and at identical intervals thereafter. The Council may also undertake reviews in the light of any relevant new developments which might warrant modification or amendment of this Agreement.

2. Amendments merely serving the purpose of adjusting to higher levels of protection of intellectual property rights achieved, and in force, in other multilateral agreements and accepted under those agreements by all Members of the MTO may be referred to the Ministerial Conference for action in accordance with Article X, paragraph 6, of the Agreement Establishing the MTO on the basis of a consensus proposal from the Council for Trade-Related Aspects of Intellectual Property Rights.

Article 72

Reservations

Reservations may not be entered in respect of any of the provisions of this Agreement without the consent of the other Members.

Article 73

Security Exceptions

Nothing in this agreement shall be construed:

(a) to require any Member to furnish any information the disclosure of which it considers contrary to its essential security interests, or

(b) to prevent any Member from taking any action which it considers necessary for the protection of its essential security interests.

   (i) relating to fissionable materials or the materials from which they are derived;

  (ii) relating to the traffic in arms, ammunition and implements of war and to such traffic in other goods and materials as is carried on directly or indirectly for the purpose of supplying a military establishment;

 (iii) taken in time of war or other emergency in international relations, or

(c) to prevent any Member from taking any action in pursuance of its obligations under the United Nations Charter for the maintenance of international peace and security.

APPENDIX II

BERNE CONVENTION FOR THE PROTECTION OF LITERARY AND ARTISTIC WORKS

(Paris Act, 24 July 1971)

The countries of the Union, being equally animated by the desire to protect, in as effective and uniform a manner as possible, the rights of authorities in their literary and artistic works, recognising the importance of the work of the Revision Conference held at Stockholm in 1967,

Have resolved to revise the Act adopted by the Stockholm Conference, while maintaining without change Articles 1 to 20 and 22 to 26 of that Act. Consequently, the undersigned Plenipotentiaries, have presented their full powers, recognised as in good and due form, have agreed as follows:

Article 1

The countries to which this Convention applies constitute a Union for the protection of the rights of authors in their literary and artistic works.

Article 2

(1) The expression 'literary and artistic works' shall include every production in its literary, scientific and artistic domain, whatever may be the mode or form of expression, such as books, pamphlets and other writings; lectures, addresses, sermons and other works of the same nature; dramatic or dramatico-musical works; choreographic works and entertainments in dumb show; musical compositions with or without words; cinematographic works to which are assimilated works expressed by a process analogous to cinematography; works of drawing, painting, architecture, sculpture, engraving and lithography; photographic works to which are assimilated works expressed by a process analogous to photography; works of applied art; illustrations, maps, plans, sketches and three-dimensional works relative to geography, topography, architecture or science.

(2) It shall, however, be a matter for legislation in the countries of the Union to prescribe that works in general or any specified categories of works shall not be protected unless they have been fixed in some material form.

(3) Translations, adaptations, arrangements of music and other alterations of a literary or artistic work shall be protected as original works without prejudice to the copyright in the original work.

(4) It shall be a matter for legislation in the countries of the Union to determine the protection to be granted to official texts of a legislative, administrative and legal nature, and to official translations of such texts.

(5) Collections of literary or artistic works such as encyclopaedias and anthologies which, by reason of the selection and arrangement of their contents, constitute intellectual creations shall be protected as such, without prejudice to the copyright in each of the works forming part of such collections.

(6) The works mentioned in this Article shall enjoy protection in all countries of the Union. This protection shall operate for the benefit of the author and his successors in title.

(7) Subject to the provisions of Article 7(4) of this Convention, it shall be a matter for legislation in the countries of the Union to determine the extent of the application of their laws to works of applied art and industrial designs and models as well as the conditions under which such works, designs and models shall be protected. Works protected in the country of origin solely as designs and models shall be entitled in another country of the Union only to such special protection as is granted in that country to designs and models; however, if no such special protection is granted in that country, such works shall be protected as artistic works.

(8) The protection of this Convention shall not apply to news of the day or to miscellaneous facts having the character of mere items of press information.

Article 2bis

(1) It shall be a matter for legislation in the countries of the Union to exclude, wholly or in part, from the protection provided by the preceding Article political speeches and speeches delivered in the course of legal proceedings.

(2) It shall also be a matter for legislation in the countries of the Union to determine the conditions under which lectures, addresses and other works of the same nature which are delivered in public may be reproduced by the press, broadcast, communicated by the public by wire and made the subject of public communication as envisaged in Article 11*bis*(1) of this Convention, when such use is justified by the informatory purpose.

(3) Nevertheless, the author shall enjoy the exclusive right of making a collection of his works mentioned in the preceding paragraphs.

Article 3

(1) The protection of this Convention shall apply to:

    (a) authors who are nationals of one of the countries of the Union, for their works, whether published or not;

    (b) authors who are not nationals of one of the countries of the Union, for their works first published in one of those countries, or simultaneously in a country outside the Union and in a country of the Union.

(2) Authors who are not nationals of one of the countries of the Union but who have their habitual residence in one of them shall, for the purposes of this Convention, be assimilated to nationals of that country.

(3) The expression 'published works' means works published with the consent of their authors, whatever may be the means of manufacture of the copies provided that the availability of such copies has been such as to satisfy the reasonable requirements of the public, having regard to the nature of the work. The performance of a dramatic, dramatico-musical, cinematographic or musical work, the public recitation of a literary work, the communication by wire or the broadcasting of literary or artistic

works, the exhibition of a work of art and the construction of a work of architecture shall not constitute publication.

(4) A work shall be considered as having been published simultaneously in several countries if it has been published in two or more countries within thirty days of its first publication.

Article 4

The protection of this Convention shall apply, even if the conditions of Article 3 are not fulfilled, to:

(a) authors of cinematographic works the maker of which has his headquarters or habitual residence in one of the countries of the Union;

(b) authors of works of architecture erected in a country of the Union or of other artistic works incorporated in a building or other structure located in a country of the Union.

Article 5

(1) Authors shall enjoy, in respect of works for which they are protected under this Convention, in countries of the Union other than the country of origin, the rights which their respective laws do now or may hereafter grant to their nationals, as well as the rights specially granted by this Convention.

(2) The enjoyment and the exercise of these rights shall not be subject to any formality; such enjoyment and such exercise shall be independent for the existence of protection in the country of origin of the work. Consequently, apart from the provisions of this Convention, the extent of protection, as well as the means of redress afforded to the author to protect his rights, shall be governed exclusively by the laws of the country where protection is claimed.

(3) Protection in the country of origin is governed by domestic law. However, when the author is not a national of the country of origin of the work for which he is protected under this Convention, he shall enjoy in that country the same rights as national authors.

(4) The country of origin shall be considered to be:

(a) in the case of works first published in a country of the Union, that country; in the case of works published simultaneously in several countries of the Union which grant different terms of protection, the country whose legislation grants the shortest term of protection;

(b) in the case of works published simultaneously in a country outside the Union and in a country of the Union, the latter country;

(c) in the case of unpublished works or of works first published in a country outside the Union, without simultaneous publication in a country of the Union, the country of the Union of which the author is a national, provided that:

(i) when these are cinematographic works the maker of which has his headquarters or his habitual residence in the country of the Union, the country of origin shall be that country, and

(ii) when these are works of architecture erected in a country of the Union or other artistic works incorporated in a building or other structure located in a country of the Union, the country of origin shall be that country.

Article 6

(1) Where any country outside the Union fails to protect in an adequate manner the works of authors who are nationals of one of the countries of the Union, the latter country may restrict the protection given to the works of authors who are, at the date of the first publication thereof, nationals of the other country and are not habitually resident in one of the countries of the Union. If the country of first publication avails itself of this right, the other countries of the Union shall not be required to grant to works thus subjected to special treatment a wider protection than that granted to them in the country of first publication.

(2) No restrictions introduced by virtue of the preceding paragraph shall affect the rights which an author may have acquired in respect of a work published in a country of the Union before such restrictions were put into force.

(3) The countries of the Union which restrict the grant of copyright in accordance with this Article shall give notice thereof to the Director General of the World Intellectual Property Organisation (hereinafter designated as the Director General) by a written declaration specifying the countries in regard to which protection is restricted, and the restrictions to which rights of authors who are nationals of those countries are subjected. The Director General shall immediately communicate this declaration to all the countries of the Union.

Article 6bis

(1) Independently of the author's economic rights, and even after the transfer of the said rights, the author shall have the right to claim authorship of the work and to object to any distortion, mutilation or other modification of, or other derogatory action in relation to, the said work, which would be prejudicial to his honour or reputation.

(2) The rights granted to the author in accordance with the preceding paragraph shall, after his death, be maintained, at least until the expiry of the economic rights, and shall be exercisable by the persons or institutions authorised by the legislation of the country where protection is claimed. However, those countries whose legislation, at the moment of their ratification of or accession to this Act, does not provide for the protection after the death of the author of all the rights set out in the preceding paragraph may provide that some of these rights may, after his death, cease to be maintained.

(3) The means of redress for safeguarding the rights granted by this Article shall be governed by the legislation of the country where protection is claimed.

Article 7

(1) The term of protection granted by this Convention shall be the life of the author and fifty years after his death.

(2) However, in the case of cinematographic works, the countries of the Union may provide that the term of protection shall expire fifty years after the work has been made available to the public with the consent of the author, or, failing such event within fifty years from the making of such a work, fifty years after the making.

(3) In the case of anonymous or pseudonymous works, the term of protection granted by this Convention shall expire fifty years after the work has been lawfully made available to the public. However, when the pseudonym adopted by the author leaves no doubt as to his identity, the term of protection shall be that provided in paragraph (1). If the author of an anonymous or pseudonymous work discloses his identity during the above-mentioned period, the term of protection applicable shall be that provided in paragraph (1). The countries of the Union shall not be required to protect anonymous or pseudonymous works in respect of which it is reasonable to presume that their author has been dead for fifty years.

(4) It shall be a matter for legislation in the countries of the Union to determine the term of protection of photographic works and that of works of applied art in so far as they are protected as artistic works; however, this term shall last at least until the end of a period of twenty-five years from the making of such a work.

(5) The term of protection subsequent to the death of the author and the terms provided by paragraphs (2), (3) and (4) shall run from the date of death or of the event referred to in those paragraphs, but such terms shall always be deemed to begin on the first of January of the year following the death or such event.

(6) The countries of the Union may grant a term of protection in excess of those provided by the preceding paragraphs.

(7) Those countries of the Union bound by the Rome Act of this Convention which grant, in their national legislation in force at the time of signature of the present Act, shorter terms of protection than those provided for in the preceding paragraphs shall have the right to maintain such terms when ratifying or acceding to the present Act.

(8) In any case the term shall be governed by the legislation of the country where protection is claimed; however, unless the legislation of that country otherwise provides, the term shall not exceed the term fixed in the country of origin of the work.

Article 7bis

The provisions of the preceding Article shall also apply in the case of a work of joint authorship, provided that the terms measured from the death of the author shall be calculated from the death of the last surviving author.

Article 8

Authors of literary and artistic works protected by this Convention shall enjoy the exclusive right of making and of authorising the translation of their works throughout the term of protection of their rights in the original works.

Article 9

(1) Authors of literary and artistic works protected by this Convention shall have the exclusive right of authorising the reproduction of these works, in any manner or form.

(2) It shall be a matter for legislation in the countries of the Union to permit the reproduction of such works in certain special cases, provided that such reproduction does not conflict with a normal exploitation of the work and does not unreasonably prejudice the legitimate interests of the author.

(3) Any sound or visual recording shall be considered as a reproduction for the purposes of this Convention.

Article 10

(1) It shall be permissible to make quotations from a work which has already been lawfully made available to the public, provided that their making is compatible with fair practice, and their extent does not exceed that justified by the purpose, including quotations from newspaper articles and periodicals in the form of press summaries.

(2) It shall be a matter for legislation in the countries of the Union, and for special agreements existing or to be concluded between them, to permit the utilisation, to the extent justified by the purpose, of literary or artistic works by way of illustration in publications, broadcasts or sound or visual recordings for teaching, provided such utilisation is compatible with fair practice.

(3) Where use is made of works in accordance with the preceding paragraphs of this Article, mention shall be made of the source, and of the name of the author if it appears thereon.

Article 10bis

(1) It shall be a matter for legislation in the countries of the Union to permit the reproduction by the press, the broadcasting or the communication to the public by wire of articles published in newspapers or periodicals on current economic, political or religious topics, and of broadcast works of the same character, in cases in which the reproduction, broadcasting or such communication thereof is not expressly reserved. Nevertheless, the source must always be clearly indicated; the legal consequences of a breach of this obligation shall be determined by the legislation of the country where protection is claimed.

(2) It shall also be a matter for legislation in the countries of the Union to determine the conditions under which, for the purpose of reporting current events by means of photography, cinematography, broadcasting or communication to the public by wire, literary or artistic works seen or heard in the course of the event may, to the extent justified by the informatory purpose, be reproduced and made available to the public.

Article 11

(1) Authors of dramatic, dramatico-musical and musical works shall enjoy the exclusive right of authorising:

    (i)   the public performance of their works, including such public performance by any means or process;

    (ii)   any communication to the public of the performance of their works.

(2) Authors of dramatic or dramatico-musical works shall enjoy, during the full term of their rights in the original works, the same rights with respect to translations thereof.

Article 11bis

(1) Authors of literary and artistic works shall enjoy the exclusive right of authorising:

    (1)   the broadcasting of their works or the communication thereof to the public by any other means of wireless diffusion of signs, sounds or images;

    (ii)   any communication to the public by wire or by re-broadcasting of the broadcast of the work, when this communication is made by an organisation other than the original one;

    (iii)   the public communication by loudspeaker or any other analogous instrument transmitting, by signs, sounds or images, the broadcast of the work.

(2) It shall be a matter for legislation in the countries of the Union to determine the conditions under which the rights mentioned in the preceding paragraph may be exercised, but these conditions shall apply only in the countries where they have been prescribed. They shall not in any circumstances be prejudicial to the moral rights of the author, nor his right to obtain equitable remuneration which, in the absence of agreement, shall be fixed by competent authority.

(3) In the absence of any contrary stipulation, permission granted in accordance with paragraph (1) of this Article shall not imply permission to record, by means of instruments recording sounds or images, the work broadcast. It shall, however, be a matter for legislation in the countries of the Union to determine the regulations for ephemeral recordings made by a broadcasting organisation by means of its own facilities and used for its own broadcasts. The preservation of these recordings in official archives may, on the ground of their exceptional documentary character, be authorised by such legislation.

Article 11ter

(1) Authors of literary works shall enjoy the exclusive right of authorising:

    (i)   the public recitation of their works, including such public recitation by any means or process;

    (ii)   any communication to the public of the recitation of their works.

(2) Authors of literary works shall enjoy, during the full term of their rights in the original works, the same rights with respect to translations thereof.

Article 12

Authors of literary or artistic works shall enjoy the exclusive right of authorising adaptations, arrangements and other alterations of their works.

Article 13

(1) Each country of the Union may impose for itself reservations and conditions on the exclusive right granted to the author of a musical work and to the author of any words, the recording of which together with the musical work has already been authorised by the latter, to authorise the sound recording of that musical work, together with such words, if any; but all such reservations and conditions shall apply only in the countries which have imposed them and shall not, in any circumstances, be prejudicial to the rights of these authors to obtain equitable remuneration which, in the absence of agreement, shall be fixed by competent authority.

(2) Recordings of musical works made in a country of the Union in accordance with Article 13(3) of the Conventions signed at Rome on June 2, 1928, and at Brussels on June 26, 1948, may be reproduced in that country without the permission of the author of the musical work until a date two years after that country becomes bound by this Act.

(3) Recordings made in accordance with paragraphs (1) and (2) of this Article and imported without permission from the parties concerned into a country where they are treated as infringing recordings shall be liable to seizure.

Article 14

(1) Authors of literary or artistic works shall have the exclusive right of authorising:

  (i)   the cinematographic adaptation and reproduction of these works, and the distribution of the works thus adapted or reproduced;

  (ii) the public performance and communication to the public by wire of the works thus adapted or reproduced;

(2) The adaptation into any other artistic form of a cinematographic production derived from literary or artistic works shall, without prejudice to the authorisation of the author of the cinematographic production, remain subject to the authorisation of the authors of the original works.

(3) The provisions of Article 13(1) shall not apply.

Article 14bis

(1) Without prejudice to the copyright in any work which may have been adapted or reproduced a cinematographic work shall be protected as an original work. The owner of copyright in a cinematographic work shall enjoy the same rights as the author of an original work, including the rights referred to in the preceding Article;

(2) (a) Ownership of copyright in a cinematographic work shall be a matter for legislation in the country where protection is claimed.

  (b) However, in the countries of the Union which, by legislation, include among the owners of copyright in a cinematographic work authors who brought contributions to the making of the work, such authors, if they have undertaken to bring such contributions, may not, in the absence of any contrary or special stipulation, object to the reproduction, distribution, public performance communication to the public by wire, broadcasting or any other communication to the public, or to the subtitling or dubbing of texts, of the work.

(c) The question whether or not the form of the undertaking referred to above should, for the application of the preceding subparagraph (b), be in a written agreement or a written act of the same effect shall be a matter for the legislation of the country where the maker of the cinematographic work has his headquarters or habitual residence. However, it shall be a matter for the legislation of the country of the Union where protection is claimed to provide that the said undertaking shall be in a written agreement or a written act of the same effect. The countries whose legislation so provides shall notify the Director General by means of a written declaration, which will be immediately communicated by him to all the other countries of the Union.

(d) By contrary or special stipulation is meant any restrictive condition which is relevant to the aforesaid undertaking.

(3) Unless the national legislation provides to the contrary, the provision of paragraph (2)(b) above shall not be applicable to authors of scenarios, dialogues and musical works created for the making of the cinematographic work, or to the principal director thereof. However, those countries of the Union whose legislation does not contain rules providing for the application of the said paragraph (2)(b) to such director shall notify the Director General by means of a written declaration, which will be immediately communicated by him to all the other countries of the Union.

Article 14ter

(1) The author, or after his death the persons or institutions authorised by national legislation, shall, with respect to original works of art and original manuscripts of writers and composers, enjoy the inalienable right to an interest in any sale of the work subsequent to the first transfer by the author of the work.

(2) The protection provided by the preceding paragraph may be claimed in a country of the Union only if legislation in the country to which the author belongs to permits, and to the extent permitted by the country where this protection is claimed.

(3) The procedure for collection and the amounts shall be matters for determination by national legislation.

Article 15

(1) In order that the author of a literary or artistic work protected by this Convention shall, in the absence of proof to the contrary, be regarded as such, and consequently be entitled to institute infringement proceedings in the countries of the Union, it shall be sufficient for his name to appear on the work in the usual manner. This paragraph shall be applicable even if this name is a pseudonym, where the pseudonym adopted by the author leaves no doubt as to his identity.

(2) The person or body corporate whose name appears on a cinematographic work in the usual manner shall, in the absence of proof to the contrary, be presumed to be the maker of the said work.

(3) In the case of anonymous and pseudonymous works, other than those referred to in paragraph (1) above, the publisher whose name appears on the work shall, in the absence of proof to the contrary, be deemed to represent the author, and in this capacity he shall be entitled to protect and enforce the authors rights. The provisions of this paragraph shall cease to apply when the author reveals his identity and establishes his claim to authorship of the work.

(4) (a) In the case of unpublished works where the identity of the author is unknown, but where there is every ground to presume that he is a national of a country of the Union, it shall be a matter for legislation in that country to designate the competent authority which shall represent the author and shall be entitled to protect and enforce his rights in the countries of the Union.

   (b) Countries of the Union which make such designation under the terms of this provision shall notify the Director General by means of a written declaration giving full information concerning the authority thus designated. The Director General shall at once communicate this declaration to all other countries of the Union.

Article 16

(1) Infringing copies of a work shall be liable to seizure in any country of the Union where the work enjoys legal protection.

(2) The provisions of the preceding paragraph shall also apply to reproductions coming from a country where the work is not protected, or has ceased to be protected.

(3) The seizures shall take place in accordance with the legislation of each country.

Article 17

The provisions of this Convention cannot in any way affect the right of the Government of each country of the Union to permit, to control, or to prohibit, by legislation or regulation, the circulation, presentation, or exhibition of any work or production in regard to which the competent authority may find it necessary to exercise that right.

Article 18

(1) This Convention shall apply to all works which, at the moment of its coming into force, have not yet fallen into the public domain in the country of origin through the expiry of the term of protection.

(2) If, however, through the expiry of the term of protection which was previously granted, a work has fallen onto the public domain of the country where protection is claimed, that work shall not be protected anew.

(3) The application of this principle shall be subject to any provisions contained in special conventions to that effect existing or to be concluded between countries of the Union. In the absence of such provisions, the respective countries shall determine, each in so far as it is concerned, the conditions of application of this principle.

(4) The preceding provisions shall also apply in the case of new accessions to the Union and to cases in which protection is extended by the application of Article 7 or by the abandonment of reservations.

Article 19

The provisions of this Convention shall not preclude the making of a claim to the benefit of any greater protection which may be granted by legislation in a country of the Union.

Article 20

The Governments of the countries of the Union reserve the right to enter into special agreements among themselves, in so far as such agreements grant to authors more extensive rights than those granted by the Convention, or contain other provisions not contrary to this Convention. The provisions of agreements which satisfy these conditions shall remain applicable.

Article 21

(1) Special provisions regarding developing countries are included in the Appendix.

(2) Subject to the provisions of Article 28(1)(b), the Appendix forms an integral part of this Act.

Article 22

(1) (a) The Union shall have an Assembly consisting of those countries of the Union which are bound by Articles 22 to 26.

    (b) The Government of each country shall be represented by one delegate, who may be assisted by alternate delegates, advisors, and experts.

    (c) The expenses of each delegation shall be borne by the Government which has appointed it.

(2) (a) The Assembly shall:

    (i) deal with all matters concerning the maintenance and development of the Union and the implementation of this Convention;

    (ii) give directions concerning the preparation for conferences of revision to the International Bureau of Intellectual Property (hereinafter designated as the International Bureau) referred to in the Convention Establishing the World Intellectual Property Organisation (hereinafter designated as the Organisation), due account being taken of any comments made by those countries of the Union which are not bound by Articles 22 to 26;

    (iii) review and approve the reports and activities of the Director General of the Organisation concerning the Union, and give him necessary instructions concerning matters within the competence of the Union;

    (iv) elect the members of the Executive Committee of the Assembly;

    (v) review and approve the reports and activities of its Executive Committee, and give instructions to such Committee;

    (vi) determine the programme and adopt the triennial budget of the Union, and approve its final accounts;

    (vii) adopt the financial regulations of the Union;

    (viii) establish such committees of experts and working groups as may be necessary for the work of the Union;

(ix)   determine which countries not members of the Union and which intergovernmental and international non-governmental organisations shall be admitted to its meetings as observers;

(x)   adopt amendments to Articles 22 to 26;

(xi)   take any other appropriate action designed to further the objectives of the Union;

(xii)   exercise such other functions as are appropriate under this Convention;

(xiii)   subject to its acceptance, exercise such rights as are given to it in the Convention establishing the Organisation.

(b) With respect to matters which are of interest also to other Unions administered by the Organisation, the Assembly shall make its decisions after having heard the advice of the Co-Ordination Committee of the Organisation.

(3) (a) Each country member of the Assembly shall have one vote.

(b) One-half of the countries members of the Assembly shall constitute a quorum.

(c) Notwithstanding the provisions of subparagraph (b), if, in any session, the number of countries represented is less than one-half but equal to or more than one-third of the countries members of the Assembly, the Assembly may make decisions but, with the exception of decisions concerning its own procedure, all such decisions shall take effect only if the following conditions are fulfilled. The International Bureau shall communicate the said decisions to the countries members of the Assembly which were not represented and shall invite them to express in writing their vote or abstention within a period of three months from the date of the communication. If, at the expiration of this period, the number of countries having thus expressed their vote or abstention attains the number of countries which was lacking for attaining the quorum in the session itself, such decisions shall take effect provided that at the same time the required majority still obtains.

(d) Subject to the provisions of Article 26(2), the decisions of the Assembly shall require two-thirds of the votes cast.

(e) Abstentions shall not be considered as votes.

(f) A delegate may represent, and vote in the name of, one country only.

(g) Countries of the Union not members of the Assembly shall be admitted to its meetings as observers.

(4) (a) The Assembly shall meet once in every third calendar year in ordinary session upon convocation by the Director General and, in the absence of exceptional circumstances, during the same period and at the same place as the General Assembly of the Organisation.

(b) The Assembly shall meet in extraordinary session upon convocation by the Director General, at the request of the Executive Committee or at the request of one-fourth of the countries members of the Assembly.

(5) The Assembly shall adopt its own rules of procedure.

Article 23

(1) The Assembly shall have an Executive Committee.

(2) (a) The Executive Committee shall consist of countries elected by the Assembly from among countries members of the Assembly. Furthermore the country on whose territory the Organisation has its headquarters shall, subject to the provisions of Article 25(7)(b), have an *ex officio* seat on the Committee

(b) The Government of each country member of the Executive Committee shall be represented by one delegate, who may be assisted by alternate delegates advisors, and experts.

(c) The expenses of each delegation shall be borne by the Government which has appointed it.

(3) The number of countries members of the Executive Committee shall correspond to one-fourth of the number of countries members of the Assembly. In establishing the number of seats to be filled, remainders after division by four shall be disregarded.

(4) In electing the members of the Executive Committee, the Assembly shall have due regard to an equitable geographical distribution and to the need for countries party to the Special Agreements which might be established in relation with the Union to be among the countries constituting the Executive Committee.

(5) (a) Each member of the Executive Committee shall serve from the close of the session of the Assembly which elected it to the close of the next ordinary session of the Assembly.

(b) Members of the Executive Committee may be re-elected, but not more than two-thirds of them.

(c) The Assembly shall establish the details of the rules governing the election country of and possible re-election of the members of the Executive Committee.

(6) (a) The Executive Committee shall:
   (i) prepare the draft agenda of the Assembly;
   (ii) submit proposals to the Assembly respecting the draft programme and triennial budget of the Union prepared by the Director General;
   (iii) approve, within the limits of the programme and the triennial budget, the specific yearly budgets and programmes prepared by the Director General;
   (iv) submit, with appropriate comments, to the Assembly the periodical reports of the Director General and the yearly audit reports on the accounts;
   (v) in accordance with the decisions of the Assembly and having regard to circumstances arising between two ordinary sessions of the Assembly, take all necessary measures to ensure the execution of the program of

the Union by the Director General;

(vi) perform such other functions as are allocated to it under this Convention.

(b) With respect to matters which are of interest also to other Unions administered by the Organisation, the Executive Committee shall make its decisions after having heard the advice of the Co-ordination Committee of the Organisation.

(7) (a) The Executive Committee shall meet once a year in ordinary session upon convocation by the Director General, preferably during the same period and same place as the Co-ordination Committee of the Organisation.

(b) The Executive Committee shall meet in extraordinary session upon convocation by the Director General, either on his own initiative, or at the request of its Chairman or one-fourth of its members.

(8) (a) Each country member of the Executive Committee shall have one vote.

(b) One-half of the members of the Executive Committee shall constitute a quorum.

(c) Decisions shall be made by a simple majority of the votes cast.

(d) Abstentions shall not be considered as votes.

(e) A delegate may represent, and vote in the name of, one country only.

(9) Countries of the Union not members of the Executive Committee shall be admitted to its meetings as observers.

(10) The Executive Committee shall adopt its own rules of procedure.

Article 24

(1) (a) The administrative tasks with respect to the Union shall be performed by the International Bureau, which is a continuation of the Bureau of the Union united with the Bureau of the Union established by the International Convention, for the Protection of Industrial Property.

(b) In particular, the International Bureau shall provide the secretariat of the various organs of the Union.

(c) The Director General of the Organisation shall be the chief executive of the Union and shall represent the Union.

(2) The International Bureau shall assemble and publish information concerning the protection of copyright. Each country of the Union shall promptly communicate to the International Bureau all new laws and official texts concerning the protection of copyright.

(3) The International Bureau shall publish a monthly periodical.

(4) The International Bureau shall, on request, furnish information to any country of the Union on matters concerning the protection of copyright.

(5) The International Bureau shall conduct studies, and shall provide services, designed to facilitate the protection of copyright.

(6) The Director General and any staff member designated by him shall participate, without the right to vote, in all meetings of the Assembly, the Executive Committee and any other committee of experts or working group. The Director General, or a staff member designated by him, shall be *ex officio* secretary of these bodies.

(7) (a) The International Bureau shall, in accordance with the directions of the Assembly and in co-operation with the Executive Committee, make the preparations for the conferences of revision of the provisions of the Convention other than Articles 22 to 26.

(b) The International Bureau may consult with intergovernmental and International non-governmental organisations concerning preparations for conferences of revision.

(c) The Director General and persons designated by him shall take part, without the right to vote, in the discussions at these conferences.

(8) The International Bureau shall carry out any other tasks assigned to it.

Article 25

(1) (a) The Union shall have a budget.

(b) The budget of the Union shall include the income and expenses proper to the Union, its contribution to the budget of expenses common to the Unions, and, where applicable, the sum made available to the budget of the Conference of the Organisation.

(c) Expenses not attributable exclusively to the Union but also to one or more other Unions administered by the Organisation shall be considered as expenses common to the Unions. The share of the Union in such common expenses shall be in proportion to the interest the Union has in them.

(2) The budget of the Union shall be established with due regard to the requirements of co-ordination with the budgets of the other Unions administered by the Organisation.

(3) The budget of the Union shall be financed from the following sources:

(i) contributions of the countries of the Union;

(ii) fees and charges due for services performed by the International Bureau in relation to the Union;

(iii) sale of, or royalties on, the publications of the International Bureau concerning the Union;

(iv) gifts, bequests, and subventions;

(v) rents, interests, and other miscellaneous income.

(4) (a) For the purpose of establishing its contribution towards the budget, each country of the Union shall belong to a class, and shall pay its annual contributions on the basis of a number of units fixed as follows:

Class I.. 25

Class II... 20

Class III 15

Class IV 10

Class V.. 5

Class VI 3

Class VIII.. 1

(b) Unless it has already done so, each country shall indicate, concurrently with depositing its instrument of ratification or accession, the class to which it wishes to belong. Any country may change class. If it chooses a lower class, the country must announce it to the Assembly at one of its ordinary sessions. Any such change shall take effect at the beginning of the calendar year following the session.

(c) The annual contribution of each country shall be an amount in the same proportion to the total sum to be contributed to the annual budget of the Union by all countries as the number of its units is to the total of the units of all contributing countries.

(d) Contributions shall become due on the first of January of each year.

(e) A country which is in arrears in the payment of its contributions shall have no vote in any of the organs of the Union of which it is a member if the amount of its arrears equals or exceeds the amount of the contributions due from it for the preceding two full years. However, any organ of the Union may allow such a country to continue to exercise its vote in that organ if, and as long as, it is satisfied that the delay in payment is due to exceptional and unavoidable circumstances.

(f) If the budget is not adopted before the beginning of a new financial period, it shall be at the same level as the budget of the previous year, in accordance with the financial regulations.

(5) The amount of the fees and charges due for services rendered by the International Bureau in relation to the Union shall be established, and shall be reported to the Assembly and the Executive Committee, by the Director General.

(6) (a) The Union shall have a working capital fund which shall be constituted by a single payment made by each country of the Union. If the fund becomes insufficient, an increase shall be decided by the Assembly.

(b) The amount of the initial payment of each country to the said fund or of its participation in the increase thereof shall be a proportion of the contribution of that country for the year in which the fund is established or the increase decided.

(c) The proportion and the terms of payment shall be fixed by the Assembly on the proposal of the Director General and after it has heard the advice of the Co-ordination Committee of the Organisation.

(7) (a) In the headquarters agreement concluded with the country on the territory of which the Organisation has its headquarters, it shall be provided that, whenever the working capital fund is insufficient, such country shall grant advances. The amount of these advances and the conditions on which they are granted shall be the subject of separate agreements, in each case, between

such country and the Organisation. As long as it remains under the obligation to grant advances, such country shall have an *ex officio* seat on the Executive Committee.

(b) The country referred to in subparagraph (a) and the Organisation shall each have the right to denounce the obligation to grant advances, by written notification. Denunciation shall take effect three years after the end of the year in which it has been notified.

(8) The auditing of the accounts shall be effected by one or more of the countries of the Union or by external auditors, as provided in the financial regulations. They shall be designated with their agreement, by the Assembly.

Article 26

(1) Proposals for the amendment of Articles 22, 23, 24, 25, and the present Article, may be initiated by any country member of the Assembly, by the Executive Committee, or by the Director General. Such proposals shall be communicated by the Director General to the member countries of the Assembly at least six months in advance of their consideration by the Assembly.

(2) Amendments of the Articles referred to in paragraph (1) shall be adopted by the Assembly. Adoption shall require three-fourths of the votes cast, provided that any amendment of Article 22, and of the present paragraph, shall require four-fifths of the votes cast.

(3) Any amendment to the Articles referred to in paragraph (1) shall enter into the force one month after written notifications of acceptance, effected in accordance with their respective constitutional processes, have been received by the Director General from three-fourths of the countries members of the Assembly at the time it adopted the amendment. Any amendment to the said Articles thus accepted shall bind all the countries which are members of the Assembly at the time the amendment enters into force, or which become members thereof at a subsequent date, provided that any amendment increasing the financial obligations of countries of the Union shall bind only those countries which have notified their acceptance of such amendment.

Article 27

(1) This Convention shall be submitted to revision with a view to the introduction of amendments designed to improve the system of the Union.

(2) For this purpose, conferences shall be held successively in one of the countries of the Union among the delegates of the said countries.

(3) Subject to the provisions of Article 26 which apply to the amendment of Articles 22 to 26, any revision of this Act, including the Appendix, shall require the unanimity of the votes cast.

Article 28

(1) (a) Any country of the Union which has signed this Act may ratify it, and, if it has not signed it, may accede to it. Instruments of ratification or accession shall be deposited with the Director General.

(b) Any country of the Union may declare in its instrument of ratification or accession that its ratification or accession shall not apply to Articles 1 to 21 and the Appendix, provided that, if such country has previously made a declaration under Article VI(1) of the Appendix, then it may declare in the said instrument only that its ratification or accession shall not apply to Articles 1 to 20.

(c) Any country of the Union which, in accordance with subparagraph (b), excluded provisions therein referred to from the effects of its ratification or accession may at any later time declare that it extends the effects of its ratification or accession to those provisions. Such declaration shall be deposited with the Director General.

(2) (a) Articles 1 to 21 and the Appendix shall enter into force three months after both of the following two conditions are fulfilled:

    (i) at least five countries of the Union have ratified or acceded to this Act without making a declaration under paragraph (1)(b),

    (ii) France, Spain, the United Kingdom of Great Britain and Northern Ireland, and the United States of America have become bound by the Universal Copyright Convention as revised at Paris on July 24, 1971.

(b) The entry into force referred to in subparagraph (a) shall apply to those countries of the Union which, at least three months before the said entry into force, have deposited instruments of ratification or accession not containing a declaration under paragraph (1)(b).

(c) With respect to any country of the Union not covered by subparagraph (b) and which ratifies or accedes to this Act without making a declaration under paragraph (1)(b), Articles 1 to 21 and the Appendix shall enter into force three months after the date on which the Director General has notified the deposit of the relevant instrument of ratification or accession, unless a subsequent date has been indicated in the instrument deposited. In the latter case, Articles 1 to 21 and the Appendix shall enter into force with respect to that country on the date thus indicated.

(d) The provisions of subparagraphs (a) to (c) do not affect the application of Article VI of the Appendix.

(3) With respect to any country of the Union which ratifies or accedes to this Act with or without a declaration made under paragraph (1)(b), Articles 22 to 38 shall enter into force three months after the date on which the Director General has notified the deposit of the relevant instrument of ratification or accession, unless a subsequent date has been indicated in the instrument deposited. In the latter case, Articles 22 to 38 shall enter into force with respect to that country on the date thus indicated.

Article 29

(1) Any country outside the Union may accede to this Act and thereby become party to this Convention and a member of the Union. Instruments of accession shall be deposited with the Director General.

(2) (a) Subject to subparagraph (b), this Convention shall enter into force with

respect to any country outside the Union three months after the date on which the Director General has notified the deposit of its instrument of accession, unless a subsequent date has been indicated in the instrument deposited. In the latter case, this Convention shall enter into force with respect to that country on the date thus indicated.

(b) If the entry into force according to subparagraph (a) precedes the entry into force of Articles 1 to 21 and the Appendix according to Article 28(2)(a), the said country shall, in the meantime, be bound, instead of by Articles 1 to 21 and the Appendix, by Articles 1 to 20 of the Brussels Act of this Convention.

Article 29bis

Ratification of or accession to this Act by any country not bound by Articles 22 to 38 of the Stockholm Act of this Convention shall, for the sole purposes of Article 14(2) of the Convention establishing the Organisation, amount to a ratification of or accession to the said Stockholm Act with the limitation set forth in Article 28(1)(b)(i) thereof.

Article 30

(1) Subject to the exceptions permitted by paragraph (2) of this Article, by Article 28(1)(b), by Article 33(2), and by the Appendix, ratification or accession shall automatically entail acceptance of all the provisions and admission to all the advantages of this Convention.

(2) (a) Any country of the Union ratifying or acceding to this Act may, subject to Article V(2) of the Appendix retain the benefit of the reservation it has previously formulated on condition that it makes a declaration to that effect at the time of the deposit of its instrument of ratification or accession.

(b) Any country outside the Union may declare, in acceding to this Convention and subject to Article V(2) of the Appendix, that it intends to substitute, temporarily at least, for Article 8 of this Act concerning the right of translation, the provisions of Article 5 of the Union Convention of 1886, as completed at Paris in 1896, on the clear understanding that the said provisions are applicable only to translations into a language in general use in the said country. Subject to Article 1(6)(b) of the Appendix, any country has the right to apply, in relation to the right of translation of works whose country of origin is a country availing itself of such a reservation, a protection which is equivalent to the protection granted by the latter country.

(c) Any country may withdraw such reservations at any time by notification addressed to the director General.

Article 31

(1) Any country may declare in its instrument of ratification or accession, or may inform the Director General by written notification at any time thereafter, that this Convention shall be applicable to all or part of those territories, designated in the declaration or notification, for the external relations of which it is responsible.

(2) Any country which has made such a declaration or given such a notification may, at any time, notify the Director General that this Convention shall cease to be applicable to all or part of such territories.

(3) (a) Any declaration made under paragraph (1) shall take effect on the same date as the ratification or accession in which it was included, and any notification given under that paragraph shall take effect three months after its notification by the Director General.

(b) Any notification given under paragraph (2) shall take effect twelve months after its receipt by the Director General.

(4) This Article shall in no way be understood as implying the recognition or tacit acceptance by a country of the Union of the factual situation concerning a territory to which this Convention is made applicable by another country of the Union by virtue of a declaration under paragraph (1).

Article 32

(1) This Act shall, as regards relations between the countries of the Union, and to the extent that it applies, replace the Berne Convention of September 9, 1886, and the subsequent Acts of revision. The Acts previously in force shall continue to be applicable, in their entirety or to the extent that this Act does not replace them by virtue of the preceding sentence, in relations with countries of the Union which do not ratify or accede to this Act.

(2) Countries outside the Union which become party to this Act shall, subject to paragraph (3), apply it with respect to any country of the Union not bound by this Act or which, although bound by this Act, has made a declaration pursuant to Article 28(1)(b). Such countries recognise that the said country of the Union, in its relations with them:

(i) may apply the provisions of the most recent Act by which it is bound, and

(ii) subject to Article 1(6) of the Appendix, has the right to adapt the protection to the level provided for by this Act.

(3) Any country which has availed itself of any of the faculties provided for in the Appendix may apply the provisions of the Appendix relating to the faculty or faculties of which it has availed itself in its relations with any other country of the Union which is not bound by this Act, provided that the latter country has accepted the application of the said provisions.

Article 33

(1) Any dispute between two or more countries of the Union concerning the interpretation or application of this Convention, not settled by negotiation, may, by any one of the countries concerned, brought before the International Court of Justice by application in conformity with the Statute of the Court, unless the countries concerned agree on some other method of settlement. The country bringing the dispute before the Court shall inform the International Bureau; the International Bureau shall bring the matter to the attention of the other countries of the Union.

(2) Each country may, at the time it signs this Act or deposits its instrument of ratification or accession, declare that it does not consider itself bound by the provisions of paragraph (1). With regard to any dispute between such country and any other country of the Union, the provisions of paragraph (1) shall not apply.

(3) Any country having made a declaration in accordance with the provisions of paragraph (2) may, at any time, withdraw its declaration by notification addressed to the Director General.

Article 34

(1) Subject to Article 29bis, no country may ratify or accede to earlier Acts of this Convention once Articles 1 to 21 and the Appendix have entered into force.

(2) Once Articles 1 to 21 and the Appendix have entered into force, no country may make a declaration under Article 5 of the Protocol Regarding Developing Countries attached to the Stockholm Act.

Article 34

(1) Subject to Article 29bis, no country may ratify or accede to earlier Acts of this Convention once Articles 1 to 21 and the Appendix have entered into force.

(2) Once Articles 1 to 21 and the Appendix have entered into force, no country may make a declaration under Article 5 of the Protocol Regarding Developing Countries attached to the Stockholm Act.

Article 35

(1) This Convention shall remain in force without limitation as to time.

(2) Any country may denounce this Act by notification addressed to the Director General. Such denunciation shall constitute also denunciation of all earlier Acts and shall affect only the country making it, the Convention remaining in full force and effect as regards the other countries of the Union.

(3) Denunciation shall take effect one year after the day on which the Director General has received the notification.

(4) The right of denunciation provided by this Article shall not be exercised by any country before the expiration of five years from the date upon which it becomes a member of the Union.

Article 36

(1) Any country party to this Convention undertakes to adopt, in accordance with its constitution, the measures necessary to ensure the application of this Convention.

(2) It is understood that, at the time a country becomes bound by this Convention, it will be in a position under its domestic law to give effect to the provisions of this Convention.

Article 37

(1) (a) This Act shall be signed in a single copy in the French and English all languages and, subject to paragraph (2), shall be deposited with the Director General.

(b) Official texts shall be established by the Director General, after consultation with the interested Governments, in the Arabic, German, Italian, Portuguese and Spanish languages, and such other languages as the Assembly may designate.

(c) In case of differences of opinion on the interpretation of the various texts, the French text shall prevail.

(2) This Act shall remain open for signature until 31 January, 1972. Until that date, the copy referred to in paragraph (1)(a) shall be deposited with the Government of the French Republic.

(3) The Director General shall certify and transmit two copies of the signed text of this Act to the Governments of all countries of the Union and, on request, to the Government of any other country.

(4) The Director General shall register this Act with the Secretariat of the United Nations.

(5) The Director General shall notify the Governments of all countries of the Union of signatures, deposits of instruments of ratification or accession and any declarations included in such instruments or made pursuant to Articles 28(l)(c), 30(2)(a) and (b), and 33(2), entry into force of any provisions of this Act, notifications of denunciation, and notifications pursuant to Articles 30(2)(c), 31(1) and (2), 33(3), and 38(1), as well as the Appendix.

Article 38

(1) Countries of the Union which have not ratified or acceded to this Act and which are not bound by Articles 22 to 26 of the Stockholm Act of this Convention may, until April 26, 1975, exercise, if they so desire, the rights provided under the said Articles as if they were bound by them. Any country desiring to exercise such rights shall give written notification to this effect to the Director General; this notification shall be effective on the date of its receipt. Such countries shall be deemed to be members of the Assembly until the said date.

(2) As long as all the countries of the Union have not become members of the Organisation, the International Bureau of the Organisation shall also function as the Bureau of the Union, and the Director General as the Director of the said Bureau.

(3) Once all the countries of the Union have become Members of the Organisation, the rights, obligations, and property, of the Bureau of the Union shall devolve on the International Bureau of the Organisation.

APPENDIX

Special Provisions Regarding Developing Countries

Article I

(1) Any country regarded as a developing country in conformity with the established practice of the General Assembly of the United Nations which ratifies or accedes to this Act, of which this Appendix forms an integral part, and which, having regard to its economic situation and its social or cultural needs does not consider itself immediately in a position to make provision for the protection of all the rights as

provided for in this Act, may, by a notification deposited with the Director General at the time of depositing its instrument of ratification or accession or, subject to Article V(1)(c), at any time thereafter, declare that it will avail itself of the faculty provided for in Article II, or of the faculty provided for in Article III, or of both of those faculties. It may, instead of availing itself of the faculty provided for in Article II, make a declaration according to Article V(1)(a).

(2) (a) Any declaration under paragraph (1) notified before the expiration of the period of ten years from the entry into force of Articles 1 to 21 and this Appendix according to Article 28(2) shall be effective until the expiration of the said period. Any such declaration may be renewed in whole or in part for periods of ten years each by a notification deposited with the Director General not more than fifteen months and not less than three months before the expiration of the ten-year period then running.

(b) Any declaration under paragraph (1) notified after the expiration of the period of ten years from the entry into force of Articles 1 to 21 and this Appendix according to Article 28(2) shall be effective until the expiration of the ten-year period then running. Any such declaration may be renewed as provided for in the second sentence of subparagraph (a).

(3) Any country of the Union which has ceased to be regarded as a developing any country as referred to in paragraph (1) shall no longer be entitled to renew its declaration as provided in paragraph (2), and, whether or not it formally withdraws its declaration, such country shall be precluded from availing itself of the faculties referred to in paragraph (1) from the expiration of the ten-year period then running or from the expiration of a period of three years after it has ceased to be regarded as a developing country, whichever period expires later.

(4) Where, at the time when the declaration made under paragraph (1) or (2) ceases to be effective, there are copies in stock which were made under a licence granted by virtue of this Appendix, such copies may continue to be distributed until their stock is exhausted.

(5) Any country which is bound by the provisions of this Act and which has deposited a declaration or a notification in accordance with Article 31(1) with respect to the application of this Act to a particular territory, the situation of which can be regarded as analogous to that of the countries referred to in paragraph (1), may, in respect of such territory, make the declaration referred to in paragraph (1) and the notification of renewal referred to in paragraph (2). As long as such declaration or notification remains in effect, the provisions of this Appendix shall be applicable to the territory in respect of which it was made.

(6) (a) The fact that a country avails itself of any of the faculties referred to in paragraph (1) does not permit another country to give less protection to works of which the country of origin is the former country than it is obliged to grant under Articles 1 to 20.

(b) The right to apply reciprocal treatment provided for in Article 30(2)(b), second sentence, shall not, until the date on which the period applicable under Article 1(3) expires, be exercised in respect of works the country of origin of which is a country which has made a declaration according to Article V(l)(a).

Article II

(1) Any country which has declared that it will avail itself of the faculty provided for in this Article shall be entitled, so far as works published in printed or analogous forms of reproduction are concerned, to substitute for the exclusive right of translation provided for in Article 8 a system of non-exclusive and non-transferable licences, granted by the competent authority under the following conditions and subject to Article IV.

(2) (a) Subject to paragraph (3), if, after the expiration of a period of three years, or of any longer period determined by the national legislation of the said country, commencing on the date of the first publication of the work, a translation of such work has not been published in a language in general use in that country by the owner of the right of translation, or with his authorisation, any national of such country may obtain a licence to make a translation of the work in the said language and publish the translation in printed or analogous forms of reproduction.

(b) A licence under the conditions provided for in this Article may also be granted if all the editions of the translation published in the language concerned are out of print.

(3) (a) In the case of translations into a language which is not in general use in one or more developed countries which are members of the Union, a period of one year be substituted for the period of three years referred to in paragraph (2)(a).

(b) Any country referred to in paragraph (1) may, with the unanimous agreement of the developed countries which are members of the Union and in which the same language is in general use, substitute, in the case of translations into that language, for the period of three years referred to in paragraph (2)(a) a shorter period as determined by such agreement but not less than one year. However, the provisions of the foregoing sentence shall not apply where the language in question is English, French or Spanish. The Director General shall be notified of any such agreement by the Governments which have concluded it.

(4) (a) No licence obtainable after three years shall be granted under this Article until a further period of six months has elapsed, and no licence obtainable after one year shall be granted this Article until a further period of nine months has elapsed

(i) from the date on which the applicant complies with the requirements mentioned in Article IV(1), or

(ii) where the identity or the address of the owner of the right of translation is unknown, from the date on which the applicant sends, as provided for in Article IV(2), copies of his application submitted to the authority competent to grant the licence.

(b) If, during the said period of six or nine months, a translation in the language in respect of which the application was made is published by the owner of the right of translation or with his authorisation, no licence under this Article shall be granted.

(5) Any licence under this Article shall be granted only for the purpose of teaching, scholarship or research.

(6) If a translation of a work is published by the owner of the right of translation or with his authorisation at a price reasonably related to that normally charged in the country for comparable works, any licence granted under this Article shall terminate if such translation is in the same language and with substantially the same content as the translation published under the licence. Any copies already made before the licence terminates may continue to be distributed until their stock acuity provided.

(7) For works which are composed mainly of illustrations, a licence to make and publish a translation of the text and to reproduce and publish the illustrations may be granted only if the conditions of Article III are also fulfilled.

(8) No licence shall be granted under this Article when the author has withdrawn from circulation all copies of his work.

(9) (a) A licence to make a translation of a work which has been published in printed or analogous forms of reproduction may also be granted to any broadcasting organisation having its headquarters in a country referred to in paragraph (1), upon an application made to the competent authority of the country by the said organisation, provided that all the following conditions are met:

    (i) the translation is made from a copy made and acquired in accordance with the laws of the said country;

    (ii) the translation is only for use in broadcasts intended exclusively for teaching or for the dissemination of the results of specialised technical or scientific research to experts in a particular profession;

    (iii) the translation is used exclusively for the purposes referred to in condition (ii) through broadcasts made lawfully and intended for recipients on the territory of the said country, including broadcasts made through the medium of sound or visual recordings lawfully and exclusively made for the purpose of such broadcasts;

    (iv) all uses made of the translation are without any commercial purpose.

(b) Sound or visual recordings of a translation which was made by a broadcasting organisation under a licence granted by virtue of this paragraph may, for the purposes and subject to the conditions referred to in subparagraph (a) and with the agreement of that organisation, also be used by any other broadcasting organisation having its headquarters in the country whose competent authority granted the licence in question.

(c) Provided that all of the criteria and conditions set out in subparagraph (a) are met, a licence may also be granted to a broadcasting organisation to translate any text incorporated in an audio-visual fixation where such fixation was itself prepared and published for the sole purpose of being used in connection with systematic instructional activities.

(d) Subject to subparagraphs (a) to (c), the provisions of the preceding paragraphs shall apply to the grant and exercise of any licence granted under this paragraph.

Article III

(1) Any country which has declared that it will avail itself of the faculty provided for in this Article shall be entitled to substitute for the exclusive right of reproduction provided for in Article 9 a system of non-exclusive and non-transferable licences, granted by the competent authority under the following conditions and subject to Article IV.

(2) (a) If, in relation to a work to which this Article applies by virtue of paragraph (7), after the expiration of

    (i) the relevant period specified in paragraph (3), commencing on the date of first publication of a particular edition of the work, or

    (ii) any longer period determined by national legislation of the referred to in paragraph (1), commencing on the same date,

copies of such edition have not been distributed in that country to the general public or in connection with systematic instructional activities, by the owner of the right of reproduction or with his authorisation, at a price reasonably related to that normally charged in the country for comparable works, any national of such country may obtain a licence to reproduce and publish such edition at that or a lower price for use in connection with systematic instructional activities.

  (b) A licence to reproduce and publish an edition which has been distributed as described in subparagraph (a) may also be granted under the conditions provided for in this Article if, after the expiration of the applicable period, no authorised copies of that edition have been on sale for a period of six months in the country concerned to the general public or in connection with systematic instructional activities at a price reasonably to that normally charged in the country for comparable works.

(3) The period referred to in paragraph (2)(a)(i) shall be five years, except that:

    (i) for works of the natural and physical sciences, including mathematics, and of technology, the period shall be three years;

    (ii) for works of fiction, poetry, drama and music, and for art books the period shall be seven years.

(4) (a) No licence obtainable after three years shall be granted under this Article until a period of six months has elapsed

    (i) from the date on which the applicant complies with the requirements mentioned in Article IV(1), or

    (ii) where the identity or the address of the owner of the right of reproduction is unknown, from the date on which the applicant sends, as provided for in Article IV(2), copies of his application submitted to the authority competent to grant the licence.

(b) Where licences are obtainable after other periods and Article IV(2) is applicable, no licence shall be granted until a period of three months has elapsed origin from the date of the dispatch of the copies of the application.

(c) If, during the period of six or three months referred to in subparagraphs (a) and (b), a distribution as described in paragraph 2(a) has taken place no licence shall be granted under this Article.

(d) No licence shall be granted if the author has withdrawn from circulation all copies of the edition for the reproduction and publication of which the licence has been applied for.

(5) A licence to reproduce and publish a translation of a work shall not granted under this Article in the following cases:

(i) where the translation was not published by the owner of the right of translation or with his authorisation, or

(ii) where the translation is not in a language in general use in the country in which the licence is applied for.

(6) If copies of an edition of a work are distributed in the country referred to in paragraph (1) to the general public or in connection with systematic instructional activities, by the owner of the right of reproduction or with his authorisation, at a price reasonably related to that normally charged in the country for comparable works, any licence granted under this Article shall terminate if such edition is in the same language and with substantially the same content as the edition which was published under the said licence. Any copies already made before the licence terminates may continue to be distributed until their stock is exhausted.

(7) (a) Subject to subparagraph (b), the works to which this Article applies shall be limited to works published in printed or analogous forms of reproduction.

(b) This Article shall also apply to the reproduction in audio-visual form of lawfully made audio-visual fixations including any protected works incorporated therein and to the translation of any incorporated text into a language in general use in the country in which the licence is applied for, always provided that the audio-visual fixations in question were prepared and published for the sole purpose of being used in connection with the systematic instructional activities.

Article IV

(1) A licence under Article II or Article III may be granted only if the applicant, in accordance with the procedure of the country concerned, establishes either that he has requested, and has been denied, authorisation by the owner of the right to make and publish the translation or to reproduce and publish the edition, as the case may be, or that, after due diligence on his part, he was unable to find the owner of the right. At the same time as making the request, the applicant shall inform any national or international information centre referred to in paragraph (2).

(2) If the owner of the right cannot be found, the applicant for a licence shall send, by registered airmail, copies of his application, submitted to the authority competent to grant the licence, to the publisher whose name appears on the work and to any

national or international information centre which may have been designated, in a notification to that effect deposited with the Director General, by the Government of the country in which the publisher is believed to have his principal place of business.

(3) The name of the author shall be indicated on all copies of the translation or reproduction published under a licence granted under Article II or Article III. The title of the work shall appear on all such copies. In the case of a translation, the original title of the work shall appear in any case on all the said copies.

(4) (a) No licence granted under Article II or Article III shall extend to the export of copies, and any such licence shall be valid only for publication of the translation or of the reproduction, as the case may be, in the territory of the country in which it has been applied for.

   (b) For the purposes of subparagraph (a), the notion of export shall include the sending of copies from any territory to the country which, in respect of that territory, has made a declaration under Article 1(5).

   (c) Where a governmental or other public entity of a country which has granted a licence to make a translation under Article II into a language other than English, French or Spanish sends copies of a translation published under such licence to another country, such sending of copies shall not, for the purposes of subparagraph (a), be considered to constitute export if all of the following conditions are met:

      (i) the recipients are individuals who are nationals of the country whose competent authority has granted the licence, or organisations grouping such individuals;

      (ii) the copies are to be used only for the purpose of teaching, scholarship or research;

      (iii) the sending of the copies and their subsequent distribution to recipients is without any commercial purpose; and

      (iv) the country to which the copies have been sent has agreed with the country whose competent authority has granted the licence to allow the receipt, or distribution, or both, and the Director General has been notified of the agreement by the Government of the country in which the licence has been granted.

(5) All copies published under a licence granted by virtue of Article II or Article III shall bear a notice in the appropriate language stating that the copies are available for distribution only in the country or territory to which the said licence applies.

(6) (a) Due provision shall be made at the national level to ensure:

      (i) that the licence provides, in favour of the owner of the right of translation or of reproduction, as the case may be, for just compensation that is consistent with standards of royalties normally operating on licences freely negotiated between persons in the two countries concerned, and

      (ii) payment and transmittal of the compensation: should national currency regulations intervene, the competent authority shall make all efforts, by the use of international machinery, to ensure transmittal in internationally convertible currency or its equivalent.

(b) Due provision shall be made by national legislation to ensure a correct translation of the work, or an accurate reproduction of the particular edition, as the case may be.

Article V

(1) (a) Any country entitled to make a declaration that it will avail itself of the faculty provided for in Article II may, instead, at the time of ratifying or acceding to this Act:

> (i) if it is a country to which Article 30(2)(a) applies, make a declaration under that provision as far as the right of translation is concerned;
>
> (ii) if it is a country to which Article 30(2)(a) does not apply, and even if it is not a country outside the Union, make a declaration as provided for in Article 30(2)(b), first sentence.

(b) In the case of a country which ceases to be regarded as a developing country as referred to in Article 1(1), a declaration made according to this paragraph be effective until the date on which the period applicable under Article 1(3) expires.

(c) Any country which has made a declaration according to this paragraph may not subsequently avail itself of the faculty provided for in Article II even if it withdraws the said declaration.

(2) Subject to paragraph (3), any country which has availed itself of the faculty provided for in Article II may not subsequently make a declaration according to paragraph (1).

(3) Any country which has ceased to be regarded as a developing country as referred to in Article 1(1) may, not later than two years prior to the expiration of the period applicable under Article 1(3), make a declaration to the effect provided for in Article 30(2)(b), first sentence, notwithstanding the fact that it is not a country outside the Union. Such declaration shall take effect at the date on which the period applicable under Article 1(3) expires.

Article VI

(1) Any country of the Union may declare, as from the date of this Act, and at any time before becoming bound by Articles 1 to 21 and this Appendix:

> (i) if it is a country which, were it bound by Articles 1 to 21 and this Appendix, would be entitled to avail itself of the faculties referred to in Article 1(1), that it will apply the provisions of Article II or of Article III or of both to works whose country of origin is a country which, pursuant to (ii) below, admits the application of those Articles to such works, or which is bound by Articles 1 to 21 and this Appendix; such declaration may, instead of referring to Article II, refer to Article V;
>
> (ii) that it admits the application of this Appendix to works of which it is the country of origin by countries which have made a declaration under (i) above or a notification under Article 1.

(2) Any declaration made under paragraph (1) shall be in writing and shall be deposited with the Director General. The declaration shall become effective from the date of its deposit.

APPENDIX III

PARIS CONVENTION FOR THE PROTECTION OF INDUSTRIAL PROPERTY OF 20 MARCH 1883

(As revised at Brussels on 14 December 1900, at Washington on 2 June 1911, at the Hague on 6 November 1925, at London on 2 June 1934, at Lisbon on 31 October 1958, and at Stockholm on 14 July 1967.)

Article 1

[Establishment of the Union; Scope of Industrial Property]*

(1) The countries to which this Convention applies constitute a Union for the protection of industrial property.

(2) The protection of industrial property has as its object patents, utility models, industrial designs, trademarks, service marks, trade names, indications of source or appellations of origin, and the repression of unfair competition.

(3) Industrial property shall be understood in the broadest sense and shall apply not only to industry and commerce proper, but likewise to agricultural and extractive industries and to all manufactured or natural products, for example, wines, grain, tobacco leaf, fruit, cattle, minerals, mineral waters, beer, flowers, and flour.

(4) Patents shall include the various kinds of industrial patents recognized by the laws of the countries of the Union, such as patents of importation, patents of improvement, patents and certificates of addition, etc.

Article 2

[National Treatment for Nationals of Countries of the Union]

(1) Nationals of any country of the Union shall, as regards the protection of industrial property, enjoy in all the other countries of the Union the advantages that their respective laws now grant, or may hereafter grant, to nationals; all without prejudice to the rights specially provided for by this Convention. Consequently, they shall have the same protection as the latter, and the same legal remedy against any infringement of their rights, provided that the conditions and formalities imposed upon nationals are complied with.

(2) However, no requirement as to domicile or establishment in the country where protection is claimed may be imposed upon nationals of countries of the Union for the enjoyment of any industrial property rights.

(3) The provisions of the laws of each of the countries of the Union relating to judicial and administrative procedure and to jurisdiction, and to the designation of an address for service or the appointment of an agent, which may be required by the laws on industrial property are expressly reserved.

---

*· Articles have been given titles to facilitate their identification. There are no titles in the signed (French) text.

Article 3

[Same Treatment for Certain Categories of Persons as for Nationals of Countries of the Union]

Nationals of countries outside the Union who are domiciled or who have real and effective industrial or commercial establishments in the territory of one of the countries of the Union shall be treated in the same manner as nationals of the countries of the Union.

Article 4

[A to I. *Patents, Utility Models, Industrial Designs, Marks, Inventors' Certificates: Right of Priority* - G. *Patents*: Division of the Application]

A　(1)　Any person who has duly filed an application for a patent, or for the registration of a utility model, or of an industrial design, or of a trademark, in one of the countries of the Union, or his successor in title, shall enjoy, for the purpose of filing in the other countries, a right of priority during the periods hereinafter fixed.

　　(2)　Any filing that is equivalent to a regular national filing under the domestic legislation of any country of the Union or under bilateral or multilateral treaties concluded between countries of the Union shall be recognized as giving rise to the right of priority.

　　(3)　By a regular national filing is meant any filing that is adequate to establish the date on which the application was filed in the country concerned, whatever may be the subsequent fate of the application.

B.　(1)　Consequently, any subsequent filing in any of the other countries of the Union before the expiration of the periods referred to above shall not be invalidated by reason of any acts accomplished in the interval, in particular, another filing, the publication or exploitation of the invention, the putting on sale of copies of the design, or the use of the mark, and such acts cannot give rise to any third-party right or any right of personal possession. Rights acquired by third parties before the date of the first application that serves as the basis for the right of priority are reserved in accordance with the domestic legislation of each country of the Union.

C.　(1)　The periods of priority referred to above shall be twelve months for patents and utility models, and six months for industrial designs and trademarks.

　　(2)　These periods shall start from the date of filing of the first application; the day of filing shall not be included in the period.

　　(3)　If the last day of the period is an official holiday, or a day when the Office is not open for the filing of applications in the country where protection is claimed, the period shall be extended until the first following working day.

　　(4)　A subsequent application concerning the same subject as a previous first application within the meaning of paragraph (2), above, filed in the same country of the Union, shall be considered as the first application, of which the filing date shall be the starting point of the period of priority, if, at the time of filing the subsequent application, the said previous application has been withdrawn, abandoned, or refused, without having been laid open to public inspection and without leaving any rights outstanding, and if it has not yet served as a basis for claiming a right of priority. The previous application may not thereafter serve as a basis for claiming a right of priority.

D. (1) Any person desiring to take advantage of the priority of a previous filing shall be required to make a declaration indicating the date of such filing and the country in which it was made. Each country shall determine the latest date on which such declaration must be made.

(2) These particulars shall be mentioned in the publications issued by the competent authority, and in particular in the patents and the specifications relating thereto.

(3) The countries of the Union may require any person making a declaration of priority to produce a copy of the application (description, drawings, etc) previously filed. The copy, certified as correct by the authority which received such application, shall not require any authentication, and may in any case be filed, without fee, at any time within three months of the filing of the subsequent application. They may require it to be accompanied by a certificate from the same authority showing the date of filing, and by a translation.

(4) No other formalities may be required for the declaration of priority at the time of filing the application. Each country of the Union shall determine the consequences of failure to comply with the formalities prescribed by this Article, but such consequences shall in no case go beyond the loss of the right of priority.

(5) Subsequently, further proof may be required. Any person who avails himself of the priority of a previous application shall be required to specify the number of that application; this number shall be published as provided for by paragraph (2), above.

E. (1) Where an industrial design is filed in a country by virtue of a right of priority based on the filing of a utility model, the period of priority shall be the same as that fixed for industrial designs.

(2) Furthermore, it is permissible to file a utility model in a country by virtue of a right of priority based on the filing of a patent application, and vice versa.

F. No country of the Union may refuse a priority or a patent application on the ground that the applicant claims multiple priorities, even if they originate in different countries, or on the ground that an application claiming one or more priorities contains one or more elements that were not included in the application or applications whose priority is claimed, provided that, in both cases, there is unity of invention within the meaning of the law of the country.

With respect to the elements not included in the application or applications whose priority is claimed, the filing of the subsequent application shall give rise to a right of priority under ordinary conditions.

G. (1) If the examination reveals that an application for a patent contains more than one invention, the applicant may divide the application into a certain number of divisional applications and preserve as the date of each the date of the initial application and the benefit of the right of priority if any.

(2) The applicant may also, on his own initiative, divide a patent application and preserve as the date of each divisional application the date of the initial application and the benefit of the right of priority, if any. Each country of the Union shall have the right to determine the conditions under which such division shall be authorized.

H. Priority may not be refused on the ground that certain elements of the invention for which priority is claimed do not appear among the claims formulated in the application in the country of origin, provided that the application documents as a whole specifically disclose such elements.

I. (1) Applications for inventors' certificates filed in a country in which applicants have the right to apply at their own option either for a patent or for an inventor's certificate shall give rise to the right of priority provided for by this Article, under the same conditions and with the same effects as applications for patents.

(2) In a country in which applicants have the right to apply at their own option either for a patent or for an inventor's certificate, an applicant for an inventor's certificate shall, in accordance with the provisions of this Article relating to patent applications, enjoy a right of priority based on an application for a patent, a utility model, or an inventor's certificate.

Article 5

[D. Patents, Utility Models, Marks, Industrial Designs: Marking]

D. No indication or mention of the patent, of the utility model, of the registration of the trademark, or of the deposit of the industrial design, shall be required upon the goods as a condition of recognition of the right of protection.

Article 5bis

[All Industrial Property Rights: Period of Grace for the Payment of Fees for the Maintenance of Rights; *Patents*: Restoration]

(1) A period of grace of not less than six months shall be allowed for the payment of the fees prescribed for the maintenance of industrial property rights, subject, if the domestic legislation so provides, to the payment of a surcharge.

Article 5^quinquies

[Industrial Designs]

Industrial designs shall be protected in all the countries of the Union.

Article 11

[Inventions, Utility Models, Industrial Designs, Marks: Temporary Protection at Certain International Exhibitions]

(1) The countries of the Union shall, in conformity with their domestic legislation, grant temporary protection to patentable inventions, utility models, industrial designs, and

trademarks, in respect of goods exhibited at official or officially recognized international exhibitions held in the territory of any of them.

(2) Such temporary protection shall not extend the periods provided by Article 4. If, later, the right of priority is invoked, the authorities of any country may provide that the period shall start from the date of introduction of the goods into the exhibition.

(3) Each country may require, as proof of the identity of the article exhibited and of the date of its introduction, such documentary evidence as it considers necessary.

Article 12

[Special National Industrial Property Services]

(1) Each country of the Union undertakes to establish a special industrial property service and a central office for the communication to the public of patents, utility models, industrial designs, and trademarks.

(2) This service shall publish an official periodical journal. It shall publish regularly:

(a) the names of the proprietors of patents granted, with a brief designation of the inventions patented;

(b) the reproductions of registered trademarks.

Article 13

[Assembly of the Union]

(1) (a) The Union shall have an Assembly consisting of those countries of the Union which are bound by Articles 13 to 17.

(b) The Government of each country shall be represented by one delegate, who may be assisted by alternate delegates, advisors, and experts.

(c) The expenses of each delegation shall be borne by the Government which has appointed it.

(2) (a) The Assembly shall:

(i) deal with all matters concerning the maintenance and development of the Union and the implementation of this Convention;

(ii) give directions concerning the preparation for conferences of revision to the International Bureau of Intellectual Property (hereinafter designated as the 'International Bureau') referred to in the Convention establishing the World Intellectual Property Organization (hereinafter payment designated as 'the Organization'), due account being taken of any comments made by those countries of the Union which are not bound by Articles 13 to 17;

(iii) review and approve the reports and activities of the Director-General of the Organization concerning the Union, and give him all necessary instructions concerning matters within the competence of the Union;

(iv) elect the members of the Executive Committee of the Assembly;

(v) review and approve the reports and activities of its Executive Committee, and give instructions to such Committee;

(vi) determine the program and adopt the triennial budget of the Union, and approve its final accounts;

(vii) adopt the financial regulations of the Union;

(viii)   establish such committees of experts and working groups as it deems appropriate to achieve the objectives of the Union;

(ix)   determine which countries not members of the Union and which intergovernmental and international non-governmental organizations shall be admitted to its meetings as observers

(x)   adopt amendments to Articles 13 to 17;

(xi)   take any other appropriate action designed to further the objectives of the Union;

(xii)   perform such other functions as are appropriate under this Convention;

(xiii)   subject to its acceptance, exercise such rights as are given to it in the Convention establishing the Organization.

(b)   With respect to matters which are of interest also to other Unions administered by the Organization, the Assembly shall make its decision after heaving heard the advice of the Co-ordination Committee of the Organization.

(3)   (a)   Subject to the provisions of subparagraph *(b),* a delegate may represent one country only.

(b)   Countries of the Union grouped under the terms of a special agreement in a common office possessing for each of them the character of a special national service of industrial property as referred to in Article 12 may be jointly represented during discussions by one of their number.

(4)   (a)   Each country member of the Assembly shall have one vote.

(b)   One-half of the countries members of the Assembly shall constitute a quorum.

(c)   Notwithstanding the provisions of subparagraph (b), if, in any session, the number of countries represented is less than one-half but equal to or more than one-third of the countries members of the Assembly, the Assembly may make decisions but, with the exception of decisions concerning its own procedure, all such decisions shall take effect only if the conditions set forth hereinafter are fulfilled. The International Bureau shall communicate the said decisions to the countries members of the Assembly which were not represented and shall invite them to express in writing their vote or abstention within a period of three months from the date of the communication. If, at the expiration of this period, the number of countries having thus expressed their vote or abstention attains the number of countries which was lacking for attaining the quorum in the session itself, such decision shall take effect provided that at the same time the required majority still obtains.

(d)   Subject to the provisions of Article 17(2), the decisions of the Assembly shall require two-thirds of the votes cast

(e)   Abstentions shall not be considered as votes.

(5)   (a)   Subject to the provisions of subparagraph (b), a delegate may vote in the name of one country only.

(b)   The countries of the Union referred to in paragraph (3)(h) shall, as a general rule, endeavour to send their own delegations to the sessions of the

Assembly. If, however, for exceptional reasons, any such country cannot send its own delegation, it may give to the delegation of another such country the power to vote in its name, provided that each delegation may vote by proxy for one country only.

Such power to vote shall be granted in a document signed by the Head of State or the competent Minister.

(6) Countries of the Union not members of the Assembly shall be admitted to the meetings of the latter as observers.

(7) (a) The Assembly shall meet once in every third calendar year in ordinary session upon convocation by the Director-General and, in the absence of exceptional circumstances, during the same period and at the same place as the General Assembly of the Organization.

(b) The Assembly shall meet in extraordinary session upon convocation by the Director-General, at the request of the Executive Committee or at the request of one-fourth of the countries members of the Assembly.

(8) The Assembly shall adopt its own rules of procedure.

Article 14

[Executive Committee]

(1) The Assembly shall have an Executive Committee.

(2) (a) The Executive Committee shall consist of countries elected by Assembly from among countries members of the Assembly. Furthermore, the country on whose territory the Organization has its headquarters shall, subject to the provisions of Article 16(7)(b), have an *ex officio* seat on the Committee.

(b) The Government of each country member of the Executive Committee shall be represented by one delegate, who may be assisted by alternate delegates, special advisors, and experts.

(c) The expenses of each delegation shall be borne by the Government which has appointed it.

(3) The number of countries members of the Executive Committee shall correspond to one-fourth of the number of countries members of the Assembly.

In establishing the number of seats to be filled, remainders after division by four shall be disregarded.

(4) In electing the members of the Executive Committee, the Assembly shall have due regard to an equitable geographical distribution and to the need for countries party to the Special Agreements established in relation with the Union to be among the countries constituting the Executive Committee.

(5) (a) Each member of the Executive Committee shall serve from the close of the session of the Assembly which elected it to the close of the next ordinary session of the Assembly.

(b) Members of the Executive Committee may be re-elected, but only up to a maximum of two-thirds of such members.

(c) The Assembly shall establish the details of the rules governing the election and possible re-election of the members of the Executive Committee.

(6) (a) The Executive Committee shall:

   (i) prepare the draft agenda of the Assembly;

   (ii) submit proposals to the Assembly in respect of the draft program and triennial budget of the Union prepared by the Director-General;

   (iii) approve, within the limits of the program and the triennial budget, the shall, as specific yearly budgets and programs prepared by the Director-General;

   (iv) submit, with the appropriate comments, to the Assembly the periodical reports of the Director-General and the yearly audit reports on the accounts;

   (v) take all necessary measures to ensure the execution of the program of the Union by the Director-General, in accordance with the decisions of the, Assembly and having regard to circumstances arising between two ordinary sessions of the Assembly;

   (vi) perform such other functions as are allocated to it under this Convention

(b) With respect to matters which are of interest also to other Unions administered by the Organization, the Executive Committee shall make its decisions after having heard the advice of the Co-ordination Committee of the Organization.

(7) (a) The Executive Committee shall meet once a year in ordinary session upon convocation by the Director-General, preferably during the same period and at the same place as the Co-ordination Committee of the Organization.

(b) The Executive Committee shall meet in extraordinary session upon convocation by the Director-General, either on his own initiative, or at the request of its Chairman or one-fourth of its members.

(8) (a) Each country member of the Executive Committee shall have one vote.

(b) One-half of the members of the Executive Committee shall constitute a quorum.

(c) Decisions shall be made by a simple majority of the votes cast.

(d) Abstentions shall not be considered as votes.

(e) A delegate may represent, and vote in the name of, one country only.

(9) Countries of the Union not members of the Executive Committee shall be admitted to its meeting as observers.

(10) The Executive Committee shall adopt its own rules of procedure.

Article 15

[International Bureau]

(1) (a) Administrative tasks concerning the Union shall be performed by the International Bureau, which is a continuation of the Bureau of the Union united with the Bureau of the Union established by the International Convention for the Protection of Literary and Artistic Works.

(b) In particular, the International Bureau shall provide the secretariat of the various organs of the Union.

(c) The Director-General of the Organization shall be the chief executive of the Union and shall represent the Union.

(2) The International Bureau shall assemble and publish information concerning the protection of industrial property. Each country of the Union shall promptly communicate to the International Bureau all new laws and official texts concerning the protection of industrial property. Furthermore, it shall furnish the International Bureau with all the publications of its industrial property service of direct concern to the protection of industrial property which the International Bureau may find useful in its work.

(3) The International Bureau shall publish a monthly periodical.

(4) The International Bureau shall, on request, furnish any country of the Union with information on matters concerning the protection of industrial property.

(5) The International Bureau shall conduct studies, and shall provide services designed to facilitate the protection of industrial property.

(6) The Director-General and any staff member designated by him shall participate, without the right to vote, in all meetings of the Assembly, the Executive Committee, and any other committee of experts or working group. The Director-General, or a staff member designated by him, shall be *ex officio* secretary of these bodies.

(7) (a) The International Bureau shall, in accordance with the directions of the Assembly and in co-operation with the Executive Committee, make the preparations for the conferences of revision of the provisions of the Convention other than Articles 13 to 17.

(b) The International Bureau may consult with intergovernmental and international non-governmental organizations concerning preparations for conferences of revision.

(c) The Director-General and persons designated by him shall take part, without the right to vote, in the discussions at these conferences.

(8) The International Bureau shall carry out any other tasks assigned to it.

Article 16

[Finances]

(1) (a) The Union shall have a budget.

(b) The budget of the Union shall include the income and expenses proper to the Union, its contribution to the budget of expenses common to the Unions, and, where applicable, the sum made available to the budget of the Conference of the Organization.

(c) Expenses not attributable exclusively to the Union but also to one or more other Unions administered by the Organization shall be considered as expenses common to the Unions. The share of the Union in such common expenses shall be in proportion to the interest the Union has in them.

(2) The budget of the Union shall be established with due regard to the requirements of co-ordination with the budgets of the other Unions administered by the Organization.

(3) The budget of the Union shall be financed from the following sources:

    (i)   contributions of the countries of the Union;

    (ii) fees and charges due for services rendered by the International Bureau in relation to the Union;

    (iii) sale of, or royalties on, the publications of the International Bureau concerning the Union;

    (iv) gifts, bequests, and subventions;

    (v) rents, interests, and other miscellaneous income.

(4) (a) For the purpose of establishing its contribution towards the budget, each country of the Union shall belong to a class, and shall pay its annual contributions on the basis of a number of units fixed as follows:

Class I 25

Class 11 20

Class III.. 15

Class IV 10

Class V... 5

Class VI 3

Class VII.. 1

(b) Unless it has already done so, each country shall indicate, concurrently with depositing its instrument of ratification or accession, the class to which it wishes to belong. Any country may change class. If it chooses a lower class, the country must announce such change to the Assembly at one of its ordinary sessions. Any such change shall take effect at the beginning of the calendar year following the said session.

(c) The annual contribution of each country shall be an amount in the same proportion to the total sum to be contributed to the budget of the Union by all countries as the number of its units is to the total of the units of all contributing countries.

(d) Contributions shall become due on the first of January of each year.

(e) A country which is in arrears in the payment of its contributions may not exercise its right to vote in any of the organs of the Union of which it is a member if the amount of its arrears equals or exceeds the amount of the contributions due from it for the preceding two full years. However, any organ of the Union may allow such a country to continue to exercise its right to vote in that organ if, and as long as, it is satisfied that the delay in payment is due to exceptional and unavoidable circumstances.

(f) If the budget is not adopted before the beginning of a new financial period, it shall be at the same level as the budget of the previous year, as provided in the financial regulations.

(5) The amount of the fees and charges due for services rendered by the International Bureau in relation to the Union shall be established, and shall be reported to the Assembly and the Executive Committee, by the Director-General.

(6) (a) The Union shall have a working capital fund which shall be constituted by a single payment made by each country of the Union. If the fund becomes insufficient, the Assembly shall decide to increase it.

(b) The amount of the initial payment of each country to the said fund or of its participation in the increase thereof shall be a proportion of the contribution of that country for the year in which the fund is established or the decision to increase it is made.

(c) The proportion and the terms of payment shall be fixed by the Assembly on the proposal of the Director-General and after it has heard the advice of the Co-ordination Committee of the Organization.

(7) (a) In the headquarters agreement concluded with the country on the territory of which the Organization has its headquarters, it shall be provided that, whenever the working capital fund is insufficient, such country shall grant advances. The amount of these advances and the conditions on which they are granted shall be the subject of separate agreements, in each case, between such country and the Organization. As long as it remains under the obligation to grant advances, such country shall have an *ex officio* seat on the Executive Committee.

(b) The country referred to in subparagraph (a) and the Organization shall each have the right to denounce the obligation to grant advances, by written notification. Denunciation shall take effect three years after the end of the year in which it has been notified.

(8) The auditing of the accounts shall be effected by one or more of the countries of the Union or by external auditors, as provided in the financial regulations. They shall be designated, with their agreement, by the Assembly.

Article 17

[Amendment of Articles 13 to 17]

(1) Proposals for the amendment of Articles 13, 14, 15, 16, and the present Article, may be initiated by any country member of the Assembly, by the Executive Committee, or by the Director-General. Such proposals shall be communicated by the Director-General to the member countries of the Assembly at least six months in advance of their consideration by the Assembly.

(2) Amendments to the Articles referred to in paragraph (1) shall be adopted by the Assembly. Adoption shall require three-fourths of the votes cast, provided that any amendment to Article 13, and to the present paragraph, shall require four-fifths of the votes cast.

(3) Any amendment to the Articles referred to in paragraph (1) shall enter into force one month after written notifications of acceptance, effected in accordance with their respective constitutional processes, have been received by the Director-General from three-fourths of the countries members of the Assembly at the time it adopted

the amendment. Any amendment to the said Articles thus accepted shall bind all the countries which are members of the Assembly at the time the amendment enters into force, or which become members thereof at a subsequent date, provided that any amendment increasing the financial obligations of countries of the Union shall bind only those countries which have notified their acceptance of such amendment.

Article 18

[Revision of Articles 1 to 12 and 18 to 30]

(1) This Convention shall be submitted to revision with a view to the introduction of amendments designed to improve the system of the Union.

(2) For that purpose, conferences shall be held successively in one of the countries of the Union among the delegates of the said countries.

(3) Amendments to Articles 13 to 17 are governed by the provisions of Article 17.

Article 19

[Special Agreements]

It is understood that the countries of the Union reserve the right to make separately between themselves special agreements for the protection of industrial property, in so far as these agreements do not contravene the provisions of this Convention.

Article 20

[Ratification or Accession by Countries of the Union; Entry Into Force]

(1) (a) Any country of the Union which has signed this Act may ratify it, and, if it has not signed it, may accede to it. Instruments of ratification and accession shall be deposited with the Director-General.

(b) Any country of the Union may declare in its instrument of ratification or accession that its ratification or accession shall not apply:

(i) to Articles 1 to 12, or
(ii) to Articles 13 to 17.

(c) Any country of the Union which, in accordance with subparagraph (b), has excluded from the effects of its ratification or accession one of the two groups of Articles referred to in that subparagraph may at any later time declare that it extends the effects of its ratification or accession to that group of Articles. Such declaration shall be deposited with the Director-General.

(2) (a) Articles 1 to 12 shall enter into force, with respect to the first ten countries of the Union which have deposited instruments of ratification or accession without making the declaration permitted under paragraph (1)(b)(i), three months after the deposit of the tenth such instrument of ratification or accession.

(b) Articles 13 to 17 shall enter into force, with respect to the first ten countries of the union which have deposited instruments of ratification or accession without making the declaration permitted under paragraph (1)(b)(ii), three months after the deposit of the tenth such instrument of ratification or accession.

(c) Subject to the initial entry into force, pursuant to the provisions of subparagraphs (a) and (b), of each of the two groups of Articles referred to in paragraph (1)(b)(i) and (ii), and subject to the provisions of paragraph (1)(b), Articles 1 to 17 shall, with respect to any country of the Union, other than those referred to in subparagraphs (a) and (b), which deposits an instrument of ratification or accession or any country of the Union which deposits a declaration pursuant to paragraph (1)(c), enter into force three months after the date of notification by the Director-General of such deposit, unless a subsequent date has been indicated in the instrument or declaration deposited. In the latter case, this Act shall enter into force with respect to that country on the date thus indicated.

(3) With respect to any country of the Union which deposits an instrument of ratification or accession, Articles 18 to 30 shall enter into force on the earlier of the dates on which any of the groups of Articles referred to in paragraph (1)(b) enters into force with respect to that country pursuant to paragraph (2)(a, (b), or (c).

Article 21

[Accession by Countries Outside the Union; Entry Into Force]

(1)1 Any country outside the Union may accede to this Act and thereby become a member of the Union. Instruments of accession shall be deposited with the Director-General.

(2) (a) With respect to any country outside the Union which deposits its instrument of accession one month or more before the date of entry into force of any provisions of the present Act, this Act shall enter into force, unless a subsequent date has been indicated in the instrument of accession, on the date upon which provisions first enter into force pursuant to Article 20(2)(a) or (b); provided that:

   (i) if Articles 1 to 12 do not enter into force on that date, such country shall, during the interim period before the entry into force of such provisions, and in substitution therefor, be bound by Articles 1 to 12 of the Lisbon Act,
   (ii) if Articles 13 to 17 do not enter into force on that date, such country shall, during the interim period before the entry into force of such provisions, and in substitution therefor, be bound by Articles 13 and 14(3), (4), and (5) of the Lisbon Act.

If a country indicates a subsequent date in its instrument of accession, this Act shall enter into force with respect to that country on the date thus indicated.

(b) With respect to any country outside the Union which deposits its instrument of accession on a date which is subsequent to, or precedes by less than one month, the entry into force of one group of Articles of the present Act, this Act shall, subject to the proviso of subparagraph (a), enter into force three months after the date on which its accession has been notified by the Director-General, unless a subsequent date has been indicated in the instrument of accession. In the latter case, this Act shall enter into force with respect to the country on the date thus indicated.

(3) With respect to any country outside the Union which deposits its instrument of accession after the date of entry into force of the present Act in its entirety, or less than one month before such date, this Act shall enter into force three months after the date on which its accession has been notified by the Director-General, unless a subsequent date has been indicated in the instrument of accession. In the latter case, this Act shall enter into force with respect to that country on the date thus indicated.

Article 22

[Consequences of Ratification or Accession]

Subject to the possibilities of exceptions provided for in Articles 20(1)(b) and 28(2), ratification or accession shall automatically entail acceptance of all the clauses and admission to all the advantages of this Act.

Article 23

[Accession to Earlier Acts]

After the entry into force of this Act in its entirety, a country may not accede to earlier Acts of this Convention.

Article 24

[Territories]

(1) Any country may declare in its instrument of ratification or accession, or may inform the Director-General by written notification any time thereafter, that this Convention shall be applicable to all or part of those territories, designated in the declaration or notification, for the external relations of which it is responsible.

(2) Any country which has made such a declaration or given such a notification may, at any time, notify the Director-General that this Convention shall cease to be applicable to all or part of such territories.

(3) (a) Any declaration made under paragraph (1) shall take effect on the same date as the ratification or accession in the instrument of which it was included, and any notification given under such paragraph shall take effect three months after its notification by the Director-General.

(b) Any notification given under paragraph (2) shall take effect twelve months after its receipt by the Director-General.

Article 25

[Implementation of the Convention on the Domestic Level]

(1) Any country party to this Convention undertakes to adopt, in accordance with its constitution, the measures necessary to ensure the application of this Convention.

(2) It is understood that, at the time a country deposits its instrument of ratification or accession, it will be in a position under its domestic law to give effect to the provisions of this Convention.

Article 26

[Denunciation]

(1) This Convention shall remain in force without limitation as to time.

(2) Any country may denounce this Act by notification addressed to the Director-General. Such denunciation shall constitute also denunciation of all earlier Acts and shall affect only the country making it, the Convention remaining in full force and effect as regards the other countries of the Union.

(3) Denunciation shall take effect one year after the date on which the Director-General has received the notification.

(4) The right of denunciation provided by this Article shall not be exercised by any country before the expiration of five years from the date upon which it becomes a member of the Union.

Article 27

[Application of Earlier Acts]

(1) The present Act shall, as regards the relations between the countries to which it applies, and to the extent that it applies, replace the Convention of Paris of March 20, 1883, and the subsequent Acts of revision.

(2) (a) As regards the countries to which the present Act does not apply, or does not apply in its entirety, but to which the Lisbon Act of October 31 1958, applies, the latter shall remain in force in its entirety or to the extent that the present Act does not replace it by virtue of paragraph (1).

(b) Similarly, as regards the countries to which neither the present Act, nor portions thereof, nor the Lisbon Act applies, the London Act of June 2, 1934, shall remain in force in its entirety or to the extent that the present Act does not replace it by virtue of paragraph (1).

(c) Similarly, as regards the countries to which neither the present Act, nor portions thereof, nor the Lisbon Act, nor the London Act applies, the Hague Act of November 6, 1925, shall remain in force in its entirety or to the extent that the present Act does not replace it by virtue of paragraph (1).

(3) Countries outside the Union which become party to this Act shall apply it with respect to any country of the Union not party to this Act or which, although party to this Act, has made a declaration pursuant to Article 20(1)(b)(i). Such countries recognize that the said country of the Union may apply, in its relations with them, the provisions of the most recent Act to which it is party.

Article 28

[Disputes]

(1) Any dispute between two or more countries of the Union concerning the interpretation or application of this Convention, not settled by negotiation, may, by any one of the countries concerned, be brought before the International Court of Justice by application in conformity with the Statute of the Court, unless the countries concerned agree on some other method of settlement. The country

bringing the dispute before the Court shall inform the International Bureau; the Bureau of International Bureau shall bring the matter to the attention of the other countries of the Union.

(2) Each country may, at the time it signs this Act or deposits its instrument of ratification or accession, declare that it does not consider itself bound by the provisions of paragraph (1). With regard to any dispute between such country and any other country of the Union, the provisions of paragraph (1) shall not apply.

(3) Any country having made a declaration in accordance with the provisions of paragraph (2) may, at any time, withdraw its declaration by notification addressed to the Director-General.

Article 29

[Signatures, Languages, Depository Functions]

(1) (a) This Act shall be signed in a single copy in the French language and shall be deposited with the Government of Sweden.

(b) Official texts shall be established by the Director-General, after consultation with the interested Governments, in the English, German, Italian, Portuguese, Russian and Spanish languages, and such other languages as the Assembly may designate.

(c) In case of differences of opinion on the interpretation of the various texts, the French text shall prevail.

(2) This Act shall remain open for signature at Stockholm until January 13, 1968.

(3) The Director-General shall transmit two copies, certified by the Government of Sweden, of the signed text of this Act to the Governments of all countries of the Union and, on request, to the Government of any other country.

(4) The Director-General shall register this Act with the Secretariat of the United Nations.

(5) The Director-General shall notify the Governments of all countries of the Union of signatures, deposits of instruments of ratification or accession and any declarations included in such instruments or made pursuant to Article 20(1)(c), entry into force of any provisions of this Act, notifications of denunciation, and notifications pursuant to Article 24.

Article 30

[Transitional Provisions]

(1) Until the first Director-General assumes office, references in this Act to the International Bureau of the Organization or to the Director-General shall be deemed to be references to the Bureau of the Union or its Director respectively. (

(2) Countries of the Union not bound by Articles 13 to 17 may, until five years after the entry into force of the Convention establishing the Organization, exercise, if they so desire, the rights provided under Articles 13 to 17 of this Act as if they were bound by those Articles. Any country desiring to exercise such rights shall give written notification to that effect to the Director-General; such notification shall be effective

from the date of its receipt. Such countries shall be deemed to be members of the Assembly until the expiration of the said period.

(3) As long as all the countries of the Union have not become Members of the Organization, the International Bureau of the Organization shall also function as the Bureau of the Union, and the Director-General as the Director of the said Bureau.

(4) Once all the countries of the Union have become Members of the Organization, the rights, obligations, and property, of the Bureau of the Union shall devolve on the International Bureau of the Organization.

IN WITNESS WHEREOF the undersigned, being authorised thereto, have provisions signed this present Act.

DONE at Stockholm on 14 July, 1967.

APPENDIX IV

NICE CLASSIFICATION (6TH ED)
LIST OF CLASSES OF GOODS AND SERVICES

Class 1

Chemicals used in industry, science and photography, as well as in agriculture, horticulture and forestry; unprocessed artificial resins, unprocessed plastics; manures; fire extinguishing compositions; tempering and soldering preparations; chemical substances for preserving foodstuffs; tanning substances; adhesives used in industry.

Class 2

Paints, varnishes, lacquers; preservatives against rust and against deterioration of wood; colorants; mordants; raw natural resins; metals in foil and powder form for painters, decorators, printers and artists.

Class 3

Bleaching preparations and other substances for laundry use; cleaning, polishing, scouring and abrasive preparations; soaps; perfumery, essential oils, cosmetics, hair lotions; dentifrices.

Class 4

Industrial oils and greases; lubricants; dust absorbing, wetting and binding compositions; fuels (including motor spirit) and illuminants; candles, wicks.

Class 5

Pharmaceutical, veterinary and sanitary preparations; dietetic substances adapted for medical use, food for babies; plasters, materials for dressings; material for stopping teeth, dental wax; disinfectants; preparations for destroying vermin; fungicides, herbicides.

Class 6

Common metals and their alloys; metal building materials; transportable buildings of metal; materials of metal for railway tracks; non-electric cables and wires of common metal; ironmongery, small items of metal hardware; pipes and tubes of metal; safes; goods of common metal not included In other classes; ores.

Class 7

Machines and machine tools; motors and engines (except for land vehicles); machine coupling and transmission components (except for land vehicles); agricultural implements; incubators for eggs.

Class 8

Hand tools and implements (hand operated); cutlery; side arms; razors.

Class 9

Scientific, nautical, surveying, electric, photographic, cinematographic, optical, weighing, measuring, signalling, checking (supervision), life-saving and teaching apparatus and instruments; apparatus for recording, transmission or reproduction of sound or images; magnetic data carriers, recording discs; automatic vending machines and mechanisms for coin-operated apparatus; cash registers, calculating machines, data processing equipment and computers; fire-extinguishing apparatus.

Class 10

Surgical, medical, dental and veterinary apparatus and instruments, artificial limbs, eyes and teeth; orthopaedic articles; suture materials.

Class 11

Apparatus for lighting, heating, steam generating, cooking, refrigerating, drying, ventilating, water supply and sanitary purposes.

Class 12

vehicles; apparatus for locomotion by land, air or water.

Class 13

Firearms; ammunition and projectiles; explosives; fireworks.

Class 14

Precious metals and their alloys and goods in precious metals or coated therewith, not included in other classes; jewellery, precious stones; horological and chronometric instruments.

Class 15

Musical instruments.

Class 16

Paper, cardboard and goods made from these materials, not included in other classes; printed matter; bookbinding material; photographs; stationery; adhesives for stationery or household purposes; artists' materials; paint brushes; typewriters and office requisites (except furniture); instructional and teaching material (except apparatus); plastic materials for packaging (not included in other classes); playing cards; printers' type; printing blocks.

Class 17

Rubber, gutta-percha, gum, asbestos, mica and goods made from these materials and not included in other classes; plastics in extruded form for use In manufacture; packing, stopping and insulating materials; flexible pipes, not of metal.

Class 18

Leather and imitations of leather, and goods made of these materials and not included in other classes; animal skins, hides; trunks and travelling bags; umbrellas, parasols and walking sticks; whips, harness and saddlery.

Class 19

Building materials (non-metallic); non-metallic rigid pipes for building; asphalt, pitch and bitumen; non-metallic transportable buildings; monuments, not of metal.

Class 20

Furniture, mirrors, picture frames; goods (not included in other classes) of wood, cork, reed, cane, wicker, horn, bone, ivory, whalebone, shell, amber, mother-of-pearl, meerschaum and substitutes for all these materials, or of plastics.

Class 21

Household or kitchen utensils and containers (not of precious metal or coated therewith); combs and sponges; brushes (except paint brushes); brush-making materials; articles for cleaning purposes; steelwool; unworked or semi-worked glass (except glass used in building); glassware, porcelain and earthenware not included in other classes.

Class 22

Ropes, string, nets, tents, awnings, tarpaulins, sails, sacks and bags (not included in other classes); padding and stuffing materials (except of rubber or plastics); raw fibrous textile materials.

Class 23

Yarns and threads, for textile use.

Class 24

Textiles and textile goods, not included in other classes; bed and table covers.

Class 25

Clothing, footwear, headgear.

Class 26

Lace and embroidery, ribbons and braid; buttons, hooks and eyes, pins and needles; artificial flowers.

Class 27

Carpets, rugs, mats and matting, linoleum and other materials for covering existing floors; wall hangings (non-textile).

Class 28

Games and playthings; gymnastic and sporting articles not included in other classes; decorations for Christmas trees.

Class 29

Meat, fish, poultry and game; meat extracts; preserved, dried and cooked fruits and vegetables; jellies, jams, fruit sauces; eggs, milk and milk products; edible oils and fats.

Class 30

Coffee, tea, cocoa, sugar, rice, tapioca, sago, artificial coffee; flour and preparations made from cereals, bread, pastry and confectionery, ices; honey, treacle; yeast, baking-powder; salt, mustard; vinegar, sauces (condiments); spices; ice.

Class 31

Agricultural, horticultural and forestry products and grains not included in other classes; live animals; fresh fruits and vegetables; seeds, natural plants and flowers; foodstuffs for animals, malt.

Class 32

Beers; mineral and aerated waters and other non-alcoholic drinks; fruit drinks and fruit juices; syrups and other preparations for making beverages.

Class 33

Alcoholic beverages (except beers).

Class 34

Tobacco, smokers' articles; matches.

Class 35

Advertising; business management; business administration; office functions.

Class 36

Insurance; financial affairs; monetary affairs; real estate affairs.

Class 37

Building construction; repair; installation services.

Class 38

Telecommunications.

Class 39

Transport; packaging and storage of goods; travel arrangement.

Class 40

Treatment of materials.

Class 41

Education; providing of training; entertainment; sporting and cultural activities.

Class 42

Providing of food and drink; temporary accommodation; medical, hygienic and beauty care; veterinary and agricultural services; legal services; scientific and industrial research; computer programming; services that cannot be placed in other classes.

APPENDIX V

STATES PARTY TO THE MADRID AGREEMENT
(46 STATES)

Albania	Liechtenstein
Algeria	Luxembourg
Armenia	Monaco
Austria	Mongoha
Azerbaijan	Morocco
Belarus	Netherlands
Belgium	Poland
Bosnia & Herzegovina	Portugal
Bulgaria	Republic of Moldova
China	Romania
Croatia	Russian Federation
Cuba	San Marino
Czech Republic	Slovakia
Democratic People's Republic of Korea	Slovenia
Egypt	Spain
France	Sudan
Germany	Switzerland
Hungary	Tajikistan
Italy	Former Yugoslav Republic of Macedonia
Kazakstan	Ukraine
Kyrgyzstan	Uzbekistan
Latvia	Vietnam
Liberia	Yugoslavia (now Serbia)

APPENDIX VI

FIRST COUNCIL DIRECTIVE

of 21 December 1988

TO APPROXIMATE THE

LAWS OF THE MEMBER STATES RELATING TO TRADE MARKS

(89/104/EEC)

THE COUNCIL OF THE EUROPEAN COMMUNITIES,

Having regard to the Treaty establishing the European Economic Community, and in particular Article 100a thereof,

Having regard to the proposal from the Commission,

In co-operation with the European Parliament,

Having regard to the opinion of the Economic and Social Committee,[3]

Whereas the trade mark laws at present applicable in the Member States contain disparities which may impede the free movement of goods and freedom to provide services and may distort competition within the common market; whereas it is therefore necessary, in view of the establishment and functioning of the internal market, to approximate the laws of Member States;

Whereas it is important not to disregard the solutions and advantages which the Community trade mark system may afford to undertakings wishing to acquire trade marks;

Whereas it does not appear to be necessary at present to undertake full-scale approximation of the trade mark laws of Member States and it will be sufficient if approximation is limited to those national provisions of law which most directly affect the functioning of the internal market;

Whereas the Directive does not deprive the Member States of the right to continue to protect trade marks acquired through use but takes them into account only in regard to the relationship between them and trademarks acquired by registration;

Whereas Member States also remain free to fix the provisions of procedure concerning the registration, the revocation and the invalidity of trade marks acquired by registration; whereas they can, for example, determine the form of trade mark registration and invalidity procedures, decide whether earlier rights should be invoked either in the registration procedure or in the invalidity procedure or in both and, if they allow earlier rights to be invoked in the registration procedure, have an opposition procedure or an *ex officio* examination procedure or both; whereas Member States remain free to determine the effects of revocation or invalidity of trade marks;

Whereas this Directive does not exclude the application to trade marks of provisions of law of the Member States other than trade mark law, such as the provisions relating to unfair competition, civil liability or consumer protection;

Whereas attainment of the objectives at which this approximation of laws is aiming requires that the conditions for obtaining and continuing to hold a registered trade mark are, in general, identical in all Member States; whereas, to this end, it is necessary to list examples of signs which may constitute a trade mark, provided that such signs are capable of distinguishing the goods or services of one undertaking from those of other undertakings; whereas the grounds for refusal or invalidity concerning the trade mark itself for example, the absence of any distinctive character, or concerning conflicts between the trade mark and earlier rights, are to be listed in an exhaustive manner, even if some of these grounds are listed as an option for the Member States which will therefore be able to maintain or introduce those grounds in their legislation; whereas Member States will be able to maintain or introduce into their legislation grounds of refusal or invalidity linked to conditions for obtaining and continuing to hold a trade mark for which there is no provision of approximation, concerning, for example, the eligibility for the grant of a trade mark, the renewal of the trade mark or rules on fees, or related to the non-compliance with procedural rules;

Whereas in order to reduce the total number of trade marks registered and protected in the Community and, consequently, the number of conflicts which arise between them, it is essential to require that registered trade marks must actually be used or, if not used, be subject to revocation; whereas it is necessary to provide that a trade mark cannot be invalidated on the basis of the existence of a non-used earlier trade mark, while the Member States remain free to apply the same principle in respect of the registration of a trade mark or to provide that a trade mark may not be successfully invoked in infringement proceedings if it is established as a result of a plea that the trade mark could be revoked; whereas in all these cases it is up to the Member States to establish the applicable rules of procedure;

Whereas it is fundamental, in order to facilitate the free circulation of goods and services, to ensure that henceforth registered trade marks enjoy the same protection under the legal systems of all the Member States; whereas this should however not prevent the Member States from granting at their option extensive protection to those trade marks which have a reputation;

Whereas the protection afforded by the registered trade mark, the function of which is in particular to guarantee the trade mark as an indication of origin, is absolute in the case of identity between the mark and the sign and goods or services; whereas the protection applies also in case of similarity between the mark and the sign and the goods or services; whereas it is indispensable to give an interpretation of the concept of similarity in relation to the likelihood of confusion; whereas the likelihood of confusion, the appreciation of which depends on numerous elements and, in particular, on the recognition of the trade mark on the market, of the association which can be made with the used or registered sign, of the degree of similarity between the trade mark and the sign and between the goods or services identified, constitutes the specific condition for such protection; whereas the ways in which likelihood of confusion may be established, and in particular the onus of proof, are a matter for national procedural rules which are not prejudiced by the Directive;

Whereas it is important, for reasons of legal certainty and without inequitably prejudicing the interests of a proprietor of an earlier trade mark, to provide that the latter may no longer request a declaration of invalidity nor may he oppose the use of a trade mark subsequent to his own of which he has knowingly tolerated the use for a substantial length of time, unless the application for the subsequent trade mark was made in bad faith;

Whereas all Member States of the Community are bound by the Paris Convention for the Protection of Industrial Property; whereas it is necessary that the provisions of this Directive are entirely consistent with those of the Paris Convention; whereas the obligations of the Member States resulting from this Convention are not affected by this Directive; whereas, where appropriate, the second subparagraph of Article 234 of the Treaty is applicable.

HAS ADOPTED THIS DIRECTIVE;

Article 1

Scope

This Directive shall apply to every trade mark in respect of goods or services which is the subject of registration or of an application in a Member State for registration as an individual trade mark, a collective mark or a guarantee or certification mark, or which is the subject of a registration or an application for registration in the Benelux Trade Mark Office or of an international registration having effect in a Member State.

Article 2

Signs of which a trade mark may consist

A trade mark may consist of any sign capable of being represented graphically, particularly words, including personal names, designs, letters, numerals, the shape of goods or of their packaging, provided that such signs are capable of distinguishing the goods or services of one undertaking from those of other undertakings.

Article 3

Grounds for refusal or invalidity

1. The following shall not be registered or if registered shall be liable to be declared invalid:

    (a) signs which cannot constitute a trade mark;

    (b) trade marks which are devoid of any distinctive character;

    (c) trade marks which consist exclusively of signs or indications which may serve, in trade, to designate the kind, quality, quantity, intended purpose, value, geographical origin, or the time of production of the goods or of rendering of the service, or other characteristics of the goods or service;

    (d) trade marks which consist exclusively of signs or indications which have become customary in the current language or in the bona fide and established practices of the trade;

(e) signs which consist exclusively of:
- the shape which results from the nature of the goods themselves, or
- the shape of goods which is necessary to obtain a technical result, or
- the shape which gives substantial value to the goods;

(f) trade marks which are contrary to public policy or to accepted principles of morality;

(g) trade marks which are of such a nature as to deceive the public, for instance as to the nature, quality or geographical origin of the goods or service;

(h) trade marks which have not been authorised by the competent authorities and are to be refused or invalidated pursuant to Article 6*ter* of the Paris Convention for the Protection of Industrial Property, hereinafter referred to as the 'Paris Convention'.

2. Any Member State may provide that a trade mark shall not be registered or, if registered, shall be liable to be declared invalid where and to the extent that:

(a) the use of that trade mark may be prohibited pursuant to provisions of law other than trade mark law of the Member State concerned or of the Community;

(b) the trade mark covers a sign of high symbolic value, in particular a religious symbol;

(c) the trade mark includes badges, emblems and escutcheons other than those covered by Article 6*ter* of the Paris Convention which are of public interest, unless the consent of the appropriate authorities to its registration has been given in conformity legislation of the Member State;

(d) The application for registration of the trade mark was made in bad faith by the applicant.

3. A trade mark shall not be refused registration or be declared invalid in accordance with paragraph 1(b), (c) or (d) if, before the date of application for registration and following the use which has been made of it, it has acquired a distinctive character. Any Member State may in addition provide that this provision shall also apply where the distinctive character was acquired after the date of application for registration or after the date of registration.

4. Any Member State may provide that, by derogation from the preceding paragraphs, the grounds of refusal of registration or invalidity in force in that a State prior to the date on which the provisions necessary to comply with this Directive enter into force, shall apply to trade marks or which application has been made prior to that date.

Article 4

Further grounds for refusal or invalidity concerning conflicts with earlier rights

1. A trade mark shall not be registered or, if registered, shall be liable to be declared invalid:

(a) if it is identical with an earlier trade mark, and the goods or services for which the trade mark is applied for or is registered are identical with the goods or services for which the earlier trade mark is protected;

(b) if because of its identity with, or similarity to, the earlier trade mark and the identity or similarity of the goods or services covered by the trade marks, there exists a likelihood of confusion on the part of the public, which includes the likelihood of association with the earlier trade mark.

2. 'Earlier trade marks' within the meaning of paragraph 1 means:

(a) trade marks of the following kinds with a date of application for registration which is earlier than the date of application for registration of the trade mark, taking account, where appropriate, of the priorities claimed in respect of those trade marks-

    (i) Community trade marks;

    (ii) trade marks registered in the Member State or, in the case of Belgium, Luxembourg or the Netherlands, at the Benelux Trade Mark Office;

    (iii) trade marks registered under international arrangements which have effect in the Member State;

(b) Community trade marks which validly claim seniority, in accordance with the Regulation on the Community trade mark, from a trade mark referred to in (a)(ii) and (iii), even when the latter trade mark has been surrendered or allowed to lapse;

(c) applications for the trade marks referred to in (a) and (b), subject to their registration;

(d) trade marks which, on the date of application for registration of the trade mark, or, where appropriate, of the priority claimed in respect of the application for registration of the trade mark, are well known in a Member State, in the sense in which the words 'well known' are used in Article 6 *bis* of the Paris Convention;

3. A trade mark shall furthermore not be registered or; if registered, shall be liable to be declared invalid if it is identical with, or similar to, an earlier Community trade mark within the meaning of paragraph 2 and is to be, or has been, registered for goods or services which are not similar to those for which the earlier Community trade mark is registered, where the earlier Community trade mark has a reputation in the Community and where the use of the later trade mark without due cause would take unfair advantage of, or be detrimental to, the distinctive character or the repute of the earlier Community trade mark.

4. Any Member State may furthermore provide that a trade mark shall not be registered or, if registered, shall be liable to be declared invalid where, and to the extent that:

(a) the trade mark is identical with, or similar to, an earlier national trade mark within the meaning of paragraph 2 and is to be, or has been, registered for goods or services which are not similar to those for which the earlier trade mark is registered, where the earlier trade mark has a reputation in the Member State concerned and where the use of the later trade mark without due cause would take unfair advantage of, or be detrimental to, the distinctive character or the repute of the earlier trade mark;

(b) rights to a non-registered trade mark or to another sign used in the course of trade were acquired prior to the date of application for registration of the subsequent trade mark, or the date of the priority claimed for the application for registration of the subsequent trade mark and that non-registered trade mark or other sign confers on its proprietor the right to prohibit the use of a subsequent trade mark;

(c) the use of the trade mark may be prohibited by virtue of an earlier right other than the rights referred to in paragraphs 2 and 4(b) and in particular-

    (i)   a right to a name;

    (ii) a right of personal portrayal;

    (iii) a copyright;

    (iv) an industrial property right;

(d) the trade mark is identical with, or similar to, an earlier collective trade mark conferring a right which expired within a period of a maximum of three years preceding application;

(e) the trade mark is identical with, or similar to, an earlier guarantee or certification mark conferring a right which expired within a period preceding application the length of which is fixed by the Member State;

(f) the trade mark is identical with, or similar to, an earlier trade mark which was registered for identical or similar goods or services and conferred on them a right which has expired for failure to renew within a period of a maximum of two years preceding application unless the proprietor of the earlier trade mark gave his agreement for the registration of the later mark or did not use his trade mark;

(g) the trade mark is liable to be confused with a mark which was in use abroad on the filing date of the application and which is still in use there, provided that at the date of the application the applicant was acting in bad faith.

5. The Member States may permit that in appropriate circumstances registration need not be refused or the trade mark need not be declared invalid where the proprietor of the earlier trade mark or other earlier right consents to the registration of the later trade mark.

6. Any Member State may provide that, by derogation from paragraphs 1 to 5, the grounds for refusal of registration or invalidity in force in that State prior to the date on which the provisions necessary to comply with this Directive enter into force, shall apply to trade marks for which application has been made prior to that date.

Article 5

Rights conferred by a trade mark

1. The registered trade mark shall confer on the proprietor exclusive rights therein. The proprietor shall be entitled to prevent all third parties not having his consent from using in the course of trade:

(a) any sign which is identical with the trade mark in relation to goods or services which are identical with those for which the trade mark is registered;

(b) any sign where, because of its identity with, or similarity to, the trade mark and the identity or similarity of the goods or services covered by the trade mark and the sign, there exists a likelihood of confusion on the part of the public, which includes the likelihood of association between the sign and the trade mark.

2. Any Member State may also provide that the proprietor shall be entitled to prevent all third parties not having his consent from using in the course of trade any sign which is identical with, or similar to, the trade mark in relation to goods or services which are not similar to those for which the trade mark is registered, where the latter has a reputation in the Member State and where use of that sign without due cause takes unfair advantage of, or is detrimental to, the distinctive character or the repute of the trade mark.

3. The following, *inter alia*, may be prohibited under paragraphs 1 and 2:

   (a) affixing the sign to the goods or to the packaging thereof;

   (b) offering the goods, or putting them on the market or stocking them for these purposes under that sign, or offering or supplying services thereunder;

   (c) importing or exporting the goods under the sign;

   (d) using the sign on business papers and in advertising.

4. Where, under the law of the Member State, the use of a sign under the Conditions referred to in 1(b) or 2 could not be prohibited before the date on which the provisions necessary to comply with this Directive entered into force in the Member State concerned, the rights conferred by the trade mark may not be relied on to prevent the continued use of the sign.

5. Paragraphs 1 to 4 shall not affect provisions in any Member State relating to the protection against the use of a sign other than for the purposes of distinguishing goods or services, where use of that sign without due cause takes unfair advantage of, or is detrimental to, the distinctive character or the repute of the trade mark.

Article 6

Limitation of the effects of a trade mark

1. The trade mark shall not entitle the proprietor to prohibit a third party from using, in the course of trade:

   (a) his own name or address;

   (b) indications concerning the kind, quality, quantity, intended purpose, value, geographical origin, the time of production of goods or of rendering of the service, or other characteristics of goods or services;

   (c) the trade mark where it is necessary to indicate the intended purpose of a product or service, in particular as accessories or spare parts;

provided he uses them in accordance with honest practices in industrial or commercial matters.

2. The trade mark shall not entitle the proprietor to prohibit a third party from using, in the course of trade, an earlier right which only applies in a particular locality if that right is recognised by the laws of the Member State in question and within the limits of the territory in which it is recognised.

Article 7

Exhaustion of the rights conferred by a trade mark

1. The trade mark shall not entitle the proprietor to prohibit its use in relation to goods which have been put on the market in the Community under that trade mark by the proprietor or with his consent.

2. Paragraph 1 shall not apply where there exist legitimate reasons for the proprietor to oppose further commercialisation of the goods, especially where the condition of the goods is changed or impaired after they have been put on the market.

Article 8

Licensing

1. A trade mark may be licensed for some or all of the goods or services for which it is registered and for the whole or part of the Member State concerned. A license may be exclusive or non-exclusive.

2. The proprietor of a trade mark may invoke the rights conferred by that trade mark against a licensee who contravenes any provision in his licensing - contract with regard to its duration, the form covered by the registration in which the trade mark may be used, the scope of the goods or services for which the licence is granted, the territory in which the trade mark may be affixed, or the quality of the goods manufactured or of the services provided by the licensee.

Article 9

Limitation in consequence of acquiescence

1. Where, in a Member State, the proprietor of an earlier trade mark as referred to in Article 4(2) has acquiesced, for a period of five successive years, in the use of a later trade mark registered in that Member State while being aware of such use, he shall no longer be entitled on the basis of the earlier trade mark either to apply for a declaration that the later trade mark is invalid or to oppose the use of the later trade mark in respect of the goods or services for which the later trade mark has been used, unless registration of the later trade mark was applied for in bad faith.

2. Any Member State may provide that paragraph 1 shall apply *mutatis mutandis* to the proprietor of an earlier trade mark referred to in Article 4(4) (a) or an other earlier right referred to in Article 4(4) (b) or (c).

3. In the cases referred to in paragraphs 1 and 2, the proprietor of a later registered trade mark shall not be entitled to oppose the use of the earlier right, even though that right may no longer be invoked against the later trade mark.

Article 10

Use of trade marks

1. If, within a period of five years following the date of the completion of the registration procedure, the proprietor has not put the trade mark to genuine use in the Member State in connection with the goods or services in respect of which it is registered, or if such use has been suspended during an uninterrupted period of five years, the trade mark shall be subject to the sanctions provided for in this Directive, unless there are proper reasons for non-use.

2. The following shall also constitute use within the meaning of paragraph 1:

   (a) use of the trade mark in a form differing in elements which do not alter the distinctive character of the mark in the form in which it was registered;

   (b) affixing of the trade mark to goods or to the packaging thereof in the Member State concerned solely for export purposes.

3. Use of the trade mark with the consent of the proprietor or by any person who has authority to use a collective mark or a guarantee or certification mark shall be deemed to constitute use by the proprietor.

4. In relation to trade marks registered before the date on which the provisions necessary to comply with this Directive enter into force in the Member State concerned:

   (a) where a provision in force prior to that date attaches sanctions to non-use of a trade mark during an uninterrupted period, the relevant period of five years mentioned in paragraph 1 shall be deemed to have begun to run at the same time as any period of non-use which is already running at that date;

   (b) where there is no use provision in force prior to that date, the periods of five years mentioned in paragraph 1 shall be deemed to run from that date at the earliest.

Article 11

Sanctions for non use of a trade mark in legal or administrative proceedings

1. A trade mark may not be declared invalid on the ground that there is an earlier conflicting trade mark if the latter does not fulfil the requirements of use set out in Articles 10(1), (2) and (3) or in Article 10(4), as the case may be.

2. Any Member State may provide that registration of a trade mark may not be refused on the ground that there is an earlier conflicting trade mark if the latter does not fulfil the requirements of use set out in Article 10(1), (2) and (3) or in Article 10(4), as the case may be.

3. Without prejudice to the application of Article 12, where a counterclaim for revocation is made, any Member State may provide that a trade mark may not be successfully invoked in infringement proceedings if it is established as a result of a plea that the trade mark could be revoked pursuant to Article 12(1).

4. If the earlier trade mark has been used in relation to part only of the goods or services for which it is registered, it shall, for purposes of applying paragraphs 1, 2 and 3, be deemed to be registered in respect only of that part of the goods or services.

Article 12

Grounds for revocation

1. A trade mark shall be liable to revocation if, within a continuous period of five years, it has not been put to genuine use in the Member State in connection with the goods or services in respect of which it is registered, and there are no proper reasons for non-use; however, no person may claim that the proprietor's rights in a trade mark should be revoked where, during the interval between expiry of the five-year period and filing of the application for revocation, genuine use of the trade mark has been

started or resumed; the commencement or resumption of use within a period of three months preceding the filing of the application for revocation which began at the earliest on expiry of the continuous period of five years of non-use, shall, however, be disregarded where preparations for the commencement or resumption occur only after the proprietor becomes aware that the application for revocation may be filed.

2. A trade mark shall also be liable to revocation if, after the date on which it was registered:

   (a) in consequence of acts or inactivity of the proprietor it has become the common name in the trade for a product or service in -respect of which it is registered;

   (b) in consequence of the use made of it by the proprietor of the trade mark or with his consent in respect of the goods or services for which it is registered, it is liable to mislead the public, particularly as to the nature, quality or geographical origin of those goods or services.

Article 13

Grounds for refusal or revocation or invalidity relating to only some of the goods or services

Where grounds for refusal of registration or for revocation or invalidity of trade mark exist in respect of only some of the goods or services for which that trade mark has been applied for or registered, refusal of registration or revocation or invalidity shall cover those goods or services only.

Article 14

Establishment a posteriori of invalidity or revocation of a trade mark

Where the seniority of an earlier trade mark which has been surrendered or allowed to lapse, is claimed for a Community trade mark, the invalidity or revocation of the earlier trade mark may be established a *posteriori.*

Article 15

Special provisions in respect of collective marks, guarantee marks and certification marks

1. Without prejudice to Article 4, Member States whose laws authorise the registration of collective marks or of guarantee or certification marks may provide that such marks shall not be registered, or shall be revoked or declared invalid, on grounds additional to those specified in Articles 3 and 12 where the function of those marks so requires.

2. By way of derogation from Article 3(1) (c), Member States may provide that signs or indications which may serve, in trade, to designate the geographical origin of the goods or services may constitute collective, guarantee or certification marks. Such a mark does not entitle the proprietor to prohibit a third party from using in the course of trade such signs or indications, provided he uses them in accordance with honest practices in industrial or commercial matters; in particular, such a mark may not be invoked against a third party who is entitled to use a geographical name.

Article 16

National provisions to be adopted pursuant to this Directive

1. The Member States shall bring into force the laws, regulations and administrative provisions necessary to comply with this Directive not later than [31 December 1992].[1] They shall immediately inform the Commission thereof.

2. Acting on a proposal from the Commission, the Council, acting by qualified majority, may defer the date referred to in paragraph 1 until 31 December 1992 at the latest.

3 Member States shall communicate to the Commission the text of the main provisions of national law which they adopt in the field governed by this Directive.

Article 17

Addressees

This Directive is addressed to the Member States.

---

[1] Words in para (1) substituted by Council Decision 92/10/EEC of 19 December 1991, Art 1.

APPENDIX VII

COUNCIL REGULATION

of 14 July 1992

ON THE

PROTECTION OF GEOGRAPHICAL INDICATIONS AND DESIGNATIONS OF ORIGIN FOR AGRICULTURAL PRODUCTS AND FOODSTUFFS

(EEC) 2081/92

THE COUNCIL OF THE EUROPEAN COMMUNITIES,

Having regard to the Treaty establishing the European Economic Community, and in particular Article 43,

Having regard to the proposal from the Commission, Having regard to the opinion of the European Parliament, Having regard to the opinion of the Economic and Social Committee,

Whereas the production, manufacture and distribution of agricultural products and foodstuffs play an important role in the Community economy;

Whereas, as part of the adjustment of the common agricultural policy the diversification of agricultural production should be encouraged so as to achieve a better balance between supply and demand on the markets; whereas the promotion of products having certain characteristics could be of considerable benefit to the rural economy, in particular to less-favoured or remote areas, by improving the incomes of farmers and by retaining the rural population in these areas;

Whereas, moreover, it has been observed in recent years that consumers are tending to attach greater importance to the quality of foodstuffs rather than to quantity; whereas this quest for specific products generates a growing demand for agricultural products or foodstuffs with an identifiable geographical origin;

Whereas in view of the wide variety of products marketed and of the abundance of information concerning them provided, consumers must, in order to be able to make the best choice, be given clear and succinct information regarding the origin of the product;

Whereas the labelling of agricultural products and foodstuffs is subject to the general rules laid down in Council Directive 79/112/EEC of 18 December 1978 on the approximation of the laws of the Member States relating to the labelling, presentation and advertising of foodstuffs [*OJ L33, 8 February 1979, p 1, as amended*]; whereas, in view of their specific nature, additional special provisions should be adopted for agricultural products and foodstuffs from a specified geographical area;

Whereas the desire to protect agricultural products or foodstuffs which have an identifiable geographical origin has led certain Member States to introduce 'registered designations of origin'; whereas these have proved successful with producers, who have secured higher incomes in return for a genuine effort to improve quality, and with consumers, who can purchase high quality products with guarantees as to the method of production and origin;

Whereas, however, there is diversity in the national practices for implementing registered designations or origin and geographical indications; whereas a Community approach should be envisaged; whereas a framework of Community rules on protection will permit the development of geographical indications and designations of origin since, by providing a more uniform approach, such a framework will ensure fair competition between the producers of products bearing such indications and enhance the credibility of the products in the consumers' eyes;

Whereas the planned rules should take account of existing Community legislation on wines and spirit drinks, which provide for a higher level of protection;

Whereas the scope of this Regulation is limited to certain agricultural products and foodstuffs for which a link between product or foodstuff characteristics and geographical origin exists; whereas, however, this scope could be enlarged to encompass other products or foodstuffs;

Whereas existing practices make it appropriate to define two different types of geographical description, namely protected geographical indications and protected designations of origin;

Whereas an agricultural product or foodstuff bearing such an indication must meet certain conditions set out in a specification;

Whereas to enjoy protection in every Member State geographical indications and designations of origin must be registered at Community level; whereas entry in a register should also provide information to those involved in trade and to consumers;

Whereas the registration procedure should enable any person individually and directly concerned in a Member State to exercise his rights by notifying the Commission of his opposition;

Whereas there should be procedures to permit amendment of the specification, after registration, in the light of technological progress or withdrawal from the register of the geographical indication or designation of origin of an agricultural product or foodstuff if that product or foodstuff ceases to conform to the specification on the basis of which the geographical indication or designation of origin was granted;

Whereas provision should be made for trade with third countries offering equivalent guarantees for the issue and inspection of geographical indications or designations of origin granted on their territory;

Whereas provision should be made for a procedure establishing close co-operation between the Member States and the Commission through a Regulatory Committee set up for that purpose,

HAS ADOPTED THIS REGULATION:

Article 1

1. This Regulation lays down rules on the protection of designations of origin and geographical indications of agricultural products intended for human consumption

referred to in Annex II to the Treaty and of the foodstuffs referred to in Annex I to this Regulation and agricultural products listed in Annex II to this Regulation.

However) this Regulation shall not apply to wine products or to spirit drinks.

Annex I may be amended in accordance with the procedure set out in Article 15.

2. This Regulation shall apply without prejudice to other specific Community provisions.

3. Council Directive 83/189/EEC of 28 March 1983 laying down a procedure for the provision of information in the field of technical standards and regulations [OJ L109, 26 April 1983, p 1, as amended] shall not apply to the designations of origin and geographical indications covered by this Regulation.

Article 2

1. Community protection of designations of origin and of geographical indications of agricultural products and foodstuffs shall be obtained in accordance with this Regulation.

2. For the purposes of this Regulation;

    (a) designation of origin: means the name of a region, a specific place or, in exceptional cases, a country, used to describe an agricultural product or a foodstuff:

        - originating in that region, specific place or country, and

        - the quality or characteristics of which are essentially or exclusively due to a particular geographical environment with its inherent natural and human factors, and the production, processing and preparation of which take place in the defined geographical area;

    (b) geographical indications: means the name of a region, a specific place or, in exceptional cases, a country, used to describe an agricultural product or a foodstuff:

        - originating in that region, specific place or country, and

        - which possesses a specific quality, reputation or other characteristics attributable to that geographical origin and the production and/or processing and/or preparation of which take place in the defined geographical area.

3. Certain traditional geographical or non-geographical names designating an agricultural product or a foodstuff originating in a region or a specific place, which fulfil the conditions referred to in the second indent of paragraph 2(a) shall also be considered as designations of origin.

4. By way of derogation from Article 2(a), certain geographical designations shall be treated as designations of origin where the raw materials of the products concerned come from a geographical area larger than or different from the processing area, provided that:

        - the production area of the raw materials is limited,

        - special conditions for the production of the raw materials exist, and

-      there are inspection arrangements to ensure that those conditions are adhered to.

5. For the purposes of paragraph 4, only live animals, meat and milk may be considered as raw materials. Use of other raw materials may be authorized in accordance with the procedure laid down in Article 15.

6. In order to be eligible for the derogation provided for in paragraph 4, the designations in question may be or have already been recognized as designations of origin with national protection by the Member State concerned, or, if no such scheme exists, have a proven, traditional character and an exceptional reputation and renown.

7. In order to be eligible for the derogation provided for in paragraph 4, applications for registration must be lodged within two years of the entry into force of this Regulation.

   (c) the definition of the geographical area and, if appropriate, details indicating compliance with the requirements in Article 2(4);

   (d) evidence that the agricultural product or the foodstuff originates in the geographical area, within the meaning of Article 2(2)(a) or (b), whichever is applicable;

   (e) a description of the method of obtaining the agricultural product or foodstuff and, if appropriate, the authentic and unvarying local methods;

   (f) the details hearing out the link with the geographical environment or the geographical origin within the meaning of Article 2(2)(a) or (b),˙whichever is applicable;

   (g) details of the inspection structures provided for in Article 10;

   (h) the specific labelling details relating to the indication PDO or PGI, whichever is applicable, or the equivalent traditional national indications;

   (i) any requirements laid down by Community and/or national provisions.

Article 5

1. Only a group or, subject to certain conditions to be laid down in accordance with the procedure provided for in Article 15, a natural or legal person, shall be entitled to apply for registration.

    For the purposes of this Article, 'Group' means any association, irrespective of its legal form or composition, of producers and/or processors working with the same agricultural product or foodstuff. Other interested parties may participate in the group.

2. A group or a natural or legal person may apply for registration only in respect of agricultural products or foodstuffs which it produces or obtains within the meaning of Article 2(2)(a) or (b).

3. The application for registration shall include the product specification referred to in Article 4.

4. The application shall be sent to the Member State in which the geographical area is located.

5. The Member State shall check that the application is justified and shall forward the application, including the product specification referred to in Article 4 and other documents on which it has based its decision, to the Commission, if it considers that it satisfies the requirements of this Regulation.

   If the application concerns a name indicating a geographical area situated in another Member State also, that Member State shall be consulted before any decision is taken.

6. Member States shall introduce the laws, regulations and administrative provisions necessary to comply with this Article.

Article 6

1. Within a period of six months the Commission shall verify, by means of a formal investigation, whether the registration application includes all the particulars provided for in Article 4.

   The Commission shall inform the Member State concerned of its findings.

2. If, after taking account of paragraph I, the Commission concludes that the name qualifies for protection, it shall publish in the *Official Journal of the European Communities* the name and address of the applicant, the name of the product, the main points of the application, the references to national provisions governing the preparations, production or manufacture of the product and, if necessary, the grounds for its conclusions.

3. If no statement of objections is notified to the Commission in accordance with Article 7) the name shall be entered in a register kept by the Commission entitled Register of protected designations of origin and protected geographical indications', which shall contain the names of the groups and the inspection bodies concerned.

4. The Commission shall publish in the *Official Journal of the European Communities*.

   - the names entered in the Register,
   - amendments to the Register made in accordance with Article 9 and 11.

5. If, in the light of the investigation provided for in paragraph 1, the Commission concludes that the name does not qualify for protection, it shall decide, in accordance with the procedure provided for in Article 15, not to proceed with the publication provided for in paragraph 2 of this Article.

   Before publication as provided for in paragraphs 2 and 4 and registration as provided for in paragraph 3, the Commission may request the opinion of the Committee provided for in Article 15.

Article 7

1. Within six months of the date of publication in the *Official Journal of the European Communities* referred to in Article 6(2), any Member State may object to the registration.

2. The competent authorities of the Member States shall ensure that all persons who can demonstrate a legitimate economic interest are authorized to consult the application. In addition and in accordance with the existing situation in the Member States, the Member States may provide access to other parties with a legitimate interest.

3. Any legitimately concerned natural or legal person may object to the proposed registration by sending a duly substantiated statement to the competent authority of the Member State in which he resides or is established. The competent authority shall take the necessary measures to consider these comments or objection within the deadlines laid down.

4. A statement of objection shall be admissible only if it:

    - either shows non-compliance with the conditions referred to in Article 2,

    - or shows that the proposed registration of a name would jeopardize the existence of an entirely or partly identical name or trade mark or the existence of products which are legally on the market at the time of publication of this regulation in the *Official Journal of the European Communities*,

    - or indicates the features which demonstrate that the name whose registration is applied for is generic in nature.

5. Where an objection is admissible within the meaning of paragraph 4, the Commission shall ask the Member States concerned to seek agreement among themselves in accordance with their internal procedures within three months. If:

    (a) agreement is reached, the Member States in question shall communicate to the Commission all the factors which made agreement possible together with the applicant's opinion and that of the objector. Where there has been no change to the information received under Article 5, the Commission shall proceed in accordance with Article 6(4). If there has been a change, it shall again initiate the procedure laid down in Article 7;

    (b) no agreement is reached, the Commission shall take a decision in accordance with the procedure laid down in Article 15, having regard to traditional fair practice and of the actual likelihood of confusion. Should it decide to proceed with registration, the Commission shall carry out publication in accordance with Article 6(4).

Article 8

The indications PDO, PGI or equivalent traditional national indications may appear only on agricultural products and foodstuffs that comply with this Regulation.

Article 9

The Member State concerned may request the amendment of a specification, m particular to take account of developments in scientific and technical knowledge or to redefine the geographical area.

The Article 6 procedure shall apply *mutatis mutantdis.*

The Commission may, however, decide, under the procedure laid down in Article 15, not to apply the Article 6 procedure in the case of a minor amendment.

Article 10

1. Member States shall ensure that not later than six months after the entry into force of this Regulation inspection structures are in place, the function of which shall be to

ensure that agricultural products and foodstuffs bearing a protected name meet the requirements laid down in the specifications.

2. An inspection structure may comprise one or more designated inspection authorities and/or private bodies approved for that purpose by the Member State. Member States shall send the Commission lists of the authorities and/or bodies approved and their respective powers. The Commission shall publish those particulars in the *Official Journal of the European Communities*.

3. Designated inspection authorities and/or approved private bodies must offer adequate guarantees of objectivity and impartiality with regard to all producers or processors subject to their control and have permanently at their disposal the qualified staff and resources necessary to carry out inspection of agricultural products and foodstuffs bearing a protected name.

   If an inspection structure uses the services of another body for some inspections, that body must offer the same guarantees. In that event the designated inspection authorities and/or approved private bodies shall, however, continue to be responsible *vis-a-vis* the Member State for all inspections.

   As from 1 January 1998, in order to be approved by the Member States for the purpose of this Regulation, private bodies must fulfil the requirements laid down in standard EN 45011 of 26 June 1989.

4. If a designated inspection authority and/or private body in a Member State establishes that an agricultural product or a foodstuff bearing a protected name of origin in that Member State does not meet the criteria of the specification, they shall take the steps necessary to ensure that this Regulation is complied with. They shall inform the Member State of the measures taken in carrying out their inspections. The parties concerned must be notified of all decisions taken.

5. A Member State must withdraw approval from an inspection body where the criteria referred to in paragraphs 2 and 3 are no longer fulfilled. It shall inform the Commission, which shall publish in the *Official Journal of the European Communities* a revised list of approved bodies.

6. The Member States shall adopt the measures necessary to ensure that a producer who complies with this Regulation has access to the inspection system.

7. The costs of inspections provided under this Regulation shall be borne by the producers using the protected name.

Article 11

1. Any Member State may submit that a condition laid down in the product specification of an agricultural product or foodstuff covered by a protected name has not been met.

2. The Member State referred to in paragraph 1 shall make its submission to the Member State concerned. The Member State concerned shall examine the complaint and inform the other Member State of its findings and of any measures taken.

3. In the event of repeated irregularities and the failure of the Member States concerned to come to an agreement, a duly substantiated application must be sent to the Commission.

4. The Commission shall examine the application by consulting the Member States concerned. Where appropriate, having consulted the committee referred to in Article 15, the Commission shall take the necessary steps. These may include cancellation of the registration.

Article 12

1. Without prejudice to international agreements, this Regulation may apply to an agricultural product or foodstuff from a third country provided that:

   - the third country is able to give guarantees identical or equivalent to those referred to in Article 4,

   - the third country concerned has inspection arrangements equivalent to those laid down in Article 10,

   - the third country concerned is prepared to provide protection equivalent to that available in the Community to corresponding agricultural products for foodstuffs coming from the Community.

2. If a protected name of a third country is identical to a Community protected name, registration shall be granted with due regard for local and traditional usage and the practical risks of confusion.

   Use of such names shall be authorized only if the country of origin of the product is clearly and visibly indicated on the label.

Article 13

1. Registered names shall be protected against:

   (a) any direct or indirect commercial use of a name registered in respect of products not covered by the registration in so far as those products are comparable to the products registered under that name or insofar as using the name exploits the reputation of the protected name;

   (b) any misuse, imitation or evocation, even if the true origin of the product is indicated or if the protected name is translated or accompanied by an expression such as 'style', 'type', 'method', 'as produced in', 'imitation' or similar;

   (c) any other false or misleading indication as to the provenance, origin, nature or essential qualities of the product, on the inner or outer packaging, advertising material or documents relating to the product concerned, and the packing of the product in a container liable to convey a false impression as to its origin;

   (d) any other practice liable to mislead the public as to the true origin of the product.

   Where a registered name contains within it the name of an agricultural product or foodstuff which is considered generic, the use of that generic name on the appropriate agricultural product or foodstuff shall not be considered to be contrary to (a) or (b) in the first sub-paragraph.

2. However, Member States may maintain national measures authorizing the -use of the expressions referred to in paragraph 1(b) for a period of not more than five years after the date of publication of this Regulation, provided that:

- the products have been marketed legally using such expressions for at

- least five years before the date of publication of this Regulation, the labelling clearly indicates the true origin of the product.

However, this exception may not lead to the marketing of products freely on the territory of a Member State where such expressions are prohibited.

3. Protected names may not become generic.

Article 14

1. Where a designation of origin or geographical indication is registered in accordance with this Regulation, the application for registration of a trade mark corresponding to one of the situations referred to in Article 13 and relating to the same type of product shall be refused, provided that the application for registration of the trade mark was submitted after the date of the publication provided for in Article 6(2).

Trade marks registered in breach of the first sub-paragraph shall be declared invalid.

This paragraph shall also apply where the application for registration of a trade mark was lodged before the date of publication of the application for registration provided for in Article 6(2), provided that publication occurred before the trade mark was registered.

2. With due regard for Community law, use of a trade mark corresponding to one of the situations referred to in Article 13 which was registered in good faith before the date on which application for registration of a designation of origin or geographical indication was lodged may continue notwithstanding the registration of a designation of origin or geographical indication, where there are no grounds for invalidity or revocation of the trade mark as provided respectively by Article 3(1)(c) and (g) and Article 12(2)(b) of First Council Directive 89/104/EEC of 21 December 1988 to approximate the laws of the Member States relating to trade marks .

3. A designation of origin or geographical indication shall not be registered where, in the light of a trade mark's reputation and renown and the length of time it has been used, registration is liable to mislead the consumer as to the true identity of the product.

Article 15

The Commission shall be assisted by a committee composed of the representatives of the Member States and chaired by the representative of the Commission.

The representative of the Commission shall submit to the committee a draft of the measures to be taken. The committee shall deliver its opinion on the draft within a time limit which the chairman may lay down according to the urgency of the matter. The opinion shall be delivered by the majority laid down in Article 148(2) of the Treaty in the case of decisions which the Council is required to adopt on a proposal from the Commission. The votes of the representatives of the Member States within the committee shall be weighted in the manner set out in that Article. The chairman shall not vote.

The Commission shall adopt the measures envisaged if they are in accordance with the opinion of the committee.

If the measures envisaged are not in accordance with the opinion of the committee, or if no opinion is delivered, the Commission shall, without delay, submit to the Council a proposal relating to the measures to be taken. The Council shall act by a qualified majority.

If, on the expiry of a period of three months from the date of referral to the Council, the Council has not acted, the proposed measures shall be adopted by the Commission.

Article 16

Detailed rules for applying this Regulation shall be adopted in accordance with the procedure laid down in Article 15.

Article 17

1. Within six months of the entry into force of the Regulation, Member States shall inform the Commission which of their legally protected names or, in those Member States where there is no protection system, which of their names established by usage they wish to register pursuant to this Regulation.
2. In accordance with the procedure laid down in Article 15, the Commission shall register the names referred to in paragraph 1 which comply with Articles 2 and 4. Article 7 shall not apply. However, generic names shall not be added.
3. Member States may maintain national protection of the names communicated in accordance with paragraph 1 until such time as a decision on registration has been taken.

Article 18

This Regulation shall enter into force twelve months after the date of its publication in the *Official Journal of the European Communities*.

Note: Regulation (EEC) 2081/92 was published in the Official Journal on 24 July 1992.

This Regulation shall be binding in its entirety and directly applicable in all Member States.

Done at Brussels, 14 July 1992.

Annex I

Foodstuffs referred to in Article 1(1)

- Beer,
- Natural mineral waters and spring waters,
- Beverages made from plant extracts,
- Bread, pastry, cakes, confectionery, biscuits and other baker's wares,
- Natural gums and resins.

Annex II

Agricultural products referred to in Article 1(1)

- Hay
- Essential oils.

Index

PRS
see **Performing Rights Society**
pseudonymous works
duration of copyright, 10.10, 10.16
public domain information
see **confidentiality**
public domain texts, 10.18, 10.19, 16.24
public interest, 23.40-23.48
public lending right, 20.14
public order or morality
exceptions to patentability, 2.14, 2.27,
2.48, 3.38
EPO guidelines, 3.38
public policy or morality
trade marks contrary to, 29.19-29.21
public safety
State use of patented inventions, 8.50
trade marks contrary to, 29.20
public speeches
copyright in, 11.06, 11.25-11.27
transcripts, 11.26, 11.27
publication, 3.49
see also **non-prejudicial disclosures**
copyright infringement, 16.06
patent applications, 4.34-4.37
sound recordings, 12.02
trade mark applications, 33.19
publishing rights, 9.03-9.06, 19.01
see also **copyright**

quia timet **injunction**, 18.30, 31.46

racing cards, 11.07
radio broadcasts
see **broadcasts**
radio listings, 11.07
Radio Telefis Eireann
see **RTE**
railway guides, 11.07
railway timetables, 11.11, 11.20
raw materials, 6.16
readings, 17.13
recitations, 17.13
recombinant DNA technology, 3.37
recording rights, 15.38
see also **sound recordings**

mechanical rights, 17.18
non-voluntary licences, 17.18-17.19
private recordings, 17.14
Red Cross, 29.29
regional patent, 2.69
regional patent treaties, 2.69
see also **European Patent
Convention**
Register of Business Names, 25.04
Register of Patent Agents, 1.06
Register of Trade Marks, 33.76
registered designs
see **industrial designs**
Registrar of Companies, 25.02
remedies
see also **Account of Profit; Anton
Piller Order; damages; injunction**
breach of confidence, 23.50-23.63
copyright infringement, 18.01-18.35
patent infringement, 6.56-6.97
tort, in, 24.01-24.51
see also **passing off**
trade mark infringement, 31.39-31.62
renewal fees
patents
see **patent applications**
rental and lending rights
collecting societies, 9.21
EU Directive, 12.14-12.15, 20.12-20.15
exclusions, 20.12, 20.13
Geneva Treaties, 20.34
performers' rights, 12.15, 20.15
public lending rights, 20.12, 20.13
repair, 17.21
Community design, 22.42, 22.43
patented product, 6.04
reporting of current events
copyright infringement, defence to, 17.08
reproduction
adaptation, 16.12
archival exceptions, 17.14, 17.15, 17.17
artistic works, 16.05
collecting societies, 9.21
computer programs, parts of, 13.10-13.14
copyright infringement, 16.05
criticism or review, for, 17.06, 17.07